The I-Series

Microsoft® Access 2002

Introductory

Stephen Haag
University of Denver

James T. Perry
University of San Diego

Merrill Wells
University of Denver

Boston Burr Ridge, IL Dubuque, IA Madison, WI New York San Francisco St. Louis
Bangkok Bogotá Caracas Kuala Lumpur Lisbon London Madrid Mexico City
Milan Montreal New Delhi Santiago Seoul Singapore Sydney Taipei Toronto

McGraw-Hill Higher Education

A Division of The ***McGraw-Hill*** *Companies*

The I-Series: Microsoft Access 2002, Introductory

Published by McGraw-Hill/Irwin, an imprint of The McGraw-Hill Companies, Inc. 1221 Avenue of the Americas, New York, NY 10020.

Some ancillaries, including electronic and print components, may not be available to customers outside the United States.

This book is printed on acid-free paper.

1 2 3 4 5 6 7 8 9 0 WEB/WEB 0 9 8 7 6 5 4 3 2 1

ISBN 0-07-247030-5

Publisher: *George Werthman*
Sponsoring editor: *Dan Silverburg*
Developmental editor: *Melissa Forte*
Manager, Marketing and Sales: *Paul Murphy*
Project manager: *Scott Scheidt*
Production supervisor: *Rose Hepburn*
Senior designer: *Jennifer McQueen and Mary Christianson*
Senior producer, Media technology: *David Barrick*
Lead supplement producer: *Marc Mattson*
Cover freelance design/illustration: *Asylum Studios*
Interior freelance design: *Asylum Studios*
Compositor: *GAC Indianapolis*
Typeface: *10/12 New Aster*
Printer: *Webcrafters, Inc.*

Library of Congress Cataloging-in-Publication Data

Haag, Stephen.
Microsoft Access 2002: introductory / Stephen Haag, James T. Perry, Merrill Wells.
p. cm. (I-series)
ISBN 0-07-247030-5 (alk. paper)
1. Database management. 2. Microsoft Access. I. Perry, James T. II. Wells, Merrill. III. Title
QA76.9.D3 H23 2002
005.75'65—dc21 2001052132

http://www.mhhe.com

about McGraw-Hill/Irwin

INFORMATION TECHNOLOGY AT MCGRAW-HILL/IRWIN

At McGraw-Hill Higher Education, we publish instructional materials targeted at the higher education market. In an effort to expand the tools of higher learning, we publish texts, lab manuals, study guides, testing materials, software, and multimedia products.

At McGraw-Hill/Irwin (a division of McGraw-Hill Higher Education), we realize that technology has created and will continue to create new mediums for professors and students to use in managing resources and communicating information to one another. We strive to provide the most flexible and complete teaching and learning tools available as well as offer solutions to the changing world of teaching and learning.

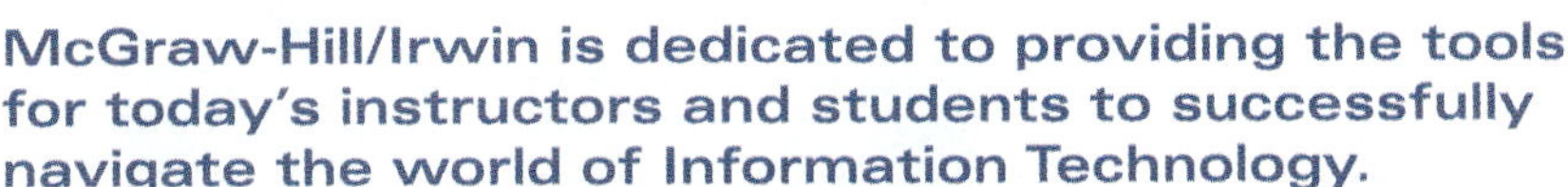

- **SEMINAR SERIES**—McGraw-Hill/Irwin's Technology Connection seminar series offered across the country every year demonstrates the latest technology products and encourages collaboration among teaching professionals.

- **MCGRAW-HILL/OSBORNE**—This division of The McGraw-Hill Companies is known for its best-selling Internet titles, *Internet & Web Yellow Pages* and the *Internet Complete Reference*. For more information, visit Osborne at www.osborne.com.

- **DIGITAL SOLUTIONS**—McGraw-Hill/Irwin is committed to publishing digital solutions. Taking your course online doesn't have to be a solitary adventure, nor does it have to be a difficult one. We offer several solutions that will allow you to enjoy all the benefits of having your course material online.

- **PACKAGING OPTIONS**—For more information about our discount options, contact your McGraw-Hill/Irwin sales representative at 1-800-338-3987 or visit our Web site at www.mhhe.com/it.

THE I-SERIES PAGE

By using the I-Series, students will be able to learn and master applications skills by being actively engaged—by *doing*. The "I" in I-Series demonstrates Insightful tasks that will not only Inform students, but also Involve them while learning the applications.

How will The I-Series accomplish this for you?

Through relevant, real-world chapter opening cases.

Through tasks throughout each chapter that incorporate steps and tips for easy reference.

Through alternative methods and styles of learning to keep the student involved.

Through rich, end-of-chapter materials that support what the student has learned.

I-Series titles include:

- Microsoft Office XP, Volume I
- Microsoft Office XP, Volume I Expanded
- Microsoft Office XP, Volume II
- Microsoft Word 2002 (Brief, Introductory, Complete Versions) 12 Chapters
- Microsoft Excel 2002 (Brief, Introductory, Complete Versions) 12 Chapters
- Microsoft Access 2002 (Brief, Introductory, Complete Versions) 12 Chapters
- Microsoft PowerPoint 2002 (Brief, Introductory Versions) 8 Chapters
- Microsoft Windows 2000 (Brief, Introductory, Complete Versions) 12 Chapters
- Microsoft Windows XP and Bonus Books to come!

To accompany the series: The I-Series Computing Concepts text (Introductory, Complete Versions)

For additional resources, visit the I-Series Online Learning Center at www.mhhe.com/i-series/

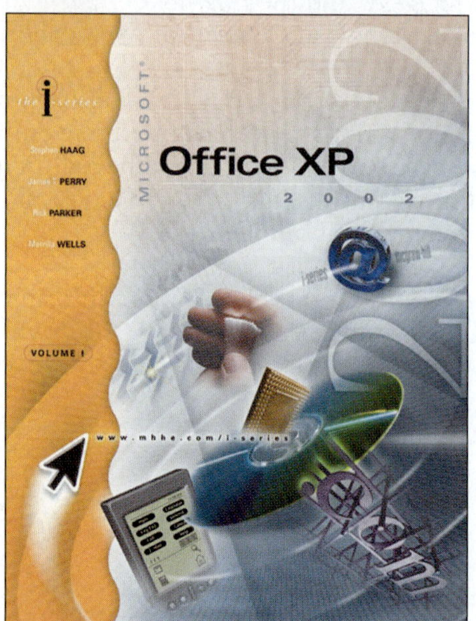

GOALS/PHILOSOPHY

The I-Series applications textbooks strongly emphasize that students learn and master applications skills by being actively engaged—by *doing*. We made the decision that teaching how to accomplish tasks is not enough for complete understanding and mastery. Students must understand the importance of each of the tasks that lead to a finished product at the end of each chapter.

Approach

The I-Series chapters are subdivided into sessions that contain related groups of tasks with active, hands-on components. The session tasks containing numbered steps collectively result in a completed project at the end of each session. Prior to introducing numbered steps that show how to accomplish a particular task, we discuss why the steps are important. We discuss the role that the collective steps play in the overall plan for creating or modifying a document or object, answering students' often-heard questions, "Why are we doing these steps? Why are these steps important?" Without an explanation of why an activity is important and what it accomplishes, students can easily find themselves following the steps but not registering the big picture of what the steps accomplish and why they are executing them.

I-Series Applications for 2002

The I-Series offers three levels of instruction. Each level builds upon knowledge from the previous level. With the exception of the running project that is the last exercise of every chapter, chapter cases and end-of-chapter exercises are independent from one chapter to the next, with the exception of Access. The three levels available are

Brief Covers the basics of the Microsoft application and contains Chapters 1 through 4. The Brief textbooks are typically 200 pages long.

Introductory Includes chapters in the Brief textbook plus Chapters 5 through 8. Introductory textbooks typically are 400 pages long and prepare students for the Microsoft Office User Specialist (MOUS) Core Exam.

Complete Includes the Introductory textbook plus Chapters 9 through 12. The four additional chapters cover advanced level content and are typically 600 pages long. Complete textbooks prepare students for the Microsoft Office User Specialist (MOUS) Expert Exam. The Microsoft Office User Specialist program is recognized around the world as the standard for demonstrating proficiency using Microsoft Office applications.

In addition, there are two compilation volumes available.

Office I Includes introductory chapters on Windows and Computing Concepts followed by Chapters 1 through 4 (Brief textbook) of Word, Excel, Access, and PowerPoint. In addition, material from the companion Computing Concepts book is integrated into the first few chapters to provide students an understanding of the relationship between Microsoft Office applications and computer information systems.

Office II Includes introductory chapters on Windows and Computing Concepts followed by Chapters 5 through 8 from each of the Introductory-level textbooks including Word, Excel, Access, and PowerPoint. In addition, material from the companion Computing Concepts book is integrated into the introductory chapters to provide students a deeper understanding of the relationship between Microsoft Office applications and computer information systems. An introduction to Visual Basic for Applications (VBA) completes the Office II textbook.

Approved Microsoft Courseware

Use of the Microsoft Office User Specialist Approved Courseware logo on this product signifies that it has been independently reviewed and approved to comply with the following standards: Acceptable coverage of all content related to the Microsoft Office Exams entitled Microsoft Access 2002, Microsoft Excel 2002, Microsoft PowerPoint 2002, and Microsoft Word 2002, and sufficient performance-based exercises that relate closely to all required content, based on sampling of the textbooks. For further information on Microsoft's MOUS certification program, please visit Microsoft's Web site at www.microsoft.com.

about the authors

STEPHEN HAAG

Stephen Haag is a professor and Chair of Information Technology and Electronic Commerce and the Director of Technology in the University of Denver's Daniels College of Business. Stephen holds a B.B.A. and an M.B.A. from West Texas State University and a Ph.D. from the University of Texas at Arlington. Stephen has published numerous articles appearing in such journals as *Communications of the ACM, The International Journal of Systems Science, Applied Economics, Managerial and Decision Economics, Socio-Economic Planning Sciences,* and the *Australian Journal of Management.*

Stephen is also the author of 13 other books including *Interactions: Teaching English as a Second Language* (with his mother and father), *Case Studies in Information Technology, Information Technology: Tomorrow's Advantage Today* (with Peter Keen), and *Excelling in Finance.* Stephen is also the lead author of the accompanying *I-Series: Computing Concepts* text, released in both an Introductory and Complete version. Stephen lives with his wife, Pam, and their four sons, Indiana, Darian, Trevor, and Elvis, in Highlands Ranch, Colorado.

JAMES PERRY

James Perry is a professor of Management Information Systems at the University of San Diego's School of Business. Jim is an active instructor who teaches both undergraduate and graduate courses. He holds a B.S. in mathematics from Purdue University and a Ph.D. in computer science from The Pennsylvania State University. He has published several journal and conference papers. He is the co-author of 56 textbooks and trade books such as *Using Access with Accounting Systems, Building Accounting Systems, Understanding Oracle, The Internet,* and *Electronic Commerce.* His books have been translated into Dutch, French, and Chinese. Jim worked as a computer security consultant to various private and governmental organizations including the Jet Propulsion Laboratory. He was a consultant on the Strategic Defense Initiative ("Star Wars") project and served as a member of the computer security oversight committee.

RICK PARKER

Rick Parker received his bachelor's degree from Brigham Young University. He received his Ph.D. in animal physiology at Iowa State University. After completing his Ph.D., he and his wife, Marilyn, and their children moved to Edmonton, Alberta, Canada, where he completed a post-doctorate at the University of Alberta. He accepted a position as a research and teaching associate at the University of Wyoming, Laramie, Wyoming.

Rick developed a love for the power and creativity unleashed by computers and software. After arriving at the College of Southern Idaho, Twin Falls, in 1984, he guided the creation and development of numerous college software courses and software training programs for business and industry. He also led the conversion of an old office occupations technical program into a business computer applications program, which evolved into an information technology program. During the early adoption of computers and software by the college, Rick wrote in-house training manuals and taught computer/software courses.

Rick currently works as a professional-technical division director at the College of Southern Idaho. As director, he supervises faculty in agriculture, information technology and drafting, and electronics programs. He is the author of four other textbooks.

MERRILL WELLS

The caption next to **Merrill Wells'** eighth grade yearbook picture noted that her career goal was to teach college and write books. She completed an MBA at Indiana University and began a career as a programmer. After several years of progressive positions in business and industry, she returned to academia, spending 10 years as a computer technology faculty member at Red Rocks Community College and then becoming an information technology professor at the University of Denver, Daniels College of Business. She completed her first published book in 1993 and began presenting at educational seminars in 1997. Other publications include *An Introduction to Computers, Introduction to Visual Basic,* and *Programming Logic and Design.*

about the i-series—key features

Each textbook features the following:

Did You Know Each chapter has six or seven interesting facts—both about high tech and other topics.

Sessions Each chapter is divided into two or three sessions.

Chapter Outline Provides students with a quick map of the major headings in the chapter.

Chapter and MOUS Objectives At the beginning of each chapter is a list of 5 to 10 action-oriented objectives. Any chapter objectives that are also MOUS objectives indicate the MOUS objective number also.

Chapter Opening Case Each chapter begins with a case. Cases describe a mixture of fictitious and real people and companies and the needs of the people and companies. Throughout the chapter, the student gains the skills and knowledge to solve the problem stated in the case.

Introduction The chapter introduction establishes the overview of the chapter's activities in the context of the case problem.

Another Way and Another Word Another Way is a highlighted feature providing a bulleted list of steps to accomplish a task, or best practices—that is, a better or faster way to accomplish a task such as pasting a format onto an Excel cell. Another Word, another highlighted box, briefly explains more about a topic or highlights a potential pitfall.

Step-by-Step Instructions Numbered step-by-step instructions for all hands-on activities appear in a distinctive color. Keyboard characters and menu selections appear in a **special format** to emphasize what the user should press or type. Steps make clear to the student the exact sequence of keystrokes and mouse clicks needed to complete a task such as formatting a Word paragraph.

Tips Tips appear within a numbered sequence of steps and warn the student of possible missteps or provide alternatives to the step that precedes the tip.

Task Reference and Task Reference Round-Up Task References appear throughout the textbook. Set in a distinctive design, each Task Reference contains a bulleted list of steps showing a generic way to accomplish activities that are especially important or significant. A Task Reference Round-Up at the end of each chapter summarizes a chapter's Task References.

MOUS Objectives Summary A list of MOUS objectives covered in a chapter appears in the chapter objectives and the chapter summary.

Making the Grade Short answer questions appear at the end of each chapter's sessions. They test a student's grasp of each session's contents, and Making the Grade answers appear at the end of each book so students can check their answers.

Rich End-of-Chapter Materials End-of-chapter materials incorporating a three-level approach reinforce learning and help students take ownership of the chapter. Level One, review of terminology, contains a fun crossword puzzle that enforces review of a chapter's key terms. Level Two, review of concepts, contains fill-in-the blank questions, review questions, and a Jeopardy-style create-a-question exercise. Level Three is Hands-on Projects.

Hands-on Projects Extensive hands-on projects engage the student in a problem-solving exercise from start to finish. There are six clearly labeled categories that each contain one or two questions. Categories are Practice, Challenge!, On the Web, E-Business, Around the World, and a Running Project that carries throughout all the chapters.

We understand that, in today's teaching environment, offering a textbook alone is not sufficient to meet the needs of the many instructors who use our books. To teach effectively, instructors must have a full complement of supplemental resources to assist them in every facet of teaching, from preparing for class to conducting a lecture to assessing students' comprehension. The **I-Series** offers a complete supplements package and Web site that is briefly described below.

INSTRUCTOR'S RESOURCE KIT

The Instructor's Resource Kit is a CD-ROM containing the Instructor's Manual in both MS Word and .pdf formats, PowerPoint Slides with Presentation Software, Brownstone test-generating software, and accompanying test item files in both MS Word and .pdf formats for each chapter. The CD also contains figure files from the text, student data files, and solutions files. The features of each of the three main components of the Instructor's Resource Kit are highlighted below.

Instructor's Manual Featuring:

- Chapter learning objectives per chapter
- Chapter outline with teaching tips
- Annotated Solutions Diagram to provide Troubleshooting Tips, Tricks, and Traps
- Lecture Notes, illustrating key concepts and ideas
- Annotated Syllabus, depicting a time table and schedule for covering chapter content
- Additional end-of-chapter projects
- Answers to all Making the Grade and end-of-chapter questions

PowerPoint Presentation

The PowerPoint presentation is designed to provide instructors with comprehensive lecture and teaching resources that will include

- Chapter learning objectives followed by source content that illustrates key terms and key facts per chapter
- FAQ (frequently asked questions) to show key concepts throughout the chapter; also, lecture notes, to illustrate these key concepts and ideas
- End-of-chapter exercises and activities per chapter, as taken from the end-of-chapter materials in the text
- Speaker's Notes, to be incorporated throughout the slides per chapter
- Figures/screen shots, to be incorporated throughout the slides per chapter

PowerPoint includes presentation software for instructors to design their own presentation for their course.

Test Bank

The I-Series Test Bank, using Diploma Network Testing Software by Brownstone, contains over 3,000 questions (both objective and interactive) categorized by topic, page reference to the text, and difficulty level of learning. Each question is assigned a learning category:

- Level 1: Key Terms and Facts
- Level 2: Key Concepts
- Level 3: Application and Problem-Solving

The types of questions consist of 40 percent Identifying/Interactive Lab Questions, 20 percent Multiple Choice, 20 percent True/False, and 20 percent Fill-in/Short Answer Questions.

ONLINE LEARNING CENTER/ WEB SITE

The Online Learning Center that accompanies the I-Series is accessible through our Information Technology Supersite at http://www.mhhe.com/catalogs/irwin/it/. This site provides additional review and learning tools developed using the same three-level approach found in the text and supplements. To locate the I-Series OLC/Web site directly, go to www.mhhe.com/i-series. The site is divided into three key areas:

- **Information Center** Contains core information about the text, the authors, and a guide to our additional features and benefits of the series, including the supplements.

- **Instructor Center** Offers instructional materials, downloads, additional activities and answers to additional projects, answers to chapter troubleshooting exercises, answers to chapter preparation/post exercises posed to students, relevant links for professors, and more.
- **Student Center** Contains chapter objectives and outlines, self-quizzes, chapter troubleshooting exercises, chapter preparation/post exercises, additional projects, simulations, student data files and solutions files, Web links, and more.

RESOURCES FOR STUDENTS

Interactive Companion CD This student CD-ROM can be packaged with this text. It is designed for use in class, in the lab, or at home by students and professors and combines video, interactive exercises, and animation to cover the most difficult and popular topics in Computing Concepts. By combining video, interactive exercises, animation, additional content, and actual "lab" tutorials, we expand the reach and scope of the textbook.

SimNet XPert **SimNet XPert** is a simulated assessment and learning tool. It allows students to study MS Office XP skills and computer concepts, and professors to test and evaluate students' proficiency within MS Office XP applications and concepts. Students can practice and study their skills at home or in the school lab using SimNet XPert, which does not require the purchase of Office XP software. SimNet XPert will contain new features and enhancements for Office XP, including:

***NEW!* Live Assessments! SimNet *XP*ert** now includes live-in-the-application assessments! One for each skill set for Core MOUS objectives in Word 2002, Excel 2002, Access 2002, and PowerPoint 2002 (total of 29 Live-in-the-Application Assessments). Multiple tasks are required to complete each live assessment (about 100 tasks covered).

***NEW!* Computer Concepts Coverage! SimNet *XP*ert** now includes coverage of computer concepts in both the Learning and the Assessment sides.

***NEW!* Practice or Pretest Questions! SimNet *XP*ert** has a separate pool of 600 questions for practice tests or pretests.

***NEW!* Comprehensive Exercises! SimNet *XP*ert** offers comprehensive exercises for each application. These exercises require the student to use multiple skills to solve one exercise in the simulated environment.

ENHANCED!* More Assessment Questions! SimNet *XPert includes over 1,400 assessment questions.

***ENHANCED!* Simulated Interface!** The simulated environment in **SimNet *XP*ert** has been substantially deepened to more realistically simulate the real applications. Now students are not graded incorrect just because they chose the wrong sub-menu or dialog box. The student is not graded until he or she does something that immediately invokes an action.

DIGITAL SOLUTIONS FOR INSTRUCTORS AND STUDENTS

PageOut PageOut is our Course Web Site Development Center that offers a syllabus page, URL, McGraw-Hill Online Learning Center content, online exercises and quizzes, gradebook, discussion board, and an area for student Web pages. For more information, visit the PageOut Web site at www.pageout.net.

Online Courses Available OLCs are your perfect solutions for Internet-based content. Simply put, these Centers are "digital cartridges" that contain a book's pedagogy and supplements. As students read the book, they can go online and take self-grading quizzes or work through interactive exercises.

Online Learning Centers can be delivered through any of these platforms:

McGraw-Hill Learning Architecture (TopClass)

Blackboard.com

College.com (formerly Real Education)

WebCT (a product of Universal Learning Technology)

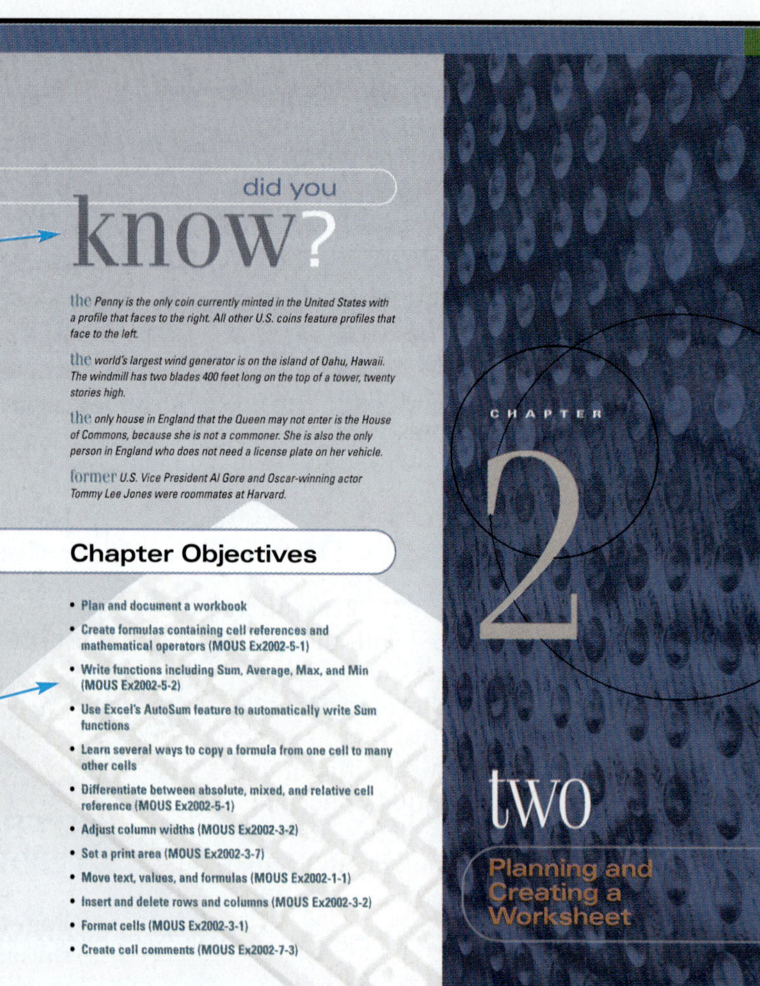
did you know?

the Penny is the only coin currently minted in the United States with a profile that faces to the right. All other U.S. coins feature profiles that face to the left.

the world's largest wind generator is on the island of Oahu, Hawaii. The windmill has two blades 400 feet long on the top of a tower, twenty stories high.

the only house in England that the Queen may not enter is the House of Commons, because she is not a commoner. She is also the only person in England who does not need a license plate on her vehicle.

former U.S. Vice President Al Gore and Oscar-winning actor Tommy Lee Jones were roommates at Harvard.

Chapter Objectives

- Plan and document a workbook
- Create formulas containing cell references and mathematical operators (MOUS Ex2002-5-1)
- Write functions including Sum, Average, Max, and Min (MOUS Ex2002-5-2)
- Use Excel's AutoSum feature to automatically write Sum functions
- Learn several ways to copy a formula from one cell to many other cells
- Differentiate between absolute, mixed, and relative cell reference (MOUS Ex2002-5-1)
- Adjust column widths (MOUS Ex2002-3-2)
- Set a print area (MOUS Ex2002-3-7)
- Move text, values, and formulas (MOUS Ex2002-1-1)
- Insert and delete rows and columns (MOUS Ex2002-3-2)
- Format cells (MOUS Ex2002-3-1)
- Create cell comments (MOUS Ex2002-7-3)

CHAPTER 2 two

Planning and Creating a Worksheet

Did You Know?

A unique presentation of text and graphics introduce interesting and little-known facts.

Chapter Objectives

Each chapter begins with a list of competencies covered in the chapter.

Task Reference

Provides steps to accomplish an especially important task.

task reference

Changing Relative References to Absolute or Mixed References

- Double-click the cell containing the formula that you want to edit or click the cell and then press **F2**
- Move the insertion point, a vertical bar, to the left of the cell reference you want to alter
- Press function key **F4** repeatedly until the absolute or mixed reference you want appears
- Press **Enter** to complete the cell edit procedure

Making the Grade

Short-answer questions appear at the end of each session and answers appear at the end of the book.

SESSION 2.1 **making the grade**

1. Explain how AutoSum works and what it does.
2. Suppose you select cell A14 and type D5+F5. What is stored in cell A14: text, a value, or a formula?
3. You can drag the ________, which is a small black square in the lower-right corner of the active cell, to copy the cell's contents.
4. Evaluation of a formula such as =D4+D5*D6 is governed by order of precedence. Explain what that means in general and then indicate the order in which Excel calculates the preceding expression.
5. Suppose Excel did not provide an AVERAGE function. Show an alternative way to compute the average of cell range A1:B25 using the other Excel statistical functions.

Copying a formula from one cell to many cells:

1. Click cell **G4** to make it the active cell. The cell's formula, =F4/B4, appears in the formula bar
2. Click **Edit** on the menu bar and then click **Copy** to copy the cell's contents to the Clipboard. Notice that a dashed line encloses the cell whose contents are on the Clipboard

tip: *You can press* ***Ctrl+C*** *instead of using the Copy command. Those of you who keep your hands on the keyboard may favor this keyboard shortcut.*

3. Click and drag cells **G5** through **G8** to select them. They are the target range into which you will paste the cell G4's contents
4. Click **Edit** on the menu bar and then click **Paste.** Excel copies the Clipboard's contents into each of the cells in the selected range and then adjusts each cell's formula to correspond to its new location. Notice that the Paste Options Smart Tag appears below and to the right of cell G8 (see Figure 2.16). The Paste Options Smart Tag provides several formatting and copying options in its list. You can access the options by clicking the Smart Tag list arrow

FIGURE 2.16
Copied formulas' results

tip: *You can press* ***Ctrl+*** ... *paste the Clipboard's conte...*

5. Press **Escape** to cl... line from the sourc... and view the formu...

Step-by-Step Instruction

Numbered steps guide you through the exact sequence of keystrokes to accomplish the task.

Tips

Tips appear within steps and either indicate possible missteps or provide alternatives to a step.

hands-on projects

practice

LEVEL THREE

...' Work Hours

...r Wexler's Tool and ...age a group of five ...r group has a differ... record on a weekly ...ch employee works, ..., and percentage of ...at each employee's ...ing the information ...icient way to record ... Alan Gin, the com...r, wants you to pre...report your group's ...ges. You create a ...and wages.

...Wages.xls and

...on sheet and then ...ove to that work-

...all the employees'

...ve row 1: Click cell ..., and release the ...he Menu bar and

...he range and type

...click cell **C1,** type ...e **Wages,** click cell

12. Click cell **E3** and type the formula that represents the employee's percentage of the total wages: **=D3/D$8*100**
13. Copy the formula in cell E3 to the cell range **E4:E7**
14. Select cell range **A1:E8,** click **Format,** click **AutoFormat,** select the **Simple** format, and click **OK**
15. Select cell range **E3:E7** and click the **Decrease Decimal** button enough times to reduce the displayed percentages to two decimal places
16. Click cell **A10** and type your first and last names
17. Set the left, right, top, and bottom margins to two inches
18. Either execute **Print** or execute **Save As,** according to your instructor's direction

2. Creating an Invoice

As office manager of Randy's Foreign Cars, one of your duties is to produce and mail invoices to customers who have arranged to pay for their automobile repairs up to 30 days after mechanics perform the work. Randy's invoices include parts, sales tax on parts, and labor charges. State law stipulates that customers do not pay sales tax on the labor charges. Only parts are subject to state sales tax. State sales tax is 6 percent. Create and print an invoice whose details appear below.

End-of-Chapter Hands-on Projects

A rich variety of projects introduced by a case lets you put into practice what you have learned. Categories include Practice, Challenge, On the Web, E-Business, Around the World, and a running case project.

Screen Shots

Screen shots show you what to expect at critical points.

anotherword

... about Smart Tags

Microsoft Office Smart Tags are a set of buttons that are shared across the Office applications. The buttons appear when needed, such as when Excel detects you may have made an error in an Excel formula, and gives the user appropriate options to change the given action or error.

Another Way/ Another Word

Another Way highlights an alternative way to accomplish a task; Another Word explains more about a topic.

task reference roundup

Task	Location	Preferred Method
Writing formulas	EX 2.9	• Select a cell, type **5**, type the formula, press **Enter**
Modifying an AutoSum cell range by pointing	EX 2.11	• Press an arrow key repeatedly to select leftmost or topmost cell in range, press and hold **Shift**, select cell range with arrow keys, release **Shift**, press **Enter**
Writing a function using the Paste Function button	EX 2.17	• Select a cell, click **Paste Function**, click a function category, click a function name, click **OK**, complete the Formula Palette dialog box, click **OK**
Copying and pasting a cell or range of cells	EX 2.21	• Select source cell(s), click **Edit**, click **Copy**, select target cell(s), click **Edit**, click **Paste**
Copying cell contents using a cell's fill handle	EX 2.23	• Select source cell(s), drag the fill handle to the source cell(s) range, release the mouse button

Task Reference RoundUp

Provides a quick reference and summary of a chapter's task references.

APPROVED COURSEWARE

What does this logo mean?

It means this courseware has been approved by the Microsoft® Office User Specialist Program to be among the finest available for learning *Microsoft Word 2002, Microsoft Excel 2002, Microsoft Access 2002, and Microsoft PowerPoint 2002*. It also means that upon completion of this courseware, you may be prepared to become a Microsoft Office User Specialist. The I-Series Microsoft Office XP books are available in three levels of coverage: Brief level, Intro level, and the Complete level. The I-Series Introductory books are approved courseware to prepare you for the MOUS level 1 exam. The I-Series Complete books will prepare you for the expert level exam.

What is a Microsoft Office User Specialist?

A Microsoft Office User Specialist is an individual who has certified his or her skills in one or more of the Microsoft Office desktop applications of Microsoft Word, Microsoft Excel, Microsoft PowerPoint®, Microsoft Outlook® or Microsoft Access, or in Microsoft Project. The Microsoft Office User Specialist Program typically offers certification exams at the "Core" and "Expert" skill levels.* The Microsoft Office User Specialist Program is the only Microsoft approved program in the world for certifying proficiency in Microsoft Office desktop applications and Microsoft Project. This certification can be a valuable asset in any job search or career advancement.

More Information:

To learn more about becoming a Microsoft Office User Specialist, visit www.mous.net

To purchase a Microsoft Office User Specialist certification exam, visit www.DesktopIQ.co

To learn about other Microsoft Office User Specialist approved courseware from McGraw-Hill/Irwin, visit http://www.mhhe.com/catalogs/irwin/cit/mous/index.mhtml

.

* The availability of Microsoft Office User Specialist certification exams varies by application, application version and language. Visit www.mous.net for exam availability.

acknowledgments

The authors want to acknowledge the work and support of the seasoned professionals at McGraw-Hill. Thank you to George Werthman, publisher, for his strong leadership and a management style that fosters innovation and creativity. Thank you to Dan Silverburg, sponsoring editor, who is an experienced editor and recent recruit to the I-Series. Dan quickly absorbed a month's worth of information in days and guided the authors through the sometimes-difficult publishing maze. Our special thanks go to Melissa Forte, developmental editor, who served, unofficially, as a cheerleader for the authors. The hub of our editorial "wheel," Melissa shouldered more than her share of work in the many months from prelaunch boot camp to bound book date. We are grateful to Gina Huck, developmental editor, for her dedication to this project. From the project's inception, Gina has guided us and kept us on track. Sarah Wood, developmental editor, paid attention to all the details that required her special care.

Thank you to Valerie Bolch, a University of San Diego graduate student, who did a wonderful job of creating some of the end-of-chapter exercises and tech editing the Excel manuscript. Ron Tariga, also a graduate student at the University of San Diego, helped categorize and display several Office XP toolbar buttons. Stirling Perry, a University of San Diego undergraduate student, took screen shots of all of the Office XP toolbar buttons and organized them into logical groups. Wendi Whitmore, a University of San Diego undergraduate student, provided screen shots of Office 2000 toolbars, prior to the release of Office XP. Many thanks to Linda Dillon, who provided creative input and feedback for the PowerPoint end-of-chapter materials. Also, the labor of Carolla McCammack in tech editing many of the Access chapters has been invaluable.

Thank you to Marilyn Parker, Rick's partner for 32 years, for her help, support, and tolerance. She helped with some of the manuscript details, supported Rick's need for time, and tolerated his emotional absence. Rick's sons, Cole, Morgan, Spence, and Sam, were patient and helpful during the time required for all the steps in the production of this book. All of them filled in and did "his" chores at times as they tolerated his distractions. Also, thanks to Mali Jones for her excellent technical editing.

We all wish to thank all of our schools for providing support, including time off to dedicate to writing: University of San Diego, University of Denver, and the College of Southern Idaho.

If you would like to contact us about any of the books in the I-Series, we would enjoy hearing from you. We welcome comments and suggestions that we might incorporate into future editions of the books. You can e-mail book-related messages to us at i-series@mcgraw-hill.com. For the latest information about the I-Series textbooks and related resources, please visit our Web site at www.mhhe.com/i-series.

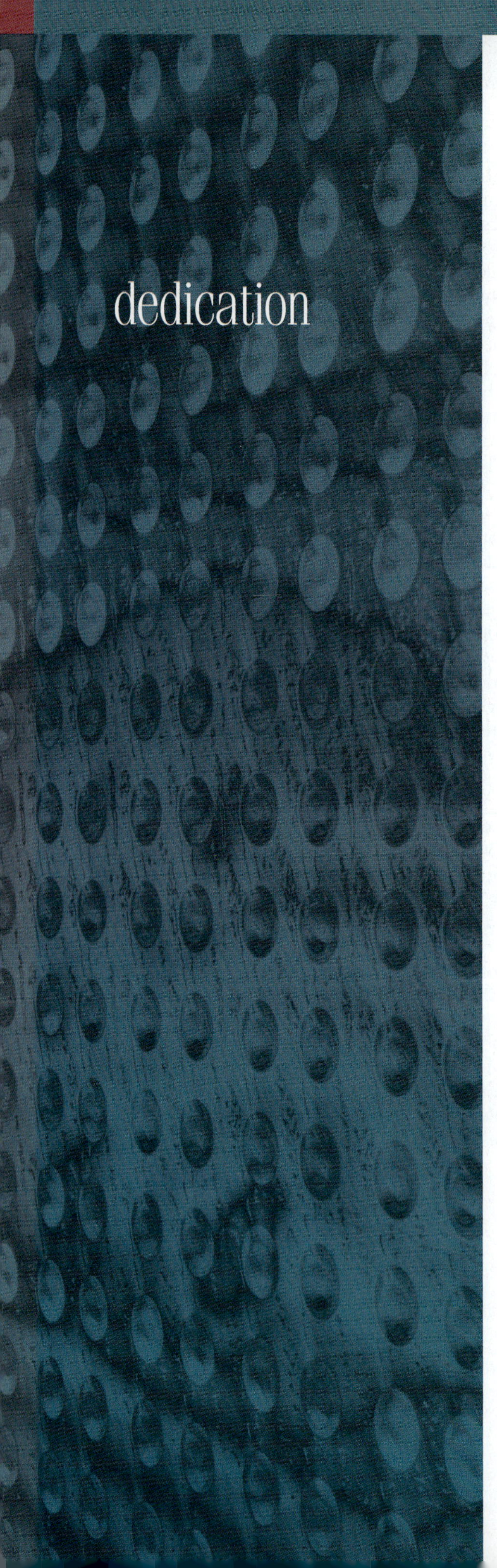

TO my wonderful family:

Rick, Daniel, Dusty, Tori, Evan, Connor and Gage

For all that they do to support me when writing isn't easy and to celebrate the times when it goes well.

M.W.

brief contents

table of contents

did you

know?

the *"XP" in Microsoft Office XP stands for "experience"—specifically, an exciting new set of experiences enabled by this new release?*

Microsoft *was created by Paul Allen and Bill Gates in 1975 in Albuquerque, New Mexico, long before they moved their offices to Redmond, Washington?*

Allen *and Gates developed a version of the BASIC computer language for the first personal computer, known as the Altair 8800?*

the *inventor of the Altair 8800, Dr. Ed Roberts, is now a family physician in Cochran, Georgia?*

Dr. *Roberts coined the phrase "personal computer" since it was the first computer designed for personal use?*

what *was the basic configuration of the Altair 8800?*
(see www.mhhe.com/i-series for the answer)

Chapter Objectives

In this chapter you will:

- **Be introduced to the Office XP suite**
- **Find out what new features exist in Office XP**
- **Become familiar with the different versions of Office XP and which four applications are included in all versions**
- **Learn about the common screen elements such as the title bar, menu bar, and toolbars**
- **Learn how to switch between two or more open applications**
- **Learn how to use Office XP's newest features: the task pane and smart tags**
- **Become familiar with how to get help in an application**
- **Learn how to customize your Office Assistant**
- **Learn about the newest Help features: Answer Wizard and Ask a Question**

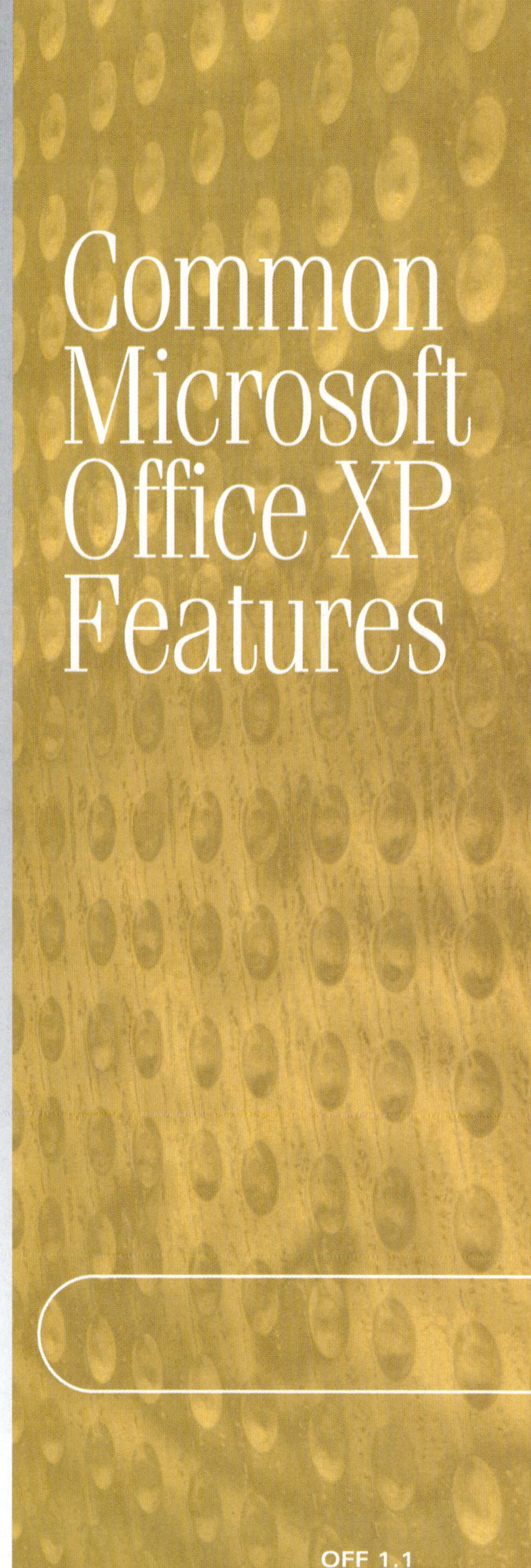

Common Microsoft Office XP Features

CHAPTER OUTLINE:

1.1 Introducing Microsoft Office XP

INTRODUCTION

Office XP is the newest version of the popular Microsoft integrated application suite series that has helped personal computer users around the world to be productive and creative. Specifically, an ***application*** is a program that is designed to help you accomplish a particular task, such as creating a slide-show presentation using PowerPoint. An ***integrated application suite,*** like Office XP, is a collection of application programs bundled together and designed to allow the user to effortlessly share information from one application to the next.

SESSION 1.1 INTRODUCING MICROSOFT OFFICE XP

There are several versions of Office XP available to users with a diversity of personal and business needs. They include the Standard edition, the Professional edition, the Professional Special edition, and the Developer edition. Each edition comes with a collection of different programs, but all include the basic applications of Word, Excel, Outlook, and PowerPoint, which is the collection known as the ***Standard edition***. The ***Professional edition*** adds Access to the collection, whereas the ***Professional Special edition*** includes Access, FrontPage, and Publisher. A summary of some of the more popular applications available in Office XP is listed in Figure 1.1.

FIGURE 1.1
Application programs available in Microsoft Office XP

Office XP Application	Summary of What the Program Does
Word 2002	Word is a general-purpose word-processing tool that allows users to create primarily text-based documents, such as letters, résumés, research papers, and even Web pages.
Excel 2002	Excel is an electronic spreadsheet tool that can be used to input, organize, calculate, analyze, and display business data.
PowerPoint 2002	PowerPoint is a popular presentation tool that allows users to create overhead transparencies and powerful multimedia slide shows.
Access 2002	Access is a relational database tool that can be used to collect, organize, and retrieve large amounts of data. With a database you can manipulate the data into useful information using tables, forms, queries, and reports.
Outlook 2002	Outlook is a desktop information management tool that allows you to send and receive e-mail, maintain a personal calendar of appointments, schedule meetings with co-workers, create to-do lists, and store address information about business/personal contacts.
FrontPage 2002	FrontPage is a powerful Web publishing tool that provides everything needed to create, edit, and manage a personal or corporate Web site, without having to learn HTML.
Publisher 2002	Publisher is a desktop publishing tool that provides individual users the capability to create professional-looking flyers, brochures, and newsletters.

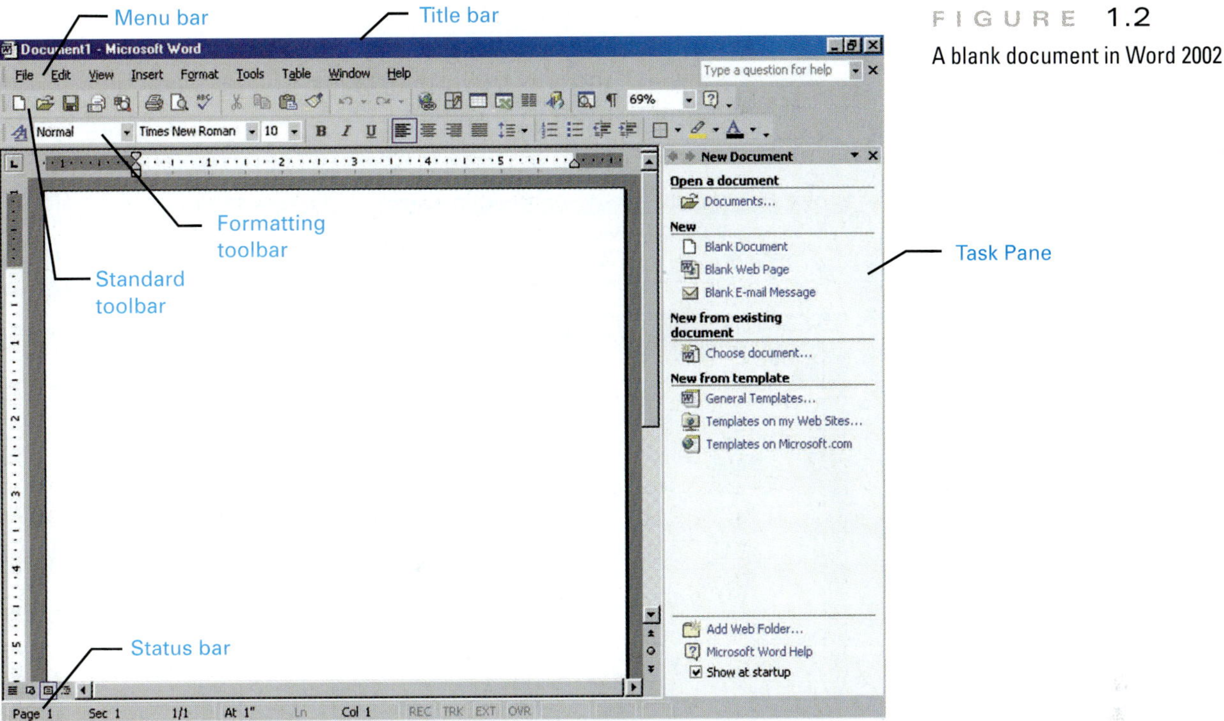

FIGURE 1.2
A blank document in Word 2002

Identifying Common Screen Elements

When you open two or more of the Microsoft applications, you will notice the similarities in the programs. This design is done intentionally so that as you learn to use one application, you will be able to quickly navigate through the remaining Office XP programs. When you first open Word, you will find a blank document as seen in Figure 1.2. In this exercise you will get to preview a blank document in Word and a blank workbook in Excel. Notice the common features of the two programs as you work with them. These features will be explained over the next few pages.

anotherword

. . . on the Office XP Suite

Collectively, the programs are officially referred to as ***Microsoft Office XP,*** but individually each application is referred to as version 2002.

Opening multiple applications in Office XP:

1. Click the **Start**  button on the taskbar to display the pop-up menu
2. Move your cursor up the menu and stop on **Programs.** Another menu will appear listing all the programs available on your computer
3. Locate **Microsoft Word** in the program list and click it. After a few seconds you should see a blank document as previously seen in Figure 1.2. Now compare the screen layout with that found in Excel
4. Click the **Start** button, then point to **Programs,** once again

5. This time locate and click **Microsoft Excel** in the program list. After a few seconds you will see a blank workbook, similar to the one found in Figure 1.3

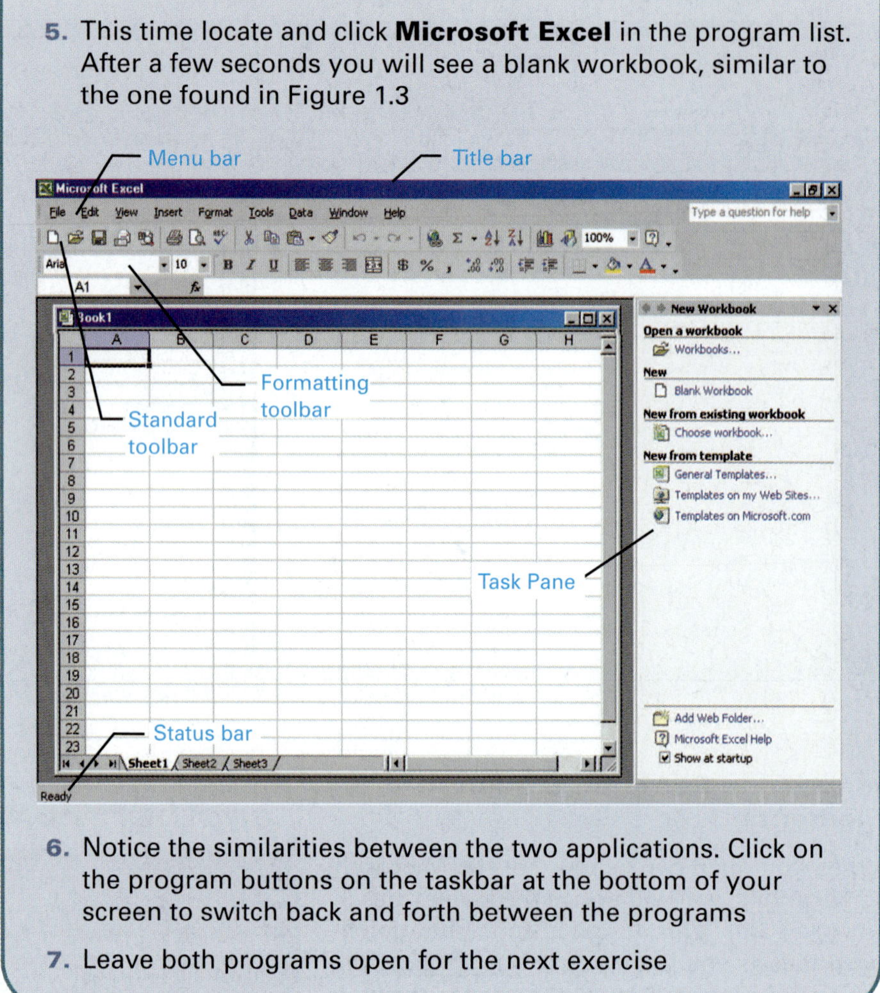

FIGURE 1.3
A blank workbook in Microsoft Excel

6. Notice the similarities between the two applications. Click on the program buttons on the taskbar at the bottom of your screen to switch back and forth between the programs

7. Leave both programs open for the next exercise

anotherway

. . . . to switch between applications

You also can switch between applications by using what is known as the Alt+Tab sequence. Press and hold the **Alt** key, then press **Tab** one time. Let go of both keys when you see the gray box in the middle of your screen displaying program icons. This will allow you to quickly cycle back and forth through any open programs.

Title Bar, Menu Bar, and Toolbars

As you examine the Word and Excel programs, you will notice that each application contains similar elements such as a title bar, a menu bar, a toolbar, and a status bar. The ***title bar*** at the top of each screen displays the application's icon, the title of the document you are working on, and the name of the application program you are using.

The ***menu bar*** displays a list of key menu options available to you for that particular program. In addition to a few program-specific menu items, all of the Office XP applications generally will contain the identical menu options of File, Edit, View, Insert, Tools, Window, and Help. To use these menus, you simply click one time on the desired menu, and a submenu will then appear with additional options.

On the third row of each application is the ***toolbar,*** which is a collection of commonly used shortcut buttons. A single click on a toolbar button activates a program feature that also can be found in one of the menu options. Most office applications will display the ***Standard toolbar,*** which contains the popular icons such as Cut, Copy, and Paste. The table displayed in Figure 1.4 shows a list of these common buttons and their functions.

Another popular toolbar found in Office XP applications is the ***Formatting toolbar,*** which allows you to change the appearance of text,

New		Opens a new blank document, workbook, presentation, or database.
Open		Opens a previously created document, workbook, presentation, or database.
Save		Allows you to quickly save your work. The first time you save, you will be prompted for a file name and location.
E-mail		New to Office XP, this button lets you quickly send the existing document as an email message.
Print		Prints a document.
Cut		Removes selected information from your document and temporarily places it on the Clipboard.
Copy		Duplicates selected information and places it on the Clipboard.
Paste		Copies information on the Clipboard to the current document.
Undo Typing		Reverses the last action or keystroke taken. This is a great safety net for those uh-oh type mistakes!

FIGURE 1.4
Standard toolbar buttons and their function

such as bold, italicize, or underline. There are many toolbars available to display and some will appear as you use certain features in Office applications.

anotherway

. . . to activate a menu option

You also can activate a menu option by using shortcut key strokes. In the menu you will notice that one letter of each option is underlined. These designated letters can be used in conjunction with the Alt key to quickly access a menu task. For example, you can press **Alt+F+S** to save your file.

Task Panes, Clipboard, and Smart Tags

Most of the Office XP applications include a new feature known as the ***Task Pane*** as shown in Figure 1.5. This window allows you to access important tasks from a single, convenient location, while still working on your document. With the Task Pane window you can open files, view your clipboard, perform searches, and much more. By default, when you open an Office XP application, the Task Pane window is displayed to allow the user to open a file. As you select various functions of the application, the contents of the task pane will automatically change. You can close the task pane at any time by clicking on the close button, and redisplay the window by selecting it from the View menu.

One of the options available on the task pane is the ***Clipboard,*** which is a temporary storage location for selected text. In Office XP, you can actually view the contents of up to 24 items that have been cut or copied to the clipboard. This is a very powerful tool that will allow you to collect 24 sets of data and then let you quickly paste those data to a new location or document. When you paste any of the clipboard contents to your document, a Smart Tag button will appear next to the text. This smart tag, known as the ***Paste Options button,*** will prompt the user (when clicked) with additional features such as allowing you to paste with or without the original text formatting. There are additional ***smart tag buttons*** that appear as needed to provide options for completing a task quickly. In this next exercise you will get to practice using the Task Pane, Clipboard, and Paste Options smart tag button.

anotherword

. . . on the Clipboard

It is important to note that the Clipboard contents are available to all applications and not just the original application from where it was extracted.

FIGURE 1.5
Task Pane in Microsoft Word

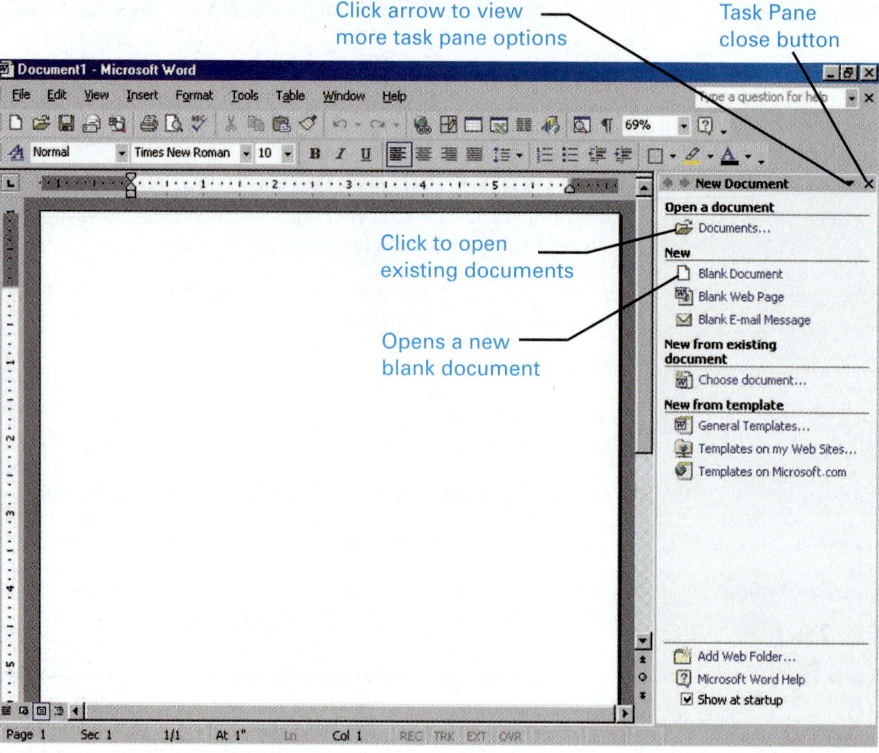

Working with the Task Pane

1. In the Excel application, type **Hello Office XP!** in cell A1 and press **Enter**
2. Click cell A1 and then change the font size of the text to size **22.** Click the **Italic** button on the Formatting toolbar to italicize your text as shown in Figure 1.6
3. Click the **Copy** button on the Standard toolbar. This will copy the contents of cell A1 to the clipboard
4. Press **Alt+Tab** to switch back to the Word program
5. Click the **Paste** button and press **Enter.** The text should appear in the blank document exactly as it was typed and italicized
6. At the top of the Task Pane window, click the **drop-down menu arrow** and select **Clipboard** from the drop-down list. You can now view the Clipboard task pane and the text that was copied to it
7. In the Clipboard Contents task pane, click on the **Hello Office XP!** item as indicated in Figure 1.7. This will paste the text a second time into your document

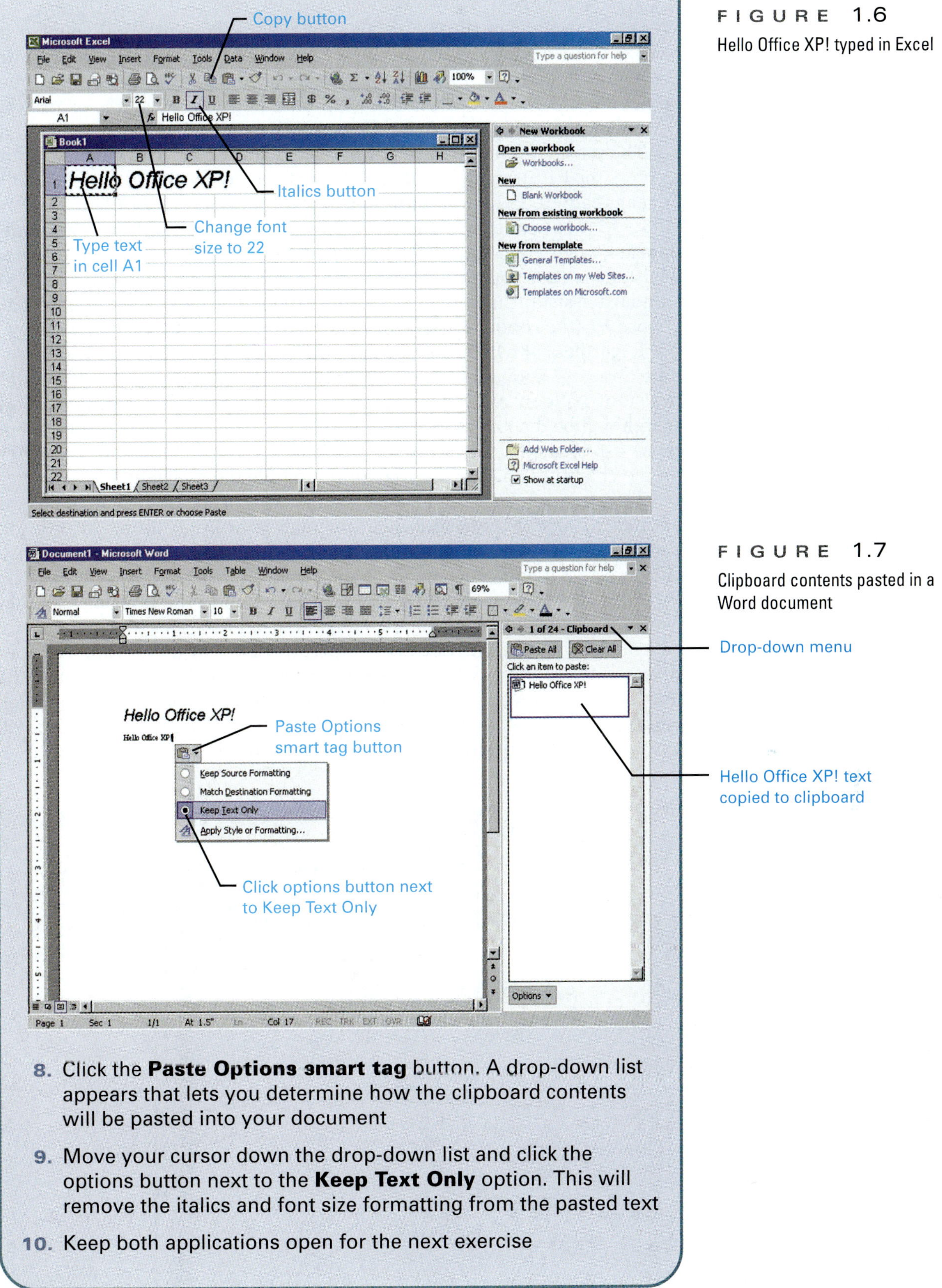

FIGURE 1.6
Hello Office XP! typed in Excel

FIGURE 1.7
Clipboard contents pasted in a Word document

8. Click the **Paste Options smart tag** button. A drop-down list appears that lets you determine how the clipboard contents will be pasted into your document
9. Move your cursor down the drop-down list and click the options button next to the **Keep Text Only** option. This will remove the italics and font size formatting from the pasted text
10. Keep both applications open for the next exercise

Getting Help

When you use any of the Office XP applications, you may find yourself in need of some assistance. There are several ways to obtain help, and fortunately for the user, they are once again consistent across the applications. To get help, the user can use the Help menu option, press F1, or use the Office Assistant, Answer Wizard, or Ask a Question text box.

The most common way of getting help is to use the Help menu option or press the F1 function key. If you do ask for help, an ***Office Assistant*** will appear ready to help you with your question as shown in Figure 1.8. In Office XP applications, the Office Assistant is hidden by default and only appears when Help is activated. One of the fun aspects about the Office Assistant is that you can select your favorite character to help you. The standard assistant is known as ***Clippit*** (the paper clip), but you also can choose ***F1*** (the robot), ***Links*** (the cat), or ***Rocky*** (the dog), among others.

Regardless of which one you use, once you request help and your assistant appears, you must then type in your help question in the Office Assistant balloon and click on the Search button. The results of your search will be displayed in a Help window for you to review or print. For those users who prefer not to use an Office Assistant, you can right-click on the character and choose the option to hide the assistant.

The ***Answer Wizard,*** located in the Microsoft Help dialog box, is another means of requesting help through your application. In order to use the Answer Wizard, you must first hide the Office Assistant and then click on Help menu. Once the Help dialog box is displayed, simply click on the Answer Wizard tab and type in your question in the text box. Another way to get help without using the Office Assistant is to use the new feature called ***Ask a Question.*** Located in the top-right corner of your window, this is perhaps the most convenient method for getting help because the user simply has to key in a search topic in the text box and press enter, without having to launch the Answer Wizard or Office Assistant. You will get to practice requesting help in the next exercise.

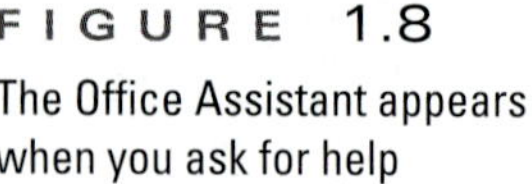

FIGURE 1.8
The Office Assistant appears when you ask for help

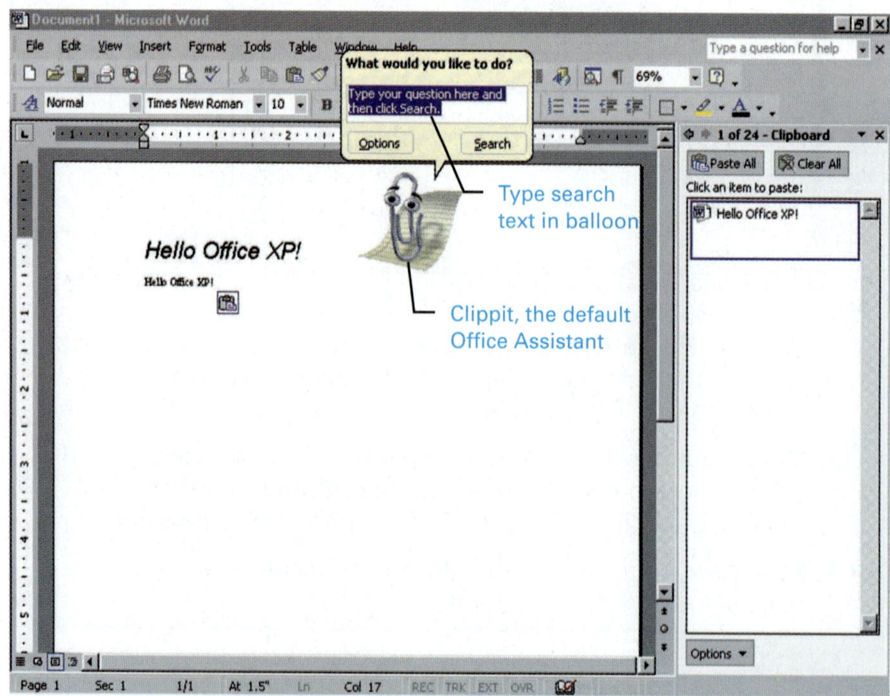

To get help:

1. In your Word document or Excel workbook, press the **F1** function key. This should activate your Office Assistant to the screen

tip: *If the office assistant does not appear, click on the **Help** menu and select **Show the Office Assistant***

2. In the Office Assistant balloon, type **Speech Recognition,** then click the **Search button**
3. In the next balloon that appears, click the **About Speech Recognition** bullet. This will open up the Microsoft Help window with the speech recognition search results as shown in Figure 1.9. Press the **ESC** key on your keyboard to remove the Office Assistant balloon

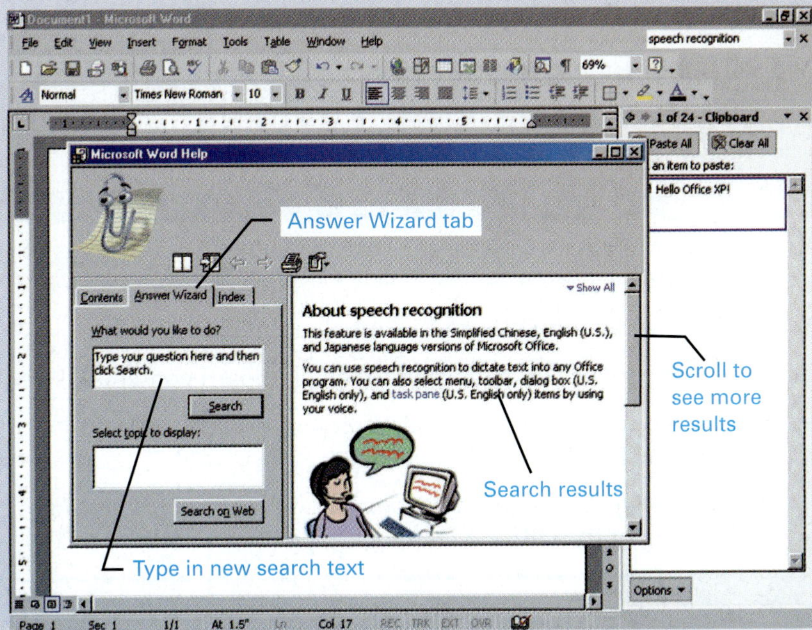

FIGURE 1.9
Results of search displayed in Microsoft help window

4. After looking over your search results, click the **Close** button of the Help window
5. Right-click the **Office Assistant** and, in the menu that pops up, select **Choose Assistant**
6. Click either the **Back** or **Next** button in the Office Assistant dialog box as shown in Figure 1.10 until you find an assistant that you like, and then click **OK**
7. Right-click the **Office Assistant** again, and this time select **Hide.** This will hide the Office Assistant until you request help again
8. **Close** any open documents and programs

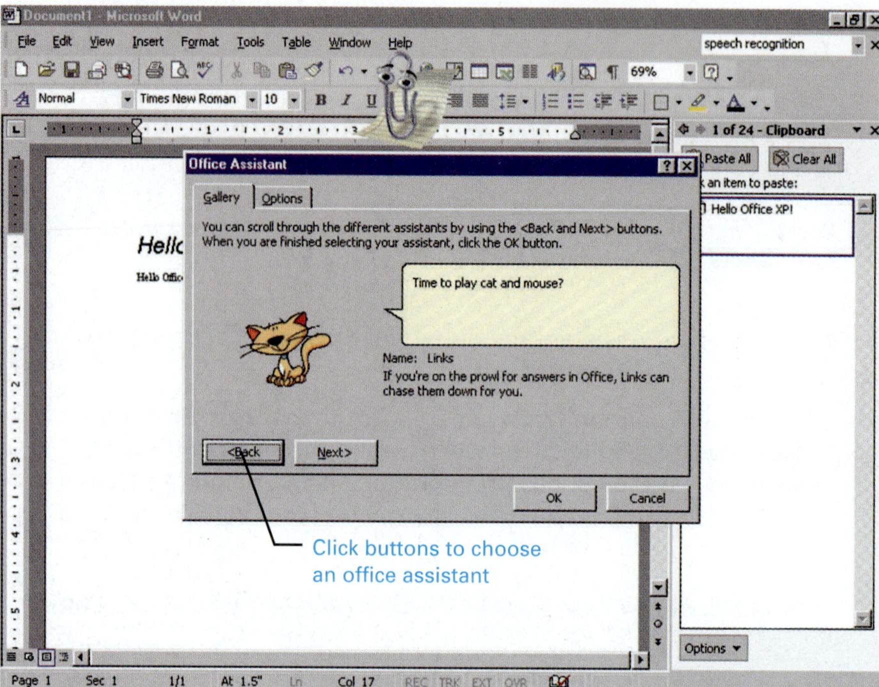

FIGURE 1.10
Office Assistant dialog box

SESSION 1.1

making the grade

1. What four application programs are available in all versions of Office XP?
2. What is the default Office Assistant character?
3. How many items can be posted to the clipboard contents?
4. Which two toolbars are the most frequently used in all applications?
5. What is the quickest and most convenient method for getting help in any of the Office XP applications?

SUMMARY

In this chapter you have been introduced to the common elements of Microsoft's newest integrated application suite, known as Office XP. Regardless of which version of the program you are using, you always will have access to the Word, Excel, PowerPoint, and Outlook applications. As you learn to navigate through these applications, you will notice many similarities that allow the user to easily adapt from one application to the next. These common features include the title bar, the menu bar, and toolbars. You learned that the standard and formatting toolbars are the most commonly used toolbars in Office XP, but that there also are many toolbars available for users to select from or that automatically appear when completing a task.

Through the exercises in this chapter, you learned how to use one of Office XP's newest features, the task pane. This window allows the user quick access to various task sequences such as opening a file, viewing the Clipboard contents, performing a search, and inserting clip art. While the

Clipboard is not new to Microsoft products, it is more powerful in this version because it allows the user to post up to 24 different items in its contents. Finally, when in desperate need of answers, the user can always turn to the many help modes of Office XP. You can use one of the customized Office Assistants such as Clippit, use the Answer Wizard in the Help dialog box, or use the Ask a Question text box to find a quick solution to a problem.

task reference roundup

Task	Page #	Preferred Method
Switch between applications	OFF 1.3	• Press **Alt+Tab**
Copy and Paste using Clipboard task pane	OFF 1.5	• Highlight/select text to be copied
		• Click the **Copy** button on the toolbar
		• Place cursor in desired paste location
		• Click on item in Clipboard task pane to paste
Obtaining Help	OFF 1.8	• Press **F1** or click **Office Assistant**

review of terminology

CROSSWORD PUZZLE

Across

2. The dog Office Assistant
6. Office XP version that consists of Word, Excel, PowerPoint, and Outlook
7. Relational database tool that can be used to collect, organize, and retrieve large amounts of data
8. Is located in the Help dialog box and provides another means of requesting help
10. A popular presentation tool that allows users to create multimedia slide shows
11. Temporary storage location for up to 24 items of selected text that has been cut or copied
13. This window allows you to view clipboard contents in addition to other important tasks
14. A collection of commonly used shortcut buttons

Down

1. Toolbar that allows you to change the appearance of your text
3. The cat office assistant
4. Button that appears when you paste into your document
5. Buttons that appear as needed to provide options for completing a task quickly
9. The paper clip Office Assistant
12. Displays a list of key menu options available to you for that particular program

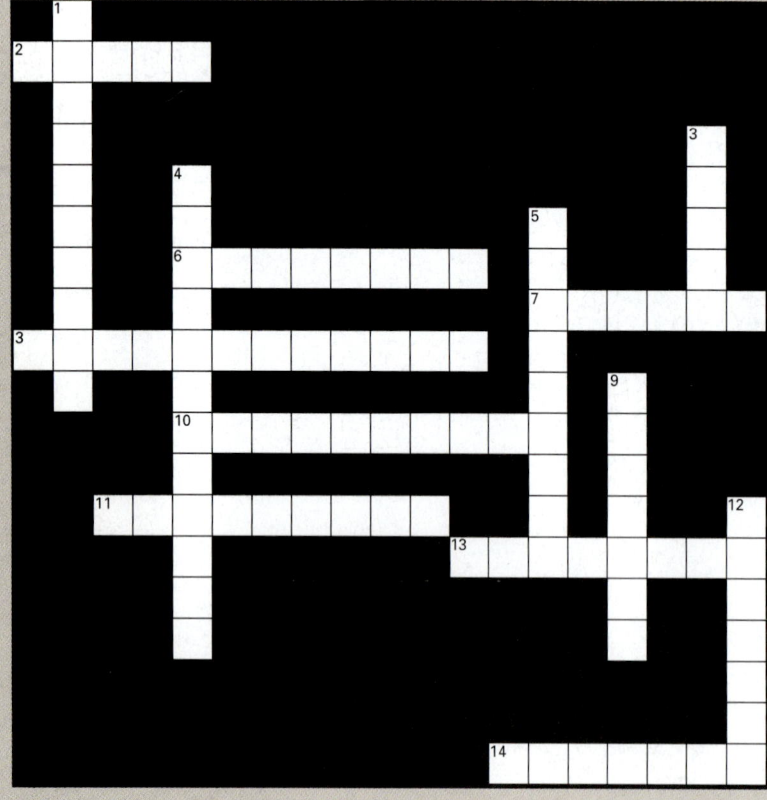

review of concepts

FILL-IN THE BLANKS

1. ___________ is the newest version of the popular Microsoft integrated application suite series.
2. An ___________ is a program that is designed to help you accomplish a particular task, such as creating a slide-show presentation.
3. By default, when you open an Office XP application, the ___________ window is displayed to allow the user to open a file.
4. The standard Office Assistant is known as __________(the paper clip), but you can also choose _________ (the robot), __________ (the Cat), or ___________ (the dog).
5. In Office XP, you can actually view the contents of up to __________ items that have been cut or copied to the clipboard.
6. A single click on a toolbar button activates a program feature that also can be found in one of the ____________ options.
7. Most office applications will display the ___________ toolbar, which contains the popular icons such as Cut, Copy, and Paste.

REVIEW QUESTIONS

1. What are some of the common features found in all Office XP applications?
2. What tools can you use to get help or search for additional information?
3. What is the Task Pane window used for?
4. What are smart tag buttons and when do you have access to them? Give an example of one.
5. What are the four basic applications that are included as part of all versions of Office XP?

MATCHING

Match the term with the related definition.

1. _____ Access 2002
2. _____ Clipboard
3. _____ Excel 2002
4. _____ Formatting toolbar
5. _____ PowerPoint 2002
6. _____ Standard toolbar
7. _____ Task pane
8. _____ Word 2002

a. A temporary storage location for up to 24 items of selected text that has been cut or copied.

b. Collection of buttons that allows you to change the appearance of text, such as bold, italicize, or underline.

c. Collection of buttons that contains the popular icons such as Cut, Copy, and Paste.

d. Electronic spreadsheet tool that can be used to input, organize, calculate, analyze, and display business data.

e. General purpose word-processing tool that allows users to create primarily text-based documents.

f. A popular presentation tool that allows users to create overhead transparencies and powerful multimedia slide shows.

g. Relational database tool that can be used to collect, organize, and retrieve large amounts of data.

h. This window allows you to access important tasks from a single, convenient location, while still working on your document.

NOTES

did you know?

a NUKE *InterNETWORK poll found that 52 percent of Internet users have cut back on watching TV in order to spend more time online; 12 percent have cut back on seeing friends.*

Time *magazine named the computer its "Man of the Year" in 1982.*

dating *back to the 1600s, thermometers were filled with brandy instead of mercury.*

a chip *of silicon a quarter-inch square has the capacity of the original 1949 ENIAC computer, which occupied a full city block.*

Bill Gates *formed a company to sell a computerized traffic counting system to cities, which made $20,000 its first year. Business dropped sharply when customers learned Gates was only 14 years old.*

a 1999 *survey of 25,500 standard English-language dictionary words found that ____ percent of them have been registered as .coms.*

to *find out how many English-language words had been registered as .coms by the middle of 1999, visit www.mhhe.com/i-series.*

Chapter Objectives

In this chapter you will:

- **Learn what relational databases are and how they function**
- **Define the terms field, record, table, and database**
- **Understand the use of primary keys, aggregate keys, and foreign keys**
- **Open Access and identify Access objects—AC2002-1-2**
- **Navigate Access records—AC2002-1-3**
- **Create an Access database using a Wizard—AC2002-1-1**

CHAPTER 1

one

Understanding Relational Databases

chapter case

PuppyParadise

Evan Gibbs is the 15-year-old proprietor of PuppyParadise, the distributor of the PoochPouch. Evan developed the PoochPouch as an entry for the annual school district Invention Convention. He and his miniature Pinscher, Gizmo, displayed the product at the convention and received several orders leading to a feature in the business segment of the local television news.

The PoochPouch is a comfortable sleeping bag for dogs. The bottom of the pouch is a zippered compartment containing pillow foam. The top is a zipper-attached quilt with a snout handle of rigid plastic sewn into the open edge so that the dog can flip it up and crawl in.

Bob Blankenship saw the PoochPouch at the convention and wanted to market it in his mall kiosks across the United States. Evan created the PuppyParadise Web site and subscribed to search engines so that people searching for dog products would hit his site. To launch his product Evan requested $1,000 from his parents for initial production. His parents agreed on the condition that one-half of his proceeds would be used to repay the $1,000 until the debt was cleared.

For the first orders, Evan handwrote the invoices, personally delivered the product, and collected checks on the spot. To project a more professional image, he decided to automate by using Word for invoices and Excel to track profits and expenses. After six months the $1,000 from his parents was completely repaid, but Evan's business requirements were more complicated.

What had started out as a bed for Evan's dog had grown into a complex organization with a need to collect and track data. Evan had stacks of paper relating to orders, fabrics, appliqués,

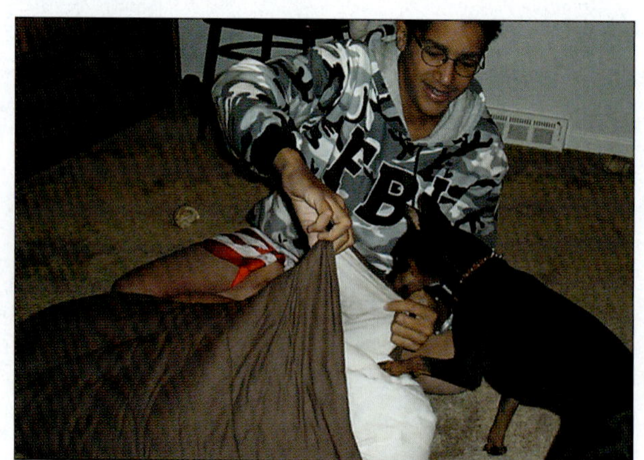

FIGURE 1.1
Evan, Gizmo and the PoochPouch

invoices, vendors, customers, seamstresses, shippers, and dogs. The problem was that finding information needed to make a business decision was onerous. Something as simple as determining how much of a particular fabric to procure based on customer order history took hours of manual searching and computation.

It is obvious to Evan that he needs the data organization and reporting capabilities of a database, but he has no experience in this area. He asks you to help him determine how best to automate data gathering and evaluation. PuppyParadise will be used throughout this book to demonstrate the data needs of an entrepreneurial business and the use of Access to develop effective data applications.

CHAPTER OUTLINE

SESSION 1.1 INTRODUCING RELATIONAL DATABASES

Before evaluating the specific needs of PuppyParadise, you decide to review your knowledge of databases. Because relational databases are the most efficient way to store and manipulate data, you will focus your research on those concepts.

USES AND BENEFITS OF RELATIONAL DATABASES

All organizations maintain and use data for day-to-day business operations, history, and performance analysis. Data are stored about members of the organization (employees, customers), products of the organization (services, goods), suppliers (vendors, consultants), and transactions (sales, purchases). The data maintained are determined by the needs of the organization. Schools keep data on employees, students, and business operations such as ordering products and paying for products and services.

Data are a valuable organizational resource. Good data and information retrieval technology can improve the organization's ability to compete in an industry, deliver products to consumers, and evaluate opportunities. The loss or contamination of an organization's data can contribute to failure.

A ***database management system (DBMS)*** is the software that is used to store data, maintain those data, and provide easy access to stored data. Good DBMSs provide users with

- Common interfaces to share data
- Software tools needed to design the storage area for data
- Facilities to maintain stored data
- Tools to create screens (forms) used to view and update data
- Query services to obtain fast answers to questions about the data
- Report generation capabilities
- Utilities to secure, back up, and restore data

Relational database management systems (RDBMSs) are a type of DBMS that store data in interrelated tables. Tables are related by sharing a common field as shown in Figure 1.2. The tblVendor and tblSoftware tables share the common field VendorCode. If you select a product like Number Crunch from tblSoftware, the VendorCode from that table can be matched to the VendorCode in tblVendor to retrieve data about Edusoft Inc., the Number Crunch vendor.

RDBMSs are flexible, reliable, and efficient because they use data storage and retrieval methodology based on mathematics. ***Data integrity*** is the term used to describe the reliability of data. Data stored in a relational database are more likely to be correct because

- They are validated as they are entered using ***data validation rules*** to ensure that entries are within appropriate bounds
- A specific piece of data such as customer name is stored only once—thereby avoiding the errors that could be introduced by making the same update to several files. Having one update point is said to reduce ***data redundancy***
- Database security ensures that only authorized people can access and update data

RELATIONAL DATABASE CONCEPTS

In the computing world where software becomes obsolete almost before it can be implemented, relational database technology is relatively old and stable. Relational database theory was developed by E. F. Codd, a researcher at IBM in the 1960s. The first RDBMS was released in the mid 1970s for IBM mainframes. Since then RDBMS software has been developed for every size computer and operating system. Better implementations and graphical user interfaces (GUIs) have been produced, but the basic technology remains the same.

FIGURE 1.2
Using related tables

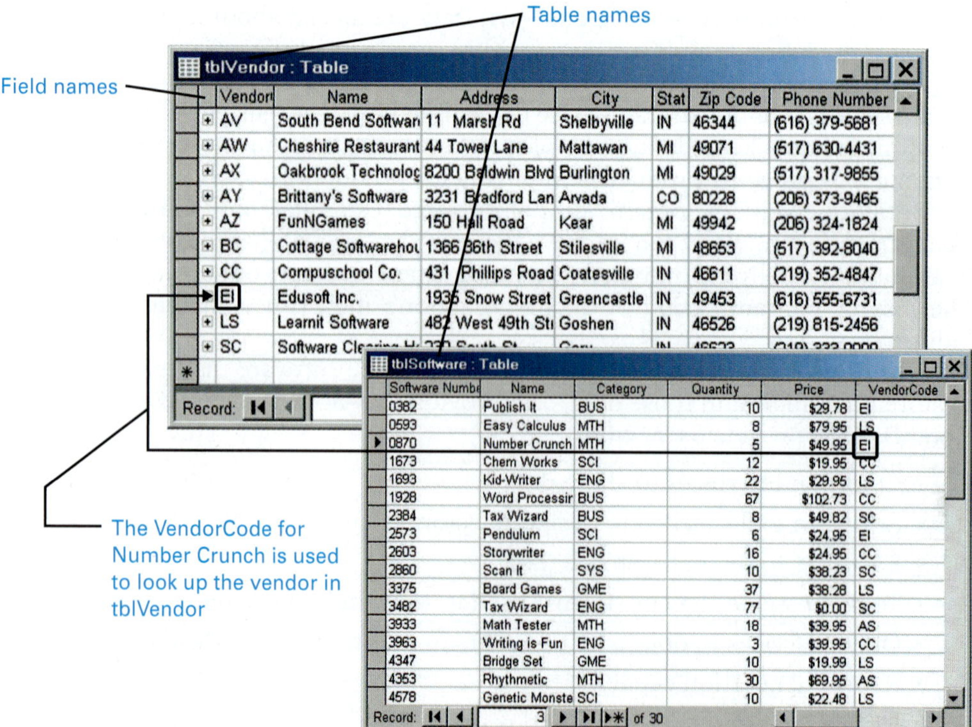
Table names
Field names
The VendorCode for Number Crunch is used to look up the vendor in tblVendor

tblVendor : Table

Vendor	Name	Address	City	Stat	Zip Code	Phone Number
AV	South Bend Softwar	11 Marsh Rd	Shelbyville	IN	46344	(616) 379-5681
AW	Cheshire Restaurant	44 Tower Lane	Mattawan	MI	49071	(517) 630-4431
AX	Oakbrook Technolog	8200 Baldwin Blvd	Burlington	MI	49029	(517) 317-9855
AY	Brittany's Software	3231 Bradford Lan	Arvada	CO	80228	(206) 373-9465
AZ	FunNGames	150 Hall Road	Kear	MI	49942	(206) 324-1824
BC	Cottage Softwarehou	1366 36th Street	Stilesville	MI	48653	(517) 392-8040
CC	Compuschool Co.	431 Phillips Road	Coatesville	IN	46611	(219) 352-4847
EI	Edusoft Inc.	1935 Snow Street	Greencastle	IN	49453	(616) 555-6731
LS	Learnit Software	482 West 49th Str	Goshen	IN	46526	(219) 815-2456
SC	Software Cle					

Record:

tblSoftware : Table

Software Numbe	Name	Category	Quantity	Price	VendorCode
0382	Publish It	BUS	10	$29.78	EI
0593	Easy Calculus	MTH	8	$79.95	LS
0870	Number Crunch	MTH	5	$49.95	EI
1673	Chem Works	SCI	12	$19.95	CC
1693	Kid-Writer	ENG	22	$29.95	LS
1928	Word Processir	BUS	67	$102.73	CC
2384	Tax Wizard	BUS	8	$49.82	SC
2573	Pendulum	SCI	6	$24.95	EI
2603	Storywriter	ENG	16	$24.95	CC
2860	Scan It	SYS	10	$38.23	SC
3375	Board Games	GME	37	$38.28	LS
3482	Tax Wizard	ENG	77	$0.00	SC
3933	Math Tester	MTH	18	$39.95	AS
3963	Writing is Fun	ENG	3	$39.95	CC
4347	Bridge Set	GME	10	$19.99	LS
4353	Rhythmetic	MTH	30	$69.95	AS
4578	Genetic Monste	SCI	10	$22.48	LS

Record: 3 of 30

RDBMSs provide a ***data definition language (DDL)*** for structuring the data tables and their relationships and a ***data access language (DAL)*** for rapidly retrieving and organizing stored data. Questions or queries are posed to a relational database using ***structured query language (SQL).*** Most database management software, including Access, provide graphical interfaces that allow users to create tables, queries, forms, and reports without knowing the underlying language.

Relations

As previously demonstrated, relational databases store data in tables. The formal name for a table is a relation. A relation (table) consists of rows and columns of related data. Each row represents the unique data for one ***entity*** (person, place, object, idea, or event) and also can be referred to as a ***record*** or tuple. Each column represents a unique property of an entity such as LastName, BirthDate, or Quantity and also can be referred to as a ***field*** or attribute. The intersection of a row and column contains data pertaining to one attribute of one entity and is called a ***data value.*** For example, $39.95 is the Price (attribute) associated with SoftwareNum 3963 (entity identifier) in Figure 1.3. A ***relational database*** is a collection of such relations.

All entries in the table for one attribute belong to the same ***domain.*** The domain is the list of all possible values of an attribute. For example, the list of all Software Names is the domain for the Name attribute in tblSoftware.

Since each cell in a table represents the value for one entity and one attribute, the order in which the columns and rows are stored is irrelevant. You can view columns and rows in any order without impacting the validity of the data. The only restriction is that a column contains only one data value and a row represents the data for one entity.

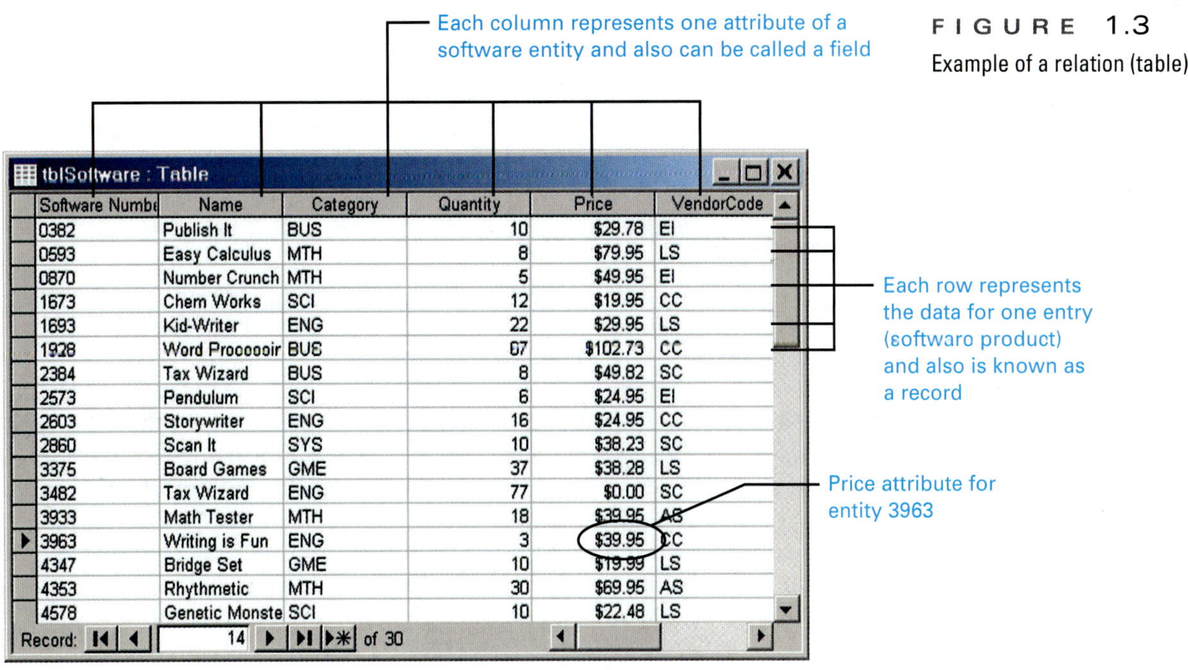
tblSoftware : Table

Software Numbe	Name	Category	Quantity	Price	VendorCode
0382	Publish It	BUS	10	$29.78	EI
0593	Easy Calculus	MTH	8	$79.95	LS
0870	Number Crunch	MTH	5	$49.95	EI
1673	Chem Works	SCI	12	$19.95	CC
1693	Kid-Writer	ENG	22	$29.95	LS
1928	Word Processoir	BUS	67	$102.73	CC
2384	Tax Wizard	BUS	8	$49.82	SC
2573	Pendulum	SCI	6	$24.95	EI
2603	Storywriter	ENG	16	$24.95	CC
2860	Scan It	SYS	10	$38.23	SC
3375	Board Games	GME	37	$38.28	LS
3482	Tax Wizard	ENG	77	$0.00	SC
3933	Math Tester	MTH	18	$39.95	AS
3963	Writing is Fun	ENG	3	$39.95	CC
4347	Bridge Set	GME	10	$19.99	LS
4353	Rhythmetic	MTH	30	$69.95	AS
4578	Genetic Monste	SCI	10	$22.48	LS

Record: 14 of 30

Each column represents one attribute of a software entity and also can be called a field
Each row represents the data for one entry (software product) and also is known as a record
Price attribute for entity 3963

FIGURE 1.3
Example of a relation (table)

Keys

Keys are table attributes that perform a special function in the relation. The ***primary key*** uniquely and minimally identifies an entity with one and only one row of data. In tblSoftware above, the field Software Number holds a unique value for each software company, identifying each as a distinct entity in the table. A primary key can identify one and only one row in the table. An error message will be generated and the update aborted by the RDBMS if a duplicate primary key is entered. To meet the minimal requirement of the primary key definition, the key must contain no unnecessary data. For example, the Software Number and Name fields could be used in combination to uniquely identify each row of data in tblSoftware; however, the combination does not meet the minimal test because Software Number alone is a unique identifier.

Sometimes there is no one attribute (column) in a table with values that can uniquely identify each row of data. In such cases the designer looks for a combination of attributes that can act as the table primary key. When multiple columns of data are used for the primary key, the result is a ***composite key.*** As an example, a composite key is advisable when storing data about U.S. cities. The city name alone is not sufficient since multiple U.S. cities carry the same name (for example, Bloomington, IN, and Bloomington, IL). In this case, both the city and state columns would be required for a unique key.

In many instances, there are multiple attributes in the table that each could serve as the primary key of that table. Each attribute that could be defined as the primary key is called a ***candidate key.*** One of the candidate keys is assigned as the primary key and the others are called ***alternate keys.*** In tblSoftware Software Number and Name each uniquely and minimally identifies one row in the table and is therefore a candidate key. Software Number was named the primary key, so Name remains an alternate key.

A ***foreign key*** is used to match the values from one table to those in another table. VendorCode in tblSoftware is a foreign key that matches values in the tblVendor VendorCode attribute. In tblVendor VendorCode is the primary key. Most designers will give the same name to attributes stored in multiple tables so it is obvious that they are really the same attribute.

Because there are so many types of keys, the word *key* used alone can seem ambiguous, but it is not. When the word *key* is used without identifying the type of key (i.e., foreign key), it always means the primary key.

Relationships

When a foreign key from a table is used to link to the data in another table, it is called ***joining.*** Join relationships take one of the three forms discussed in the following paragraphs.

One-to-one (abbreviated 1:1) relationships exist when one row of the first table matches to one and only one row of the second table and both tables have the same primary key. One-to-one relationships are very rare because such closely related data would normally be stored in a single table. When table requirements exceed Access's limit of 255 columns per table, two tables with a one-to-one relationship are created to hold all of the data. Security and privacy issues also can cause closely related data to be stored in multiple tables. For example, in the medical community some

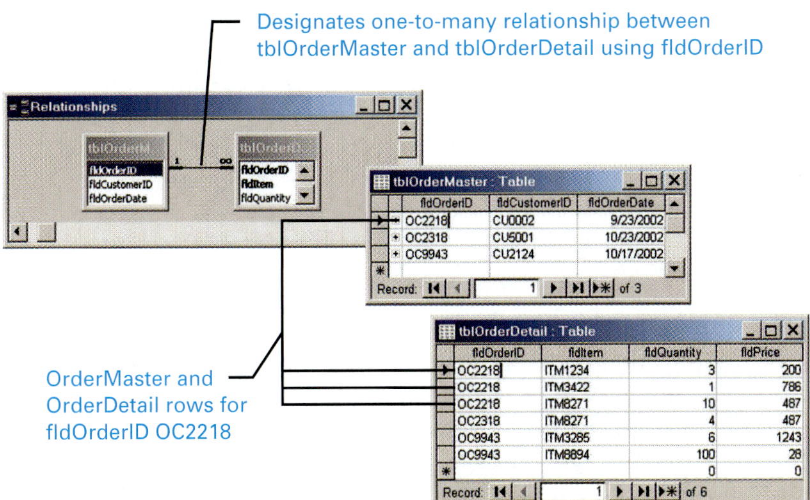

FIGURE 1.4

Orders database demonstrating one-to-many relationship

patient data must be reported and some must be held private. Even though all of the data are for patients, it makes sense to store the private data in a separate table and use a one-to-one relationship to join it with the more public data.

One-to-many (abbreviated 1:M or 1:∞) relationships exist when one row of the first table matches to multiple rows in the second table. One-to-many relationships are the most common. Figure 1.4 shows the tables needed to keep order information for a small business like PuppyParadise. The tblOrderMaster is used to store the static or header information of the order (**fldOrderID,** fldCustomerID, and fldOrderDate). fldOrderID is bolded in the list because it is unique for each order and has been set as the primary key. The tblOrderDetail stores information about each item that has been ordered (**fldOrderID, fldItem,** fldQuantity, fldPrice). tblOrderDetail uses a composite key of fldOrderID and fldItem since each order should contain one row per item being ordered.

Many-to-many (abbreviated M:N or ∞:∞) relationships exist when one row in the first table matches with multiple rows in the second table and one row in the second table matches with multiple rows in the first table. Many-to-many relationships can't be directly modeled in relational databases but are broken into multiple one-to-many relationships.

Relational Database Objects

In general an object is a reusable template or structure that will speed development. Relational database objects assist in developing the components for the database. All RDBMSs support table, query, report, form, index, and stored procedure objects. The ***database*** file is a container that organizes the tables, queries, forms, reports, and other objects.

The ***table*** object is the fundamental structure of a relational database management system. The function of a table object is to store data about a category of things such as employees in records (rows) and fields (columns).

The ***query*** object will allow you to formulate a question about the data stored in your tables, or a request to perform an action on the data and store it as a reusable object. A query can bring together data from multiple tables to serve as the source of data for a form, report, or data access page.

The ***form*** object allows you to create a custom interface for taking actions or for entering, displaying, and editing data in fields. A typical form, like the one in Figure 1.5, displays one row of data from a table in contrast to the default table grid that displays several rows of data.

A ***report*** object prints information formatted and organized according to your specifications. Examples of reports are sales summaries, phone lists, and mailing labels.

Indexing

When storing more than a few records in a table, it is important to optimize the table so that data can be efficiently retrieved. Conceptually, storing and accessing data in tables are straight forward, but scanning tables for values or sorting the rows for output can be very inefficient. Consider looking for a specific topic in this book like *Saving Access as HTML.* One approach would be to scan the pages of this book until you found the topic. A second approach would be to find the topic in the index and then proceed to the correct page(s). In the vast majority of searches, the index approach would provide the fastest and most complete results.

Table ***indexes*** can be applied to improve table search performance and are similar in function to the index of a book. A table index tracks where the rows for a particular value are stored in the table so that the values can be accessed without scanning through the entire table. When you have a primary key, a unique index is automatically defined for the key values. Any other fields that are frequently used to search for values or sort data are also candidates for indexing. Figure 1.6 shows the fields and indexes

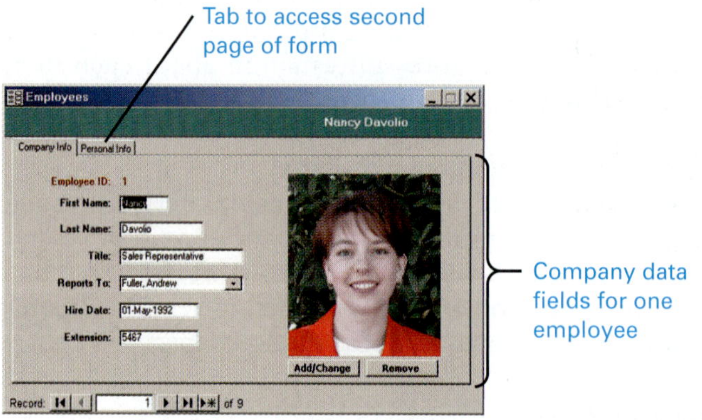

FIGURE 1.5
Tabbed form from the northwind sample database

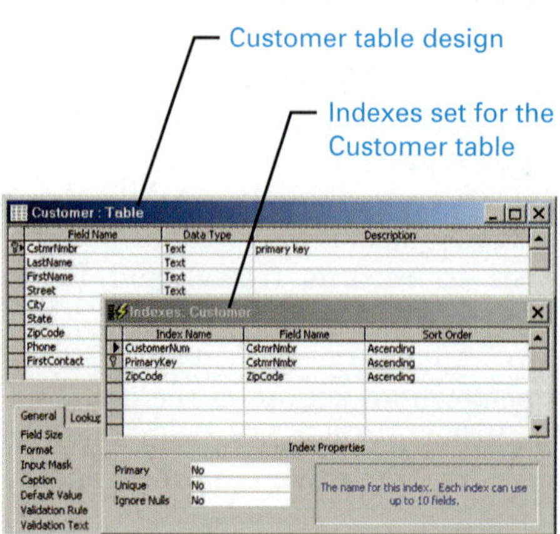

FIGURE 1.6
Indexes for the customer table

for a Customer table. Notice that indexes have been set for the PrimaryKey (CustomerNum) and ZipCode because both fields are frequently used to sort and retrieve data.

Indexes are automatically updated as table data are added or changed. There are no restrictions on the number of indexes applied to a table. Indexes can be added and deleted as they are needed using table Design view.

DATABASE MANAGEMENT SYSTEMS

Database management systems are the various software products that allow organizations to store data in a central location using a standard format. While we are concentrating on the relational database model that stores data in tables, it is important to understand where the relational model fits in the overall data storage scheme. There are also hierarchical, network, and object-oriented models for database management systems.

DBMS Models

Hierarchical and network database management system models are older and more restricted than the relational model. Both the hierarchical and network models depend on predefined data relationships, while the relational database model allows new relationships to be defined at any time. There are, however, situations where users have fixed storage and reporting requirements where the older models will outperform relational databases.

Evolving user needs and emerging technologies have given rise to object-oriented DBMS models. In addition to handling conventional rows and columns of data, an object-oriented database will store documents, diagrams, graphics, multimedia, and more. In an object-oriented database, each item stored is an ***object.*** An object is virtually anything—traditional data, a moving image, people talking, a photograph, narrative, text, music, or any combination. Objects can be accessed individually or in combination. For example a graphic and a voice recording each could be a stored object in a database. These objects could be accessed individually or combined into a new object comprised of both the graphic and sound. Regardless of what is stored and how it will be used, the idea is to have a natural-looking way to interact with all types of data.

No leader has emerged in object-oriented database technology, and most current implementations are actually object-relational databases. An object relational DBMS is a relational database that can store other objects such as graphics, video, audio, methods, and procedures describing how the objects will behave.

There are a wide variety of products that can be used to manage object-relational data access. Each product has strengths and weaknesses that should be understood before using the product. A few RDBMSs that, to one extent or another, can store objects are

- Microsoft Access—widely used on personal computers
- Microsoft SQL Server—used to share data on Microsoft NT networks
- Oracle—most popular web-commerce database
- DB2—IBM mini and mainframe data storage software

Client/Server DBMS

Besides looking at the model used to store the data, DBMSs can be divided into two basic categories: ***personal databases*** and ***client/server databases.*** Many of the same concepts apply to both DBMS categories. The differences lie largely in the amount of data that can be stored, the number of concurrent users supported, networking capabilities, and the level of data security provided.

Personal database management systems like Microsoft Access work best in single-user environments. The ideal environment is one user updating and reporting on the data from one PC. Although personal database management systems can be networked and shared, the general rule-of-thumb is that there should be no more than 10 concurrent users. If security, network traffic, or the ability to recover from system failures is important, a client/server DBMS would be a better choice.

Client/server DBMSs are designed to support multiple users in a networked environment. Powerful servers store and process large quantities of organizational data, while client PCs can request data from the server and then query, update, and report on it locally. A typical client/server application has a front end like Microsoft Access that runs on the local client workstation and a back end like Microsoft SQL Server that runs on the server. In these implementations, the front end provides the local user interface on a PC, while the back end has the power to store and process data from multiple users on a network server.

For example, the client (you at your PC) could request a listing of August computer sales. The server database holds the information for all organizational sales and must run a query to retrieve August computer sales, which it then passes to the requesting client (your computer). You now have a local copy of August computer sales that you can use your local client software to manipulate. Depending on the application, you might make changes to the local data and then the client could send updates to the server that are then applied to the organizational database.

Client/server applications are cost effective and scalable. They also can take advantage of common PC software like Microsoft Access on the client, making them easy for users to learn and use. On the down side, shared data are never as secure as centralized data stored on a mainframe.

OPENING AN ACCESS DATABASE

Access software can be opened from the Start menu or by opening an Access document directly. When an Access database file is double-clicked, Access is launched and then the database is loaded in one step.

Starting Access and opening a blank database:

1. Verify that Windows has loaded and is ready to launch programs
2. Click the **Start** button on the Windows taskbar and then pause over **Programs** to list the programs available on your computer
3. Select **Microsoft Access** to launch Access

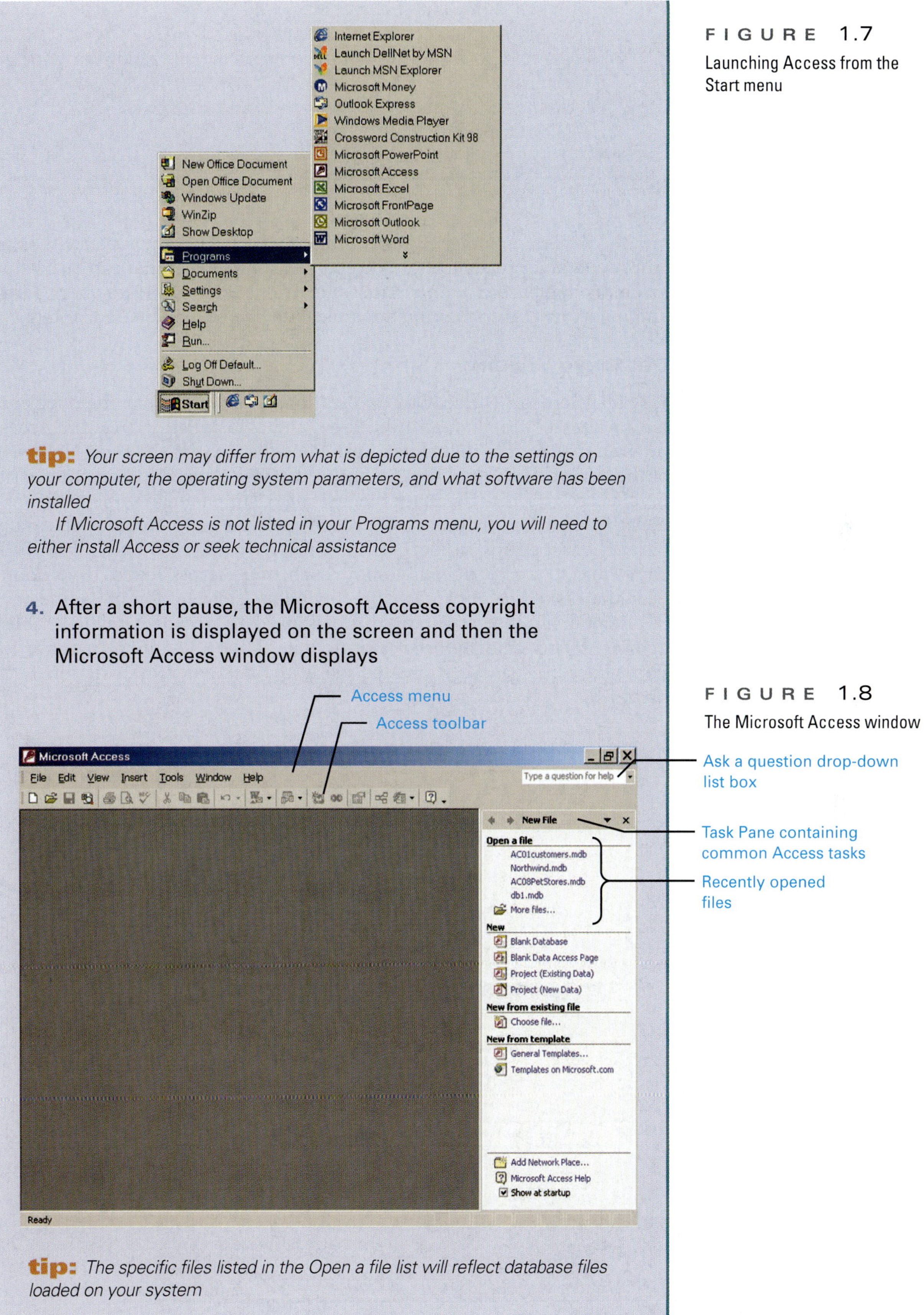

FIGURE 1.7
Launching Access from the Start menu

tip: *Your screen may differ from what is depicted due to the settings on your computer, the operating system parameters, and what software has been installed*

If Microsoft Access is not listed in your Programs menu, you will need to either install Access or seek technical assistance

4. After a short pause, the Microsoft Access copyright information is displayed on the screen and then the Microsoft Access window displays

FIGURE 1.8
The Microsoft Access window

tip: *The specific files listed in the Open a file list will reflect database files loaded on your system*

5. In the Task Pane, click **Blank Database**
   a. Use the Save in drop-down list to select a location for your database
   b. Change the default file name to **Blank.mdb**
   c. Click **Create**

The Access database, Blank.mdb, created in the previous steps is an empty container ready to store objects. The only object that can be built in an empty database is a table. After at least one table is added, query, form, and report objects to manipulate table data can be created and stored.

Database Window

Like all Microsoft Office 2002 applications, the Access opening page contains a menu, a toolbar, an Edit Pane, and a Task Pane. Once the Access program has been initiated, the Task Pane displays on the right-hand side of the screen. The initial file options in the Task Pane are to open an existing file, create a new database file, use an existing database file to create a new database, or use one of Microsoft's templates to create a new database. The last option in the Task Pane is a check box that will turn off the Task Pane so that it does not show each time Access loads. If you don't need the Task Pane, it can be closed using the close button in its title bar.

Remember that a database file is used to organize related tables, queries, forms, and reports. A prototype of the Customer database for PuppyParadise has been created using the customer information Evan provided.

Opening the Customer database:

1. Make sure that the data files for this course are in the proper drive and that Access is already open. Instructions for creating the data disk can be found at www.mhhe.com/i-series
2. Click **View,** pause over **Toolbars,** and click **Task Pane**

FIGURE 1.9
Microsoft Access open dialog box

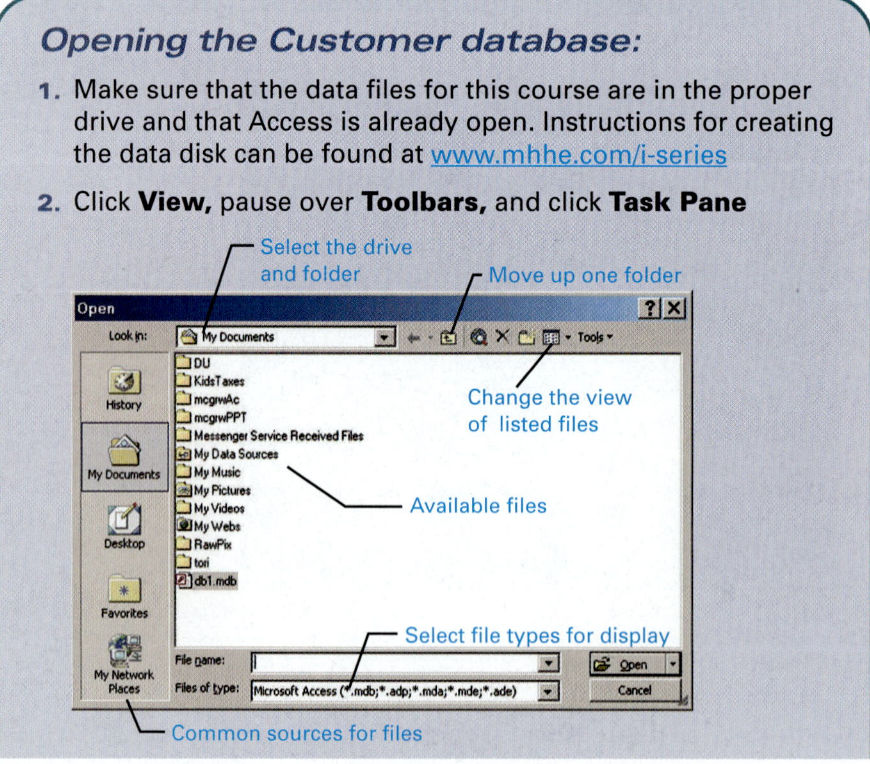

3. If the **AC01customers.mdb** database displays in the Task Pane, select it and skip to step 5
4. If the AC01customer.mdb database does not display, click the **More files** option in the Task Pane to display a standard Open file dialog box

tip: *The Open dialog box will display the files from My Documents on your computer, so the files and folders displayed will be different on each computer*

5. Click the **Look in** drop-down arrow and select the drive containing your data disk. Open the folder for Chapter 1 and select the **AC01customers.mdb** file
6. Once the file is selected, click **Open** to load the database into Access

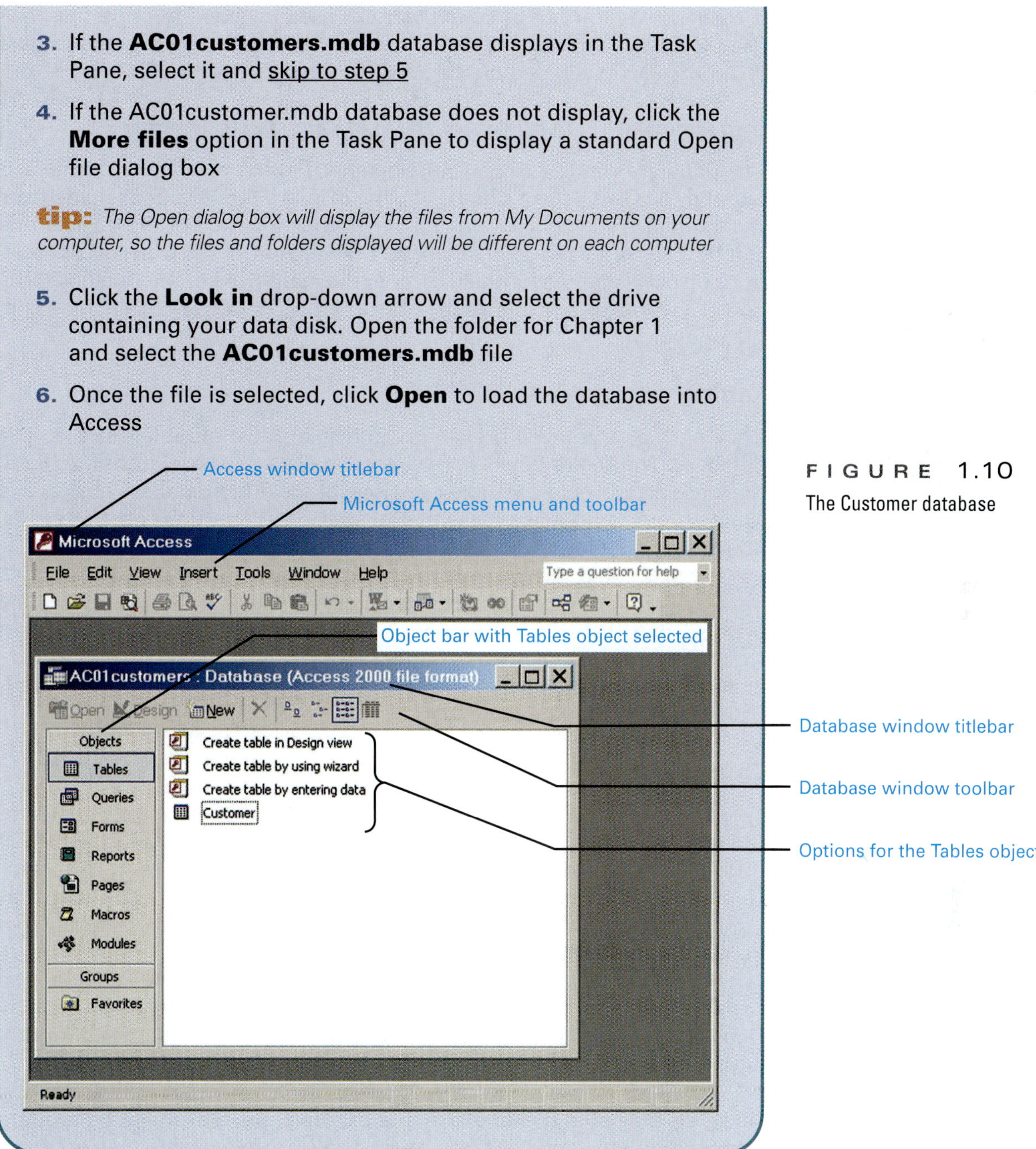

FIGURE 1.10
The Customer database

Windows and Toolbars

The Microsoft Access user interface consists of a series of windows that display inside the main ***Access window.*** As you can see in Figure 1.10, when a database is open, it displays in its own window called the ***Database window.*** Tasks that are common to all Access operations reside on the Access window, while those specific to a database are accomplished from the Database window. Other windows will be discussed as we explore more features of Access.

Each open window has a toolbar with operations that are relevant to the functions of that window. For example, the toolbar in the Database window contains options for opening and creating database tables while

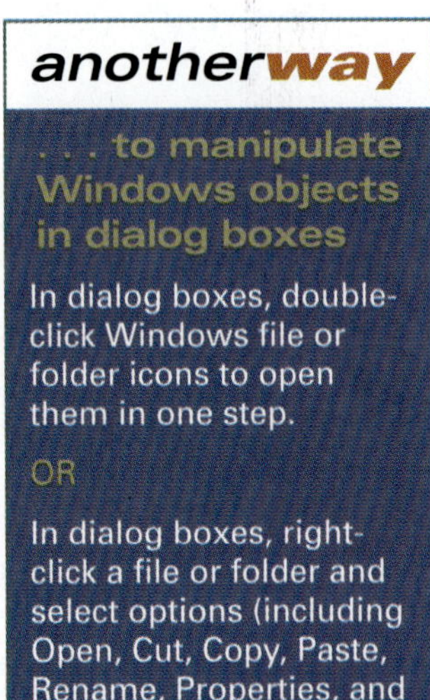
anotherway

. . . to manipulate Windows objects in dialog boxes

In dialog boxes, double-click Windows file or folder icons to open them in one step.

OR

In dialog boxes, right-click a file or folder and select options (including Open, Cut, Copy, Paste, Rename, Properties, and more) from the shortcut menu.

the Access window has common features used to open files, save files, and use the Office clipboard. The toolbar in the Access window enables and disables selections based on the needs of the active window.

IDENTIFYING ACCESS DATABASE OBJECTS

The Database window is made up of panes. The left pane holds the Objects bar and the Groups bar. The right pane displays the selections made from the left pane. The ***Objects bar*** displays icons for each of the objects that can be created for the open database. Clicking one of the Objects bar selections displays options for that object in the main pane of the Database window. The ***Groups bar*** allows the user to group database objects for easier manipulation.

Tables

Clicking Tables in the Objects bar will display a list of tables for the open database. The Tables object is the backbone of a database, meaning that if there are no tables in the database, none of the other database objects can function. It should make sense that to query (ask questions of) a table, the table and its data must already exist.

For relational databases, tables are designed using a process called normalization, their structures are defined during the table creation process, and then data are entered. Notice in Figure 1.11 that the first three options presented when the Tables object is selected are tools used to create new tables in the database. Each table that has already been built is listed below the Create table tools.

Queries

Selecting Queries from the Objects bar will display valid query options for the open database. Queries are used to view, change, and analyze data in different ways. They also can be used to select and sort data for forms, reports, and data access pages. Access provides both QBE (Query by Example) and SQL (Structured Query Language) interfaces. Several types of queries are available in Microsoft Access.

Select queries are the most common and are used to retrieve data from one or more tables. Select queries also can perform simple calculations and organize the data. Selected data can be updated or used for other processes like reporting.

Parameter queries prompt the user for criteria that will be used in selecting data from the database. For example, the user might be prompted for two dates and then the query would display sales that occurred between the dates entered.

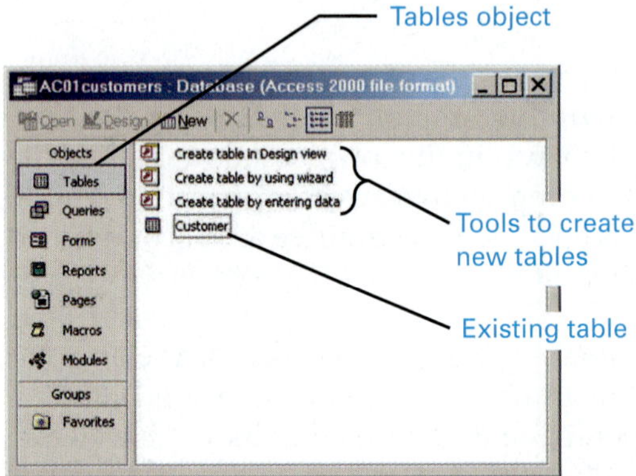

FIGURE 1.11
Selecting the tables object

Crosstab queries are used to analyze data. They group data and calculate values for each group. If you have worked with Excel, it is very similar to crosstab reporting in that application.

Action queries update the data in a database in some fashion. Action queries can be used to delete a group of records that meet a criterion, to update a group of records, to add records to an existing table, or to add records to a new table. Action queries are very powerful and are most effective when used to update or move large quantities of data. For example, suppose that your database was very large. To improve performance, you decide to move data for customers who have not purchased anything in the last year to an inactive table. You could review and move records manually or use an Action query with criteria for inactive accounts to select the records and move them to the inactive table in a single operation.

Forms

A form is a database object used primarily to enter and display database data. Forms also can be used to create a user interface for a database. Forms that create a user interface are called switchboards. A switchboard would contain options to open the tables, queries, forms, reports, and other objects of the database (see Figure 1.12). A dialog box is also a form that accepts user input and carries out an action based on the input. All forms are used to make it easier for a user to interact with the database.

Reports

The Reports object is used to display database data in print. Reports can be as simple as mailing labels or contain complex formatting and graphics. Normally a report is based on the result of a query. Using a query to select the data ensures that the report contains only the desired rows and columns.

Once the data are selected, the report design specifies how those data will be displayed. The design includes specifications for the report title, sort order, and grouping and summarizing of data. Expressions can be used to create calculations based on data values. For example, if you were creating a sales report, you might want subtotals for the sales by month or by department.

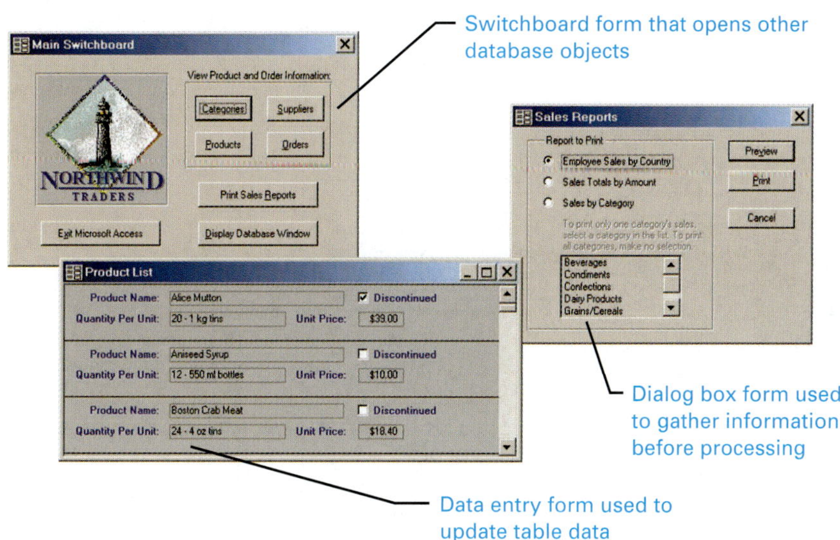

FIGURE 1.12
Examples of forms—switchboard, input, and dialog box

Pages

The Microsoft Access Pages object supports the creation and deployment of Web pages. There are three types of Web pages that are related to data in a database. How the data will be used determines which type of page should be created.

Data access pages allow a Web browser to be used to view and update table data. A data access page has a live connection to the data in your database. It can be used on an intranet or published to the Internet using DHTML (Dynamic HTML) technology.

An ***Active Server Page (ASP)*** is designed to display up-to-date read-only data. The data are selected by the server and displayed in a table format. Opening or refreshing an ASP file from a Web browser causes the page to be dynamically created from current values and sent to the browser.

Finally, ***static HTML*** pages can be used to publish a snapshot of the data. Static pages can be based on tables, queries, forms, or reports. Each object will display in a format consistent with its on-screen appearance. No user action can cause a static page to update. If the data change, you must update the HTML pages and post them to the Web again. HTML template files can be used to create a consistent publishing format for static pages.

Macros

Macros are used to automate repetitive database tasks. The basic building block of a macro is an action: a self-contained instruction or command like Open Table. Actions are selected from a drop-down list box (see Figure 1.13) and include options for manipulating tables, queries, reports, and forms.

Modules

Modules are used to customize the way tables, forms, reports, and queries in your database look and function. Modules are written in Visual Basic (VB), a programming language used to develop Windows applications. A ***module*** is a collection of Visual Basic statements and procedures that are organized and stored together to be accessed as a unit. You can create simple event procedures that are initiated by a user action such as clicking or double-clicking. Complex custom functionality also can be added with a solid understanding of programming concepts.

FIGURE 1.13
The Macro window

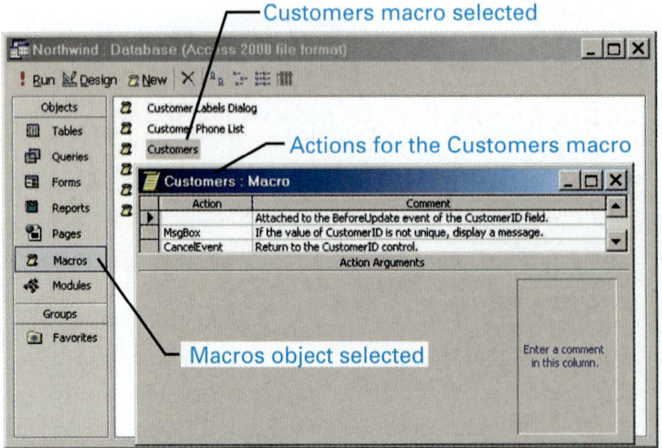

making the grade

1. RDBMS is an acronym for ________.
2. SQL (Structured Query Language) is ________.
3. Tables are joined using a shared ________.
4. A table attribute that uniquely and minimally identifies each row in the table is called a(n) ________.
5. Go back and review the PuppyParadise case at the beginning of this chapter. Considering Evan's business needs, create a list of data attributes (fields) that PuppyParadise would need to store about its customers.

SESSION 1.2 INTRODUCING MICROSOFT ACCESS

Now that you have reviewed your understanding of database management systems and opened Access, it is time to introduce Evan to Access and begin to formulate a plan for PuppyParadise. Since PuppyParadise has some standard business needs like storing customer data, it makes sense to look at customer tables first.

OPENING AN EXISTING TABLE

Tables are the central objects of a database. They store the data on which all other Access objects operate. To view or update table data, the table must be opened.

Viewing Table Data

Since relational databases store data in tables, the default layout used to display Access data is a table or ***Datasheet view.*** In the datasheet, you can move to a new row by clicking the ***record selector*** button to the left of a record. An entire column of data can be selected using the ***field selector*** button above the column. The record selector is also called a row selector and the field selector can be called the column selector.

TRADITIONAL NAVIGATION. The Tab key can be used to advance from cell to cell in the datasheet. Arrow keys also will move from cell to cell and have the added advantage of moving up and down between rows. When using keyboard navigation, the default is for the entire contents of a cell to be selected. This can be effective if you want to type and replace existing contents. If, however, you want to move character by character in a cell, you will need to choose Options from the Tools menu and change the Keyboard options to either Go to start of field or Go to end of field. You also can click in any cell using a pointing device or use the navigation buttons below the datasheet. Navigation buttons are outlined in Figure 1.14.

VOICE NAVIGATION. Access 2002 is enabled to use speech for both dictation and command control. This feature is only effective if speech recognition training has been completed (covered in general Office Topics) and you own a good microphone headset. Activate speech recognition by selecting Speech from the Tools menu. The Language Bar—shown in

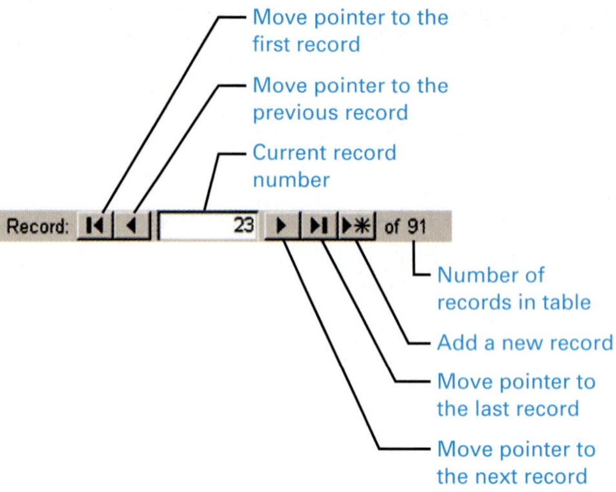

FIGURE 1.14
Datasheet navigation buttons

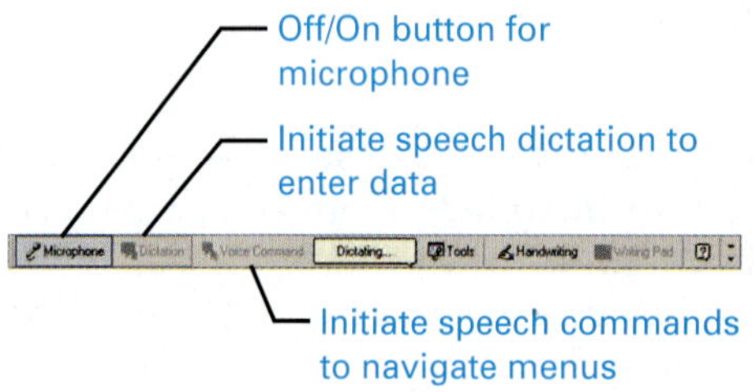

FIGURE 1.15
Language bar

Figure 1.15—will float over the Access Title Bar, allowing you to control language options.

Voice commands can be issued by choosing Voice Command from the Language Bar and speaking menu options such as File Print. Because of the complexity of the Access interface, dictation is time consuming to learn and of limited functionality. Speaking keywords such as Tab moves from cell to cell in a datasheet, but dictating data values is challenging. For example, speaking "CustmrNmbr 048" (zero four eight) results in "zer" being stored in the field because speech recognition tried to write out zero but the field only allows 3 characters. Speaking "forty-eight" places 48 in the cell when 048 is the correct value. Similar problems arise when speaking dates and phone numbers.

task reference

Opening an Access Object

- Click the type of object that you would like to open in the Database window's Objects bar
- Select the object that you would like to open
- Click the **Open** button

Opening the Customer table:

1. If you are not continuing from the previous session, start Access and open the AC01customers.mdb database. Verify that the **Tables** object is selected in the Database window

tip: *Refer to Figure 1.11 to find the Tables object*

2. Double-click the **Customer** table. The contents of the table will display in Datasheet view
3. Navigate the table data by clicking in several cells
4. Select the record for Ben Katz by clicking the record selector (the gray button before the record)
5. Select the State column by clicking the column selector (the gray button above the data labeled State)
6. Click in any cell and use the Tab and Shift+Tab keys to navigate forward and backward through the cells

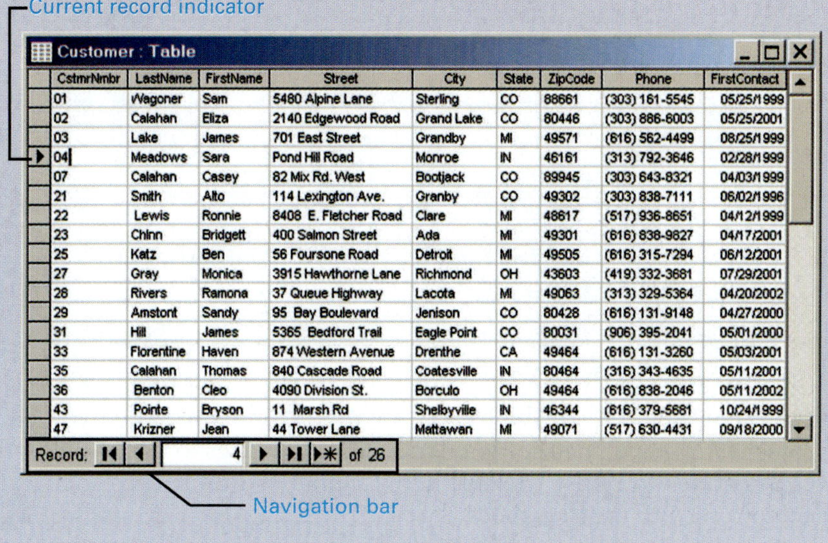

CstmrNmbr	LastName	FirstName	Street	City	State	ZipCode	Phone	FirstContact
01	Wagoner	Sam	5480 Alpine Lane	Sterling	CO	88661	(303) 161-5545	05/25/1999
02	Calahan	Eliza	2140 Edgewood Road	Grand Lake	CO	80446	(303) 886-6003	05/25/2001
03	Lake	James	701 East Street	Grandby	MI	49571	(616) 562-4499	08/25/1999
04	Meadows	Sara	Pond Hill Road	Monroe	IN	46161	(313) 792-3646	02/28/1999
07	Calahan	Casey	82 Mix Rd. West	Bootjack	CO	89945	(303) 643-8321	04/03/1999
21	Smith	Alto	114 Lexington Ave.	Granby	CO	49302	(303) 838-7111	06/02/1996
22	Lewis	Ronnie	8408 E. Fletcher Road	Clare	MI	48617	(517) 936-8651	04/12/1999
23	Chinn	Bridgett	400 Salmon Street	Ada	MI	49301	(616) 838-9827	04/17/2001
25	Katz	Ben	56 Foursone Road	Detroit	MI	49505	(616) 315-7294	06/12/2001
27	Gray	Monica	3915 Hawthorne Lane	Richmond	OH	43603	(419) 332-3681	07/29/2001
28	Rivers	Ramona	37 Queue Highway	Lacota	MI	49063	(313) 329-5364	04/20/2002
29	Amstont	Sandy	95 Bay Boulevard	Jenison	CO	80428	(616) 131-9148	04/27/2000
31	Hill	James	5365 Bedford Trail	Eagle Point	CO	80031	(906) 395-2041	05/01/2000
33	Florentine	Haven	874 Western Avenue	Drenthe	CA	49464	(616) 131-3260	05/03/2001
35	Calahan	Thomas	840 Cascade Road	Coatesville	IN	80464	(316) 343-4635	05/11/2001
36	Benton	Cleo	4090 Division St.	Borculo	OH	49464	(616) 838-2046	05/11/2002
43	Pointe	Bryson	11 Marsh Rd	Shelbyville	IN	46344	(616) 379-5681	10/24/1999
47	Krizner	Jean	44 Tower Lane	Mattawan	MI	49071	(517) 630-4431	09/18/2000

FIGURE 1.16
The customer table

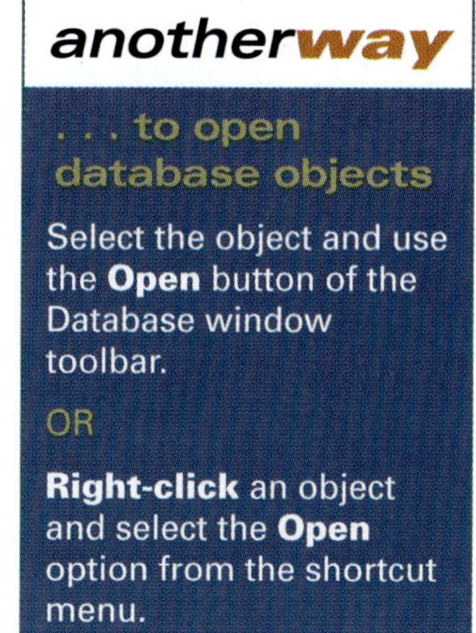

anotherway
. . . to open database objects
Select the object and use the **Open** button of the Database window toolbar.
OR
Right-click an object and select the **Open** option from the shortcut menu.

Adjusting Column Widths and Row Heights

Besides navigating table data, you can adjust the appearance of datasheet contents. When the datasheet loads, default sizes for rows and columns are used. Often the column is larger or smaller than the data it contains. Resizing the columns and rows will make the data more readable.

Changing Customer table column widths and row heights:

1. Verify that the Customer table is open in Datasheet view
2. Place the pointer on the right edge of the State field selector until the pointer has left- and right-pointing arrows, as demonstrated in Figure 1.17
3. Click and drag the State column until it is just wide enough to display the data
4. To allow Access to automatically size a column based on the data it contains, double-click the right edge of the field selector. Use this method to adjust the width of the Street column

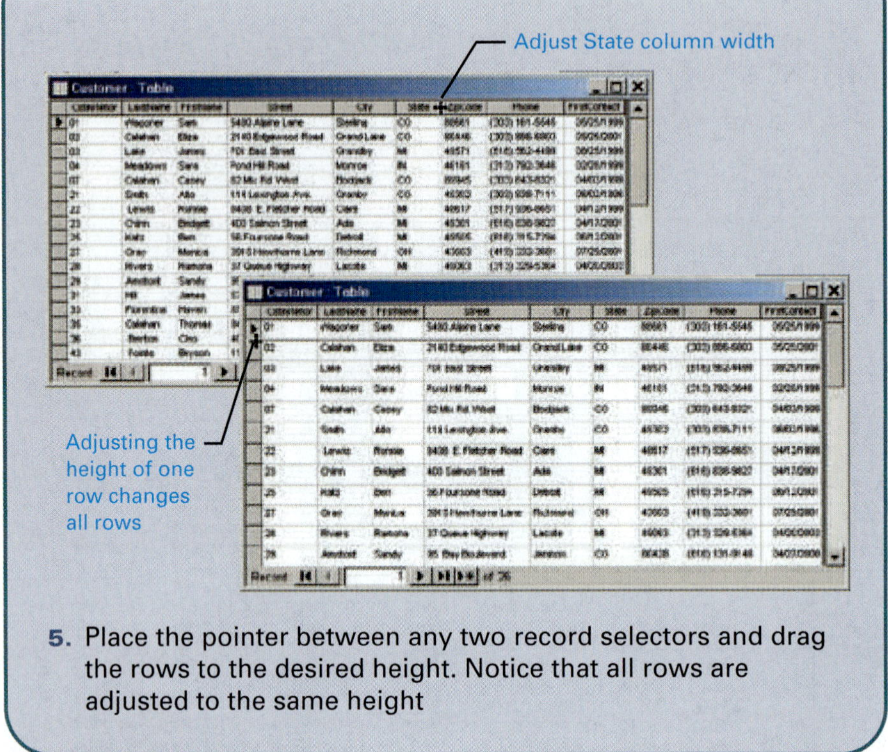
Adjust State column width
Adjusting the height of one row changes all rows

5. Place the pointer between any two record selectors and drag the rows to the desired height. Notice that all rows are adjusted to the same height

FIGURE 1.17
Adjusting column widths and row heights

Changes to the column and row dimensions cannot be reversed with the Undo command from the toolbar or the Edit menu. When you close the datasheet, you will be prompted to save the changes to the layout of the table. Select Yes to retain the size adjustments, No to discard them, and Cancel to return to the datasheet.

Printing Table Data

Access print features are very similar to those of other Office products. There are two common methods for printing Access objects:

- Click the Print button on the toolbar to print an open datasheet or other open object. If there is no datasheet open, the Print button will cause the selected object to print.
- Alternatively, you can use the Print option of the File menu, which will open the Print dialog box. The Print dialog box provides options for setting up your output page, changing the printer, controlling printer properties, and printing multiple copies.

The toolbar's Print Preview button is an excellent way to verify the content and format of output before printing. The Print Preview toolbar contains options to control the zoom (magnification) of the output and the number of pages that display for review and to change the printer setup. If you have made and saved formatting changes such as column widths or fonts to the datasheet, they will be reflected in the printed output.

Viewing Table Design

The ***Design view*** for a table displays the attributes of each field in the table called the table structure. Design view can be used to build tables from scratch or make changes to the design of existing tables. You and Evan will take a look at the design of the PuppyParadise Customer table prototype.

Displaying the Customer table's design:

1. If the Customer table is open, close it. From the Database window, select **Table** from the Object bar and **Customer** from the main pane
2. Click the **Design view** button from the Database window toolbar

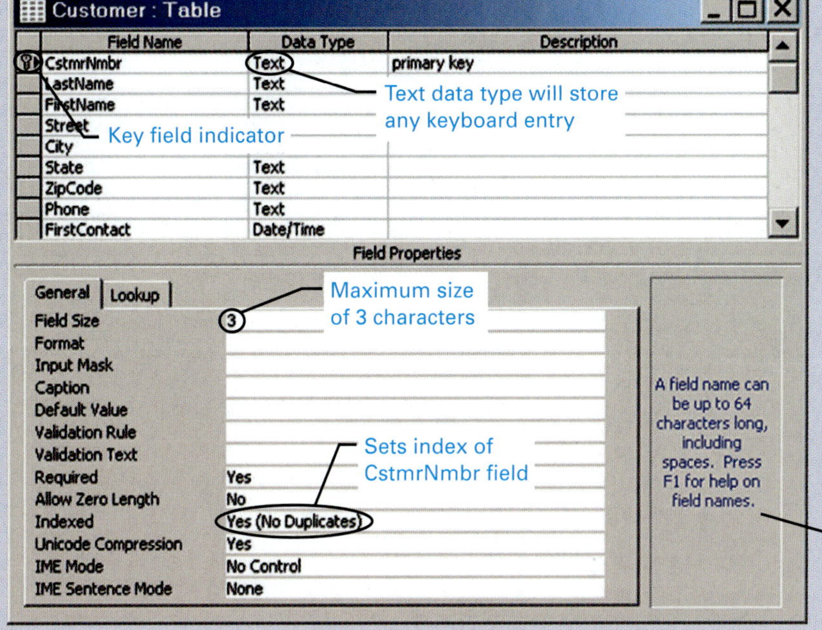

FIGURE 1.18
Customer table design view

3. Review the attributes of the CstmrNmbr field

In table Design view, the key icon in the selector indicates that it is the primary key. The Text data type means that it will accept any text entered (letters, numbers, or punctuation), a Field Size of 3 denotes that a maximum of three characters can be stored, and an Indexed value of Yes indicates that the field has been indexed.

> **anotherword**
>
> **. . . on changing views**
>
> Many Access objects support multiple views like the table object. The Design view allows you to see and update the table design while the Datasheet view allows you to see and update the stored data. You can move easily from one object view to another using the View button on the toolbar. The View button is a drop-down button that will display the valid views for the open or selected object. The two most common views are Datasheet and Design.

Printing Table Design

It is a good idea to keep paper documentation outlining the design of your tables. Printing table design cannot be accomplished using the Print option of the File menu, as you would expect. Special tools are used to analyze and document the design of Access objects. The documentation feature of the Database Analyzer includes the ability to print table designs.

Printing the Customer table's design:

1. From the **Tools** menu, select **Analyze** and then **Documenter**

tip: *No particular object or view is necessary for this operation*

2. The Documenter dialog box will display to allow you to select the object to be documented and the options for the documentation

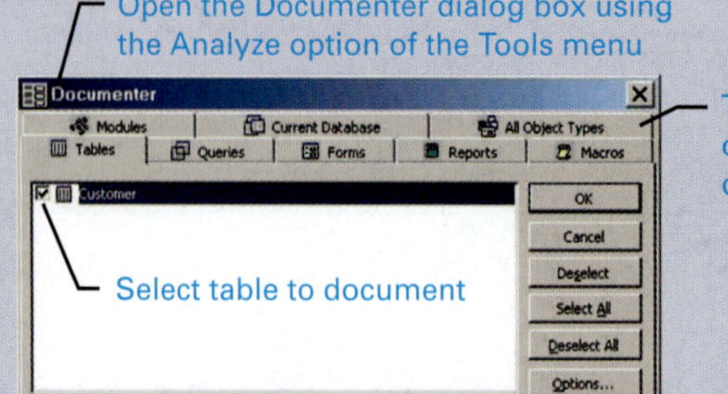

FIGURE 1.19
Printing Customer table design

3. Verify that the **Tables** tab is selected and **check** the Customer table checkbox

tip: *The table to be documented must be checked; highlighting is not sufficient*

4. Click the **Options** button to display the Print Table Definition dialog box. The options selected here determine what documentation will print for the Customer table. The default values are shown in Figure 1.20
5. Click **OK** to exit the Print Table Definition dialog box

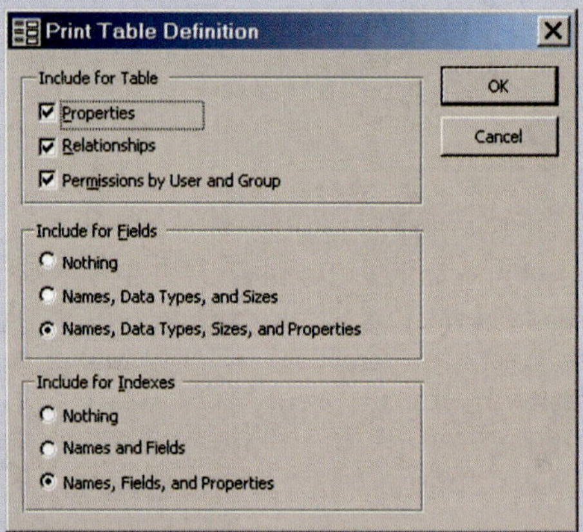

FIGURE 1.20
Print Table Definition dialog box settings

6. Click **OK** in the Documenter dialog box to generate a preview copy of the documentation
7. Select **Print** from the **File** menu and complete the Table Design Print as you would print any other document

USING ACCESS WIZARDS

Wizards are helpful applets in Office that walk users through complex tasks. The Wizards installed on your computer are determined by the options selected when Access was installed. To work along with the instructions in the section, you will need the Wizards for creating tables, forms, queries, and reports. If these Wizards are not present, run the installation again or seek technical assistance.

task reference

Activating Access Wizards

- Click the object (Queries, Forms, Reports) whose Wizard you would like to access in the Database window's Objects bar
- Click **New** in the Database window's toolbar
- The available Wizards will be listed
- Select the Wizard and respond to its questions

The Simple Query Wizard

The Simple Query Wizard allows columns (fields) to be specified for retrieval from one or more tables in a database. Simple calculations such as count, sum, or average can be added to the results. This Wizard does not allow criteria for selecting specific rows of data, so all rows of the table(s) are included in the return set.

The Simple Query Wizard displays a series of dialog boxes requesting the information needed to complete the query. Each Wizard dialog box contains navigation buttons that will allow you to move to the previous dialog box (Previous), move to the next dialog box (Next), cancel the operation (Cancel), or complete the task with the data entered so far (Finish).

Querying the Customer table:

1. Verify that the Customer database is open and contains a Customer table with data
2. Click **Queries** in the Objects bar and then select **New** from the Database window toolbar

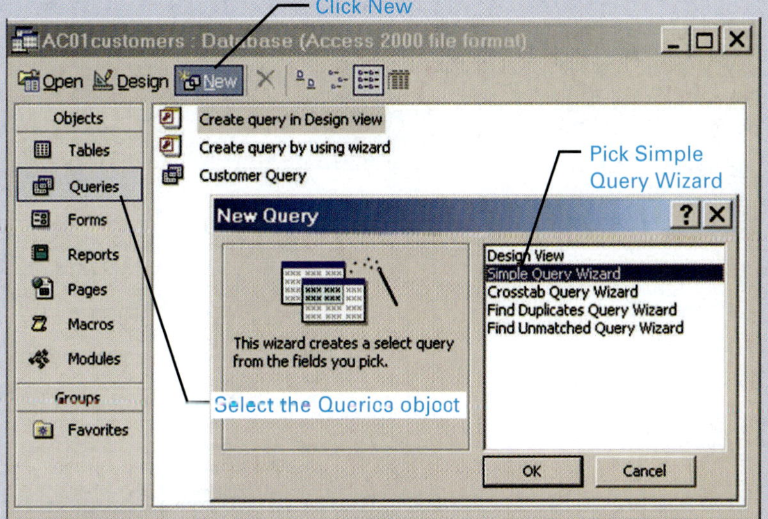

FIGURE 1.21
Simple Query Wizard

3. Select **Simple Query Wizard** from the New Query dialog box, and then click **OK.** The Simple Query Wizard dialog box will display
4. The Simple Query Wizard will prompt for the information needed to create a query. Use the Tables/Queries drop-down list box to select the **Customer** table

5. Practice using the selector buttons outlined in Figure 1.19 to select and unselect fields for the query. For this query, select the **CstmrNmbr, LastName, FirstName,** and **Phone** columns and then click **Next**

FIGURE 1.22
Select table and fields for query

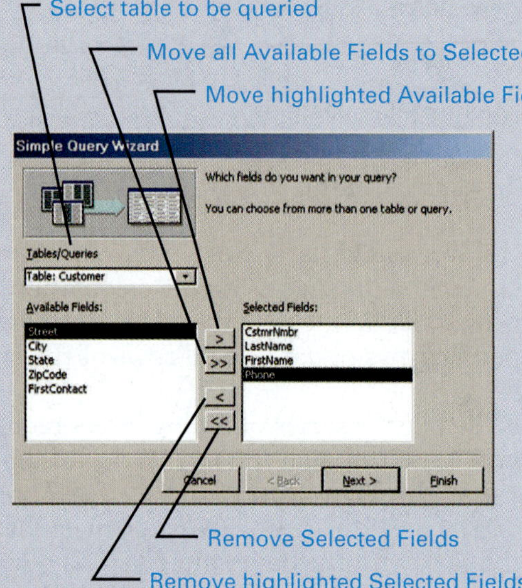

6. The next dialog box allows the creation of a custom title for your query output. The default of Customer Query does not need to be changed. Click **Finish**

7. The query results are displayed in Datasheet view and can be manipulated, formatted, updated, or printed using the same techniques as when reviewing an entire table in Datasheet view

FIGURE 1.23
Customer query results

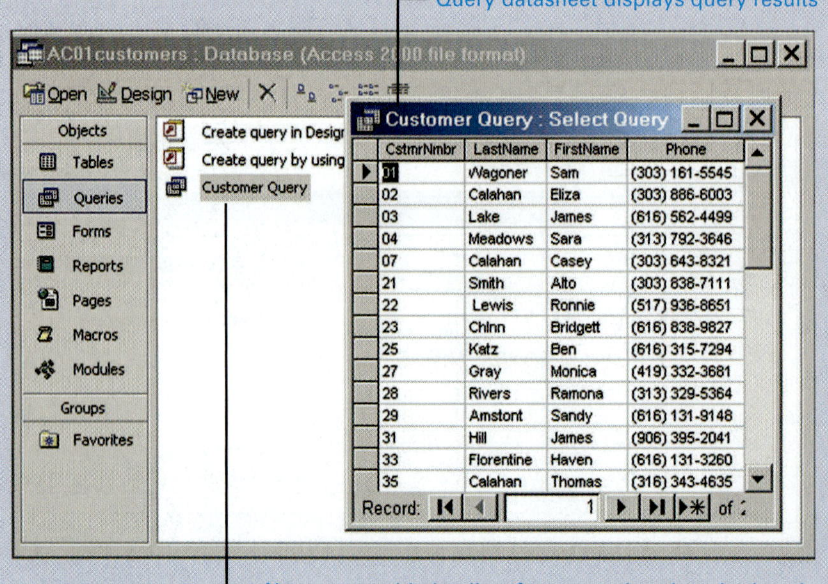

CstmrNmbr	LastName	FirstName	Phone
01	Wagoner	Sam	(303) 161-5545
02	Calahan	Eliza	(303) 886-6003
03	Lake	James	(616) 562-4499
04	Meadows	Sara	(313) 792-3646
07	Calahan	Casey	(303) 643-8321
21	Smith	Alto	(303) 838-7111
22	Lewis	Ronnie	(517) 936-8651
23	Chinn	Bridgett	(616) 838-9827
25	Katz	Ben	(616) 315-7294
27	Gray	Monica	(419) 332-3681
28	Rivers	Ramona	(313) 329-5364
29	Amstont	Sandy	(616) 131-9148
31	Hill	James	(906) 395-2041
33	Florentine	Haven	(616) 131-3260
35	Calahan	Thomas	(316) 343-4635

8. Close the datasheet and notice that Customer Query has been added to the list of Queries

another way

. . . to initiate the Simple Query Wizard

Once the Queries object is selected, double-click on Create query by using Wizard. The Simple Query Wizard dialog box will open in one step.

The query results are not saved, but the query criteria are stored for future use. A saved query can be reopened by double-clicking the title. By default, the query results are displayed in order by CstmrNmbr since it is the primary key. To change the order of the output, click anywhere in the field that you want to sort and click either the ***Sort Ascending*** or ***Sort Descending*** toolbar button.

Evan wants to use the query results as a phone book of his customers, so it makes more sense for the records to be sorted by the customer's name. To change the record order, you will need to sort by both the customer's last and first names. When sorting by multiple fields, the fields must be contiguous and in order of their importance to the sort. LastName is the primary sort field for this query and must appear before the secondary sort field, FirstName.

To change the order of the columns, select the column using the Field selector and drag the selected column to its new location. For this phone book, the column order should be LastName, FirstName, Phone, and CstmrNmbr.

Sorting the Query results:

1. **Open** Customer Query created in the previous steps
2. Change the order of the columns by clicking the **Field Descriptor** to select the column, and then click and drag the Field Descriptor to its new location. Repeat this process until the column order is LastName, FirstName, Phone, and CstmrNmbr

tip: *The Field Descriptor is the box with the field name above each column of data*

3. Place the cursor in the LastName field and click the **Sort Descending** button on the toolbar
4. Notice that while the data are sorted correctly by last name, the first names are not correctly ordered. The Calahans are not sorted by their first names. If you click in FirstName and sort, the data are no longer sorted by LastName
5. To sort both fields simultaneously, use the Field Selectors to select both the FirstName and LastName columns by clicking and dragging across both Field Selectors
6. When both the FirstName and LastName columns are selected, click the **Sort Ascending** button on the toolbar
7. Now that the data are arranged as Evan wanted, it can be printed using the **Print** button of the Access toolbar
8. When you close the sorted query results, you will be prompted to save the layout changes that you have made. Choose **Yes** so that the next run of the Customer Query will be sorted as Evan wants

FIGURE 1.24
Reordering customer query results

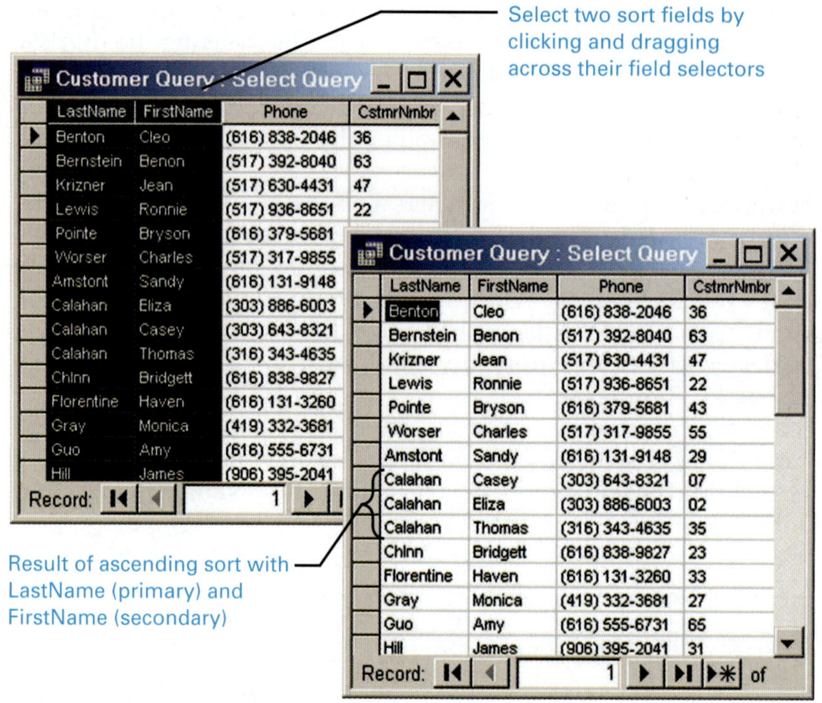
Select two sort fields by clicking and dragging across their field selectors
Result of ascending sort with LastName (primary) and FirstName (secondary)

The Form Wizard

Forms are primarily used to display or update database data on a computer screen. There are two ways to create simple forms. AutoForm is the fastest and most efficient when you want a form displaying all fields from a single table. The Form Wizard will create more complex forms involving multiple tables and formatting.

Using AutoForm:

1. Verify that the Customer database is open and that the Customer table contains data
2. Click **Forms** in the Objects bar, and then select **New** from the Database window toolbar to open the New Form dialog box
3. Each of the five AutoForm Wizards produces the form in a different layout. Datasheet is the default form with which you have already worked. Select **AutoForm: Columnar** to produce a single-column form
4. Select the **Customer** table from the drop-down list and click **OK**
5. Repeat the process for **AutoForm: Tabular**. Compare the results of the two types of AutoForms
6. Use the Close button in the Form toolbar to close the tabular AutoForm, naming it **CustomerTabular**

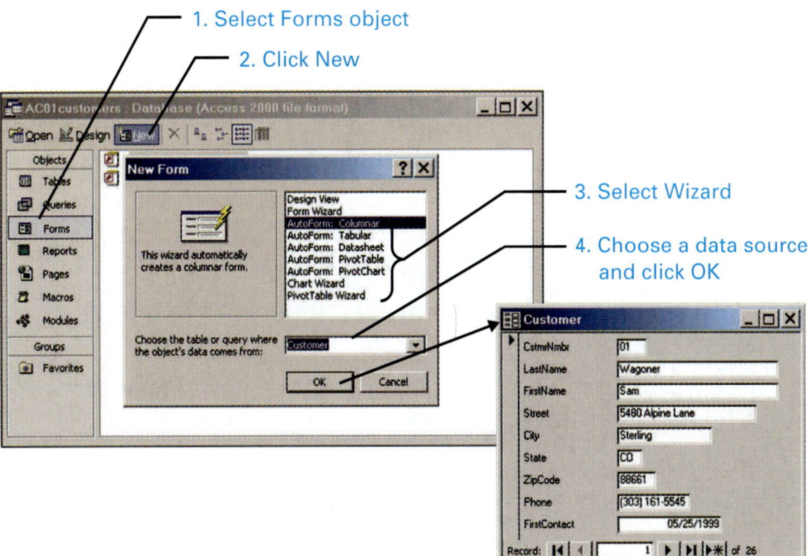

FIGURE 1.25
AutoForm results

Save any form specifications that will be used in the future. Forms also can be printed. Clicking the Printer button on the toolbar will print out all records in the table. Choosing Print from the File menu provides options to print all or a subset of the records.

Printing Forms with data:

1. Verify that the columnar AutoForm created in the previous step is open
2. Use the navigation bar to move to the fourth record
3. From the Access menu select **File** and then **Print** to open the Print dialog box
4. The Print Range options determine what records print. All will print all table records. Pages From will print the specified range and Selected Record(s) will print the current selection. Choose **Selected Record(s)** to print the fourth record

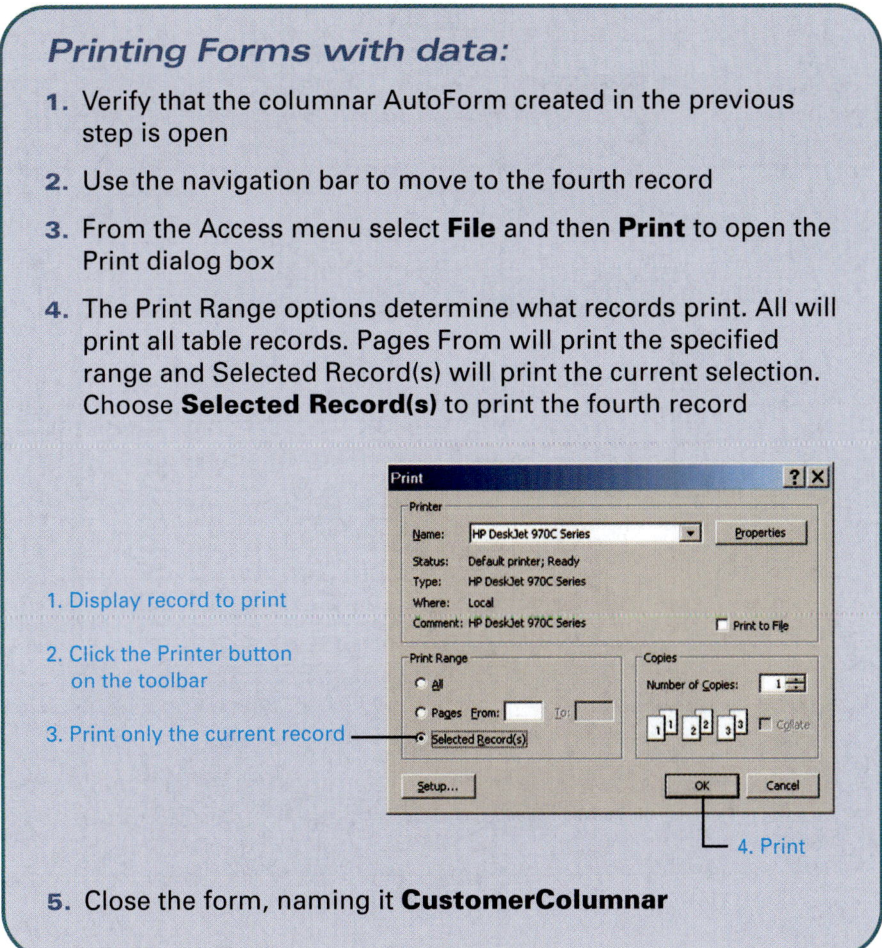

FIGURE 1.26
Printing forms with data

5. Close the form, naming it **CustomerColumnar**

The Report Wizard

Reports are primarily used to consolidate and format data for printing. There are two types of report Wizards available. The AutoReport Wizard creates default reports from one table or query. The Report Wizard will create multitable reports with calculations and custom formatting.

Using the Report Wizard:

1. Verify that the Customer database is open and that the Customer table contains data
2. Click **Reports** in the Objects bar and then select **New** from the Database window toolbar. The New Report dialog box will open
3. Click **AutoReport: Tabular** to create a report in rows and columns
4. Select the **Customer** table from the drop-down list and click **OK**

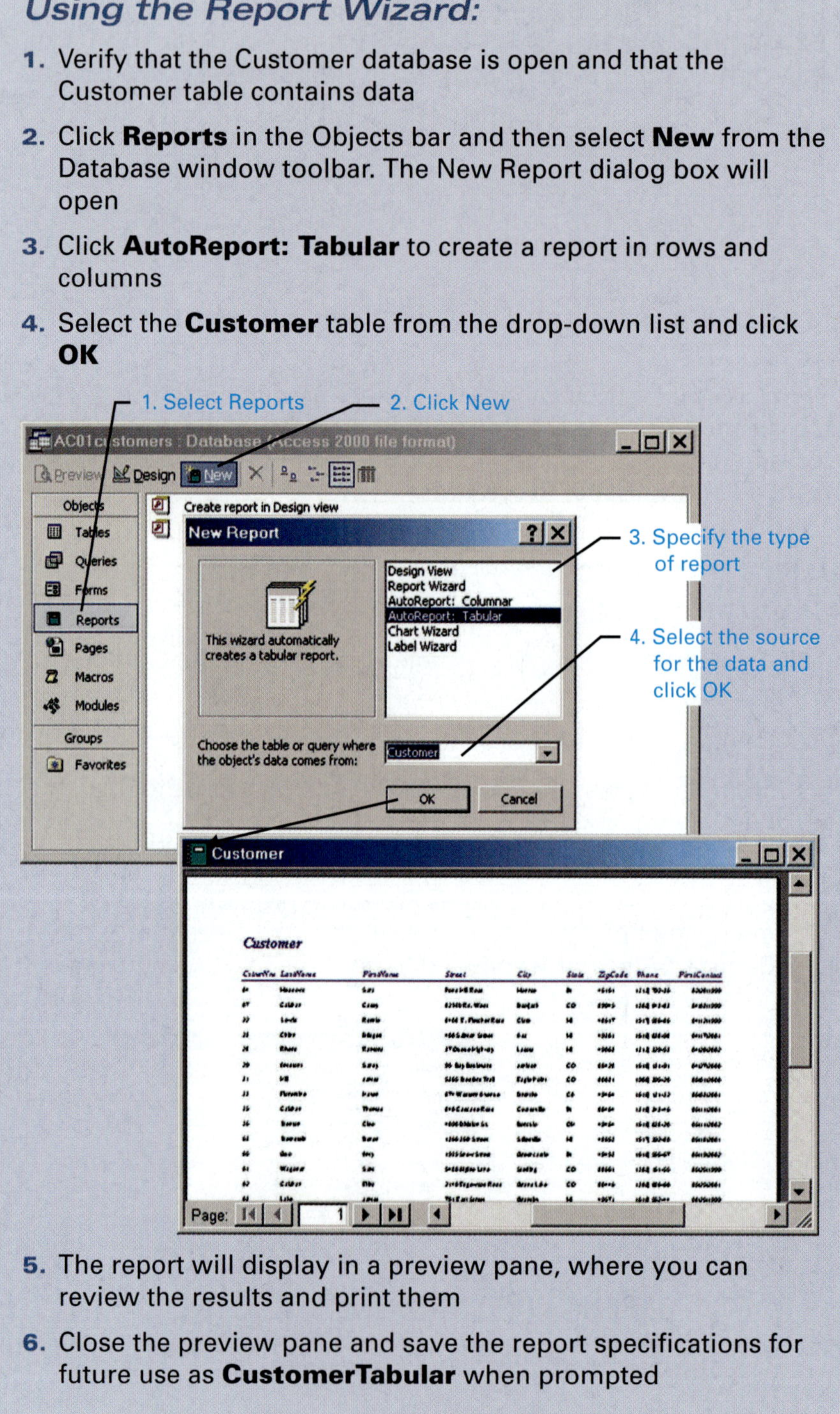

FIGURE 1.27
Report Wizard results

5. The report will display in a preview pane, where you can review the results and print them
6. Close the preview pane and save the report specifications for future use as **CustomerTabular** when prompted

The Create Table Wizard

The Create Table Wizard provides a collection of business and personal database tables to be used as the basis for creating your table.

Using the Create Table Wizard:

1. Verify that the Customer database is open
2. Click **Tables** in the Objects bar, double-click **Create table by using Wizard** to open it without viewing the intermediate dialog boxes

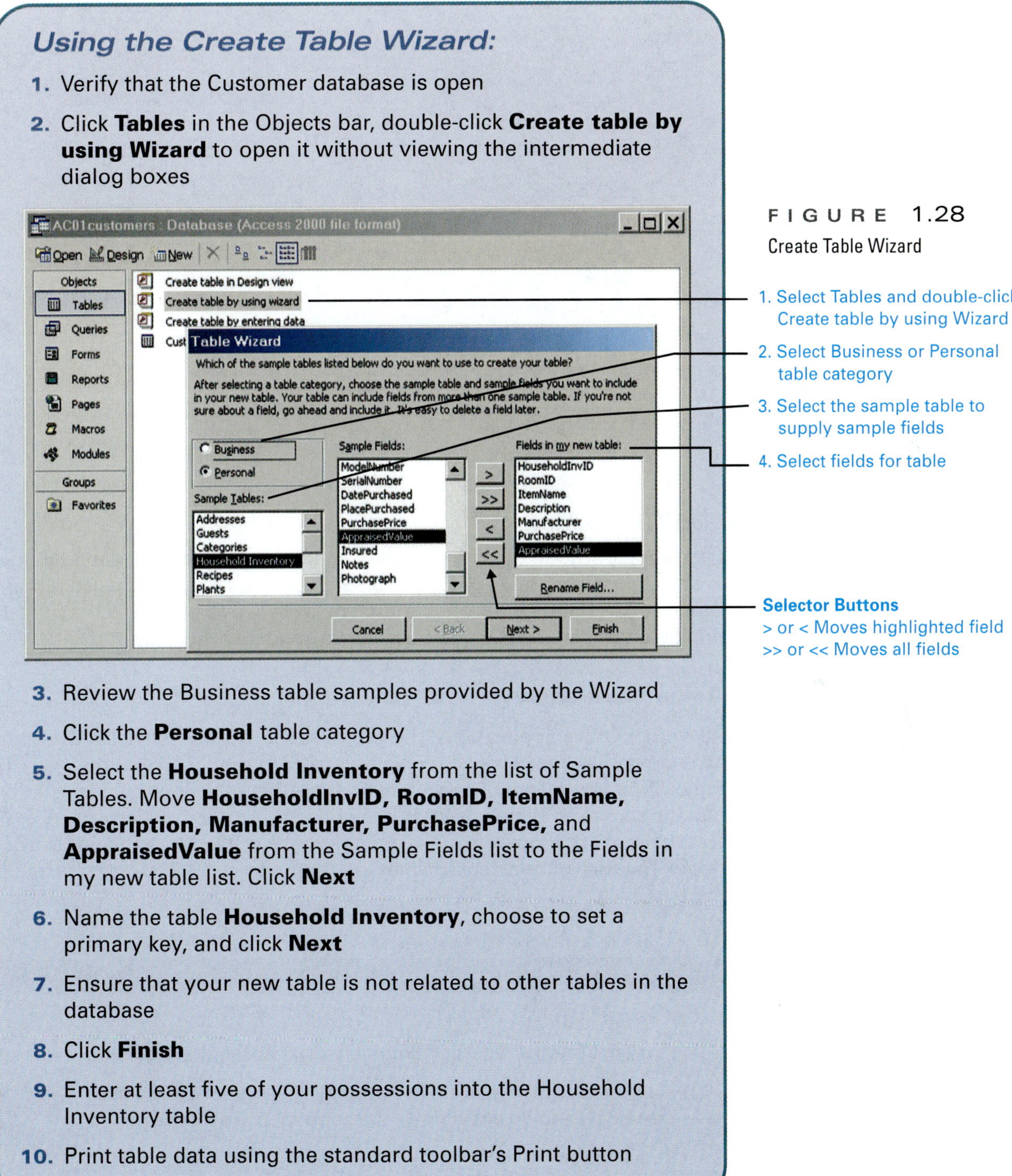

FIGURE 1.28
Create Table Wizard

3. Review the Business table samples provided by the Wizard
4. Click the **Personal** table category
5. Select the **Household Inventory** from the list of Sample Tables. Move **HouseholdInvID, RoomID, ItemName, Description, Manufacturer, PurchasePrice,** and **AppraisedValue** from the Sample Fields list to the Fields in my new table list. Click **Next**
6. Name the table **Household Inventory**, choose to set a primary key, and click **Next**
7. Ensure that your new table is not related to other tables in the database
8. Click **Finish**
9. Enter at least five of your possessions into the Household Inventory table
10. Print table data using the standard toolbar's Print button

It is important to remember that the Create Table Wizard uses templates to build the fields of a new table. All field names and properties can be customized to suit the current use.

FIGURE 1.29

Create Table Wizard (continued)

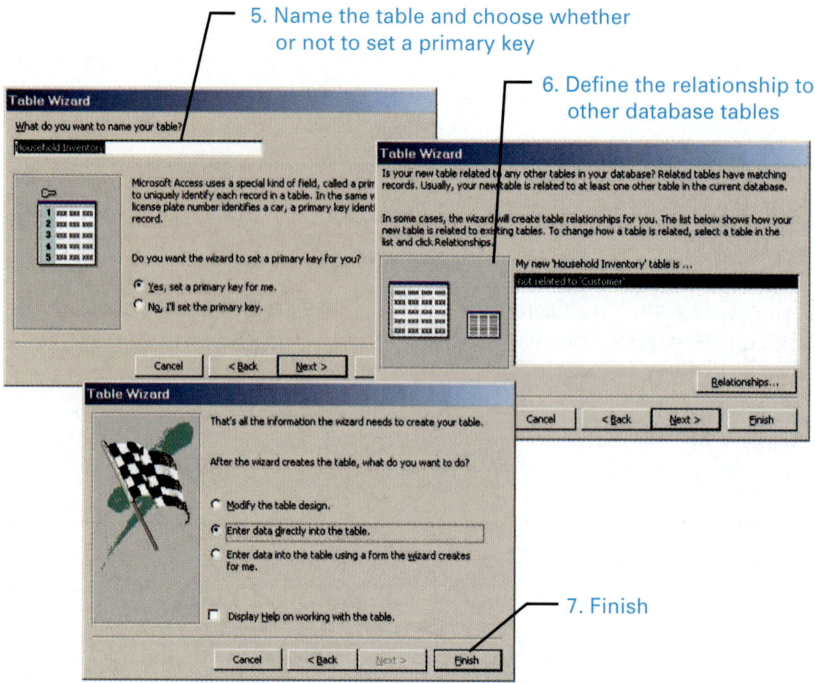

GETTING HELP

Even people who work with Access on a daily basis need direction on how to accomplish new tasks or those that are not frequently performed. Access supports several methods of obtaining help. The technique selected for getting help depends on the question being posed and the work style.

Ask a Question

Like other Office applications, the Access menu bar has the Ask a Question drop-down list box. This is an effective way to request help on a specific topic. Type in a question and press Enter. A list of related topics will display, as shown in Figure 1.30. When you select a topic, Microsoft Access Help opens with more selections, which can be clicked to bring up instructions. The instructions can display on your screen as you work through them in Access.

task reference

Getting Help

- Click in the Ask a Question drop-down text box in the Access menu
- Type in keywords relevant to your topic. Full sentences are not necessary and do not improve the performance of the search
- Press **Enter**
- Select from the topics provided or adjust the keywords and search again

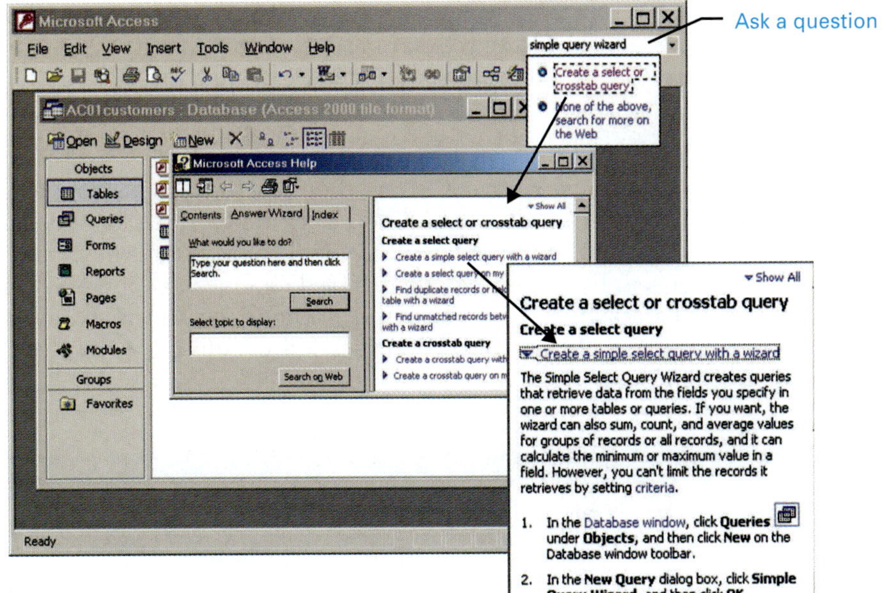

FIGURE 1.30
Getting help

Once Microsoft Access Help is initiated, the Contents and Index tabs display as well as the default Answer Wizard tab. The Contents tab works like the table of contents for a book, allowing users to select a topic. Selecting an entire topic can be helpful when you need more than just a series of steps to complete a task. The Index tab provides a way to search the document index for keywords. A list of keywords is provided or you can enter your own.

The Office Assistant

Dropping down the Help menu in the Access window displays a complete list of help options. The available options are to start help, initiate the Office Assistant, view Sample Databases, access help on the Web, or use the What's This tool.

The What's This tool is activated from the toolbar button and changes the pointer to an arrow and a question mark. With this tool active, point and click on any interface component and receive a brief description of its function and operation. What's This closes after one interface item is described.

The Office Assistant is the animated interface to Microsoft Office Help and can be initiated by pressing F1, choosing Microsoft Access Help from the Help menu, or choosing Show the Office Assistant from the Help menu (see Figure 1.31). Regardless of how the assistant is initiated, typing a question and clicking Search will open Microsoft Access Help (shown in Figure 1.30) with topics related to your search.

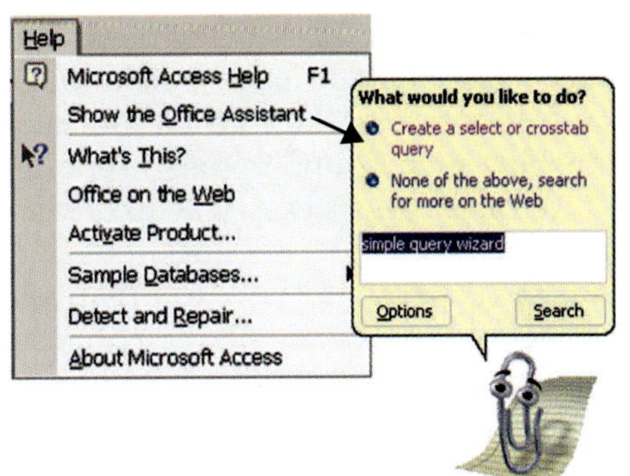

FIGURE 1.31
Help menu and Office Assistant

Right-clicking the Office Assistant displays options that control how the assistant works. The visual presentation gallery includes Merlin the magician, a robot, a cat, and a dog. If he is left active and set to do so, the assistant will provide tips as you work. He can also be hidden or disabled.

EXITING ACCESS

Exiting Access is accomplished by choosing the Close button of the main Access window. The Exit option of the File menu also will close Access. Regardless of the exit method employed, all open objects will be closed before Access is closed. If you have made unsaved changes to open objects such as a table or datasheet, you will be prompted to save or abandon changes. When all open objects have been successfully closed, Access will close.

SESSION 1.2

making the grade

1. Access database objects include ______, ______, and ______.
2. T F Changes made in the Datasheet view such as widening columns are automatically saved when the view is closed.
3. Describe the purpose of the Documenter (Tools|Analyze|Documenter) menu option.
4. Create a query from the PuppyParadise Customer table that will be used to create mailing labels. The query results should include the customer's full name and complete street address. The records should be sorted by ZipCode.

SESSION 1.3 SUMMARY

Relational database management systems are powerful data storage and retrieval technologies. Data stored in RDBMSs have reduced data redundancy and increased data integrity and use data validation rules to improve data reliability.

Raw data are stored in tables where they can be accessed and manipulated using Queries, Forms, and Reports objects. Each table column represents an attribute or field of an entity. For example, Gender is a common column in a table storing data about employees. All of the attributes for one entity are stored in a row or record, so all data stored for one employee is in the same row. All of the possible values of an attribute are called its domain. Indexes are used to speed data access and sort output.

Ideally each table should have a primary key that uniquely and minimally identifies each row of data. Social Security Number is the most likely primary key when storing data about people. Tables are joined to each other using shared fields. A field that can be used to join to another table is called a foreign key. When tables are joined, they have definable relationships such as one-to-one or one-to-many.

Wizards are an easy way to create simple queries, forms, and reports. Queries are a way to ask questions of the database data by specifying what data to retrieve and how to organize them. Queries also can be used to update multiple rows of data in one step. Forms are a user-friendly way to view and update data on a computer screen. Reports allow you to format data for printing.

Database objects support multiple views. Personal preference and the operation to be performed determine the view to be used. For example, a table's Datasheet view is used to view, navigate, and maintain data while the Design view is used to change the structure of the table.

Visit www.mhhe.com/i-series/ to explore related topics.

MOUS OBJECTIVES SUMMARY

- AC2002-1-1—Create Access databases using the Wizard
- AC2002-1-2—Open database objects in multiple views
- AC2002-1-3—Navigate among records

task reference roundup

Task	Page #	Preferred Method
Opening an Access object	AC 1.18	• Click the type of object that you would like to open in the Database window's Objects bar
		• Select the object that you would like to open
		• Click the **Open** button
Activating Access Wizards	AC 1.23	• Click the object (Queries, Forms, Reports) whose Wizard you would like to access in the Database window's Objects bar
		• Click **New** in the Database window's toolbar
		• The available Wizards will be listed
		• Select the Wizard and respond to its questions
Getting Help	AC 1.30	• Click in the Ask a Question drop-down text box in the Access menu
		• Type in keywords relevant to your topic. Full sentences are not necessary and do not improve the performance of the search
		• Press **Enter**
		• Select from the topics provided or adjust the keywords and search again

CROSSWORD PUZZLE

Across

3. Synonym for a table row
8. Storing duplicate data
9. Synonym for a table column
12. Synonym for a table
15. Object used to ask questions of the data
16. Set of all possible values for an attribute
17. Acronym for database management system

Down

1. Key that uniquely identifies each row of table data
2. A key that could have been set as the primary key
4. A key used to join tables
5. Term for the validity of data
6. Combining data from multiple tables
7. A data _______ is stored in a table cell
10. The primary relational database object
11. Stored procedures that walk you through common tasks
13. Person, place, thing, or event about which data is being collected
14. The language used to query relational databases

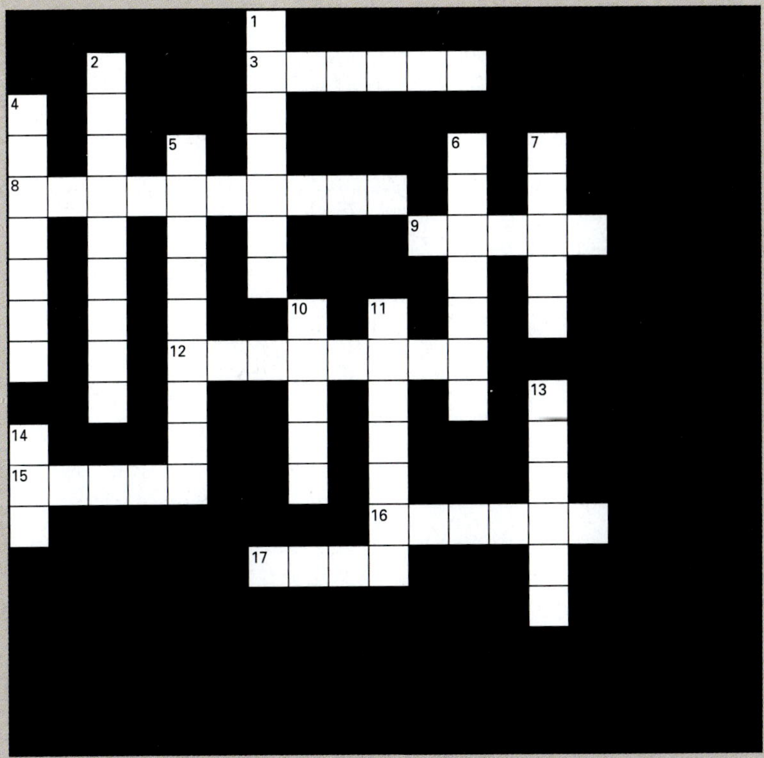

review of concepts

FILL-IN

1. The Access object used to create printed output is the _______ object.
2. Database _______ ensures that only authorized people can access and update database data.
3. _______ is the language used to define the structure of a database table.
4. When using the Simple Query Wizard, the _______ button will add the current field to those that will appear in the query answerset.
5. The _______ is one way to obtain help in Access.
6. A(n) _______ key is a field that could have been defined as the primary key but was not.

REVIEW QUESTIONS

Each of the following topics should be addressed in one to three paragraphs.

1. Discuss at least two ways to open an Access database.
2. Discuss the benefits and difficulties of using database management systems.
3. How does reduced data redundancy decrease errors in database data?
4. Outline at least two Customer data queries that might benefit PuppyParadise.

CREATE THE QUESTION

For each of the following answers, create the question.

ANSWER	QUESTION
1. They are specific to each Access object and appear at the top of a window.	_______________
2. Setting a primary key automatically creates the first one for a table.	_______________
3. The object that allows you to create a custom user interface to display and manipulate data.	_______________
4. A reusable template that will speed the development of Access database components such as tables and queries.	_______________
5. The Table view used to change the Table structure.	_______________

FACT OR FICTION

For each of the following, determine whether the statement is fact, fiction, or both and present your arguments for that conclusion.

1. Relational databases are the only databases in use by today's businesses.
2. The Office Assistant is the only way to obtain Access help.
3. The Query Datasheet toolbar can be displayed while viewing a form.
4. A query is another way to store data.
5. The Print button can be used to print the design of a table.
6. The Simple Query Wizard allows you to select columns that will be returned by a query, but not the rows.

practice

Working with a Database for Curbside Recycling

Curbside Recycling is a Muncie, Indiana, recycling organization that picks up recyclables from homeowners. Neighborhoods subscribe to the service so that pickup is cost effective. Curbside provides special containers to subscribers for sorting recyclables: a blue container for paper products and a purple container for aluminum, plastic, and glass products.

Subscribers place their recycling containers on the curb for biweekly pickup. Each recycling container is weighed before being emptied. Curbside drivers carry handheld recording devices used to track each pickup. Subscribers receive quarterly profit-sharing checks based on their contributions. If Curbside does not make a profit, subscribers don't get paid for their recyclables. If Curbside makes a profit, subscribers share in that profit. Curbside has asked you to help develop a database that will effectively track subscribers using the data downloaded from the drivers' devices. Eventually, there will be multiple tables in the database. The Customers table will hold static customer information such as name, address, and phone. The CustomerRecords table holds data about each recyclable pickup. It currently contains test data and is the one with which you will be working.

1. Make sure that you have access to the data from your data disk
2. Start Access and open the **AC01CurbsideRecycling.mdb** database from your Chapter One files
3. Open the **CustomerRecords** table, add records for yourself and a friend covering at least three pickup dates each
4. Sort the datasheet rows by EmployeeID, SrvcDate, and CustID. Print the result
5. Make the following updates to existing data:

   CustId 2, SvcDate 11/22/2002 WeightOther should be updated to **17**

   CustID 20, SvcDate 11/22/2002 WeightOther should be updated to **26**
6. Sort the CustomerRecords datasheet. Use EmployeeId as the primary sort and WeightOther as the secondary sort. Print the results and save the format changes to the table
7. Use the Simple Query Wizard to create a report containing EmployeeID, WeightPaper, and WeightOther. When prompted, choose Summary and set the Summary Options to Sum WeightPaper and WeightOther. The report should display one row of totals for each employee
8. Save and print the query
9. Use AutoForm: Columnar to create a data entry form. Display the 10/15/2002 record for customer 80 and print it. Save the form
10. Use the Report Wizard to create a tabular report. Save and print the result
11. If your work is complete, exit Access; otherwise continue to the next assignment

challenge!

Tracking Employees at Little White School House

Samuel Mink is the director of the Little White School House, a small private mountain community school. There are 142 students from preschool through grade 6. The staff consists of eight teachers, the director, a secretary, and community volunteers. Current records for the school are kept manually or in an Excel spreadsheet. Samuel would like more automation, consistency in record keeping, and reporting capabilities. You have met with Samuel and he has provided you with sample forms and a copy of the current data.

Your plan is to begin by putting employee tracking into an Access database according to the criteria listed below.

1. Use Microsoft Word to create a list of employee attributes that should be contained in the Little White School House Employee table
2. Open Access, create a new database (select Blank Database from the New category of the Task Pane) and name it **LittleWhiteSchoolHouse**
3. Use the Table Wizard to create an Employee table with a primary key. Remember that while you need to store personal data, payroll data, and contact information, this is a small organization, so all of the suggested fields are not needed
4. Enter the following data:

<your name>	Secretary	22,400
Samuel Mink	Director	58,929
Margaret Frost	Preschool teacher	31,211
Rachael Dawson	1st grade teacher	28,452
Robert Gibbs	2nd grade teacher	36,283
Randi Evans	3rd grade teacher	45,879
Asayah Muhammad	4th grade teacher	44,962
David Mackall	5th grade teacher	30,980
Kasey Johnson	Music teacher	30,281
Ennis Johnson	Art teacher	30,486

5. Add two of your friends as volunteers (0 salary) and make up the remaining data so there are no blank cells in the table
6. Sort the table by employee name and print
7. Sort the table by decreasing salary and print
8. Print the table design
9. Use the AutoForm: Columnar Wizard to create a form for this table. Print the form with the data for Asayah Muhammad showing (Figure 1.32)
10. Close the database and exit Access if your work is complete

FIGURE 1.32

Employee table form

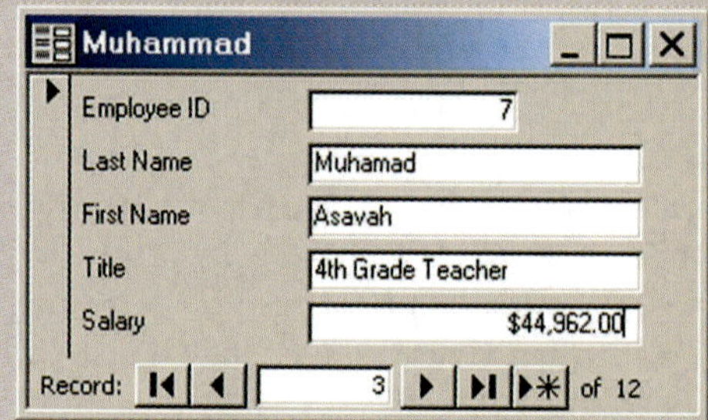

on the web

Searching for Service Organizations

The Wheeler Helping Hand Association (WHHA) is an alliance of missions, food banks, and service organizations supporting central Indiana. The goal of the group is to provide assistance to people who need food, shelter, clothing, job training, and counseling. The organization has two full-time staff to organize and coordinate hundreds of volunteers. Volunteers are the backbone of the organization, doing everything from cooking to counseling.

All supplies are donated through charitable contributions. Most of the contributions are received through churches, but there is also an annual Thanksgiving phone drive and a new Internet contributions site. The Internet contributions site has two purposes. The first is to let people know what the current needs of the organization are by posting a list of the most needed food, clothing, and services. The second is to promote the Wheeler Helping Hand vision and accept monetary contributions.

You have volunteered and have been asked to use your computer expertise to support the services being provided. You know that the Internet is a great resource and have decided to look for better ways to promote the association and support the volunteers. One of your ideas is to provide a database of Web sites that have useful services for WHHA clients. Although the clients are unlikely to have computer access, volunteers who need to be able to provide support without much training would find the information useful.

1. Use your favorite search engine to find organizations and services that could benefit the WHHA clientele
2. Record the information from at least six sites to be entered into the volunteer database
3. Open Access, create a new database (select Blank Database from the New category of the Task Pane), and name it **WHHA**
4. Use the Table Wizard to create a **Services** table:
   a. From the Suppliers Sample Table select SupplierID, SupplierName, ContactName, ContactTitle, PhoneNumber, EmailAddress, and Notes
   b. Rename (click the Rename Field button with the field selected) SupplierID to ServicesID, SupplierName to ServicesName, and EmailAddress to WebAddress
   c. Set ServicesId as the primary key
5. Enter the data from your Web search in the Services table. Make up the contact data if needed and include your comments about the services and the Web site in notes. Do not leave any blank cells
6. Print the table design
7. Use the AutoForm: Tabular Wizard to create a form for the Services table named **WHHA.** Print the form with the data for your third record showing
8. Close the WHHA database and exit Access if your work is complete

e-business

Exotic Flora Price List

Exotic Flora is a worldwide consortium of small florists who provide unique fresh flower arrangements for every occasion. Each florist pays a membership fee and agrees to deliver ordered arrangements within 24 hours of payment verification. All arrangements are guaranteed to match the order and to last for at least 10 days.

The bulk of flower orders are generated through an e-storefront that accepts orders, verifies payment, and forwards the order to the appropriate florist. Forty-two percent of the profit for each order goes to the e-storefront management organization, 10 percent goes to the Exotic Flora association, and the florist who delivers the flowers keeps the remainder.

For the e-storefront to work effectively, the member florists must provide product data to the storefront managers in a convenient format. After some trial and error, the florists have settled on Access as the tool that best suits their needs. Each member florist provides a weekly table of available arrangements with the arrangement name, price, picture, availability dates, and maximum quantity that can be delivered. The e-storefront manager consolidates the Access tables provided by the various florists into a large Oracle database that is used to generate the e-storefront site.

Gabriella Juarez is a small florist in Pahoa, Hawaii, who has decided to join Exotic Flora to increase her business. She has no experience with computers and has asked you to build the database that she needs.

1. Open Access, create a new database (select Blank Database from the New category of the Task Pane), and name it **ExoticFlora**
2. Use the Table Wizard to create a Products table:
    a. From the Products sample table select ProductID, ProductName, ProductDescription, and UnitPrice
    b. From the Employees sample table select Photograph
    c. From the Events sample table select StartDate and EndDate
    d. Set ProductId as the primary key
3. Enter the following five records into the table. A comma separates the data for each column. Instructions for adding the jpg image are in the Tip

    Tropical Splash, 4 Ginger, 4 Heliconia, large and lush tropical foliage, 49.00, splash.jpg

    Tropical Delight, 3 Anthurium, 3 Ginger, 2 Birds of Paradise, 65.95, HA2.jpg

    Hearts of Fire, 12 red Anthurium with lush tropical foliage, 49.50, hearts.jpg

    Kea Mix, 6 assorted Anthurium, 2 red Ginger, 2 Birds, 3 Dembrodium, 65.78, KeaMix.jpg

    Ohanu Mix, A seasonal mix of tropical flowers including, 47.50, OhanuMix.jpg

    tip: *Click the Photograph cell, choose Object from the Insert menu, and browse to find the pictures. The actual photograph is not visible in this view. You can change the photograph by deleting the current cell contents and inserting a new photo*

4. Sort the data by product name and print
5. Print the table design
6. Use the AutoForm: Tabular Wizard to create a form for this table
    a. Open the form design and resize the picture frame to show the graphics

    tip: *Click on the Photograph object and drag the white sizing handles*

    b. Print the form with the data for Kea Tropical Mix showing
7. Close the ExoticFlora database and exit Access if your work is complete

around the world

Tracking International Trade Consultants

The Alliance for Global Commerce (AGC) is an organization that tracks and rates businesses participating in international trade. The three businessmen who founded AGC were able to navigate the various cultures and rituals participating in trades, but had a persistent problem with knowing which other traders were reliable. Since trial and error had proved costly, they started AGC.

The AGC vision was to create something like the Better Business Bureau on an international scale. Initially the three men gathered data on trade incidents necessary to support their own trade activities and then published the data in a newsletter distributed to trade, retail, and wholesale organizations. After that, the newsletter recipients reported trade incidents that were tracked and published in the newsletter. Incidents are any behavior of a trade organization that negatively impacts the viability of the trade pact. The most common incidents are failure to pay and shipments over one week late. Initially there was a concern that false incident reports would be a problem, but they proved not to be.

FIGURE 1.33
AGC form and report

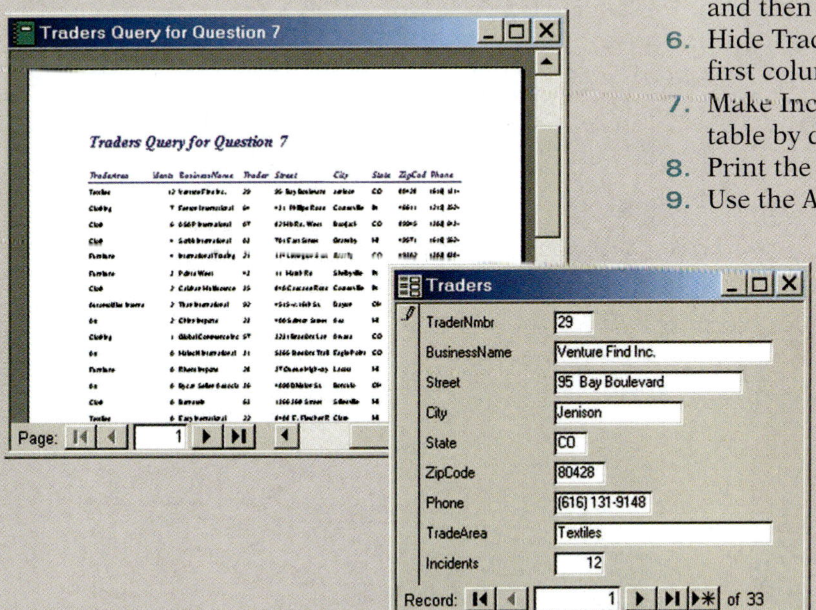

The founders now believe that as international commerce increases, the problems with unreliable and unscrupulous traders will become more prevalent, increasing the need for tracking and analysis. They have hired you to spearhead the data gathering and analysis. You have begun by building a table of traders and searching for new trade organizations.

1. Start Access and open the AC01AGC.mdb database
2. Open the Traders table and become familiar with its contents
3. Add the following data:

   South Side Imports 3850 S. Emerson Ave., Indianapolis, IN 46121, 317-786-8188 Automobiles, 0

   Titan International, 4515 W 16th St., Dayton, OH 48378, 383-484-9195, Automobiles, 2

   Auto Network, 8441 Castleton Corner Dr., Atlanta, GA 30301, 290-748-2070, Clothing, 0

   tip: *TraderNmbr values will be generated automatically. Commas are used to separate the fields and should not be entered*

4. Look in your local phone book and find four international trade businesses. Enter the data into the Traders table
5. Make TradeArea the first column, sort by it, and then print
6. Hide TraderNmbr. Make BusinessName the first column, sort by it, and then print
7. Make Incidents the first column. Sort the table by decreasing Incidents and print
8. Print the table design
9. Use the AutoForm: Columnar Wizard to create a form for this table. Print the form with the data for Chinn Imports showing
10. Use the AutoReport: Tabular Wizard to create and print a report
11. Close the AGC database and exit Access if your work is complete

running project: tnt web page design

Beginning the TnT database

TnT is a custom Web page development company founded by Victoria (Tori) Salazar and her college roommate Tonya O'Dowd. Tonya was an art major learning graphic design and Tori was a computer science major studying programming languages. The company was born when both had final projects due at the end of their second semester. Tonya was creating custom graphics and Tori was using Java to automate a Web site when they decided that they could create a killer site if they combined their talents.

Their first project was to put the college newspaper online. As a result of this project, both were hired as interns at the local newspaper.

After college, Tonya was hired as a graphic artist at a Web design company and Tori was hired as a Web software developer by a Fortune 500 company. They lived in different parts of the country but maintained contact via e-mail. After a few years Tori began picking up some extra work doing e-commerce development for fun and contracted with Tonya to create the graphics. The women liked working together and having control of what they worked on and decided to pick up more contracts. As business grew, both women quit their other jobs to concentrate on Web development.

They are frequently asked for customer references and samples of their work and it has become tedious to maintain the Web site that provides this information. Tori and Tanya ask you to develop a database that will support their business. At some point they would like to store links to their customers and the sites that they have developed and update their Web site automatically. The first step is to create the Customer table.

1. Make sure that you have access to the data disk
2. Start Access and open the **AC01TnT.mdb** database
3. Open the **tblCustomers** table in Datasheet view
4. Sort the table by Country and Customer. Print the results
5. Print the table design
6. Use the Simple Query Wizard to create a query displaying the customer, city, state, country, and phone. Sort by country and customer. Print and save
7. Add yourself and two of your friends as customers
8. Create a columnar form and print your record
9. Create a tabular report with customer name and both phone numbers sorted by customer name. Save and print
10. Close the database and exit Access if your work is complete

did you know?

according to Dennis Changon, spokesman for the International Civil Aviation Organization in Montreal, Canada, if all of the commercial planes in the world were grounded at the same time, there wouldn't be space to park them all at the gates.

Colonel Waring, New York City Street Cleaning Commissioner, was responsible for organizing the first rubbish-sorting plant for recycling in the United States in 1898.

early models of vacuum cleaners were powered by gasoline.

honey is used as a center for golf balls and in antifreeze mixtures.

the first commercial passenger airplane began flying in 1914.

focus group information compiled by CalComp revealed that _____ percent of computer users do not like using a mouse.

to find out how many computer users don't like using a mouse, visit www.mhhe.com/i-series.

Chapter Objectives

In this chapter you will:

- **Maintain table data using various methods to add records, delete records, and update field data—AC2002-5-1**
- **Learn to organize and find table data using Datasheet view—AC2002-5-3**
- **Understand how to design relational database tables**
- **Create and save Access table definitions—AC2002-2-1**
- **Use the Clipboard to copy records between tables**
- **Format datasheets—AC2002-2-4**

CHAPTER 2 two

Maintaining Your Database

chapter case

PuppyParadise

You and Evan have made a great deal of progress in evaluating the database needs of PuppyParadise. Evan's response to the Customer table prototype has been very positive and it is time to review the remaining data storage requirements of this home business.

You know that user education is critical to the success of any database development project. If you build a wonderful database but the customer doesn't know how to use it, the result is an ineffective product. To avoid this situation, the process of familiarizing Evan with Access needs to continue. You want to ensure that he is comfortable organizing, maintaining, and using the stored data. Additionally, Evan is interested in learning how to design and develop databases. He believes the ability to use databases is a critical business skill and that this understanding will help him in his study of e-commerce when he goes to college.

Evan has provided you with hard copies of the Excel and manual reports that he creates. You have evaluated these reports to determine the data requirements of PuppyParadise. Your preliminary assessment of the organization's database requirements indicates that tables for orders, products, and suppliers are needed in addition to the existing Customer table. The Orders table would hold data about each order such as order number, product, and quantity ordered. The Products table would list products with their availability (quantity on hand and time to produce). The Suppliers table would contain contact and history information for vendors that provide products and services to PuppyParadise. You and Evan will proceed with a more detailed analysis of data requirements and then develop prototypes of the new tables that you determine are necessary. You will begin by looking at the data necessary to bill customers using the sample invoice from Figure 2.1.

FIGURE 2.1

PuppyParadise customer invoice

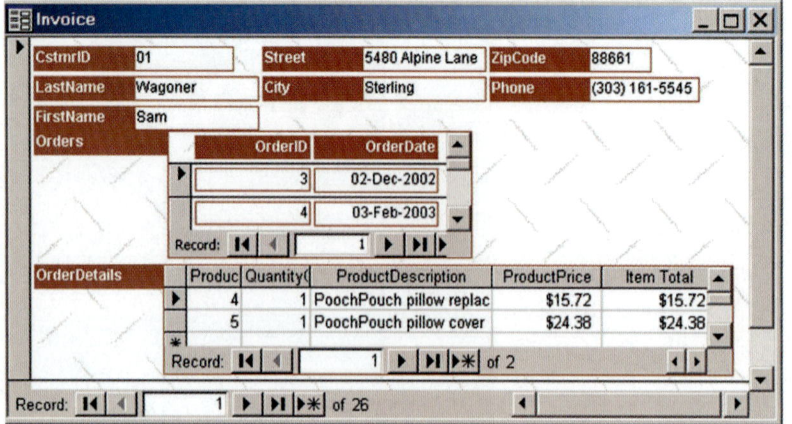

SESSION 2.1 MAINTAINING ACCESS DATA

To be effective, data stored in a database must be kept current. The process of keeping data current is called maintenance. Maintenance tasks include adding new records, removing old records, and changing values in existing records. Evan will be the only user of PuppyParadise data, so it is critical that he understands how to sort, find, and update tables.

CHAPTER OUTLINE

ORDERING, FINDING, AND ENTERING DATA

Access table data can be maintained many ways. The best way to maintain data will depend on the size of the tables, the frequency of updates, the design features that have been applied, and personal preferences. Because all Access objects support updates from the Datasheet view, you will review that method with Evan first.

Recall from the previous chapter that the Datasheet view displays stored values in a tabular format. Each row of data is a record and each column is a field. You can use the record selector to select an entire record, the field selector to select a column, and the Tab key to move from cell to cell. While this might be all the navigation that you need in a small database, the deficiencies of these methods should be obvious when contemplating the maintenance of tables containing hundreds or thousands of records.

Sorting Records

Database data are stored in what is called natural order, or the sequence the records were added to the table. By default the datasheet shows data in order by the primary key if there is one. Many times the primary key is wonderful for uniquely identifying records, but not an effective tool for humans to use in finding records. For example when you are looking for data on a specific person, you would have a hard time finding him or her by Social Security Number, the most likely primary key. However, it would be relatively easy to find him or her using the last and first names.

Finding and updating the correct row and column of data are critical to the integrity of database data. A simple way to improve your ability to find specific records in a large table of data is to sort the records in a manner related to the way they are being used. The same table data can be displayed in various sort orders that match the assorted ways that the data are used (see Figure 2.2).

Moving Table Columns

Sorting table data in Datasheet view works in much the same way as sorting query output, which was introduced in the previous chapter. The first step in changing the order of the records is typically to move the sort column(s) to the left of the datasheet to visually indicate which field has been used to order. Most users expect data to be sorted by the first column(s) displayed for a table.

Changing the column order significantly improves the usability of a datasheet and has no impact on how the data are actually stored. When the column order reflects how the data are sorted (leftmost fields) and matches the way it is used (source documents like drivers licenses), updates are much more likely to be valid.

FIGURE 2.2
Various sorts of the Customer table

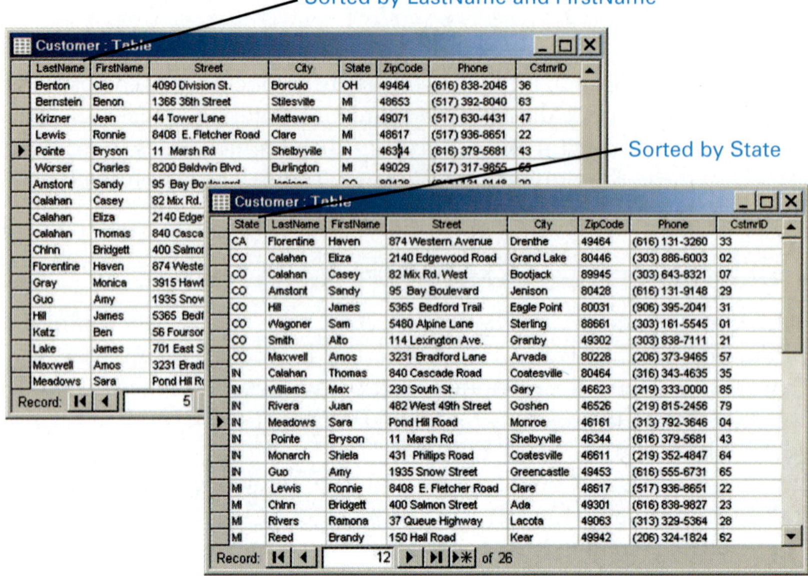

Evan lets you know that when he takes orders for a PoochPouch, he asks for the customers' name, address, city, state, zip, and then phone number. He would like the data in that order.

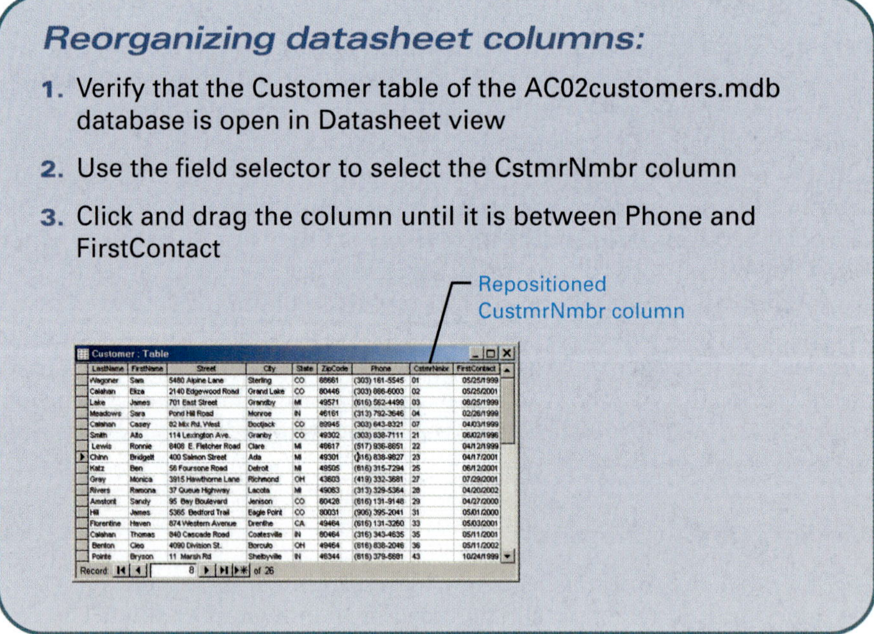

Reorganizing datasheet columns:

1. Verify that the Customer table of the AC02customers.mdb database is open in Datasheet view
2. Use the field selector to select the CstmrNmbr column
3. Click and drag the column until it is between Phone and FirstContact

FIGURE 2.3
Customer table with new column order

Organizing Records

Sorting by one field is as simple as clicking anywhere in the column and selecting the Sort Ascending or Sort Descending key from the toolbar. Unless a sort field contains unique values for each row in the table, multiple sort fields are needed to completely organize the data. For example LastName is a nonunique field that can contain multiple rows with the value, Hampton for instance. When a sort field has multiple rows with the same value in the ***primary sort*** field, a ***secondary sort*** field like

FirstName is needed to organize records. Access will allow you to select two or more adjacent columns for a sort. The order of the columns determines the importance of the field to the sort. Access will sort by the leftmost column first and then continue sorting with each of the other selected columns moving from left to right.

To achieve the desired order for the Customer table, you will need to sort by both the customer's last and first names. LastName is the primary sort field and must appear in the table before the secondary sort field, FirstName. To sort the data, select both the LastName and FirstName columns and then select the appropriate sort key button from the Access toolbar.

Sorting the Customer table:

1. Open the database AC02Customers.mdb if it is not already open
2. Open the Datasheet view of the Customer table
3. Verify that the column order is set so that LastName is the primary sort field and FirstName is the secondary sort field
4. Select both the LastName and FirstName columns and click the **Sort Ascending** button on the toolbar

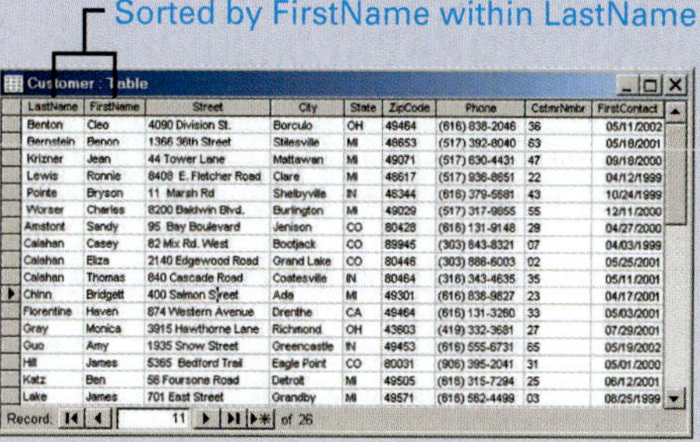

LastName	FirstName	Street	City	State	ZipCode	Phone	CstmrNmbr	FirstContact
Benton	Cleo	4090 Division St.	Borculo	OH	49464	(616) 838-2046	36	05/11/2002
Bernstein	Benon	1366 36th Street	Stilesville	MI	48653	(517) 392-8040	63	05/18/2001
Krizner	Jean	44 Tower Lane	Mattawan	MI	49071	(517) 630-4431	47	09/18/2000
Lewis	Ronnie	8408 E. Fletcher Road	Clare	MI	48617	(517) 936-8651	22	04/12/1999
Pointe	Bryson	11 Marsh Rd	Shelbyville	IN	46344	(616) 379-5881	43	10/24/1999
Worser	Charles	8200 Baldwin Blvd.	Burlington	MI	49029	(517) 317-9855	55	12/11/2000
Amstont	Sandy	95 Bay Boulevard	Jenison	CO	80428	(616) 131-9148	29	04/27/2000
Calahan	Casey	82 Mix Rd. West	Bootjack	CO	89945	(303) 843-8321	07	04/03/1999
Calahan	Eliza	2140 Edgewood Road	Grand Lake	CO	80446	(303) 886-6003	02	05/25/2001
Calahan	Thomas	840 Cascade Road	Coatesville	IN	80464	(316) 343-4635	35	05/11/2001
Chinn	Bridgett	400 Salmon Street	Ada	MI	49301	(616) 838-9827	23	04/17/2001
Florentine	Haven	874 Western Avenue	Drenthe	CA	49464	(616) 131-3260	33	05/03/2001
Gray	Monica	3915 Hawthorne Lane	Richmond	OH	43603	(419) 332-3681	27	07/29/2001
Guo	Amy	1935 Snow Street	Greencastle	IN	49453	(616) 555-6731	65	05/19/2002
Hill	James	5365 Bedford Trail	Eagle Point	CO	80031	(906) 395-2041	31	05/01/2000
Katz	Ben	56 Foursone Road	Detroit	MI	49505	(616) 315-7294	25	06/12/2001
Lake	James	701 East Street	Grandby	MI	49571	(616) 562-4499	03	08/25/1999

5. When you close the datasheet, you will be prompted to save the layout changes that you have made. Choose **Yes** so that the next time you open the Customer table it will be sorted as Evan wants

FIGURE 2.4
Reordering Customer table data

The impact of ascending and descending sorts on various types of data are represented in Figure 2.5. If you need to sort nonadjacent columns or use an ascending sort on some fields and descending sort on others, this can be accomplished in a query.

Finding Records

Access provides a Find tool for locating specific records. It can be used in many of the views of a database including the Datasheet view. Click in the column whose values will be searched and then click the Find button on the toolbar or select the Find option of the Edit menu.

The Find and Replace dialog box is used to set the criteria for a search. Valid criteria are outlined in Figure 2.6.

FIGURE 2.5
Sort behaviors

Type of Data	Ascending Sort Behavior	Descending Sort Behavior
Number	Sorts from lowest to highest value	Sorts from highest to lowest value
Text	Sorts from A to Z	Sorts from Z to A
Date	Sorts from oldest to newest date	Sorts from newest to oldest date
Time	Sorts from oldest to newest time	Sorts from newest to oldest time
Yes/No	Sorts Yes or checked first	Sorts No or unchecked first

FIGURE 2.6
Find and replace dialog box components

Criteria	Find and Replace Dialog Box Action	
Find What	Sets the value that will be matched in the search	
Look In	Determines what will be searched. The default is the active column, but you also can choose to search the entire table.	
Match	Any Part of Field	Matches if the *Find What* value is anywhere in the field
	Whole Field	Matches if the *Find What* value is all that is in the field
	Start of Field	Matches if the *Find What* value is at the start of the field
Search	All	Searches for a match in the entire *Look In* area
	Up	Searches for a match above the cursor in the *Look In* area
	Down	Searches for a match below the cursor in the *Look In* area
Match Case	Matches the case of *Find What* when clicked on	

task reference

Finding Specific Data Values

- Click in the column to search
- Click the **Find** button
- Enter the Find What criteria using data values and wildcards to create a search pattern. Remember that a question mark (?) can be used as a wildcard for one character and an asterisk (*) is a wildcard for multiple characters
- Click the **Find Next** button. If multiple rows match the Find What criteria, repeat this step until the desired row is found

The Find and Replace dialog box can be used to find and replace values. It is best to test the Find criteria and then add the Replace value so that data are not accidentally destroyed. In the next exercise you will be replacing the word "Road" with the abbreviation "Rd." in the Customer table's Street addresses column.

Finding and replacing values in the Customer table:

1. Verify that the Customer table of AC02customers.mdb database is open in Datasheet view
2. Click in the **LastName** column and activate the Find and Replace dialog box using the **Find** button on the toolbar
3. Enter **Calahan** in the Find What text box and click **Find Next.** The first Calahan occurrence should highlight. Click **Find Next** again to display the second occurrence and again to find the third occurrence

tip: *When Find Next is clicked after all occurrences of a value have been found, a dialog box displays stating "Microsoft Access finished searching the records. The search item was not found"*

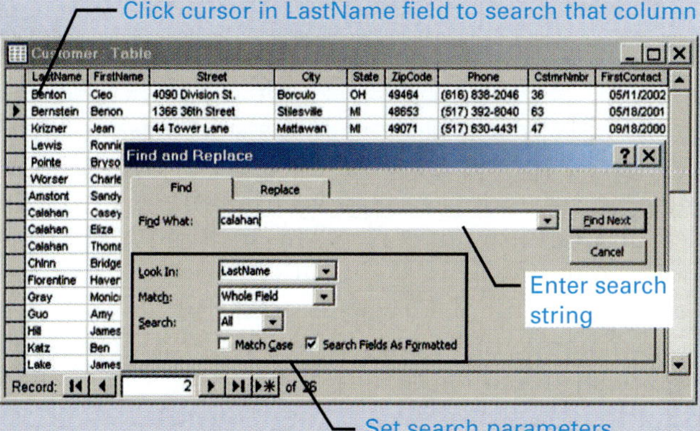
Click cursor in LastName field to search that column
Enter search string
Set search parameters

4. Click in the Street column and enter a Find What value of **Road** and set Match to **Any Part of Field.** Click **Find Next** repeatedly to step through all of the values

tip: *Be sure that only the word "Road" is being selected from the street address. When the replace is applied in the next step, it will replace everything selected—not just the Find What value. If the entire contents of the Street are being selected, double check the Match setting*

5. Now that the Find works, lets replace "Road" with the abbreviation "Rd." in all of the addresses. Click the **Replace** tab of the Find and Replace dialog box. Enter **Rd.** in the Replace With text box
6. Click **Replace All** to update all of the records at once
7. Verify that the replace worked correctly
8. Save

anotherway

. . . to initiate Access operations for the current column

Pressing **Ctrl+F** will initiate the Find and Replace dialog box for the active column.

FIGURE 2.7
Find and Replace

FIGURE 2.8
Access wildcards

Access Wildcards		
Character	*Description*	*Example*
*	Matches any number of characters; it can be used as the first or last character of a search value	wh* Finds what, who, whale, and wham
?	Matches any single alphabetic character	b?ll Finds bill, bell, ball, and bull
#	Matches any single numeric character	b#98 Finds b098, b98, and b998
[]	Matches any one of the characters contained in the brackets	b[ae]ll Finds ball and bell
	! Negates a condition	b[!ae]ll Finds bill, ball, and bull because they do not contain *a* or *e*
	- Specifies a range of conditions	B[a-g]ll Finds ball, bbll, bcll, bdll, bell, bfll, and bgll

Wildcards

When entering the Find What criteria, wildcards are used to create a pattern match (see Figure 2.8). A question mark (?) can be used to represent any single character in a pattern. Let's say, for example, that you were looking for a female Tony, but are not sure of the spelling. A search for Ton? would return both Toni and Tony. It would also return Tone, Tong, and Tons if they were stored in the field. The asterisk (*) wildcard will replace any number of characters so that searching for Ton* would return Tonaba, Toni, Tony, Tons, Tonka, Tonanbaum, and so on.

It is important to note that wildcards are not meant to be used with date, time, and numeric data types. Using wildcards with these data types can cause incomplete or erroneous data retrieval. Confusion arises because wildcards on numeric fields often appear to work and sometimes produce the correct results. Ideally wildcards are used on text data when you only know part of the value or want to find data that match a pattern.

Using wildcards to find Customer table data:

1. Verify that the Customer table of AC02customers.mdb database is open in Datasheet view
2. Click in the **Street** column and activate the Find and Replace dialog box using the **Find** button on the toolbar
3. Enter ***hill*** in the Find What area

tip: *This Find What criterion will find any street addresses containing the characters "hill"*

4. Repeatedly click **Find Next,** evaluating each found address until there are no more matches
5. Click in the **FirstName** column and activate the Find and Replace dialog box by clicking it
6. For this exercise we would like to retrieve first names with three letters. Type **???** in the Find What text box
7. Repeatedly click **Find Next,** evaluating each name found until there are no more matches
8. Click in the **State** column and activate the Find and Replace dialog box by clicking it

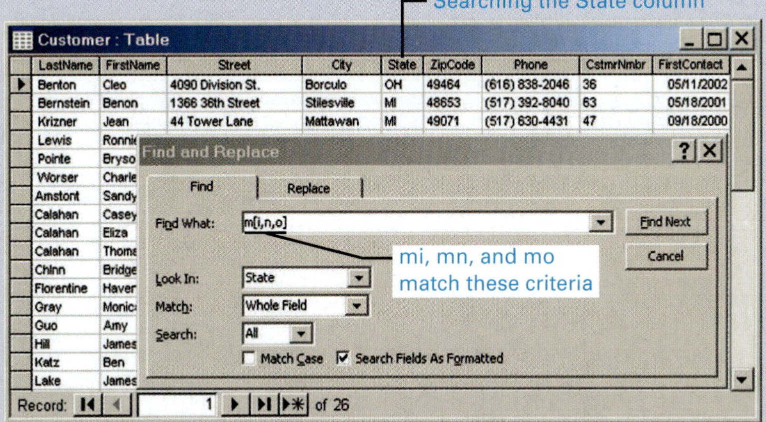

FIGURE 2.9
Find using wildcards

9. For this exercise we would like to retrieve data for the states of Michigan (MI), Missouri (MO), and Minnesota (MN), so you will need to enter **m[i,n,o]** in the Find What text box and click **Find Next.** The first matching occurrence should highlight. Click **Find Next** until you have reviewed all selected records

Adding Table Records

The order of table data display has nothing to do with the order in which it is stored. It is therefore not important to insert new records in any particular order. The primary key or a user-defined sort criterion will determine display order.

Whether a table simply needs some new records added or is empty because it has just been built, the datasheet is a simple place to create new records. When you open a table, the default is to display the data in Datasheet view. The last row displayed in the datasheet is blank with an asterisk in the record indicator, as shown in Figure 2.10.

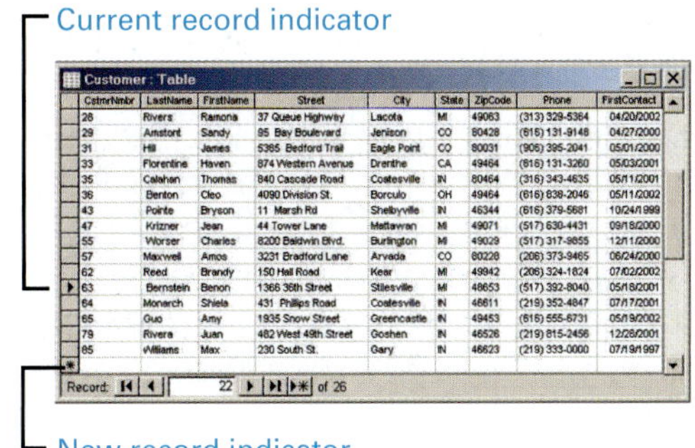

FIGURE 2.10
Customer table in Datasheet view

Clicking in the new record row will change the record indicator to an arrow, meaning that it is the current record. As you begin to enter data in the row, the record indicator changes to a pencil to point out that the record is being edited. Once the record is in edit mode, you can key in field data using the Tab key to advance to the next field and Shift+Tab to move to the previous field. Moving to the next empty record or to any other row of the datasheet will automatically save newly entered data. If a required field such as the primary key has been left blank, an error message will display.

Adding New Records to the Customer table:

1. Verify that the Customer table of the AC02customers.mdb database is open in Datasheet view. Find the current record indicator, a right-pointing arrow in the record selector
2. Click the **New Record** indicator, an * in the record selector, or toolbar button

tip: *The record indicator should convert to a pencil as you begin making modifications to indicate that the record is in edit mode*

FIGURE 2.11
New data for the Customer table

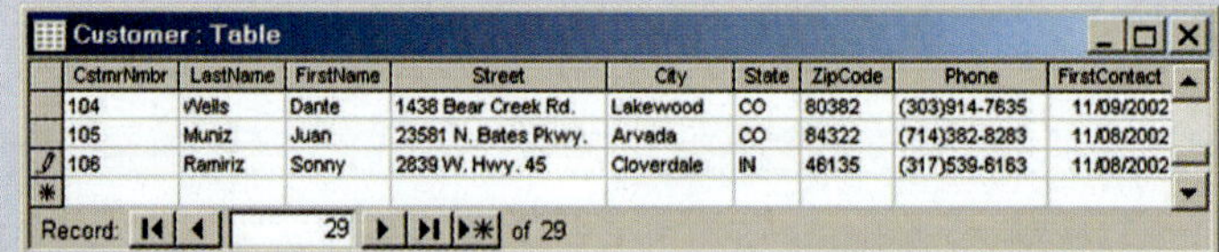

CstmrNmbr	LastName	FirstName	Street	City	State	ZipCode	Phone	FirstContact
104	Wells	Dante	1438 Bear Creek Rd.	Lakewood	CO	80382	(303)914-7635	11/09/2002
105	Muniz	Juan	23581 N. Bates Pkwy.	Arvada	CO	84322	(714)382-8283	11/08/2002
106	Ramiriz	Sonny	2839 W. Hwy. 45	Cloverdale	IN	46135	(317)539-6163	11/08/2002

3. Verify that the empty record is the current record and then enter the data in Figure 2.11 using the Tab key to move from cell to cell

tip: *Correct typing errors by using the Backspace key to delete characters to the left of the insertion point or the Delete key to remove characters to the right of the insertion point, or by double-clicking a data value to select the entire value and overtype it*

4. Add yourself as customer 108
5. Resort the table contents by LastName and FirstName and then print the table using the Print button from the toolbar

UPDATING DATA

Besides adding new records to database tables, existing data must be updated to keep them current. Customers move, changing their address information; get married or divorced, changing their name; or sometimes the original data were entered erroneously and must be corrected. Whatever the cause, deleting old data and updating existing data are critical to the integrity of a database.

Deleting Data

Database data need to be removed from tables when they are no longer useful. Unnecessary rows of data slow processing and confuse users. Most businesses do not simply delete old data because they could be useful as history or may need to be retained for legal reasons (tax and personnel data must be retained for periods specified by laws). In such cases, the data are backed up or stored to an alternate location before they are deleted from the active table.

Actually deleting a single record is a simple process. Use the record selector to highlight the record to be deleted and then press the **Del** key on the keyboard. There is also a Delete button on the toolbar, a Delete Record option in the Edit menu, and a Delete Record option in the popup menu. Once completed, the delete process cannot be reversed, so be careful to verify that you are deleting the correct record.

Deleting a record from the Customer table:

1. Verify that the Customer table of the AC02Customers.mdb database is open in Datasheet view
2. Use the record selector to choose the record for Ramona Rivers
3. Press the **delete** button on the toolbar or the **Del** key on your keyboard
4. Answer **Yes** to the warning that the delete can't be undone

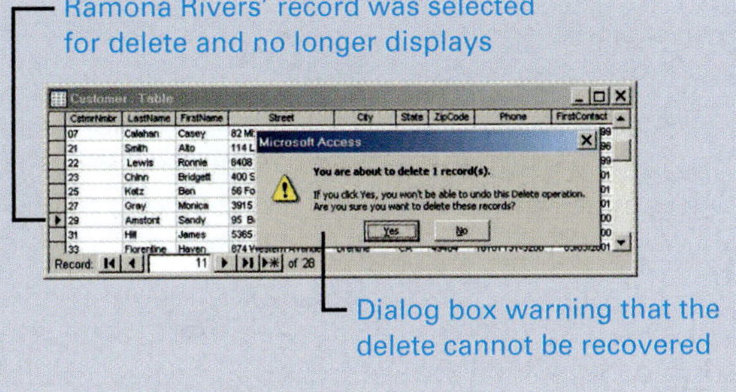
Ramona Rivers' record was selected for delete and no longer displays
Dialog box warning that the delete cannot be recovered
Microsoft Access
You are about to delete 1 record(s).
Yes
No

FIGURE 2.12
Deleting a Customer table record

Using Find to locate records for deletion is an effective way to ensure that the correct record is selected. It is also possible to delete a group of records. Use click and drag across multiple record selectors to highlight several contiguous records. Any of the previously mentioned delete methods will remove all selected records. The warning dialog box will list the number of records selected for deletion.

Modifying Data

Modifying data is the process of changing specific values in a record or records. Access navigation can be customized to simplify the editing process. When using keyboard navigation (Tab and arrow keys), the default navigation settings cause the entire contents of a cell to be selected when entered. Typing while all contents of a cell are selected will replace the entire data value. If, however, the goal is to move character by character in a cell, choose Options from the Tools menu and change the Keyboard options to either Go to start of field or Go to end of field.

In navigation mode (Tab selects the entire cell contents), using the Home and End keys will move the cursor to the first and last cell in a record, respectively. The arrow keys move the cursor from cell to cell. In edit mode (Go to start or end of field), the Home and End keys move the cursor to the beginning and end of a field. The left and right arrow keys move the cursor character-by-character within the cell.

The mouse also can be used to navigate during editing operations. Clicking an insertion point in the text of a field will allow new characters to be added to the existing data. Click and drag to select multiple characters of a data value for typeover. When editing with the mouse, each table cell is edited like a word processing document.

Using Undo

When editing records in Datasheet view, the Undo feature of Microsoft Access 2002 will allow changes to be reversed. Undo can be accessed from the Edit menu or via the toolbar button. As edits are completed, undo stores each action. All actions on a single record can be undone one at a time before they are saved using the Undo button.

Once the cursor moves to another record or the view is exited, any changes made to a record are saved to the database and undo is cleared. At that point selecting Undo Saved Record from the Edit menu will restore the original record (see Figure 2.13).

Updating with the Microsoft Office Clipboard

The Windows clipboard is a temporary storage area that will hold cut or copied information from any Windows program. Stored information can be pasted into any open Windows program. The Windows clipboard holds only one item. By contrast, the Microsoft Office Clipboard allows multiple text and graphic items from any number of Office programs to be collected and then pasted into any open Office document. For example, some text from a Microsoft Word document, some data from a Microsoft Excel spreadsheet, a bulleted list from Microsoft PowerPoint, and some text from Microsoft FrontPage or Microsoft Internet Explorer could all be copied to the MS Office Clipboard and then pasted into a Microsoft Access datasheet.

Like the Windows clipboard, the Office Clipboard works with the Cut and Copy buttons on the toolbar. The Office Clipboard, however, will hold up to 24 items. Items remain on the Office Clipboard until all Office appli-

FIGURE 2.13
Undo saved record

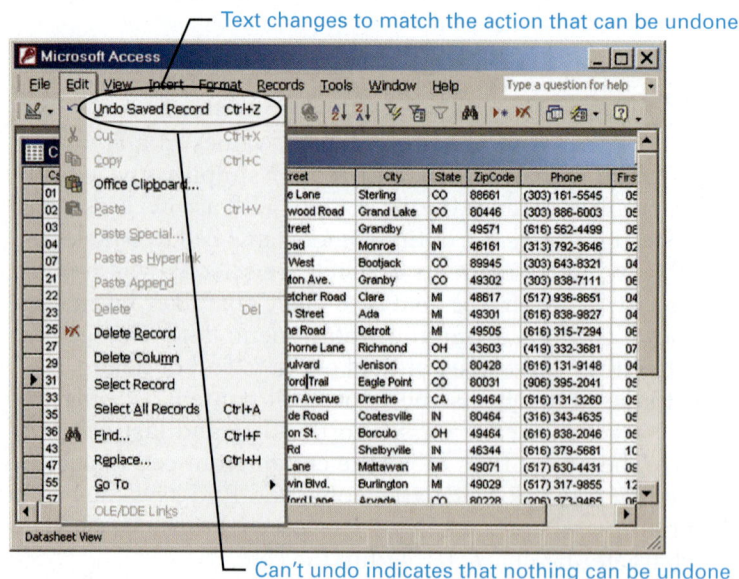

Text changes to match the action that can be undone

Can't undo indicates that nothing can be undone

cations are closed or the clipboard is cleared. The Paste button on the toolbar pastes the contents of the Windows clipboard, which is also the last entry from the Office Clipboard. The Office Clipboard opens as soon as two items are cut or copied from the same application. The contents of the Office Clipboard are viewed in the Task Pane by selecting Office Clipboard from the Edit menu or the Office Clipboard icon from the taskbar.

The Office Clipboard can be used to copy values from one row of a database table to another row or rows to speed repetitive data entry and reduce errors. The clipboard can also be used to copy entire records and move data from other Office applications. Each clipboard item carries the icon of the originating Office product (see Figure 2.14). Items can be selected and pasted individually or the Paste All button can be used to paste the entire clipboard contents at once.

Notice in Figure 2.14 that Access data are placed on the clipboard with the field name as well as the copied contents. The field name is informational and will not be pasted. The selection can be any part of a field, an entire column, multiple fields of a record, or multiple rows of a table to copy to the clipboard. When pasting data from multiple fields to a datasheet, make sure the columns match the order of the data you want to copy or move.

In the next series of steps, the Office Clipboard will be used to copy to a new table the records of customers with billing problems.

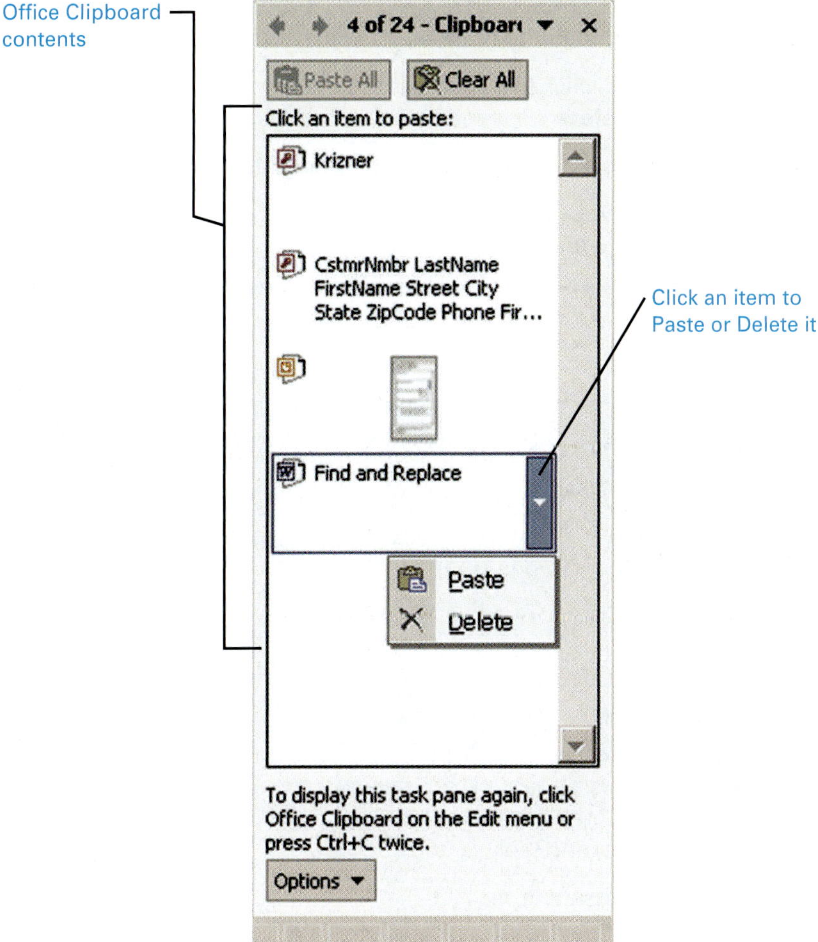

FIGURE 2.14
The Office Clipboard

task reference

Using the Office Clipboard

- Collect items to paste
  - Display the Office Clipboard by selecting **Office Clipboard** from the **Edit** menu
  - Select the item to be copied
  - Click the **Copy** or **Cut** button in the Standard toolbar
  - Continue placing items on the clipboard (up to 24) until you have collected everything that you need
- Paste collected items
  - Display the Office Clipboard if it is not already present. If the Office Clipboard option of the Edit menu is not available, you are in an application or view that does not support the Office Clipboard
  - Click or select the area where you want to place items
  - Do one of the following:
    - Select the **Paste All** button to paste the entire contents of the Office Clipboard
    - Select a clipboard item and choose **Paste** from its drop-down menu
- Remove Office Clipboard items when it is open
  - To clear one item, click the arrow next to the item you want to delete and then click **Delete**
  - To clear all clipboard contents, click the **Clear All** button
  - Placing more than 24 items on the clipboard will replace existing items beginning with the oldest item

Using the Office Clipboard with the Customer table:

1. Verify that the AC02customers.mdb database is open. Close the Customer table if it is open
2. Use the Windows clipboard to make a copy of the Customer table
   a. Select the **Customer** table in the Database window
   b. Select the **Copy** button from the Standard toolbar
   c. Select the **Paste** button from the Standard toolbar. Name the copied table **CustomerBackup** and select the **Structure Only** paste options. This will create a new table named CustomerBackup with no data
3. Open the **Customer** table

4. Select the **Office Clipboard** option of the **Edit** menu to view current clipboard contents. If necessary, click the **Clear All** button to remove existing clipboard contents
5. There are three customers—Sam Wagoner, Haven Florentine, and Jean Krizner—with billing problems whose data need to be put in the new table. Select each record and copy it to the clipboard using the Copy button
6. Close the Customer table
7. Open the **CustomerBackup** table, which should contain no records

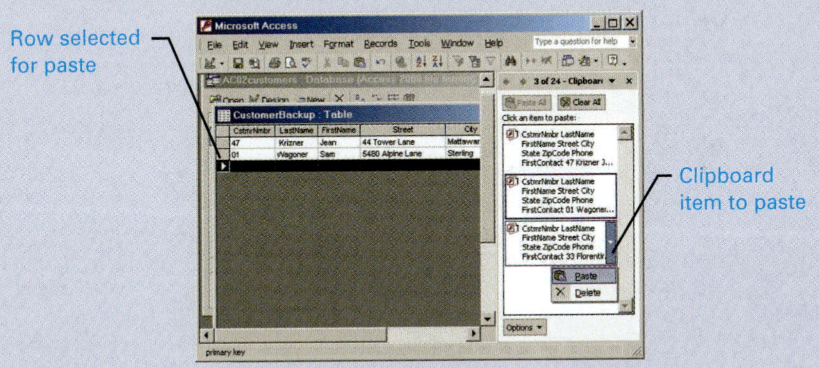

FIGURE 2.15 Pasting records from the Office Clipboard

8. Select the new record row of CustomerBackup and select the **Paste** option for the first item on the Office Clipboard. Repeat this process for the other two items on the Office Clipboard

tip: *If you get a paste error, verify that the entire row of CustomerBackup is selected before trying to paste a record from the Office Clipboard*

When pasting multiple fields, it is important for the paste area to match the size and shape of the copy area (same number of cells). When pasting multiple cells or entire rows of data, it is important for the field names of the paste area to match the field names of the copy area.

In Access only one database can be open at a time. Using the Office Clipboard it is possible to open a database, place data on the clipboard, open another database, and paste the Office Clipboard contents.

ORGANIZING A DATASHEET

Datasheets are often bigger than your computer screen, making data updates difficult. Hiding and freezing columns can improve your ability to enter data in the correct rows and columns.

Hiding and Unhiding Columns

When there are columns in a datasheet that are not relevant to the task at hand, they can be hidden. Hiding removes columns from display but does not impact the stored data. When only the needed columns are displayed, more of the table will fit on the screen, you do not have to tab through unwanted data, and only the displayed columns will print.

another*word*

. . . on Hiding and Unhiding Columns

The Unhide Columns dialog box can be activated when no columns are hidden. It is a convenient way to hide multiple columns by unchecking them. The shortcut menu containing the Unhide Columns option can be activated by right-clicking the datasheet window outside the data area (for example, in the Title bar).

task reference

Hiding and Unhiding Datasheet Columns

- Open a table, query, or form in Datasheet view
- To Hide a column
  - Click the field selector of the column to be hidden
  - Click **Hide Columns** on the **Format** menu
- To Unhide a column
  - On the **Format** menu, click **Unhide Columns**
  - Select the names of the columns to show from the Unhide Columns dialog box

Hiding and unhiding columns of the Customer table:

1. Open the Customer table of the AC02customers.mdb database in Datasheet view
2. Click the column selector for State
3. Select the **Format** menu and then select **Hide Columns.** The column will remain hidden until it is unhidden or until you close the datasheet without saving the formatting changes
4. To unhide columns, select **Unhide Columns** from the **Format** menu
5. Check the **State checkbox** in the Unhide Columns dialog box and click **Close**

Freezing and Unfreezing Columns

Freezing columns is useful when the datasheet is wider than the viewing area of your screen. As you move to the far-right columns, the leftmost columns scroll off the screen, making it difficult to determine what entities' record is being edited. Freezing the column containing entity identification information causes that column or columns to stay on the screen while scrolling through the remaining columns.

task reference

Freezing and Unfreezing Datasheet Columns

- Open a table, query, or form in Datasheet view
- Select the column(s) to freeze or unfreeze
- To Freeze column(s), select **Freeze Columns** on the **Format** menu
- To Unfreeze column(s), select **Unfreeze All Columns** on the **Format** menu

Freezing and unfreezing columns of the Customer table:

1. Verify that the Customer table of AC02customers.mdb database is open in Datasheet view
2. Narrow the datasheet to display only five columns of data by dragging its right corner to the left. Use the Tab key to navigate through a record to demonstrate that the identifying values (CstmrNmbr, LastName, FirstName) scroll out of the viewing area
3. Select both the **LastName** and **FirstName** columns by clicking and dragging across their field selectors
4. Select the **Format** menu and then select **Freeze Columns.** The LastName and FirstName columns will be moved to the first columns of the datasheet

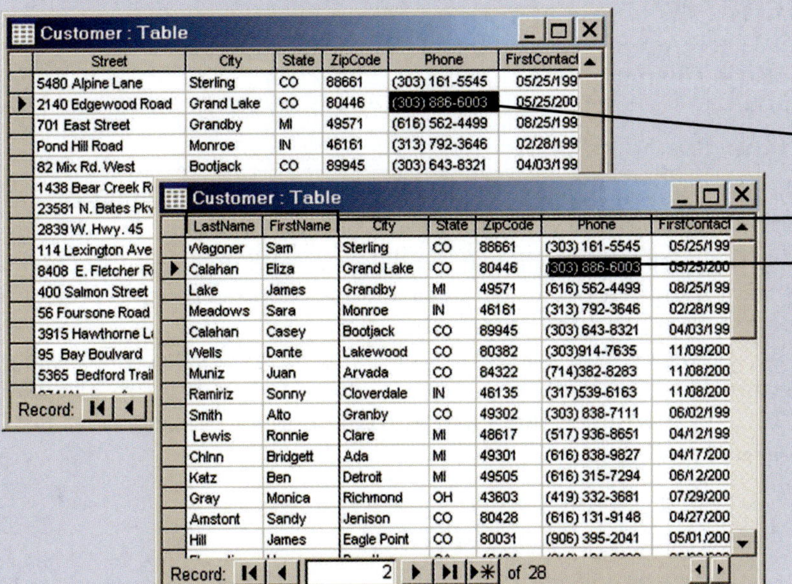

FIGURE 2.16
Unfrozen and frozen Customer table columns

Eliza Calahan's phone number without name fields frozen

Frozen fields

Eliza Calahan's name displays in the same screen as her phone number with name fields frozen

5. Tab through the columns of a record. Notice that the frozen fields stay visible while the remaining fields scroll
6. To unfreeze columns, select **Unfreeze All Columns** from the **Format** menu

making the grade

SESSION 2.1

1. What is the significance of an asterisk in the row selector of a table?
2. Discuss the use of wildcards when finding data in a table.
3. When/how are changes made to a record stored in the table?
4. Discuss the importance of column order when sorting by multiple fields.
5. T F Rows deleted from a table can be restored.
6. T F The Windows Clipboard and the Office Clipboard are the same thing.

SESSION 2.2 DESIGNING AND BUILDING A DATABASE

Now that you and Evan are comfortable with the Customer table, it is time to assess the remaining data requirements for PuppyParadise. Evan is interested in learning how to design and develop databases and has asked to work through this process with you. Involving users in the design process helps to ensure that their needs will be met by the completed database.

ASSESSING INFORMATION NEEDS

The longevity and effectiveness of a database are rooted in the quality of its design. Poorly designed databases are tedious to work with and do not effectively adapt to changing business needs. The 90/10 rule is often cited. It states that 90 percent of your effort should go into design so that only 10 percent of your effort is spent maintaining it.

Regardless of the size of the project, the first step is to assess the information needs. The formality and duration of this process are governed by the size of the project and the organization responsible for the development. There are a variety of tools and procedures that can be used to define information needs.

Outline the Mission

Identifying the mission of a database involves determining specifically what the database will and will not accomplish. To determine the mission, talk to the people who will use the database and document the tasks that they want it to perform. If there are existing reports or forms, collect them; otherwise sketch out the reports that users want.

For example, with PuppyParadise, you have reviewed all of the paper files and Excel spreadsheets currently used by Evan to run his business. The review determined that current tracking fits generally into one of the following areas:

- Tracking customer orders
- Determining product availability
- Tracking suppliers

The next step is to find out what the current system won't do that the new system needs to do. A simple way of determining requirements is to write down the business questions the database should be able to answer. Evan tells you that he is generally happy with the data he has, but it is taking too much time to find and consolidate.

The business questions he considers most important are

- What are the total sales for each month?
- What do my customers owe me?
- How many multiple-order customers do I have?
- Which suppliers provide the best service?
- What do I owe suppliers?
- How much of each product do I have available?

These questions define the outputs that are required of the PuppyParadise database and are used to determine what fields (inputs) need to be stored in database tables. The questions are also a very good start at outlining the forms, queries, and reports needed to provide answers.

Establish Table Subjects

Each table in a database contains data about only one subject (one type of entity). Divining table subjects is not always as easy as it sounds. The business questions that establish the results that are needed from the database which correspond nicely to queries, reports, and forms but do not dictate table structure. Categorizing the information into tables is done by evaluating the impacts of various table configurations on the effectiveness of the database. A formal set of steps called normalization often is used to help ensure effective table design. This session will demonstrate an informal application of normalization rules. Common sense and good judgment help in this process.

Let's consider an invoice for a customer (see Figure 2.17). The invoice would contain information such as the invoice number, invoice date, customer's name and address, product identification, product description, product price, quantity ordered, item total, tax, shipping, and invoice total. While all of these appear on one invoice, it would be problematic to store everything in one table. A customer can order multiple products at a time, which would mean that there would be a row of data for each product ordered. If a customer ordered three products, everything would be entered in the table three times. That is great for the data that change each time, but static data such as the customer's name and address would also be entered three times, significantly multiplying the chance of data entry errors. Duplication also increases maintenance by requiring multiple records to be updated if the customer moves.

To reduce the storage of duplicate data, put the data that do not change often in one table and the changing data in another. The data that do not change often are referred to as static data while frequently changing data are called transaction data. The Customer table will hold the static data about the customer. It is also apparent that a table holding data about products would be beneficial. Common shorthand used to describe tables is to list the table name with its attributes (fields) in parenthesis after it. In this notation, the primary key is underlined. Using this notation with the invoice data, we can demonstrate the tables currently being evaluated as shown in Figure 2.18.

The next step is to review the unassigned attributes to be certain that they do not belong in either the Customer or Products table. The question to ask to determine whether the field belongs in the Customer table is "Does this attribute belong to the customer?" Similarly, ask if the attribute belongs to the Products table. For all of the unassigned values shown above, the answer to both questions is no, meaning that at least one more table is needed.

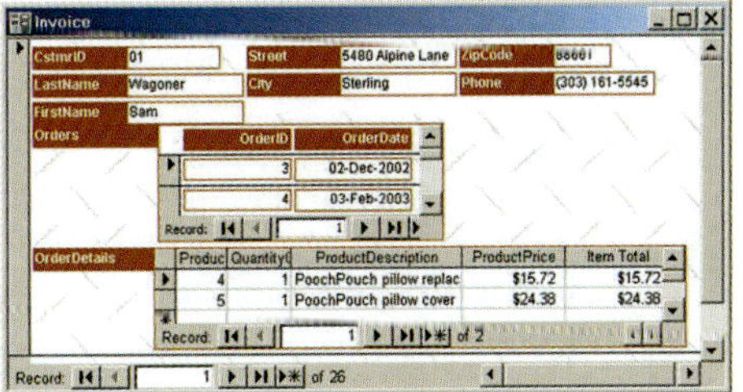

FIGURE 2.17
Customer invoice

FIGURE 2.18
First table design break out

Customer (name, address)

Products (product identification, product description, product price)

Unassigned (invoice number, invoice date, quantity ordered, item total, tax, shipping, and invoice total)

FIGURE 2.19
Table design after removing calculated values

Customer (name, address)

Products (product identification, product description, product price)

Orders (invoice number, invoice date, quantity ordered)

While the formal rules of normalization have not been presented, this informal process is achieving the same result. One further rule holds that derived or calculated data should not be stored in tables. Following that axiom, tax, shipping, and invoice total should be calculated when the invoice is created, not stored in a table, so they can be removed from consideration. The remaining unassigned attributes of invoice number, invoice date, and quantity ordered could all be considered to be order data. Each of these fields is frequently updated with information generated by customer orders. This design stage is shown in Figure 2.19.

This evaluation process needs to be completed for each output defined in the mission statement. The result will be a list of tables and possible attributes covering most of the user's requirements.

Establish Table Fields

Now that the table entities (subjects) and what they should store are established, it is time to determine exactly what attributes need to be stored in each table and how they will be named. In general, field names should be descriptive and not contain spaces or special characters. Here are some tips for defining fields:

- Each field must directly describe the subject of the table. A field that does not describe the subject belongs in another table
- Store data in their smallest logical part. It is easy to merge attributes in queries, forms, and reports, but very difficult to access part of a data value. Combined data values also make it difficult to retrieve and analyze the data. Create separate fields for each part of a person's name and address. Consider breaking up any field that you might want to access part of, such as a part number with embedded information. For easy reporting, such a part number could be broken into PartCategory and PartID, which combine to make a unique part number
- Assign a primary key field to each table. The primary key field(s) should uniquely and minimally identify a specific entity or row of data in the table. If there is no naturally occurring primary key, one should be generated. For example, because names can be duplicated in the data use either Social Security Number or a sequential number to uniquely identify each person

Applying these tips to the previous design results in creating multiple fields for the customer's name and address and adding CstmrID as the key to the customer table (see Figure 2.20).

At this point it is wise to return to the information gathered while creating the mission statement. Be sure that all of the data to create the defined outputs are assigned to a table. Further ensure that all of the questions documented for the design can be answered from the data assigned to tables.

Customer (<u>CstmrID</u>, LastName, FirstName, Street, City, State, Zip)

Products (<u>ProductID</u>, ProductDescription, ProductPrice)

Orders (<u>OrderID</u>, OrderDate, QuantityOrdered)

FIGURE 2.20
Table design with field names and primary keys assigned

Defining Relationships

The power of relational databases is their ability to rapidly locate and organize data stored in multiple tables. For example, the current design stores the data to create a customer invoice in three tables. Data from multiple tables are joined by matching values in a shared field. Those relationships have to be identified and foreign key fields added to the tables.

Decide what tables are related and then how they are related. Remember that table relationships are classified by how many records in the first table are related to how many records in the second table. One-to-many relationships are the most common and occur when one record in Table A relates to many records in Table B. For example, one customer can have many orders. In a one-to-one relationship, one record from the first table can be related to one record of the second table. One-to-one relationships are created when there are too many fields for one table, or there are fields that are blank for most of the rows.

Many-to-many relationships are the most complex because many records from one table are related to many rows in another table. For example, one customer can buy many products and one product can be purchased by many customers. Since relational databases can't directly model many-to-many relationships, a new table is added that has a one-to-many relationship with each table in the many-to-many relationship.

One way to determine relationships is to diagram them. There are usually multiple ways to set the relations in a database; choosing the best fit takes practice. Begin by drawing a rounded box for each table and placing the table name in it. Connect tables that are related with a line and label the line with a brief description of the relationship.

Figure 2.21 presents one possible model of the Customer, Products, and Orders relationships. These diagrams are read from entity to entity as shown in the Relationships figure notes.

Notice that the relationship between products and orders is many-to-many. To model this relationship, an intermediate table having a one-to-many relationship with each table in the many-to-many relationship must be added to the design. In this case, OrderDetails has been added as the intermediate table (see Figure 2.22). It has one-to-many relationships to the Orders and Products tables. Each row in OrderDetails represents one invoice line item (the order for one product). To complete the design, the primary key from the table on the one side of the relationship is added to the table on the many side as a foreign key, enabling the tables to be joined. The final design is described in Figure 2.22.

Designing a Prototype

Once the tables, fields, and relationships are designed, it is time to build a prototype for testing. Create the tables, specify the relationships, and enter some test data. The test data should be representative of the data the table will actually hold to successfully evaluate the design. Create rough drafts

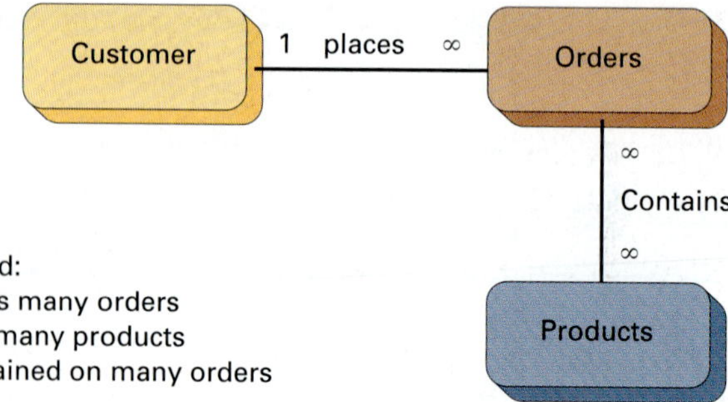

Relationships depicted:
- One customer places many orders
- One order contains many products
- One product is contained on many orders

FIGURE 2.21
Preliminary entity diagram for invoicing design

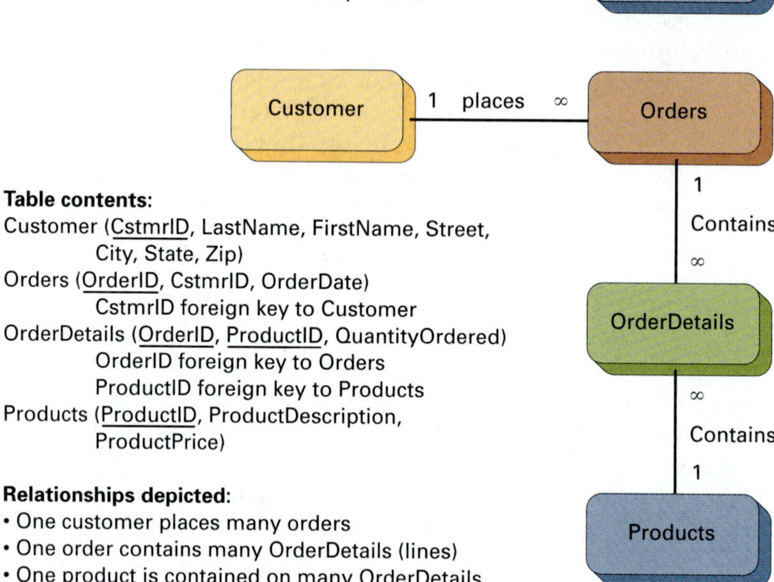

Customer
1 places ∞
Orders
1
Contains
∞
OrderDetails
∞
Contains
1
Products
Table contents:
Customer (CstmrID, LastName, FirstName, Street, City, State, Zip)
Orders (OrderID, CstmrID, OrderDate)
CstmrID foreign key to Customer
OrderDetails (OrderID, ProductID, QuantityOrdered)
OrderID foreign key to Orders
ProductID foreign key to Products
Products (ProductID, ProductDescription, ProductPrice)
Relationships depicted:
• One customer places many orders
• One order contains many OrderDetails (lines)
• One product is contained on many OrderDetails

FIGURE 2.22
Invoicing design with two one-to-many relationships replacing a many-to-many relationship

of the queries, forms, and reports to see if they contain the data needed to answer the questions outlined in the mission statement.

As you work with the prototype, note where the design can be improved. Are any data missing? Are data repeated? Are the primary keys working correctly? Can tables be joined effectively? Update the prototype and continue testing until it is ready for production.

BUILDING ACCESS TABLES USING DESIGN VIEW

In Session 1.2 a table was built using the Table Wizard. Now it's time to take a look at what is going on behind the Wizard. There are many table attributes automatically set by the Table Wizard. The attributes of a table determine how data will be stored, displayed, and processed. Field attributes include a field's name, data type, size, and key. Building tables in Design view allows control over all table attributes.

Field Names

The ***Field Name*** is used to retrieve data from a column in queries, forms, and reports. Although the design already specifies field names, it is important to understand the rules that govern name selection. In Microsoft Access field names must be unique within a table and can

- Be up to 64 characters long
- Include any combination of letters, numbers, spaces, and special characters except a period (.), an exclamation point (!), an accent grave (`), and brackets ([ ])

- Not start with a space
- Not contain control characters

Although Access allows spaces within field names, it is best to capitalize the first letter of each word and not use spaces. So while both Customer number and CustomerNumber are valid field names, CustomerNumber is the better choice. Finally, short but descriptive names are best since the assigned names will be used frequently.

Data Types

The ***Data Type*** of a field establishes what data values it can store and what other properties can be set for the field. For example, setting the OrderDate field to a Date data type ensures that only valid dates and/or times can be stored. Figure 2.23 outlines Access data types.

In addition to determining what data can be stored in a field, the Number, Date/Time, Currency, and Yes/No data types have display formats. Display formats define what the user sees as output from these fields.

You and Evan add data types to the table design as outlined in Figure 2.24.

FIGURE 2.23

Microsoft Access data type overview

Data type	Use for	Size
Text	Text or combinations of text and numbers, such as addresses. Also numbers that do not require calculations, such as phone numbers, part numbers, or postal codes	Up to 255 characters
Memo	Lengthy text and numbers, such as notes or descriptions	Up to 64,000 characters
Number	Numeric data to be used for mathematical calculations, except calculations involving money. Set the FieldSize property to define the specific Number type	Dependent on the field size chosen
Date/Time	Dates and times	8 bytes
Currency	Currency or other values with 4 or fewer decimals. Accurate to 15 digits to the left of the decimal point and 4 digits to the right. Calculations do not round	8 bytes
AutoNumber	Unique sequential (incrementing by 1) or random numbers automatically inserted when a record is added	4 bytes
Yes/No	Fields that will contain only one of two values, such as Yes/No, True/False, On/Off	1 bit
OLE Object	Objects (such as Microsoft Word documents, Microsoft Excel spreadsheets, pictures, sounds, or other binary data), created in other programs using the OLE protocol, that can be linked to or embedded	Up to 1 gigabyte (limited by disk space)
Hyperlink	Field that will store hyperlinks. A hyperlink can be a UNC path or a URL	Up to 64,000 characters
Lookup Wizard	A field that allows you to choose a list of values from another table using a combo box. Choosing this option initiates a Wizard to define this for you	The same size as the primary key field that is also the Lookup field; typically 4 bytes

FIGURE 2.24
Table design with data types

Table	Field Name	Data Type
Customer	CstmrID	Text
	LastName	Text
	FirstName	Text
	Street	Text
	City	Text
	State	Text
	Zip	Text
Orders	OrderID	AutoNumber
	CstmrID	Text
	OrderDate	Date/Time
OrderDetails	OrderID	Number
	ProductID	Number
	QuantityOrdered	Number
Products	ProductID	AutoNumber
	ProductDescription	Text
	ProductPrice	Currency

Field Sizes

The ***Field Size*** property is available for Text, Number, and AutoNumber data types. The other data types either have a fixed field size or adjust to fit the data entered. Field size determines the maximum value a field can store, how much storage space it requires, and how fast it processes. In general, use the smallest field size that will meet your needs.

For fields with a Text data type, the field size can be set from 0 to 255 characters. The default text field size is 50 characters. Text fields only store the data entered without any trailing spaces, so setting a smaller field size does not reduce storage requirements. Smaller text field sizes do improve the validity of stored data. For example, if a company has 15-character part numbers, setting the field size to 15 stops the user from entering more than 15 characters. The valid field sizes for Number data types are outlined in Figure 2.25.

If the DataType property is set to AutoNumber, the FieldSize property can be set to Long Integer or Replication ID, as outlined in Figure 2.23. AutoNumber fields are frequently used to generate unique primary keys for records without a natural primary key. It is important to note that the currency field size is not just for tracking dollars and cents. The currency field size will provide faster fixed-point calculations than either Single or Double and should be used for all noncurrency data of one to four decimal places.

The database design with field sizes added is shown in Figure 2.26.

FIGURE 2.25

Microsoft Access field sizes for number data type

Field Size	Description	Decimal Precision	Storage Size
Byte	Stores numbers from 0 to 255 (no fractions)	None	1 byte
Decimal	Stores numbers from −10^28 − 1 through 10^28 − 1	28	12 bytes
Integer	Stores numbers from −32,768 to 32,767 (no fractions)	None	2 bytes
Long Integer	(Access Default) Stores numbers from −2,147,483,648 to 2,147,483,647 (no fractions)	None	4 bytes
Single	Stores numbers from 3.402823E38 to 1.401298E−45 for negative values and from 1.401298E−45 to 3.402823E38 for positive values	7	4 bytes
Double	Stores numbers from −1.79769313486231E308 to −4.94065645841247E−324 for negative values and from 1.79769313486231E308 to 4.94065645841247E−324 for positive values	15	8 bytes
Replication ID	Globally unique identifier	N/A	16 bytes

FIGURE 2.26

Database design with field sizes

Table	Field Name	Data Type	Field Size
Customer	<u>CstmrID</u>	Text	5
	LastName	Text	30
	FirstName	Text	30
	Street	Text	30
	City	Text	30
	State	Text	2
	Zip	Text	5
Orders	<u>OrderID</u>	AutoNumber	LongInteger
	CstmrID	Text	5
	OrderDate	Date/Time	N/A
OrderDetails	<u>OrderID</u>	Number	LongInteger
	<u>ProductID</u>	Number	LongInteger
	QuantityOrdered	Number	Integer
Products	<u>ProductID</u>	AutoNumber	LongInteger
	ProductDescription	Text	30
	ProductPrice	Currency	N/A

Building a Table Definition

It's finally time to build the table definition in Access using Design view and set all of the attributes that have been outlined.

Defining a Table Field

- Click **Tables** in the Options bar
- Click the **Design view** button on the toolbar
- Enter a field name
- Select a data type
- Define other field attributes as needed

Building the Orders table:

1. Open the AC02PuppyParadise.mdb file. The Customer and Products tables have already been built
2. Click the **Tables** object in the Database window and select the **New** button on the toolbar
3. Select **Design View** from the New Table dialog box and click **OK**

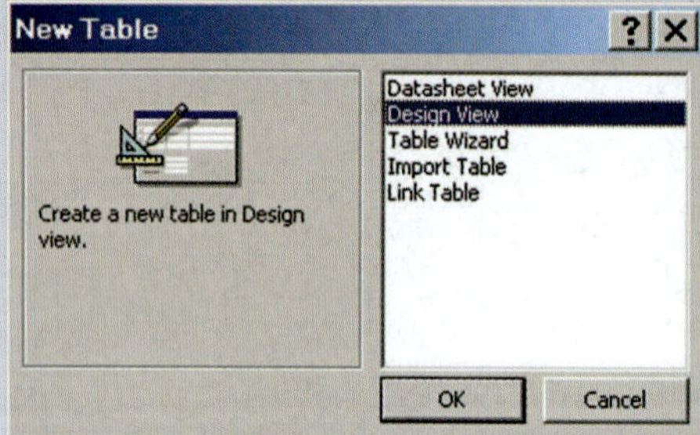

FIGURE 2.27
New table design view

4. Review the Design view grid. Note the default table name, Table1. Find the columns for Field Name, Data Type, and Description. As you create fields, the General tab at the bottom of the page will display other attributes such as Field Size
5. The first field of the Orders table is OrderID. To create that field, type **OrderID** in the Field Name column of the first row. Tab to or click in Data Type to activate the drop-down list. Select **AutoNumber** as the Data Type and leave the Field Size as **LongInteger**

tip: *The Description attribute is for the developer's notes about the design and contents of a field. The value can be up to 255 characters and will display in the Access status bar when the field is active in Datasheet view*

6. Repeat step 5 for the CstmrID field using Figure 2.28. Be sure to set the Field Size for CstmrID on the General tab

7. Repeat step 5 for the OrderDate field using Figure 2.28

Orders Table Design

Table	Field Name	Data Type	Field Size
Orders	OrderID	AutoNumber	LongInteger
	CstmrID	Text	5
	OrderDate	Date/Time	N/A

Access Orders Table Definition

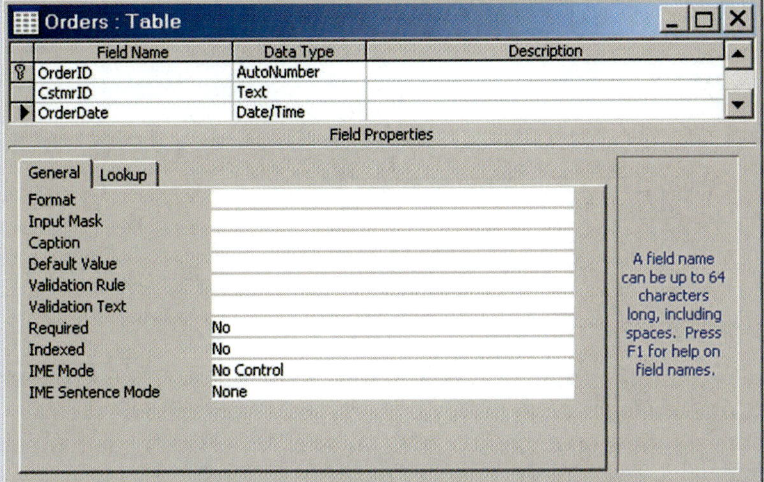

FIGURE 2.28
Field definitions for the orders table

8. Set the table primary key by clicking the record indicator for the OrderID field and then selecting the **Key** button from the Access toolbar

9. Close the Design view window and answer **Yes** to Do you want to save changes to the design of table 'Table1'?

10. Enter **Orders** in the Save As dialog box and click **OK**

FIGURE 2.29
Orders table listed in the database window

11. Verify that your new Orders table is listed in the database window

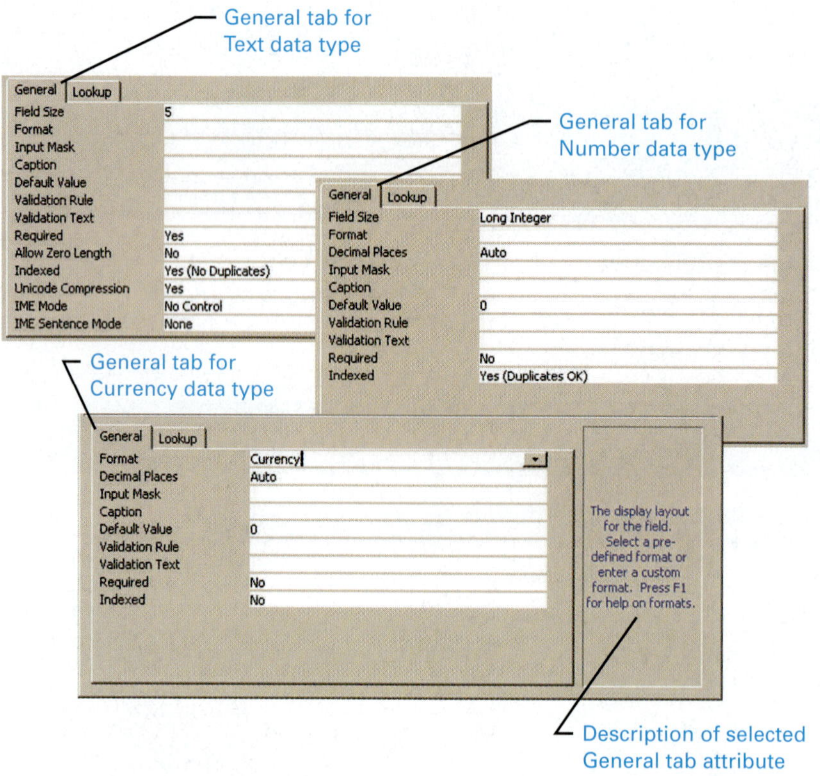

FIGURE 2.30
General tab attributes for text, number, and currency

General Tab Attributes

Let's take a look at some of the other table attributes. The attributes that display on the General tab in Design view are determined by the Data Type selection, as shown in Figure 2.30. A brief description of the selected attribute will display in the panel to the right of the General tab. Attributes that are common to all data types include Caption, Default Value, Validation, Required, and Indexed.

A field's ***Caption*** is the text that will display in forms, queries, and reports to identify the field. If you do not set the Caption, the Field Name will display. ***Default Value*** allows you to speed data entry by automatically placing the most common value in the field each time a new record is added. The user can override the default value by typing over it. ***Validation*** holds the rules that govern what data are valid for the field, which are covered in a later chapter. The ***Required*** attribute is set to yes when the field cannot be blank and no when blank entries are acceptable. ***Indexed*** is set to yes for a field when indexing by that field will improve database performance. A table's primary key is automatically indexed. In general, foreign keys also should be indexed. Other fields are indexed to address performance issues when the database is in use.

A field's ***Format*** attribute controls how data are displayed to the user. Contrast this with the Data Type and Field Size, which control how they are stored. Many Data Types have preset formats that can be selected from a drop-down list. Custom formats also can be created as they are needed. Custom Number formats use a # to represent each number in the output. For example, ###.### would cause all number values to display with three decimal places.

Custom date formats are more complex, using the symbols outlined in Figure 2.31. A Date/Time field is capable of storing both the date and time in the same field. If both are stored, the format can be set to display either one or both. Custom time formats are not covered here.

Symbol	Uses
/	Date separator
d	Formats the day of the month
	d—day of the month without leading zeroes (1–31)
	dd—day of the month in two digits (01–31)
	ddd—weekday abbreviations (Sun–Sat)
	ddddd—full weekday (Sunday–Saturday)
w	Sets week formats
	w—day of the week (1–7)
	ww—week of the year (1–53)
m	Formats the month
	m—month without leading zeroes (1–12)
	mm—two-digit month (01–12)
	mmm—month abbreviations (Jan–Dec)
	mmmm—full month name (January–December)
y	Formats the year
	yy—two-digit year (01–99)
	yyy—full year (0100–9999)

FIGURE 2.31
Custom date format symbols

Setting General tab attributes:

1. Verify that the AC02PuppyParadise.mdb file is open
2. Open the **Orders** table in Design view
3. Select the **OrderDate** field

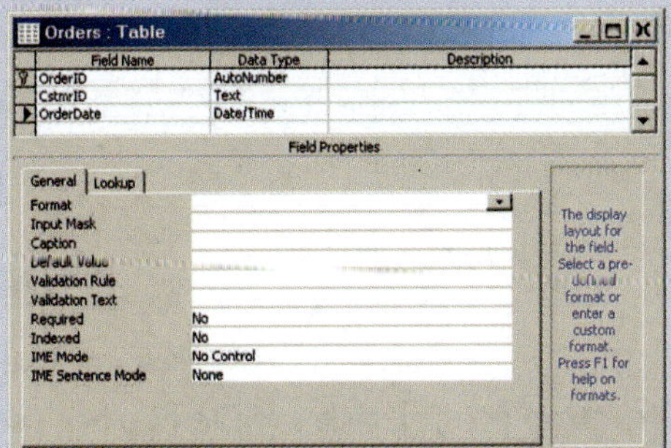

FIGURE 2.32
OrderDate format

4. Enter the custom format **dd-mmm-yyyy**. Dates entered in this field will display with a two-digit day, a three-character month abbreviation, and a four-digit year (15-Jul-2002)
5. Verify your custom format and close the design window
6. Answer **Yes** to save the design changes that you have made

If a Number field is set to Currency format (not the same as Currency field size), it will display based on the regional settings in the Windows Control Panel. Changes made to the regional settings in the Windows Control Panel will be automatically reflected in table fields set to currency format.

To complete the database prototype, the OrderDetails table must be built and table relationships defined. You will build OrderDetails in the next series of steps. Setting relationships is covered later.

Building the OrderDetails table:

1. Verify that the AC02PuppyParadise.mdb file is open
2. Open a new table by selecting **Tables** from the Object Bar and clicking **New** on the toolbar
3. Use what you have learned to build the table fields outlined in Figure 2.33

FIGURE 2.33
OrderDetails fields and attributes

Table	Field Name	Data Type	Field Size	Other Attributes
OrderDetails	OrderID	Number	LongInteger	
	ProductID	Number	LongInteger	
	QuantityOrdered	Number	Integer	Required, Default value 1

4. Click and drag over the record indicators for OrderID and ProductID to select them both. Use the key icon in the Access toolbar to set them as the composite primary key

tip: *If you are successful, both fields should have a key icon in their record selector*

5. Verify your fields and field attributes
6. Close the design window and save the table as **OrderDetails**
7. Open the **OrderDetails** table in Datasheet view. The table is now ready to hold data
8. Close OrderDetails

***another*word**

. . . on Saving Table Designs

You will be prompted to save your changes when you access another view, but you can save them at any point by clicking the Save File button on the Access toolbar.

Using Undo and Redo when Defining Tables

The Microsoft Access Undo feature has more options in Design view than it does in Datasheet view. The difference stems from the way the two views save data. Design view saves data on exit. The Datasheet view updates the database as soon as the cursor moves to a new record.

In Design view Access keeps a list of the 20 most recent actions that can be undone. The Undo button on the Access toolbar has a drop-down list that displays those actions. Clicking an action to undo will also undo all actions above the selection on the list. One action at a time can be undone by repeatedly typing Ctrl+Z.

The Redo button stores the 20 most recent undone actions. Like the Undo button, when redoing an action, the Redo button reinstates all actions above it on the list. Both the Undo and Redo lists are cleared when the view is changed.

WORKING WITH NEW TABLES

New tables have now been created using both the New Table Wizard and Table Design view. Table Design view provides the developer with much more control than using a Wizard. Many developers use the Wizard to create the first draft of a table and then use Design view to customize the table generated by the Wizard. Regardless of how you choose to build tables, the abilities to move comfortably between table views and add data are critical.

Navigating between Views

When working with Access objects, it is tedious to close the object to use a different view. Fortunately Access provides an easy way to move between views using the View button on the Access toolbar. The View button is a drop-down list box that displays valid options for the current or open object (see Figure 2.34).

Remember that the undo and redo buffers are cleared when you change views, but the clipboard is not cleared. Changes made in one view can impact data in another view. Be especially careful when changing the design of an object. The impacts of table design changes are discussed in a later chapter.

Populating New Tables

Session 2.1 covered adding, deleting, and updating records in a table. As has been noted, table Datasheet view is a simple way to enter data. Forms and queries also can be used to add and maintain table data. The clipboard can copy data that exist elsewhere and paste them into the table. Finally, data can be imported from existing documents maintained by other Office products like Excel.

Regardless of how tables are being populated, there are dangers in entering data before the entire database has been built and table relationships set. The defined relationships between tables enforce integrity of the data that are entered. With the independent tables that are in the PuppyParadise database now, an order could be entered for a customer

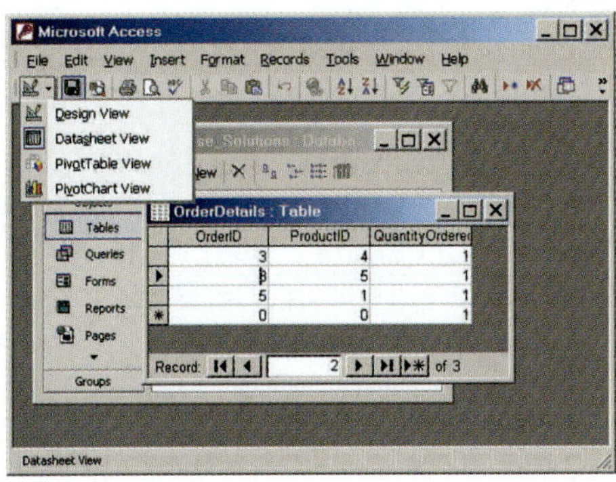

FIGURE 2.34
View button of the Access toolbar

who is not in the Customer table. Similarly an order could be entered for a product that is not in the Products table. Because building table relationships is outside the scope of this presentation, a copy of PuppyParadise.mdb has been created with the table relationships set. The relationships will keep you from entering orders for nonexistent customers and products.

The AC02PuppyParadise2.mdb prototype will be used in the remaining steps. Table relationships have been set and the Customer and Products tables have already been populated. You will be entering orders.

Populating the Orders table:

1. Open the AC02PuppyParadise2.mdb database
2. Explore the table designs using Design view—they are the same as what you built earlier in this session
3. Explore the data in the Customer and Products tables
4. Select **Relationships** from the **Tools** menu to view the table relationships that have been set up

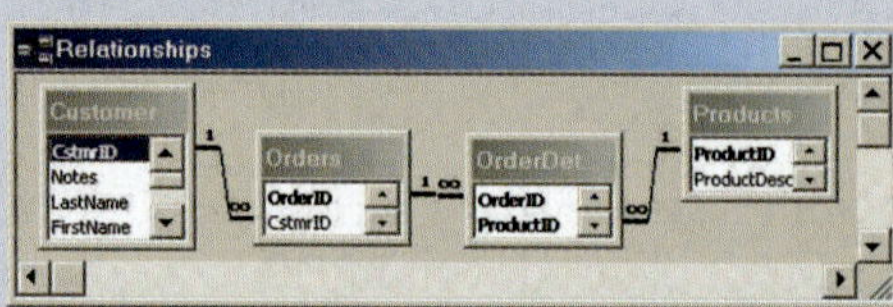

FIGURE 2.35
PuppyParadise table relationships

5. Open the **Orders** table in Datasheet view and add a record for customer 5 on 12/15/02. You will receive the error shown in Figure 2.36 because customer 5 is not in the Customer table

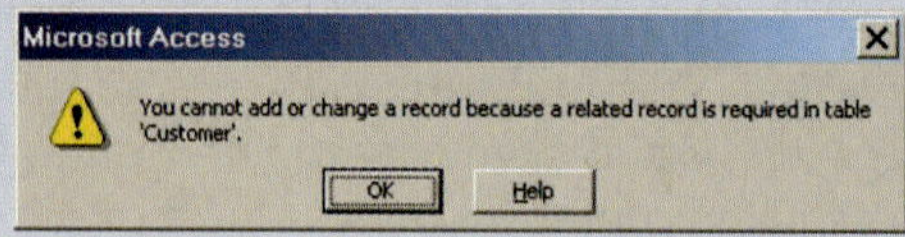

FIGURE 2.36
Table relationships being enforced

6. Enter the records shown in Figure 2.37 for customers 01 and 02 who have already been added to the Customer table

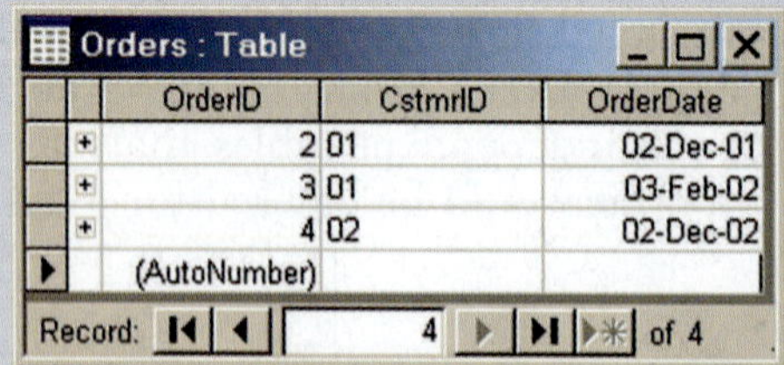
Orders : Table

OrderID	CstmrID	OrderDate
2	01	02-Dec-01
3	01	03-Feb-02
4	02	02-Dec-02
(AutoNumber)		

Record: 4 of 4

FIGURE 2.37
Records for the Orders table

7. Close the Orders table
8. Open the **OrderDetails** table. The one-to-many relationship between Orders and OrderDetails means that Orders must be entered before OrderDetails (line items) can be added for that order. If you try to add a nonexistent OrderDetail, you will receive the error shown in Figure 2.36

9. Enter the records shown in Figure 2.38. These data represent the product and quantity (invoice detail lines) for orders 03 and 05

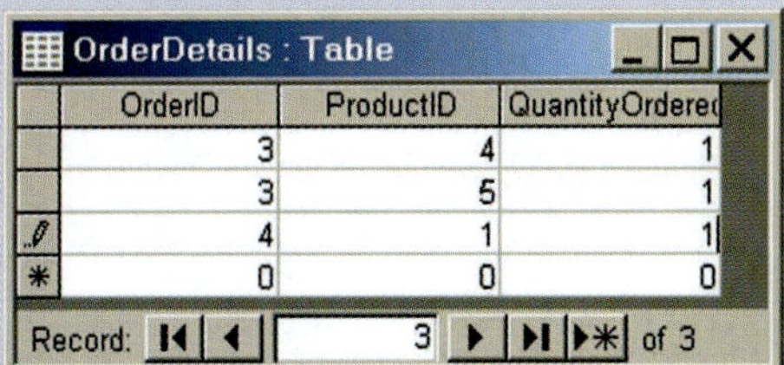
OrderID	ProductID	QuantityOrdered
3	4	1
3	5	1
4	1	1
0	0	0

Record: 3 of 3

FIGURE 2.38
Records for the OrderDetails table

10. Close the OrderDetails table
11. Open the **Customer** table. You can view all of the linked table data in a subdatasheet by clicking the plus sign in front of the customer record. The Orders and OrderDetails records for Customer 01 are shown in Figure 2.39. Review the order for customer 2

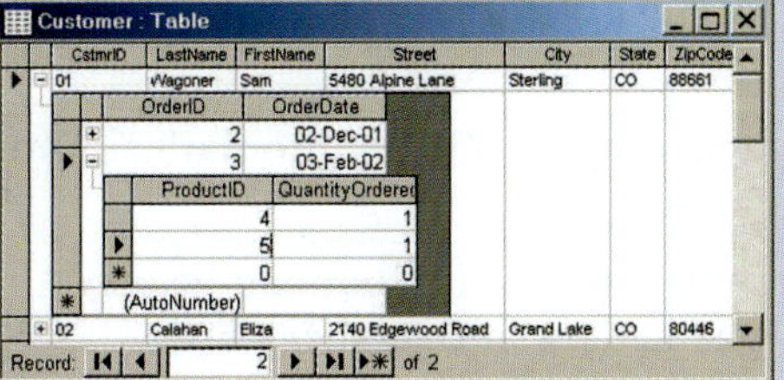

FIGURE 2.39
Orders and OrderDetails for Customer 01 shown in subdatsheet

12. Close the PuppyParadise2.mdb file

These steps demonstrated how properly designed relational databases force data to be entered in an order that is consistent with the defined relationships. The data on the one side of the relationship must always be present before data on the many side of the relationship can be added. Conversely a parent record (one side of the relationship) cannot be deleted when there are child records. You entered two orders for customer 01. The Customer record for customer 01 could not be deleted unless the Orders and associated OrderDetails were deleted first.

When relationships are built between tables, Access uses ***subdatasheets*** to display data from related tables. When viewing data from the parent or primary table in Datasheet view, a plus sign indicates that a subdatasheet can be displayed. To view the related data, click the plus sign. To remove the subdatasheet, click the minus sign.

ACCESS LIMITATIONS

The general specifications for Microsoft Access are very broad and reflect optimal implementations. The model of computer, available memory, and use of the database can reduce the maximums significantly. An Access database can

- Be up to 2 gigabytes
- Store up to 32,7678 objects such as tables, queries, forms, and reports
- Have 64 characters in an object name
- Have 14-character passwords

- Support up to 255 concurrent users

Microsoft Access tables can

- Have up to 64 characters in each field name
- Have up to 255 fields
- Be one of 2048 concurrent open tables
- Be up to 1 gigabyte
- Have 32 indexes
- Be sorted by up to 255 characters in one or more fields

SESSION 2.2

making the grade

1. When fields are listed in parentheses after the table name, how is the primary key identified?
2. T F The Format attribute controls how data values are stored in the table.
3. What is the maximum number of characters a text field can store?
4. To enter the most common value of a field automatically you would set the _____ attribute.
5. T F The Undo button on the Access toolbar can be used to undo 20 items when entering data in Datasheet view.
6. T F Currency format is dependent on the regional settings of the computer.

SESSION 2.3 SUMMARY

To keep data accurate, it must be maintained. In Datasheet view the rows and columns of a table can be reorganized to make maintenance easier without impacting the underlying table structure or data. When sorting by multiple columns, the sort columns must be adjacent and in order of their importance (primary sort field first). Columns such as the primary key can be frozen so that they remain on the screen to identify records when scrolling to the right in a datasheet to ensure updates are being made to the correct record. Columns can be hidden when they are not relevant to the current operation.

Adding, deleting, and editing existing records can easily be accomplished in Datasheet view. A NewRecord indicator (*) displays in an empty row at the bottom of a table's datasheet. Click in the NewRecord row to enter new data using the Tab key to move between table columns. Updates made to table data are saved automatically when the cursor is moved to another record—the Save File button is not needed. The Microsoft Office Clipboard operates between Office products with storage for 24 items.

Find and Replace allows both a search criterion and a replace value to be specified. By clicking the Find Next button, each occurrence of the search value can be found and replaced with the new value. Wildcards such as * and ? can be used to search for specific patterns of data such as Ton? or Ton*.

The Undo feature operates differently in the various Access views. In the Design view where the table file is not updated until you leave the view, both Undo and Redo are available for 20 actions. In table Datasheet view, Undo is available for the last action and the last record update can be reversed from the Edit menu.

Database design is critical to the development of a stable database with valid data. The 90/10 rule states that 90 percent of the time should be spent designing the database structure so that only 10 percent of the time is spent maintaining it. The design process includes outlining the mission, determining the outputs, listing fields, assigning fields to tables, defining table relationships, and building a prototype. Once the database design is complete, the tables are built by defining their fields, field attributes, and relationships.

Visit www.mhhe.com/i-series/ to explore related topics.

MOUS OBJECTIVES SUMMARY

- AC2002-1-4—Format datasheets for display
- AC2002-2-1—Create one or more tables
- AC2002-5-1—Enter and edit records in a datasheet
- AC2002-5-3—Sort records in a datasheet

task reference roundup

Task	Page #	Preferred Method
Finding Specific Data Values	AC 2.6	• Click in the column that you would like to search
		• Click the **Find** button
		• Enter the Find What criteria using the data value that you would like to find. Remember that a question mark (?) can be used as a wildcard for one character and an asterisk (*) is a wildcard for multiple characters
		• Click the **Find Next** button. If multiple rows match the Find What criteria, you may need to repeat this step until the row you are searching for is found
Office Clipboard: Collect items to paste	AC 2.14	• Display the Office Clipboard by selecting **Office Clipboard** from the **Edit** menu
		• Select the item to be copied
		• Click the **Copy** or **Cut** button in the Standard toolbar
		• Continue placing items on the clipboard (up to 24) until you have collected everything that you need
Office Clipboard: Paste collected items	AC 2.14	• Display the Office Clipboard if it is not already present. If the Office Clipboard option of the Edit menu is not available, you are in an application or view that does not support the Office Clipboard
		• Click or select the area where you want to place items
		• Do one of the following:
		• Select the **Paste All** button to paste the entire contents of the Office Clipboard
		or
		• Select a clipboard item and choose **Paste** from its drop-down menu

task reference roundup

Task	Page #	Preferred Method
Office Clipboard: Remove items	AC 2.14	When the clipboard is open • To clear one item, click the arrow next to the item you want to delete and then click **Delete**
		• To clear all clipboard contents, click the **Clear All** button
		• Placing more than 24 items on the clipboard will replace existing items beginning with the oldest item
Hiding Datasheet Columns	AC 2.16	• Open a table, query, or form in Datasheet view
		• Click the field selector of the column to be hidden
		• Click **Hide Columns** on the **Format** menu
To Unhide a Column	AC 2.16	• On the **Format** menu, click **Unhide Columns**
		• Select the names of the columns that you want to show from the Unhide Columns dialog box
Freezing and Unfreezing Datasheet Columns	AC 2.16	• Open a table, query, or form in Datasheet view
		• Select the column(s) that you want to freeze or unfreeze
		• To freeze column(s), select **Freeze Columns** on the **Format** menu
		• To unfreeze column(s) select **Unfreeze All Columns** on the **Format** menu
Defining a Table Field	AC 2.26	• Click **Tables** in the Options bar
		• Click the **Design view** button on the toolbar
		• Enter a field name
		• Select a data type
		• Define other field attributes as needed

CROSSWORD PUZZLE

Across

2. Property of a field that causes a table to be indexed by the field.
4. The second sort field is the ______ sort.
7. A field property that holds rules about what can be entered.
10. The table property that automatically adds a value to new records.
13. Holds up to 24 Office items for pasting.
14. The field identifier is its ______.

Down

1. Buffer that holds 20 reversible actions in table Design view.
2. Property of a field that presents a data entry template.
3. A model of the database for testing.
4. The place where related data display by clicking the +.
5. Property of a field that controls its default display label.
6. Property of a field that controls how data display after they are entered.
8. A field that lists valid values held in another table.
9. Statement documenting the purpose of a database during design.
11. The table on the one side of a relationship is the parent or ______ table.
11. The first sort field is the ______ sort.
12. A table column that does not scroll off the screen is said to be ______.

FILL-IN

1. The ______________ view of a table has more levels of undo than the ______________ view.
2. Access has a maximum capacity of ______________ open tables.
3. The ______________ dialog box is used to enter criteria for searching a table.

REVIEW QUESTIONS

Each of the following topics should be addressed in one to three paragraphs.

1. Explain the meaning of the following:
   Product (<u>ProductID</u>, ProductDescription, ProductPrice).
2. Explain how at least two of the rules used to assign fields to tables are used.
3. What is the process of modeling tables with a many-to-many relationship?
4. Assume that you are designing a Products table for a candy manufacturer. The fields that you are considering are CandyType, CandyFilling, CandyCost, CandyPicture, QuantityOrdered, TotalYTDProduction. How would you determine what fields to include in the table? Is there a natural primary key for this table?
5. If you were to build a database to store information on your CD collection, what fields would you consider? How many tables? What would be the key field(s)? Why?

CREATE THE QUESTION

For each of the following answers, create the question.

ANSWER	QUESTION
1. Things that you can do to improve the order of columns in Datasheet view.	______________
2. Secondary sort field.	______________
3. The entry in the Find What text box.	______________
4. ?	______________
5. When the cursor is placed in another record.	______________

FACT OR FICTION

For each of the following determine whether the statement is fact, fiction, or both and present your arguments for that conclusion.

1. An edit on a record can be undone after moving to another record and storing the edit from the second record.
2. Setting the Caption property of a field changes the label that displays with the field data without any further impact.
3. There are no problems with entering data into tables before all of the table relationships have been defined.
4. Records entered into a table are physically stored in the order that they were entered so there is no "insert" operation that places a record in a specific table location.
5. When building new tables with the New Table Wizard, you have complete control over all of the field properties.

hands-on projects

LEVEL THREE

practice

Creating BBs Shoes Database

BBs Shoes is a family-owned shoe store specializing in athletic shoes. Roberto and Benita Lopez started the store to provide name-brand shoes at a discount price. They are dedicated to being a neighborhood resource, by providing needed shoes and jobs to the neighborhood. Benita has decided that a database would help track inventory. She has asked you to build it for them.

1. Start Access and open a new blank database. If a database is already open, use the **Toolbars** option of the **View** menu to open the **Task Pane**
2. Name the database **BBsShoes.mdb**
3. Create Figure 2.40 in Design view
4. Add the data in Figure 2.41
5. Although there are not enough data to make a Find truly operational, practice using Find with wildcards. Use Find to locate all inventory stored in aisle A. What Find What value did you use? How many did you find?
6. Enter three more records with data about your favorite shoes. Give each a unique stock number and a storage location of B1
7. Update the data as follows:

   Change *Nike Tiemp 2000 D* to **Nike Tiempo 2000 D**

   Change *Rio Zoom Hardground* to **Rio Zoom Hrdgrnd**

   Use **Undo** to reverse the previous change. If you have already saved the update by moving to another record, use **Undo Saved Record** from the **Edit** menu
8. Delete the record for RZ17203
9. Hide the StockNbr column, sort by descending price, and print the result
10. What forms and reports using these data can you think of to help Benita?
11. Are there other tables that could benefit this business? What would they track?

FIGURE 2.40

Shoes table design

Field Name	Data Type	Field Size	Notes
StockNbr	Text	7	Primary key
ShoeDescription	Text	30	
ShoePrice	Currency		
QtyOnHand	Number	Integer	
Location	Text	3	Aisle and shelf location

FIGURE 2.41

Shoes table data

TeStock : Table

StockNbr	ShoeDescription	ShoePrice	QtyOnHand	Location
AG87473	Adidas Gazelle	$59.95	78	B10
AR17208	Air Roma II	$69.95	83	H1
NT17165	Nike Tiempo 2000 D	$89.95	28	F2
NT17166	Nike Tiempo 2000 M	$84.95	45	G8
PC19436	Puma Cellerator	$149.95	20	A2
PS19439	Puma Sting	$74.95	36	H4
		$0.00	0	

Record: 5 of 6

www.mhhe.com/i-series

challenge!

HealthCare2Go Employee Tracking

HealthCare2Go is a temporary services agency providing short-term employees to the medical community. Temporary employees are scattered across the United States and travel to their temporary positions. Riki Lee is charged with tracking the availability of employees and needs help building an effective database.

1. Start Access and open a new blank database. If a database is already open, use the **Toolbars** option of the **View** menu to open the **Task Pane**
2. Name the database **MedTemps.mdb**
3. Create Figure 2.42 in Design view
4. Print the table design
5. Use the Office Clipboard to copy records from the **AC02TempEmployees.mdb** table into your Employees table
6. Use Find with wildcards to locate all RNs and LPNs. What Find What value did you use? How many did you find?
7. The JobClass field is too small and has truncated data. MedTe should be **MedTech.** Change the Field Size to 10 and then use Find and Replace to change the field values. Document how you accomplished this
8. Test your update by trying to change the JobClass for Cecilia Wong to **Operations Manager.** Document the result
9. Add the data in Figure 2.43. Make up the addresses and phone numbers using your city, state, zip code, and area code. Remember that EmployeeID is generated for you
10. Sort the table data by last and first names. Order and resize the columns appropriately. Print the result

FIGURE 2.42

Employees table design

Field Name	Data Type	Field Size	Notes
EmployeeID	AutoNumber		Key
LastName	Text	25	
FirstName	Text	25	
Address	Text	30	
City	Text	30	
State	Text	2	
Zip	Text	5	
Phone	Text	10	
JobClass	Text	5	

FIGURE 2.43

Employees table data

LastName	FirstName	Phone	Classification	DateHired
Andersen	Tom	3155505000	T1	05/14/96
Anderson	Sam	2155605000	P11	01/19/98
Bartlen	Connie	8745885234	G2	07/22/01
Anderson	Nancy	8875825838	T1	10/30/95
Callaway	Lois	8795023303	T2	03/02/95
Carter	Mary Jane	3065889302	P3	07/16/95
Decett	Lana	1135638751	F1	10/22/96
Drennen	Leo	9325872193	F3	05/05/01
French	Jennifer	7735008370	G1	11/14/94
Hampton	Dan	4255575368	F1	01/14/93
Harris	Jerry	2915468297	W1	08/28/94
Ricker	Ricky	1285327321	H2	09/19/01
Werner	Paul	7615989891	L1	04/13/00
Waxman	Sue	4125933232	W3	01/15/95

on the web

Toy Purchase Statistics by Internet Research Inc.

Internet Research Inc. (IRI) is a statistical evaluation organization specializing in Internet commerce. The evaluations are based on many facets of commerce including product price, shipping costs, timely delivery, ease of Web site navigation, product quality, and return policies. The statistics generated by IRI are published on a Web site for consumers and used by Shopping Bots to rank and evaluate shopping requests entered by users.

You have been hired by IRI to maintain the statistical evaluations of toy sales sites. As a training exercise, you will gather data manually and use Access to evaluate the results. You will begin by researching toy prices and building an Access table to hold your findings. The goal is to familiarize you with the sites and tools you will be evaluating and provide an understanding of the underlying research methodologies.

1. Use a Shopping Bot such as www.mysimon.com or a search engine to find at least two sites that sell toys
   a. At your first site, determine the lowest priced Barbie (you can choose another popular toy with multiple models)
   b. Find the price for the same toy at the second site
   c. At the second site determine the highest priced Barbie
   d. Find the price for the same toy at the first site
   e. Perform the previous steps for a third toy of your choice
2. Start Access and open a new blank database. If a database is already open, use the **Toolbars** option of the **View** menu to open the **Task Pane**
3. Name the database **IRI.mdb**
4. Create the table shown in Figure 2.44 in Design view
5. Print the table design
6. Input the data from your search, use a unique key value for each record, verify your data entry, and make any necessary edits
7. Further testing of the table uncovers a need for a ReviewDate field. Add it as the last table field with an appropriate data type and format
8. Test your update by adding review dates to all of the records
9. Sort the table data by ToyName. Order the columns so that the sort field is first and adjust the column width to fit the data. Print the results
10. Sort the table data by Web site. Order the columns appropriately. Print the results

FIGURE 2.44
Toys table design

Field Name	Data Type	Field Size	Notes
ToyID	Text	3	Key
WebSite	Hyperlink		Key
ToyName	Text	25	
ToyDescription	Text	50	
Price	Currency		

e-business

SportBabies.com Product List

SportBabies.com is an online storefront selling replica sports uniforms for babies and toddlers. It carries products for all NFL, NHL, NBA, Major League Baseball, National League Baseball, and college teams. The uniforms are exact replicas of those currently worn on the field and come in standard baby and toddler sizes. Product manufacturers include Champion, Nike, Russell, and Wilson. Classic player gear is also available.

The current Web site is based on static HTML, which means that it must be manually maintained each time products and prices change. To automate this heavy maintenance project, a database is being created. The database will be maintained and generate updates to the Web site. You have been asked to build the ProductList database. You will be using NFL products for testing.

1. Start Access and open a new blank database. If a database is already open, use the **Toolbars** option of the **View** menu to open the **Task Pane**
2. Name the database **SportBabies.mdb**
3. Create the table shown in Figure 2.45 in Design view
4. Add the data in Figure 2.46
5. Add records for three non-NFL players
6. Add yourself and a friend as NBA players
7. Make League, Team, and Player the first columns of the datasheet by hiding the ProductID column. Sort by League, Team, and Player and print the result
8. Print the table design
9. Use Find with wildcards to locate records for NFL and NBA players. Document the Find criteria
10. Sort the data by descending price. Make Price the first column and print
11. Document at least three business questions that could be answered using these data

FIGURE 2.45
ProductList table design

Field Name	Data Type	Field Size	Notes
ProductID	AutoNumber		Key
League	Text	3	
Team	Text	30	
Player	Text	25	
Price	Currency		

FIGURE 2.46
ProductList data

League	Team	Player	Price
NFL	49ers	Rice	29.99
NFL	Bears	Enis	31.48
NFL	Bengals	Dillon	24.52
NFL	Bengals	Warric	28.92
NFL	Broncos	Davis	32.45
NFL	Broncos	Greese	35.32
NFL	Broncos	Price	25.68
NFL	Cowboys	Sanders	21.15
NFL	Cowboys	Galloway	21.15
NFL	Cowboys	Smith	20.44
NFL	Jets	Martin	20.44
NFL	Jets	Johnson	23.83

around the world

Getz International Travel Corporate Customers Database

Getz International Travel is the largest travel agency in the world. The organization consists of over 5,000 full-time employees working in offices in San Francisco, Los Angeles, Phoenix, Chicago, Detroit, Indianapolis, Orlando, London, Budapest, Warsaw, Taiwan, and Paris. Getz arranges every facet of travel for both domestic and international treks.

Schedules are happily arranged for individuals, small groups, and large groups of up to 300. Arrangements include airfare, tours, hotels, car rentals, and more.

The over 5,000 corporate customers are the backbone of the organization. Currently, all customers are kept in the same table. You have been assigned the task of creating a separate table for corporate customers because they are being assigned to a new division of the organization.

1. Start Access and open a new blank database. If a database is already open, use the **Toolbars** option of the **View** menu to open the **Task Pane**
2. Name the database **Getz.mdb**
3. Create the table shown in Figure 2.47 in Design view
4. Print the table design
5. Add the data in Figure 2.48. Remember that CustomerID is generated for you
6. Create a format for the CustomerID field that will cause it to display with a dash after the first two digits (03-129)
7. Due to a data entry error, you need to use Find and Replace to change all of the area codes from 313 to 303
8. Add five local businesses to the table. Use your friends' names for primary and secondary contacts
9. Sort the table data by CompanyName. Order and resize the columns appropriately. Print the results
10. Sort the table by City within State. Order the columns appropriately. Print the results
11. Create a Find that will locate Colorado records. Document the Find What criteria

FIGURE 2.47

Corporate customers table design

tblCustomers : Table

Field Name	Data Type	Description
CustomerID	Number	Customer identification number
CompanyName	Text	Company Name
Contact	Text	Contact person within company
2ndContact	Text	Secondary Contact person
Address	Text	Street address or Post Office Box
City	Text	City
State	Text	State (two character abbreviation)
ZipCode	Text	Five-digit ZIP code
PhoneNumber	Text	Telephone number
FaxNumber	Text	Facximile phone number
CreditLimit	Number	Credit Limit

FIGURE 2.48

Corporate customers table data

CustomerID	CompanyName	Contact	Address	City	State	Zip	Phone Number
20931	Sutton Attorneys	Bill Skewes	30752 Southview Dr.	Evergreen	CO	80439	(313)674-7041
2048	1st Bank	Marie Baal	3560 Evergreen Pkwy.	Evergreen	CO	80453	(313)674-7809
1768	Alpine Construction Group	James Darling	805 W 44th Ave.	Wheat Ridge	CO	80321	(313)674-1753
2718	Vision Land Consultants	Ramona Hyde	30960 Stagecoach Blvd.	Arvada	CO	80932	(313)674-3025
1873	Eye Wear Inc.	Kathleen Paduano	60605 US Hwy. 285	Pine	CO	80637	(313)674-2114

running project: tnt web page design

TnT is a custom Web page development company founded by Victoria (Tori) Salazar and Tonya O'Dowd. The background for this case was presented in Chapter 1. Go back and review it if necessary.

1. Use Windows to create a copy of AC01TnT.mdb and rename the copy **<yourname>TnT.mdb**. Replace <yourname> with your last name and first name (e.g., WellsJim)
2. Start Access and open the <yourname>TnT.mdb database
3. Open tblCustomers in Datasheet view
4. Use Find and Replace to remove the parentheses () and the dash (-) from the cusPhone and cusFax fields
5. In Design view, add a format to each field that will display the deleted characters even though they are not stored in the field
6. Create a new table in Design view
   a. The first table field is custID with a Number data type and LongInteger field size because it will join to the custID field of tblCustomers carrying an AutoNumber data type
   b. The second table field is SiteNumber with a Number data type and Integer field size
   c. The third field is URL with a Hyperlink data type
   d. Set the combination of custID and SiteNumber as the primary key
   e. Close the Design view and save the table as CustomerSites
7. You will need to build a one-to-many relationship between these two tables, since each customer can have more that one site built by TnT
   a. Open the Relationships window by right-clicking in the database window and choosing **Relationships**
   b. Right-click in the Relationships window and choose **Show Table . . .**
   c. In the Show Table window click **Add** to add the CustomerSites (it is selected by default) table to the Relationships window
   d. In the Show Table window select **tblCustomers** and click **Add** to add it to the Relationships window
   e. Close the Show Table window
   f. In the Relationships window click the custID field in CustomerSites and drag to the custID field in tblCustomers. The Edit Relationships window should open
   g. Click the checkboxes as shown in Figure 2.49 and choose **Create**
   h. A one-to-many relationship should now display in the Relationships window
   i. Close the Relationships window, saving the relationship
8. Close CustomerSites
9. Open tblCustomers and review the data you entered in the subdatasheets
10. Print both tables and exit Access

FIGURE 2.49

Edit Relationships Window settings

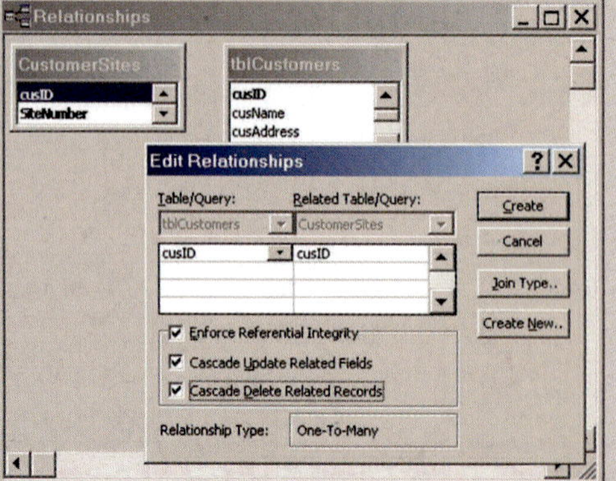

did you know?

the *scientist Anders Celsius developed a measuring scale with freezing at 100 degrees and boiling at 0 degrees. Fellow scientists waited until Celsius died to reverse the scale.*

cooking *and salad oils with an additive developed by Penn State chemical engineers performed as well as commercial oils when used to lubricate machinery, such as cars and boats.*

the *first video game was Pong, introduced in 1972 by Noel Bushnell, who then created Atari.*

in *Rome, the world's first paved streets were laid out in 170 B.C. The new streets were popular as they were functional in all types of weather and were easier to keep clean, but they amplified the city's noise level.*

to *make a daguerreotype, an early photograph, required a 15-minute average exposure time.*

33 *percent of computer data loss cases are due to human error.*

Chapter Objectives

In this chapter you will:

- **Filter data in Datasheet view—AC2002-5-4**
- **Create and run select queries—AC2002-3-1**
- **Save filters and queries**
- **Add calculations to queries—AC2002-3-2**
- **Construct and customize simple forms—AC2002-4-1 and AC2002-4-2**
- **Create, customize, and print simple reports—AC2002-7-1 and AC2002-7-3**
- **Produce mailing labels**

CHAPTER 3 three

Introducing Queries, Filters, Forms, and Reports

chapter case

PuppyParadise

Evan is facing a tough decision. PuppyParadise is taking over 100 orders per week and he is unable to keep up. He is considering the following options:

- Limiting the number of orders to what he personally can process
- Moving the business out of his house so that he can hire someone to answer the phone and process orders
- Finding a partner who will share the workload
- Selling the business

To evaluate the viability of these options, Evan needs information about his business. The only thing that he is certain of at this point is that current profits are not sufficient to support even a part-time employee. To decide how to proceed, Evan needs to evaluate the potential of his products and markets. Is the market sufficient to increase his sales volume? Can his suppliers support an increase in volume? Evan has no idea how many of his customers have not paid him, since he sends out invoices but does not have an effective way of following up. Such tracking and follow-up

FIGURE 3.1

Potential PuppyParadise queries and reports

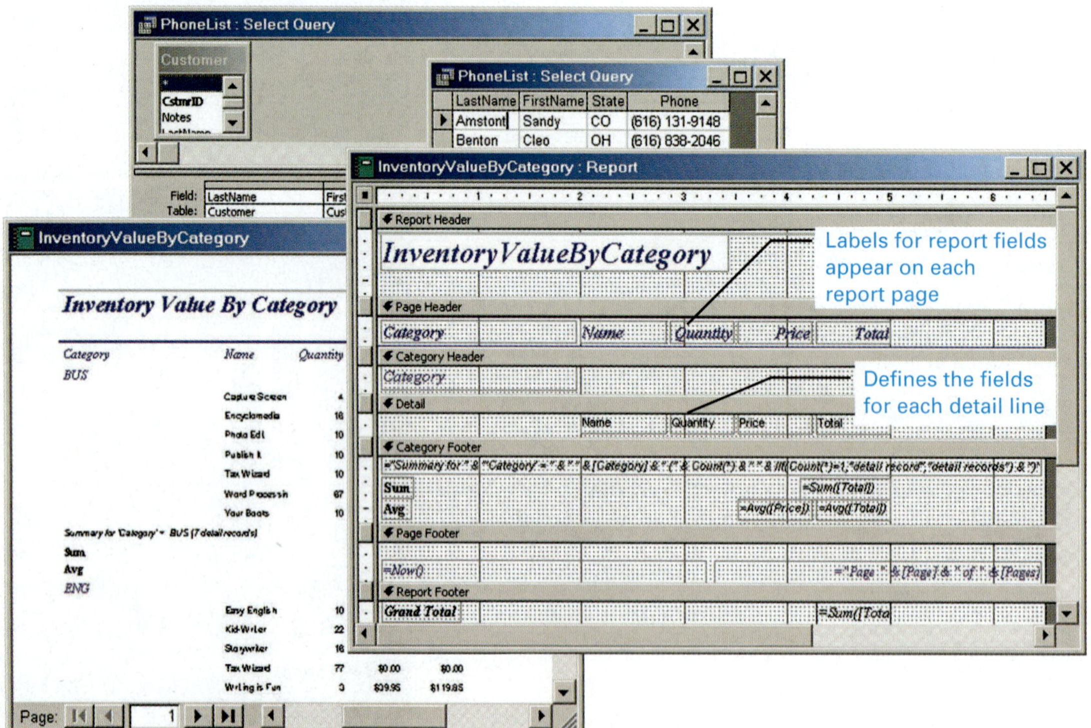

could improve his profitability. He also needs to know if there are things that he can do to cut costs, like discontinuing unprofitable products.

Although his existing data are limited and not yet entered into a database, Evan can see the potential of query and report facilities. Queries and reports can be used to organize and analyze his business data to help him make decisions. While no amount of information can guarantee the result of a decision, timely and effective information can significantly improve the likelihood of a positive outcome. Evan has asked you to build the query and reporting capabilities that will allow him to get the effective information to support his decision.

SESSION 3.1 SELECTING AND ORGANIZING DATA

Access provides an array of options for selecting and organizing data into useful information. This session evaluates the effectiveness of various filters and introduces select queries.

CHAPTER OUTLINE

SELECTING DATA WITH FILTERS

Filters are used to restrict (limit) the rows of data displayed in the current datasheet so that a subset of the data can be manipulated. An ideal time to use filters is to maintain or print only some of the rows in a table. Evan is curious about how filters can be used with PuppyParadise data. He does not understand the functionality of the various types of filters and has asked you to show him.

Introducing Filters

There are four ways to apply filters to the datasheet. The first, ***Filter by Selection,*** returns records matching the datasheet selection. The second, ***Filter by Form,*** presents an empty version of the current datasheet where match values can be typed. ***Filter for Input*** accepts a value or expression to restrict the records. The ***Advanced Filter/Sort*** window presents a design grid used to build filter criteria. Regardless of the type of filter being applied, the goal is to display only records that meet specific criteria. Creating the criteria is slightly different for each type of filter. You will show Evan an example of each type of filter using the PuppyParadise prototype database so that he gains an understanding of their utility.

Creating Filter by Selection Criteria

Filter by Selection is the most intuitive filtering tool, but also the most limited. All or part of a data value in any field can be selected to control which records will display. The selection is evaluated as described in Figure 3.2.

FIGURE 3.2
Filter by selection criteria

Selection	Action	City Field Example
Click in a field	The whole field value will be used to search that field for matches	Click in the value Berlin and only records for Berlin will be selected
Select an entire field	The whole field value will be used to search that field for matches	Select the value Berlin and only records for Berlin will be returned
Select the first character(s) of a field value	Records starting with the selected characters will be returned	Select the characters "Ber" and all records starting with Ber will be retrieved (i.e., Berlin, Berlington, Berton, etc.)
Select character(s) after the first character	Records that contain the selection anywhere will be returned	Select "er" from Berlin and all records containing er will be retrieved (i.e., Anderson, Berlin, Merlin, Waterberry, etc.)

task reference

Filter by Selection

- Open the table in Datasheet view
- Select the field and character(s) of the search criteria (see Figure 3.2)
- Click the **Filter By Selection** toolbar button to return values matching the selection

  or
- right-click and choose **Filter Excluding Selection** to filter the selection out of the data
- Evaluate the results of the filter
- Click **Remove Filter** on the Access toolbar

Filtering the Customer table:

1. Verify that the Customer table of the AC03PuppyParadise.mdb database is open in Datasheet view
2. Click in the City cell containing the value **Coatesville**
3. Click the **Filter By Selection** toolbar button
4. Click the **Remove Filter** toolbar button
5. Select **on** in any City value
6. Click the **Filter By Selection** toolbar button
7. Click the **Remove Filter** toolbar button
8. Select **G** in any City value where it is the first character
9. Click the **Filter By Selection** toolbar button

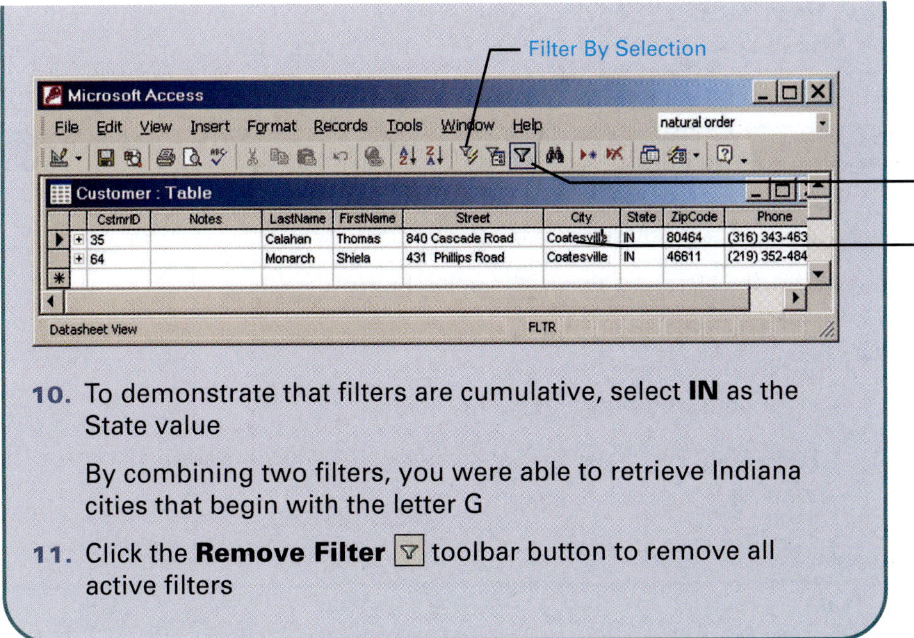

FIGURE 3.3
Filter by selection result using **Coatesville** criterion

10. To demonstrate that filters are cumulative, select **IN** as the State value

    By combining two filters, you were able to retrieve Indiana cities that begin with the letter G

11. Click the **Remove Filter** toolbar button to remove all active filters

Filters also can be used to exclude the selection. Select a value and then right-click to bring up the pop-up menu. Select ***Filter Excluding Selection*** from the pop-up menu and all records containing that value will be excluded from the datasheet.

Excluding records from the Customer table:

1. Verify that the Customer table of the AC03PuppyParadise.mdb database is open in Datasheet view
2. Click in any **CO** State value
3. Right-click on the selection to bring up the pop-up menu
4. Select **Filter Excluding Selection.** The datasheet should not display Colorado records
5. Click the **Remove Filter** toolbar button to remove all active filters

Filters are cumulative, so a second filter can be applied to the result of the first filter. The results of a filter stay in effect until *Remove Filter* is selected or the datasheet is closed.

Creating Filter by Form Criteria

Clicking Filter by Form presents a blank datasheet containing two tabs where filter values can be selected from a drop-down list box or typed manually. Unlike Filter by Selection, Filter by Form accepts multiple criteria. Conditions entered in the Look for tab must all be true to retrieve a record. The Or tab allows alternate values to be entered for the same field.

Like many Access operations, Filter by Form has its own unique toolbar that is visible only in this view. Besides the standard toolbar options such as Print, Cut, Copy, and Paste, there are also some unique toolbar options such as Open Filter and Save Filter. To leave the view, use the Close button on the Filter by Form toolbar.

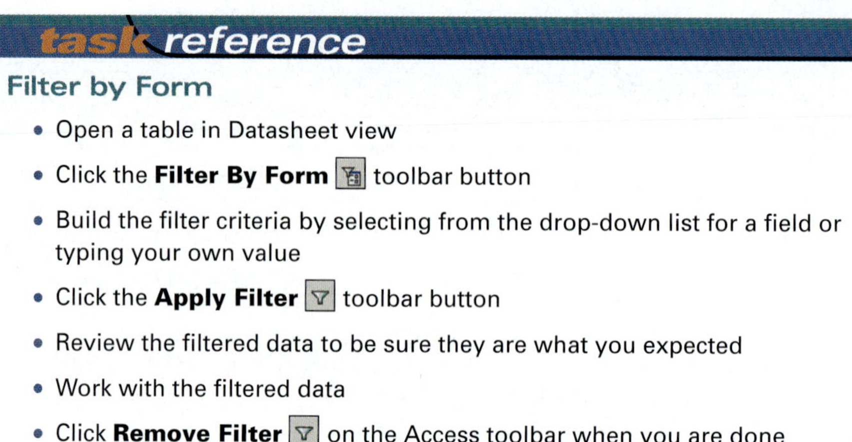

task reference

Filter by Form

- Open a table in Datasheet view
- Click the **Filter By Form** toolbar button
- Build the filter criteria by selecting from the drop-down list for a field or typing your own value
- Click the **Apply Filter** toolbar button
- Review the filtered data to be sure they are what you expected
- Work with the filtered data
- Click **Remove Filter** on the Access toolbar when you are done

Filtering the Customer table with Filter by Form:

1. Verify that the Customer table of the AC03PuppyParadise.mdb database is open in Datasheet view
2. Click the **Filter By Form** button on the Access toolbar
3. Remove any existing criteria by selecting them and pressing **Delete**
4. You want to retrieve records for customer numbers greater than five from Indiana. To accomplish this, enter the criteria shown in Figure 3.4 and click **Apply Filter**
5. Review the records to be sure that the results are what you expected

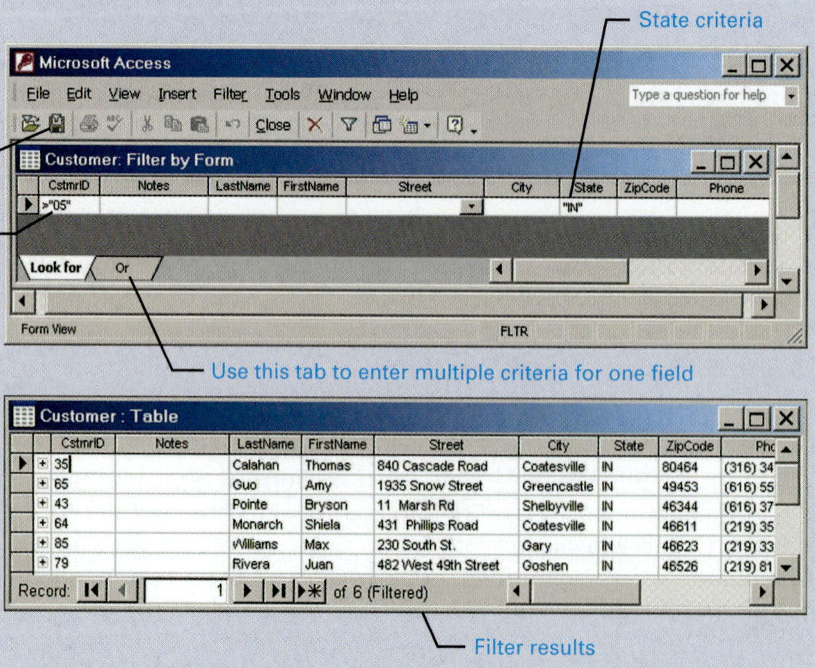

FIGURE 3.4

Filter By Form using compound criteria

State criteria

Filter by Form Toolbar

CstmrID criteria

Use this tab to enter multiple criteria for one field

Filter results

tip: *When sorting or filtering numbers stored in text fields, 0s are important. Leading 0s (005) are entered so that the numbers sort correctly. They also must be entered when filtering or the records returned will be inappropriate (5, 05, and 005 each returns a different result). You must match what is stored in the table*

6. Click the **Remove Filter** toolbar button to remove all active filters

When filtering, double quotes ("") are required around match values for fields containing text data. Access adds the double quotes for you if you forget. As you have just seen, Filter by Form uses relational operators (=, >, <, >=, <=, and <>). The equal condition is the default and does not need to be stated, as was demonstrated with the "IN" criterion for State. All other operators must precede the value in the criteria, as was demonstrated with the > "05" criterion for CstmrID. Criteria also can be entered using keywords including In, Like, and Between. More detail on building criteria will be presented in the next session.

Filtering the Customer table with an Or condition:

1. Verify that the Customer table of the AC03PuppyParadise.mdb database is open in Datasheet view
2. Click the **Filter By Form** button on the Access toolbar
3. Remove any existing criteria by selecting them and pressing **Delete**
4. You want to retrieve records for customers in Colorado, Indiana, or California. The Or tab will be used to enter each of the alternate state abbreviations. Enter **CO** in the State field of the Look for tab
5. Click the **Or** tab at the bottom of the window. Enter **IN** in the State field of the Or tab

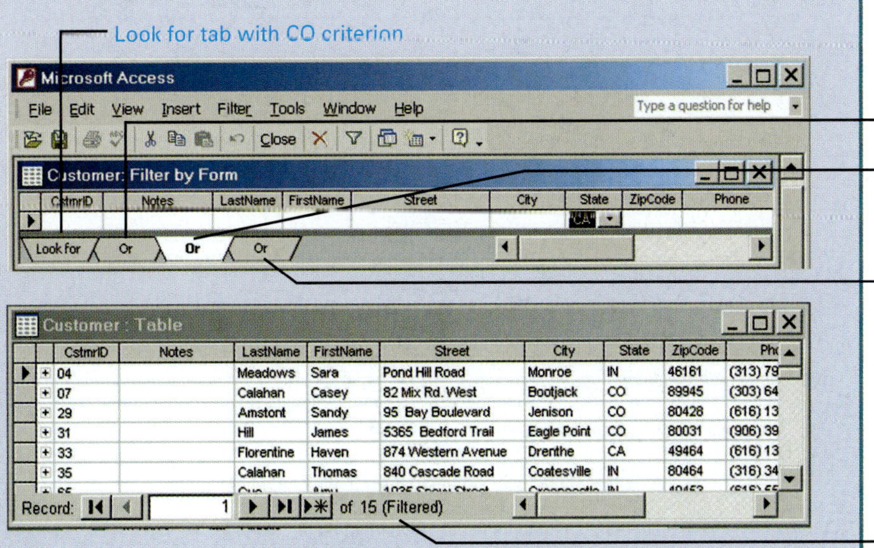

FIGURE 3.5
Filter By Form using Or criteria

6. Click the second **Or** tab and enter **CA** in its State field
7. Click the **Apply Filter** toolbar button
8. Review the records to be sure that they match the filter criteria
9. Click the **Remove Filter** toolbar button to remove all active filters

Filter by Form also can be used to see the filter criteria created by other types of filters. Did you notice that when you first opened the Filter by Form grid, it contained the criteria from the last Filter by Selection filter that you applied?

Creating Filter for Input Criteria

Filter for Input allows filter criteria to be entered from the pop-up menu. Simply right-click in the field to be filtered and type your criteria in the Filter For text box. Filter for criteria can include combinations of identifiers, operators, wildcards, and values.

task reference

Filter for Input

- Open a table in Datasheet view
- Right-click the field to be filtered
- Type the filter criteria in the Filter For text box using wildcards, operators, and values
- Press **Enter** to activate the filter
- Review the filtered data to be sure they are what you expected
- Work with the filtered data
- Click **Remove Filter** on the Access toolbar when you are done

Filtering the Customer table with Filter By Form:

1. Verify that the Customer table of the AC03PuppyParadise.mdb database is open in Datasheet view
2. Right-click in the FirstName field
3. You want to select all records for people with "am" anywhere in their first name. To accomplish this type ***am*** in the Filter For text box
4. Press **Enter** to activate the filter
5. Evaluate the filter results
6. Click **Remove Filter** on the Access toolbar

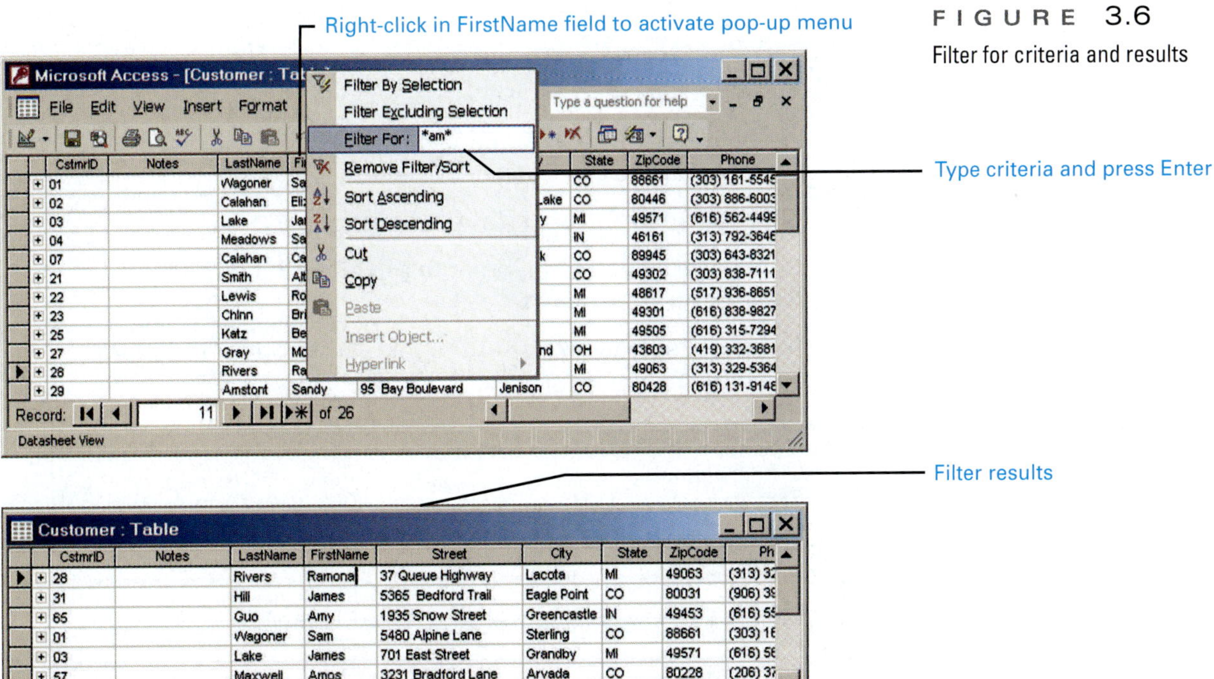
Right-click in FirstName field to activate pop-up menu
Type criteria and press Enter
Filter results

FIGURE 3.6
Filter for criteria and results

After a criterion is typed in the pop-up menu, the Tab key can be clicked instead of pressing Enter to keep the pop-up menu open and add criteria for the current field. Because filters are cumulative, opening the pop-up window for another field will accept criteria to further filter data.

Creating Advanced Filter/Sort Criteria

The Advanced Filter/Sort grid allows criteria to be entered on multiple fields and sorted in one step. The grid is very similar to the query by example grid that will be covered in the next topic.

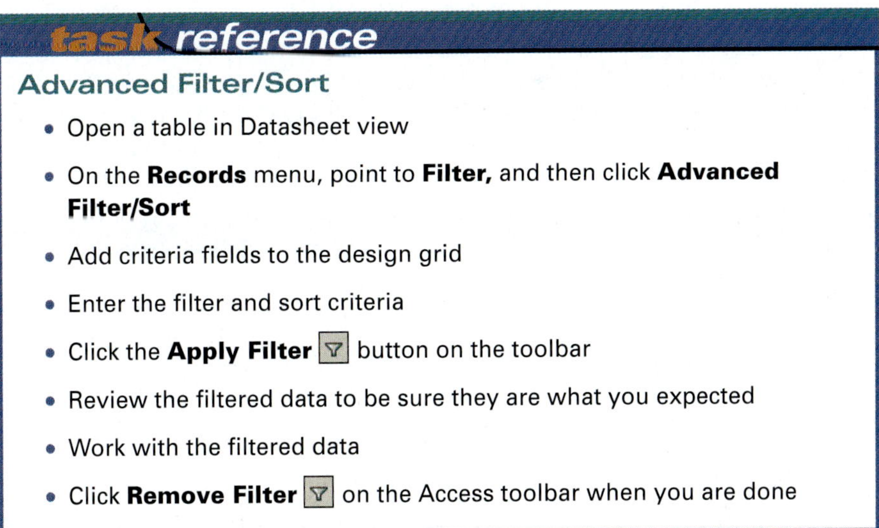

task reference

Advanced Filter/Sort

- Open a table in Datasheet view
- On the **Records** menu, point to **Filter,** and then click **Advanced Filter/Sort**
- Add criteria fields to the design grid
- Enter the filter and sort criteria
- Click the **Apply Filter** button on the toolbar
- Review the filtered data to be sure they are what you expected
- Work with the filtered data
- Click **Remove Filter** on the Access toolbar when you are done

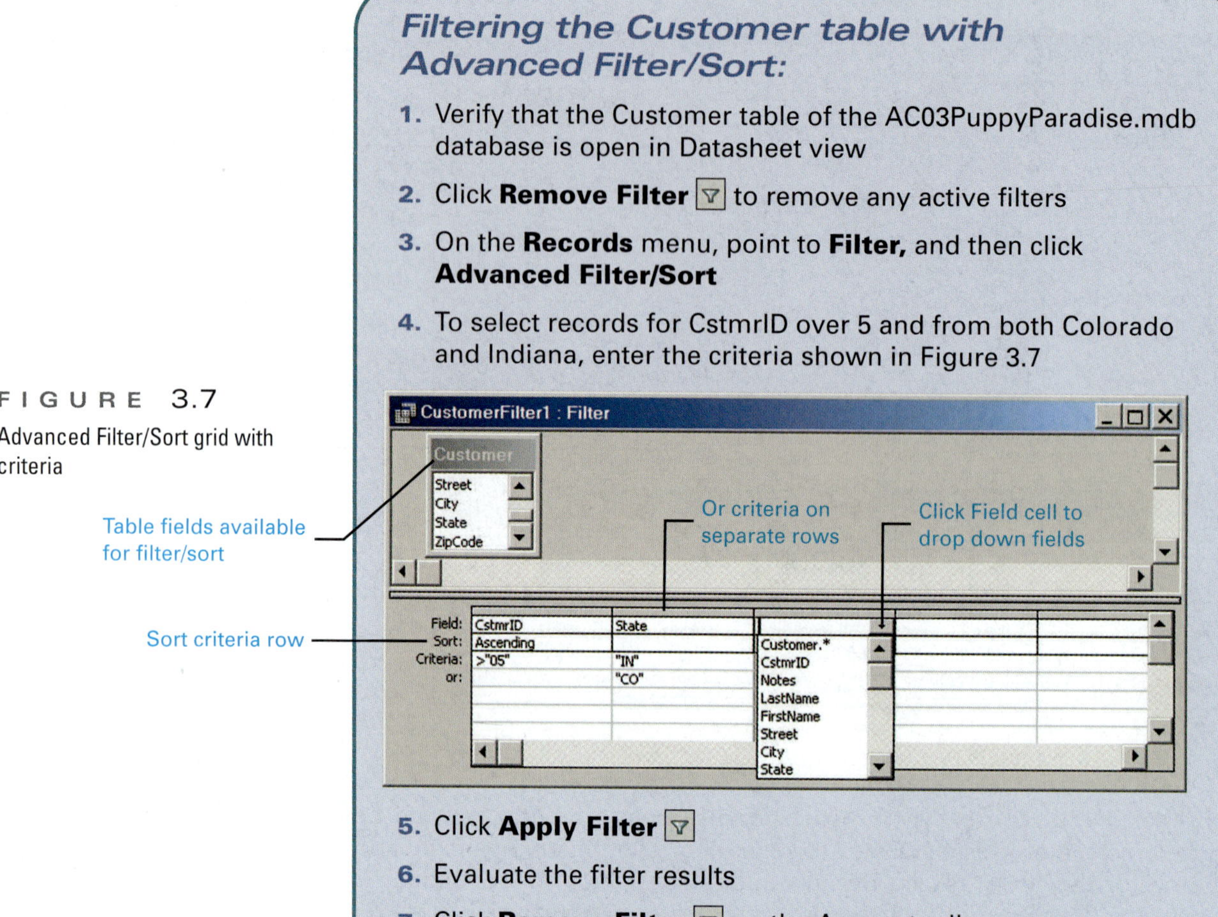

Filtering the Customer table with Advanced Filter/Sort:

1. Verify that the Customer table of the AC03PuppyParadise.mdb database is open in Datasheet view
2. Click **Remove Filter** to remove any active filters
3. On the **Records** menu, point to **Filter,** and then click **Advanced Filter/Sort**
4. To select records for CstmrID over 5 and from both Colorado and Indiana, enter the criteria shown in Figure 3.7

FIGURE 3.7
Advanced Filter/Sort grid with criteria

5. Click **Apply Filter**
6. Evaluate the filter results
7. Click **Remove Filter** on the Access toolbar

As you can easily see, the Advanced Filter/Sort is the most powerful and the most complex filtering tool. The type of filter used depends on the complexity of the filter criteria and the user's comfort with the filtering options.

Saving a Filter as a Query

Filters are not one of the Access database objects and so they cannot be stored. To remedy this situation, a filter can be saved with a table, form, or query object. In each case, a query, which is more powerful than a filter, is saved. A saved filter can be reapplied without reentering the criteria.

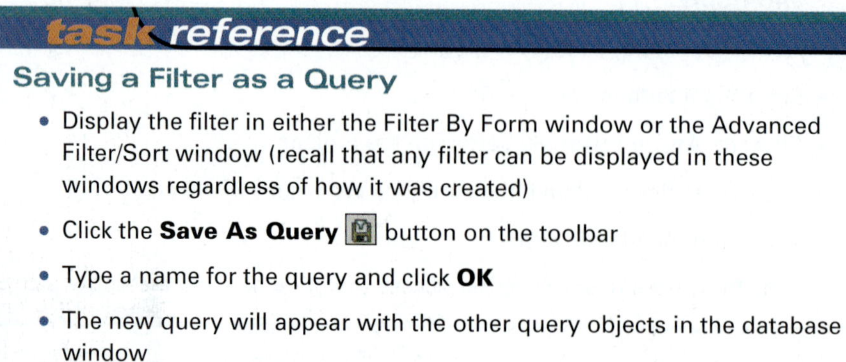

task reference

Saving a Filter as a Query

- Display the filter in either the Filter By Form window or the Advanced Filter/Sort window (recall that any filter can be displayed in these windows regardless of how it was created)
- Click the **Save As Query** button on the toolbar
- Type a name for the query and click **OK**
- The new query will appear with the other query objects in the database window

Limitations of Filters

While filters are valuable tools when selecting and organizing data, there are some significant limitations in what they can accomplish. The most obvious limitation of filtering data is that all table fields must display in the filtered result. There is no way to select specific fields or even change the order in which fields are displayed. It is true that you can manually hide fields and change column order, but that becomes tedious.

anotherword

. . . on Filters

Besides filtering data in Datasheet view, filters can be used to restrict data displayed in a form or a subdatasheet. One filter can be associated with each form so that it activates when the form is opened. This is useful when multiple users share a database and each only wants access to his or her specific data.

Finally, only one table can be filtered at a time—there is no join capability. Only one filter can be associated with a table or form; however, any number of filters can be saved as queries. The functions that are missing in filters are the strength of queries.

SELECTING DATA WITH QUERIES

Queries are used to view and analyze data in different ways. They are much more powerful than filters because they can retrieve data from multiple tables and add calculations to the results. Stored queries also can be used to select records that will be displayed in a form or report.

Introducing Queries

Queries are commonly used to support the business decision-making process. For example, Evan could use a query to profile his customers so that he can understand how to better market his products. He also could find out if he has any products that have never been purchased so that he can discontinue them or which customers have not been billed so that he can send them invoices (see Figure 3.8).

To answer such questions, the necessary data must be stored in one or more tables in the database. For example, the current PuppyParadise database could not provide much information on who Evan's customers are

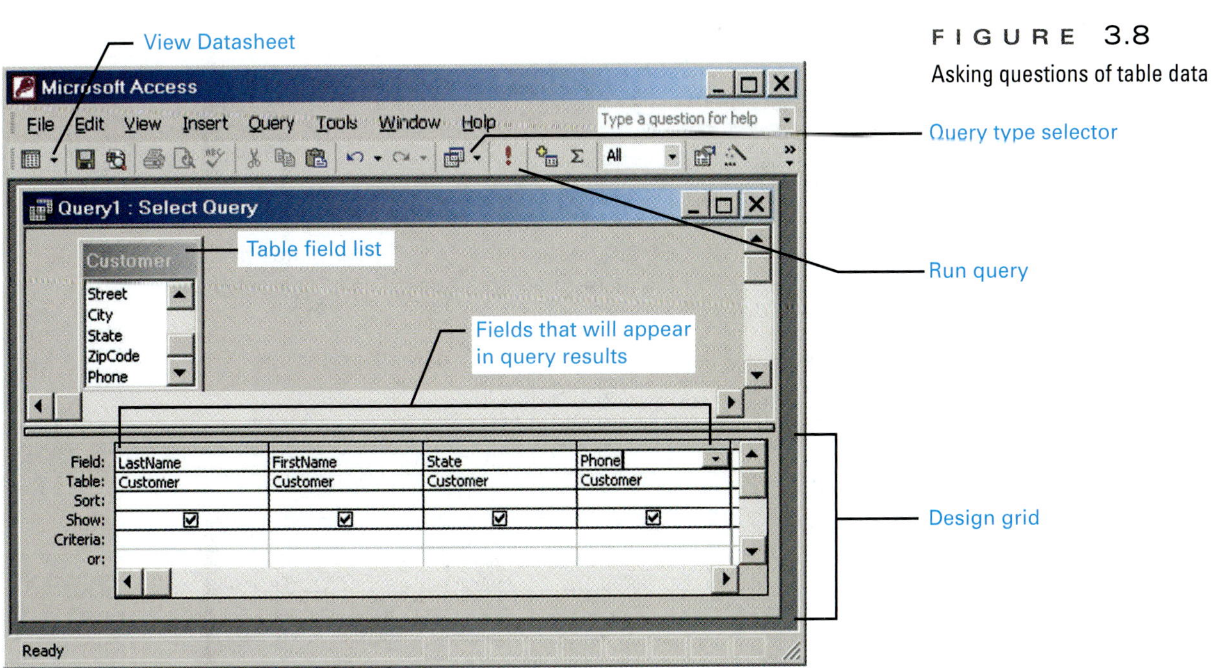

FIGURE 3.8
Asking questions of table data

because no data is stored about the customer's gender, age group, income, or other factors that are generally used to set advertising strategy.

The most common type of query is a select query. Select queries retrieve data from one or more tables and display the results in Datasheet view. Once displayed, the records can be updated. Select queries can

- Display selected rows of data
- Display selected columns of data
- Sort query results
- Calculate within records (e.g., calculate gross pay for each employee record)
- Group records and create subtotals (e.g., subtotal expenses for each department)
- Calculate totals such as sums, counts, and averages

You have already created a query using a Wizard. As with other Wizards, the Simple Query Wizard asks questions and produces a query based on your answers but does not allow access to the full scope of query capabilities. Informational queries are better developed in query Design view.

Specifying Simple Query Criteria

In query Design view a query by example (QBE) grid is used to enter question criteria. The ***design grid*** is used to provide examples of the information to be retrieved and Access will select all data matching the criteria. Since the most popular type of query is a select query, that is the QBE default.

One of the queries that Evan is interested in building is a phone list for his customers. On the phone list, he wants the customer's full name, state, and phone number. This is a select query that you will create in query Design view.

task reference

Create a Select Query

- Select the **Queries** object from the Database window
- Click **New** from the toolbar
- Select the **Design view** button from the New Query dialog box and click **OK**
- Double-click the name of each table that contains relevant data from the Show Table dialog box
- Double-click each table field that is to be contained in the query result to place it in the Field row of the design grid. The order of the columns is the order of the output
- Enter sort criteria in the Sort row of the design grid
- Enter selections in the Criteria row of the design grid
- Click the **Datasheet view** button on the toolbar to see the query results
- Click the **Design view** button on the toolbar to update the query criteria
- Click the **Save** button to save the query criteria

Creating a Customer table query:

1. Close the Customer table of the AC03PuppyParadise.mdb database
2. Select the **Queries** object from the Database window
3. Click **New** on the toolbar
4. Select **Design view** from the New Query dialog box and click **OK**
5. Double-click on the **Customer** table in the Show Table dialog box to add it to the design grid

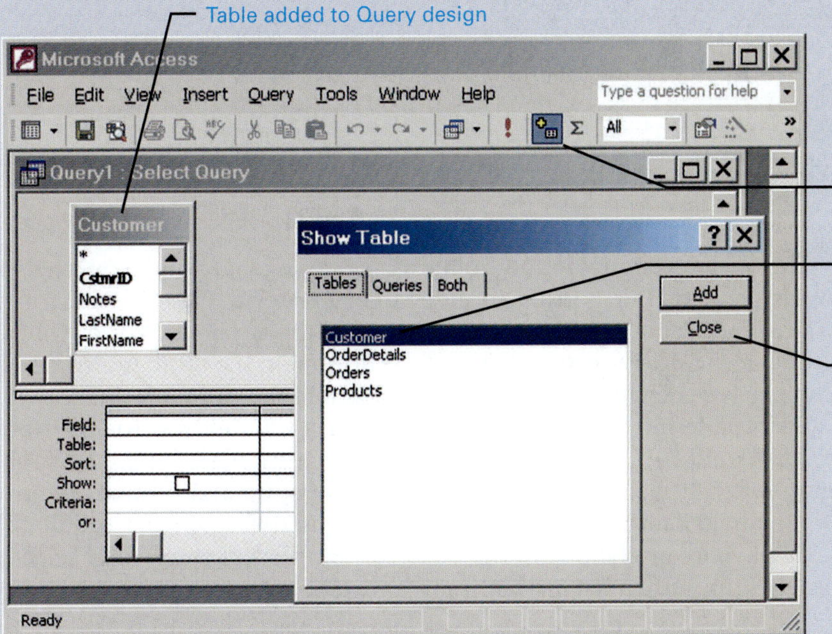

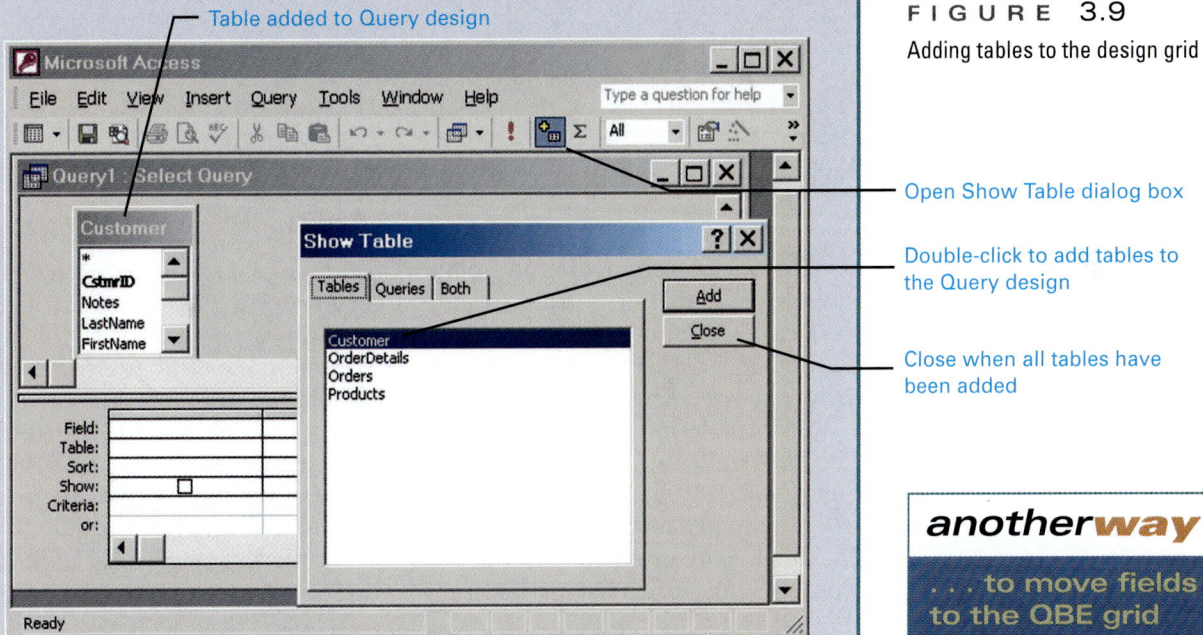

FIGURE 3.9
Adding tables to the design grid

6. Click **Close** in the Show Table dialog box
7. Double-click the **LastName, FirstName, State,** and **Phone** fields from the Customer table field list, adding each to the Field row of the design grid

tip: *If you place an undesired field in the design grid by mistake, delete it by clicking the cursor on the bar above the field to select the column. When the column is selected, press the **Delete** key to remove the column from the grid*

If fields are selected in the wrong order, move a column by clicking the cursor on the bar above the field to select the column. When the column is selected, click and drag it to the desired location

8. Click the **Datasheet view** button to see the query results
9. Click the **Design view** button to return to the query Design view

anotherway

. . . to move fields to the QBE grid

Double-click on the title bar of the field list to select all fields in a table. Drag the selected fields to the Field row of the QBE grid. Access will place each field in its own column of the grid. To move multiple fields from a table simultaneously, select the first field from the table and then hold down the Ctrl key while selecting the other fields. When you have selected all of the desired fields, drag the selection to the Field row of the QBE grid. Access will place each field in its own column in the order that they appear in the table.

FIGURE 3.10
Phone List query results

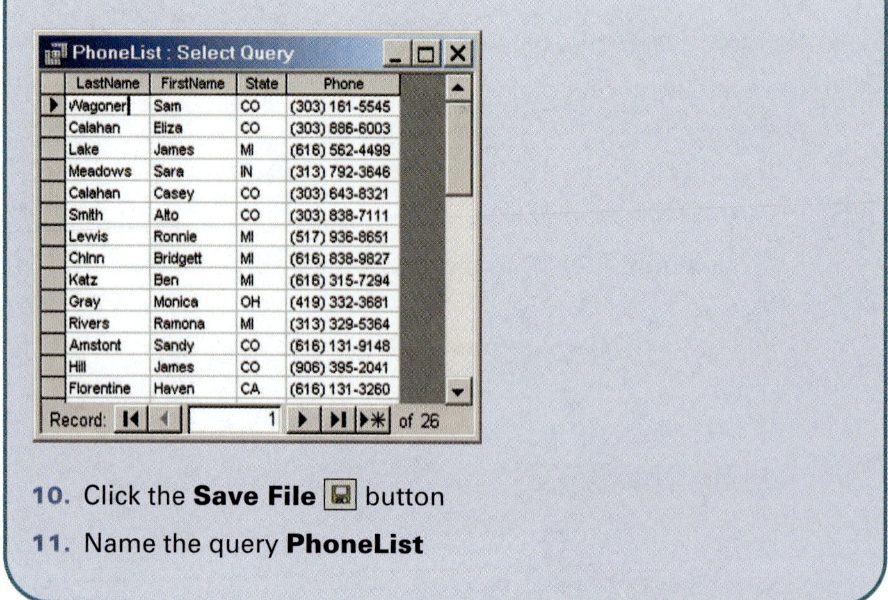

PhoneList : Select Query

LastName	FirstName	State	Phone
Wagoner	Sam	CO	(303) 161-5545
Calahan	Eliza	CO	(303) 886-6003
Lake	James	MI	(616) 562-4499
Meadows	Sara	IN	(313) 792-3646
Calahan	Casey	CO	(303) 643-8321
Smith	Alto	CO	(303) 838-7111
Lewis	Ronnie	MI	(517) 936-8651
Chinn	Bridgett	MI	(616) 838-9827
Katz	Ben	MI	(616) 315-7294
Gray	Monica	OH	(419) 332-3681
Rivers	Ramona	MI	(313) 329-5364
Amstont	Sandy	CO	(616) 131-9148
Hill	James	CO	(906) 395-2041
Florentine	Haven	CA	(616) 131-3260

Record: 1 of 26

10. Click the **Save File** button
11. Name the query **PhoneList**

The query Design window contains the tables that will be queried and the design grid that is used to enter query criteria. The title bar of the Design window contains the query name and the type of query, or Query1: Select Query by default. The Query Type button on the toolbar also reflects the query type as well as allowing the selection of a different query type.

Each table in the Design window displays the field list for that table. The first option of each table field list is the asterisk (*) wildcard (see Figure 3.11). To be included in the query results, the fields must be moved from the field list to the design grid. Clicking and dragging a field, double-clicking a field, or clicking in the Field row of the design grid and selecting from the drop-down list are alternative ways to move fields into the design

FIGURE 3.11
Designing a query

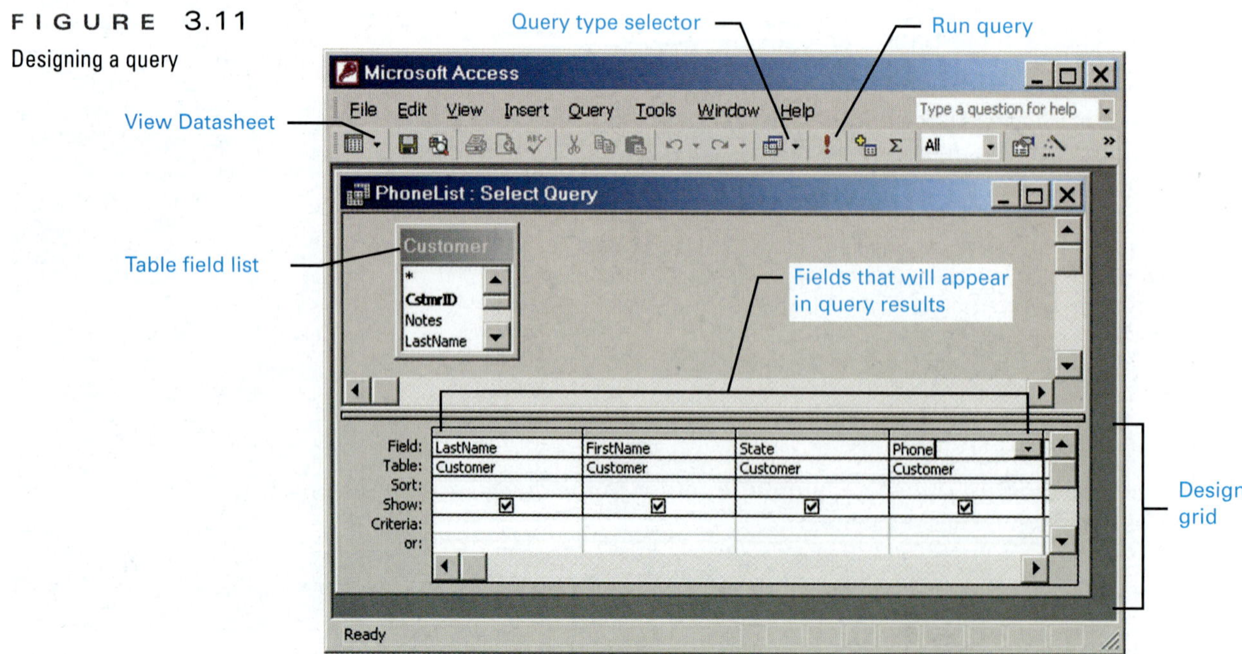

grid. Placing the wildcard (*) in the design grid causes all fields from that table to be included in the output. The order of field columns in the design grid determines their order in the query results.

Each column in the design grid contains a field and the selection criteria for that field. Query criteria include Sort, Show, Criteria, and or. Sort allows ascending or descending sorts on each field. If sorts are set on multiple fields, the leftmost is primary. Show determines whether the field is visible in the query results. Criteria is a selection value similar to that entered in a filter. The or row allows the entry of alternative criteria for a field.

The query results can be viewed at any time by clicking the Datasheet view button. Clicking the Design view button will return to the design grid. It is important to remember that the datasheet displayed from a query is a temporary subset of the data. Updates made to data in the query datasheet are applied to the table data.

Modifying Datasheet Appearance

As with the table datasheet, query results displayed in query Datasheet view can be formatted for better viewing. Columns can be hidden or reordered or have their width adjusted. Formats can be saved with the query or abandoned on exit.

The appearance of a datasheet can be modified for readability, or to visually distinguish it from other datasheets, using the Datasheet Formatting toolbar (see Figure 3.12). Turn on the toolbar by selecting Formatting (Datasheet) from the Toolbars option of the View menu. Formatting toolbar options apply to the entire datasheet—not just the selection.

Figure 3.12 demonstrates Access's datasheet formatting capabilities. The point size (8 is the default), background color, text color, and line color have all been modified. The options were not selected for visual appeal but for ease of identification.

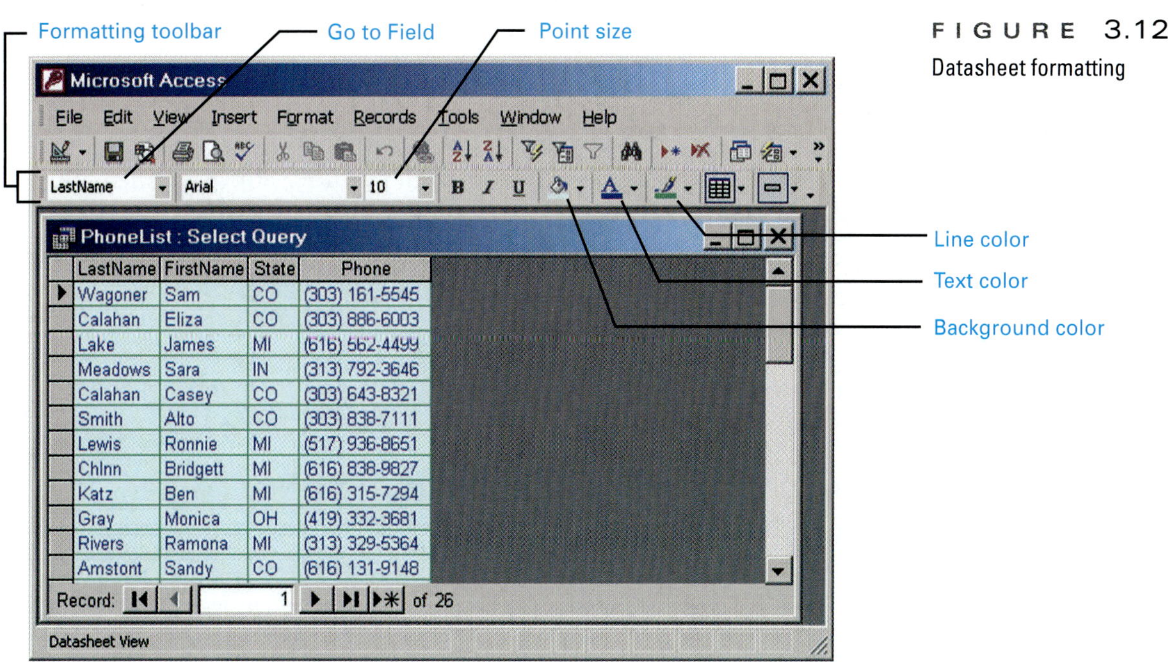

FIGURE 3.12
Datasheet formatting

Formatting the Customer table query:

1. Verify that the PhoneList query of the AC03PuppyParadise.mdb database is open in Datasheet view
2. Activate the Formatting toolbar by selecting **Formatting (Datasheet)** from the **Toolbars** option of the **View** menu
3. Select **Phone** from the Go to Field box to place the cursor in the Phone field
4. Change the font to **Century Gothic** and the point size to **10**
5. Choose background, text, and line colors that you think look appealing
6. Click the **Print** button to print the results
7. Close the Datasheet window without saving the formatting

Sorting Query Data

Sorting data is critical to making it simple to use. The current PhoneList query is in order by CstmrID, because it is the primary key of the source table. Most users would expect a phone list to be in order by LastName and FirstName so a phone number could be easily retrieved.

There are two ways to sort query results. The first is to use the Sort Ascending and Sort Descending buttons on the toolbar. This technique works exactly as presented in the discussion about sorting table datasheets. It is simple but has the drawback of not being stored as part of the query criteria. Each time the query is opened, the sort process must be applied.

Fortunately, the QBE grid has a sort row that allows the sort order for the query results to be part of the query. This sort will be stored as part of the query and therefore automatically will be applied each time the query is opened. Evan would always like the PhoneList to open sorted by LastName and FirstName, so you will add those criteria to the QBE grid.

Sorting the Customer table query:

1. Verify that the PhoneList query of the AC03PuppyParadise.mdb database is open in Design view
2. Verify that the field order is LastName and then FirstName so that LastName is the primary sort and FirstName is the secondary sort
3. Add Ascending to the Sort criteria of each field as shown in Figure 3.13
4. Click the **Datasheet view** button to see the query result
5. Click the **Design view** button to return to the query Design view
6. Click the **Save File** button to save the sort criteria with the query

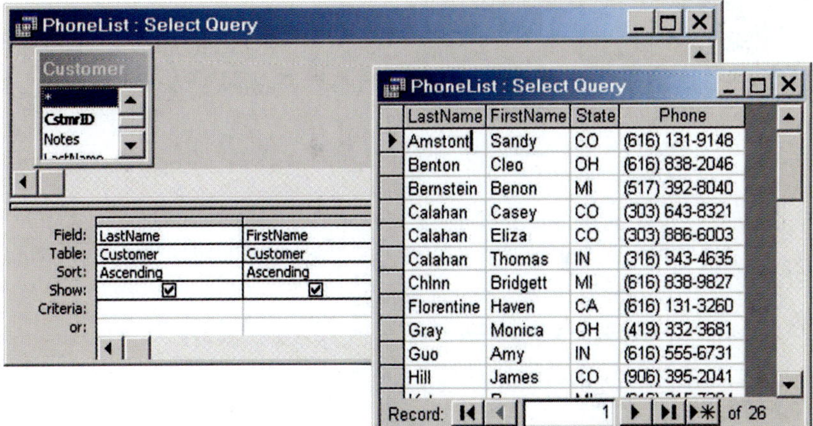

FIGURE 3.13
The PhoneList query with sort criteria

anotherway

. . . to run a query

The instructions for viewing query results have used the Design view button, which automatically runs the query. The Run query button on the toolbar will accomplish the same task.

making the grade

SESSION 3.1

1. What happens when part of a field is selected and then Filter by Selection is applied?
2. T F Filters restrict the columns that display for the filtered table.
3. How can you exclude a value from the results of a filter?
4. T F Filters remain in effect until another filter is executed.
5. What is the purpose of Or in filters?
6. What is the benefit of saving a filter as a query?

SESSION 3.2 SELECTING AND CALCULATING WITH QUERIES

Queries are a powerful analytical tool that will allow complete control over which fields and records from a table or tables display. In this session power will be added to select queries by entering record selection criteria and performing simple calculations.

SELECTING RECORDS IN QUERIES

Query record selection criteria are entered in the Criteria rows of the QBE grid using conditions. Conditions define how records will be selected and are placed in the field to which they will be applied. A typical condition uses a relational operator and a value, such as > 30000 in the Salary field, to tell Access which records to include in the query result. All records for which the condition is true will be incorporated into the query result.

FIGURE 3.14
Relational operators

Operator	Function	Example
=	Returns records that match the value exactly. It is optional because it is the Access default	"CA" #11/23/02#
>	Returns records with values greater than the condition value	> 30000 > "Collins"
>=	Returns records with values greater than or equal to the condition value	>= 30000 >= "Collins"
<	Returns records with values less than the condition value	< 45 < "Simes"
<=	Returns records with values less than or equal to the condition value	<= 89 <= "Sam"
<>	Returns records that are not equal to the condition value	<> 4 <> "Smith"
Between	Returns records with values between the two stated values. Both values are included in the result	Between 12 And 28 Between "e" And "k"
In	Returns records with values that match those in the condition list	In ("Jan", "Mar", "Sep") In (1998, 2001)
Like	Returns records with values that match the pattern stated with wildcards	Like "Pren*"

Relational operators were briefly presented in the discussion on filters. Figure 3.14 gives a more complete presentation on the meaning of the various comparison operators.

The Software database contains tables of data about the software inventory of a small retailer and the vendors that sell each software product. It is ideal for practicing selection queries and implementing calculations.

Selecting Software table records:

1. Open the AC03Software.mdb database
2. Open tblSoftware and familiarize yourself with the data
3. Select the **Queries** object from the Database window
4. Click **New** on the toolbar
5. Select **Design view** on the New Query dialog box and click **OK**
6. Double-click on the tblSoftware table in the Show Table dialog box to add it to the design grid
7. Click **Close** in the Show Table dialog box

8. You'll start by creating a price list. Place Name, Category, Quantity, and Price in the Field row of the QBE grid
9. Click the **Datasheet view** button to see the query results
10. Return to **Design view**
11. Suppose that the policy is to reorder software when there are fewer than 10 copies on hand. Enter the criterion **< 10** in the Quantity column to list software that needs to be reordered
12. Click the **Datasheet view** button to see the query results

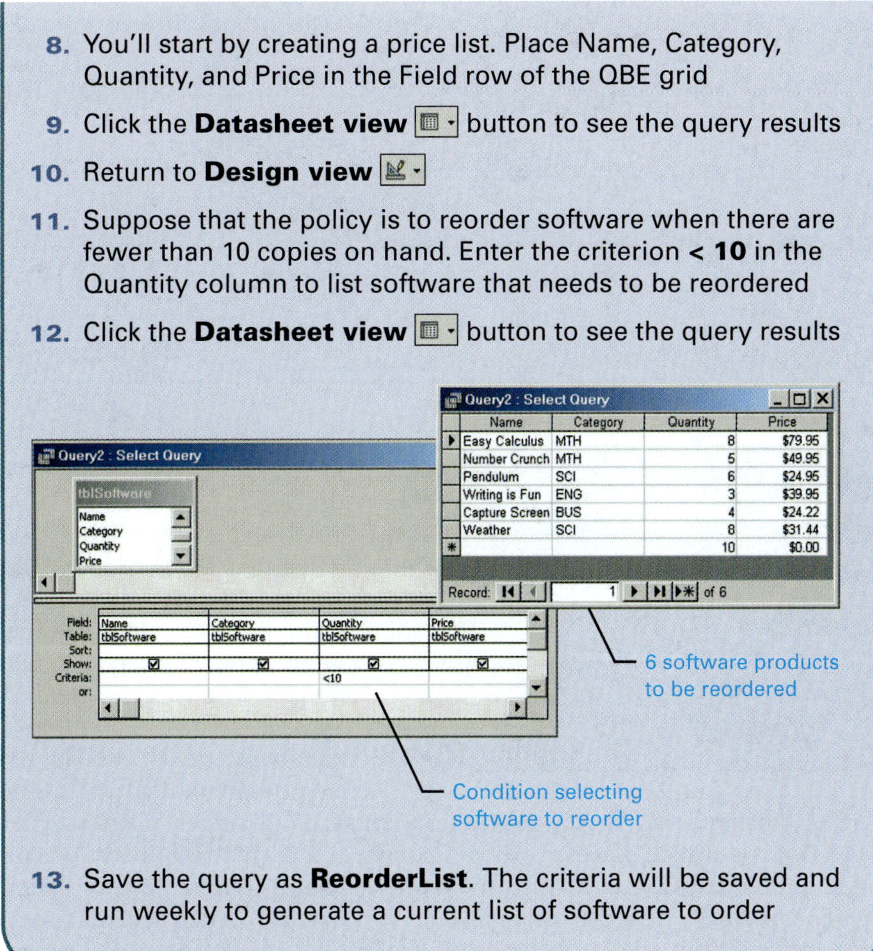

FIGURE 3.15
Software reorder query

13. Save the query as **ReorderList**. The criteria will be saved and run weekly to generate a current list of software to order

The less than (<) relational operator was used to state the condition in the previous example, but any of the other operators could have been applied. The operator is determined by the question that is being posed. Suppose that the normal inventory for each software product is 50 copies. There are currently several software products with inventory above that quantity because of a special shipment. We need to promote those items by reducing their price. The query criterion that would return this list is >50 in the Quantity field. If you want to know what software is purchased from Software Clearing House (SC), a criterion of SC in the VendorCode of the Software table would return that list. Remember that the equal (=) sign is optional when stating equality conditions.

When stating queries, delimiters are required for each match value. The data type of the field being matched determines the appropriate delimiter, as shown in Figure 3.16. Access QBE adds these delimiters to conditions entered without them.

ADDING CALCULATIONS TO QUERIES

When the PuppyParadise database was designed, the calculated fields were purposely not stored. One of the rules of normalization precludes storing calculated values because they can be recreated with current data each time a report or query is run.

FIGURE 3.16
Data type delimiters

Data Type	Delimiter	Example
Number, Currency, AutoNumber	None	>5302.28
Text	Double quotes ("") delimit text match values	"Miller"
Date/Time	Pound signs (##) delimit date and time values	<#3/30/02#
Yes/No	Keywords True/False or Yes/No are used to select data in Yes/No fields	Yes

FIGURE 3.17
Mathematical order of precedence

Order	Operation	
1	–	Negation (as in –1)
2	^	Exponentiation
3	*, /	Multiplication and division
4	+, –	Addition and subtraction

Calculated Fields

To calculate a value for each row of data in a table, you must add a ***calculated field*** to the QBE grid. A calculated field holds a mathematical expression whose results will be displayed in the field. A typical expression contains database fields, constants, and mathematical operators. The database fields in an expression must be Number, Currency, or Date/Time data type. Access does not support mathematical operations on other data types. Constants must be numeric values such as 8238 or 0.36.

The mathematical operators are +, –, *, /, and ^. When several operators are used in a single formula, the algebraic order of precedence outlined in Figure 3.17 applies. If a formula contains operators with the same precedence—for example, if a formula contains both a multiplication and division operator—the operators are evaluated from left to right. To change the order of evaluation, enclose the part of the formula to be calculated first in parentheses.

A calculated field can be entered directly into the Field row of a QBE grid, or the ***Expression Builder*** can be used to select the components of the calculation. Because the space in the QBE grid is fairly small, a large text box called a ***Zoom box*** can be opened to provide greater visibility for complicated expressions. Click in a Field cell of the QBE grid and then press Ctrl+F2 to open a Zoom box.

task reference

Create an Expression Using Expression Builder

- Click in the Field row of the QBE grid column that will display the calculation
- Click the **Build** button in the query Design toolbar
- Select expression elements and operators to create the desired calculation
- Click **OK** to place the calculation in the QBE grid

The software database contains data about the price and quantity on hand for each software title. The inventory value of each product was not stored but can be calculated for queries and reports. Inventory value provides information needed to answer questions about the value of a company or where costs could be cut in the current system.

Creating an expression field with the Expression Builder:

1. Verify that the AC03Software.mdb database is open
2. Select the **Queries** object from the Database window
3. Double-click **Create query in Design view** to open the QBE grid and Show Table dialog box
4. Double-click on the **tblSoftware** table in the Show Table dialog box to add it to the design grid
5. Click **Close** in the Show Table dialog box
6. Place **Name, Category, Quantity,** and **Price** in the Field row of the QBE grid
7. Click in the empty Field row to the right of Price and activate the **Expression Builder**

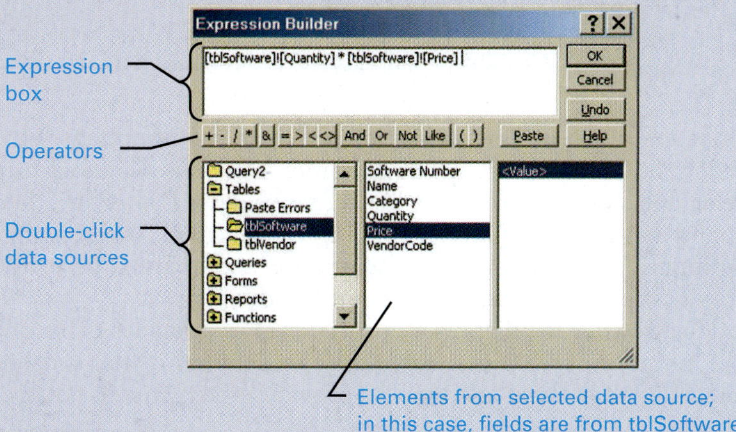

FIGURE 3.18
Expression Builder

8. Double-click **Tables,** then **tblSoftware** to list the fields that will be used in the calculation
9. Build the expression by double-clicking **Quantity,** clicking the **multiplication** button, and then double-clicking **Price**

tip: *If you make a mistake, you can make edits directly in the Expression box. Notice that Access includes the table name with each field so that you can perform calculations involving multiple tables. Square brackets [] enclose table and field names*

10. Click **OK** to close the Expression Builder and place the expression in the QBE grid

FIGURE 3.19
Expression in QBE grid

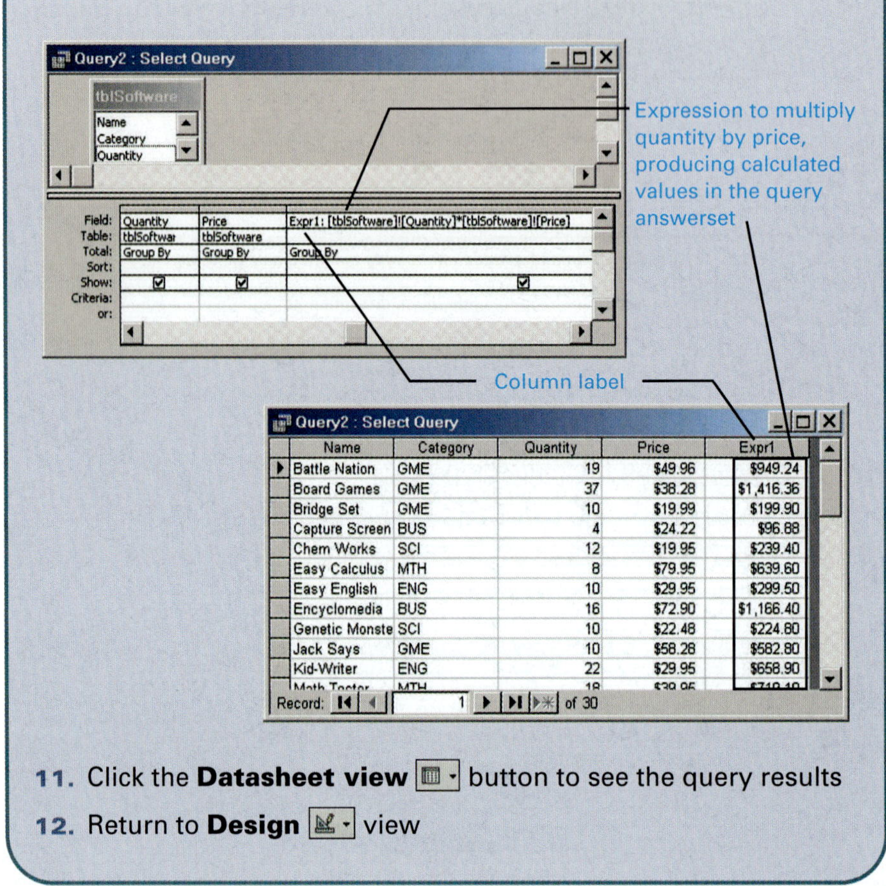

11. Click the **Datasheet view** button to see the query results
12. Return to **Design** view

Notice that the Expression Builder has a folder of functions. Functions are predefined calculations for common operations. Available functions include calculating the difference between two dates (DateDiff), determining a loan payment (Pmt), and averaging values (Avg). When using a predefined function, the appropriate calculation values must be provided in the correct order, a task that Expression Builder supports.

Notice also that the Expression Builder always places extra punctuation ([]!) in the expression. Access requires a field name that is used as the column heading for every column and provides one if you do not. Consider the following expression.

```
Expr1: [tblSoftware]![Quantity]*[tblSoftware]![Price]
```

The colon (:) separates the column heading from the expression. The default column heading is Expr1 for the first expression, Expr2 for the second, and so on. If you provide a value to the left of the colon, it will be used. The exclamation point (!) is the delimiter or separator that differentiates between the table name and the field name. The table name is optional unless there are fields from different tables with the same name. For example tblSoftware!VendorCode and tblVendor!VendorCode need the table name to differentiate the two fields. The square brackets [] are only required when there are spaces in a field or table name, so VendorCode does not require them, but [Vendor Code] does. You may choose to eliminate the extra punctuation or leave it since it only impacts the readability of an expression not the performance.

Creating an expression by typing:

1. Return to the previous query design
2. Verify that **Name, Category, Quantity,** and **Price** from the **tblSoftware** table are in the design grid
3. Select and delete the expression built with Expression Builder
4. Click in the empty Field row to the right of Price and type **Total:Quantity*Price**

tip: *When field names are unique, the table name does not need to be included in the expression. The value to the left of the colon (:) is the column label. Square brackets [] are only required when field or table names contain spaces, but Access will add them*

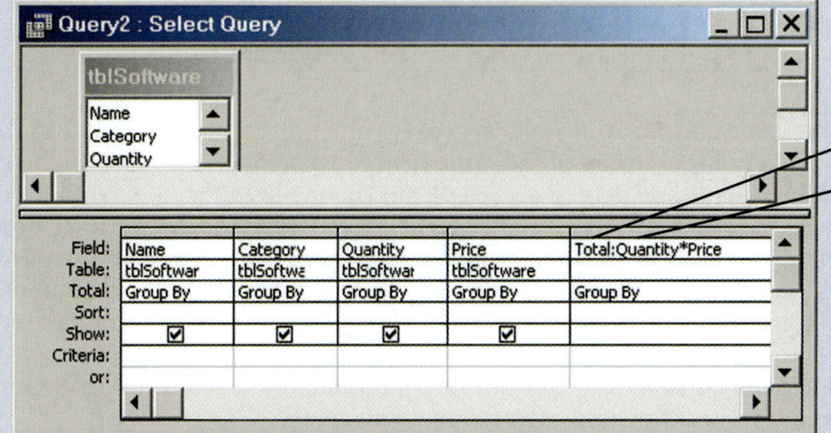

FIGURE 3.20
Typed expression in QBE grid

5. Click the **Datasheet view** button to see the query results
6. Close the query and save it as **InventoryValue**

For short, well-defined calculations, typing in the expression is usually faster than using the Expression Builder and results in less expression punctuation. It is important to know when the punctuation must be included. To recap the earlier discussion:

- The colon (:) separates the column heading from the expression
- The exclamation point (!) separates a table name from its field name. The table name is only required if you are using fields with the same name
- The square brackets [] are required to enclose both field names and table names that contain spaces

Aggregate Operations

Aggregate operations are used to calculate summary data such as averages and sums. These operations make use of the predefined functions mentioned in the previous topic and are outlined in Figure 3.21. ***Aggregate functions*** can be applied to all of the data in a table or any subset specified

FIGURE 3.21
Aggregate functions

Aggregate Function	Use	Data Types
Sum	Totals the field values for selected records	AutoNumber, Currency, Date/Time, and Number
Avg	Averages the field values for selected records	AutoNumber, Currency, Date/Time, and Number
Count	Counts the number of selected records	AutoNumber, Currency, Date/Time, Memo, Number, OLE Object, Text, and Yes/No
Max	Returns the highest field value	AutoNumber, Currency, Date/Time, Number, and Text
Min	Returns the lowest field value	AutoNumber, Currency, Date/Time, Number, and Text

by the query. Because only one aggregate function can be applied to a table column, multiple copies of the same field must be placed in the design grid to achieve multiple aggregate operations on one field.

Suppose our software retailer wants to know how many software products he carries (Count Name), the average number of copies on hand (Avg Quantity), the total number of software products on hand (Sum Quantity), the average inventory cost of a product (Avg Quantity*Price), and the total inventory cost (Sum Quantity*Price). Such information is valuable when determining the cost of adding new products or discontinuing existing products. The following steps produce this query.

Summarizing selected data with aggregate functions:

1. Verify that the AC03Software.mdb database is open
2. Open a new query in Design view with **tblSoftware** as the table being queried
3. Create the QBE fields outlined in Figure 3.22
4. Click the **Totals** Σ button to insert the Total row into the QBE grid
5. In the Total row, select the aggregate function for each column, as shown in Figure 3.22
6. Click the **Datasheet view** button to see the query results
7. Double-click the column borders to resize them
8. Return to **Design view**
9. Change the Field row for name to read **Nbr of Products: Name** to customize the field heading
10. Click the **Datasheet view** button to see the revised query results

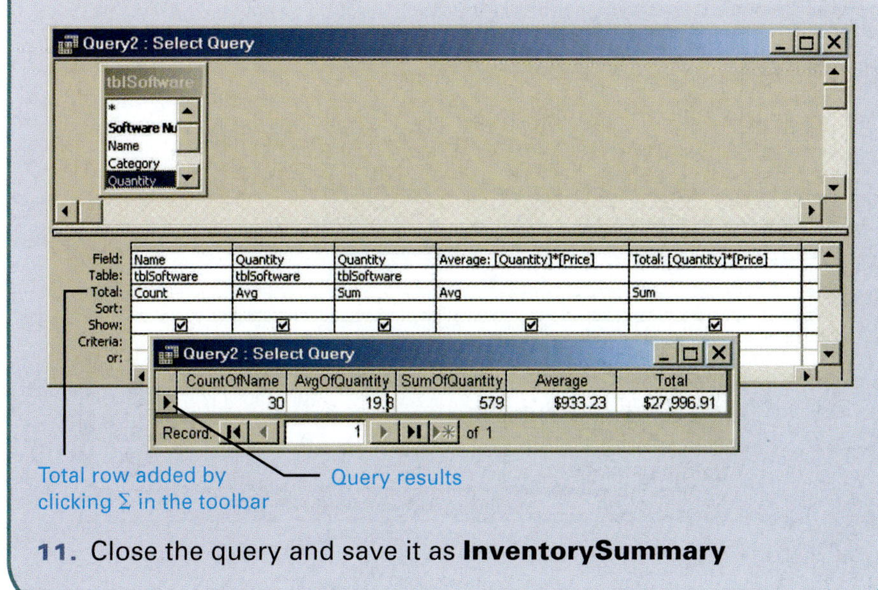

FIGURE 3.22
Aggregate functions assigned to each field

11. Close the query and save it as **InventorySummary**

Notice that Access created a unique field heading for each column by combining the aggregate function with the field name. The default name can be overridden by providing your own column headings before the colon in the field name, as demonstrated in the previous steps.

Record Group Calculations

Another calculation requirement is to create subtotals for specific groups of records. Returning to tblSoftware, we could use record group calculations to determine statistics for each vendor. Record group calculations are accomplished using the ***Group By*** operator in the Total row of a query.

Summarizing grouped data:

1. Verify that the AC03Software.mdb database is open
2. Open the **InventorySummary** query in Design view
3. To the right of the last field, add the field VendorCode, select the VendorCode column, and drag it until it is the leftmost column
4. Verify that the Total row of VendorCode is set to Group By since we want summaries for each vendor
5. Click the **Datasheet view** button to see the query results
6. Double-click the column borders to resize them
7. Select **Save As** from the **File** menu and name the revised query **VendorCodeSummary**

Once a query has been saved, it is listed as a Query object in the Database window. Only the query specifications are saved, so the next time the query is run, all calculations will be computed based on the current table data. Running a saved query is as simple as double-clicking its name.

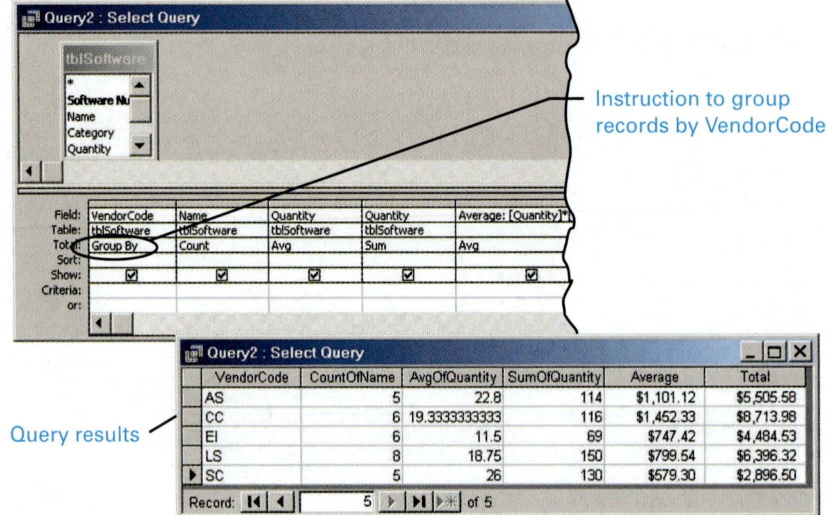

VendorCode	CountOfName	AvgOfQuantity	SumOfQuantity	Average	Total
AS	5	22.8	114	$1,101.12	$5,505.58
CC	6	19.3333333333	116	$1,452.33	$8,713.98
EI	6	11.5	69	$747.42	$4,484.53
LS	8	18.75	150	$799.54	$6,396.32
SC	5	26	130	$579.30	$2,896.50

FIGURE 3.23
Using Group By to summarize data by VendorCode

SESSION 3.2

making the grade

1. What methods could be used to return a contiguous range of values in a query?
2. T F Relational operators include +, −, *, and /.
3. What tool(s) can be used to create an expression?
4. When using aggregate functions, how many rows will be in the query results?

SESSION 3.3 BUILDING SIMPLE FORMS AND REPORTS

The default form and report capabilities of Access were introduced in Chapter 1 to demonstrate the use of these database objects. Now it's time to explore some of the valuable features of forms and reports.

CREATING AND USING FORMS

A form is an Access object like a query, meaning that its design is specified, saved, and then run against current data on demand. Access forms are used to organize and display data on the screen in a more effective format than Datasheet view. Typically, forms display only one record at a time.

Like queries, forms support multiple views: Design view, where the form layout and content can be altered; and ***Form view,*** where the data are displayed for maintenance, selection, printing, and other data update and analysis tasks.

Building Forms

There are five types of AutoForm Wizards that work like the tabular and columnar forms explored in the first chapter. Each AutoForm Wizard will allow one table and a form layout to be specified, but nothing more. The ***Form Wizard*** allows fields to be selected from one or more tables and the display format to be specified, and then it creates the form based on that input. Finally a form can be created in Design view with control over fields, formats, and calculations. Let's start by creating a form based on the InventoryQuery just created.

Using the Form wizard:

1. Verify that the AC03Software.mdb database is open
2. In the Database window, select the **Forms** object and **Create form by using wizard,** then select **New**
3. Select **Form Wizard** and click **OK**

tip: *There is no need to select a table before entering the Form Wizard as you did with AutoForm*

4. Fields for this query can be selected from any existing tables and queries. Select **Query: InventoryValue** from the Tables/Queries drop-down list
5. Use the >> button to select all of the fields for the form and click **Next**
6. Click on each of the Layout options and preview the result. Select **Columnar** for this form and click **Next.** A sample of the layout appears on the left side of the dialog box
7. Preview all of the styles and then select **Sumi Painting** and click **Next**
8. Name your form **InventoryValue** and then click **Finish**

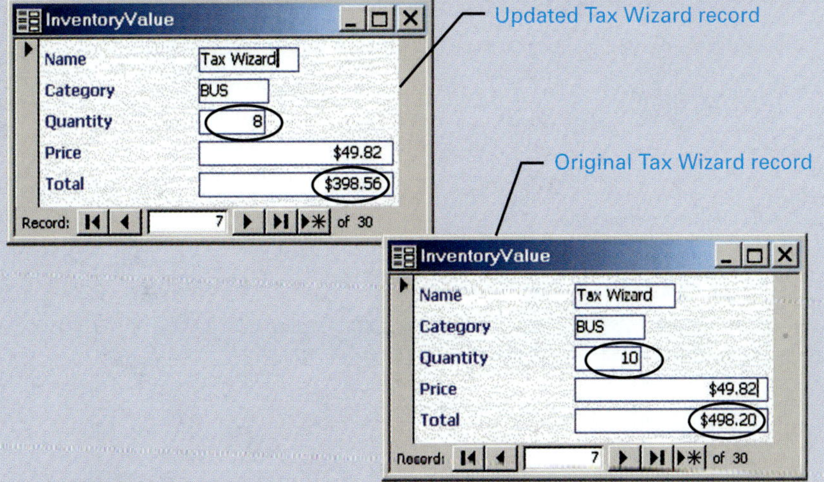

FIGURE 3.24
Completed form displaying the Tax Wizard record

9. Use the Navigation bar to move through the data to the **Tax Wizard** record
10. Notice that the Tax Wizard Total value is $498.20. Change the Quantity to **8,** move to the next record, and then back to the Tax Wizard record. Notice that the Total has also updated
11. Click the **Print Preview** button to see how your forms would print is you clicked the **Print** button. The Print option of the File menu contains options for printing only the current record or a range of records

As was just demonstrated, forms can be used to maintain the data in a database. Calculated fields (expressions) display in the form but cannot be updated. Calculation values are automatically updated when edits made to the expression fields are saved (when you move to another row of data).

Finding, editing, and deleting data are accomplished with the same techniques used in table Datasheet view. The same Sort, Filter, Find, New Record, and Delete buttons appear on the toolbar. Sorts can be applied to change the presentation order. Filters allow a subset of the data to be manipulated and Find will find records that meet a criterion. As when editing data in the datasheet, deletes cannot be undone.

Customizing Forms

Forms created with the Wizard can be modified in Design view. Developers frequently create the first cut of a form with the Wizard and customize to achieve the desired result.

task reference

Modify the Format of a Form

- Open the form in Design view
- Click the **AutoFormat** button in the Form Design toolbar
- Select from the same formats that were available in the Wizard

Changing the AutoFormat of the InventoryValue form:

1. Open the **InventoryValue** form in Design view
2. Select the **AutoFormat** button from the Form Design toolbar
3. Select the format that appeals to you

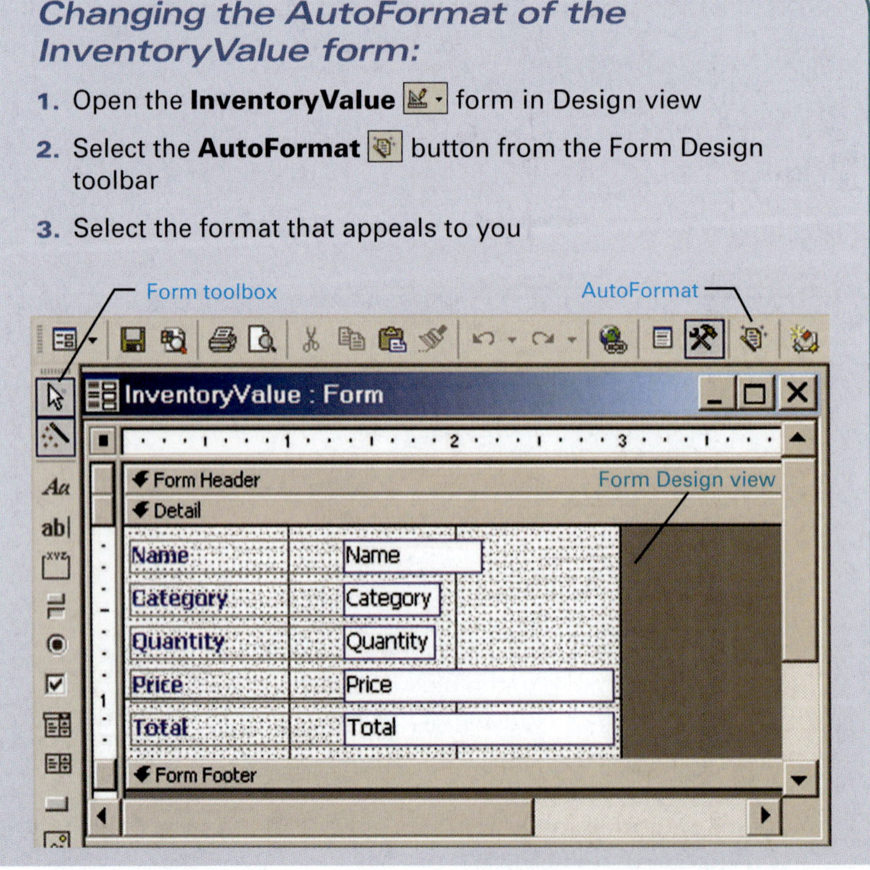

FIGURE 3.25
InventoryValue form in Design view

4. Click the **Options** button. You can choose portions of the format to apply. Click each option to see the impact
5. Click the **Form view** button to see the full impact
6. Move back and forth between Design view and Form view until you get the effect you desire
7. Save your changes

A word of caution: when using forms that do not display all of the fields of a table, users can update only the displayed fields, which can cause problems with finding and entering the data later on.

PRODUCING REPORTS

Reports are used to effectively format and print data from tables and queries. All aspects of a report can be customized, including formatting and graphics.

The Report Wizards

The AutoReport Wizard was introduced in Chapter 1 to provide an overview of what the report object does. Like tables, queries, and forms, the report object stores the criteria for creating a report.

When a report opens, the saved report criteria are run against current data. Data displayed in a report can be drawn directly from a table, a group of related tables, or a query. Expressions can be used to calculate values for every record, subtotals for groups of records, or report totals. Charts and graphics also can be added.

The AutoReport Wizard presented in Chapter 1 is the most restrictive way to create a report. It allows you to select only one table or query as the data source and uses a default layout. The Report Wizard is very similar to the Form Wizard. It will allow you to choose fields from multiple tables and queries, control the order of those fields, define calculations, and select a report layout.

Using the Report Wizard:

1. Verify that the AC03Software.mdb database is open
2. In the Database window select the **Reports** object, then double-click **Create report by using wizard** (the fastest way to start the Report Wizard)
3. Fields for this query can be selected from any existing tables and queries. Select **Query: InventoryValue** from the Tables/Queries drop-down list
4. Use the >> button to select all of the fields for the form and click **Next**
5. Grouping will create subtotals. This report needs to be grouped by software category. Select **Category** from the list of available fields and click the > selection button to group by Category and then click **Next**

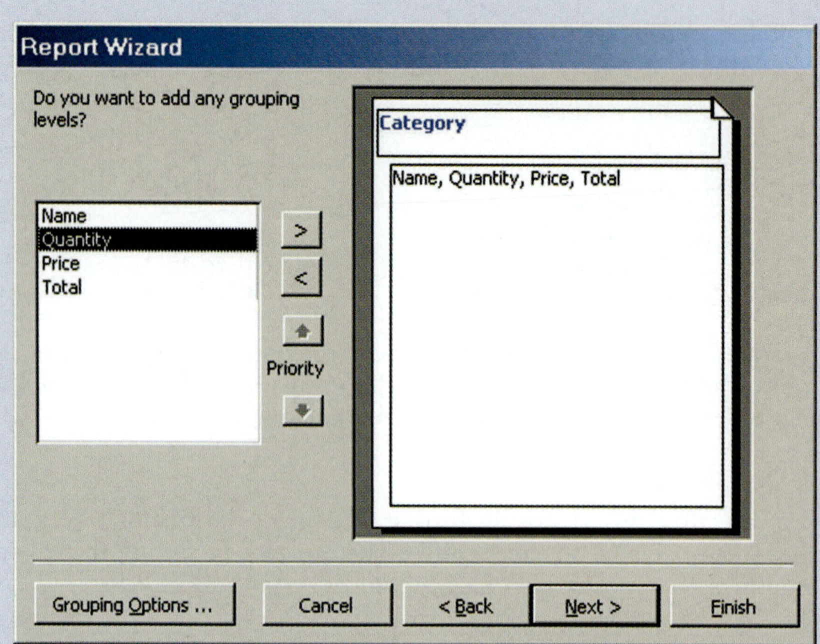

FIGURE 3.26
Category added as a group to the form

6. Select **Name** from the first sort list to cause the software to be sorted by name within Category. Click on **Summary Options** to add summary calculations

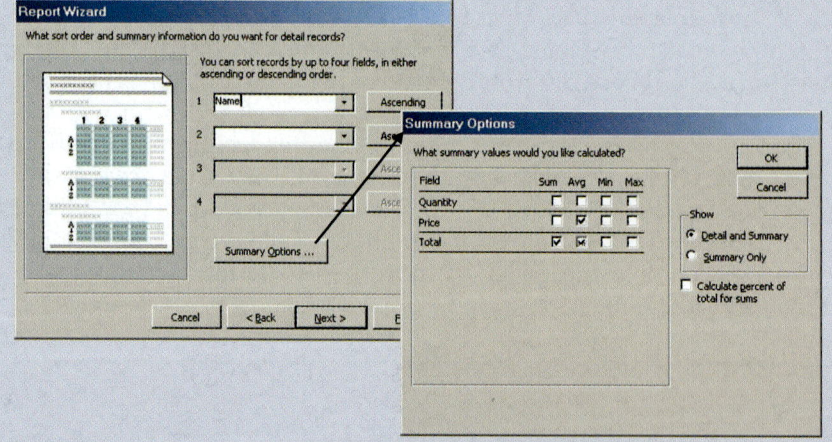

FIGURE 3.27
Setting grouping and summary options

7. For the Price field, click on **Avg** to calculate average price by category (the group you set). For the Total field, click on both **Sum** and **Avg** to calculate both the total inventory value by category and the average inventory value by category. Click **OK** in the Summary Options dialog box and then **Next** in the Report Wizard dialog box
8. Explore the various sort layouts by clicking each and reviewing the sample. Select **Stepped** and click **Next**
9. Explore the styles by clicking each and reviewing the sample. Select **Corporate** and press **Next**
10. Name the report **InventoryValueByCategory,** verify that **Preview the report** is selected, and click **Finish**

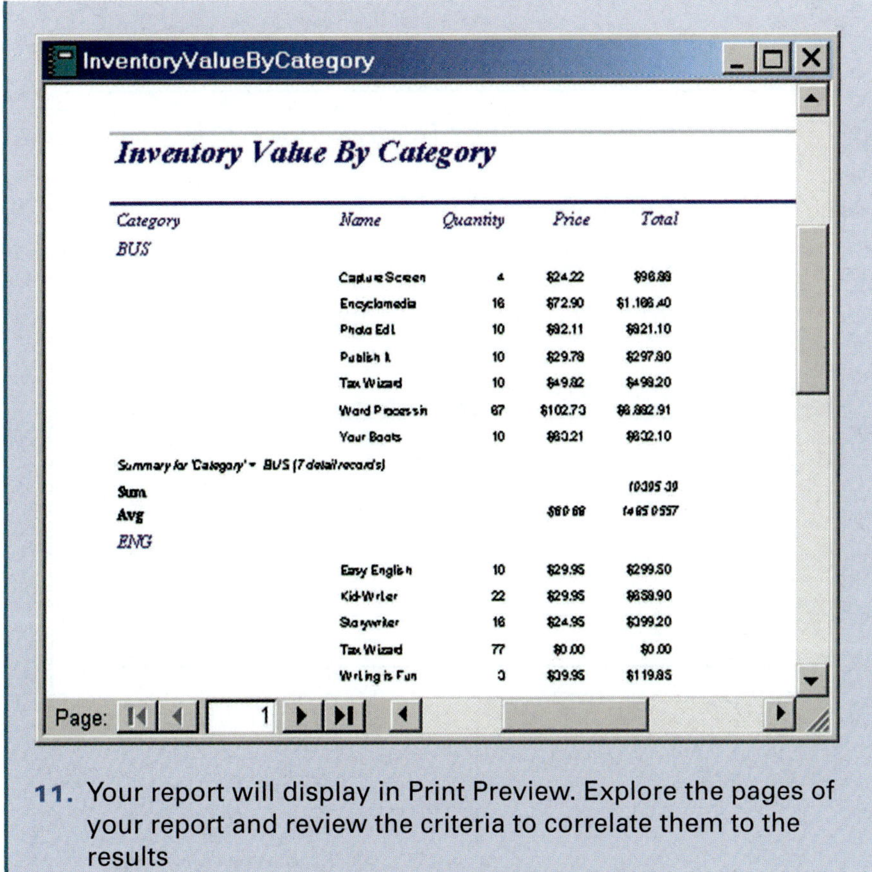

FIGURE 3.28
Completed InventoryValueByCategory report

11. Your report will display in Print Preview. Explore the pages of your report and review the criteria to correlate them to the results

Grouping records is an important concept. Reports without grouping cannot contain subtotals. When records are grouped, the group value (Category in our example) is used to create a header that appears above the records of that group. A group footer is also created to contain any summary statistics for the group. Up to 10 fields can be grouped with summary statistics for any or all of the 10.

The Report Wizard displays option buttons to ***Show Detail and Summary*** records or Summary Only records as the report is being built. Detail reports display each row from the selected input, like the report just created. Summary reports display only the summary statistics, for example, the Category footer from the previous report.

Formatting Reports

To format reports, it is necessary to use Design view. The simplest change is to choose another AutoFormat. This process is the same as changing the AutoFormat of a form.

task reference

Modify the Format of a Report

- Open the report in Design view
- Click the **AutoFormat** button in the Report Design toolbar
- Select from the same formats that were available in the Wizard

Changing the AutoFormat of the InventoryValueByCategory report:

1. Open the **InvertoryValueByCategory** report in Design view
2. Select the **AutoFormat** button from the Form Design toolbar
3. Preview the available formats (they are the same as those presented in the Wizard) and select the format that appeals to you

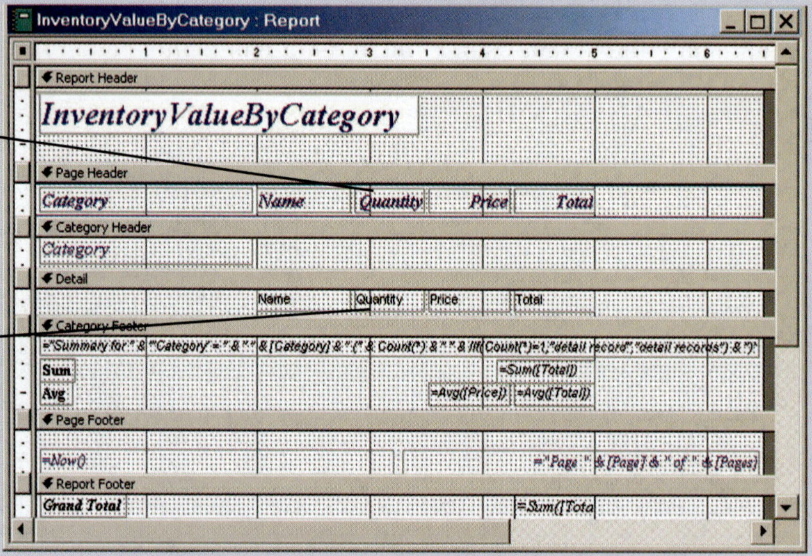

FIGURE 3.29
InventoryValueByCategory report in Design view

Labels for report fields appear on each report page

Defines the fields for each detail line

4. Click the **Options** button. You can choose portions of the format to apply. Click each option to see the impact
5. The **Customize** button allows you to save your custom format
6. Click the **Form view** button to see the full impact
7. Move back and forth between Design view and Form view until you get the effect you desire
8. Save your changes

Access forms and reports consist of objects called controls. Each control performs a specific task. For example, a label displays text; a text box displays the value of a field and accepts input from the user. In Design view, you can see that each field is composed of two controls: a label that holds the field's caption and a text box that will display the field's value.

All of the objects displayed on a form or report can be modified. Modifications include altering the labels, moving labels and text boxes, and adding new objects. To add objects, use the toolbox containing Controls and the Control Wizards.

Adding descriptive column names is accomplished by editing the labels on the form or report. To edit a label, select it and click an insertion point. Once the text is changed, the label may need to be resized to properly display the complete content. The InventoryByCategory report should be updated with labels that better describe the data.

Changing the labels of the InventoryValueByCategory report:

1. Open the **InventoryValueByCategory** report in Print Preview . Notice that the report title would look better with spaces and that the complete software title does not always display (Word Processin)
2. Change to **Design view**
3. In the Report Header, select the title (InventoryValueByCategory). Insert spaces between the words and lengthen the text box so that all of the title is displayed
4. Use **Print Preview** to evaluate your changes
5. Return to **Design view**
6. Select the Quantity, Price, and Total labels in the report's Page Header section and the Quantity, Price, and Total text boxes in the Detail section by holding down the Shift key after the first selection

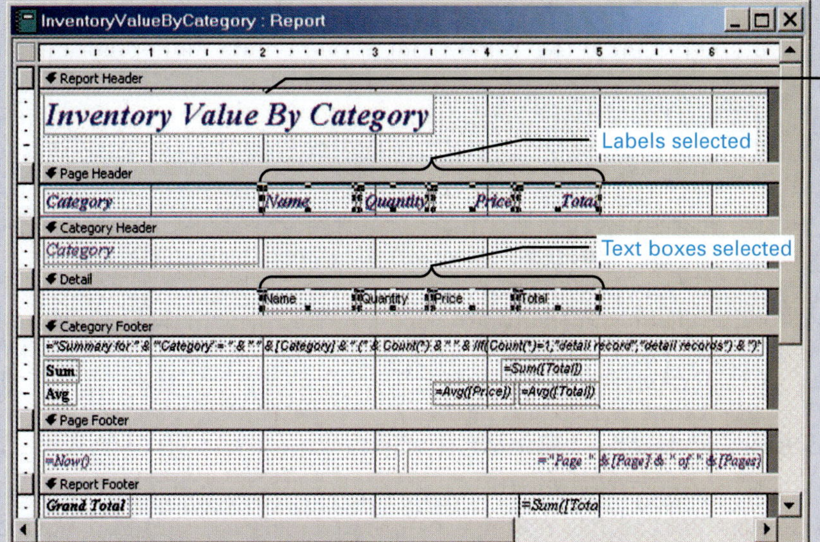

FIGURE 3.30
Labels and corresponding text boxes selected

7. The selected labels and text boxes need to be moved to the right so that the Name column can be expanded to display "Word Processing." Drag the selection to the right until the left side of Quantity is on the heavy grid line
8. Select the Name label and Name text box. Drag the right border to expand it two grid marks
9. Move back and forth between Design view and Form view until you get the effect you desire
10. Click the Save button to save your changes

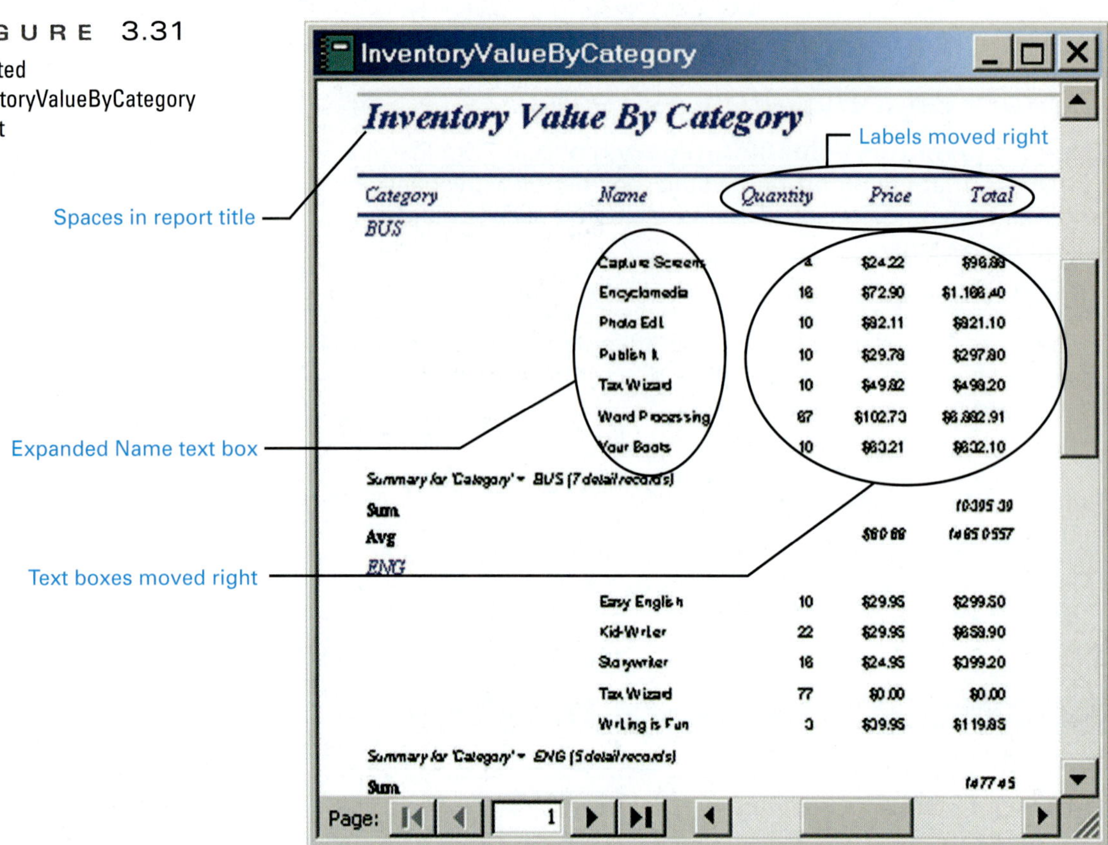

FIGURE 3.31 Updated InventoryValueByCategory report

Notice that in Design view, the report title is placed in the Report Header section of the design, causing it to appear once at the beginning of the report. The labels for a field appear in the page header section, causing them to appear once at the top of each page of the report. The text boxes that will display the values of a field appear in the Detail section of the report, which repeats for each value.

Producing Mailing Labels

Producing mailing labels is a common business task made easy by Access. The Report Wizard has options to format labels for standard business forms (available from office supply stores).

Making mailing labels for software venders:

1. Verify that the AC03Software.mdb database is open
2. In the Database window, click the **Reports** object and then **New**
3. Select the **Label Wizard** and **tblVendor** as the data source and click **OK**
4. The next step selects the type of mailing label. We will use **Avery, J8162,** a popular label type, and click **Next**
5. Select Arial **10** point as the label font and click **Next**

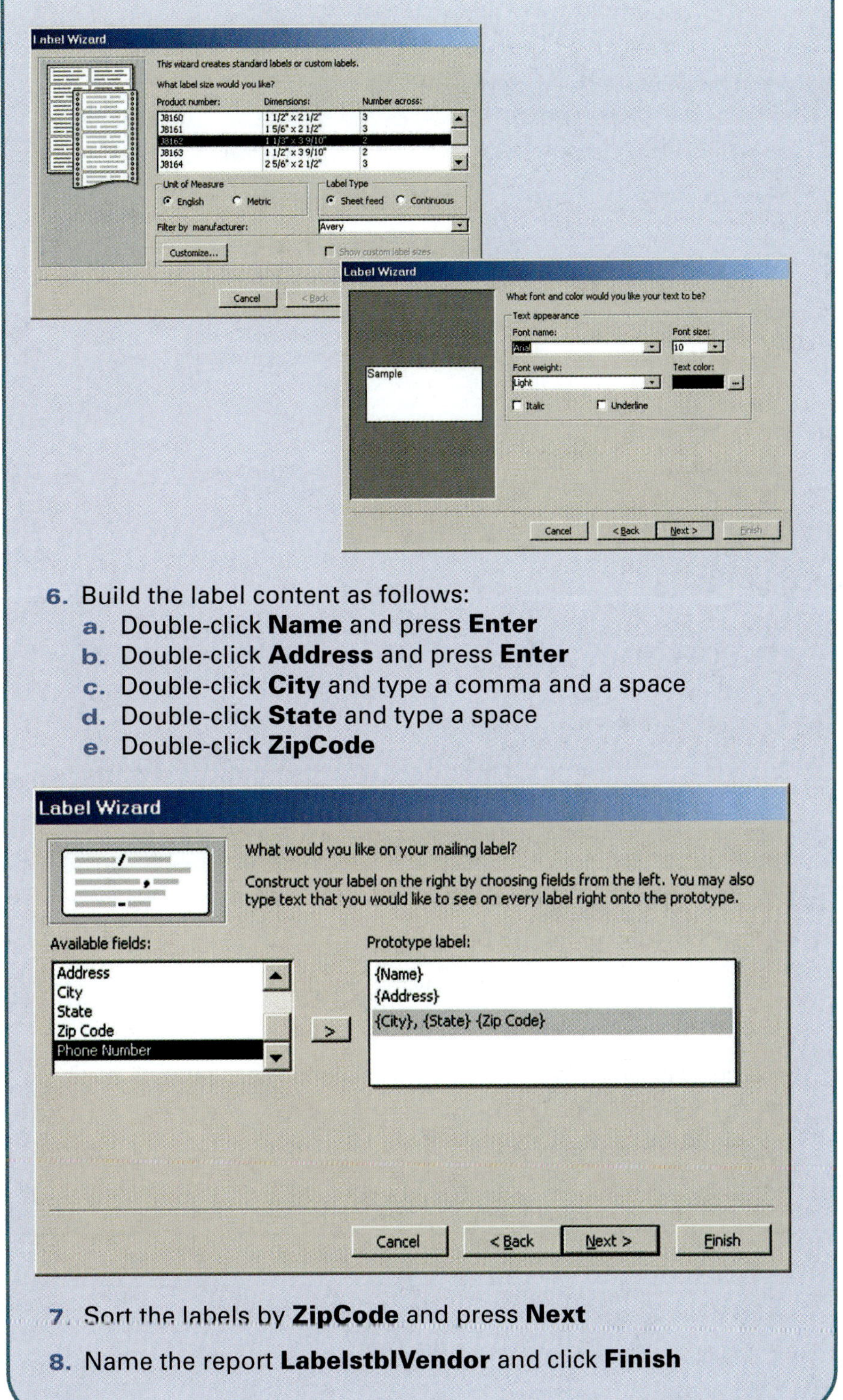

FIGURE 3.32
Selecting label type and font

6. Build the label content as follows:
   a. Double-click **Name** and press **Enter**
   b. Double-click **Address** and press **Enter**
   c. Double-click **City** and type a comma and a space
   d. Double-click **State** and type a space
   e. Double-click **ZipCode**

FIGURE 3.33
Formatting the mailing label

7. Sort the labels by **ZipCode** and press **Next**
8. Name the report **LabelstblVendor** and click **Finish**

ADDING GRAPHICS TO REPORTS AND FORMS

Although graphics do not usually add to the functionality of a report or form, they do improve visual appeal. They also can promote brand identity or distinguish one type of form or report from another. Graphics are added to reports and forms with the same technique, so only a form example is provided.

FIGURE 3.34
Mailing labels in Print Preview

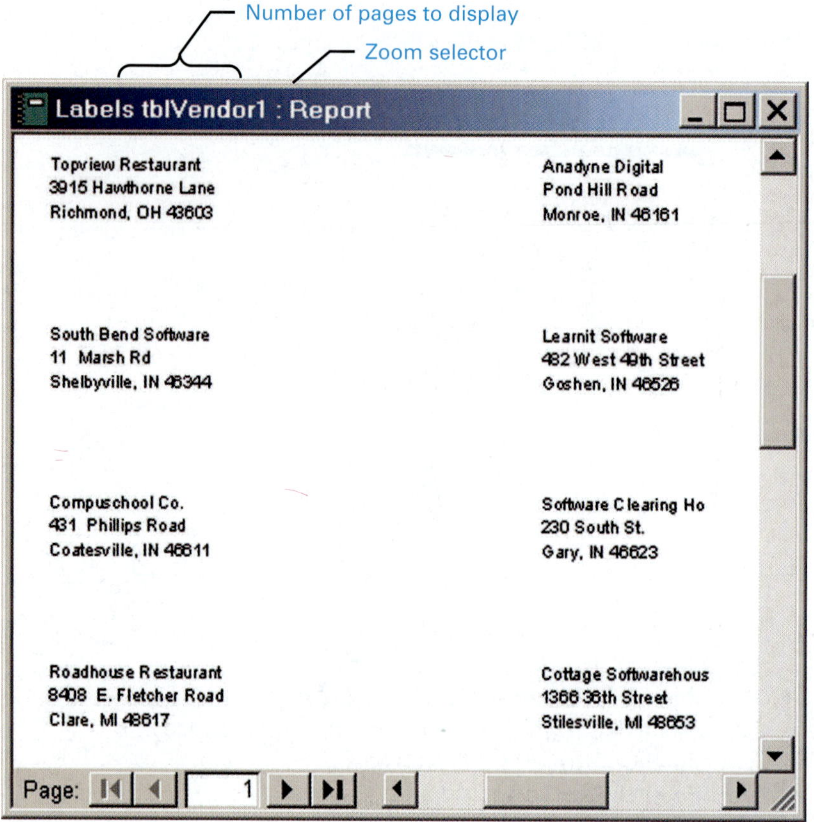

task reference

Add a Graphic to a Report or Form

- Open the report or form in Design view
- Select the section that is to display the graphic
- Select **Picture** from the **Insert** menu
- Navigate to the folder containing the image and change the file type selector to the image file type
- Select the file and click **OK**
- Move and size the image as needed

Adding a Graphic to InventoryValueByCategory:

1. Verify that the AC03Software.mdb database is open
2. Open **InventoryValueByCategory** in Design view
3. Click the Report Header (you must click the report or form section where you want the graphic to appear)
4. Select **Picture** from the **Insert** menu
5. Change the Files of type setting to **.tif**

6. Select the **AC03Computer.tif** file from the Chapter 3 data files list and click **OK**

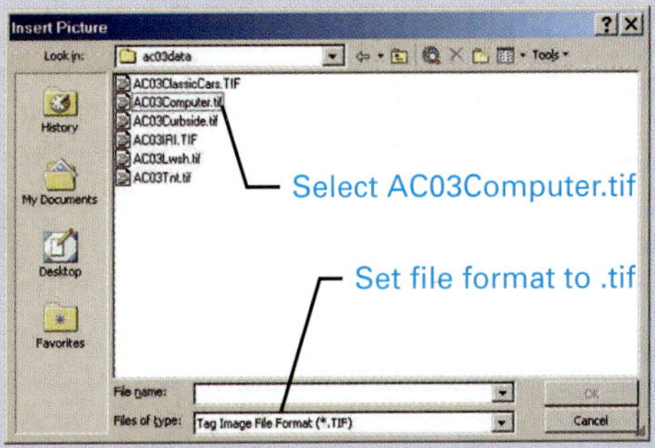

FIGURE 3.35
Selecting a picture

7. The image loads over the report title. Select the report title and drag it to the right of the image until all of the text displays and it is aligned with the bottom of the image

8. Use Print Preview to see the result

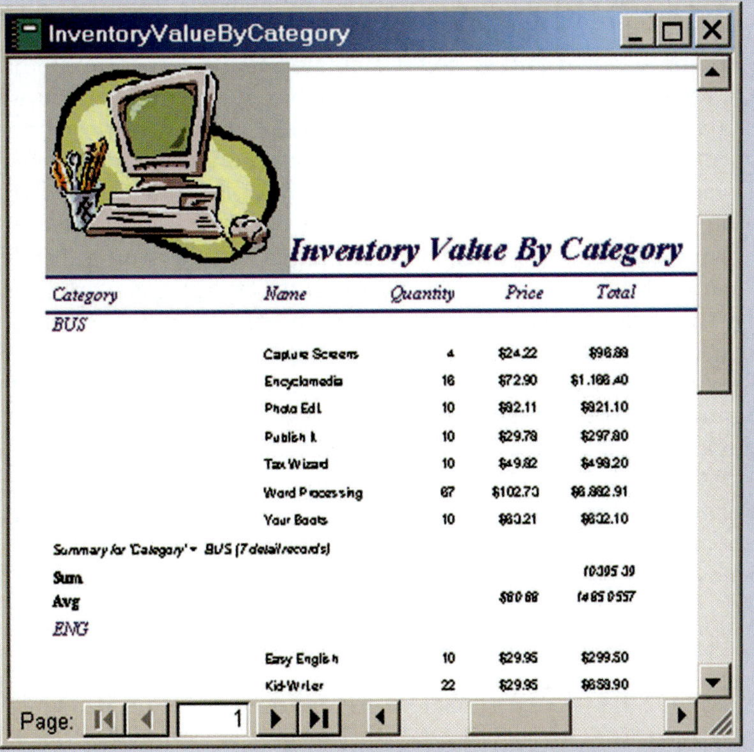

FIGURE 3.36
Form with image in the Report Header section

9. Save changes to the report and close Access

making the grade

SESSION 3.3

1. When would you use a form? A report?
2. T F Forms cannot display data from a query.
3. What is the difference between the > and the >> buttons used to select fields in Access queries?
4. Why and how would you add an expression to a query?
5. What is the difference between a field label and a field text box in the Design view of reports and forms?
6. Describe grouping in reports.

SESSION 3.3 SUMMARY

Access provides an array of options for selecting and organizing data into useful information. The strength of relational databases lies in the simplicity and flexibility of the analytical tools provided.

Filters are used to restrict rows of data to work with a subset of a table. The simplest filter is Filter by Selection, which allows the selection of all or part of a datasheet value and then retrieves records that match the selection. Filter by Form, Filter for Input, and Advanced Filter/Sort are other filtering tools. Each filtering tool has a different interface and provides progressively more functionality. Filter Excluding Selection allows the selected value to be excluded from the filter return set. Filters are cumulative and remain in effect until specifically removed. Filters must be saved as a query to be reusable.

Select queries are a more powerful data analysis tool that can retrieve and organize data from multiple tables. With queries, both columns and rows can be selected and sorted. Calculated fields can compute based on data in detail records or summarize data based on defined groups. Query criteria are built in a query by example (QBE) grid. Relational operators are used to state the conditions to retrieve records. Query results can be formatted for better viewing by changing the column width and adjusting the font.

Forms can be used to display and maintain data from multiple tables and queries. Find, sort, edit, delete, and filter operations work in forms in exactly the same way that they do in datasheets. Deleted records cannot be retrieved.

Reports are used to format printed output based on table data. Data from multiple tables and queries can be grouped, sorted, and summarized before printing. The print can include only detail records, detail and summary records, or only the summary records.

Forms and reports are similar in Design view. Each section of a form or report has a specific function, such as to format the detail record. Graphics can be added to forms and reports from the Insert menu.

MOUS OBJECTIVES SUMMARY

- AC2002-3-1—Creating Select queries using the Simple Query Wizard
- AC2002-3-1—Adding a calculated field to queries in query Design view
- AC2002-4-1—Creating forms using the Form Wizard
- AC2002-4-1—Creating auto forms
- AC2002-4-2—Modifying the properties of a form and/or specific controls on a form
- AC2002-5-1—Entering records using a form
- AC2002-5-4—Filtering datasheets by form
- AC2002-5-4—Filtering datasheets by selection
- AC2002-7-1—Creating and formatting reports using the Report Wizard
- AC2002-7-3—Previewing a report
- AC2002-7-3—Printing a report

task reference roundup

Task	Page #	Preferred Method
Filter by Selection	AC 3.4	• Open the table in Datasheet view
		• Select the field and character(s) of the search criteria (see Figure 3.2)
		• Click the **Filter By Selection** toolbar button to return values matching the selection
		or
		• right-click and choose **Filter Excluding Selection** to filter the selection out of the data
		• Evaluate the results of the filter
		• Click **Remove Filter** on the Access toolbar
Filter by Form	AC 3.6	• Open a table in Datasheet view
		• Click the **Filter By Form** toolbar button
		• Build the filter criteria by selecting from the drop-down list for a field or typing your own value
		• Click the **Apply Filter** toolbar button
		• Review the filtered data to be sure they are what you expected
		• Work with the filtered data
		• Click **Remove Filter** on the Access toolbar when you are done
Filter for Input	AC 3.8	• Open a table in Datasheet view
		• Right-click the field to be filtered
		• Type the filter criteria in the Filter For text box using wildcards, operators, and values
		• Press **Enter** to activate the filter
		• Review the filtered data to be sure they are what you expected
		• Work with the filtered data
		• Click **Remove Filter** on the Access toolbar when you are done
Advanced Filter/Sort	AC 3.9	• Open a table in Datasheet view
		• On the **Records** menu, point to **Filter** and then click **Advanced Filter/Sort**
		• Add criteria fields to the design grid
		• Enter the filter and sort criteria
		• Click the **Apply Filter** button on the toolbar
		• Review the filtered data to be sure they are what you expected
		• Work with the filtered data
		• Click **Remove Filter** on the Access toolbar when you are done
Saving a Filter as a Query	AC 3.10	• Display the filter in either the Filter By Form window or the Advanced Filter/Sort window (recall that any filter can be displayed in these windows regardless of how it was created)
		• Click the **Save As Query** button on the toolbar

task reference roundup

Task	Page #	Preferred Method
		• Type a name for the query and click **OK**
		• The new query will appear with the other query objects in the Database window
Create a Select Query	AC 3.12	• Select the **Queries** object from the Database window
		• Verify that **Create query in Design view** is selected
		• Click **New** on the toolbar
		• Select the **Design view** button from the New Query dialog box and click **OK**
		• Double-click the name of each table that contains relevant data from the Show Table dialog box
		• Double-click each table field that is to be contained in the query result to place it in the Field row of the design grid. The order of the columns is the order of the output
		• Enter sort criteria in the Sort row of the design grid
		• Enter selections in the Criteria row of the design grid
		• Click the **Datasheet view** button on the toolbar to see the query results
		• Click the **Design view** button on the toolbar to update the query criteria
		• Click the **Save** button to save the query criteria
Create an Expression Using Expression Builder	AC 3.20	• Click in the Field row of the QBE grid column that will display the calculation
		• Click the **Build** button in the Query Design toolbar
		• Select expression elements and operators to create the desired calculation
		• Click **OK** to place the calculation in the QBE grid
Modify the Format of a Form	AC 3.28	• Open the form in Design view
		• Click the **AutoFormat** button in the Form Design toolbar
		• Select from the same formats that were available in the Wizard
Modify the Format of a Report	AC 3.31	• Open the report in Design view
		• Click the **AutoFormat** button in the Report Design toolbar
		• Select from the same formats that were available in the Wizard
Add a Graphic to a Report or Form	AC 3.36	• Open the report or form in Design view
		• Select the section that is to display the graphic
		• Select **Picture** from the Insert menu
		• Navigate to the folder containing the image and change the file type selector to the image file type
		• Select the file and click **OK**
		• Move and size the image as needed

CROSSWORD PUZZLE

Across

1. Filter ____________ does not return the selected value
4. Filter ____________ uses values selected in the datasheet
6. Predefined calculations
7. ____________ operators such as + and / are used in calculations
9. View used to edit the structure of tables, forms, and reports
10. Results in a calculated value
11. Walks you through creating a multitable form
15. Menu option used to put a graphic in a form or report
17. Used to set a query field whose change in value will trigger subtotals
18. Type of function used to summarize data

Down

2. Query field containing an expression
3. Wildcard that indicates all of the fields of a table are to display in a query result
5. Expression ____________ aids in building expressions
8. Operators used to enter record retrieval conditions
12. Wizard formatting tool
13. The place where query criteria are entered
14. Expanded area for entering expressions
16. Report option to add subtotals

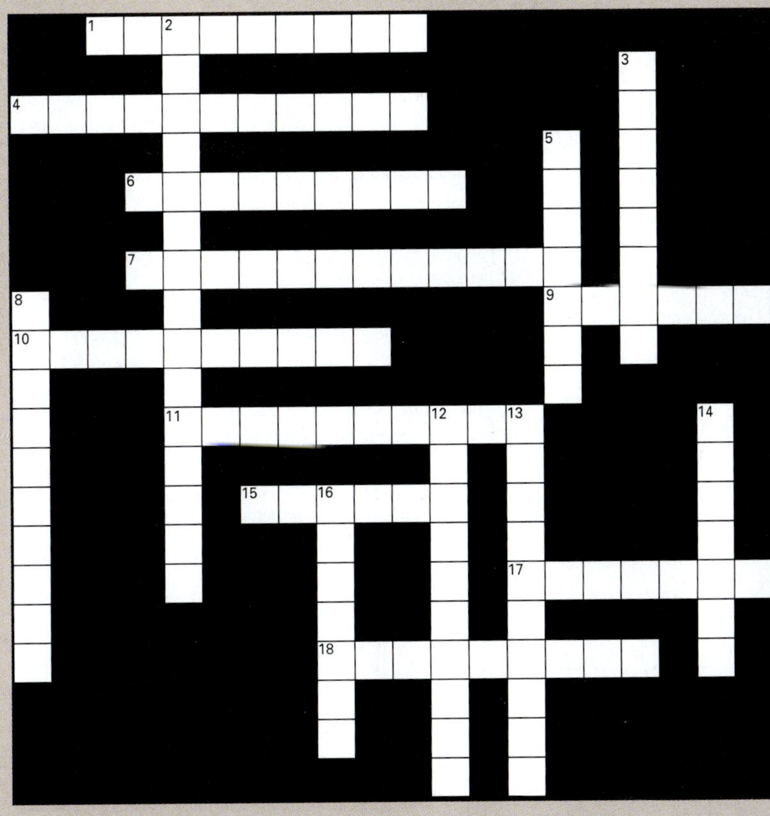

FILL-IN

1. Graphics are placed in a form or report using the ________ menu.
2. The title of a report that appears only on the first page is placed in the ________ section of the design.
3. A field from a table or query is comprised of a ________ control and a ________ control when displayed on a form.
4. When using Wizards ________ determines the background and text color applied.
5. The Form Wizard allows you to select from a list of fields in a table or query. The field list displayed is determined by ________.

REVIEW QUESTIONS

Each of the following topics should be addressed in one to three paragraphs.

1. Discuss what you would need to do to create mailing labels for the dog owners in the Clients table of the Westside Vet Clinic database.
2. Discuss the difference between detail and summary reports and when you would use each.
3. How do you decide to what groups to apply summary statistics in a grouped report?
4. In a table containing a record for each class a student has taken this semester, how would you calculate the student's GPA? The record consists of the student ID, class ID, class credits, and a score representing the letter grade (0 = F, 1 = D, 2 = C, 3 = B, 4 = A).

CREATE THE QUESTION

For each of the following answers, create the question.

ANSWER	QUESTION
1. It doesn't have to be stated in query criteria because it is the default.	________
2. They can only operate on all fields of one table.	________
3. The only way to retrieve such a record is to restore it from a backup made prior to the update.	________
4. Double-clicking a field in the field list, clicking and dragging a field from the field list, and selecting from a drop-down list box are all ways to do this.	________
5. Doing this will cause all of the fields of a table to be displayed in the output without placing each field in the QBE grid.	________

FACT OR FICTION

For each of the following, determine whether the statement is fact, fiction, or both and present your arguments for that conclusion.

1. In the expression Extended Total:Quantity*Price, the colon (:) is optional.
2. Aggregate functions can only be applied to the entire contents of a table or query.
3. The query, form, and report objects of a database store only specifications that can be used to recreate the object, not data.
4. The Form Wizard is one of the five types of AutoForms.

practice

Creating Filters, Forms, Queries, and Reports for Curbside Recycling

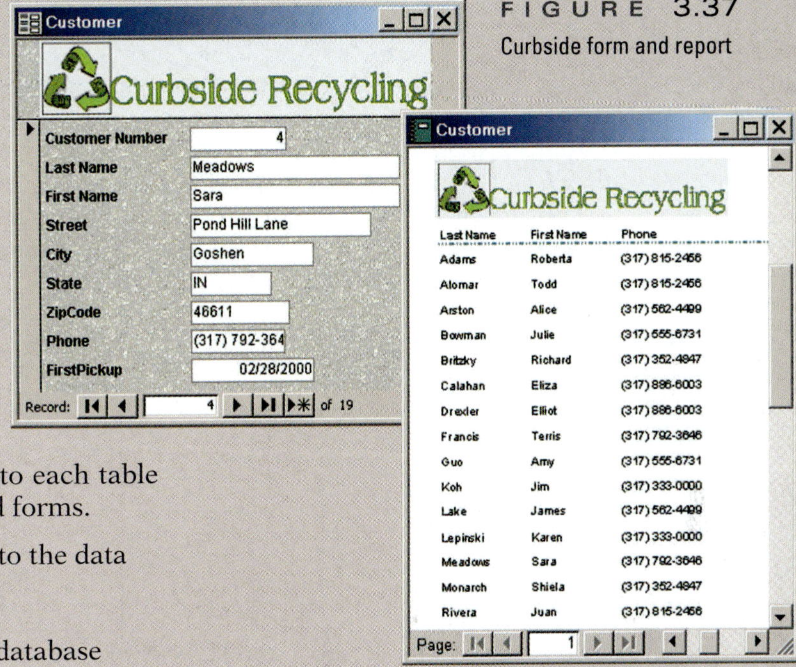

FIGURE 3.37
Curbside form and report

Curbside Recycling was introduced as a Hands-on Project in Chapter 1; review the organization's background if needed. You have added the CustomerRecords table to Curbside's database prototype. The Customers table holds static customer information such as name, address, and phone. The CustomerRecords table holds data about each recyclable pickup. Enough test data have been added to each table to test filtering, queries, reports, and forms.

1. Make sure that you have access to the data from your data disk
2. Start Access and open the **AC03CurbsideRecycling.mdb** database from your Chapter 3 files
3. Use a filter to select records for customers who had their first pickup in May of 2000
   a. Document the filtering method you used. (Hint: Two Filter by Selection filters are required; only one Filter by Form filter is required.)
   b. Sort the filtered data by customer's name and print the result
4. Use a filter to
   a. Select all customers who live on a street that has "hill" anywhere in the street address
   b. Save the filter as a query named **HillCustomers**
5. Create a form (see Figure 3.37) to be used to enter new customers and update existing customers. The columnar form should
   a. Contain all of the Customer table data
   b. Use the SandStone AutoFormat
   c. Display the logo in AC03Curbside.tif (located with the Chapter 3 data files) in the Form Header
   d. Use spaces and complete words in the field labels (e.g., CstmrNmbr changes to Customer Number)
   e. Print the form displaying the record for Alice Arston
   f. Save the form as **Customers**
6. Create a report to be used as a customer phone list. The report should
   a. Contain only the fields LastName, FirstName, and Phone
   b. Be sorted by the full customer name
   c. Use the Casual AutoFormat
   d. Display the logo in **AC03Curbside.tif** (located with the Chapter 3 data files) in the Report Header. Select and delete the default title
   e. Have the column widths narrowed to better fit the data (see Figure 3.37)
7. Use a query on CustomerRecords to determine the total and average weights of Paper and other products each customer has had picked up
   a. Print the query results
   b. Save the query as **CstmrWeights**
8. Create a detailed report with summary records displaying the Average and Total of Paper and Other weights from the CustomerRecords table. Save the report as **CstmrWeights**
9. If your work is complete, exit Access; otherwise continue to the next assignment

challenge!

Tracking Employees at Little White School House

Little White School House was introduced as a Challenge project in Chapter 1; review the organization's background if needed. You are in the process of converting the existing spreadsheets into database tables. You have cleaned up some of the data, but the transition is not going well because the spreadsheet data have not been normalized. Samuel Mink is anxious to see the reporting capabilities of Access before paying for a complete conversion. You have successfully converted a subset of the spreadsheet containing student data into a table called Students in the AC03lwsh.mdb. The StdntID is an AutoNumber field because the school has only used names in the past.

FIGURE 3.38

Little White School House form and report

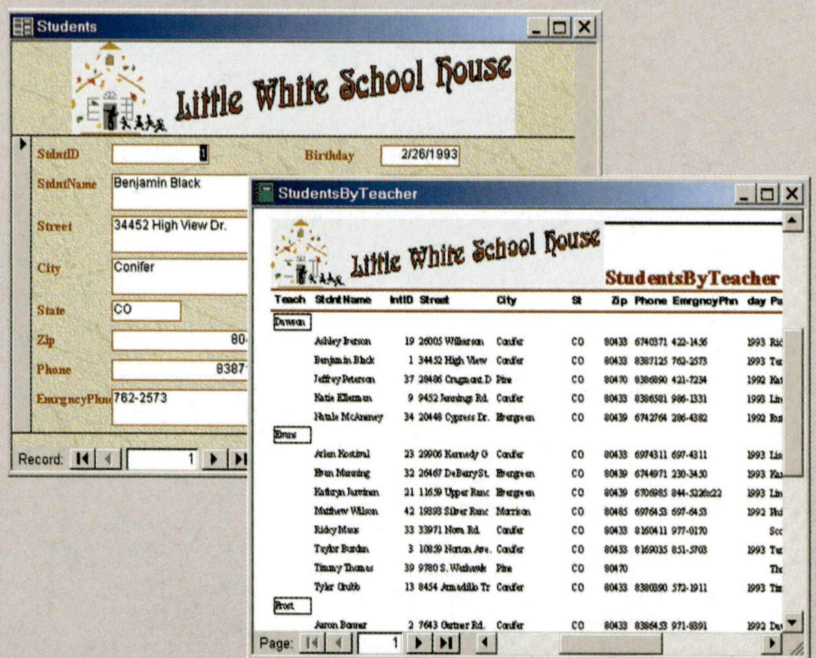

1. Retrieve your **LittleWhiteSchoolHouse** database
2. Import the Students table from AC03lwsh.mdb
   a. Use the **Import** option of **Get External Data** from the **File** menu
   b. Select **AC03lwsh.mdb** and click **Import**
   c. Select the **Students** table and click **OK**
3. Review the Students table data to become familiar with them. Notice that the student's name still needs to be broken up into two fields
4. Use a filter to select only students from Pine
   a. Print the result
   b. Save the filter as a query named **Pine**
5. Create a form that can be used to enter new students and update existing student records. The form should
   a. Use columnar format
   b. Use the Expedition AutoFormat
   c. Display the logo in **AC03lwsh.tif** (located with the Chapter 3 data files) in the Form Header
   d. Print the form displaying the record for Ricky Maus
   e. Save the form as **Students**
6. Create a query that counts the number of students on each bus. The query should display one row per bus. Save the query as **BusCount**
7. Create a report that lists students grouped by their teacher. The report should
   a. Display all fields
   b. Sort by student name
   c. Use Landscape orientation
   d. Use Bold AutoFormat
   e. Display the logo in **AC03lwsh.tif** (located with the Chapter 3 data files) in the Form Header
   f. Be saved as **StudentsByTeacher**
8. Close the database and exit Access if your work is complete

on the web

Toy Purchase Statistics by Internet Research Inc.

Internet Research Inc. (IRI) is a statistical evaluation organization specializing in Internet commerce that was introduced in Chapter 2. You have been asked to maintain statistical information on the various Web sites selling tops. The statistics are used to rank the sites and aid Shopping Bots in their searches for products. As a training exercise you have been manually retrieving price comparison information. You still need to retrieve a few more pieces of data and then you will be ready to create reports with groups and calculations to evaluate what you have gathered.

1. Use a Shopping Bot like www.mysimon.com or a search engine to find at least two sites that sell popular toys (www.eToys.com and www.ToysRUs.com are good sites, but there are many others). Select a video or computer game that you would like to purchase for a relative or friend
   a. Determine the price of the game at the first site
   b. Find the price for the same game at the second site
   c. Repeat this process for another game
2. Add your new research to the data that already exist in the AC03IRI.mdb database Toys table
3. Use a filter to select only Barbie items
   a. Print the result
   b. Save the filter as a query named **Barbie**
4. Create a form that can be used to enter new toy data and update existing Toys records. The form should
   a. Use columnar format
   b. Use the Expedition AutoFormat
   c. Display the logo in **AC03IRI.tif** (located with the Chapter 3 data files) in the Form Header
   d. Print the form displaying one of the computer game records
   e. Save the form as **Toys**
5. Create a query that counts the number of prices for each Web site. The query should display one row per Web site. Save the query as **SiteCount**

FIGURE 3.39
IRI Report

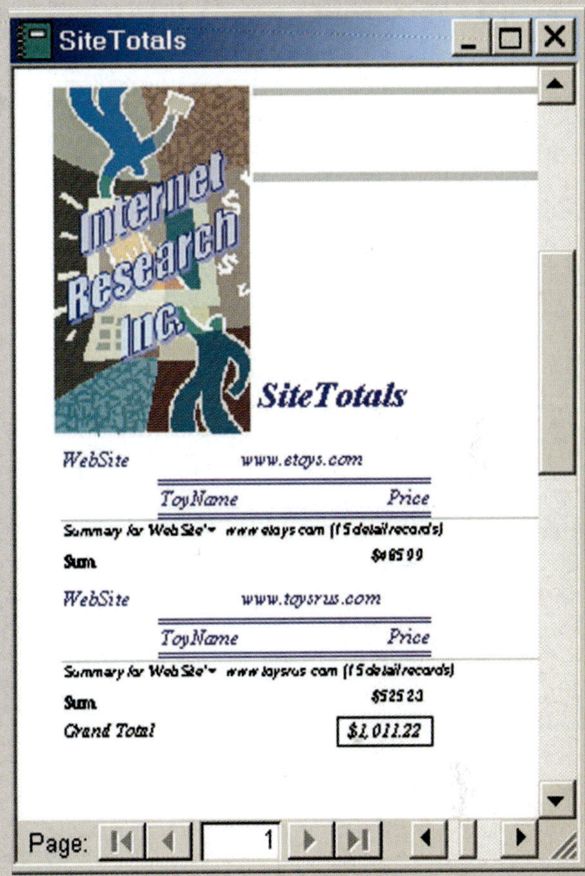

6. Create a report that lists ToyName grouped by Web site. The report should
   a. Display all fields except ToyID
   b. Sum all of the prices for a Web site
   c. Display only the summary records
   d. Use the Align Left Layout
   e. Use the Corporate AutoFormat
   f. Display the logo in **AC03IRI.tif** (located with the Chapter 3 data files) in the Form Header
   g. Be saved as **SiteTotals**
7. Close the database and exit Access if your work is complete

e-business

ScaleClassics.com Product Lists

Ricardo (Rico) Juarez runs a body shop that specializes in restoring classic cars. Rico owns three classics and began collecting scale models when his wife put her foot down and said no to building more garage space for his cars.

Although Rico frequently used the Internet and email, he had never considered starting an e-business. The Scale Classics Web site began as a technology class project for Rico's son Marcel. Marcel created a basic text and graphics informational site. Rico liked the site, but wanted a complex site dedicated to the serious collector. He envisioned a storefront, auction house, and collector's forums and had been unable to find such a site in his online searches. Rico hired a local consultant to build the site, found a processing house to manage orders and payments, and began shipping scale models from the body shop.

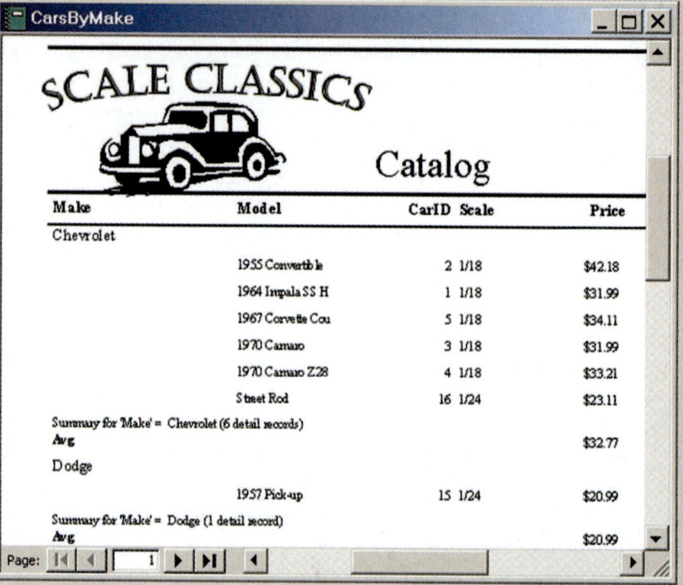

FIGURE 3.40
Average car price by model

The storefront is largely for American classic cars, which come in 1/18, 1/24, 1/43, and 1/64 scale. Popular foreign cars are also available. Rico has hired you to maintain the Product List and product analysis, which is in Access.

1. Retrieve the **Ac03Cars.mdb** database
2. Review the **Catalog** table data to become familiar with them
3. Use find and replace to correct the spelling of Chevrolet
4. Use a filter to select any record with "coupe" in the model name
   a. Print the result
   b. Save the filter as a query named **Coupe**
5. Create a form that can be used to enter new classics and update existing records. The form should
   a. Use columnar format
   b. Use the SandStone AutoFormat
   c. Display the logo in **AC03ClassicCars.tif** (located with the Chapter 3 data files) in the Form Header
   d. Print the form displaying the record for the Dodge 1957 Pick-up
   e. Save the form as **Cars**
6. Create a query to select the models that cost less than $35. The query should display all of the table fields and sort the result from the highest to the lowest price. Save the query as **LT35**
7. Create a report listing classic cars grouped by their make. The report should
   a. Display all fields
   b. Sort by the model
   c. Calculate the average price for each make
   d. Use the Formal AutoFormat
   e. Display the logo in **AC03ClassicCars.tif** (located with the Chapter 3 data files) in the Form Header
   f. Be saved as **CarsByModel**
8. Close the database and exit Access if your work is complete

around the world

Tracking the World's Population

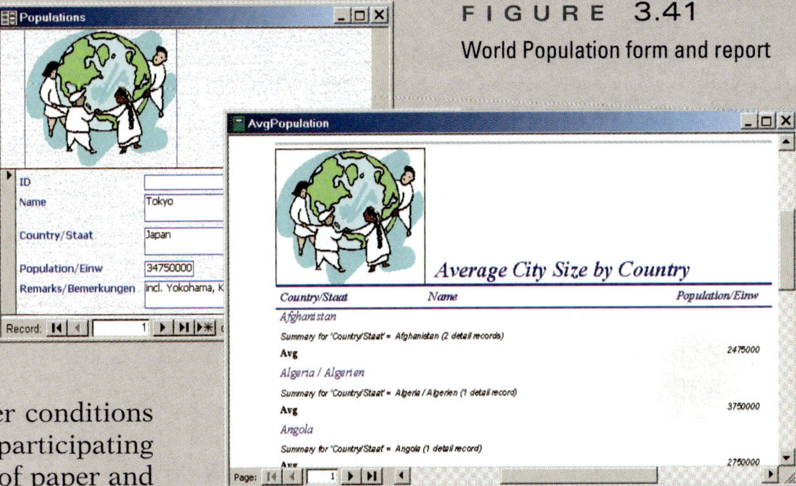

FIGURE 3.41
World Population form and report

Brandon Pryor is a middle school geography and civics teacher who is trying to make far-away places seem real to his students. Each of his students has an e-mail pen pal in another country and has researched his or her lineage and reported on one of the countries of his or her ancestors.

His classes participate in a Web forum by posting daily weather conditions and events. The name of each participating school has been entered on a sheet of paper and placed into a lottery box. Every day, the class draws a school from the lottery box and then spends time reviewing the information recorded by those students.

The next project is geared toward helping students understand the size of other cities in the world. Mr. Pryor has created an Access database of world populations for the students to analyze. You are assisting Mr. Pryor and his students in this process.

1. Open the **Cities** table of the **AC03Populations.mdb** database
2. Mr. Pryor's students are in Denver, Colorado, so the first task is to find out how many people live there. Use Filter by Form to determine the population of Denver and print the results
3. Now that you know how large Denver is, use separate filters to determine what cities around the world are the same size, larger, and smaller. Print each result
4. Use a query with an aggregate function to determine the smallest city in the table. Display only the city name and population. Print the results and save the query as **SmallestCity**

   tip: *Use the Count function on the city name and other appropriate functions for the remaining fields*

5. Now use a query to determine the largest city. Print the results of and save the query as **LargestCity**
6. Create a form for entering and maintaining the population data. The form must
   a. Use the Sumi Painting AutoFormat
   b. Contain a map or world graphic from the Clip Art gallery in the header

   tip: *Use the **Object** option of the **Insert** menu. Click **Microsoft Clip Art Gallery** as the Object Type and browse for your image*

   c. In Design view, adjust the size and position of the text boxes as needed
   d. Save the form as **PopulationUpdate**
7. Average the city population in each country to determine which country has the largest cities. Create a report containing the city, country, and population
   a. Group the data by country
   b. Sort by city name and average the population. Display summary rows only
   c. Use Corporate AutoFormat
   d. Add the Clip Art used in the form
8. Close the database and Access if your work is complete

LEVEL THREE

running project: tnt web design

Querying TnT Customer Data

The TnT database now consists of two related tables. The tblCustomers table holds the static data about the organization's customers. The CustomerSites table contains the URLs for the sites TnT has built. The CustomerSites table has a lookup field for the customer name so that you do not have to remember CustomerID values when entering data. Tori is very pleased with the progress that you are making on the TnT database. She has asked for a copy of the database so that she can begin exploring its design and content.

1. Start Access and open the **<yourname>TnT.mdb** database
2. Use a filter to select non-United States records. Print the result and save the filter as a query named **OutsideUSA**
3. Create a columnar form that can be used to enter and update customer data. The form should
   a. Include all customer data
   b. Use a columnar format
   c. Use the Industrial AutoFormat
   d. Display the logo from the file **AC03TnT.tif** in the Form Header
   e. Print the form with the record for Ross & Homer
   f. Save the form as **CustomerUpdate**
4. Create a query that lists the customer name and address (excluding other fields) by country, state, and city. Print the result. Save the query as **CityList**
5. Tori wants a phone list for U.S. customers. Create a phone list report named **PhoneListByState** that
   a. Includes the state, customer name, and phone information only
   b. Sorts by state and customer name
   c. Uses the **Corporate** AutoFormat
   d. Displays the logo from the file **AC03TnT.tif** in the Report Header
6. Create mailing labels with the following attributes:
   a. Use Avery 31017 labels
   b. Contain the customer's full name and address properly formatted
   c. Use 12-point Garamonde font
   d. Change the text color to dark blue
   e. Print one page of labels
   f. Save the report as **CustomerLabels**
7. Close the database and exit Access if your work is complete

FIGURE 3.42

CityList query

Query1 : Select Query

cusCountry	cusState	cusCity	cusID	cusName	cusAddress	cusPostalCode
Brazil		São Paulo	1	Comércio Mineiro	Av. Dos Lusíadas, 23	05432-043
Canada	BC	Vancouver	31	Bacchus Wine Cellars	1900 Oak St.	V3F 2K1
Canada	Québec	Montréal	32	Mère Paillarde	43 rue St. Laurent	H1J 1C3
USA	AK	Layfield	25	Cash & Carry	45 Medigas Rd	12345
USA	AL	Trenton	6	Bakertime Mobile	759 East 31 Ave	22345
USA	AZ	Sandy Row	9	Harper & Ronick	288 Landsdowne	32345
USA	CA	Creston	4	MMB Holdings	4090 Lethbridge	42345
USA	CA	El Rio	11	Silver Cloud	111 Rand Avenue	42345
USA	CO	Stoney Bluff	8	Summit Supply	Ridgeway Connector	80217
USA	CT	Nicola	13	DesJardins	808 Seymour	52345
USA	FL	Riverside	14	Omega Distributions	32 Merrit Ave	62345
USA	GA	Hampton	27	Ross & Homer	33 Little River Road	72345
USA	KY	Southgate	16	Dalhousie Inc.	2233 Southgate Avenue	82345

Record: 1 of 32

did you know?

an *ostrich's eye is bigger than its brain.*

Maine *is the only U.S. state that borders only one other state.*

in *the world of dolls, Midge Hadley was Barbie's® best friend in the 1960s.*

the *U.S. Congress passed a law in 1832 requiring all American citizens to spend one day each year fasting and praying.*

Antarctica *is the only continent without any reptiles or snakes.*

the *first product to have a bar code on its package was _____.*

Chapter Objectives

In this chapter you will:

- **Build, run, and save compound queries using In, Like, Between, And, and Or**
- **Understand and use Crosstab queries**
- **Modify Access table definitions by adding fields, deleting fields, and changing field properties—AC2002-2-4**
- **Add an input mask to a field—AC2002-2-2**
- **Create Lookup fields—AC2002-2-3**
- **Schedule and execute database backups**
- **Repair damaged databases—AC2002-1-5**

CHAPTER 4

four

Compound Queries and Database Utilities

chapter case

PuppyParadise

Evan has found the select queries you and he created very useful. He now knows that his sales volume is greater than he had thought and that only a handful of his bills have not been paid. He was able to calculate the average monthly income and expense for PuppyParadise and to project future income and expenses. PuppyParadise is continuing to grow and Evan is no closer to making a decision about how to handle the volume and money issues. Simple select queries are nice, but they don't provide the analytical power needed to understand the purchasing behavior of his customers. It is important to understand current purchasing behavior to project future purchases with reasonable accuracy.

To understand who buys his products and in what quantities, Evan needs to learn to create queries with multiple conditions. Using multiple conditions, data retrieved can be restricted using several values or a combination of values from multiple fields. For example, he would like to analyze sales from the last quarter and compare them to the previous quarter. That would require selecting records in three-month groups.

Evan also would like to cross-tabulate data to see the relationship between two values simultaneously. Crosstab queries will allow Evan to analyze sales by month and state in one table or sales by date and product concurrently.

Databases are critical to the operation of the organization using them. When data are lost, the ability to bill customers, order products, and support the decision-making process also is lost. An important aspect of using a database is to know how to properly back up and restore tables or the entire database. Tables should be backed up before major update operations to protect against data loss and scheduled backups should be implemented to reduce the likelihood of lost revenue.

FIGURE 4.1

First quarter 2001 PuppyParadise sales

Query1 : Select Query

OrderID	CstmrID	OrderDate	QuantityOrdered	ProductDescription
25	Benton	30-Jan-2001	1	PoochPouch- applique
8	Lewis	14-Feb-2001	1	PoochPouch- applique
8	Lewis	14-Feb-2001	1	PoochPouch- pattern
33	Monarch	28-Feb-2001	20	PoochPouch- applique
33	Monarch	28-Feb-2001	20	PoochPouch- pattern
33	Monarch	28-Feb-2001	20	PoochPouch- no pattern
10	Lake	03-Mar-2001	1	PoochPouch- pattern
10	Lake	03-Mar-2001	1	PoochPouch- no pattern
(Number)				

Record: 1 of 8

FIGURE 4.2

Sales by Product and State

ProductByStateCrosstab : Crosstab Query

ProductDescription	Total Of QuantityOrdered	CA	CO	IN	MI	OH
PoochPouch- applique	142	15	36	69	16	6
PoochPouch blanket	40		12	1	27	
PoochPouch- no pattern	405		86	96	128	95
PoochPouch- pattern	129		35	75	14	5
PoochPouch pillow cover	11		11			
PoochPouch pillow replacement	8		3		5	

Record: 1 of 6

SESSION 4.1 USING QUERIES TO ANALYZE DATA

Queries are the central tool in the database arsenal providing the ability to perform complex analysis on table data. Besides creating analytical information to support the decision-making process, queries allow appropriate data to be retrieved before creating formal reports. Queries also can be used to calculate totals or select data for forms when a user's access is restricted to a subset of the data. In the previous chapter, simple queries were used to retrieve rows and columns of data based on one condition. Most of the time, you will need to use multiple conditions when retrieving data.

SPECIFYING COMPLEX QUERY CRITERIA

Compound queries specify multiple conditions for data retrieval. The conditions can be as simple as using a list of values or as complicated as connecting a series of expressions and controlling their order of evaluation.

Selecting Records with In, Between, and Like

Using the Between, In, and Like conditional operators was briefly introduced in the previous chapter but requires further exploration. Each of these operators allows a specific group of match values to be stated for a table field. Between provides an upper and lower selection limit. All values between those limits will be selected, including the limits. So a condition of Between 12 And 14 will retrieve records with values of 12, 13, and 14.

Evan wants to retrieve sales information for the first quarter of 2001 so that he can compare it to the current quarter. You will create the first quarter query using an existing query.

Selecting Customer table records with Between:

1. Verify that the AC04PuppyParadise.mdb database is open
2. Select the **Queries** object in the Database window
3. Double-click **Create query in Design view** (this is a faster way to initiate a Design view query)
4. Click the **Queries** tab of the Show Table dialog box
5. Add **CustomerOrdersJoin** to the query design grid and choose **Close** in the Show Table dialog box
6. Add all of the fields to the design grid

tip: *Double-click in the title bar of CustomerOrdersJoin, click on the selected fields, and then drag them to the field row of the first query grid column*

7. Enter the condition **Between #1/1/2001# And #3/31/2001#** in the Criteria row of the OrderDate field to retrieve first quarter data

tip: *You do not have to enter the #s around the date values. Access will insert them*

8. Add an ascending sort to the OrderDate field

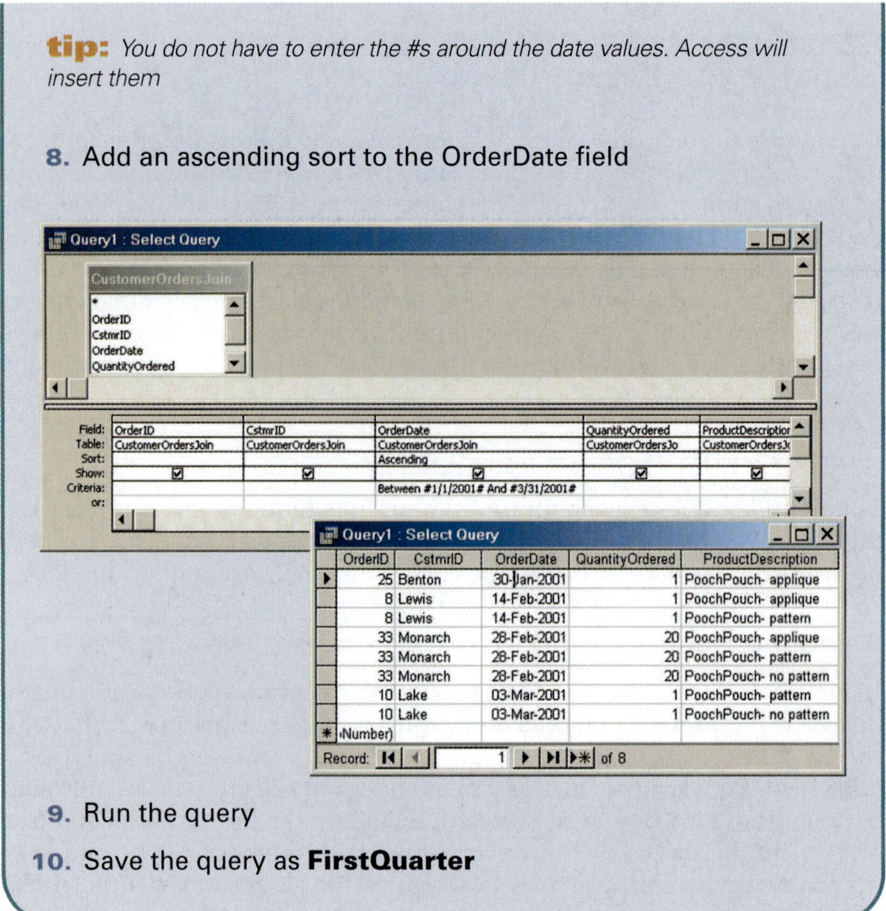

FIGURE 4.3
Selecting first quarter sales data

9. Run the query
10. Save the query as **FirstQuarter**

As was just demonstrated, an existing query can be used as the data source for other queries. In this case, the original query joined the data from three tables and then a new query was built to select first quarter data from the results of the join query.

The In operator allows a list of match values to be specified. This is effective when the match values are not logically grouped. For example In ("CA","CO","IN") would retrieve records for California, Colorado, and Indiana. The parentheses are a required part of the condition syntax for the In condition. Double quotes are a required delimiter when entering match values for Text datatype fields. Suppose that Evan needs a list of customers that live in Coatesville, Greencastle, and Monroe, Indiana.

Selecting Customer table records with In:

1. Close any open windows except the Database window in AC04PuppyParadise.mdb
2. Select the **Queries** object in the Database window
3. Double-click on **Create query in Design view**
4. Add the **Customer** table to the query design and **Close** the Show Table dialog box

5. Put all of the fields except CstmrID and Notes in the design grid
6. Enter the criteria **In ("Coatesville","Greencastle","Monroe")** in the City field
7. Because all of the cities are in Indiana, it is not necessary to display the State field. Click the Show checkbox for State off

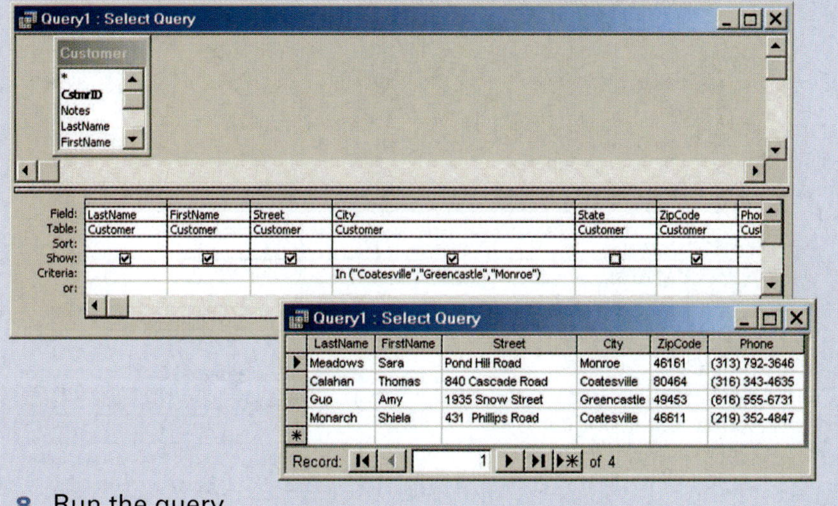

FIGURE 4.4
Customers from Coatesville, Greencastle, and Monroe

8. Run the query
9. Save the query as **INCustomers**

Each field in the QBE grid has a Show checkbox. When the checkbox is checked, values for that field will be displayed in the query results. When the checkbox is unchecked, the field will not display in the query results.

The Like operator allows a pattern to be matched using wildcards. Wildcards are designed to be used with Text fields and can provide haphazard results with other data types. Recall that the wildcards are ? to replace one character, * to replace multiple characters, and # to replace one numeral.

Let's assume that Evan needs to talk to a customer, but can't remember the full name or that customer's city. He believes that the city name starts with or contains Grand. You could use the condition Like "*grand*" to retrieve all records with the word "grand" anywhere in the city.

Selecting Customer table records with Like:

1. Verify that the AC04PuppyParadise.mdb database is open
2. Select the **Queries** object from the Database window
3. Double-click **Create query in Design view** to open the QBE grid and Show Table dialog box
4. Double-click on the **Customer** table in the Show Table dialog box to add it to the design grid

5. Click **Close** in the Show Table dialog box
6. Place **LastName, FirstName,** and **City** in the Field row of the QBE grid

FIGURE 4.5
Customer records for cities containing grand

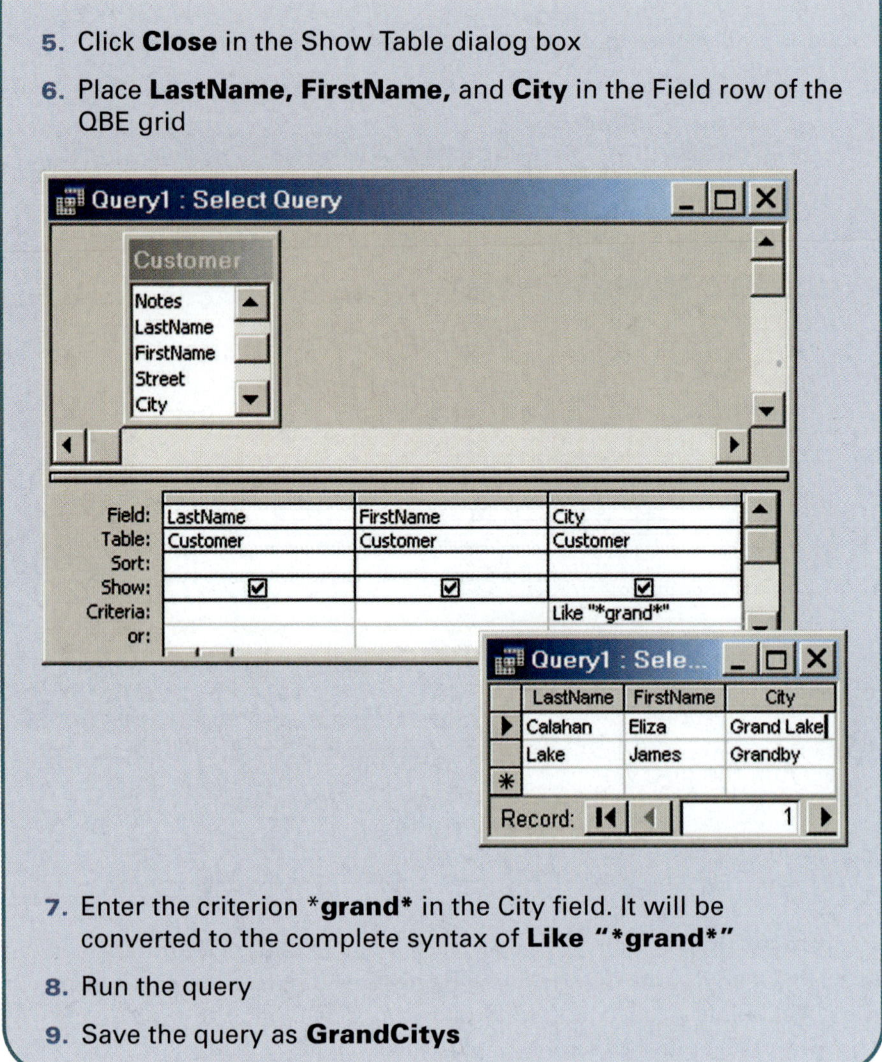

7. Enter the criterion ***grand*** in the City field. It will be converted to the complete syntax of **Like "*grand*"**
8. Run the query
9. Save the query as **GrandCitys**

In addition to selecting values that are In, Between, and Like, users often need to apply multiple selection criteria in a query. For example, to retrieve female employees who make less than $15 per hour would require a criterion for selecting records by gender and a criterion for selecting records by hourly rate. The next section discusses how to place these conditions in the query design grid.

Using Logical Operators

Logical operators are used to join multiple criteria for selecting records. Conditions can be joined with ***And*** or ***Or***. Use ***And*** to join two or more conditions when all of the conditions must be true to retrieve the record. Use ***Or*** to join two or more conditions when any of the conditions can be true to retrieve the record.

When using the QBE grid, conditions placed in the same row are connected with And, while those places in separate rows are connected with Or. Take a look at the conditions demonstrated in Figure 4.6.

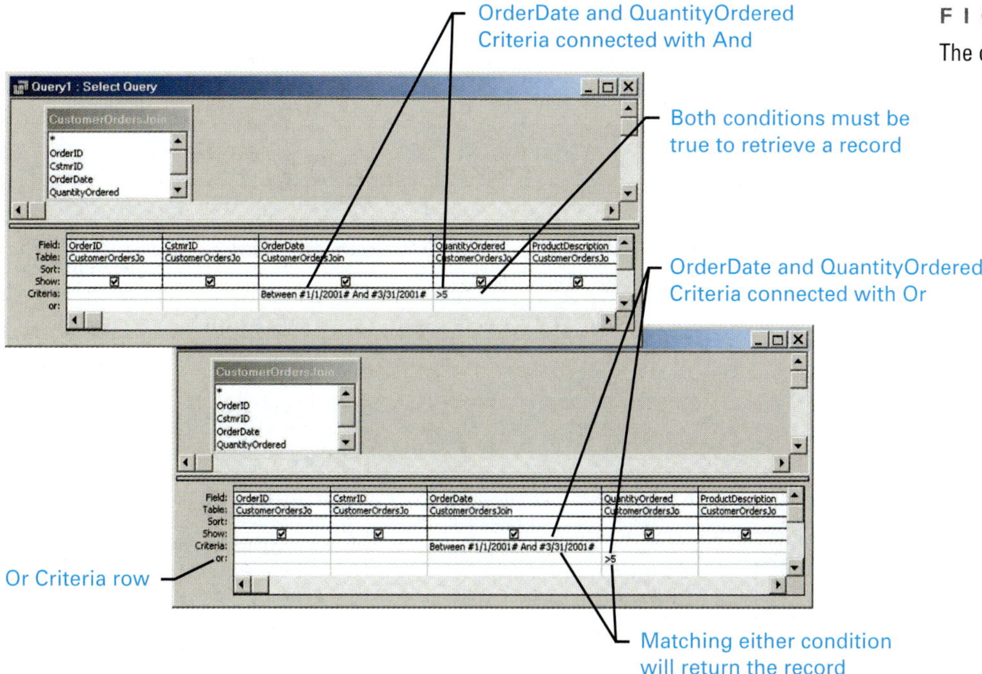
OrderDate and QuantityOrdered Criteria connected with And
Both conditions must be true to retrieve a record
OrderDate and QuantityOrdered Criteria connected with Or
Or Criteria row
Matching either condition will return the record

FIGURE 4.6

The operation of And and Or

Selecting Customer table records with compound criteria:

1. Verify that the AC04PuppyParadise.mdb database is open
2. Select the **Queries** object in the Database window
3. Double-click **Create query in Design view**
4. Click the **Queries** tab of the Show Table dialog box
5. Add **CustomerOrdersJoin** to the query design grid and choose **Close** in the Show Table dialog box
6. Add all of the fields to the design grid
7. Enter the condition **Between #1/1/2001# And #3/31/2001#** in the OrderDate field's Criteria row to retrieve first quarter data
8. In the same Criteria row enter **>5** in the QuantityOrdered column

tip: *Refer to Figure 4.6*

9. Run the query to view the results and then return to Design view
10. Delete the >5 condition for QuantityOrdered and enter >5 in the Or row of QuantityOrdered

tip: *Refer to Figure 4.6*

11. Run the query

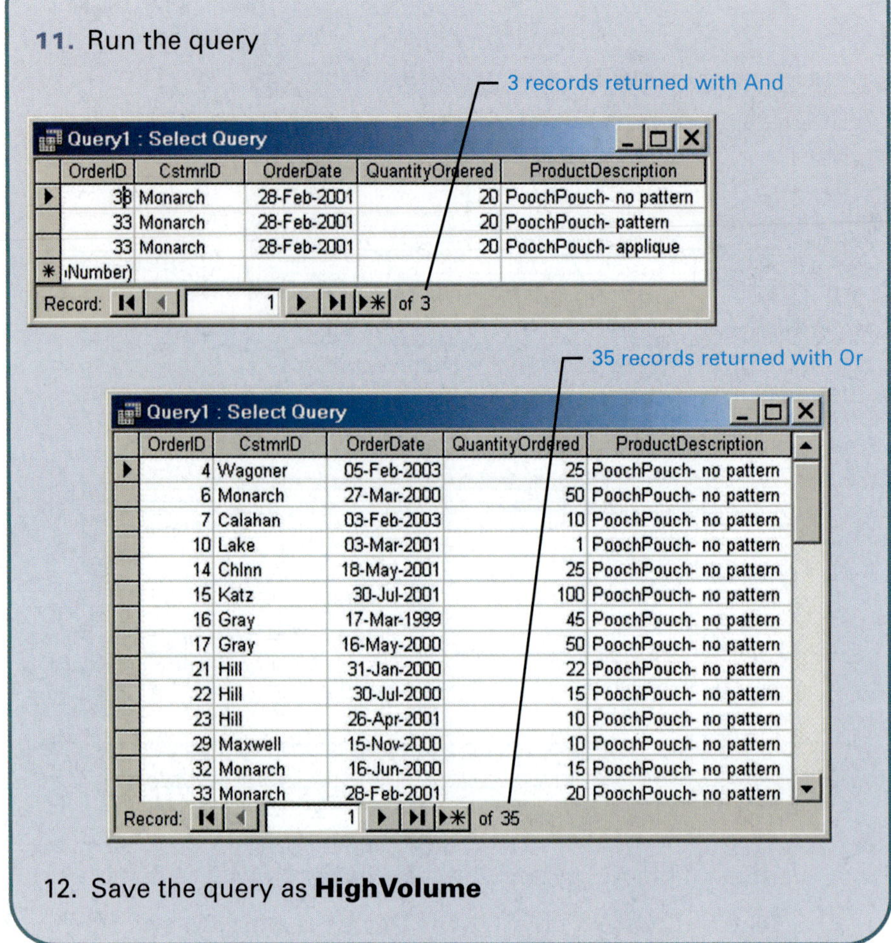

OrderID	CstmrID	OrderDate	QuantityOrdered	ProductDescription
33	Monarch	28-Feb-2001	20	PoochPouch- no pattern
33	Monarch	28-Feb-2001	20	PoochPouch- pattern
33	Monarch	28-Feb-2001	20	PoochPouch- applique
Number)				

Record: 1 of 3

OrderID	CstmrID	OrderDate	QuantityOrdered	ProductDescription
4	Wagoner	05-Feb-2003	25	PoochPouch- no pattern
6	Monarch	27-Mar-2000	50	PoochPouch- no pattern
7	Calahan	03-Feb-2003	10	PoochPouch- no pattern
10	Lake	03-Mar-2001	1	PoochPouch- no pattern
14	Chlnn	18-May-2001	25	PoochPouch- no pattern
15	Katz	30-Jul-2001	100	PoochPouch- no pattern
16	Gray	17-Mar-1999	45	PoochPouch- no pattern
17	Gray	16-May-2000	50	PoochPouch- no pattern
21	Hill	31-Jan-2000	22	PoochPouch- no pattern
22	Hill	30-Jul-2000	15	PoochPouch- no pattern
23	Hill	26-Apr-2001	10	PoochPouch- no pattern
29	Maxwell	15-Nov-2000	10	PoochPouch- no pattern
32	Monarch	16-Jun-2000	15	PoochPouch- no pattern
33	Monarch	28-Feb-2001	20	PoochPouch- no pattern

Record: 1 of 35

FIGURE 4.7
Results of And and Or compound queries

12. Save the query as **HighVolume**

As was just demonstrated, compound conditions connected with And retrieve fewer records because both conditions must be true to return a row. Connecting conditions with Or retrieves more records because only one of the conditions has to be true to return the row. It is important to correctly use And and Or to retrieve valid query results.

Using the Not Operator

The ***Not*** logical operator negates a condition to select nonmatching values. Not can be placed in front of any condition created with any of the other operators (=, >, <, >=, <=, <>). For example, the condition Not > 10 would retrieve records where the value of that field is less than or equal to 10.

Selecting Customer table records with Not:

1. Verify that the AC04PuppyParadise.mdb database is open
2. Select the **Queries** object from the Database window
3. Click the **InCustomers** query and then click the **Design view** button to open the design

4. Place **Not** in front of the In condition

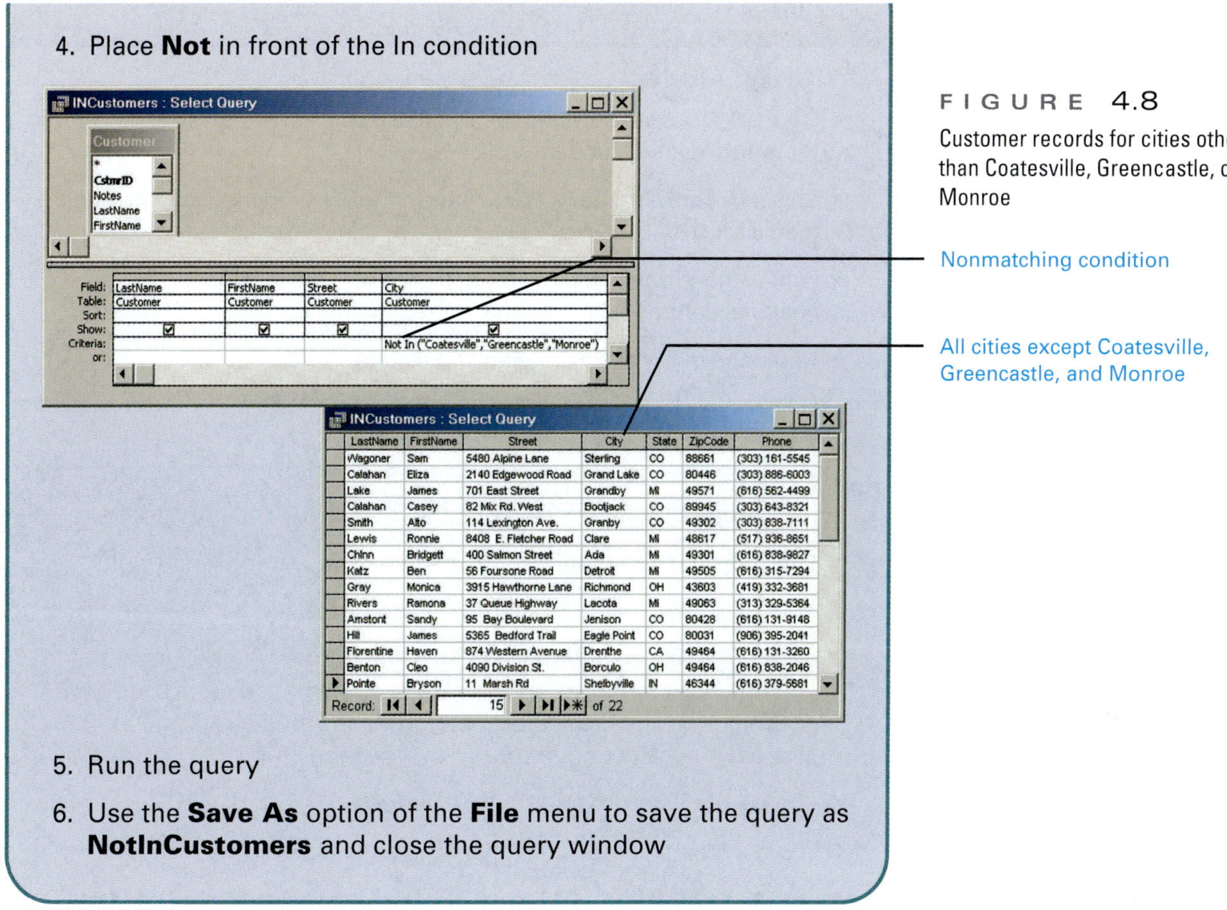

LastName	FirstName	Street	City	State	ZipCode	Phone
Wagoner	Sam	5480 Alpine Lane	Sterling	CO	88661	(303) 161-5545
Calahan	Eliza	2140 Edgewood Road	Grand Lake	CO	80446	(303) 886-6003
Lake	James	701 East Street	Grandby	MI	49571	(616) 562-4499
Calahan	Casey	82 Mix Rd. West	Bootjack	CO	89945	(303) 643-8321
Smith	Alto	114 Lexington Ave.	Granby	CO	49302	(303) 838-7111
Lewis	Ronnie	8408 E. Fletcher Road	Clare	MI	48617	(517) 936-8651
Chinn	Bridgett	400 Salmon Street	Ada	MI	49301	(616) 838-9827
Katz	Ben	56 Foursone Road	Detroit	MI	49505	(616) 315-7294
Gray	Monica	3915 Hawthorne Lane	Richmond	OH	43603	(419) 332-3681
Rivers	Ramona	37 Queue Highway	Lacota	MI	49063	(313) 329-5364
Amstont	Sandy	95 Bay Boulevard	Jenison	CO	80428	(616) 131-9148
Hill	James	5365 Bedford Trail	Eagle Point	CO	80031	(906) 395-2041
Florentine	Haven	874 Western Avenue	Drenthe	CA	49464	(616) 131-3260
Benton	Cleo	4090 Division St.	Borculo	OH	49464	(616) 838-2046
Pointe	Bryson	11 Marsh Rd	Shelbyville	IN	46344	(616) 379-5681

FIGURE 4.8

Customer records for cities other than Coatesville, Greencastle, or Monroe

5. Run the query

6. Use the **Save As** option of the **File** menu to save the query as **NotInCustomers** and close the query window

The previous example also demonstrated how to modify an existing query and save the modification with a new name. It is often easier to use this technique than it would be to create a new query from scratch.

ANALYZING DATA USING CROSSTAB QUERIES

Select queries retrieve specified data and create groups and calculations based on those data. Using this methodology, data can only be grouped vertically to create sums, averages, and other calculations. ***Crosstab queries*** are used to calculate and organize data for easier analysis of more complex problems. Crosstab queries perform calculations such as sum, average, or count and then group them by two types of information—one down the left side of the datasheet and another across the top.

Crosstab queries can be created using the Crosstab Query Wizard or in Query Design view. Which field will be used as the column heading (across the top of the datasheet) and which field will be used as the row heading (down the left side of the datasheet) must be specified to let Access know how to group the data. The available aggregate functions include Sum, Ave, Count, Min, and Max.

PuppyParadise sells multiple products. Evan wants to know which product sells best in each state. This query will list PuppyParadise products down the left side and states across the top. The Sum function will total each product by state. Crosstab queries can be created using the Crosstab Query Wizard or in Design view. Since the Wizard is simpler you will start there.

task reference

Crosstab Query

- Click the **Queries** object in the Database window, select **Create query by using wizard,** and then click **New**
- Select **Crosstab Query Wizard** from the New Query dialog box and then click **OK**
- Follow the Wizard's instructions to choose the data source, row heading, column heading, and aggregate functions for the query
- Name the query and then view the results

Analyzing sales with a crosstab query:

1. Verify that the AC04PuppyParadise.mdb database is open
2. Select the **Queries** object from the Database window
3. Double-click the **CustomerStateJoin** query and review the result. Notice that many of the products have multiple rows for each state. The crosstab query will sum these into one value for each product and state
4. Close the CustomerStateJoin window
5. Click **New** to open the New Query dialog box
6. In the New Query dialog box, click **Crosstab Query Wizard** and select **OK**

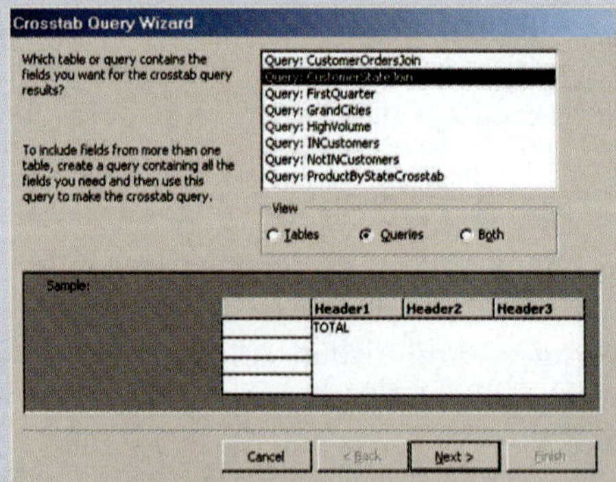

FIGURE 4.9
Selecting a query for the crosstab data source

7. Click the **Queries** option button and then select the **CustomerStateJoin** query and click **Next**
8. Select **ProductDescription** as the row heading and click **Next**
9. Select **State** as the column heading and then click **Next**
10. Select **QuantityOrdered** as the field and **Sum** as the function and then click **Next**
11. Name the query **ProductByStateCrosstab** and click **Finish**

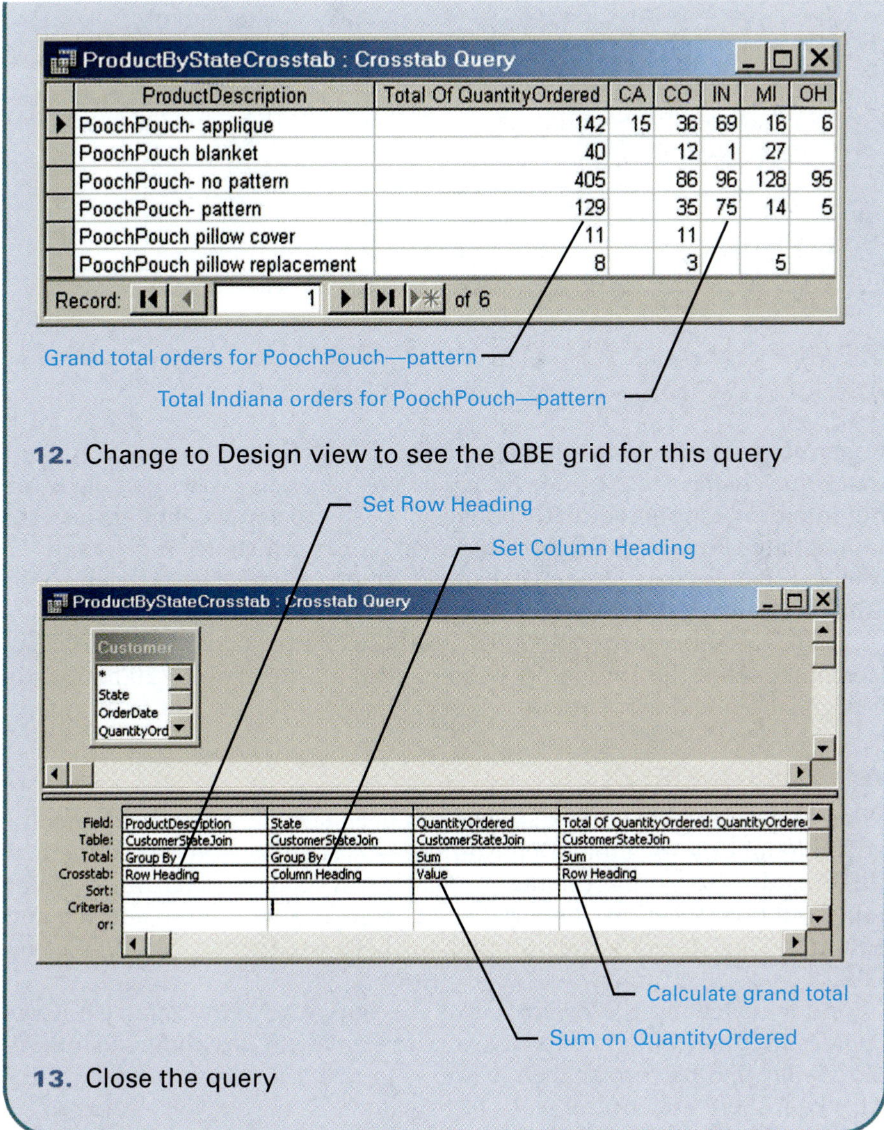

FIGURE 4.10
Crosstab results

12. Change to Design view to see the QBE grid for this query

FIGURE 4.11
Crosstab query in Design view

13. Close the query

This query will allow Evan to analyze the sales of each of his products by state. Notice that Access uses different icons for each type of query in the Database window. Figure 4.12 shows Select and Crosstab query icons. As you add other types of queries to the database, more icons will display. The icons are representative of the query operation being performed.

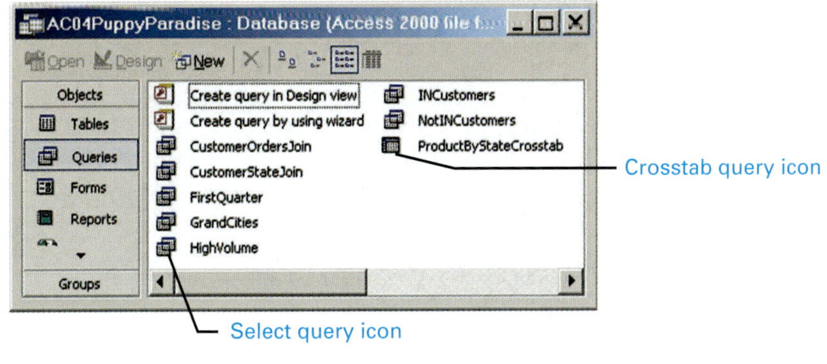

FIGURE 4.12
Query icons

SESSION 4.1

making the grade

1. Describe the use of the Like operator.
2. What condition would return all Game (GME) software from tblSoftware?
3. What are the benefits of using crosstab queries?
4. How many conditions can be included in the Between operator?

SESSION 4.2 MODIFYING TABLE DEFINITIONS

Regardless of how well a database prototype has been designed, it is likely that some changes to the table design will be necessary. After databases are put into production, required changes in business and technology necessitate updates. Before changing table design, it is critical to understand the impacts changes may have on existing data. It is always best to back up the database before undertaking structural changes.

Table modifications are most easily accomplished in Design view. Remember that the Undo and Redo operations store up to 20 actions in Design view, making it easier to correct errors.

ADDING A FIELD

When a necessary piece of data has not been stored, a new field must be added to an existing table. Determining which table should hold the new field requires revisiting the design process. Once it is determined which table will hold the field, table Datasheet view can be used to add the new column using steps that are similar to those used when building a new table.

After reviewing the prototype of the PuppyParadise database, Evan decides that he would like to have a field to make notes about customers. He would like to record their comments and the names of their pets. Although there are several ways to provide this ability, you decide to try adding a memo field to the Customer table.

Adding a Memo field to the Customer table:

1. If it is not already open, open the AC04PuppyParadise.mdb database
2. Activate the **Customer** table in Design view
3. Although the order of fields in a table is not critical, there is often logic in their placement. Evan would like the notes field at the end of the record, so click in the empty row after Phone and enter the data for a field named **Notes** with a **Memo** data type
4. No other fields are required for the table to be functional, but we will add a dummy field to be deleted in the next series of steps

5. Click on the **Notes** field that you just added, then select the **Rows** option of the **Insert** menu to add a new field between Phone and Notes
6. Type **Dummy** as the Field Name and leave the default Text data type
7. Click the **Datasheet view** button on the Access toolbar to view the results. You will be prompted to save your changes. Answer **Yes**

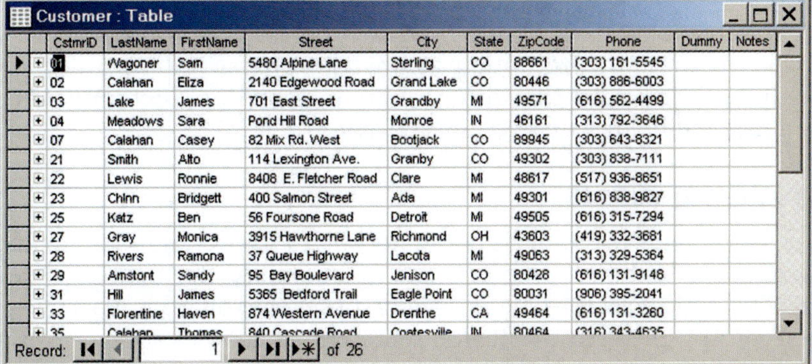

Customer : Table

CstmrID	LastName	FirstName	Street	City	State	ZipCode	Phone	Dummy	Notes
01	Wagoner	Sam	5480 Alpine Lane	Sterling	CO	88661	(303) 161-5545		
02	Calahan	Eliza	2140 Edgewood Road	Grand Lake	CO	80446	(303) 886-6003		
03	Lake	James	701 East Street	Grandby	MI	49571	(616) 562-4499		
04	Meadows	Sara	Pond Hill Road	Monroe	IN	46161	(313) 792-3646		
07	Calahan	Casey	82 Mix Rd. West	Bootjack	CO	89945	(303) 643-8321		
21	Smith	Alto	114 Lexington Ave.	Granby	CO	49302	(303) 838-7111		
22	Lewis	Ronnie	8408 E. Fletcher Road	Clare	MI	48617	(517) 936-8651		
23	Chinn	Bridgett	400 Salmon Street	Ada	MI	49301	(616) 838-9827		
25	Katz	Ben	56 Foursone Road	Detroit	MI	49505	(616) 315-7294		
27	Gray	Monica	3915 Hawthorne Lane	Richmond	OH	43603	(419) 332-3681		
28	Rivers	Ramona	37 Queue Highway	Lacota	MI	49063	(313) 329-5364		
29	Amstont	Sandy	95 Bay Boulevard	Jenison	CO	80428	(616) 131-9148		
31	Hill	James	5365 Bedford Trail	Eagle Point	CO	80031	(906) 395-2041		
33	Florentine	Haven	874 Western Avenue	Drenthe	CA	49464	(616) 131-3260		
35	Calahan	Thomas	840 Cascade Road	Coatesville	IN	80464	(316) 343-4635		

Record: 1 of 26

FIGURE 4.13

Notes and Dummy fields added to Customer table

anotherword

. . . on Adding Fields to Table Design

When it makes sense to add a new table field between existing table fields, a new row is added to the design grid. To insert a row, select the row for the new field and select **Rows** from the Access **Insert** menu. Right-clicking the row to activate the shortcut menu also will provide an Insert Rows option.

It is essential to make design changes like adding a field as early in the life of a table as possible. When an empty field is added, it can be overwhelming to gather and enter the data for the existing records.

DELETING A FIELD

Deleting a field from a table is as simple as deleting a record from a table, but the repercussions are much more involved. Deleting a field in a database that already contains data deletes all of the values held in the field. Delete operations can be undone as long as Design view is active but become permanent after changing views.

Deleting a field from the Customer table:

1. If it is not already open, open the AC04PuppyParadise.mdb database
2. Activate the **Customer** table in Design view

anotherway

. . . to select the data type of a field

When working with table designs, it can be time consuming to move from typing to selecting with the mouse. Access allows you to keep your hands on the keyboard. For example, when entering a new table field, type the Field Name and then press Tab to move to the Data Type. Type the first character of the Data Type (m for memo, n for number, and so on). Access will complete the entry and you can Tab to the next field.

3. Select the **Dummy** field using the record selector
4. Press the **Delete** key on your keyboard
5. Use the **Undo** button to undo the delete
6. Use the **Redo** button to delete the Dummy field again
7. Change to Datasheet view to review the results. Save the table design changes when prompted

The delete operation on the Dummy field is permanent because you changed views. As a precaution against destroying valuable data, it is strongly recommended that you back up tables in production databases before deleting fields from the table design.

MOVING A FIELD

The order of fields in a table is not important to its overall functionality, so they can move without impacting data functionality. The field order set by the table definition is the default column order that displays when viewing data. Typically, the leftmost field(s) represents the table's primary key and other fields are in order by how they are used.

Moving a field in the Customer table:

1. If it is not already open, open the AC04PuppyParadise.mdb database
2. Activate the **Customer** table in Design view
3. Select the **Notes** field by clicking its record indicator
4. Click and drag to move the Notes field between CustomerID and LastName

tip: *During the drag process, a line across the record indicator and data grid represents where the field will be dropped. If you missed on the first drag attempt, repeat steps 3 and 4 until Notes is positioned properly*

5. Change to **Datasheet view** to review the results. Save the table design changes when prompted
6. Change back to **Design view** and restore Notes to its original position of the last field in the table

All database objects allow you to control the order of the fields displayed, thereby overriding the field order of the table design.

CHANGING FIELD ATTRIBUTES

Of all of the table design updates, changing field properties is the most likely to destroy needed data and/or invalidate other database objects. Changing the Field Name can produce invalid results in objects that refer to fields by name, including Queries, Forms, Reports, and Modules. Making a field smaller will truncate existing data if they exceed the new size. Altering the Data Type causes Access to perform a conversion from the original type to the new type that can result in loss of data. A message will display when Access detects conversion errors so the user can choose to cancel or continue the process. Access does not detect all conversion errors. Making fields larger or changing other field attributes has little impact on the validity of the database.

Changing field properties in the Products table:

1. If it is not already open, open the AC04PuppyParadise.mdb database
2. Activate the **Products** table in Design view
3. Select the **ProductDescription** field. When entering the Products data, Evan discovered that the ProductDescription field was not long enough for a full product description. He would like it expanded to 40 characters
4. Change the Field Size from 30 to **40**
5. Click the **Save file** button on the Access toolbar to save your work

After making changes to table field attributes that might impact the validity of data held in the tables, it is recommended that the table be thoroughly tested and its data validated before placing it in production.

BUILDING LOOKUP FIELDS

A ***lookup field*** is a tool to ease data entry. Rather than requiring users to remember important values that identify customers and orders, a lookup field displays the list of possible values. Evan is having difficulty entering orders because he often mistypes the CustId. He has asked for a lookup field that will access valid CustIds and reduce errors. Since he doesn't remember CustIds, he would rather select a customer's name and have Access store the correct CustID.

task reference

Creating a Lookup Field

- Remove any existing table relationships based on the lookup fields. The most likely relationship is one-to-many where the child (many sides of the relationship) table will look up the key value of the parent table (one side of the relationship)
- Open the child table and change the Data Type of the foreign key field to Lookup Wizard
- Follow the Lookup Wizard instructions

Setting a lookup field for customers in the Orders table:

1. If it is not already open, open the AC04PuppyParadise.mdb database
2. Activate the **Orders** table in Design view

tip: *The one-to-many CstmrID relationship between the Customer and Orders tables has already been removed for you*

3. Select the Data Type of CstmrID and change it to Lookup Wizard
4. The Lookup Wizard will prompt you through the rest of the process. In the first Lookup Wizard screen, select **I want the lookup column to look up the values in a table or query.** And then click **Next**

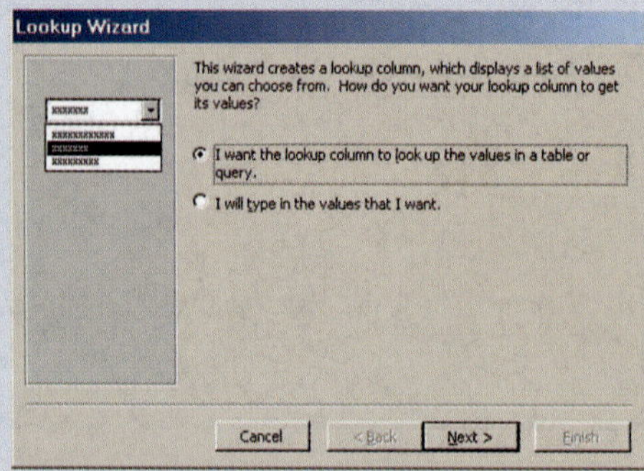

FIGURE 4.14
Lookup Wizard opening screen

5. In the second Wizard screen, choose the **Customer** table as the source of your lookup data and click **Next**
6. In the third Wizard screen, select the **CstmrID, LastName,** and **FirstName** fields using the field selector buttons (>, >>, <, <<). CstmrID must be selected because it is the shared column between the tables identifying the foreign key. FirstName and LastName are the identifying fields that Evan wants to use to look up the CstmrID. Click **Next**

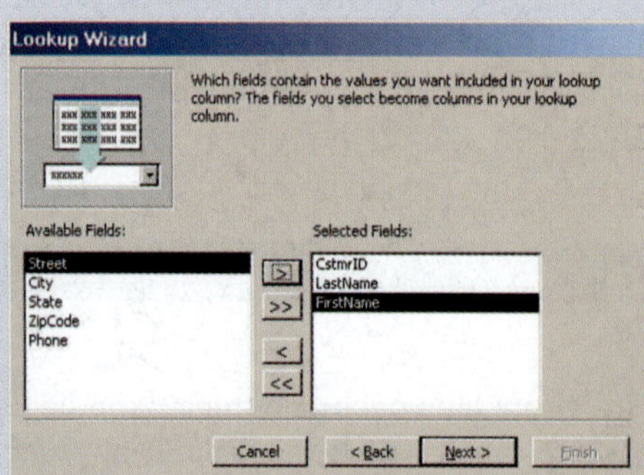

FIGURE 4.15
The third Lookup Wizard screen

7. The next Wizard screen allows you to hide the CstmrID (key) column and adjust the width of the lookup column
   a. Check **Hide key column** so that CstmrID does not display
   b. Double-click on the right border of each field selector to adjust the column width to the width of the data and click **Next**

8. The final Wizard screen asks you to name the lookup column. The default, CstmrID is fine, so just click **Finish.** You will be prompted to save the table changes; choose **Yes**

9. Change to Datasheet view. The CstmrID field will now display the customer's name but stores CstmrID. When you enter a new record, a list of valid customer names will be presented

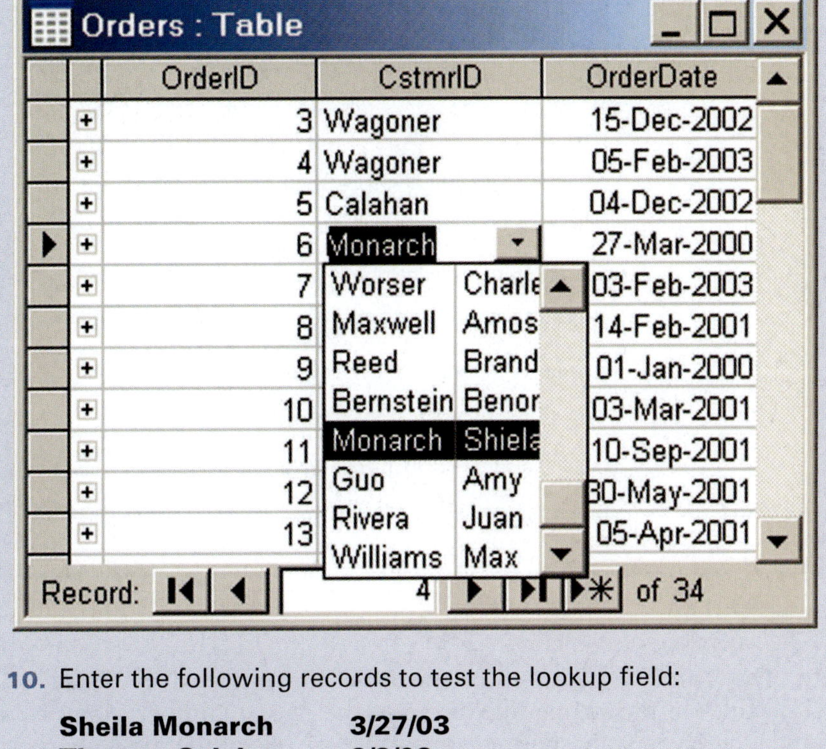

FIGURE 4.16
The Orders Table with CstmrID Lookup Field

10. Enter the following records to test the lookup field:

Sheila Monarch	**3/27/03**
Thomas Calahan	**2/3/03**

11. Close the Orders table

With the lookup field set, each new customer added to the Customer table will automatically be added to the list for the Orders table. You also can create lookup lists that contain a fixed set of values. Lookup lists should only be used when the values are limited and don't change. For example, a lookup list of salutations (Mr., Mrs., Ms.) would be appropriate.

CREATING INPUT MASKS

Field templates or ***input masks*** improve data entry for Text, Date, Number, and Currency field types. The input mask provides a pattern of input for the user to follow. For example, a Text field to store phone numbers would allow the user to enter any character from the keyboard but would not force the user to enter the area code. Applying an Input Mask would present the user with a template like (___)___-___ and require that all 10 digits of the phone number be entered.

A string of characters is entered into the input mask property to tell Access what to display to the user as a template and what to accept as valid

FIGURE 4.17
Input Mask definition characters

Character	Description
0	Required digit (0–9); no plus (+) or minus (−) sign
9	Optional digit; no plus (+) or minus (−) sign
#	Optional digit; plus (+) or minus (−) sign allowed
L	Required letter (A–Z)
?	Optional letter (A–Z)
A	Required letter or digit
a	Optional letter or digit
&	Required character or space
C	Optional character or space
.,:;-/	Placeholders and separators
<	Causes all characters that follow to be converted to lowercase
>	Causes all characters that follow to be converted to uppercase
!	Causes Input Mask to display from right to left
\	Used to display any of the characters in this table as a literal
Password	Creates a password entry text box with all entries displayed as *

input. The syntax used to enter the mask are outlined in Figure 4.17. Literal values in the string, like the ( ) in the phone number example, are entered where you want them to appear. To use one of the mask characters like the # sign, precede it with a backslash (\#).

task reference

Creating an Input Mask

- Open a table in Design view
- Select the field for which you want to define an input mask
- From the General tab select the **Input Mask** property and either
- Click the **Build** button and follow the Input Mask Wizard instructions (Text and Date fields only)

or

- Type the input mask definition (Numeric and Currency masks must be entered manually)

Setting an input mask for the OrderDate field:

1. If it is not already open, open the AC04PuppyParadise.mdb database
2. Open the **Orders** table in Design view
3. Click in the **OrderDate** field
4. In the General tab click the **Input Mask** text box and click the ellipsis to initiate the Input Mask Wizard

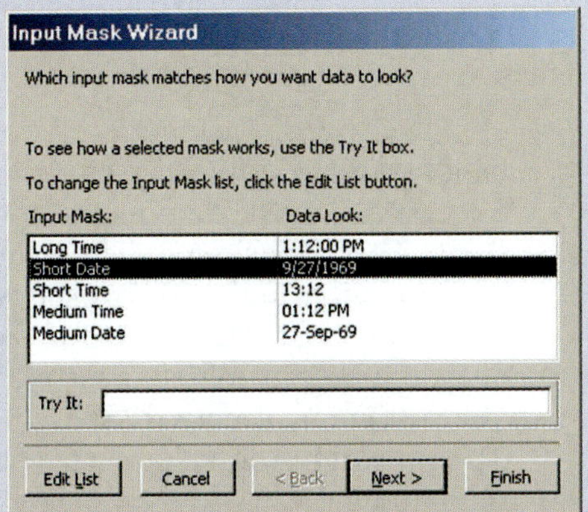

FIGURE 4.18
Input Mask Wizard

5. Select the **Short Date** format and click **Next**
6. Review the input mask created and the placeholder characters. Without updating them, click **Next,** and then click **Finish**

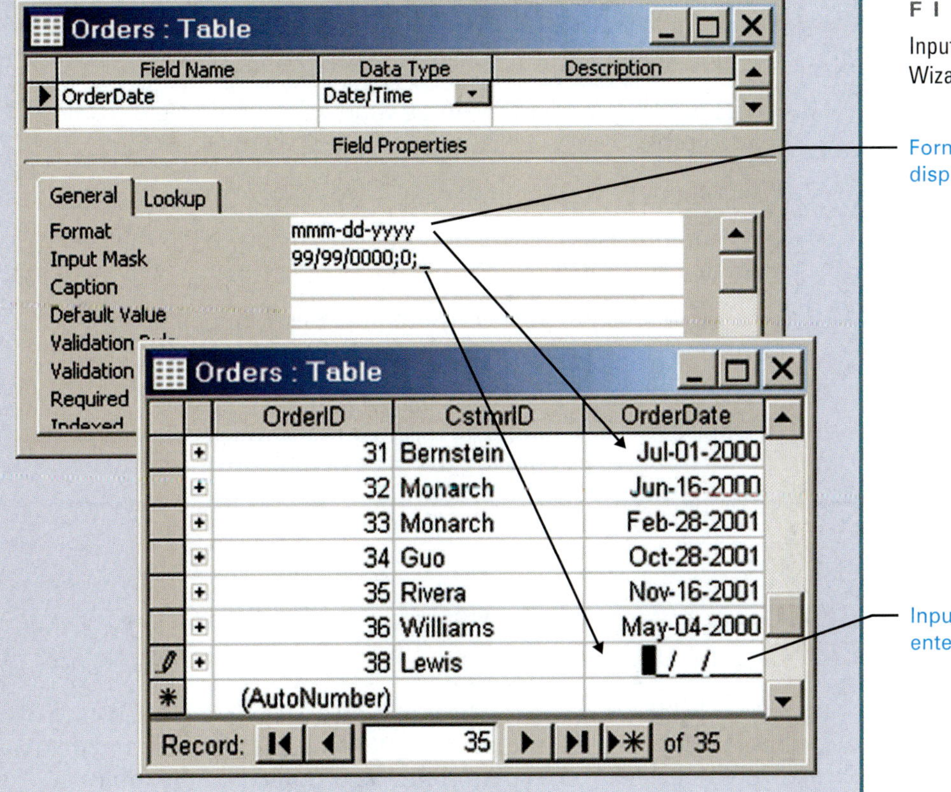

FIGURE 4.19
Input Mask created by the Wizard

Format controls the display of existing data

Input Mask for entering new data

7. Switch to Datasheet view, saving your changes
8. Enter a new record for Ronnie Lewis using today's date. Notice that the template displayed by the input mask is replaced by the Format display when entry is complete
9. Try entering a month of 15 in Sheila Monarch's record. You will receive an error
10. Close the Orders table

anotherword

. . . on Input Masks and Formats

At first glance, input masks and formats are similar field properties, but really serve different purposes. A Format property controls how the data display to the user, but does not control how they are entered or stored. To control how data are entered, use an input mask. An input mask ensures that the data match the format and values you define. When both properties are defined for a field, Microsoft Access uses the input mask when you are adding or editing data and the format when data are displayed. It is important that the results of these settings don't conflict.

The Input Mask Wizard supplies a list of standard input masks such as the Short Date mask demonstrated in the steps. These masks provide a template for data entry and perform simple data validation tasks like testing for the entry of a valid month. When these masks are not sufficient, a custom mask is built using the definition characters outlined in Figure 4.17.

SESSION 4.2

making the grade

1. When is the table Design view Undo buffer cleared?
2. A ______________ field retrieves valid values for a field from a related table.
3. What happens when you delete a field from a table structure?
4. T F Input masks control how data are displayed to the user after they are entered.
5. What are some possible conversion issues when changing a field from single to integer? Refer to Figure 2.25 for Number data type specifications.
6. In Datasheet view, data from related tables can be displayed in a ______________ by clicking the plus sign before a record.

SESSION 4.3 REPAIRING, BACKING UP, AND CONVERTING A DATABASE

As an Access database is used, it becomes larger. Each data item and database object added increase the file size. Deleting data records and database objects does not release the space that was occupied by that object.

COMPACTING AND REPAIRING A DATABASE

Access combines the processes of compacting and repairing a database into a single operation. ***Compacting*** is the process of releasing unused space from a database. Access compacts the database by reorganizing all database objects so that they take the least amount of space possible. The process is similar to defragmenting your hard drive. Besides reducing the size of the database, compacting improves database performance because well-organized data can be read and written faster. This process is also referred to as ***optimizing*** a database.

Compacting an older version of a database in Access 2001 does not convert the database to the new file format. There is a separate utility for converting database files to other versions.

AutoNumber fields are not adjusted for deleted records during the compact process, unless the deletions occurred at the end of the table (the last AutoNumbers generated). So deletion of any record that is not the last table record does not impact AutoNumbers. Such deleted numbers will not be generated again. When deletions occur at the end of the table, the AutoNumber value is reset so that the next generated number will be one greater than the AutoNumber value of the last undeleted record.

When Access is able to detect a problem with a database, a prompt to ***repair*** the damage is issued. Normally, Access will detect file corruptions when trying to load a database. Since Access cannot detect all file corruptions, it is important to compact and repair databases regularly. In addition, if a file begins to behave unpredictably, compact and repair it manually.

Access can repair most of the errors introduced during normal operation, but cannot repair certain user errors. For example, Access can repair a table index that has become corrupted by deleted records, but Access cannot repair queries or forms that refer to a table or query that has been deleted by the user.

In general, Access can repair corruption in

- A table
- The structure of a database or table
- A form, report, or module

When Access shuts down unexpectedly, significant problems can be introduced to the database if maintenance operations were underway. For example, if you were in the process of changing a record but Access was unable to complete the process, the table or tables involved become corrupted. To remedy this situation, when Access restarts it creates a copy of the file that was open when the shutdown occurred. The copy is named filename_Backup.mdb, where filename is the name of the database file that was open during the crash. Access then attempts to compact and repair the original file.

task reference

Compact and Repair the Open Database

- If the open database begins to behave erratically, on the **Tools** menu, point to **Database Utilities,** and then click **Compact and Repair Database**

Compacting and repairing the PuppyParadise database:

1. Verify that the AC04PuppyParadise.mdb database is open
2. On the **Tools** menu, point to **Database Utilities,** and then click **Compact and Repair Database**

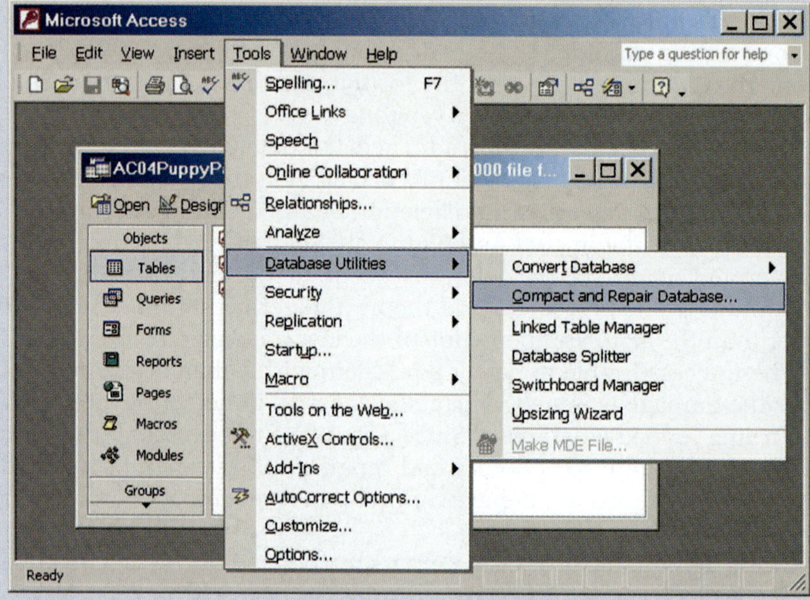

FIGURE 4.20
Manually Compact and Repair the open database

3. If the process completed successfully, no messages will display. If the process was unsuccessful, a message will display and you will need to restore from your most recent database backup
4. Continue with your other database tasks

Compact and repair can also be used on a database that is not open. This method has the advantage of allowing the compacted database to be stored in another file, maintaining both the original and the compacted file.

task reference

Compact and Repair an Unopened Database

- Access must be running with no open database
- On the **Tools** menu, point to **Database Utilities,** and then click **Compact and Repair Database**
- In the **Database to Compact From** dialog box, specify the Access file you want to compact, and then click **Compact**
- In the **Compact Database Into** dialog box, specify a name, drive, and folder for the compacted Access file
- Click **Save**

Compacting and repairing the unopened PuppyParadise database:

1. Verify that Access is running with no open databases. If the AC04PuppyParadise.mdb or another database is still open, click the Close button on the title bar of the Database window to close it
2. On the **Tools** menu, point to **Database Utilities,** and then click **Compact and Repair Database**
3. In the **Database to Compact From** dialog box, click on **AC04PuppyParadise.mdb,** and then click **Compact**
4. In the **Compact Database Into** dialog box, specify a name, drive, and folder for the compacted Access file

tip: *If you use the same name, drive, and folder, and the Access database is compacted successfully, Microsoft Access replaces the original file with the compacted version*

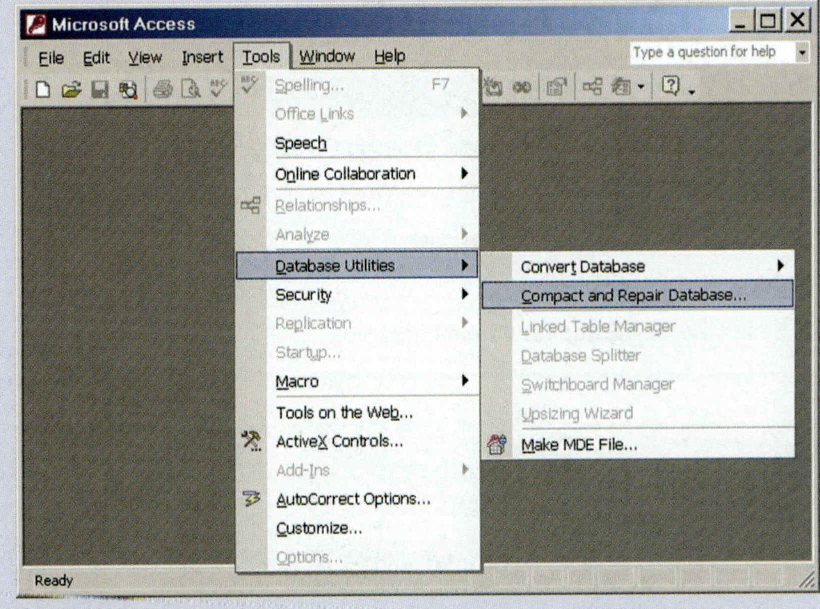

FIGURE 4.21
Compact and Repair an unopened database

5. If the process completed successfully, no messages will display. If the process was unsuccessful, a message will display and you will need to restore from your most recent database backup
6. Continue with your other database tasks

Compacting into another file is one way to create copies of a database that can be used to restore a damaged database after maintenance. The most common use is to create a current snapshot of the database just before performing tasks that could result in invalid data. For example, a query to adjust the pay rate of all employees could destroy the entire contents of the table if it contained an error. Creating a snapshot just before running the query will allow you to return to the prequery condition without much effort.

You also can create backups of individual database objects such as a table, query, or form by creating a blank database and then importing the backup objects from the original database. If only one table of the database could be damaged by the planned maintenance, this method would allow only that table to be backed up and restored. Restoring the damaged table is as simple as importing the backup copy.

COMPACTING A DATABASE AUTOMATICALLY

Since corrupted databases can lead to loss of data, queries, forms, and reports, it is important to compact and repair Access files regularly. Several generations of backup also should be maintained so that an unrepairable database can be restored to an earlier version. The most common user errors that cause database corruption are turning off the computer without closing Access or removing the disk (usually the A: or other removable disk) that Access is using before closing Access. Obviously avoiding these mistakes reduces the likelihood of database corruption.

Access automatically checks a file when it is being opened and will repair it if needed. You will not be prompted to compact the database if it is not performing optimally. Access also can be set to compact and repair the open Access file each time it is closed.

task reference

Setting Automatic Compact and Repair

- Open the Access database that you want to compact automatically
- On the **Tools** menu, click **Options**
- Click the **General** tab
- Select the **Compact on Close** check box

Setting the Automatic Compact and Repair option for AC04PuppyParadise.mdb:

1. Open the AC04PuppyParadise.mdb database so that its Compact on Close property can be set
2. On the **Tools** menu, click **Options**
3. Click the **General** tab

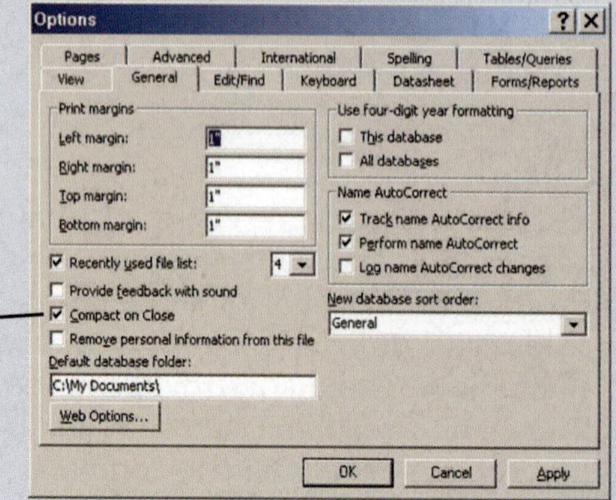

FIGURE 4.22
Automatically Compact and Repair databases

4. Click the **Compact on Close** option and click **OK**
5. AC04PuppyParadise.mdb will now compact and repair each time it is closed

tip: *You can stop the compact and repair process by pressing Ctrl+Break or Esc*

It is important to note that ***Compact on Close*** is a property of the database, not a property of Access. As such it must be set for each database for which you want to automate this process.

AUTOMATICALLY REPAIR OFFICE PROGRAMS

The same problems that can cause databases to corrupt also can damage Microsoft Office programs. All Office products later than 2000 offer a ***Detect and Repair*** facility that will notify the user when this happens and reinstall the affected software.

task reference

Setting Detect and Repair for Microsoft Office

- On the **Help** menu, click **Detect and Repair**
- To restore the program shortcuts to the Windows **Start** menu, make sure the **Restore my shortcuts while repairing** check box is selected (see Figure 4.23)
- Click **Start**

This procedure detects and repairs problems such as missing files and registry settings associated with all installed Microsoft Office programs. It will not repair personal files such as spreadsheets or documents. If the Detect and Repair command does not fix the problem, you might need to reinstall Microsoft Office.

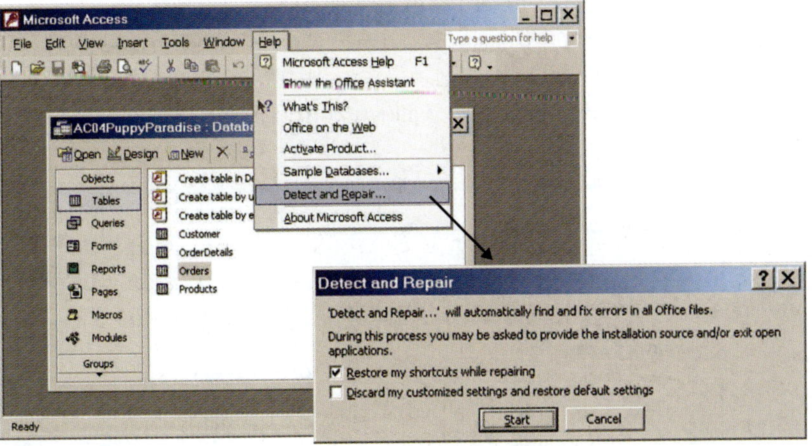

FIGURE 4.23
Microsoft Office Detect and Repair

BACKING UP AND RESTORING A DATABASE

Database backups are critical in organizations that rely on data for their operation. Besides creating backups before performing tasks that could destroy data, it is important to have regularly scheduled backups to protect against other types of loss.

Remember that data are valuable and should be protected against unforeseen events. The volume of updates to data determines how often database backups are needed. Any changes made to the database since the last backup will need to be reapplied to make it current. The question you need to ask yourself is "How much maintenance am I willing to repeat?" Weekly backups are the most common, but daily backups are not at all unusual for critical data with a high maintenance volume.

It is important to note that documentation also must be maintained for backups to be effective. You must know what updates have been made to your database since the last backup so that these can be reapplied.

Catastrophes such as floods, fires, and other acts of nature are not frequent but also should be considered when creating a backup plan. The simplest way to protect against such devastating problems is to store backups at an offsite location. This can be as simple as taking a copy of the backup home or sending it to another company site.

Backups can be created manually using the copy facility of Windows Explorer, but this becomes tedious and relies on your memory. It is better to use backup software such as Microsoft Windows 2000 Backup and Recovery Tools. Such tools are designed to complete backups of multiple files on a scheduled basis, are optimized for restoring all or part of a particular backup process, and can back up to multiple disks, CDs, and/or networked drives.

There are many backup software packages available with a variety of features. The following steps will demonstrate creating a backup using Microsoft Windows 2000 Backup and Recovery Tools because it is free with Windows 2000. If you are not running Windows 2000, you will not be able to complete these steps.

task reference

Backup and Restore Using Microsoft Windows 2000 Backup and Recovery Tools

- Click the Windows **Start** button, **Programs, Accessories, System Tools,** and then **Backup**
- Select the **Backup Wizard** to walk you through creating a backup of your file(s). Be sure to carefully explore all of the options. The Advanced button will allow you to set the type of backup and the schedule for backups
- Select the **Restore Wizard** to walk you through restoring all or part of a backup

Backing up AC04PuppyParadise.mdb with Microsoft Windows 2000 Backup and Recovery Tools:

1. Close the AC04PuppyParadise.mdb database if it is open. Make sure that you have a blank diskette for this process

2. Click the Windows **Start** button, **Programs, Accessories, System Tools,** and then **Backup**
3. Click the **Backup Wizard**
   a. Click **Next** on the opening Wizard page to continue
   b. Select **Back up selected files, drives, or network data** and then click **Next**

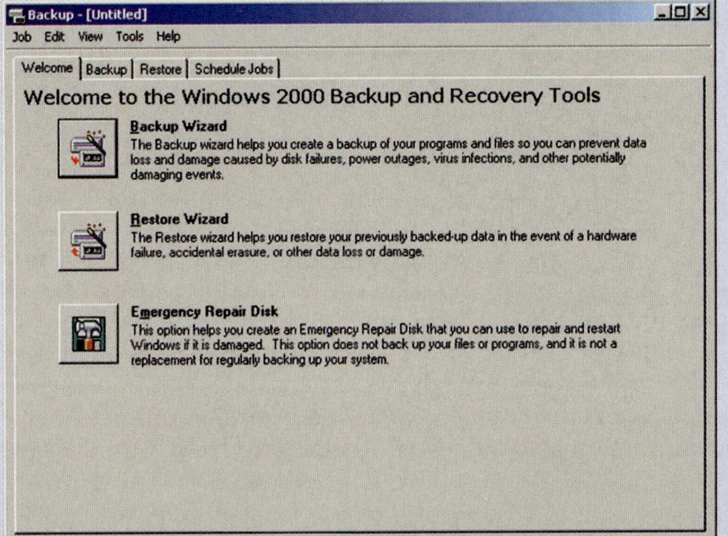

FIGURE 4.24
Microsoft Windows 2000 Backup Wizard

   c. Select the drive and path of the AC04PuppyParadise.mdb file and click **Next**

tip: *If the files are not displaying in the right panel, double-click on the folder in the left panel. Be sure that the check box in front of the PuppyParadise file name is clicked. You can click multiple files and folders for backup*

   d. Select the **A:** drive (or the appropriate drive for your backup) as the backup drive, name the file **PuppyParadise.bkf,** and click **Open**
   e. Click **Next** to move to the next Wizard dialog box
   f. Explore the Advanced options by clicking the **Advanced** command button. There are options to select the type of backup and schedule regular backups

tip: *Normal backups store all files that have been selected for backup, while Incremental backups only store those with changes*

   g. Click **Next** to move to the next Wizard dialog box
   h. Check the **Verify data after backup** check box and click **Next**
   i. Click **Next** on the Media Options dialog box
   j. Verify the label and then click **Next** on the Backup Label dialog box
   k. Click **Next** on the When to Backup dialog box. Alternatively, you can set a schedule to back up later or perform scheduled backups
   l. Click **Finish** to complete the backup
4. Close the backup window

Restoring a file or files from the backup is a simpler process. Initiate the software that was used to create the backup, select the archive file, select the file(s) to restore, and then click finish (see Figure 4.25). The most difficult part is ensuring that the correct file(s) is selected. Remember that the restore process overwrites the production files. If you accidentally restore the wrong file, there is no way to recover the maintenance applied to the file since the last backup. It is a good idea to rename the existing files before restoring from backup.

CONVERTING DATABASES

Access cannot update database designs from earlier versions. When a database that was created in an earlier version of Access is opened, a notice that the database must be converted before making changes is issued (see Figure 4.26). The Enable the database option will open the database without converting it. Enabled databases allow users to view and change data and run existing forms, queries, and reports but not change the design of database objects. Since the database format has not been converted, the database will still function in the earlier version of Access.

If the database will be used only in the current version of Access, better database performance is achieved by converting it. If, however, there is still a need to use the database in an older version of Access, enable it in the current version by opening it without converting it. In this case, modi-

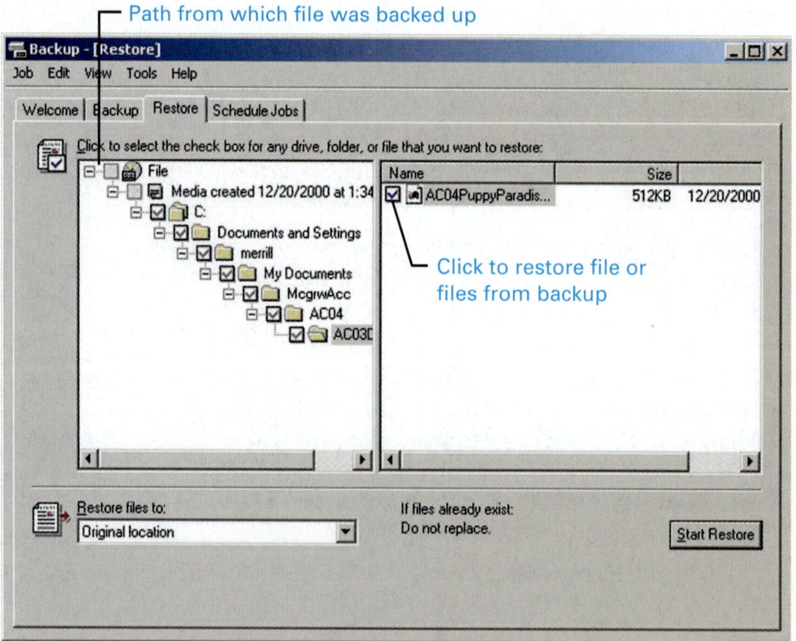

FIGURE 4.25
Selecting files to restore from Windows 2000 Backup and Recovery Tools

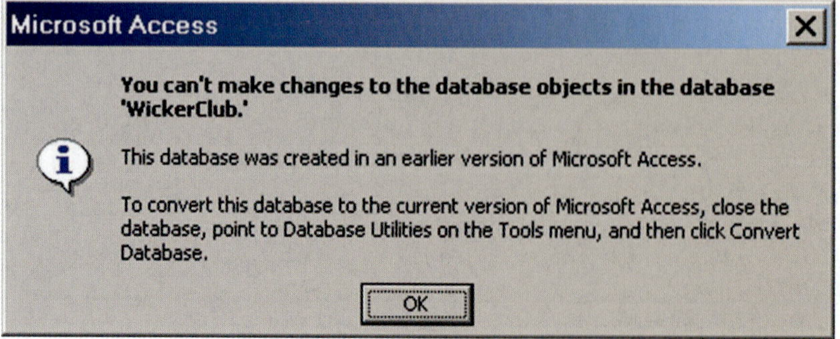

FIGURE 4.26
Conversion notification

fications to the design of database objects must be made in the original Access version. Once the database is open, it can still be converted using the Tools menu, as demonstrated in Figure 4.27.

Sometimes different parts of the same organization are using different Access versions, resulting in a need for multiple versions of the same database. Files created in the current version of Access can be converted to the file format of previous Access versions back to Access 97 (see Figure 4.28). Bear in mind that converting to a previous Access version will cause the database to lose all of the functionality that is specific to newer versions of Access.

Knowing how and when to convert databases means that you can work on the same database with different versions of Access, making your work more portable.

making the grade

SESSION 4.3

1. Why should you back up a database?
2. How do you decide when to convert a database to a newer version of Access?
3. What is the difference between compacting and repairing a database?
4. What is the purpose of Detect and Repair?

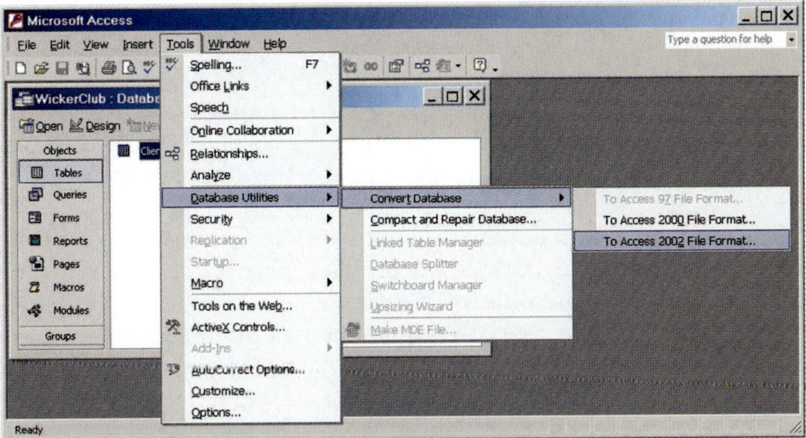

FIGURE 4.27
Converting an open database to a newer version

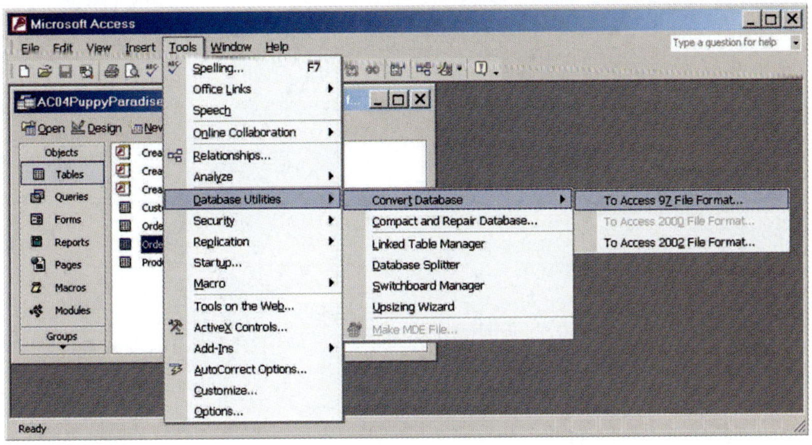

FIGURE 4.28
Converting to a previous access version

SESSION 4.4 SUMMARY

Effective analysis of the data held in a relational database often requires creating queries with complex conditions. Multiple criteria can be applied to one field using the In, Between, and Like conditional operators. The In operator is used to submit a list of match values. The Between operator supplies an upper and lower limit for values that will be retrieved. All records with values between the upper and lower limit—including the limit values—will be retrieved. The Like operator is used to submit a pattern match for a field selection value.

Pattern matches make use of wildcards to state the criteria. The * wildcard is used to represent any number of characters, the ? wildcard is used to represent a single character, and the # wildcard is used to represent a single numeral. The Like operator is designed to work with Text fields and provides haphazard results with other field types.

The And and Or operators provide another way to enter compound conditions. When the And logical operator combines two conditions, both conditions must be true for the record to be retrieved. When the Or logical operator combines two conditions, one or both conditions can be true to retrieve a record. The words And and Or can be entered into Criteria for a field to state multiple conditions for that field or they can be used to join criteria for multiple fields. When the conditions are in different fields and on the same Criteria row, the conditions are joined with And. When the conditions are on different Criteria rows, the conditions are joined with Or. The Not logical operator is used to negate a condition for a field. For example Not =6 would retrieve records that do not contain the value 6.

Crosstab queries are used to calculate and organize data by two variables. The row and column headings are defined and then set the aggregate function used to calculate the values displayed.

Great care should be taken when modifying the field attributes of tables that contain production data, since such changes could result in permanent data loss. Lookup fields and input masks can be added to the field properties of a table definition. Both properties improve the validity of data.

Finally Compacting and Repairing a database frees unused space from the database to optimize its performance. The repair process fixes structural problems with database objects. A strategy for backing up and restoring critical databases is necessary to reduce the risk of data loss.

Visit www.mhhe.com/i-series/ to explore related topics.

MOUS OBJECTIVES SUMMARY

- AC2002-1-5—Use Access tools to maintain and repair databases
- AC2002-2-2—Add a predefined input mask to a field
- AC2002-2-3—Create lookup fields
- AC2002-2-4—Modify field properties

task reference roundup

Task	Page #	Preferred Method
Crosstab Query	AC 4.10	• Click the **Queries** object in the Database window, select **Create query by using wizard**, and then click **New**
		• Select **Crosstab Query Wizard** from the New Query dialog box and then click **OK**
		• Follow the Wizard's instructions to choose the data source, row heading, column heading, and aggregate functions for the query
		• Name the query and then view the results
Creating a Lookup Field	AC 4.15	• Verify the relationship between the table that will have the lookup field and the table where the field is being looked up. The most likely relationship is one-to-many, where the child (many sides of the relationship) table will look up the key value of the parent table (one side of the relationship)
		• Open the child table and change the Data Type to **Lookup Wizard**
		• Follow the Lookup Wizard instructions
Creating an Input Mask	AC 4.18	• Open a table in Design view
		• Select the field for which you want to define an input mask
		• From the General tab select the **Input Mask** property and either
		• Click the **Build** button and follow the Input Mask Wizard instructions (Text and Date fields only)
		or
		• Type the input mask definition (Numeric and Currency masks must be entered manually)
Compact and Repair the Open Database	AC 4.21	• On the **Tools menu,** point to **Database Utilities**, and then click **Compact and Repair Database**
Compact and Repair an Unopened Database	AC 4.22	• Access must be running with no open database
		• On the **Tools** menu, point to **Database Utilities**, and then click **Compact and Repair Database**
		• In the **Database to Compact From** dialog box, specify the Access file you want to compact, and then click **Compact**
		• In the **Compact Database Into** dialog box, specify a name, drive, and folder for the compacted Access file
		• **Click** Save
Setting Automatic Compact and Repair	AC 4.24	• Open the Access database that you want to compact automatically
		• On the **Tools** menu, click **Options**
		• Click the **General** tab
		• Select the **Compact on Close** check box
Setting Detect and Repair for Microsoft Office	AC 4.25	• On the **Help** menu, click **Detect and Repair**

task reference roundup

Task	Page #	Preferred Method
		• To restore the program shortcuts to the Windows **Start** menu, make sure the **Restore my shortcuts while repairing** check box is selected
		• Click **Start**
Backup and Restore using Microsoft Windows 2000 Backup and Recovery Tools	AC 4.26	• Click the Windows **Start** button, **Programs**, **Accessories**, **System Tools,** and then **Backup**
		• Select the **Backup Wizard** to walk you through creating a backup of your file(s). Be sure to carefully explore all of the options. The Advanced button will allow you to set the type of backup and the schedule for backups
		• Select the **Restore Wizard** to walk you through restoring all or part of a backup

CROSSWORD PUZZLE

Across

2. Removes empty space from a database
5. Query that summarizes data on two values
8. *, ?, #
10. Operator that submits a pattern match
11. And, Or, and Not are examples of ________ operators
13. Operator that submits an upper and lower limit
14. Negates a condition

Down

1. Setting to automate compacting—Compact on ________
3. Activities to improve performance
4. >, <, and = are examples of ________ operators
6. Combines conditions when both must be true
7. Combines conditions when only one must be true
9. Office facility to keep software performing properly
12. Operator that submits a list of match values

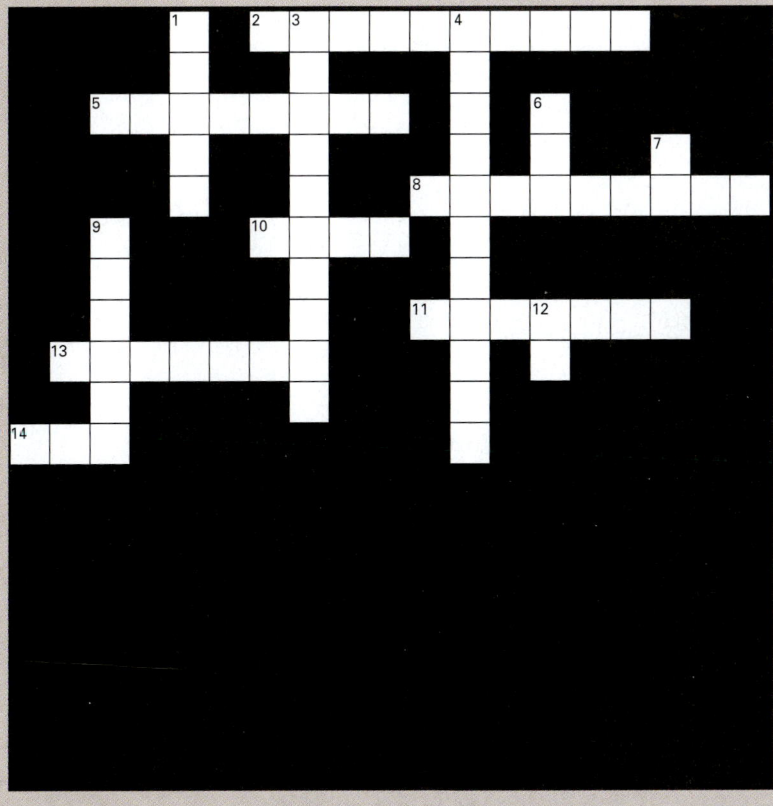

FILL-IN

1. The ______ operator would be used to select records containing the values Life, Love, and Death.
2. The value that appears across the top of a crosstab query is the ________.
3. The condition that would be used to select values Smith and Smyth is ________.
4. The oldest version of Access to which a current database can be converted is ________.
5. Compact on Close is a property of ________.

REVIEW QUESTIONS

Each of the following topics should be addressed in one to three paragraphs.

1. What should you do if your database begins to behave erratically?
2. When should a snapshot backup be created?
3. What criteria would select records where the JobDescription is manager and the Salary is over 35000?
4. Why would you compact a database into another file?
5. How are select queries and crosstab queries the same?

CREATE THE QUESTION

For each of the following answers, create the question.

ANSWER	QUESTION
1. Like "C?ndy?".	________
2. Clicking this allows a field to be used for selection criteria, but does not display in the result.	________
3. Between 7 And 9	________
4. ?	________
5. Shutting off your computer without closing Access properly.	________

FACT OR FICTION

For each of the following, determine whether the statement is fact, fiction, or both and present your arguments for that conclusion.

1. It is not necessary to Compact and Repair a database each time it is used.
2. Not > 10 is the only way to enter this condition.
3. Like "5/##/01" will match all May values in a date field.
4. Creating copies of databases using Windows copy is an effective way to back up databases.
5. You should always convert databases to the newest version of Access.
6. AutoNumber fields are always reset when the database is compacted.
7. Changes made to a table's design have no impact on data already stored in the table.
8. Input masks improve data entry by displaying a template for user entry and restricting the type of data accepted in each input position.
9. When changing field attributes for tables that already contain data, the only way to recover from data errors caused by the changes is to restore to a ________ of the table that you created.
10. Explain the difference between moving a field in Datasheet and Design view.

hands-on projects

practice

Merrill Middle School Software Tracking

Merrill Middle School maintains an inventory of its software in an Access database. To date no analysis of the data has been completed. There is no centralized purchasing and no one knows just exactly how much software they have, where it is stored, or what it cost. You have been asked to prepare some queries to help determine what policies should be set about software purchases.

1. Start Access and open the **AC04Merrill.mdb** database
2. Open the Software table and review the data to become familiar with them
3. Create a query in Design view that selects the English software that has been purchased from Learnit Software (LS)
   a. Enter **ENG** in the Criteria row of Category
   b. Enter **LS** in the Criteria row of Vendor (entering an And condition)
   c. Save the query as **LearnIt**
4. The administration has decided to begin by checking software that is valued at over $500. Since you believe that the bulk of software expense is in the business area, you will create a query for business software valued at over $500
   a. Open a new query in Design view
   b. Add the InventoryValue query to the query design grid and add all of its fields to the Field row of the query
   c. Place **BUS** and **>500** in the Criteria row of the appropriate columns to create an And condition
   d. Run the query
   e. Save the query as **BusOver500**
5. Since the school purchases up to five evaluation copies of each software title, you need to look at software in the other (nonbusiness) categories where there are more than five copies
   a. Open a new query in Design view
   b. Add the InventoryValue query to the query design grid and add all of its fields to the Field row of the query
   c. Place **ENG, MTH, SYS,** and **SCI** in separate rows of the Category column to create Or conditions
   d. **>5** needs to be entered in each of the corresponding Quantity rows to create an And condition for each Category value
   e. Run the query
   f. Save the query as **NonBus1**
6. There are often multiple ways to accomplish the same task. Here is a second and more efficient way to create the previous query
   a. Open a new query in Design view
   b. Add the InventoryValue query to the query design grid and place all of its fields in the Field row of the query
   c. Place **Not Bus** in the Criteria row of Category
   d. Place **>5** in the Criteria row of Quantity (creating an And condition with Not Bus)
   e. Run the query. The results should be the same as the previous query
   f. Save the query as **NonBus2**
7. Close the database and Access if you have competed your work

FIGURE 4.29

English software from Learnit

LearnIt : Select Query

Software Number	Name	Category	Quantity	Price	VendorCode
1693	Kid-Writer	ENG	22	$29.95	LS
5950	Easy English	ENG	10	$29.95	LS
			10	$0.00	

Record: 3 of 3

FIGURE 4.30

Nonbusiness software from Learnit

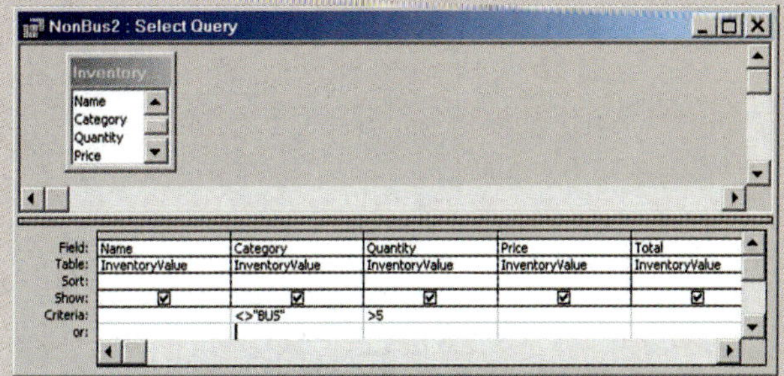

challenge!

More Queries for Curbside Recycling

Curbside Recycling maintains a database of customers and their recyclable pickups. You have been asked to create some queries to help evaluate their business.

1. Start Access and open **AC04CurbsideRecycling.mdb**
2. Run the **CustomerDetails** query and review the results. This query joins the data from the two tables to create a complete record for each recyclable pickup
3. Curbside is considering implementing a minimum pickup weight to improve its profit margin. Management would like to know how many customers have less than 10 pounds of each type of recyclable
   a. Open a new query in Design view and create a query using the name, street address, and weight fields from CustomerDetails
   b. Enter the criteria that will select rows with less than 10 pounds in either recyclable field
   c. Now alter the query to retrieve records with less than 10 pounds in both recyclable categories
   d. Save the query as **LowVolume**
4. Curbside employees are concerned about the impacts of repeatedly lifting the recyclables. You have been asked to determine how much each employee lifts per day
   a. Run the **TotalWeight** query that has been created for you and review its results
   b. Create a new crosstab query using the Wizard
   c. Use the TotalWeight query as the data source with service date as the row headings and employee ID as the column heading and sum total weight
   d. Run the query and save it as **SumTotalWeightCrosstab**
   e. Edit the SumTotalWeightCrosstab in Design view to find the Max value of Total Weight
   f. Use the **Save As** option of the File menu to save the modified query as **MaxTotalWeightCrosstab**
5. Close the database and Access if you have competed your work

FIGURE 4.31

Pickups with less than 10 pounds in either recyclable

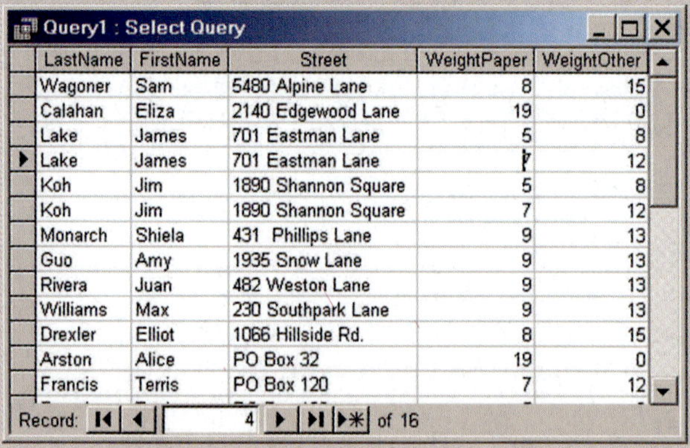

Query1 : Select Query

LastName	FirstName	Street	WeightPaper	WeightOther
Wagoner	Sam	5480 Alpine Lane	8	15
Calahan	Eliza	2140 Edgewood Lane	19	0
Lake	James	701 Eastman Lane	5	8
Lake	James	701 Eastman Lane	7	12
Koh	Jim	1890 Shannon Square	5	8
Koh	Jim	1890 Shannon Square	7	12
Monarch	Shiela	431 Phillips Lane	9	13
Guo	Amy	1935 Snow Lane	9	13
Rivera	Juan	482 Weston Lane	9	13
Williams	Max	230 Southpark Lane	9	13
Drexler	Elliot	1066 Hillside Rd.	8	15
Arston	Alice	PO Box 32	19	0
Francis	Terris	PO Box 120	7	12

Record: 4 of 16

FIGURE 4.32

Total weight by service date and employee

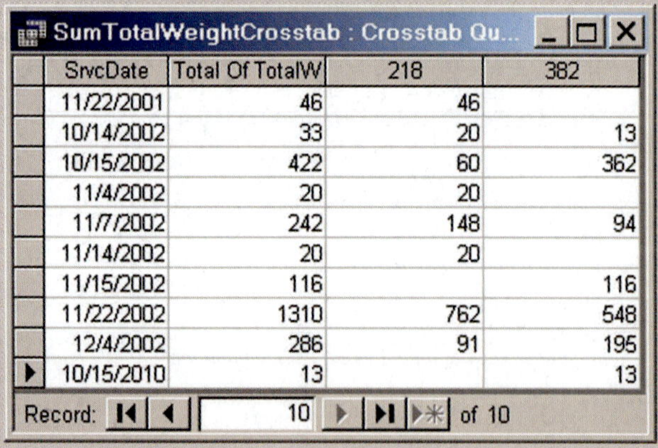

SumTotalWeightCrosstab : Crosstab Qu...

SrvcDate	Total Of TotalW	218	382
11/22/2001	46	46	
10/14/2002	33	20	13
10/15/2002	422	60	362
11/4/2002	20	20	
11/7/2002	242	148	94
11/14/2002	20	20	
11/15/2002	116		116
11/22/2002	1310	762	548
12/4/2002	286	91	195
10/15/2010	13		13

Record: 10 of 10

FIGURE 4.33

Max weight by service date and employee

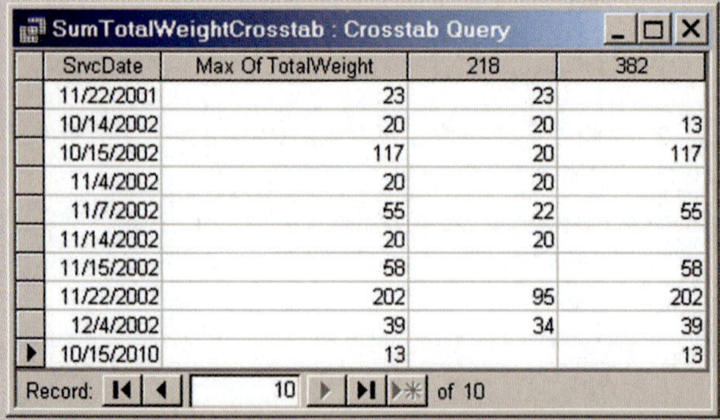

SumTotalWeightCrosstab : Crosstab Query

SrvcDate	Max Of TotalWeight	218	382
11/22/2001	23	23	
10/14/2002	20	20	13
10/15/2002	117	20	117
11/4/2002	20	20	
11/7/2002	55	22	55
11/14/2002	20	20	
11/15/2002	58		58
11/22/2002	202	95	202
12/4/2002	39	34	39
10/15/2010	13		13

Record: 10 of 10

on the web

Toy Purchase Statistics by Internet Research Inc.

Internet Research Inc. (IRI) is a statistical evaluation organization specializing in Internet commerce that was introduced in Chapter 2. You are gathering data from the Internet on Web sites that sell toys and using Access to evaluate them.

1. Use a Shopping Bot like www.mysimon.com or a search engine to find at least two sites selling popular toys (www.eToys.com and www.ToysRUs.com are good sites, but there are many others). Select and compare bicycle prices
   a. Determine the price of a model of bike at the first site
   b. Find the price for the same model at the second site
   c. Repeat this process for another bike
2. Add your new research to the data that already exist in the AC03IRI.mdb database Toys table

tip: *If you did this exercise in Chapter 3, use your updated copy of the database; otherwise go to the Chapter 3 data files and retrieve the original version*

3. Sometimes you want to convert data in a table to display with different row and column headings. This can be accomplished with a crosstab query
4. Create a new crosstab query with the Wizard
   a. Use the **Toys** table as the data source
   b. Make ToyName the row headings and Web site the column headings
   c. Display Price in the cells using the Sum function (since there is only one record per toy/Web site combination, the aggregate function will not do anything, but you must select one anyway)
   d. Click off the check box to include row sums so there is no Total column in the result
   e. Run the query. Your results should resemble those shown in Figure 4.34
   f. Save the Query as **PriceByToyAndSite**
5. Create a query in Design view that finds all products with Barbie in the ToyName. Sort the results by ToyName and Price. Save the query as **BarbieProducts**
6. Modify the query from step 5 to retrieve Barbie products that cost under $25. Save the query as **BarbieLT25**
7. Close the database and exit Access if your work is complete

FIGURE 4.34

Price by product and Web site

PriceByToyAndSite : Crosstab Query

ToyName	www_etoys_com	www_toysrus_com
Barbie Airplane	$68.99	$59.99
Barbie Family House	$49.28	$58.92
Celebration Barbie	$37.99	$36.99
Cool Blading Barbie	$22.50	$22.12
Cool Clips Barbie	$15.28	$15.87
Ferrari Barbie	$42.28	$39.99
Game Boy Army Men	$29.95	$32.99
Game Boy Asteroids	$23.32	$24.87
Game Boy Mario Golf	$31.15	$31.99
Game Boy Perfect Dark	$32.50	$59.99
Generation Girl Barbie	$21.64	$21.88
Princess Bride Barbie	$23.38	$22.99
Rose Barbie	$52.12	$53.27

Record: 2 of 15

e-business

Tracking Photographs for SportsPix

SportsPix is a digital photography operation that specializes in taking pictures of youth sports teams. Ray Damask and Grace Bishop began photographing sports teams when their nephew was playing soccer at the local YMCA. They shoot individual and team pictures for baseball, softball, soccer, football, volleyball, tennis, and martial arts. Three other photographers pitch in during peak demand periods. On a busy day, they can shoot hundreds of children with their teams, resulting in over 10,000 customers in a year.

Tracking customer receipts is easy since all packages are paid for when the photographs are shot. Customers can preview their pictures on the Web and submit an order for the shots that they want included in their package. The biggest problem is keeping effective records on who is in each photograph, to which team they belong, when the photograph was shot, and where the photograph was shot. You have developed a prototype of a Photographs table that you believe will help Ray and Grace. You have selected some test data from the information that they provided and entered it into the table. Perform the following tests to ensure the effectiveness of this solution.

1. Make sure that you have access to the data from your data disk
2. Start Access and open the **AC04SportsPix.mdb** database from your chapter four files
3. Open the **Photographs** table and add records for yourself and two of your friends. You should all be on the same team and have had your pictures taken at the same time and at the same location. Use Film ID 5443
4. Create a query that will select all fields for photographs from 8/14/2001 at 9 AM. Use Team as the primary sort and Subject Name as the secondary sort. Print the results and save the query as **DateTime**
5. Use the Simple Query Wizard to create a query that contains the Subject Name, Date, Film ID, and Photo #. Select records with Film ID values **5385, 4638,** and **5443.** Sort the query datasheet by Subject Name and print the result. Save the query as **FilmID**. Print the query datasheet
6. Create a crosstab query to document the number of subjects photographed by date and time. Make Date the row header and Time the column header. Use the Count function on Subject Name. Save the query as **DateTimeCrosstab**
7. If your work is complete exit Access; otherwise continue to the next assignment

around the world

Tracking the World's Population

Brandon Pryor's middle school class is still working on ways to evaluate the population of the worlds' largest cities. The students have a pretty good idea of how large these cities are compared to their hometown, but now they need to understand how the cities are related to each other.

1. Open the **Cities** table of the **AC04Populations.mdb** database

   tip: *If you did this exercise in Chapter 3, use your updated copy of the database*

2. Create a query in Design view that will select all records with Korea in the country name. Sort the results by City and save the query as **Korea**
3. Create a query that will select cities with populations between 15 and 35 million. Sort by descending population and name the query **35M**
4. The class is looking for a Middle East city but cannot remember the full name. They believe that it starts with al. Write a query that will help them find the correct city. Save the query as **MiddleEast**
5. Create a query that will select cities in South America (Argentina, Bolivia, Brazil, Chile, Ecuador, Peru, and Venezuela). Sort the results by Country and City. Save the query as **SouthAmerica**

   tip: *The countries have both English and German names displayed, so you will need to match for both or use wildcards*

6. Modify the previous query to select only ABC Powers (Argentina, Brazil, and Chile). ABC Powers are the nations striving to maintain peace in South and Central America. The alliance was formed to protect against aggressive policies of the United States prior to World War II. Save the query as **ABCPowers**
7. Create a query that will select all cities in North America. Sort the result from largest to smallest city. Save the query as **NorthAmerica**
8. With the world's largest population, China also has the greatest number of large cities. Create a query that will select all cities in China and order them by decreasing population. Save the query as **China**
9. Since the database contains the German names for countries as well as the English names, the students decide to see how large the cities in Germany are. Create a query that will display German cities sorted by ascending population. Save the query as **Germany**
10. Close the database and Access if your work is complete

FIGURE 4.35
German cities population

Germany : Select Query

Name	ID	Country/Staat	Population/Einw
Hannover	368	Germany / Deutschland	1025000
Nürnberg	363	Germany / Deutschland	1050000
Düsseldorf	262	Germany / Deutschland	1350000
Mannheim	208	Germany / Deutschland	1625000
Köln	183	Germany / Deutschland	1850000
München	180	Germany / Deutschland	1900000
Frankfurt (am Main)	176	Germany / Deutschland	1950000
Hamburg	125	Germany / Deutschland	2550000
Stuttgart	117	Germany / Deutschland	2650000
Berlin	64	Germany / Deutschland	4150000
Essen	37	Germany / Deutschland	6050000

Record: 11 of 11

running project: tnt web design

More Analysis of TnT Table Data

The TnT database now consists of three related tables. The tblCustomers table holds the static data about the organization's customers. The CustomerSites table contains the URLs for the sites TnT has built. The CustomerSites table has a lookup field for the customer name so that you do not have to remember CustomerID values when entering data. TnT's employees are listed in the Employees table. CustomerSites is related to both the Customers table and the Employees table. The employee listed in the CustomerSites table is the one who managed the Web site development project.

1. Start Access and open the **AC04TnT.mdb** database
2. Open each table and review the data
3. Create a query based on the Employees table that will list all of the employees who are either programmers or scripters. Order the data by JobClass, LastName, and FirstName. Save the query as **ContentDevelopers**
4. Modify the previous query to select programmers and scripters who live in Washington (WA). Save the query as **WAContentDevelopers**
5. There is an employee that you know as Jim, but you are not sure how he has been entered into the database. It could be Jim, Jimmy, or James. Create a query to search for this person. Save the query as **JimSearch**
6. The first seven employees of TnT are the project managers. The site table lists the company, the URL, and the employee number of the project manager. Tori wants a table that outlines what companies each project manager has worked with. Create a crosstab query that displays company name as the row header, employee number as the column header, and counts the site number (so that it just displays that number). Do not display a totals column. Save the query as **ProjectManagersCrosstab**
7. Create a report with the previous query as the datasource. Display the logo from AC04Tnt.tif in the report header. Save the report as **ProjectManagers**
8. Set this database up to automatically compact on exit. Document the steps used to accomplish this

FIGURE 4.36
Report based on crosstab query

TnT Web Pages

Project Managers

custID	1	2	3	4	5	6
Comércio Mineiro				1		
FairWeather Ent		1	1			
Halston & Co.					1	
MMB Holdings			2			
Bakertime Mobile	2					
Classic Accents		1		1		
Summit Supply					1	

did you know?

a goldfish is the only animal that can see both infrared and ultraviolet light.

there are more than 50,000 earthquakes throughout the world each year.

the highest place people have settled in the United States is Climax, Colorado, at 11,360 feet above sea level.

in reality, electric lightbulbs existed 50 years prior to Thomas Edison's 1879 U.S. patent date.

it really can be too cold to snow! During very cold weather, the capacity of the air to contain moisture is reduced and most of the vapor is deposited as frost, resulting in extremely low humidity. In these conditions snow cannot form.

"within ten to twenty years' time we could have a robot that will completely eliminate all routine operations around the house and remove the drudgery from human life," said mechanical engineering professor M. W. Thring, in _____ (year).

Chapter Objectives

- **Build a form in Design view—MOUS AC2002-2-1**
- **Modify an existing form in Design view**
- **Understand the Form toolbox**
- **Create a report in Design view—MOUS AC2002-4-1**
- **Summarize report data—MOUS AC2002-4-3**
- **Preview and print reports—MOUS AC2002-7-3**

CHAPTER 5 five

Customizing Forms and Reports

chapter case

PuppyParadise

Evan Gibbs is the 15-year-old proprietor of PuppyParadise, the distributor of the PoochPouch, a comfortable sleeping bag for dogs. He and his miniature Pinscher, Gizmo, displayed the product at the annual Invention Convention. The convention led to several orders and a feature in the Business segment of the local television news. After that his products were picked up by a nationwide mall distributor and are also circulated through a Web storefront.

Although Evan started out tracking his business manually, he soon decided to use Microsoft Office products to give his business a more professional image. He began to use Word for invoices, Excel for financial tracking, and Access to store data about his customers, orders, and products. Evan was very comfortable with Word and Excel, but his need to collect and track data using Access exceeded his understanding, so he asked you to help.

You and Evan have worked diligently to evaluate the data storage and reporting needs of PuppyParadise. The result is an Access database with tables to track customers, products, and orders. The database also contains a number of select queries to analyze quarterly sales, unpaid invoices, and product demand. A crosstab query to tabulate sales by month and state has let Evan know how his products sell in each state over time. Simple reports have been developed to document the status of sales and products.

While all of this is helpful to Evan, he needs more complex analytical information to effectively run his business. He wants friendlier forms that will require custom development using the Form Design view. These forms will be used to maintain

FIGURE 5.1
PuppyParadise custom output

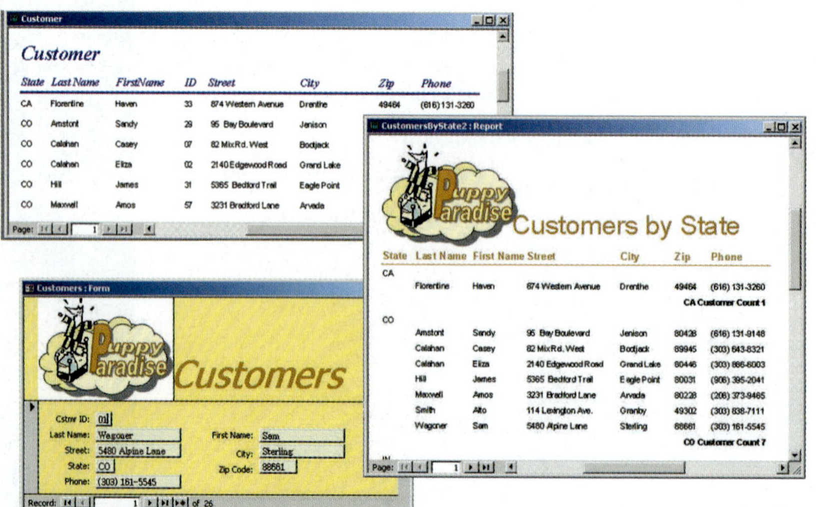

data, select records for evaluation, and print with headers and footers. More powerful reporting to calculate, sort, group, and summarize PuppyParadise data is also needed.

Evan knows that no amount of information can guarantee the result of a decision, but timely and effective information can significantly improve the likelihood of a positive outcome. He expects to improve his decision-making ability by learning more ways to effectively use Access form and report facilities.

SESSION 5.1 MAINTAINING DATA WITH FORMS

The form object is used to create a custom screen interface used to enter and display database data. Forms also create user interfaces called *switchboards* that open other forms and reports in the database, and custom dialog boxes to accept user input and carry out an action based on the input.

Most forms are bound to one or more tables or queries referred to as the form's ***record source.*** All of the fields from the underlying tables and queries do not need to be included in the form.

DEFINING A FORM IN FORM DESIGN VIEW

You already have created forms using form Wizards and modified the result by adding images. It's time to take a look at how forms work from the ground up. The design of a form stores all of the specifications for the appearance and function of the form including information about its underlying record source. Calculations are stored in the form's design and executed just before data are displayed to the user. The data displayed in the form (except calculations) are stored and/or retrieved from its underlying record source.

Form Design View

Forms are built using graphical objects called controls. Each control has a special purpose. A ***Label*** control is used to display descriptive text to the user. A ***Text Box*** control is used to enter and display data from the record source or execute and display a calculated value. These underlying controls were introduced in the previous chapter when Form Design view was used to add a graphic to the AutoForm Wizard form. Customizing an AutoForm is often the fastest way to develop a usable product.

When a new form is created in Design view (see Figure 5.2), you begin with an empty form and a toolbox containing the tools (controls) needed to create the form elements. Controls are added to the form to build the desired functionality. Since the developer is in complete control of the format, it is always best to have an idea of the operation and design of the end product before beginning.

To design a form, decide what fields need to be included. If the fields are from different tables, it is often better to create a query that joins the tables and selects the appropriate records. After documenting the fields to be included, organize a layout for those fields and any other necessary

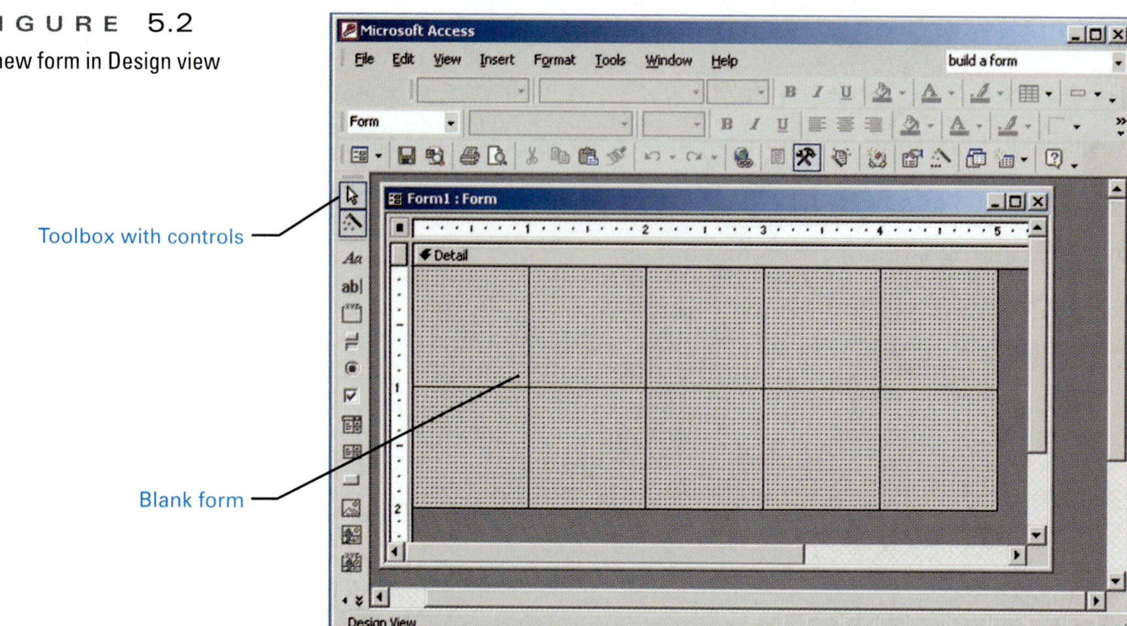

FIGURE 5.2
A new form in Design view

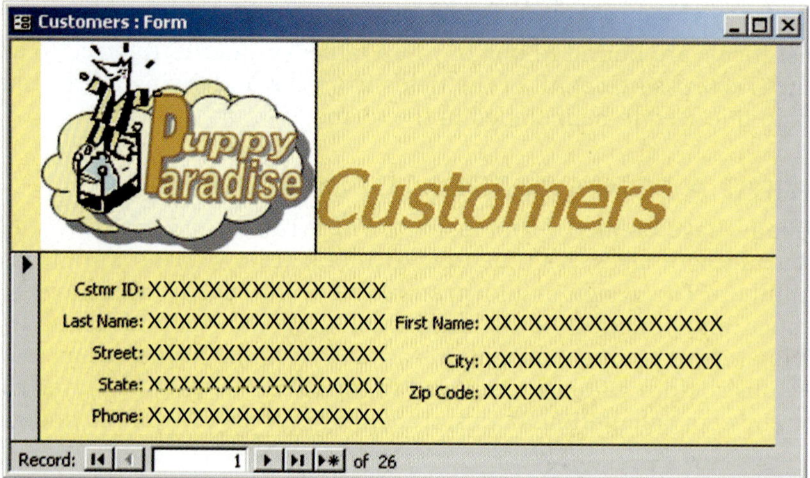

FIGURE 5.3
Customers Form Design

elements that are to be included such as a logo. Figure 5.3 shows a sample form design for PuppyParadise Customers input.

The design reflects the complete layout of the form including titles, graphics, captions, and field length. In the design shown, the field captions appear as Evan wants to see them on the form. Xs are used to indicate the placement and the length of the data display area. When the form is built, the captions will be in Label controls and the data values will be displayed in Text Box controls. The PuppyParadise logo will reside in an Image control and the form title will be entered in a Label control. Since you have a good idea of the data and its layout for the Customers form, it is time to start building it.

The Form Toolbox and Field List

The Form toolbox is a special toolbar with all of the controls that can be added to a form. If you forget what a Toolbox button is, display a Screen Tip by pausing the mouse pointer over it. Like all toolbars, the toolbox can be displayed or removed from display using the View menu. It also can be anchored or unanchored by dragging its title bar.

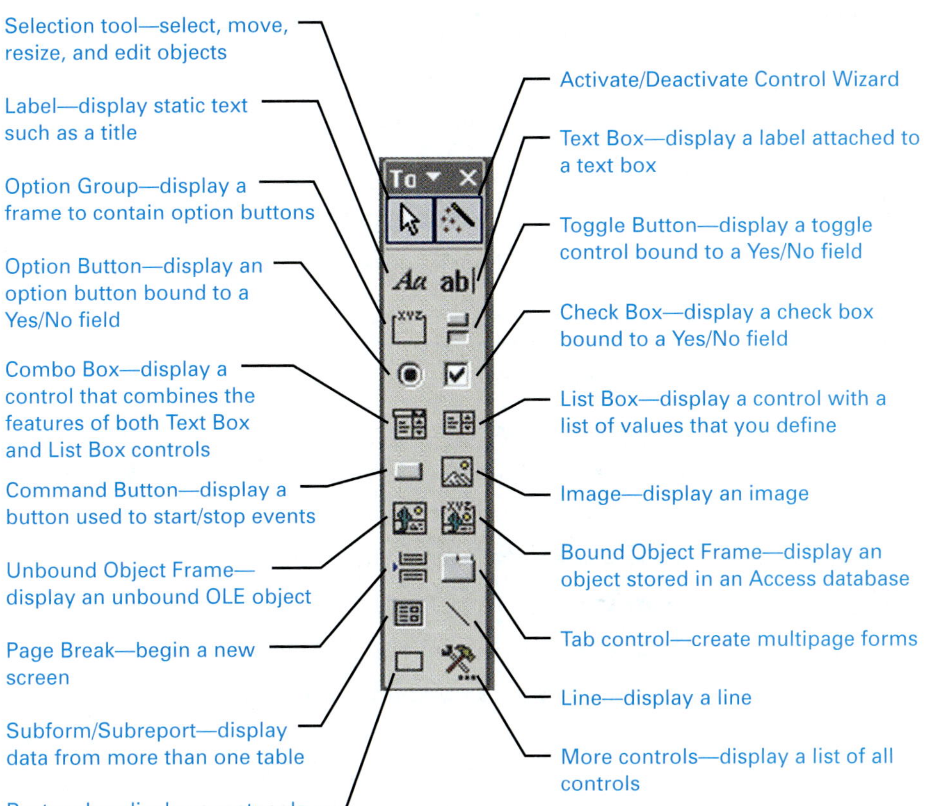

FIGURE 5.4
The Form toolbox

When a control is placed on the form, its *properties* are set, to direct what it will display and how it will appear on the form. A few of the properties that can be set will alter a control's background color, foreground color, and font. Controls and their uses are outlined in Figure 5.4.

Form controls are classified as bound, unbound, or calculated. ***Bound*** controls display data from a record source and are said to be bound to a field in the underlying table or query. Bound controls are typically added using the Field List dialog box rather than the toolbox. ***Unbound*** controls are not linked to a record source and so display fixed data such as the title of a form, instructions, or labels for other form elements. A ***calculated*** control stores the instructions on how to complete the calculation using one or more fields of the record source and displays the calculated value.

The simplest way to create a bound control is to open the Field List dialog box for the record source using the Field List button of the Form Design toolbar. With the Field List dialog box open, select a field and drag it to the form surface. Repeat this process for each field that is to display on the form. Bound controls can be rearranged on the form by dragging until they are positioned where you would like.

Bound controls created in this fashion will consist of a text box to display the field value and a label to hold a caption. The Caption property of a Label displays the Caption value set for the field in the table design. The Field Name is the default Caption property value and will display in the label when no custom value is set.

Building a Form

Evan likes using the Customer form to enter new customers, but he believes that the format could be improved. Rather than customize the existing form, you decide to rebuild it in Design view to get some practice with building forms from scratch.

Open a New Form in Design View

- In the Database window of an open database, click the **Forms** object
- Click the **New** button on the Database Window toolbar
- In the New Form dialog box, click **Design View**
- Select the table or query that will be the record source for the form and click **OK**

Creating the Customer form in Design view:

1. Open the **AC05PuppyParadise.mdb** database
2. Select the **Forms** object from the Database window
3. Click the **New** button on the Database Window toolbar
4. Verify that **Design view** is selected from the list of ways to create forms
5. Select **Customer** as the source of data for this form and click **OK**

tip: *If your screen is missing the ruler, grid, or toolbox, use the View menu to add them. The toolbox may be floating or anchored without impacting functionality. Drag the toolbox title bar to anchor or unanchor it*

FIGURE 5.5

Customer form Design view

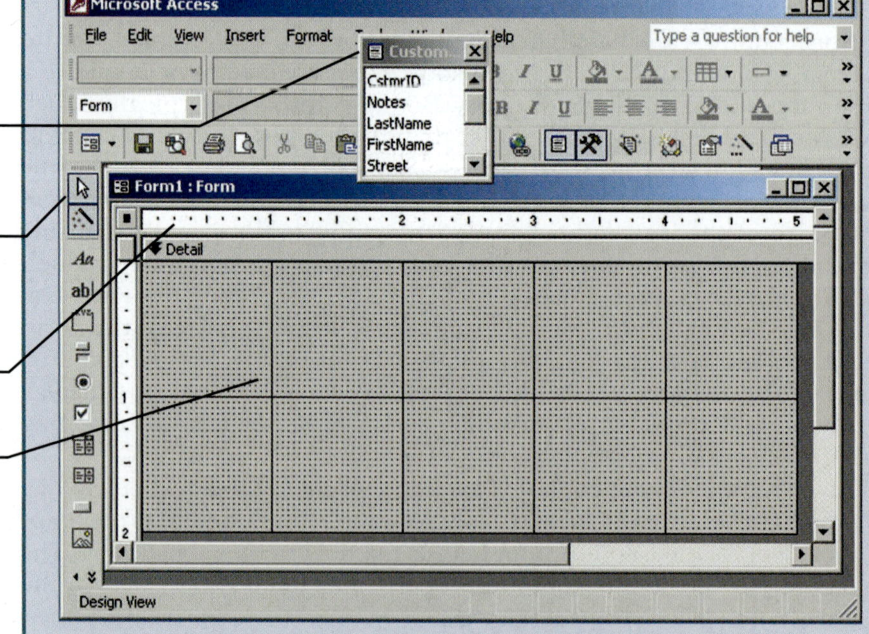

6. Select all of the fields in the Field List dialog box by double-clicking its title bar

tip: *If the field list is not displaying, click the Field List button on the Form Design toolbar*

7. Drag the selected fields to the form

tip: *Your form should generally match the appearance shown, but fields do not need to be positioned exactly since they will be moved to their final locations later*

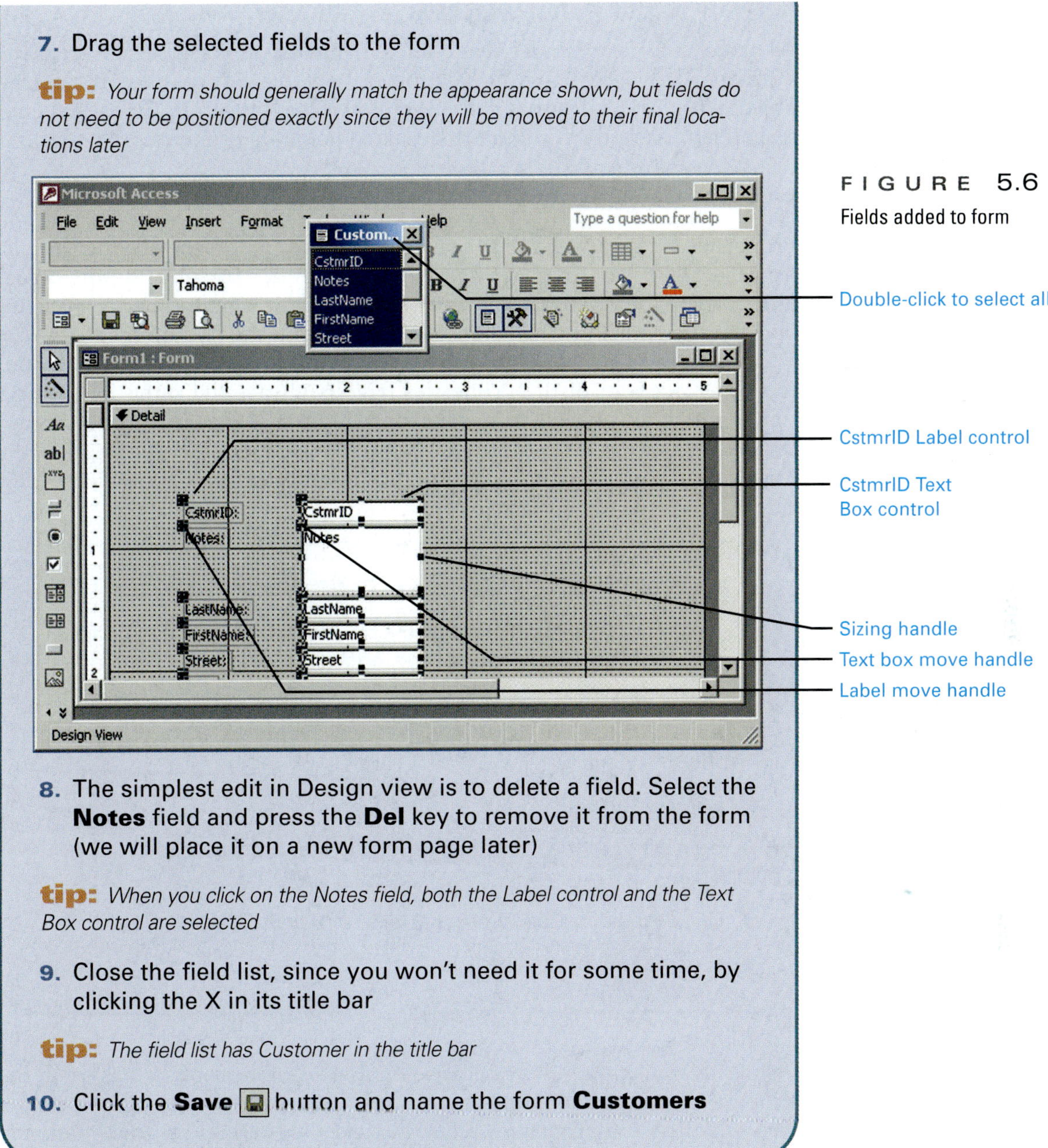

FIGURE 5.6
Fields added to form

8. The simplest edit in Design view is to delete a field. Select the **Notes** field and press the **Del** key to remove it from the form (we will place it on a new form page later)

tip: *When you click on the Notes field, both the Label control and the Text Box control are selected*

9. Close the field list, since you won't need it for some time, by clicking the X in its title bar

tip: *The field list has Customer in the title bar*

10. Click the **Save** button and name the form **Customers**

You now have created a blank form and added bound controls that will display data from the form's record source, the Customer table. Fields from the Field List dialog box can be added one at a time or in groups. To select multiple fields, click the first field and then hold down the Ctrl key as you click the other fields. As you experienced, double-clicking the Field List title bar will select all fields in the list. Once the fields are selected, drag and drop them on the form Detail section.

The form Detail section can be resized by dragging its borders. This is often necessary to make the form fit the controls it will display. The grid that displays in the Detail section is to help position the controls effectively. The rulers that appear at the top and left sides of the Detail section are to assist in positioning controls and also indicate the actual dimensions of the form. The Undo button can always be used to undo changes made to the Detail section or a control.

MODIFYING PROPERTIES

All objects have ***properties*** that control behavior. In Form Design view, the developer has access to all object properties, providing full control. One object with properties that can be set is the form itself. In turn, each control added to the form can be customized using its properties.

Form Properties

Properties are set using the ***Properties pages*** for an object (see Figure 5.7). An object's Properties pages can be opened either by selecting the object and clicking the Properties button on the Form Design toolbar or by right-clicking the object and selecting Properties from the pop-up menu.

The properties that can be set are specific to each type of object, but the general layout of the Properties page is always the same. The object that owns the Properties pages is listed in the title bar; the properties are divided by type on tabbed pages. The first Properties page to present is the Format page, which contains properties about how the object will display.

Changing form properties:

1. Verify that the **AC05PuppyParadise.mdb** database is open and that the **Customers** form created in the previous steps is in Design view
2. Right-click on the form and select **Properties** from the pop-up menu
3. Click in the Back Color property
4. Select the ellipse to the right of the current Back Color property
5. Click the second (yellow) square and click **OK**
6. Close the Properties pages

The form is now yellow because the Back Color property was set in the Properties pages. Changing the size of the form by dragging its borders also sets the form properties related to size. This could be done manually in the Properties pages, but it is easier to drag the borders. You can change the properties of the controls on a form by moving them, changing their size, or setting other properties on the Properties pages.

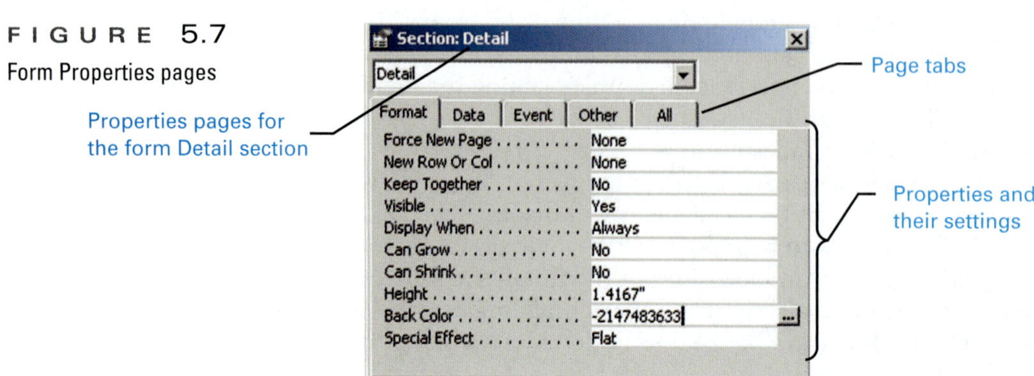

FIGURE 5.7
Form Properties pages

Adjusting Controls on a Form

Both a Label and a Text Box control represent each field from the table. Since developers typically want to manipulate both at the same time, both are selected when either one is clicked. The square ***handles*** that appear on a selected control can be used to resize it. A selected control can be moved to a new position on the form using drag and drop. The Text Box and Label controls for a field move in concert unless a move handle is used. The largest square (top left) on a Label or Text Box is called the ***move handle*** and will allow each component of the bound control to be moved independently.

Multiple controls on a form can be selected and operated on simultaneously. To select multiple controls, click and drag a selection box around the controls or click the first control and then hold down the Shift key while selecting subsequent controls. Once the controls are selected, resize, move, or set properties such as the background color.

task reference

Select and Move Form Controls

- Select the control to be operated on by clicking it. The Shift key can be used to select multiple controls
- Drag the control(s) to the new location. Use the large move handle to independently move components of a bound control

Repositioning Customers form controls:

1. Verify that the **AC05PuppyParadise.mdb** database is open and that the **Customers** form created in the previous steps is in Design view
2. First let's organize the work area. Click in the CstmrID text box to select the field and then drag it to the position shown in Figure 5.8

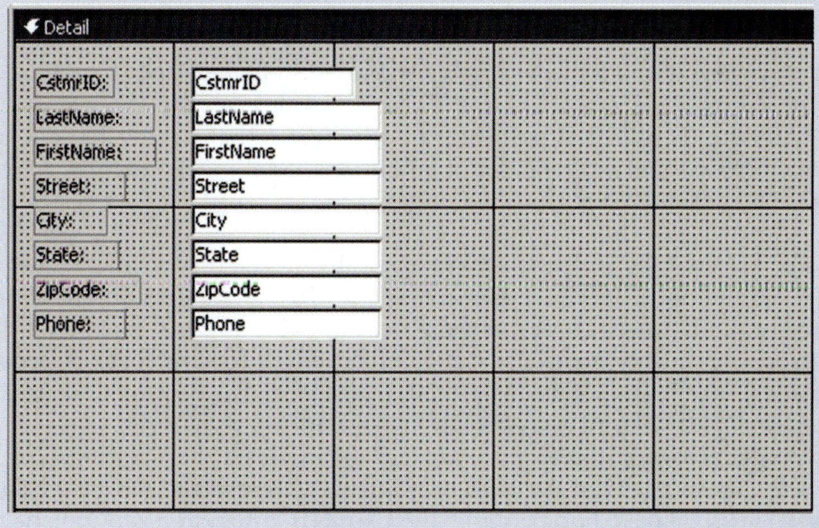

FIGURE 5.8
Repositioned Customers controls

3. Click and drag a selection box around the remaining fields and position them as shown in Figure 5.8

4. Now let's put the fields where Evan wants them. Select **FirstName** and drag it until it is on the same line and to the right of LastName

tip: *If something is selected that you don't want, deselect it by clicking on the form surface away from any control. The mouse pointer changes to a hand when you can drag the selection*

5. Select **Street** and move it up until it is under LastName
6. Select **City** and move it to the right of Street, aligned with FirstName
7. Select **State** and move it up until it is under Street
8. Select **ZipCode** and move it to the right of State, aligned with City
9. Select **Phone** and move it up until it is under State
10. Drag the borders of the Detail pane to reduce its size, as shown in Figure 5.9

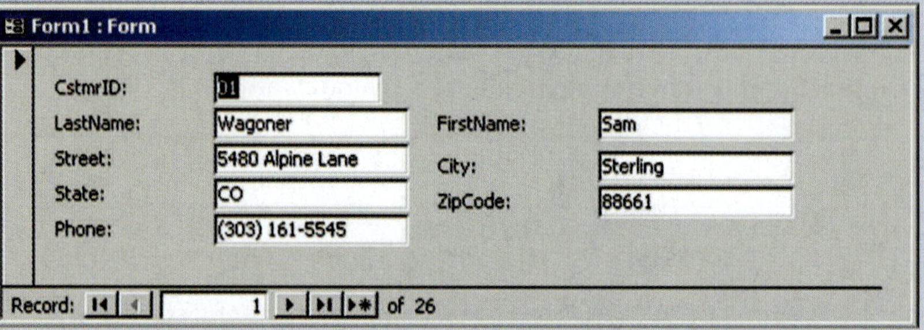

FIGURE 5.9
Customers Form view

11. Click the **Form view** button to preview the results

Click the **Design view** button and click the **Save** button to save the form as **Customers**

When moving fields it is important to notice the mouse pointer's shape. A hand with all of the fingers extended indicates that the selection can be moved to a new location. This will drag both the label and text box of a bound control. A pointing hand indicates that a move handle has been accessed to move the parts of a bound control independently. A two-headed arrow indicates that a ***sizing handle*** is being used to resize the control.

The field names from the table are usually picked for technical reasons and are often not what the user wants to see. To change the content of any label, set the Caption property of the field in Table Design. The benefit of setting this property is that its value is the default for any form or report created. A label can be directly edited, but this is effective for the current object only and will not be reflected in other forms or reports.

After previewing the form, Evan has decided that he wants spaces in the field labels. The fields need to be adjusted to match the size of the data that they will display. For example, the CstmrID, State, and ZipCode fields are much too large for their data. He would also like the labels to be right-justified and closer to the text boxes to make the relationship easier to view. These changes will require setting the properties of the Label controls.

task reference

Set Control Properties

- Right-click the control to open the pop-up menu
- Select **Properties** from the pop-up menu
- Select the appropriate Properties tab (usually Format)
- Navigate to the property and change its setting

Changing labels:

1. Verify that the **AC05PuppyParadise.mdb** database is open with the **Customers** form created in the previous steps in Design view
2. Click an insertion point in the CstmrID label and add a space between Cstmr and ID

tip: *With the label selected, use the I-beam to click an insertion point between the r and I. When this is successful, the label background becomes white and a blinking insertion point appears. This text edit area behaves like a little word processor*

3. Repeat this process for LastName, FirstName, and ZipCode

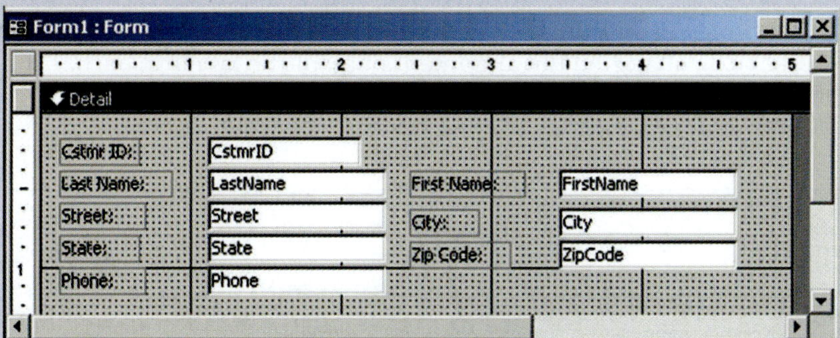

FIGURE 5.10
New labels for the Customers form

4. Now let's put the fields where Evan wants them. Use the **Shift** key with a mouse click to select every label on the form
   a. Right-click on a selected label and choose **Properties** from the pop-up menu
   b. Scroll down to Text Align and choose **Right**

tip: *All labels should be right-justified. If they are not, check your selection and try step 4b again*

   c. Close the Multiple Selection dialog box

5. Since the labels are in the correct position, you will move the text boxes to be closer to the labels. Select the CstmrID text box and use the move handle to reposition it until only one grid line shows between the label and the text box

FIGURE 5.11
Repositioned labels for the Customers form

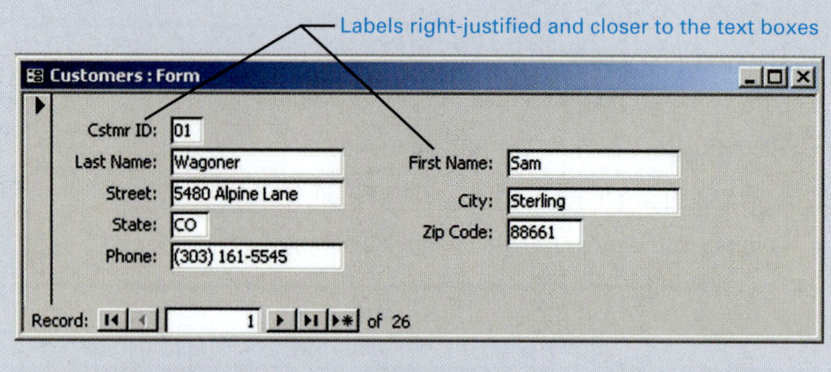

6. Repeat this process for all of the other labels
7. Select the text box for CstmrID and use the sizing handles to reduce its size to display about three characters
8. Check your results in Form view and adjust the field width as needed to properly display the data

tip: *You will need to move through the records and view the field with various data values to ensure that you have correctly modified the width*

9. Repeat this process for State and ZipCode
10. Save your changes

anotherway

. . . to change label text

The text displayed in a Label control is a property of that control. All properties, including the displayed text, can be changed from the Properties pages. Right-click on the label to activate the shortcut menu and select Properties to open the Properties pages. Set the Caption property to control the displayed text.

The properties of multiple selected objects can be set simultaneously. When working on multiple objects, the selected objects must be of the same type (e.g., changing the alignment of all of the labels in earlier steps). In the next steps you will simultaneously modify the properties of all of the text boxes on the form, by changing their Back Color and Font.

Changing text boxes:

1. Verify that the **AC05PuppyParadise.mdb** database is open and that the **Customers** form created in the previous steps is in Design view
2. Select all of the text boxes on the form by holding down the Shift key as you click
3. Open the Properties pages by clicking the **Properties** button from the toolbar (the shortcut menu also can be used)
4. Click in the **Font Name** property and select **Batang**

tip: *You will need to scroll down to find the Font property in the Format tab. If you do not have Batang, select another font. All available properties are in alphabetical order on the All tab. Move the Properties pages by dragging the title bar to see the results of your changes*

5. Click in the **Back Color** property and then click the ellipse
6. In the Color dialog box select the **Define Custom Colors** button to create a custom color for the text box backgrounds

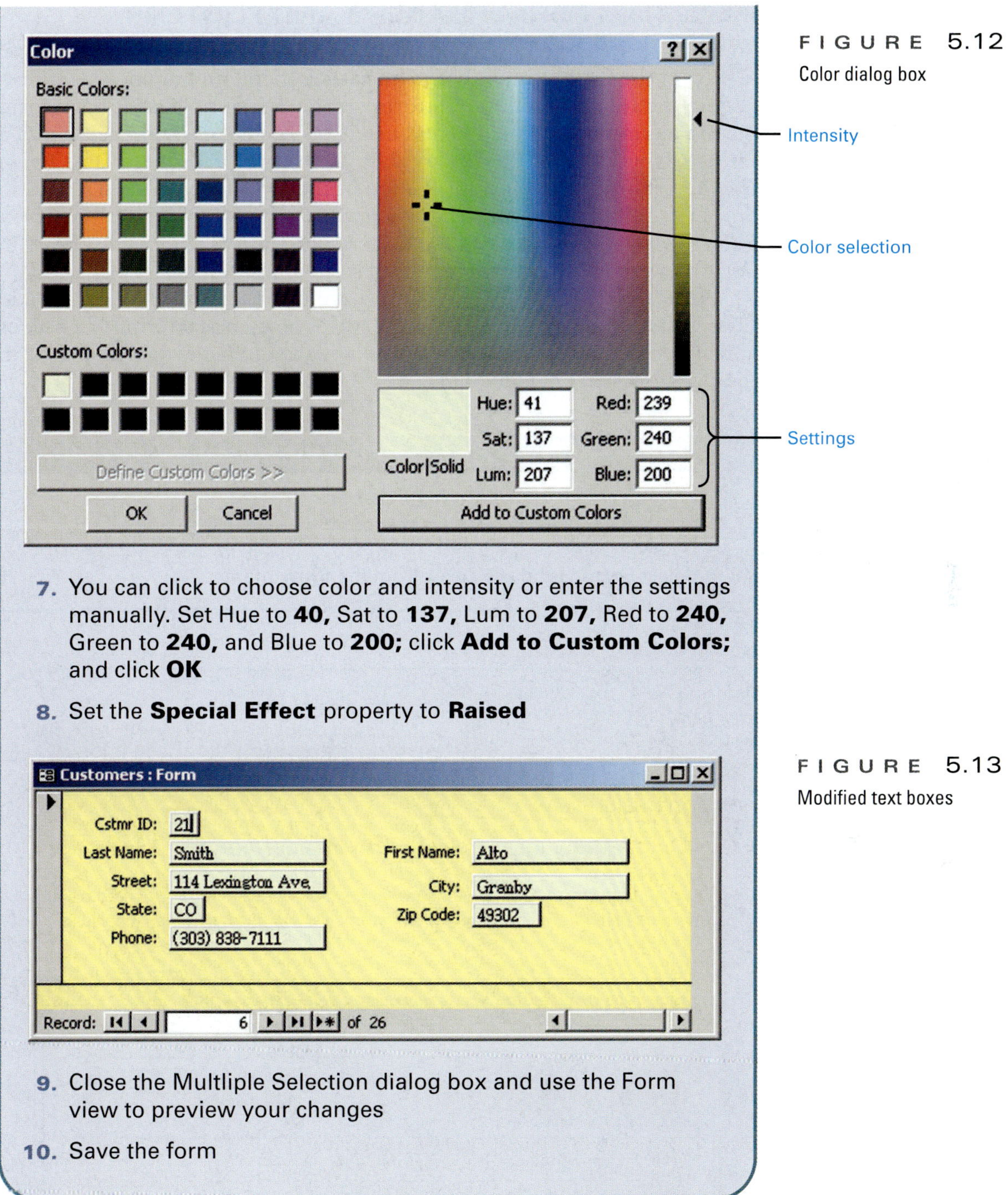

FIGURE 5.12
Color dialog box

7. You can click to choose color and intensity or enter the settings manually. Set Hue to **40,** Sat to **137,** Lum to **207,** Red to **240,** Green to **240,** and Blue to **200;** click **Add to Custom Colors;** and click **OK**
8. Set the **Special Effect** property to **Raised**

FIGURE 5.13
Modified text boxes

9. Close the Multiple Selection dialog box and use the Form view to preview your changes
10. Save the form

Although color adds interest and draws the eye, use color sparingly when creating forms that will be used frequently. The Microsoft Access default colors are used throughout the Office suite and users understand how the various colors are normally applied. Using these defaults can make your application easier to learn. In addition, color viewed over time can increase eye fatigue, making the screen harder to read.

If you do use color, be consistent in its application. The same color should always mean the same thing. Make sure that the contrast between the background color and the text color is sufficient for easy readability. In general, pale backgrounds with dark text are the most effective.

INSERTING FORM HEADERS AND FOOTERS

So far in this chapter, form modifications have been made to the Detail section of the form. Recall that in an earlier chapter a graphic was inserted into the Header section of a form created using a Wizard. Each form section has a specific function and behavior. The ***Form Detail section*** of a form is typically used to display data from a record source. The ***Form Header section*** will appear at the top of the form when it is displayed in Form view and at the beginning of a printed selection of forms. The ***Form Footer section*** will appear at the bottom of a form when it is displayed in Form view and at the end of a printed selection of forms.

Form Header and Footer sections are characteristically used to add titles, instructions, and buttons to the top or bottom of a form. The header and footer contents are static—they do not change as the data displayed in the Detail section changes.

Show Form Headers and Footers

- Open a form in Design view
- Select **Form Header/Footer** from the **View** menu

Adding Form Header/Footer:

1. Verify that the **AC05PuppyParadise.mdb** database is open and that the **Customers** form created in the previous steps is in Design view
2. On the **View** menu select **Form Header/Footer**

tip: *If both the Header and Footer sections do not display, drag the border of the Form Design window and expand it until all three form sections display*

FIGURE 5.14
Customers form with Header and Footer sections

Section bars

Section selectors

Customers : Form

Form Header

Detail

Cstmr ID: Cst
Last Name: LastName
Street: Street
State: Stat
Phone: Phone
First Name: FirstName
City: City
Zip Code: ZipCode

Form Footer

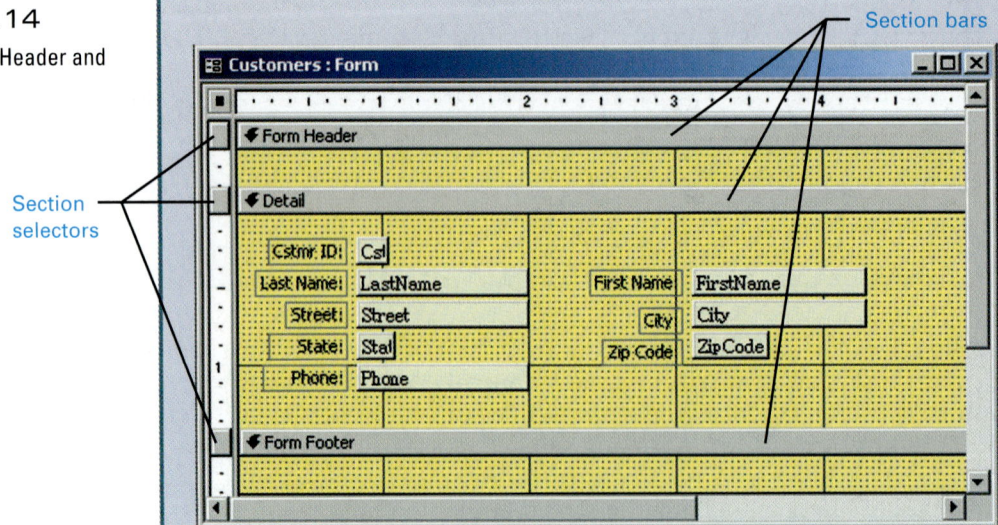

3. Use Form view to preview the changes

Deselecting Form Header/Footer on the View menu will remove both sections from the form along with any controls they contain. Either the Section selectors or Section bars (see Figure 5.14) can be used to select a form section. Once a section is selected, it can be operated on by adding controls or setting its properties.

anotherword

. . . on Form Headers and Footers

Headers and footers can only be added and removed together. If you don't want both a header and a footer, you can set the Visible property of the section that you don't want to No, or set its Height property to 0.

To complete Evan's design of the Customers form, you need to add the logo and form title. These are unbound controls that will be placed in the form header. The logo will be placed in an Image control and the form title will be in a Label control. These controls are available from the toolbox.

task reference

Add Toolbox Controls to a Form

- Open a form in Design view
- If necessary, activate the toolbox using the **Toolbox** button on the Form Design toolbar
- Verify that the Toolbox **Control Wizards** button is depressed (a blue outline will show around it)
- Click the toolbox control that is to be added to the form
- Click in the form section that will contain the control
- Set the control's properties by entering its contents, sizing, moving, and using the Properties pages

Adding content to the form header:

1. Verify that the **AC05PuppyParadise.mdb** database is open and that the **Customers** form created in the previous steps is in Design view
2. Select the **Image control** button from the toolbox and then click in the form header to activate the Control Wizard

tip: *If the Wizard does not activate, delete the Image control, click the Control Wizard button in the toolbox to activate Wizards, and repeat step 2*

3. The Image Control Wizard will open the Insert Image dialog box. Navigate to the data files for this chapter and select **AC05PupLogo.tif**. The logo shown in Figure 5.15 should display in the Image control
4. Click the **Label control** button in the toolbox and click in the form header next to the image
5. Type **Customers** (there is no Label Control Wizard)

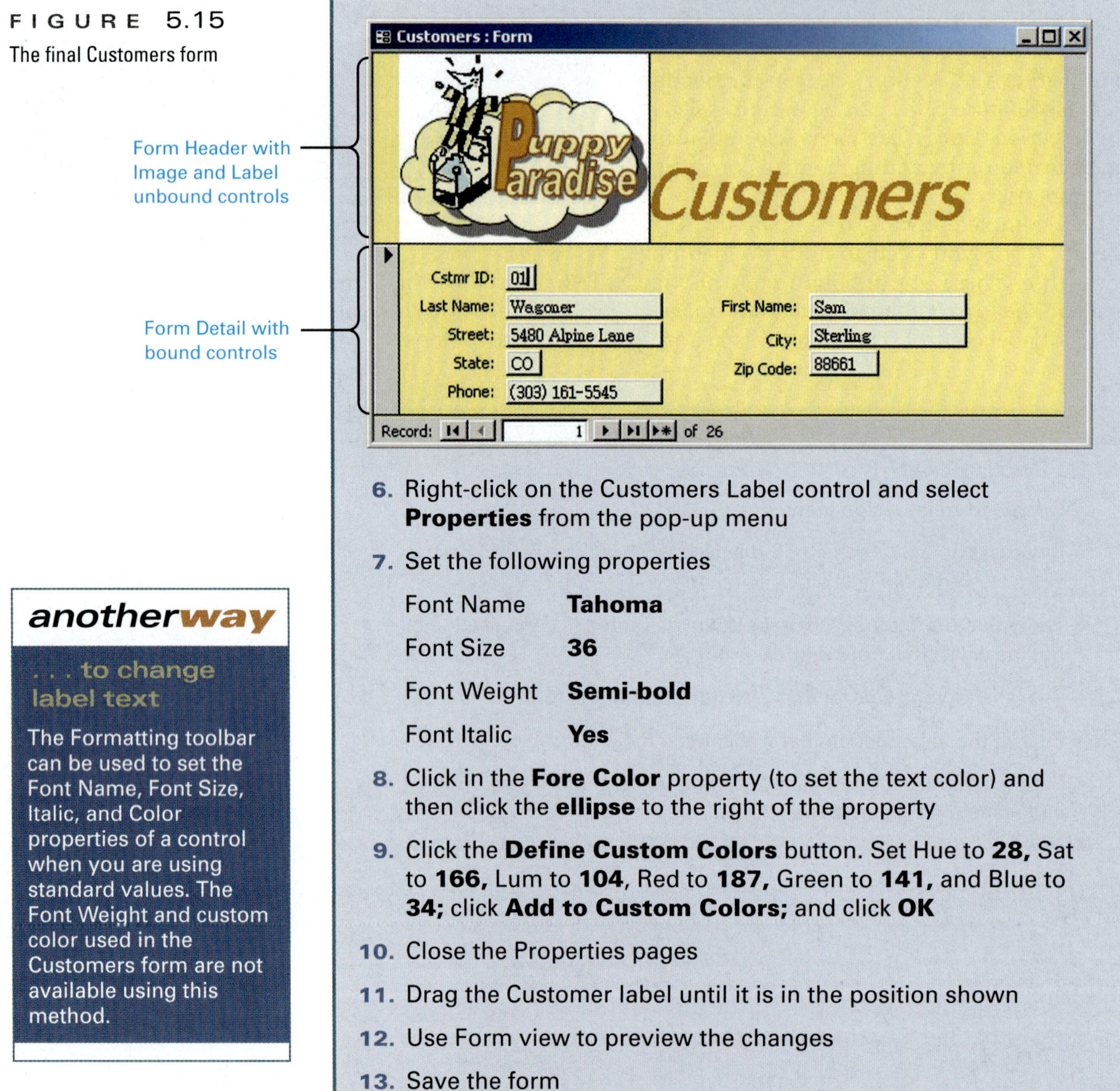

FIGURE 5.15
The final Customers form

6. Right-click on the Customers Label control and select **Properties** from the pop-up menu
7. Set the following properties

Font Name	**Tahoma**
Font Size	**36**
Font Weight	**Semi-bold**
Font Italic	**Yes**

8. Click in the **Fore Color** property (to set the text color) and then click the **ellipse** to the right of the property
9. Click the **Define Custom Colors** button. Set Hue to **28,** Sat to **166,** Lum to **104**, Red to **187,** Green to **141,** and Blue to **34;** click **Add to Custom Colors;** and click **OK**
10. Close the Properties pages
11. Drag the Customer label until it is in the position shown
12. Use Form view to preview the changes
13. Save the form

anotherway

. . . to change label text

The Formatting toolbar can be used to set the Font Name, Font Size, Italic, and Color properties of a control when you are using standard values. The Font Weight and custom color used in the Customers form are not available using this method.

In the previous steps, adding an Image control to the form initiated the Image Control Wizard. The complex controls in the toolbox have ***Control Wizards*** designed to walk users through the process of building the control's content. The Control Wizards button on the toolbox will enable and disable these Wizards. Figure 5.16 indicates which controls have Wizards available.

As controls are added to a form, they are actually layered so that the most recently added control is on the top layer. This layering is called ***z-order.*** You may notice as you adjust the position and size of controls that one may be on top of another. For example, in the Customers form header, the label is in front of the image because it was added last. To change the

Button Name	Control Wizard?	Button Name	Control Wizard?
Bound Object Frame	Yes	Option Button	Yes
Check Box	Yes	Option Group	Yes
Combo Box	Yes	Page Break	No
Command Button	Yes	Rectangle	No
Control Wizards	No	Select Objects	No
Image	Yes	Subform/Subreport	Yes
Label	No	Tab Control	No
Line	No	Text Box	No
List Box	Yes	Toggle Button	Yes
More Controls	No	Unbound Object Frame	Yes

FIGURE 5.16
Toolbox Control Wizards availability

z-order of a control, use cut and paste to remove it from its current layer and paste it to the top layer.

NAVIGATING DATA WITH FORMS

Besides using forms to page through data in the underlying record source (table or query), users need to be able to navigate directly to a specific record or records to perform maintenance. Forms already have been used to view data and print the current record, but it is also possible to use Find to navigate to a specific record and filters to create a subset of data to work on. Find and filters in Form view work in the same fashion as was covered in Datasheet view.

Finding Data with Forms

By default, a form displays all of the data in the underlying record source (table or query). When there are hundreds or even thousands of records, it can be an arduous task to find the ones that you want to work on without some helpful database tools.

Access provides a Find tool for locating and updating specific records. It can be used in many of the views of a database including the Form view. Click in the field containing the values to be searched, and then click the Find button on the toolbar. The Find and Replace dialog box is used to set the criteria for a search. Valid criteria are outlined in Figure 5.17.

When entering the Find What criteria, wildcards play an important role. A question mark (?) can be used to match any single character and the asterisk (*) wildcard will replace any number of characters. The Find and Replace dialog box also can be used to replace values that have been found. It is best to test the Find and then add the replace value so that data are not accidentally destroyed.

FIGURE 5.17
Find and Replace dialog box components

Find and Replace Dialog Box		
Critieria	***Action***	
Find What	Sets the value that will be matched in the search	
Look In	Determines what will be searched. The default is the active column, but you also can choose to search the entire table.	
Match	Any Part of Field	Matches if the *Find What* value is anywhere in the field
	Whole Field	Matches if the *Find What* value is all that is in the field
	Start of Field	Matches if the *Find What* value is at the start of the field
Search	All	Searches for a match in the entire *Look In* area
	Up	Searches for a match above the cursor in the *Look In* area
	Down	Searches for a match below the cursor in the *Look In* area
Match Case	Matches the case of *Find What* when clicked on	

Finding form records:

1. Verify that the **AC05PuppyParadise.mdb** database is open and that the **Customers** form created in the previous steps is in Form view
2. Select the **LastName** field and click the **Find** button on the toolbar
3. Enter ***g*** in the Find What criteria to find all last names containing the letter g, and click **Find Next**
4. Repeat clicking **Find Next** until no more matches are found

tip: *Wagoner, Gray, and Guo should all be found*

5. Close the Find dialog box

Filtering Form Records

Recall from the datasheet filtering discussion that there are four ways to apply filters. The first, Filter by Selection, returns records that match the value selected in the form. The second, Filter by Form, presents an empty version of the current form where match values can be typed. Filter for Input accepts a value or expression used to restrict the records and the Advanced Filter/Sort window presents a design grid used to create criteria from scratch. Regardless of the type of filter being applied, the goal is to select only records that meet the stated criteria. Creating the criteria is slightly different for each type of filter.

Filtering form records:

1. Verify that the **AC05PuppyParadise.mdb** database is open and that the **Customers** form created in the previous steps is in Form view
2. Navigate to the first record if necessary
3. Navigate to a record containing Wagoner and select the **g** (this is the same as *g*) and click **Filter By Selection** in the toolbar

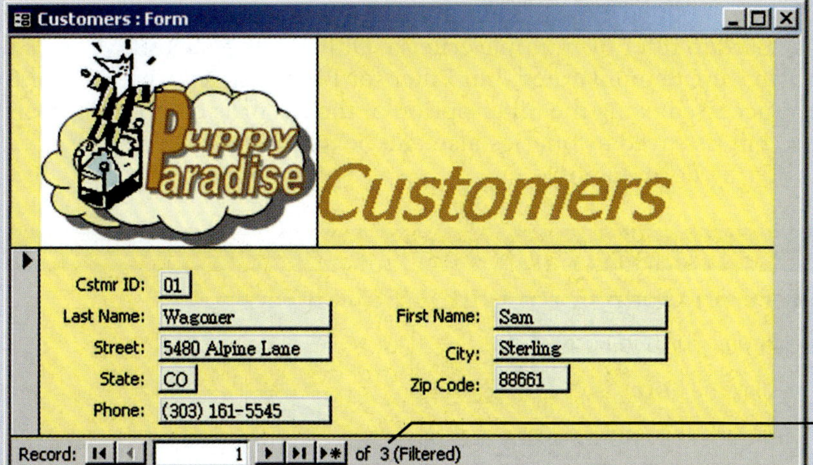

FIGURE 5.18
Filtered records by **g**

4. Use the navigation buttons to explore the filtered records
5. Use the **Remove Filter** button to return to the entire record set
6. Click the **Filter By Form** button. Like "*g*" should display as the current criteria
7. Click the **OR** tab and add the condition **s*** (Access will convert this to Like "s*") as a Last Name criterion
8. Click the **Apply Filter** button

tip: *Gray, Guo, Smith, and Wagoner should all be found*

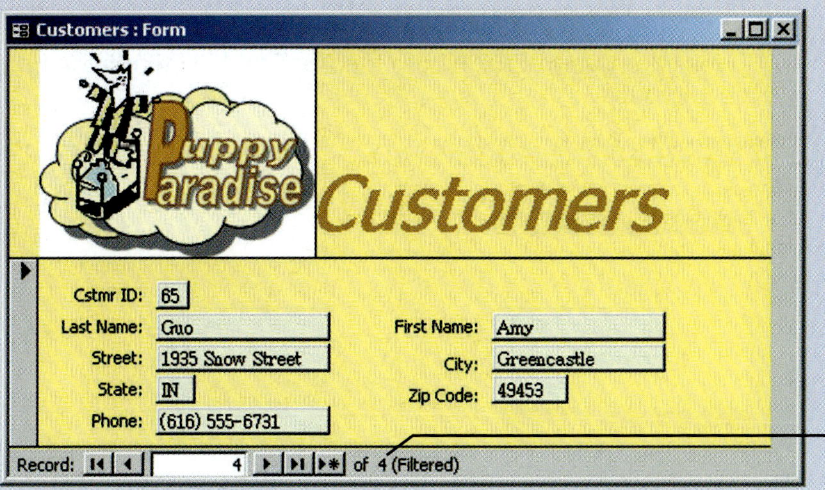

FIGURE 5.19
Filtered records by ***g* and s***

9. Use the navigation buttons to explore the filtered records
10. Use the **Save As Query** button and name the query **LastNameFilter**
11. Use the **Remove Filter** button to return to the entire record set

A filter can be saved as a query for reuse by clicking the Save As Query button on the Filter/Sort toolbar. Filter by Form and Filter for Input both can be used to filter by multiple criteria. Only Filter by Selection and Filter by Form were demonstrated, but Filter for Input and Advanced Filter/Sort can be accessed using the Filter option of the Records menu or the pop-up menu. Filters saved as queries also can be applied to an open form using the Filter by Form facility.

task reference

Query an Open Form with a Saved Filter

- Open a form in Form view
- Click the **Filter By Form** button
- Click the **Load From Query** button
- Select the query to be applied and click **OK**
- Click the **Apply Filter** button

Querying an open form:

1. Verify that the **AC05PuppyParadise.mdb** database is open and that the **Customers** form created in the previous steps is in Form view
2. Click the **Filter By Form** button
3. Click the **Load From Query** button
4. Choose **LastNameFilter** from the Applicable Filter dialog box and click **OK**

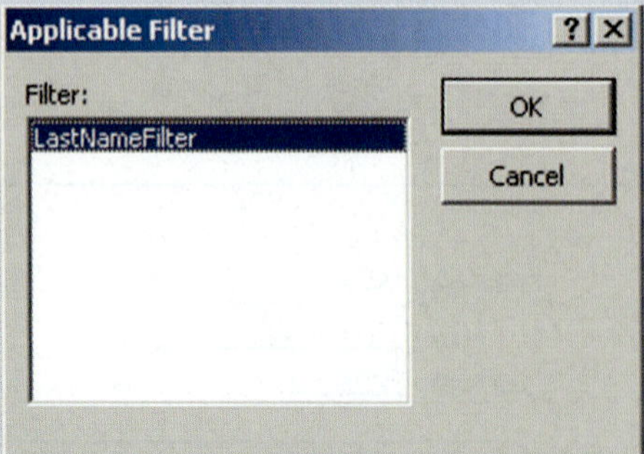

FIGURE 5.20
Applicable Filter dialog box

5. Click the **Apply Filter** button

Using Forms to Maintain Data and Print Selected Records

Forms are built to display and maintain data. Besides creating a custom interface, forms allow control over the subset of data being operated on. Recall that the form itself is based on a record source, which is a table or query. If the record source is a table, all records from that table can initially be viewed, maintained, or printed in the form. If the record source is a query, only the records selected by the query are available to the form.

When a filter or query is applied to the record source, a subset of the data matching the criteria is returned. Until the query or filter is removed, all operations are processed against the subset of data, which impacts the data that are available for maintenance, printing, and other operations.

One of the simplest mistakes to make is to forget to remove a query or filter and then apply another criterion. For example, if a filter to select Ohio customers is applied and then a filter for orders over $100, the result will be Ohio customers who ordered over $100 of goods. If the intent was to give a discount to all orders over $100, customers who are not from Ohio would be missed.

Printing all of the records in the record source is accomplished using the Print button on the toolbar. When forms were first introduced, you learned to use the Print dialog box activated from the File menu to print the current record using the Selected Records option. To print a specific subset of the data such as customers who ordered replacement parts, filter for that subset and then use the Print button to print the selected records.

making the grade SESSION 5.1

1. What would you do to change the alignment of all the labels on a form?
2. Describe the difference between bound and unbound controls.
3. What are object properties and why do you set them?
4. Why would you use Form Design view rather than a Wizard to create a form?

SESSION 5.2 COMPLEX REPORTS

The report object allows the creation of a custom hard copy output based on the data in one or more database tables. Printed output can be created using each of the database objects (forms, tables, and queries) that have already been explored, but the report object provides the greatest power and flexibility for creating printed output. Printed output from the other database objects is often used for internal analytical reporting, but when a report goes outside a department or organization, a formal report is usually created using the report object. Public reports, billing statements, and mailing labels are common organizational reports that could use the improved visual impact provided by custom reports.

DEFINING A REPORT IN REPORT DESIGN VIEW

Creating a report in Design view provides complete control of all of the report elements and their properties, making Design view much more powerful than using a Wizard. While the Report Design view is very similar to Form Design view, the process of building a report is more complex.

Report Sections

Reports can have up to seven types of sections (see Figure 5.21). The exact number of sections is determined by the report layout. The controls placed in the ***Report Detail section*** will appear once for each record in the underlying record source. The ***Group Header/Footer sections*** appear before and after each group of records. Group Header/Footer sections can be added individually or in pairs for each level of grouping in the report. The ***Page Header/Footer sections*** appear at the top and bottom of each report page. The ***Report Header/Footer sections*** are added in pairs and appear at the beginning and end of the report.

Each section has a ***Selection bar*** that can be adjusted to resize the section. Empty sections can have their size set to 0 or their Visible property set to No so that they do not display in the final report. If, for example, your report needs a Report Header but not a Report Footer, you could set the Report Footer size to 0.

The Report Header section normally contains the title of the report with the date and any other information that will print once at the beginning of the report. The Page Header contains information that should appear at the top of each page such as a page number, column headings for the report fields, and a reduced report title. The Group Header indicates the field or fields that will control data summaries.

The Group Footer section holds the summary that will be printed at the end of each detail group. For example, the order total would be printed each time the OrderNumber (group field) changes. The Page Footer section is used for page numbers and other information that needs to print at the bottom of every report page. If a report has both a Page Footer and a Report Footer, the print order of the last page is Report Footer and then Page Footer. The Report Footer section normally holds information that will be printed only once at the end of the report such as grand totals and report footnotes.

Since the Report Design view is complex, it is important to design a report before attempting to build it. One significant difference between designing forms and reports is that forms generally display one record per

FIGURE 5.21
Report sections

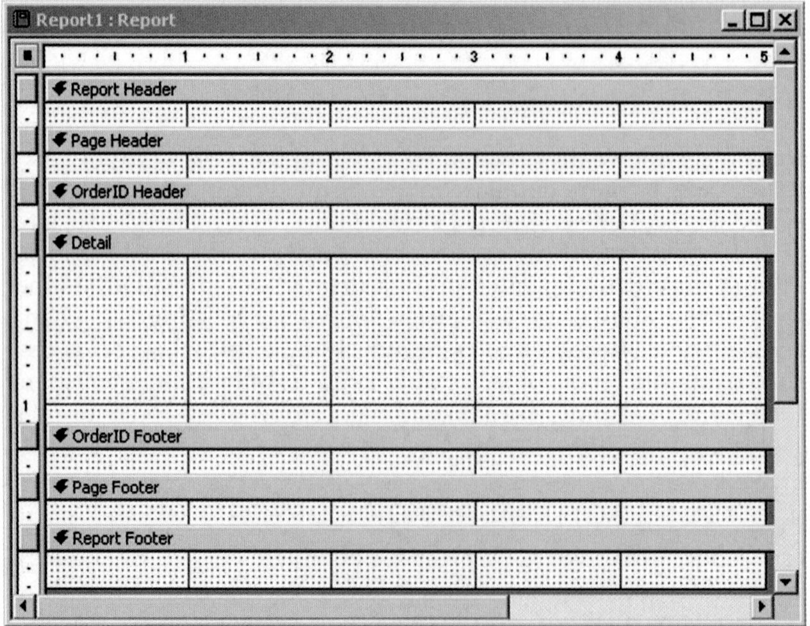

page in columns, while reports generally display several records of data per printed page in rows.

Start the report design with the Detail section by outlining where the rows of data will display. Decide what fields need to be included for each record. After documenting what fields are to be included, choose a layout for those fields and any other elements that are to be included such as a calculation or a graphic. The Detail section repeats for each record, so only one line of output needs to be specified. Figure 5.22 shows a sample form design for PuppyParadise Customers input.

Headers are generally easier to design than footers, so let's look at those next. Most reports have a title. If your title is to appear only once at the beginning of the report, place it in the Report header. If your title is to appear on every page, place it in the Page header. Some reports place a large-font title in the Report header and a small-font title in the Page header so that the report is identified on every page without wasting page space.

Report and Page headers can contain any other static data that your report requires. Candidates for these sections include page numbers, the report date, prepared by information, a report overview, and the company logo. The Page header should contain the column labels that identify the data in the Detail section. Group headers and footers will be discussed in the Calculating and Summarizing Data topic. Place the remaining information in the header that prints with the desired frequency. When a report contains both a Report header and a Page header, the Report header prints first on the initial report page.

Footers are pretty straightforward when there are no calculations involved. Place page numbers, explanatory text, legend of symbols, and preparation and use notes in the footer that prints with the frequency needed.

The design reflects the complete layout of the report including titles, graphics, captions, and field lengths. In the design shown, the field captions appear as Evan wants to see them on the report and Xs are used to

FIGURE 5.22
Customers report design

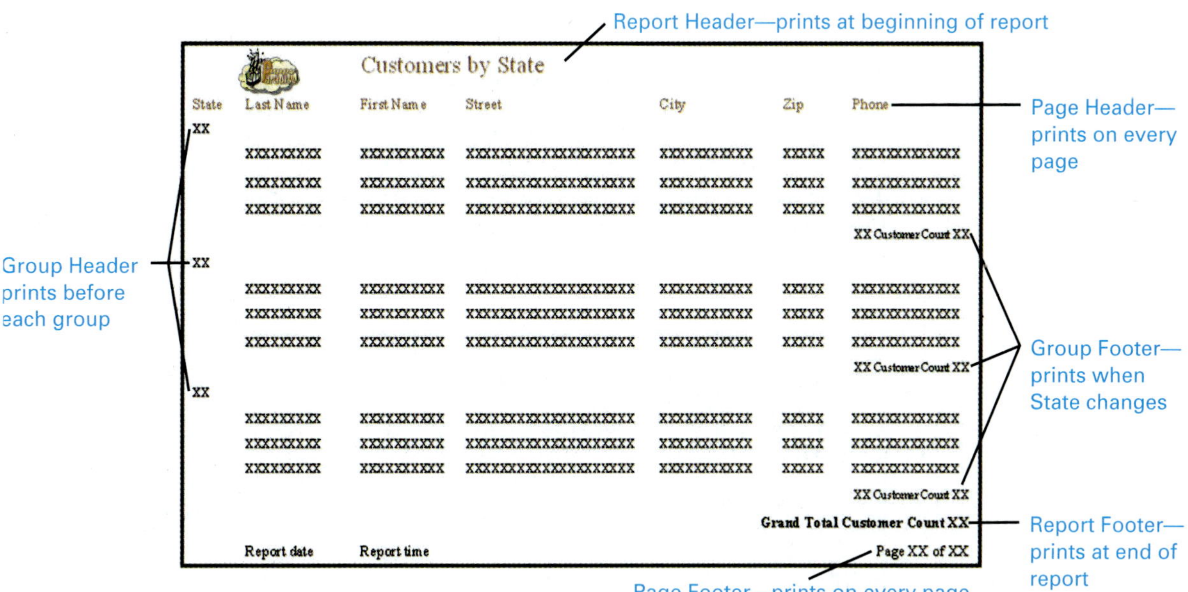

indicate where the data will display and the length of the data display area. The fields placed in the Detail section will print for each record in the record source and are depicted on the design as the repeated lines within each state group. The notations with the figure indicate the contents of the other report sections.

In Report Design view, field captions will be in Label controls and the field data will be displayed in Text Box controls. The data are grouped by state and a count of customers in each state is displayed. The PuppyParadise logo will display in an Image control and the form title will be entered in a Label.

Since a common development technique is to build a report using the AutoReport Wizard and then to customize it in Design view, it is important to understand how the Wizard behaves. The Wizard places the title provided in the Report Header section. The date and page numbers are placed in the Page Footer. The field names are used as column headings and are placed in the Page Header when there is no grouping.

Whether the report is developed completely in Report Design view or was customized after the Wizard created the first cut, it is called a ***custom report.*** Custom reports are more time consuming to create and maintain and should be used only when the Wizard cannot create the output that is needed.

The Report Toolbox and Field List

The toolbox used in Report Design view is the same as that used in Form Design view. Recall that the toolbox can be positioned anywhere on the screen and has Screen Tips that can be activated and deactivated using the View menu. The toolbar buttons are presented in Figure 5.4 if you need to review them.

When a control is placed in a report section, its properties direct what it will display and how it will appear. The Data properties of a bound control (those linked to a record source) are set to direct what field it will display. Data properties are set automatically when the record source Field List is used to add the control to your report or when the first cut of the report is created with the Wizard. Control Wizards with step-by-step instructions are available for the more complex toolbox options. Figure 5.16 outlines the availability of Control Wizards.

Customizing an AutoReport Wizard Form

To become familiar with the Report Design view, we'll start with a simple report on the PuppyParadise Customer table that has been built for you. The Wizard was used to create a report that will display all of the Customer fields except Notes in order by customer name within state. The report was saved as AutoReportCustomer.

Customizing the Customer AutoReport:

1. Verify that the **AC05PuppyParadise.mdb** database is open
2. In the Database window, select the **Reports** object and the **AutoReportCustomer** report, and click the **Design View** button

3. Explore the report design. Notice that some fields are too wide and some too narrow (Street and PhoneNumber do not completely display)

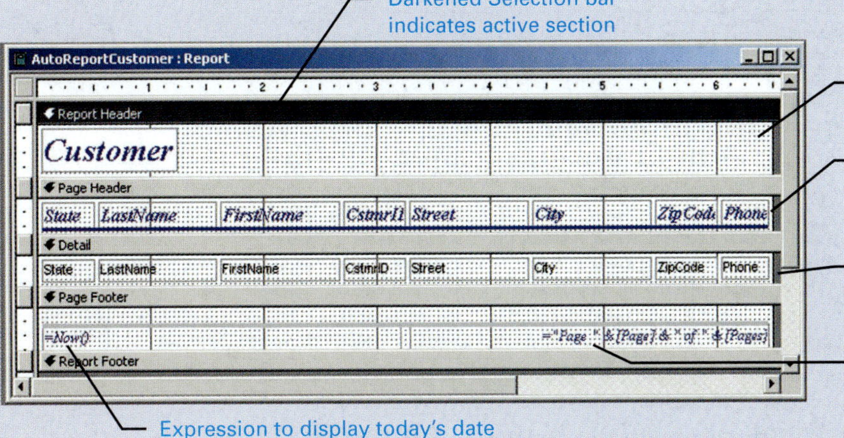

FIGURE 5.23
AutoReportCustomer

4. Use the **Print Preview View** button to preview the report and then return to Design view
5. Modify the field labels as follows

LastName	**Last Name**
FirstName	**First Name**
CstmrID	**ID**
ZipCode	**Zip**

tip: *Click an insertion point in the label and then make corrections*

6. Use the sizing handles to reduce the size of the Label and text box controls associated with State, Last Name, First Name, ID, City, and Zip

tip: *Use the View and Design buttons to move between Report views and verify the validity of your results. Each field should display all of the heading and data without too much space left over*

7. Use the move handle to adjust the positions of Last Name, First Name, ID, and Street, removing the extra space between them caused by reducing field sizes
8. Use the sizing handles to increase the size of Street until all of its data display on every detail row of the report
9. Move City, Zip, and Phone to adjust for the resizing, as shown in Figure 5.24
10. Resize Phone so that it will display the complete phone number
11. Edit the title to read **Customers by State**
12. Preview your results and save your changes when you are satisfied

FIGURE 5.24
Edited AutoReportCustomer

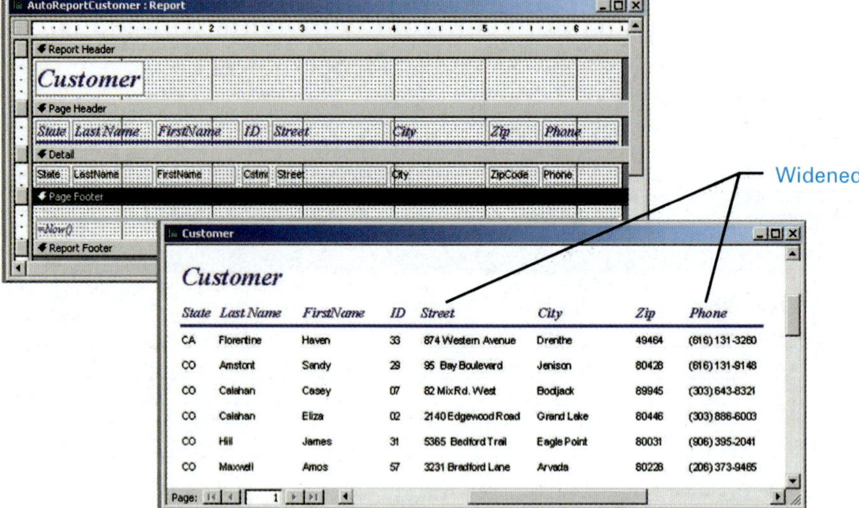

another**way**

. . . to resize a control

Controls also can be resized using the Format menu. Select the control(s) to be resized and then select **Size** from the **Format** menu. The **To Fit** option will adjust the selected controls to the size of the data they will display.

In this process the contents of the Report Header, Page Header, and Detail sections of this simple report were edited. The Page Footer contains expressions that will be discussed later. The Report Footer has been set to a Height of 0 so that it will not display.

Building a Form in Design View

Let's build a Customers by State Report in Design view. The CstmrsByState query has already been prepared as the record source to simplify the process.

task reference

Create a Report in Design View

- In the Database window click the **Reports** object and click the **New** button
- Click **Design View** as the way to develop the report, select the record source from the drop-down list, and click **OK**

Building the Customer report in Design view:

1. Verify that the **AC05PuppyParadise.mdb** database is open
2. In the Database window, select the **Reports** object and click the **New** button
3. In the New Report dialog box, select **Design view,** select **CstmrsByState** as the record source, and click **OK**
4. Double-click on the title bar of the Field List to select all of the fields from the record source table, drag the fields to the Detail section of the report, and drop them

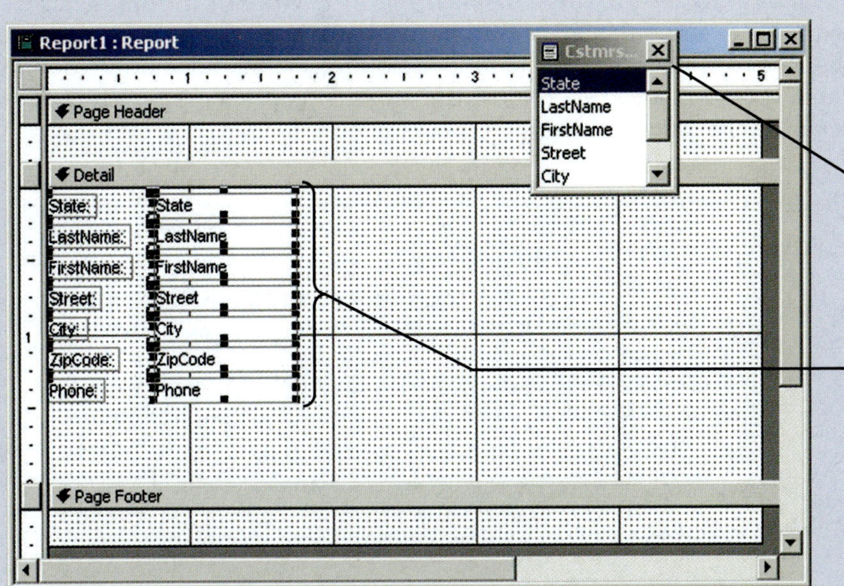

FIGURE 5.25
Customer fields placed in the Detail section

5. Click on the design background to deselect the fields and then close the Field List since it won't be used again
6. Use Shift to select all of the labels with field headings and use Cut to remove them from the Detail section
7. Click the **Page Header bar** and paste the labels there
8. With all of the labels selected, activate the Properties pages and change the Font Size to **10** points, Font Weight to **bold,** and Fore Color to the custom brown previously developed
9. Organize the labels in the Page Header and the text boxes in the Detail section as shown in Figure 5.26

FIGURE 5.26
Page Header and Detail section

tip: *Remember to use View options to preview your results. Use move handles and size handles to adjust the position and size of controls. Get the labels and text boxes as close as you can to the positions shown. We'll work on exact alignment in the next set of steps*

10. Reduce the size of the Details section by dragging the Page Footer Selection bar up until there is just enough room for the text boxes
11. Use the **View** button to preview the results. Make any needed adjustments to column widths
12. Save the report as **CustomerByState2**

In Figure 5.26 the text displaying in the column headings has been changed to match the labels that Evan wants. You still need to apply those changes to your report. By default, a colon (:) is included after each field name. You will need to remove the colons, add spaces, and abbreviate headings that are too long.

Editing label Captions:

1. Verify that the **AC05PuppyParadise.mdb** database is open and that **CustomerByState2** is open in Design view
2. Click on the **State** label and use the **Properties** button to open its Properties pages
3. Remove the colon from the **Caption** property
4. Use the drop-down list at the top of the Properties pages to move to the next label (LastName)

tip: *The text box controls are represented by the field name of the data they will contain. Labels are numbered beginning with Label01*

5. Edit this label to remove the colon (:); add spaces between words
6. Repeat this process for FirstName, Street, City, State, and Phone
7. Use the drop-down list at the top of the Properties pages to select the **ZipCode**
8. Remove the colon from the **Caption** and edit it to read **Zip**
9. Preview and save your changes

You also could have clicked in each label and edited the Captions directly. Use whichever method you prefer. Working in the Properties pages can be easier when you are setting multiple properties or working on multiple controls. Editing in the form is simpler when you are changing the Caption of a label or two.

The foundation of the final report is complete, but the controls need to be aligned exactly before moving on to the other report sections. Access provides an *Align* command that allows multiple controls to be selected and aligned to each other or to the grid. A row of objects can be aligned by their top edges (Align Top) or their bottom edges (Align Bottom). A column of objects can be aligned by their left edges (Align Left) or right edges (Align Right). Once the controls are aligned to each other, drag them as a unit to their exact report position.

For the Customer by State report to look professional, the rows need to be straight and the headings need to align exactly over the data. The Align command is the way to make that happen.

Aligning Customer report controls:

1. Verify that the **AC05PuppyParadise.mdb** database is open and that **CustomerByState2,** created in the previous steps, is open in Design view
2. Select all of the Label controls in the Page Header section by clicking the first control and then holding down the Shift key to select the remaining controls
3. Activate the **Format** menu, choose **Align,** and then click **Top** to align the tops of the selected controls

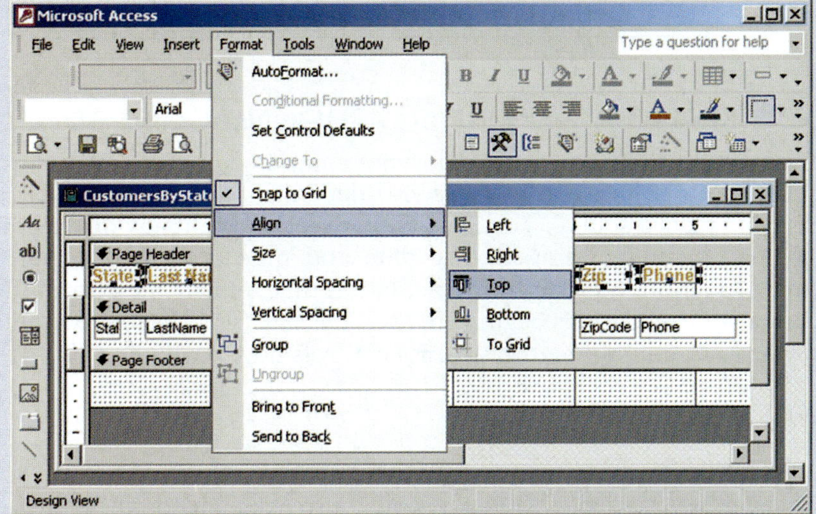

FIGURE 5.27
Aligning control tops

4. Now that the labels are aligned to each other, move them (they are already selected) to the top of the Header section
5. Repeat this process to align the text box controls and place them at the top of the Details section
6. Select the State label and hold down the Shift key and select the State text box
7. Activate the **Format** menu, choose **Align,** and then click **Left** to align the left sides of the controls
8. Adjust the position of both controls if necessary
9. Repeat steps 6 through 8 for the remaining Header/Detail pairs as needed to make your report look like Figure 5.28
10. Preview and save the report

Now that the detail portion of the report is complete, it is time to add the contents of the Page Footer and the Report Header.

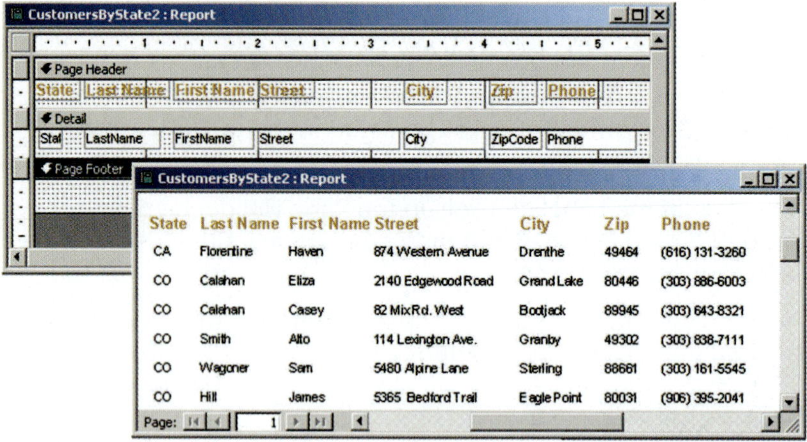

FIGURE 5.28
Aligned report

ADDING AND MODIFYING UNBOUND CONTROLS

The remaining elements of the report are composed of unbound controls. Recall that unbound controls are not dependent on the values in the underlying record source. The Page Footer section is already on the form, so we will begin building it. The date and time are added using the *=Now()* function, a predefined calculation that returns the current date and time. All calculations begin with an equal sign (=). The format applied to the text box containing the =Now() controls how it will display.

Building the Page Footer

The Page Header was added to the form to contain the field labels. When the header was added, the Page Footer also was added since they are paired. The report that Evan designed has the report date, time, and page number at the bottom of each page or in the Page Footer.

Adding the Customer report date and time:

1. Verify that the **AC05PuppyParadise.mdb** database is open and that **CustomerByState2,** created in the previous steps, is open in Design view
2. If the toolbox is not displaying, select the **Toolbox** button to activate it
3. Select the **Text Box** ab| tool from the toolbox and click in the Page Footer

tip: *The label displays the word Text with a number. Your number may be different since it reflects what you have been doing in your session*

4. Select the label and press **Del** since the report doesn't need it
5. Select the text box (it says unbound) and use the move handle to move it to the left side of the report, as shown in Figure 5.29
6. Click in the text box and type =**Now()** and use the View button to preview your changes

FIGURE 5.29
Text box with Label added to Page Footer

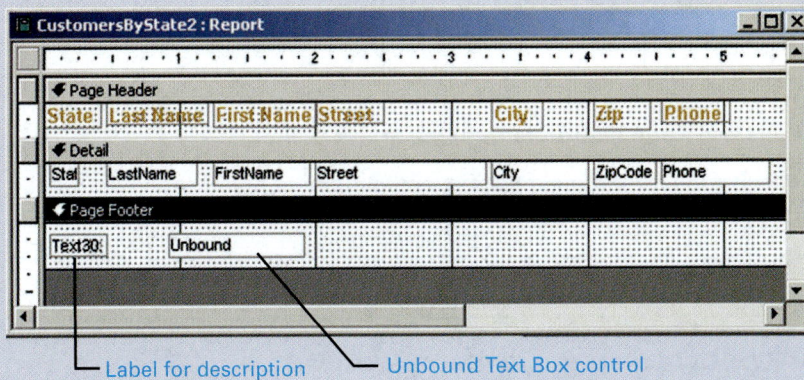

Label for description — Unbound Text Box control

tip: *You will need to scroll to the bottom of the report. Both the date and time should display in one text box until the format is changed*

7. Select the text box and use **Ctrl+C** to place it on the Clipboard
8. Select the Page Footer and use **Ctrl+V** to paste a second copy of the text box in the footer
9. Position the second copy to the right of the first
10. Click the leftmost text box, use the **Properties** button to activate the Properties pages, and set the Format property to **Long Date**
11. Set the Format property of the second text box to **Medium Time** and the Text Align property to **Left**

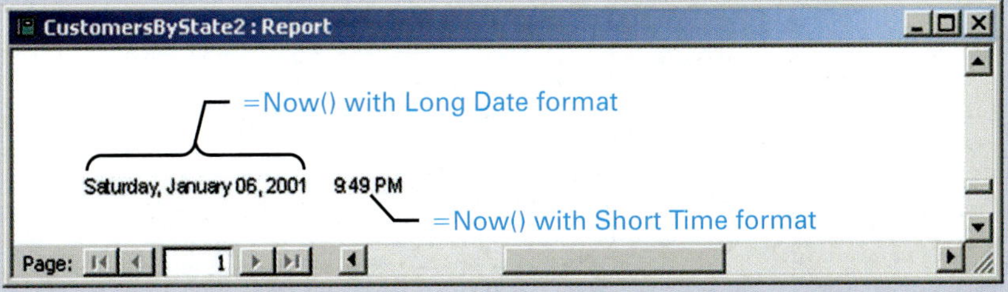

FIGURE 5.30
Date and time in Page Footer

=Now() with Long Date format — =Now() with Short Time format

12. Use the View button to preview your changes and make any needed adjustments to the position and size of the text boxes
13. Save the report

Two text boxes with the =Now() calculation were used to display the date and time so that they could be formatted the way that Evan wanted them. Whenever this report is printed, the =Now() function will retrieve the current system date and time. The text box format will cause the first text box to display a long date and the second to display a medium date.

Page numbers are added to a report in a similar fashion with an unbound control and a function. The text box and function can be entered manually or from the Insert menu. Regardless of how the page function is added, it automatically places the correct page number on each page of the report.

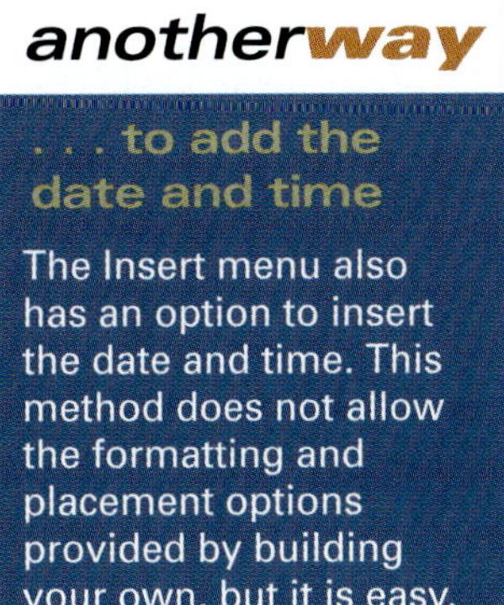
anotherway
. . . to add the date and time
The Insert menu also has an option to insert the date and time. This method does not allow the formatting and placement options provided by building your own, but it is easy.

task reference

Add Page Numbers to a Report in Design View

- Display the report in Design view
- Choose **Page Numbers** from the **Insert** menu
- Select the formatting, position, and alignment options that you want and click **OK**

Adding page numbers to the Customer report:

1. Verify that the **AC05PuppyParadise.mdb** database is open and that **CustomerByState2,** created in the previous steps, is open in Design view
2. Choose **Page Numbers** from the **Insert** menu
3. Choose the following options:

   Page N of M

   Bottom of Page [Footer]

   Alignment—Right

   Show Number on First Page—Checked

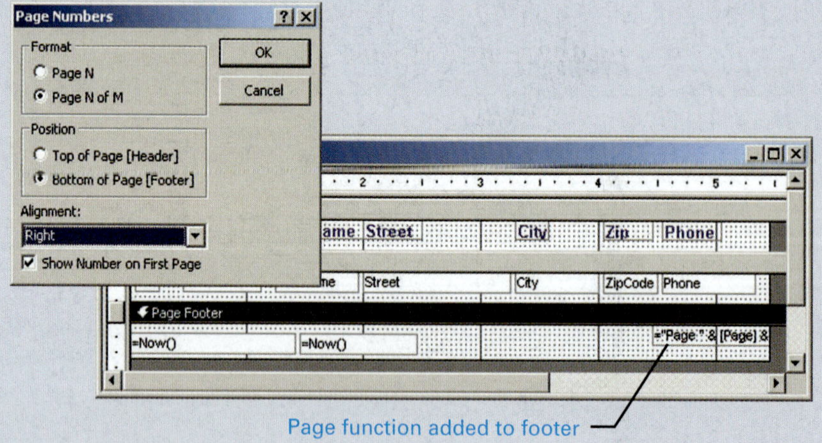

FIGURE 5.31
Page Numbers dialog box

4. Click **OK**
5. Use the View button to preview the results
6. Save the report

Any other information that is to print at the bottom of each report page can be added using the methods demonstrated.

Building the Report Header

To complete the basic report, the Report Header section will need to be added to hold the report title. Recall that a Report Header appears only once at the beginning of a report. The title will be entered in a Label and formatted with an increased font size and color.

Adding the Report Header to the Customer report:

1. Verify that the **AC05PuppyParadise.mdb** database is open and that **CustomerByState2,** created in the previous steps, is open in Design view
2. Click the **View** menu option and select **Report Header/ Footer** to add the sections to the report
3. If the toolbox is not displaying, select the **Toolbox** button to activate it
4. Select the **Image** tool from the toolbox and click the Report Header

tip: *If the Image Control Wizard does not initiate, click the Control Wizards button in the toolbox*

5. Navigate to the files for this chapter and chose **AC05PupLogo.tif** as the graphic to display
6. Select the **Label** tool from the toolbox and click in the Report Header to the right of the logo
7. Type **Customers by State**

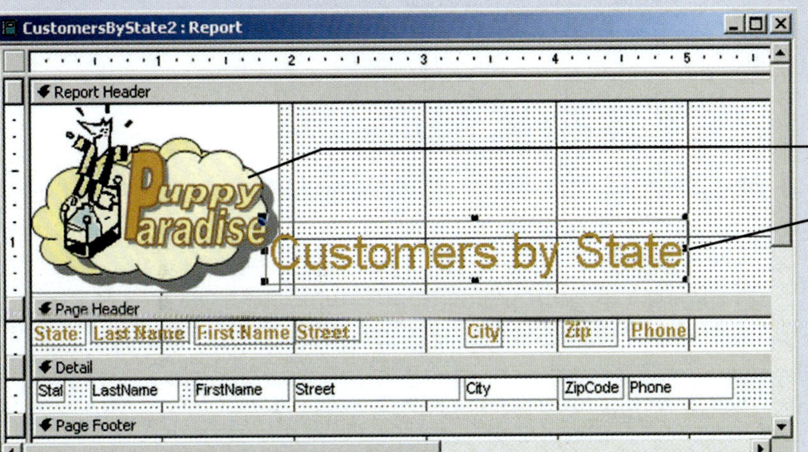

FIGURE 5.32
Report header

8. Select the title label and open the Properties pages, set the Font Size to **26,** and the Fore Color to the custom brown previously added to the palette
9. Choose **To Fit** from the **Size** option of the **Format** menu to expand the label
10. Use the View button to preview the results
11. Save the report

It should now be apparent that creating and using custom colors is easy when they are added to the palette. Custom colors can greatly enhance the professional look of any report.

Adding Separators

The AutoReport Wizard places lines to separate the data from the column headings and page footer. The Line control is used to add such separators to your report. Like other report objects, the properties of the line determine how it displays.

Adding Separators to the Customer report:

1. Verify that the **AC05PuppyParadise.mdb** database is open and that **CustomerByState2,** created in the previous steps, is open in Design view
2. Use the Detail section border to expand the height of the Page Header section to make space for the line
3. Click the **Line** tool on the Drawing toolbar
4. Click in the Page Header section below the column headers, hold down the Shift key, and drag the line the full width of the report

tip: *Holding down the Shift key while dragging a line keeps the line straight. You can use this technique when resizing the line too*

5. Activate the Line's Properties pages
   a. Set the Border Color to the custom brown that you have developed
   b. Set the Border Width to 1 pt
   c. Close the Properties dialog box
6. Use the Report Footer border to expand the height of the Page Footer section making room for the line
7. Select the Line tool and hold down the Shift key while dragging a line above the Page Footer controls
8. Activate the Line's Properties pages and set the Border Color to the custom brown that you have developed and the Border Width to 1 pt
9. Use the View button to preview the results and adjust the lines to match the left and right margins of the data
10. Save the report

Evan would like the report to present the data in order by state and customer name. He also wants the number of customers in each state counted.

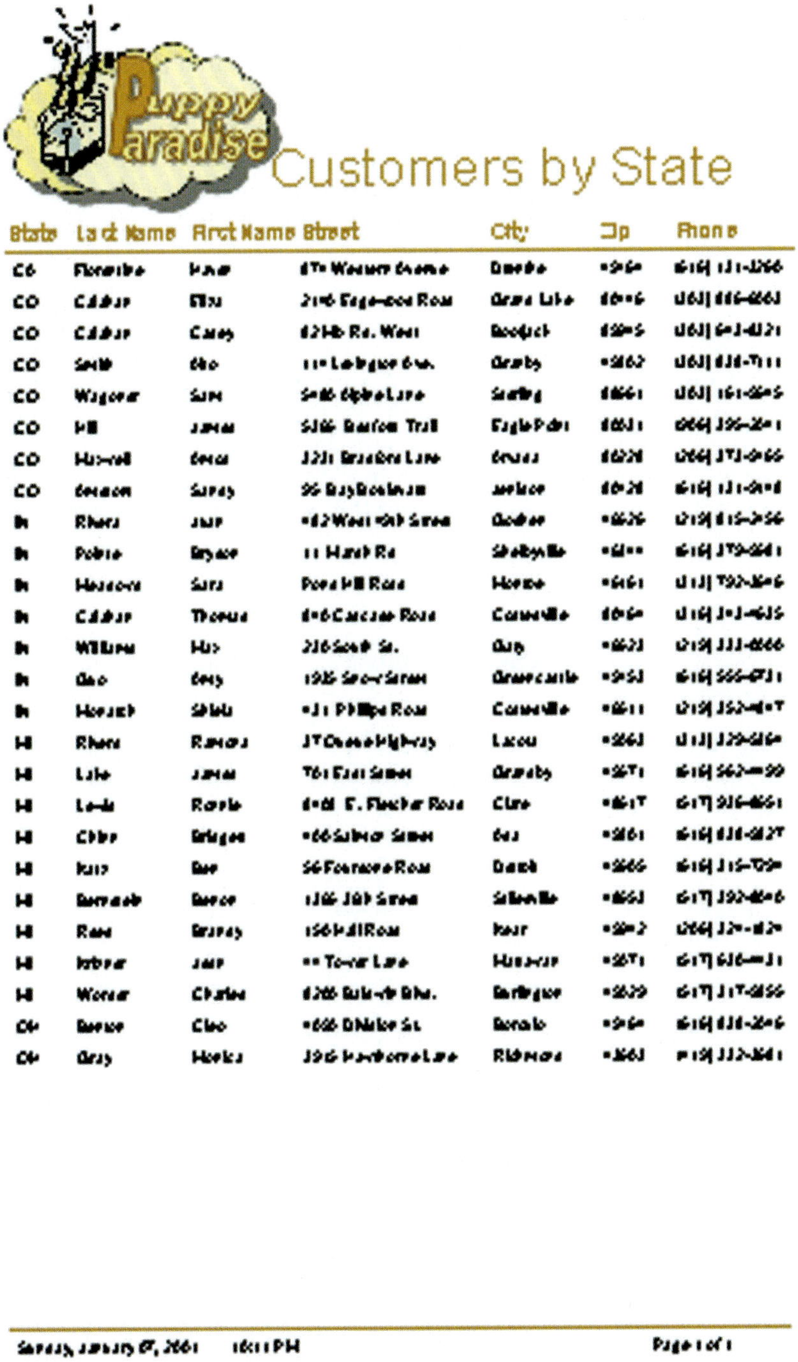

Puppy Paradise Customers by State

State	Last Name	First Name	Street	City	Zip	Phone
CO	[illegible]	[illegible]	[illegible]	[illegible]	[illegible]	[illegible]
CO	[illegible]	[illegible]	[illegible]	[illegible]	[illegible]	[illegible]
CO	[illegible]	[illegible]	[illegible]	[illegible]	[illegible]	[illegible]
CO	[illegible]	[illegible]	[illegible]	[illegible]	[illegible]	[illegible]
CO	[illegible]	[illegible]	[illegible]	[illegible]	[illegible]	[illegible]
CO	[illegible]	[illegible]	[illegible]	[illegible]	[illegible]	[illegible]
CO	[illegible]	[illegible]	[illegible]	[illegible]	[illegible]	[illegible]
CO	[illegible]	[illegible]	[illegible]	[illegible]	[illegible]	[illegible]
IN	[illegible]	[illegible]	[illegible]	[illegible]	[illegible]	[illegible]
IN	[illegible]	[illegible]	[illegible]	[illegible]	[illegible]	[illegible]
IN	[illegible]	[illegible]	[illegible]	[illegible]	[illegible]	[illegible]
IN	[illegible]	[illegible]	[illegible]	[illegible]	[illegible]	[illegible]
IN	[illegible]	[illegible]	[illegible]	[illegible]	[illegible]	[illegible]
IN	[illegible]	[illegible]	[illegible]	[illegible]	[illegible]	[illegible]
IN	[illegible]	[illegible]	[illegible]	[illegible]	[illegible]	[illegible]
MI	[illegible]	[illegible]	[illegible]	[illegible]	[illegible]	[illegible]
MI	[illegible]	[illegible]	[illegible]	[illegible]	[illegible]	[illegible]
MI	[illegible]	[illegible]	[illegible]	[illegible]	[illegible]	[illegible]
MI	[illegible]	[illegible]	[illegible]	[illegible]	[illegible]	[illegible]
MI	[illegible]	[illegible]	[illegible]	[illegible]	[illegible]	[illegible]
MI	[illegible]	[illegible]	[illegible]	[illegible]	[illegible]	[illegible]
MI	[illegible]	[illegible]	[illegible]	[illegible]	[illegible]	[illegible]
MI	[illegible]	[illegible]	[illegible]	[illegible]	[illegible]	[illegible]
MI	[illegible]	[illegible]	[illegible]	[illegible]	[illegible]	[illegible]
OH	[illegible]	[illegible]	[illegible]	[illegible]	[illegible]	[illegible]
OH	[illegible]	[illegible]	[illegible]	[illegible]	[illegible]	[illegible]

[illegible] Page 1 of 1

FIGURE 5.33
Line Separators Added to Page Header and Footer

CALCULATING AND SUMMARIZING DATA

The Design view of Access reports can be used to sort, group, and calculate. The Sorting and Grouping button on the toolbar activates the Sorting and Grouping dialog box where field(s) can be selected or expressions built that will control the order of data presentation. These fields also can be used to group data, to keep records with the same value together, or to calculate subtotals.

Calculating Totals

The simplest calculations involve totaling or counting all of the values of a field. The =***Sum()*** function is used to calculate the total of numeric fields. The =***Max()*** and =***Min()*** functions will return the maximum or minimum value of a numeric or date field. The =***Count()*** function can be used to count the number of entries in either numeric or text fields. The Report Footer section is the most likely place for grand totals, since it prints once at the end of the report.

For the PuppyParadise report, Evan wants a total count of his customers so the =Count() function will be used. The equal (=) sign indicates that the text box will display a calculated value. Count is the name of the function that controls the calculation. A field name is included in the parenthesis to tell Access what to count. In this case, it is not terribly important which of the fields is counted, but we'll use `=Count(LastName)` to count the number of LastName entries in the table. The basic syntax for applying a function is =functionname(field) where field indicates what is to be operated on, like `=Count(LastName)`.

Adding a report total (Count) to the Customer report:

1. Verify that the **AC05PuppyParadise.mdb** database is open and that **CustomerByState2,** created in the previous steps, is open in Design view
2. Click the **Text Box** [ab|] tool
3. Click in the right half of the Report Footer to add a text box and its associated label
4. Click in the label and type **Grand Total Customer Count**
5. Click in the text box and type =**Count(LastName)**

FIGURE 5.34
Total count of customers

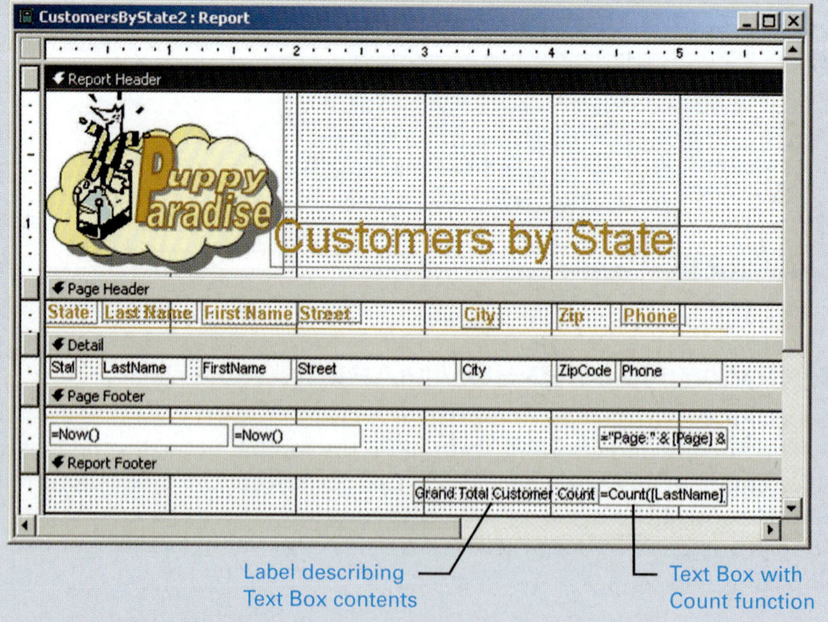

6. Use the View button to preview the results

tip: *The Report Footer will appear after the last record but before the Page Footer on the last page of the report*

7. Save the report

One text box is added to the Report Footer for each Grand Total calculation being specified. In a report calculating customer charges, possible calculations include the grand total charge (=Sum), the minimum charge (=Min), and the maximum charge (=Max). Including all three calculations would require adding three text boxes with the appropriate expression in each.

anotherword

. . . on Building Expressions

Access comes with a large library of built-in functions. If you do not remember a function or its exact syntax, the Expression Builder can be used to build the correct expression. Just click in the text box and activate the Expression Builder using the Builder button on the toolbar. The most common functions used in reports are classified as SQL Aggregate, which includes Sum, Count, Min, Max, and Avg. Selecting the function and clicking the Help button in Expression Builder will provide help topics related to that function.

Sorting and Grouping Data

The ability to sort and group data was introduced with the Report Wizard. As expected, sorting controls the order that data are presented in the report. Grouping controls what groups of data are used for page breaks or subtotals. For example, to create a count of customers in each state, the records will be grouped by state. When grouping is applied to a field or fields, the records also must be sorted by those field(s) so that the data to be grouped always present together in the report.

The Sorting and Grouping dialog box allows the selection of a field or fields that will control the presentation order of the report. Each field selected can be further specified to control its sort order and grouping properties. If Grouping Properties are not specified for a selected field, a sort on that field is created. If Grouping Properties are set, either a Group Header, a Group Footer, or both are added to the report design. The contents of the Group Header and Footer must be specified using the techniques covered for other components of the report design.

task reference

Control Sorting and Grouping in a Report

- Display the report in Design view
- Click the **Sorting and Grouping** button on the toolbar
- Use the Field/Expression drop-down list box to select each field that you want to use to sort or group data. Each selected Field/Expression will be on a different line of the grid
- Select the Sort order for each Field/Expression listed. The order of multiple fields determines their priority in the sort
- Select the grouping option(s) for each field
- Close the Sorting and Grouping dialog box
- Add the necessary controls and content to any Group Headers and Footers created

Adding Sorting and Grouping to the Customer report:

1. Verify that the **AC05PuppyParadise.mdb** database is open and that **CustomerByState2,** created in the previous steps, is open in Design view
2. Click the **Sorting and Grouping** button on the toolbar
3. Use the drop-down list box to select **State** as the first sort field, **LastName** as the second, and **FirstName** as the third

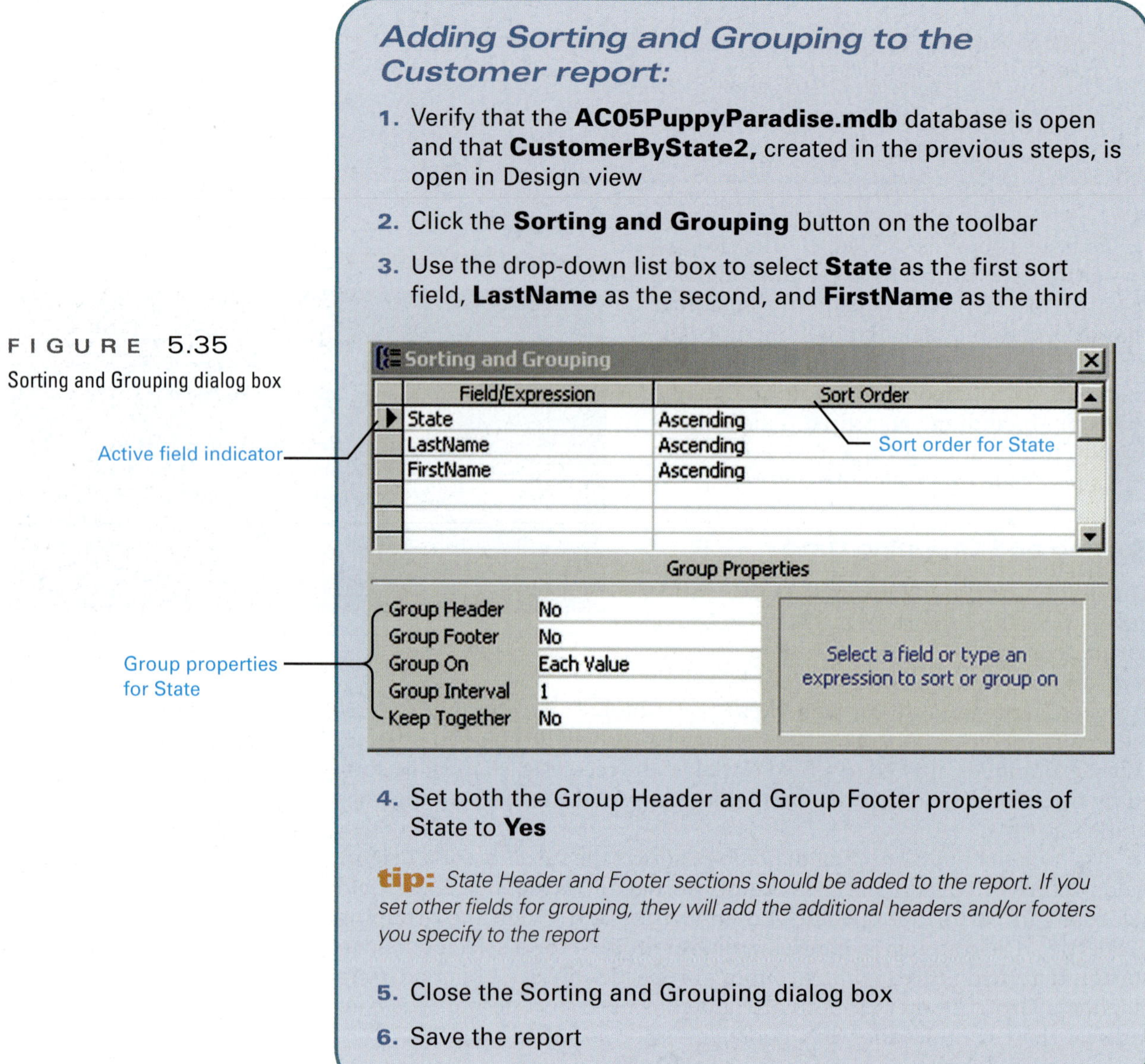

FIGURE 5.35
Sorting and Grouping dialog box

4. Set both the Group Header and Group Footer properties of State to **Yes**

tip: *State Header and Footer sections should be added to the report. If you set other fields for grouping, they will add the additional headers and/or footers you specify to the report*

5. Close the Sorting and Grouping dialog box
6. Save the report

Now both the Group Header and Group Footer sections for State need to have their contents defined. A Group Header usually contains the field that identifies the group, in this case State. Since the header prints at the beginning of each new group, placing State in the Group Header section will cause it to print once at the beginning of each new state, rather than repeating the state on every detail line.

The Group Footer usually contains the calculations for the group and any group-specific text. For Evan's report, the Group Footer will contain the count of customers in a state. This is the same calculation as was entered in the Report Footer section, but in the Group Footer it will be printed at the end of each state and zeroed to begin counting the next state.

Adding State Header and Footer content:

1. Verify that the **AC05PuppyParadise.mdb** database is open and that **CustomerByState2,** created in the previous steps, is open in Design view
2. Click the **State** field in the Detail section and use the **Cut** button to place it on the clipboard
3. Click the **State Header** bar and use the **Paste** button to place the State field in this section
4. Click the **Text Box** ab| tool and then click in the **State Footer** to the right of center
5. Delete the label, leaving only the text box (it contains the text "unbound")
6. Type =**State & " Customer Count " & Count(LastName)**

tip: *Be sure to type the space before and after Customer Count. You can expand the text box using the sizing handles so that you can see the entire expression. Access will convert the statement to* `=[State]&"CustomerCount"&Count([LastName])`

7. Using the Formatting toolbar, set the State Footer text box properties to **Bold** and **Align Right**

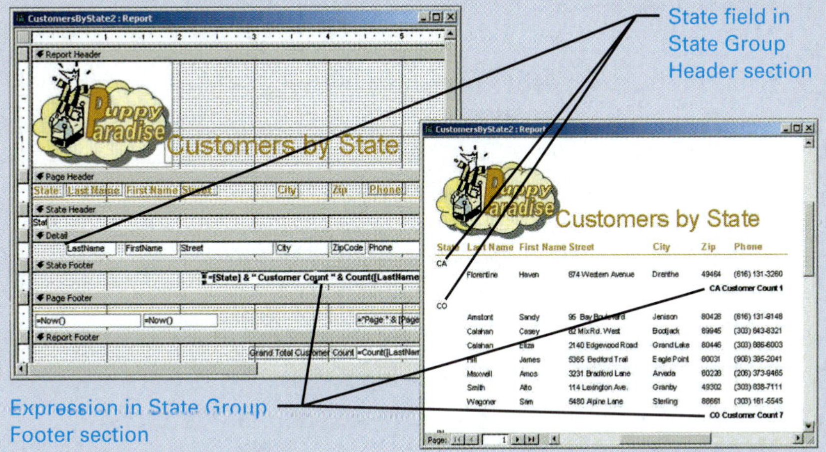

FIGURE 5.36
Completed Customer by State report

8. Use the View button to preview the report and return to Design view
9. Save the report

Add one text box to the Group Footer for each group calculation that is being specified. The ampersand (&) operator is used to ***concatenate*** different parts of an expression. When double quotes (") are included in an expression, the values between the double quotes will display exactly as entered, including spaces. There are no double quotes around field names because they will be replaced with the current field value. For example, `=LastName&", "&FirstName` would cause the value of LastName, a comma and a space, and the value of FirstName to display in a text box.

The expression used in Evan's report was `=State&"Customer Count"&Count(LastName)`. This expression causes the current value of State to print, followed by a space, the text Customer Count, another space, and the result of the expression Count(LastName).

Hiding Duplicate Report Values

After previewing the report, Evan decides that he does not want State in the Group Header section taking up a whole line of the report. He would like State displayed on the first line of each group. To accomplish this, you will need to put State back in the Detail section of the report, remove the State Header, and format State so that duplicate values do not display.

Hiding duplicate State values:

1. Verify that the **AC05PuppyParadise.mdb** database is open and that **CustomerByState2,** created in the previous steps, is open in Design view
2. Click the **State** field in the State Header section and use the **Cut** button to place it on the Clipboard
3. Click the **Detail** bar and use the **Paste** button to place the State field in this section
4. Click the **Sorting and Grouping** button
   a. Set the Group Header property of State to **No**
   b. Close the Sorting and Grouping dialog box
5. Click **State** and use the **Properties** button to activate its Properties pages
   a. Set the Hide Duplicates property to **Yes**
   b. Close the Properties dialog box
6. Using the Formatting toolbar, set the State Footer text box properties to **Bold** and **Align Right**
7. Use the View button to preview the report and return to Design view
8. Save the report as **CustomersByState3**

Two final versions of the CustomersByState report have been created. One that uses the Group Header to display the group identification and a second that hides duplicate values in the group field (State). The advantage of hiding duplicates is that more data display on a report page. The advantage of using the Group Header is that it can make the beginning of a group easier to identify.

Lines, boxes, and other formatting can be added to make the groups on your report more clear. Formatting is a matter of preference, but in general keep it simple. Don't use too many colors, lines, or unnecessary indents that can detract from the purpose of the report.

CustomersByState2 : Report

Customers by State

State	Last Name	First Name	Street	City	Zip	Phone
CA	Florentine	Haven	874 Western Avenue	Drenthe	49464	(616) 131-3260
					CA Customer Count 1	
CO	Amstont	Sandy	95 Bay Boulevard	Jenison	80428	(616) 131-9148
	Calahan	Casey	82 Mix Rd. West	Bootjack	89945	(303) 643-8321
	Calahan	Eliza	2140 Edgewood Road	Grand Lake	80446	(303) 886-6003
	Hill	James	5365 Bedford Trail	Eagle Point	80031	(906) 395-2041
	Maxwell	Amos	3231 Bradford Lane	Arvada	80228	(206) 373-9465
	Smith	Alto	114 Lexington Ave.	Granby	49302	(303) 838-7111
	Wagoner	Sam	5480 Alpine Lane	Sterling	88661	(303) 161-5545
					CO Customer Count 7	
IN	Calahan	Thomas	840 Cascade Road	Coatesville	80464	(316) 343-4635
	Guo	Amy	1935 Snow Street	Greencastle	49453	(616) 555-6731
	Meadows	Sara	Pond Hill Road	Monroe	46161	(313) 792-3646

Page: 1

FIGURE 5.37
Updated Customer by State report

PREVIEWING AND PRINTING REPORTS

The Print Preview view button on the toolbar has been used throughout the steps to evaluate design changes in a WYSIWYG (what you see is what you get) environment. Print Preview is also used to set up the printer before printing. The Setup button opens a dialog box with settings for page margins, page orientation, alternate printers, paper source, and other printer-specific options. The settings available from Setup are specific to your software configuration and printer installation, so the options beyond setting margins and page orientation will vary from computer to computer.

Both the magnifier glass and the percent drop-down list box control the zoom of your preview. The three buttons between the zoom controls set the view to one page, two pages, or multiple pages of the report. When uncertain about the function of a button, pause the cursor over it to view Screen Tips. The OfficeLinks button is used to send the report design to other Office products such as Word and Excel. The Print button will send the report directly to the printer without any further options.

Reports have a third view, Layout Preview, that also can be used to view the impact of design changes. A Layout Preview shows only a few sample records to evaluate the overall impact of design updates without reviewing multiple pages of output.

making the grade

SESSION 5.2

1. Describe the function of the Detail section of a report.
2. How do you decide whether to place a calculation in the Report Footer or a Group Footer?
3. What is the difference between a control's sizing handle and its move handles?
4. How do you determine what control to use when building a report?

SESSION 5.3 SUMMARY

Access form and report objects are designed to support different output needs. The form object is used to create screen output used to view and update data. The report object is used to create formal printed output. The output from all Access objects can be printed, but the report object is specifically designed to format printed output. Both forms and reports are bound to a record source such as a table or query.

Controls are the building blocks used to build both forms and reports. The toolbox is a special toolbar that contains controls. The Field List dialog box displays all of the fields from the record source. Bound controls are those that display data from the record source fields. Unbound controls are those that display data not bound to the record source such as report titles, logos, and lines.

The Design views used to develop both custom forms and reports are very similar. The main design area is called the Detail section. Controls added to the detail section most commonly display data from the underlying record source. Text Box controls are used to display fields and calculations. Label controls are used to display text that doesn't change such as the report title or field headings. A Line control is used to draw lines on a form or report. The Image control will display a variety of image formats.

The easiest way to add a bound control is to drag fields from the Field List. The bulk of bound controls are placed in the Detail section of a form or report. Unbound controls are added to a form or report by clicking the tool in the Toolbox and then clicking the surface where the control is to display. For simple controls such as a Label, use the Properties button to activate the Properties pages. The properties of an object control what and how it displays. More complex controls such as the Image control have Control Wizards for step-by-step instructions on setting control properties.

Visit www.mhhe.com/i-series/ to explore related topics.

MOUS OBJECTIVES SUMMARY:

- Create a form in Design View—AC2002-2-1
- Create and modify reports—AC2002-4-1
- Add Subreport controls to Access reports—AC2002-4-2
- Sort and group data in reports—AC2002-4-3

task reference roundup

Task	Page #	Preferred Method
Open a new form in Design view	AC 5.5	• In the Database window of an open database, click the **Forms** object
		• Click the **New** button on the Database window toolbar
		• In the New Form dialog box, click **Design View**
		• Select the table or query that will be the record source for the form and click **OK**

task reference roundup

Task	Page #	Preferred Method
Select and move form controls	AC 5.9	• Select the control to be operated on by clicking it. The Shift key can be used to select multiple controls
		• Drag the control(s) to the new location. Use the large move handle to independently move components of a bound control
Set control properties	AC 5.11	• Right-click the control to open the pop-up menu
		• Select **Properties** from the pop-up menu
		• Select the appropriate Properties tab (usually Format)
		• Navigate to the property and change its setting
Show Form Headers and Footers	AC 5.14	• Open a form in Design view
		• Select **Form Header/Footer** from the **View** menu
Add Toolbox controls to a design	AC 5.15	• Open a form or report in Design view
		• If necessary, activate the toolbox using the **Toolbox** button on the Form Design toolbar
		• Verify that the toolbox **Control Wizards** button is depressed (a blue outline will show around it)
		• Click the toolbox control that is to be added to the form
		• Click in the Form section that will contain the control
		• Set the control's properties using the Properties pages activated with the Properties button
Query an open form with a saved filter	AC5.20	• Open a form in Form view
		• Click the **Filter By Form** button
		• Click the **Load From Query** button
		• Select the query to be applied and click **OK**
		• Click the **Apply Filter** button
Create a report in Design view	AC 5.26	• In the Database window click the **Reports** object and click the **New** button
		• Click **Design View** as the way to develop the report, select the record source from the drop-down list, and click **OK**
Add page numbers to a report in Design view	AC 5.32	• Display the report in Design view
		• Choose **Page Numbers** from the **Insert** menu
		• Select the formatting, position, and alignment options that you want and click **OK**

task reference roundup

Task	*Page #*	*Preferred Method*
Control Sorting and Grouping in a Report	AC 5.37	• Display the report in Design view
		• Click the **Sorting and Grouping** button on the toolbar
		• Use the Field/Expression drop-down list box to select each field that you want to use to sort or group data. Each selected Field/Expression will be on a different line of the grid
		• Select the Sort order for each Field/Expression listed. The order of multiple fields determines their priority in the sort
		• Select the grouping option(s) for each field
		• Close the Sorting and Grouping dialog box
		• Add the necessary controls and content to any Group Headers and Footers created

CROSSWORD PUZZLE

Across

1. The table or query providing data.
3. The handle that allows a control to be resized.
5. The most likely place for a report title.
6. The most likely place for fields from the field list.
8. The order in which objects stack.
9. =________ returns the minimum value.
12. Section that displays at the bottom of each form.
14. Type of control that displays the result of an expression.
15. Type of control that displays data from the record source.
17. Attributes of an object that can be set to control it.
18. =________ returns the system date and time.

Down

2. Walks you through the process of setting up a complex control.
4. An area in a form or report design.
7. The act of joining strings using the ampersand (&) operator.
10. Used to size and move the selected object.
11. The ________ handle allows bound controls to move independently.
13. =________ returns the largest value.
16. =________ returns the number of values.

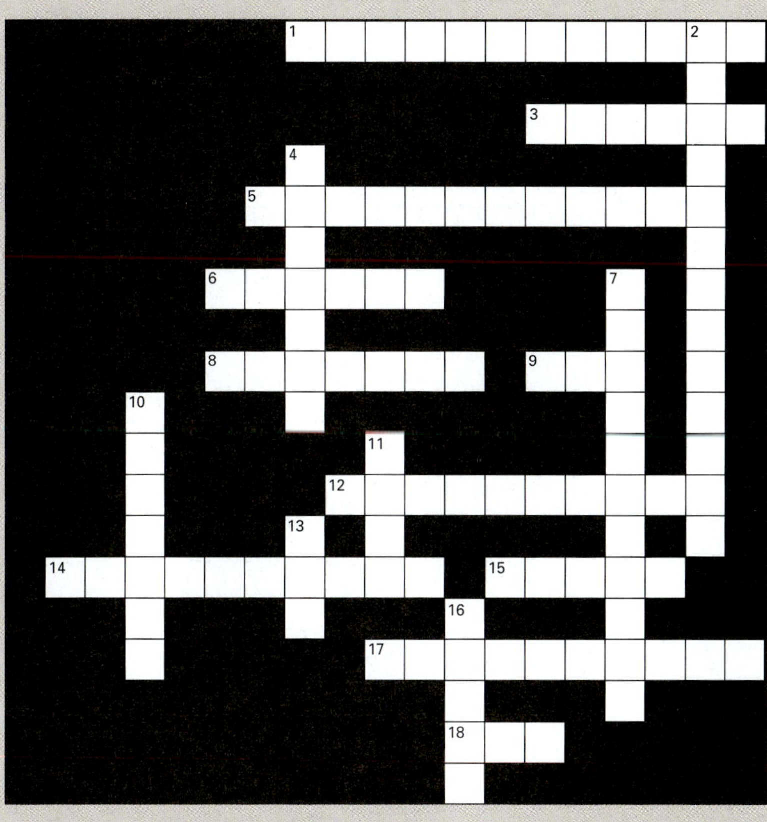

review of concepts

FILL-IN

1. Use the ________ key to select multiple controls on a form or report.
2. The ________ property controls the font color of text.
3. The squares that allow you to resize and move controls are called ________ .
4. Sections are added to report or form design using the ________ menu.
5. Use ________ to remove controls from a section so that they can be pasted into a new section.

REVIEW QUESTIONS

Each of the following topics should be addressed in one to three paragraphs.

1. When setting properties for multiple controls, what governs the controls that you can choose?
2. Why should you add a custom color to the palette?
3. Explain the use of grouping in reports.
4. Discuss all of the ways that you can control what records print from a form.
5. Explain why both the form and report objects are needed in Access.

CREATE THE QUESTION

For each of the following answers, create the question.

ANSWER	QUESTION
1. Click the Wizard button on the toolbar.	________________
2. Controls	________________
3. Sections, controls, toolbox, grid, and ruler to name a few	________________
4. Caption, Fore Color, Font Name, Font Weight, and Font Size to name a few	________________
5. The most efficient way is to use the Field List	________________

FACT OR FICTION

For each of the following, determine whether the statement is fact, fiction, or both and present your arguments for that conclusion.

1. You must set properties for every control added to a report or form.
2. Only calculations can be included in the expression for a calculated control.
3. A calculated control stores the instructions on how to calculate a value, not a precise value.
4. The toolbox must always appear anchored to the left of the Design window.
5. The only way to align controls on a form or report is to use the ruler and grid.

practice

Forms and Reports for Cyberia Coffee Shop

Cyberia Coffee Shop is a Barona, California, neighborhood coffee shop. Besides serving gourmet coffee, Cyberia dishes up sandwiches and desserts. Local bands, Internet connections, and floor-to-ceiling books on every wall provide entertainment. Li Houng, the proprietor, has decided that a database would be helpful in the acquisition of new books. Although customers rarely buy books, they do disappear or fall apart from use. Li needs a way to keep track of what books he has so that he doesn't pick up duplicates. You will use the Wizards and then Design view to create a custom form and report.

1. Start Access and open **AC05Cyberia.mdb**
2. Select the **Form** object and double-click on **Create form by using wizard**
3. Select the **Books** table, move all fields to the Selected Fields list, and click **Next**
4. Select **Columnar** and click **Next**
5. Select **Sumi Painting** and click **Next**
6. Click **Finish** and then use the **View** button to change to Design view
7. Use the Detail Selector bar to expand the height of the form header
8. Click the **Image** control and then click in the Form Header
9. Navigate to the files for this chapter and select **Cyberia.tif**
10. Position the logo in the top left corner and adjust the size of the Form Header to the logo size
11. Save the form as **Books**
12. Create a report that groups the records by author
    a. Select the **Report** object and double-click on **Create report by using wizard**
    b. Move all of the fields to the Selected Fields list and click **Finish**
    c. Click the **View** button to switch to Design view
    d. Select the Books label and move it to the right
    e. Click the **Image** tool, click in the Report Header, navigate to the files for this chapter, and select **Cyberia.tif**
    f. Move the label Books until it is positioned overlapping the logo
    g. Use **Cut** and **Paste** to move the label to the foreground
    h. Set the label properties to 36 point, bold, italic
    i. Save the report as **BooksByAuthor**

FIGURE 5.38
Books form and report

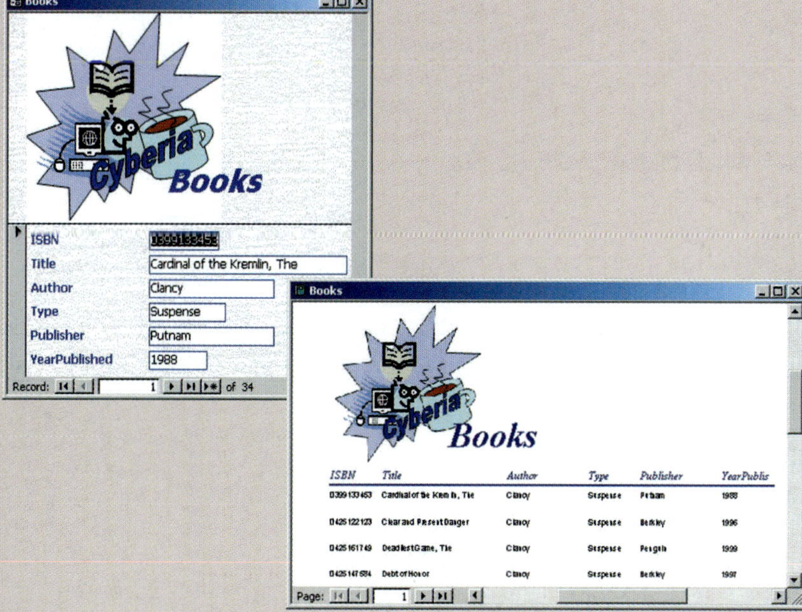

challenge!

Sorting and Grouping for Cyberia Coffee Shop

Cyberia Coffee Shop was introduced in the Practice exercise for this chapter. You have developed a form and simple report to help Li Houng track his book purchases. Now he would like some more complex reports for his customers. He would like reports that his customers can use to find books by a specific author or in a particular category. You will develop these reports from scratch in Design view.

1. Start Access and open **AC05Cyberia.mdb**
2. Open a new blank report on the books table in Design view
3. Use the Field List to place all of the Books fields into the Detail section of the report and close the Field List
4. Select all of the labels and cut them out of the Detail section; select the Page Header section and paste them there
5. Edit the labels to remove the colons (:) and make them all dark blue
6. Add the Report Header/Footer sections and use the Image control to place **AC05Cyberia.tif** in the top left corner of the Report Header
7. Add a label with the properties that cause the text Report Title to display in Times New Roman, 36 point, italic, and dark blue
8. Size the label appropriately
9. Save this part of the design as **GroupByTemplate.** We will use it to develop a grouped report in later steps
10. Save the report as **BooksByAuthor** and make the following adjustments to the design
    a. Change the title to Books By Author and adjust the size of the label
    b. Arrange the Page Header and Detail sections to display Author, Title, Type, Publisher, Year Published, and ISBN in that order. Align all controls and reduce the sizes of the Page Header and Detail sections
    c. Use the Sorting and Grouping dialog box to sort by Author and then Title. Display a Group Footer for Author
    d. Use the Properties of the Author control to hide duplicate values
    e. Add a calculated control to the Author Footer that displays an appropriate message and the count of books by each author
    f. Save the report
11. Return to the GroupByTemplate and make the following changes
    a. Save the report as **BooksByCategory**
    b. Change the report title and field order (Type, Title, Author, YearPublished, Publisher, ISBN)
    c. Count the number of reports in each category

FIGURE 5.39

Books GroupByTemplate and BooksByAuthor report

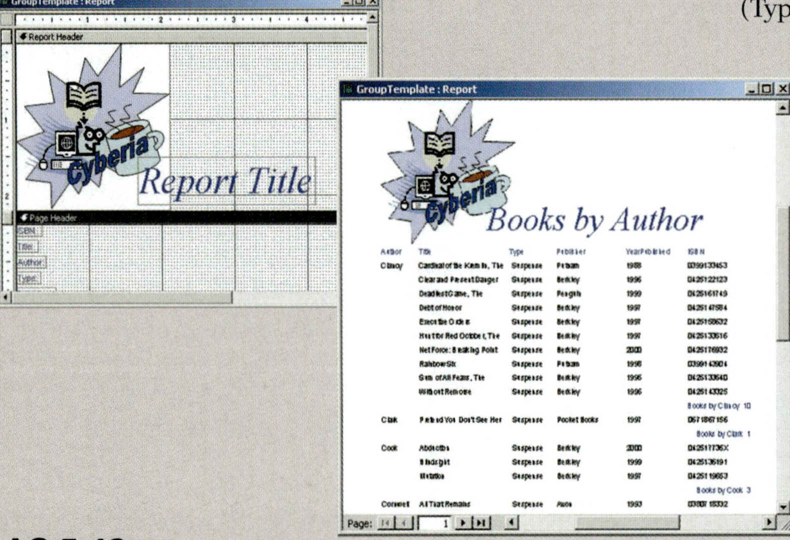

on the web

Terra Patrimonium Agricultural Chemicals Customer Analysis

Terra Patrimonium (Latin for land of our fathers) is a company that provides agricultural chemicals, supplies, and services to farmers. Vaughn Michaels, the president and founder, is experienced at using Excel and accounting software but has asked you to help create the database forms and reports needed to support the organization.

1. To prepare for this exercise, use a search engine to find three farm pictures (I found some at www.farmpictures.com) that are representative of healthy corn, barley, soy bean, or sorghum crops
2. Start Access and open **AC05TerraPatrimonium.mdb**
3. Create a new form in Design view to display healthy crops using Terra Patrimonium chemicals. The form will be placed on the Web later
   a. Use an Image control to display the image **AC05TerraPatrimonium.tif** at the top left of the form
   b. Use a Label control to insert **Bountiful Terra Patrimonium Crops** as a title below the logo
   c. Use Image controls to insert and arrange your pictures
   d. Save the form as **Bounty**
4. Create the form shown in Figure 5.40, save it as **CstmrInput,** and use the form to add the following data

Greg Mendenhall	**2481 W. State Rd 1000, Monrovia, IA 65738**
Kerry Preston	**68888 S State Rd 115, Red Oak, IA 61828**
Lonnie McCammack	**14486 E IA265, Creston, IA 61828**
George McCammack	**20281 E IA265, Creston, IA 61828**
Gordon Foss	**74589 South IA 71, Morton Mills, IA 61826**
Randy Knetzer	**RR 12, Box 217, Osceola, IA 63871**
Michael Knudson	**2829 Hwy 2 East, Mount Ayr, IA 61627**
Bob Kalahari	**RR 2 Box 105, Knoxville, IA 61726**
Joseph Kabassa	**RR 2 Box 162, Knoxville, IA 61726**
Jason Van Horne	**RR 12 Box 189, Osceola, IA 63871**
Dominic Black	**RR 1, Box 98, Osceola, IA 63871**

5. Make up a phone number for each customer added in 4
6. Use Design view to create the report shown in Figure 5.40 and save it as **PhoneList**
7. Close the TerraPatrimonium database and exit Access if your work is complete

FIGURE 5.40

CstmrInput form

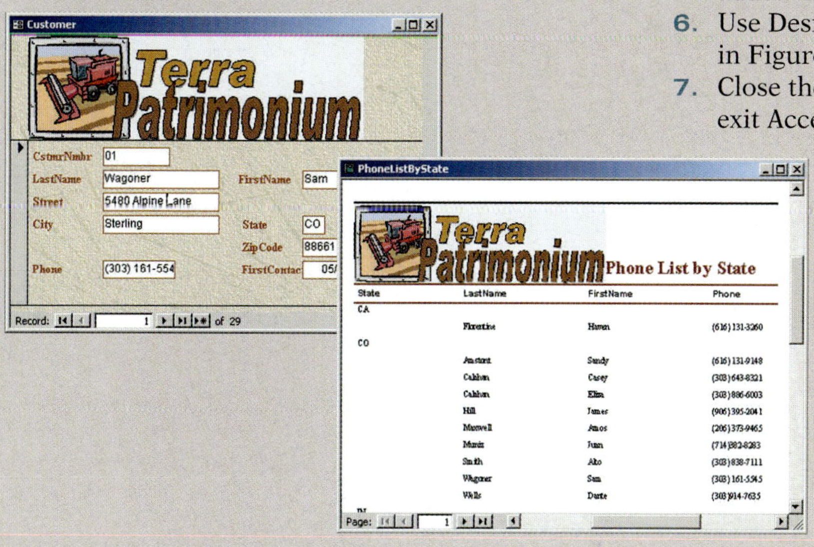

e-business

Previewing SportsPix Photographs on the Web

SportsPix is a digital photography operation that specializes in taking pictures of youth sports teams. Ray Damask and Grace Bishop began photographing sports teams when their nephew was playing soccer at the local YMCA. They shoot individual and team pictures for baseball, softball, soccer, football, volleyball, tennis, and martial arts. You have developed a prototype of a Photographs table that you believe will help Ray and Grace. You have selected some test data from the information that they provided and entered it into the table. Create the form and report outlined to ensure the effectiveness of this solution.

1. Start Access and open the **AC05SportsPix.mdb** database
2. Create the form depicted in Figure 5.41 for the **Photographs** table
   a. The logo is **AC05Sportspix.tif**
   b. Set the form properties to make the background light blue
   c. Set the Border Style property of all of the text boxes to Solid and the Border Color to a complementary blue
   d. Align all controls
   e. Adjust the size of all controls and form sections to fit the data
   f. Save the form as **PhotoInput**
3. Open the **Photographs** form and add records for yourself and two of your friends. You should all be on the same team and have had your pictures taken at the same time and at the same location. Use Film Id 5443
4. Create the report shown in Figure 5.41 for the **Photographs** table. This report will become a Web page that will allow photographs to be previewed and purchased
   a. Add the logo (**AC05Sportspix.tif**), lines, and colors shown
   b. Add a Group Header for Location and a Group Footer for Team
      i. Set the properties of both Location and Team to suppress duplicate values
      ii. Count the Subjects for each team in the Group Footer
   c. Format Time to ShortTime and ensure that the text box is large enough to display all of the date
   d. Place the report date and Page XX of XX in the Page Footer
   e. Save the report as **PhotosByLocationAndTeam**
5. If your work is complete, exit Access; otherwise continue to the next assignment

FIGURE 5.41

Photographs form and report

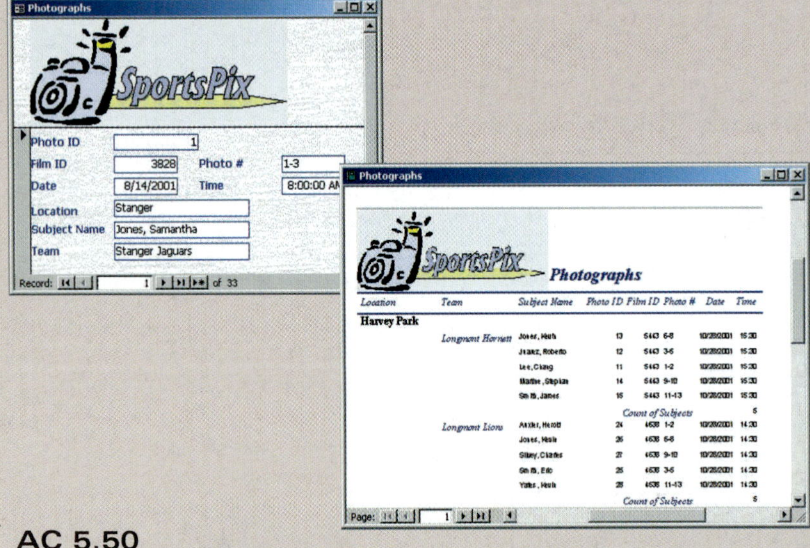

around the world

TechRocks Seminars Forms and Reports

TechRocks Seminars is an organization of independent seminar facilitators who provide onsite technical training to large businesses around the world. The facilitators build curriculum that is marketed by TechRocks. TechRocks books the seminars, arranges facilities, enrolls participants, and collects the money. While the facilitators are not employees of TechRocks, they provide the service that is marketed and their skills and schedules need to be available to all TechRocks offices.

Aisha Jackson has been charged with tracking facilitators and their classification. She has asked you to help develop the reports that will be placed on the company's Web site for use by all of the organization's offices in scheduling seminars.

1. Start Access and open the **AC05Seminars.mdb** database
2. Create a data entry form for the Facilitators table
   a. Add the **AC05TechRocks.tif** logo to the Form Header
   b. Set the form background color to a blue that complements the logo
   c. Organize and align all controls for effective use and full data display
   d. Save the form as **FacilitatorsInput**
3. Use the Enrollment table to create a report listing the students currently enrolled in each seminar
   a. The field order is Seminar ID, Last Name, First Name, Phone Number, and Student Number
   b. Adjust all controls to display all of their contents
   c. Adjust the color and content of the column headings as shown in Figure 5.42
   d. Align all controls
   e. Add a gray line under the column headings
   f. Use Sorting and Grouping to sort by Seminar ID, Last Name, and First Name. Add a Group Footer for Seminar ID
   g. Suppress the display of duplicate Seminar ID values
   h. Add a text box with the expression **=[Seminar ID] & " students " & Count([Last Name])** to the Seminar ID Footer

   tip: *Make sure to include the spaces. In this table the field names have spaces and so must be enclosed in square brackets []. The spaces before and after students in " students " prints the spaces after the Seminar ID and before the student count*

   i. Place the report date, time, and Page XX of XX in the Page Footer. Format the date and time to long format
   j. Set the Visible property of the Report Footer to **No**
   k. Place **AC05TechRocks.tif** in the Report Header and add the three labels (one for each word)
   l. Set the position and color of the title labels as shown
   m. Save the report as **StudentsBySeminar**
4. If your work is complete, exit Access; otherwise continue to the next assignment

FIGURE 5.42

Students by Seminar report

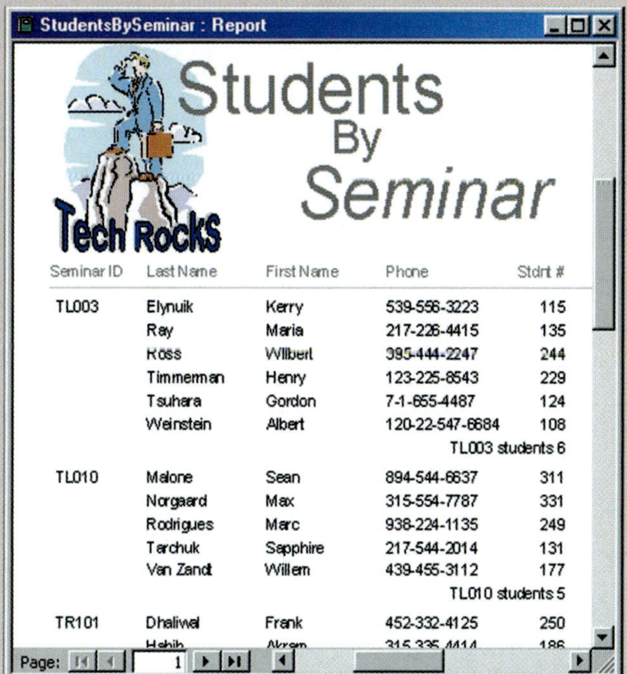
StudentsBySeminar : Report

Students By Seminar

Seminar ID	Last Name	First Name	Phone	Stdnt #
TL003	Elynuik	Kerry	539-556-3223	115
	Ray	Maria	217-226-4415	135
	Ross	Wilbert	395-444-2247	244
	Timmerman	Henry	123-225-8543	229
	Tsuhara	Gordon	7-1-655-4487	124
	Weinstein	Albert	120-22-547-6684	108
				TL003 students 6
TL010	Malone	Sean	894-544-6637	311
	Norgaard	Max	315-554-7787	331
	Rodrigues	Marc	938-224-1135	249
	Tarchuk	Sapphire	217-544-2014	131
	Van Zandt	Willem	439-455-3112	177
				TL010 students 5
TR101	Dhaliwal	Frank	452-332-4125	250

running project: tnt web design

Custom Forms and Reports for TnT

As TnT grows, so does the complexity of its database. Tori and Tonya now have over 65 employees and several hundred customers. Employees and projects are spread across the United States, so it is becoming critical to have simple data entry and reporting.

1. Start Access and open the **AC05TnT.mdb** database. Familiarize yourself with each table if necessary
2. Create a custom form for the Employees table
   a. Use the format shown in Figure 5.43

   tip: *You will need to add Label controls for the Name and Address headers in the Detail section*

   b. Use the **Rectangle** tool to group the data as shown. The Border Width is **Hairline** and the Fore Color is **gray**
   c. Set the Visible property of the Form Footer to **No**
   d. Add the TnT logo from **AC05TnT.tif**
   e. Use two labels (one for each word) to add the form title. Make it 28 point, bold, italic, and dark blue
   f. Save the form as **EmployeeUpdate**
3. Create a custom report for the Employees table
   a. The Detail line contains Job Class, Last Name, First Name, State, and Phone
   b. Adjust the headings, align and size all controls, and set the headings to dark blue
   c. Use Sorting and Grouping to sort the data by JobClass, LastName, and FirstName
   d. Set the Properties of JobClass to Hide Duplicates
   e. Create a Report Header containing the TnT logo and three labels (one for each word) with the report title
   f. Create a Page Footer with the report date (mm/dd/yyyy), military time at the left margin, Page XX of XX at the right margin, and a blue line above it
      i. Employees is 28 point, bold, italic, and dark blue
      ii. By is 24 point, italic, and dark blue
      iii. Job Classification is 22 point, italic, and dark blue
   g. Set the Visible property of the Report Footer to **No**
   h. Save the report as **EmployeesByJobClass**
4. If your work is complete, exit Access; otherwise continue to the next assignment

FIGURE 5.43

Employee Update form

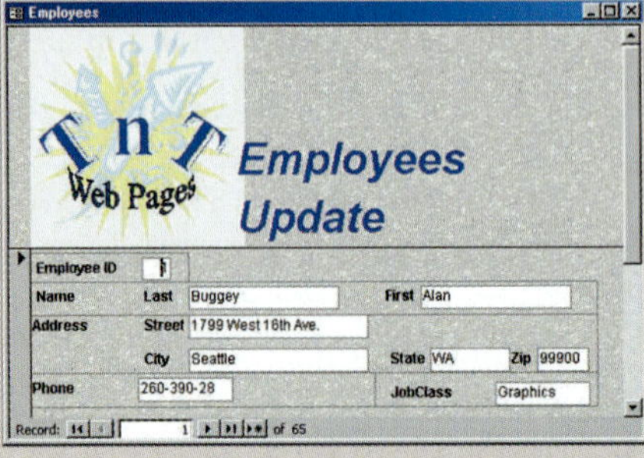

FIGURE 5.44

Employees by Job Classification report

did you
know?

the *average person takes seven minutes to fall asleep.*

the *dial tone of a normal telephone is in the key of F.*

"live *so that you wouldn't mind selling your pet parrot to the town gossip."*—Will Rogers

cutting *an onion releases a passive sulfur compound created by propanethiol S-oxide gas and enzymes contained in the onion. When this upwardly mobile gas encounters the water produced by the tear ducts in our eyelids, it produces sulfuric acid.*

quicksand *is buoyant. Anything or anyone who steps into it can float much higher than is possible in water alone.*

in *1908 __________ predicted "No flying machine will ever fly from New York to Paris."*

Chapter Objectives

- Review the types of table relationships
- Build table relationships in the Relationships window—AC2002-6-1
- Change the properties of table relationships including join type and referential integrity—AC2002-6-2, AC2002-5-2
- Query multiple tables
- Create and use multitable custom forms including subdatasheets and subforms—AC2002-2-3
- Create multitable custom reports

CHAPTER

6 six

Defining Table Relationships

chapter case

PuppyParadise

The data, forms, and reports for PuppyParadise are shaping up nicely. Evan is very comfortable entering data, running queries, and printing reports. He has enjoyed learning about the Design view of reports and forms. He even likes manipulating the controls and properties in Design view to make everything look attractive. Evan is an accomplished user of the database that you have set up, but he wants to be able to develop his own databases so that he is no longer dependent on your expertise.

Although Evan was very involved in every stage of developing the current database and even built some of the components with your help, he does not understand how to set up tables, relationships, queries, forms, and reports for himself. He has lots of questions about how things really work such as:

- What records are retrieved when I use multiple tables in a Select query?
- How can I maintain the data from all of the PuppyParadise tables at once?
- Why can't I add an order and then enter the Customer data?
- How do I know when to index a field or group of fields?
- Why would I use a query to build a form or report instead of just going directly to the tables involved?
- What is stopping me from modifying and deleting records for customers that have been entered with errors?
- In the beginning you talked about SQL being the language of relational databases. I haven't seen it, so where is it?

You and Evan sit down and develop a plan to answer his questions and improve his comfort level with the inner workings of Access. Since Evan is very comfortable working with single tables, you will start with table relationships and how they impact queries, forms, and reports. Figure 6.1 displays some of the components that will be used in this process.

FIGURE 6.1

Relating and indexing PuppyParadise tables

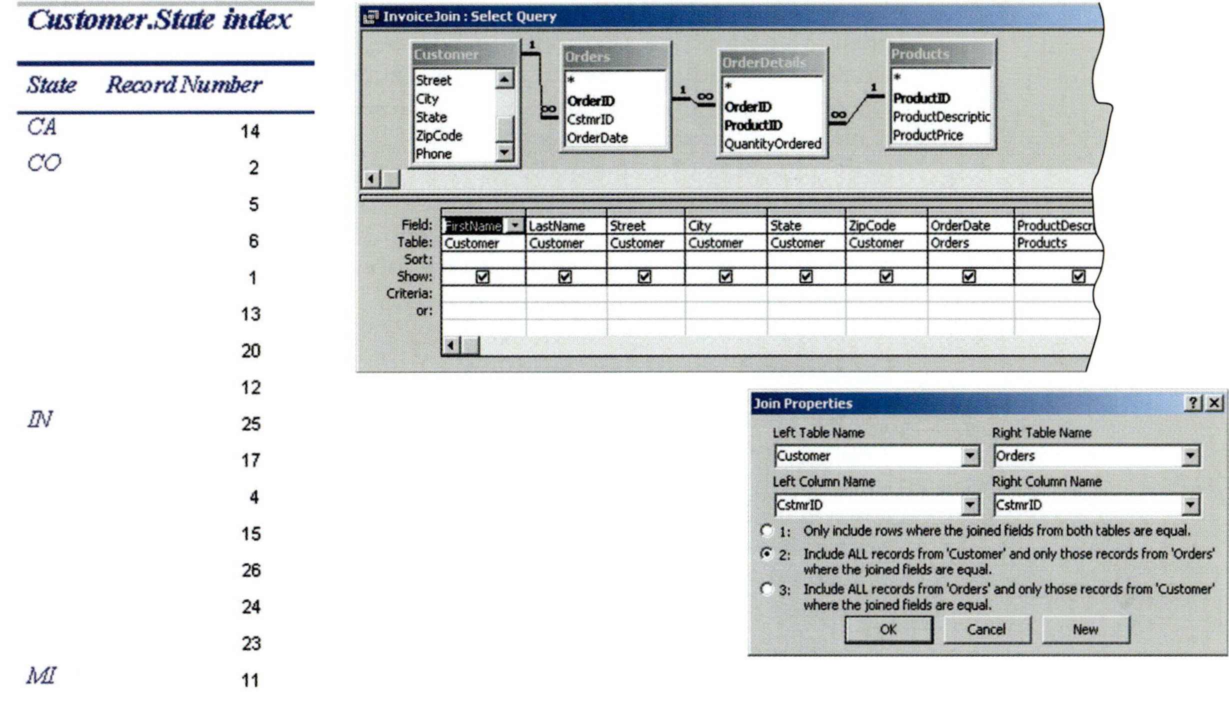

Customer.State index

State	Record Number
CA	14
CO	2
	5
	6
	1
	13
	20
	12
IN	25
	17
	4
	15
	26
	24
	23
MI	11

SESSION 6.1 RELATING TABLES

Chapter 1 introduced the concepts and terminology of relational database management systems. Subsequent chapters presented methods of using these database objects (tables, queries, forms, and reports) to view and manipulate the data held in a single table.

Chapter 2 discussed how to properly design relational databases using a common-sense version of the more formal normalization rules. Data are placed in multiple tables to reduce redundancy and increase integrity. Defining common table fields (Foreign Keys) so that data from multiple tables could be joined using queries was presented as an integral component of effective design.

The focus of this chapter is learning to build and use table relationships. It is not enough to create table designs with common fields in related tables. Like all other database objects, relationships have properties. The properties of each relationship must be correctly defined for the relationship to behave as expected.

CHAPTER OUTLINE

UNDERSTANDING TYPES OF RELATIONSHIPS

Table relationships fall into one of three general categories: one-to-one (1:1), one-to-many (1:∞), or many-to-many (∞:∞). This notation identifies how many records in the first table are related to how many records in the second table. Thus, the one-to-many notation means that one record from the ***primary table*** is related to many records in the ***related table.*** In the

PuppyPardise database, one customer can place many orders, so the relationship between the Customer and Orders tables is one-to-many.

Many-to-many relationships must be broken into multiple one-to-many relationships in the design phase of relational database development. Many-to-many relationships between tables are accommodated in databases by adding a junction table. A junction table contains the primary key columns of the two tables to be related. A one-to-many relationship from the primary key columns of each of those two tables is then created to the matching columns in the junction table. In PuppyParadise the relationship between Orders and Products would be a many-to-many relationship. One order can involve multiple products and one product can appear on multiple orders. OrderDetails is a junction table containing the primary key from both Orders and Products.

Understanding Relationships

To build a relationship, two tables must share a common field, but the fields do not have to carry the same name. The fields must carry the same Data Type and Field Size. Since all many-to-many relationships are broken down at design time, only one-to-one or one-to-many relationships will be defined in an active relational database. One-to-one relationships are rare so we will concentrate on one-to-many relationships.

Access provides the ***Relationships window*** to define, view, and edit table relationships. In a properly designed database, every table is related to at least one other table in the database. Some tables can be related to multiple tables. It is also possible to relate a table to itself. It is important to know which table is the primary table when building relationships.

task reference

View Table Relationships

- Click the **Relationships** button on the Database toolbar
- If relationships exist, they will be displayed. If there are no current relationships, you can add tables and build relationships between them

Viewing PuppyParadise relationships:

1. Verify that the **AC06PuppyParadise.mdb** database is open
2. Click the **Relationships** button on the Database toolbar

tip: *It does not matter what database object is active during this process*

3. Leave the Relationships window open so that you can refer to it as it is being discussed

The Relationships window for PuppyParadise shows a field list for each table with relationship lines depicting how the tables are related to each other. The notation on the relationship line indicates the type of relationship and which table is primary in the relationship. For example, the Customer.CstmrID (CstmrID field of the Customer table) field defines a

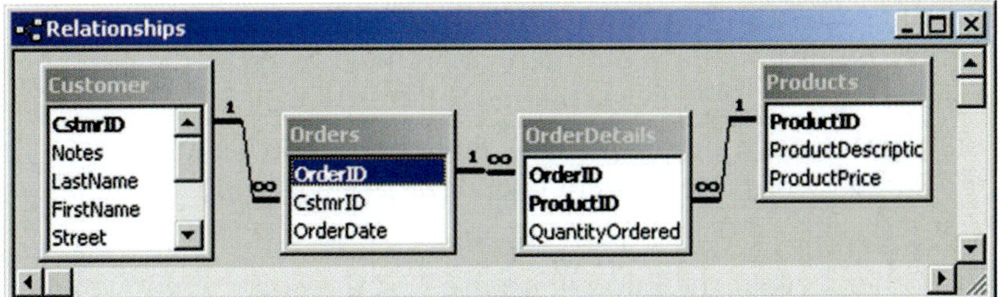

FIGURE 6.2
PuppyParadise table relationships

one-to-many relationship with the Orders.CstmrID (CstmrID field of the Orders table). The Customer table is primary in this relationship since it is on the one side, meaning that each Customer.CstmrID record can link to multiple Orders.CstmrID records.

The Customer table is related to one other database table, Orders. The Orders table, however, is related to both the Customer and the OrderDetails tables. Orders is the related table in the Customer/Orders relationship and the primary table in the Orders/OrderDetails relationship. When speaking of related table pairs, it is customary to list the primary table first.

Think about invoices or bills that you have received. They contain your name, address, an order or invoice number, and each product that you ordered with a description and a quantity. Take a look at the PuppyParadise relationships and find all of the components needed for an invoice. It should be clear by now that without the ability to join tables, users would be restricted to working with the data from each table independently. In such an environment, PuppyParadise would not be able to combine data from the Customer, Orders, and Products tables to create an invoice since the Customer table holds the customer's name and address, the Orders table contains the order quantity, and the Products table holds descriptions of each product.

The PuppyParadise invoice needs fields from each of the tables. Let's look at the relationships from a business perspective to understand what they mean in practice. Here are the PuppyParadise relationships from left to right in the Relationships window:

- One customer can place multiple orders
- One order can have multiple details (products and quantities)
- One product can appear on multiple order details

Ideally relationships are defined before any data are placed in the related table, but there is nothing in Access to prevent adding or editing relationships in an active database. Adding or changing the properties of relationships is governed by the rules of referential integrity. Your efforts to add or edit relationships also will be governed by these rules.

Referential Integrity

The rules of referential integrity govern table relationships and are sometimes referred to as parent/child rules. These rules prevent "orphans" such as an OrderDetail for a product that is not in the Products table or an order for a CstmrID that is not in the Customer table. For a relationship to be valid,

- The primary record must exist before a secondary record of that foreign key can be added to the related table (parent key must exist before the child can use that key)

- Changing the value of the primary table field that governs the relationship is not allowed if there are related records (the parent cannot be removed while it still has children)
- Deleting the record in the primary table is not allowed if there are related records (the parent cannot be deleted while it still has children)

Take another look at the PuppyParadise Relationships window. What referential integrity means in practice is that the record on the one side of the relationship must exist before any related records can be added on the many side. For example, in the PuppyParadise database, the Customer table record defining a new customer must be created before an Order can be added for that customer. For an OrderDetails record to be created, both the OrderID must exist in the Orders table and the ProductID must exist in the Products table.

Further, the parent record cannot be deleted or its key value changed while there are still related child records. In PuppyParadise, a customer cannot be deleted or assigned a new CstmrID in the Customer table while there are orders for that CstmrID in the Orders table.

Cascade Update and Delete

Double-clicking on a relationship line will open the Edit Relationships dialog box, which displays the properties of that relationship. When table relationships are defined, an option is provided to not enforce referential integrity (a very bad idea for data integrity). When referential integrity is enforced, there are options on how it is enforced.

The referential integrity options are check boxes shown in Figure 6.3 that are labeled:

- Enforce Referential Integrity, which should always be checked
- Cascade Update Related Fields
- Cascade Delete Related Records

When ***Cascade Update Related Fields*** is checked, any changes made to the key value of the primary table also will be applied to records in the related table. With this option, if you need to change a CstmrID for some

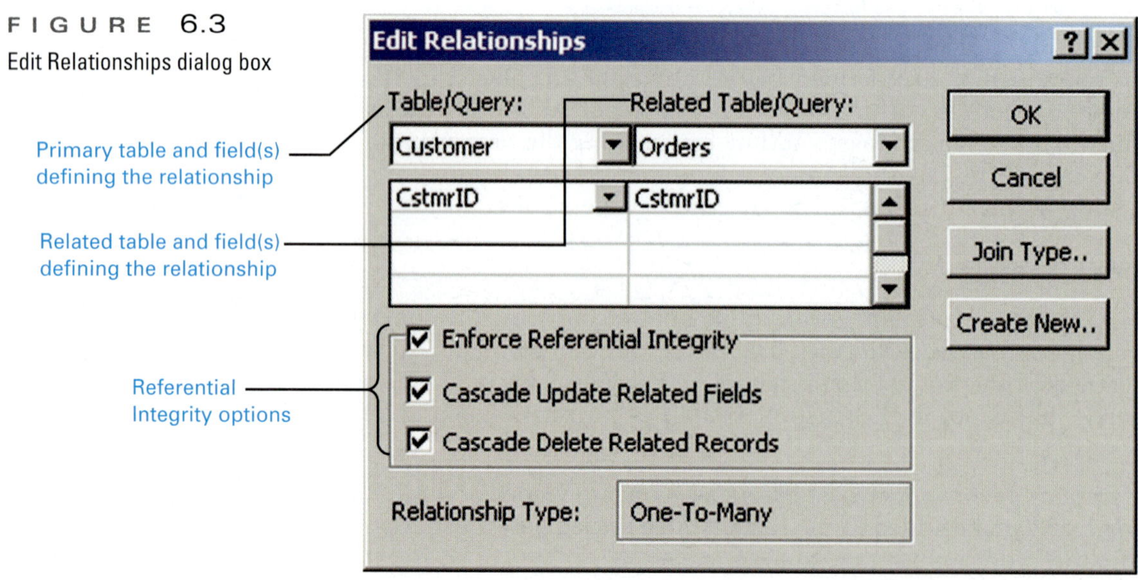

FIGURE 6.3
Edit Relationships dialog box

reason, making the change in the Customer table would also update the CstmrID of related child records in the Orders table.

Selecting the ***Cascade Delete Related Records*** check box will cause related records to be deleted when the primary record is deleted. In PuppyParadise, deleting a customer from the Customer table will also delete all orders for that customer. Cascade deletes are not always a good idea since it would allow a customer and all of the customer's orders to be deleted without verifying each delete.

task reference

View Relationship Properties

- Click the **Relationships** button on the Database toolbar
- If relationships exist, they will be displayed. If there are no current relationships, you can add tables and build relationships between them
- Double-click the relationship line that you would like to view
- The Edit Relationships dialog box displays the properties of that relationship

Viewing PuppyParadise relationship properties:

1. Verify that the **AC06PuppyParadise.mdb** database is open
2. If you are not currently viewing the Relationships window, click the **Relationships** button on the Database toolbar
3. Double-click the one-to-many relationship line between Customer and Orders

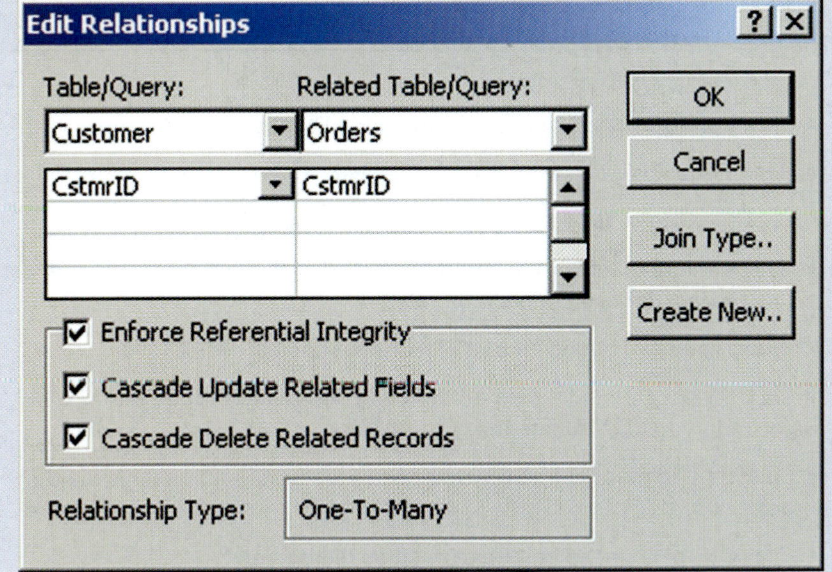

FIGURE 6.4
Customer/Orders Edit Relationships dialog box

4. Notice that the common field is named CstmrID in both tables, the referential integrity is enforced, and both cascade updates and deletes are activated

5. Close the Edit Relationships dialog box
6. Double-click one of the other relationships and review its properties
7. Close **AC06PuppyParadise.mdb**

Now that existing relationships have been explored, let's take a look at how to build new relationships.

CREATING RELATIONSHIPS IN ACCESS

Building a new database table involves defining fields and their attributes. After the table definitions are complete, relationships between tables in the same database can be built using common table fields. This task is accomplished using the Relationships window.

One-to-One

One-to-one relationships exist when one record in the primary table is related to no more than one record in the related table. Normally the data in the related table would be part of the primary table, so these relationships are not common. They are created when the data in the related tables are used infrequently or when the primary table size exceeds the Access limit, causing the table to be split.

Both tables in a one-to-one relationship have the same primary key. When a relationship is created from the primary key of one table to the primary key of another table, a one-to-one relationship is defined. We'll demonstrate this by creating a relationship between the PuppyParadise Customer table and a dummy table created for this purpose, CustomerPart2.

task reference

Create a Relationship

- Click the **Relationships** button on the Database toolbar
- If relationships exist, they will be displayed
- Click the **Show Table** button on the toolbar
- Select the table that you want to relate and click the **Add** button. Repeat this process for each table to be related
- When you have added all of the necessary tables, click **Close**
- Click the primary table field of the relationship and drag to the secondary field to initiate the relationship
- Select the referential integrity options in the Edit Relationships dialog box
- Click **OK** to close the Edit Relationships dialog box
- Repeat this process for any other relationships to be built
- Close the Relationships window

Building a one-to-one relationship:

1. Verify that the **AC06PuppyParadiseRelationships.mdb** database is open

tip: *Be sure to open the Relationships version of this database so that you can build relationships from scratch*

2. Use the **Relationships** button from the toolbar to activate the Relationships window. No relationships should display
3. Click the **Show Tables** button from the toolbar to display the list of tables that can be related
4. Make sure that the **Customer** table is selected and click the **Add** button
5. Select the **CustomerPart2** table and click the **Add** button again to add the second table of customer data
6. **Close** the Show Table dialog box
7. Click **Customer.CstmrID** and drag to **CustomerPart2.CstmrID** to open the Edit Relationships dialog box for this relationship

tip: *Recall that the notation Customer.CstmrID identifies the table.field*

8. Click on all of the referential integrity options to enforce referential integrity and activate cascade updates and deletes

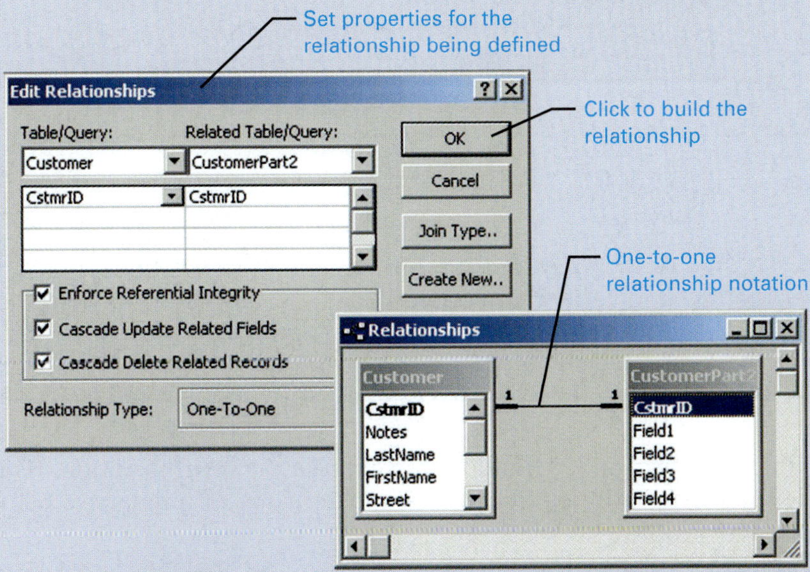

FIGURE 6.5
One-to-one relationship

9. Click **Create**
10. Close the Relationships window and click **Yes** to save your changes

This relationship was created for demonstration purposes and is not functional for PuppyParadise. A relationship sometimes needs to be deleted from a production database because it was created in error, or is no longer needed. Delete a relationship in the Relationships window by clicking the relationship line and clicking the Del key.

Since the CustomerPart2 table is not needed, both the table and the relationship just built will be deleted. Deleting either table in the relationship also deletes the relationship. A table can be deleted from the Tables object list in the Database window or from the Relationships window. Deleting the table from the Database window permanently removes it from the database.

Deleting a table and its associated relationships:

1. Verify that the **AC06PuppyParadiseRelationships.mdb** database is open
2. In the Database window, click on the **Tables** object
3. Select the **CustomerPart2** table and click **Del;** respond **Yes** to the delete prompt

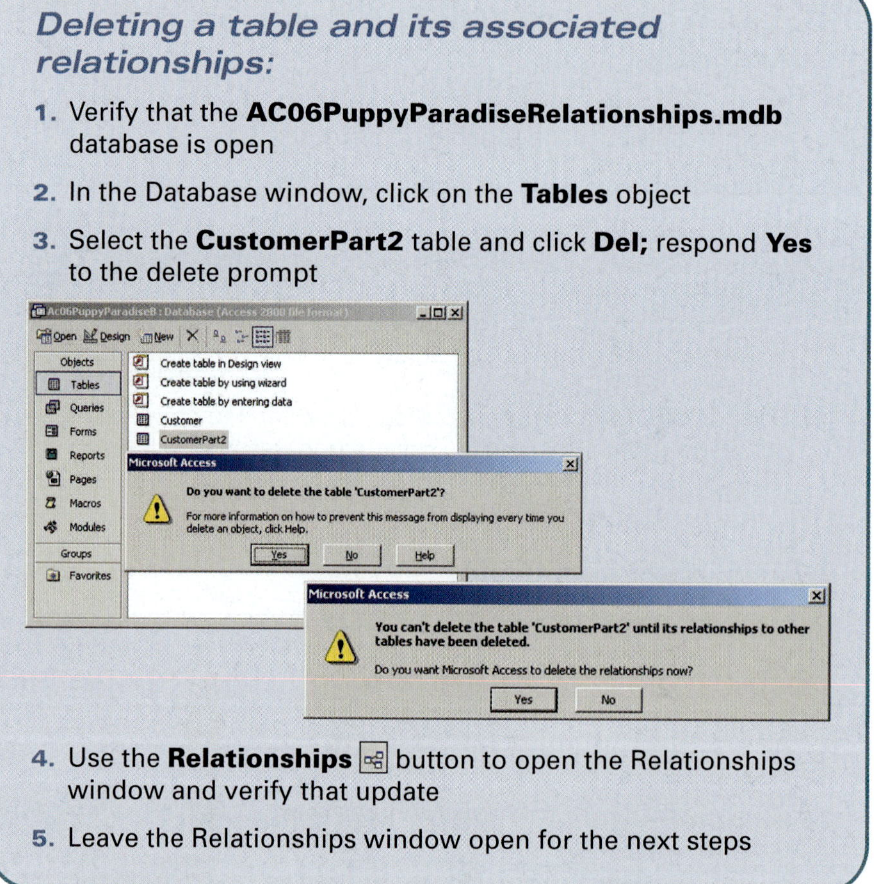

FIGURE 6.6
Deleting a table and its relationships

4. Use the **Relationships** button to open the Relationships window and verify that update
5. Leave the Relationships window open for the next steps

Table deletes cannot be undone, so execute them with caution. Using Windows Backup utilities to create a backup copy of a database before deleting tables is advisable.

One-to-Many

One-to-many relationships, when one record in the primary table can be related to multiple records in the related table, are the most common relationship type. Creating a one-to-many relationship is very similar to the technique just reviewed to create one-to-one relationships.

Both tables in a one-to-many relationship have the same field or foreign key. This shared field cannot be the primary key of the related (second) table. Clicking the field in the primary table and dragging it to the related field in the second table opens the Edit Relationships window. Set the relationship properties, most importantly referential integrity, and click Create to build the relationship.

Building a one-to-many relationship:

1. Verify that the **AC06PuppyParadiseRelationships.mdb** database is open

tip: *Be sure to open the Relationships version of this database so that you can build relationships from scratch*

2. Use the **Relationships** button on the toolbar to activate the Relationships window
3. Click the **Show Tables** button on the toolbar to display the list of tables that can be related
4. Add the tables **Customer, Orders, OrderDetails,** and **Products** (in that order) to the Relationships window

tip: *You can drag the Title bar of a table to move it in the Relationships window*

5. Click and drag a relationship from **Customer.CstmrID** to **Orders.CstmrID**

tip: *If you miss and build the relationship between the wrong fields, select the relationship line and press **Del***

6. Check all three referential integrity options and click **Create**
7. Repeat steps 5 and 6 for the **Orders.OrderID** and **OrderDetails.OrderID** relationship. A one-to-many relationship is created because OrderDetails has a compound key
8. Repeat steps 5 and 6 for **Products.ProductID** and **OrderDetails.ProductID**

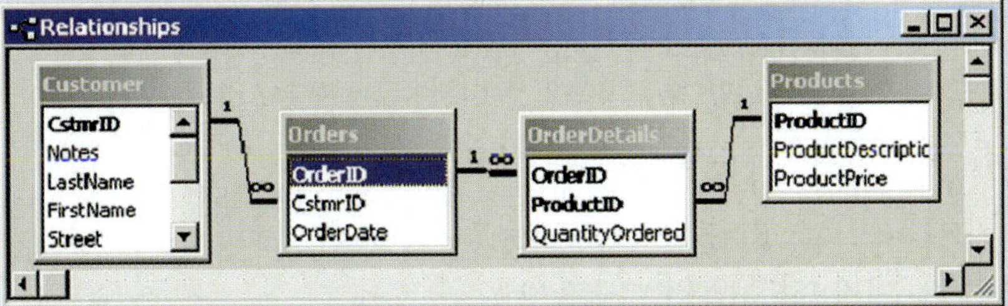

FIGURE 6.7
PuppyParadise table relationships

9. Compare your results with Figure 6.7 and make any necessary changes
10. Close the Relationships window

Although the type of relationship is not directly specified, the fields used and the direction of the drag-and-drop operation control how the relationship is built. The field at the starting point of the drag operation should always be the primary (one side) of the relationship even though the relationships often will be built correctly if the direction is reversed.

Dragging from the primary key field of one table to the primary key field of another table will create a one-to-one relationship, reflecting the fact that key fields can contain only one occurrence of each value. Dragging from the primary key field of one table to a nonkey field in another table builds a one-to-many relationship with the key field's table as primary since it can contain only one occurrence of each key value. When dragging from a nonkey field to a nonkey field, the direction of the drag operation determines which table is primary in the relationship.

The PuppyParadise OrderDetails table has a compound key using both OrderID and ProductID. Since the relationships built with the Orders and Products tables only use part of the compound key, they are one-to-many.

Any attempt to create a relationship between tables that already contain data will fail if the existing data violate the referential integrity rules selected. For example, trying to relate the Customer and Orders tables would fail if there were orders in the Orders table for a customer that was not in the Customer table. When all violations are repaired in the existing data, the relationships can be edited to enforce referential integrity rules for all new data entry.

BUILDING AND USING INDEXES

Microsoft Access uses indexes to find and sort records faster. Access uses indexes in a table as you use an index in a book: to find data, it looks up the location of the data in the index. Indexes can be based on a single field or on multiple fields. Multiple-field indexes are used to distinguish between records in which the first field may have the same value such as LastName and FirstName.

Single-Field Indexes

Access automatically creates indexes on primary key fields defined in the Design view of a table. Foreign key fields used to define table relationships in the Relationships window are also automatically indexed. Additional indexes are created to improve database performance.

Consider indexing large tables with fields that are searched frequently, sorted, or used to join tables. Indexing does require extra storage space and does not improve the performance of all database operations, so they should not be overused. When database performance needs to be improved, consider indexing fields with the following qualities:

- The field's data type is Text, Number, Currency, or Date/Time (OLE data types can't be indexed)
- Frequent searches are executed for values stored in the field
- The field is frequently used to sort
- The field contains many different values (if most of the values are the same, an index does not significantly improve performance)

When two or more fields are used frequently in combination such as LastName and FirstName, it makes sense to create a multiple-field index containing both fields. Such an index can provide dramatic performance improvements for large tables. Up to 10 fields can be included in a multiple-field index.

In the PuppyParadise database, the most frequent searches will involve the Customer table. Several Customer table forms, queries, and reports use the State field to order the results, so State is a prime candidate for indexing. Normally, database performance would be tracked before creating an index to determine whether or not indexing produced the desired results.

An index should improve the search, sort, and query performance or be removed and other ways to improve performance evaluated.

One way to track performance is to ask users to document response times and their satisfaction with specific operations such as a query or report. This is a subjective measure, but can be effective. Microsoft Access provides a tool to analyze database performance that will be covered in a later session. The Performance Analyzer suggests updates that could improve database performance with no indication of the degree of improvement likely. Third-party vendors provide the most comprehensive performance tools that can be used to verify execution and response times before and after indexing.

Creating an index actually creates an index table, similar to Figure 6.8, telling Access which records in the table belong to each index value. When an operation is performed using the index, Access is able to look up values in the index and then move directly to the associated table records. Figure 6.8 shows a portion of the index for the State field of the Customer table. In a query that retrieves CA records, Access will use the index to retrieve only record 14 of the Customer table. This is much faster than searching every record in the Customer table for a match.

Customer.State index

State	Record Number
CA	14
CO	2
	5
	6
	1
	13
	20
	12
IN	25
	17
	4
	15
	26
	24
	23
MI	11

Customer table records for CO

FIGURE 6.8
A portion of the Customer.State index

task reference

Index a Table Field

- Open the table in **Design view**
- Select the field to be indexed from the Field Name column
- Set the Indexed field property to **Yes (Duplicates OK)** or **Yes (No Duplicates)**
- Close the table design and save the changes

Indexing Customer.State:

1. Verify that the **AC06PuppyParadiseRelationships.mdb** database is open
2. Open the Design view of the Customer table
3. Select CstmrID and notice the Indexed property setting
4. Select the **State** field
5. Set the Indexed property of State to **Yes (Duplicates OK)**

tip: *Yes (No Duplicates) would be used if there were no records in the table with the same index value. The primary key of a table would have an Indexed value of Yes (No Duplicates)*

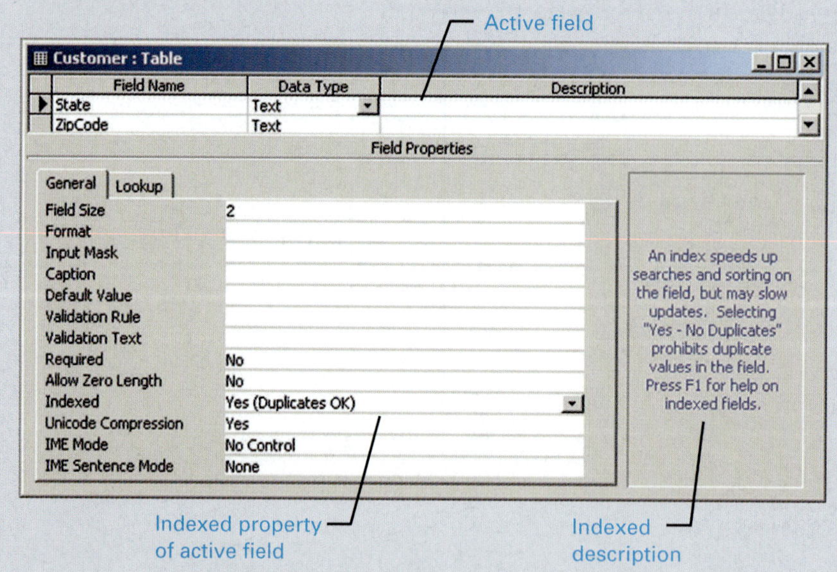

FIGURE 6.9
Customer.State indexed property

6. Close the Design view and save your changes

Indexes created automatically, such as the primary key index, cannot be deleted. Deleting other indexes simply requires setting the Indexed property of the field to No. Since the data held in each database are unique, there is no standard increase in performance gained from indexing. Additionally, an index that does not improve performance with the current data may be beneficial as more data are stored.

task reference

Delete an Index

- Open the table in **Design view**
- Select the field whose index is to be removed from the Field Name column
- Set the Indexed field property to **No** (this does not impact the field or its data)
- Close the table design and save the changes

anotherway

. . . to set and delete indexes

Indexes also can be created, updated, and deleted using the Indexes button from the Design view of a table. Since this is the only way to set multifield indexes, it is covered in that topic.

There are two disadvantages to adding indexes. Since creating an index actually adds a new table to a database, it enlarges the size of the database. Second, when values are added or changed in an indexed field, the index also must be updated, slowing the overall update process. Indexes should be monitored and retained only if they improve sort, select, and query performance.

Multiple-Field Indexes

As was mentioned, ***multiple-field indexes*** are created when fields are used in combination to sort or search a table. The most common example of LastName and FirstName exists in the PuppyParadise Customer table. Multifield indexes cannot be set in the table design, but are set in the Indexes dialog box that can only be accessed from the Design view of a table.

task reference

View the Indexes of a Table

- Open the table in **Design view**
- Click the **Indexes** button of the toolbar
- Click an index to review its properties

Viewing Customer table indexes:

1. Verify that the **AC06PuppyParadiseRelationships.mdb** database is open
2. Open the Design view of the Customer table
3. Click the **Indexes** button from the toolbar
4. Click on each index to review its properties

The Customer table should have three indexes. The PrimaryKey index was created by Access when CstmrID was set as the primary key field. The CustomerNum index also was created by Access to be used as a Foreign Key when linking to other tables. The State index was built in the previous steps. Selecting an index in the Indexes dialog box and pressing the Del key will delete that index from the database.

FIGURE 6.10
Customer table indexes

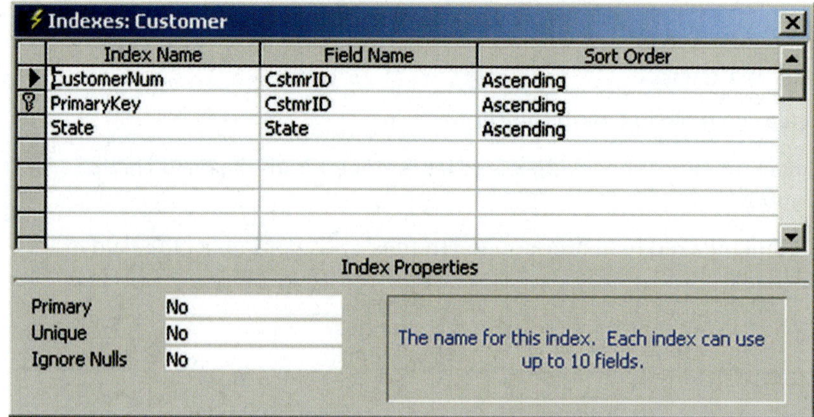

Index Name	Field Name	Sort Order
CustomerNum	CstmrID	Ascending
PrimaryKey	CstmrID	Ascending
State	State	Ascending

Index Properties

Primary No
Unique No
Ignore Nulls No

The name for this index. Each index can use up to 10 fields.

Setting a multifield Customer table index:

1. Verify that the **AC06PuppyParadiseRelationships.mdb** database is open
2. Open the Design view of the Customer table
3. Click the **Indexes** button from the toolbar
4. In the first empty Index Name type **WholeName**

tip: *Index names can be anything that you want, but something reflecting the field(s) involved usually works best*

5. In the Field Name column, click the arrow and select **LastName,** the first field for the index
6. In the Field Name column of the next row, click the arrow and select **FirstName,** the second field for the index

tip: *This step can be repeated to add up to 10 fields to the index*

7. Select the sort order for each index field. Ascending, the default, is correct for this index
8. Close the Indexes window
9. Close the Customer table Design view, saving your changes

Remember that indexing is only one way to improve database performance; Compact and Repair is another. The only way to know if indexing has made operations more efficient is to monitor those operations.

SESSION 6.1

making the grade

1. How would you view existing table relationships?
2. What is the relevance of the direction of the drag operation that creates a new relationship?
3. Why is referential integrity important?
4. Why are indexes important?

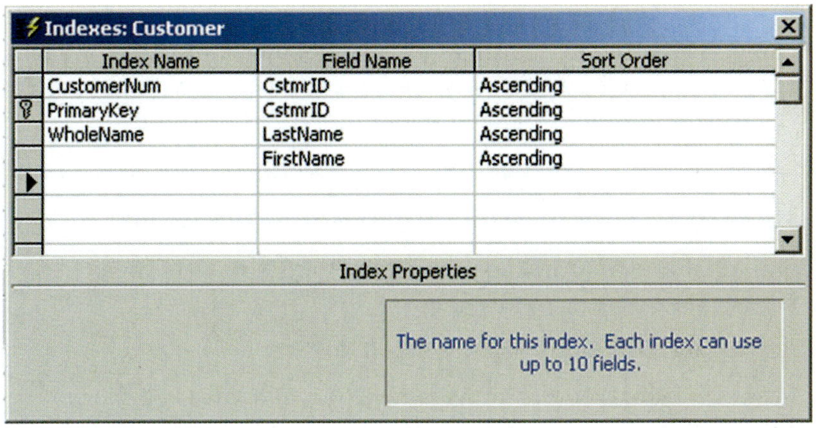

Index Name	Field Name	Sort Order
CustomerNum	CstmrID	Ascending
PrimaryKey	CstmrID	Ascending
WholeName	LastName	Ascending
	FirstName	Ascending

Index Properties

The name for this index. Each index can use up to 10 fields.

FIGURE 6.11
WholeName Customer table index

SESSION 6.2 CREATING OUTPUT WITH RELATED TABLES

You have been using data in related tables without an understanding of how these operations are really accomplished. When table relationships are properly defined, creating a query, form, or report using data from multiple tables is simply a matter of selecting the fields and arranging them as you would like.

CONSTRUCTING MULTITABLE QUERIES

Combining the data from two or more tables is usually accomplished using a query and is called joining the tables. Access supports three types of joins. The most common join is called an ***inner join*** and is the default join operation.

Inner Join

Joining the data from multiple tables can be accomplished by matching records with a common value. Typically the values being matched are in fields with defined relationships. For example, matching OrderDetails. ProductID to Product.ProductID would allow retrieval of the Product. ProductDescription using a defined relationship. Existing relationships are displayed as join lines in the query grid and display the one-to-many notation when referential integrity is enforced. Even if no relationships have been defined between the tables selected for a query, Microsoft Access will infer a relationship if they contain fields with the same name.

Sometimes data from unrelated tables are needed. In this case, there is no field that will connect the data in one table to another table, so one or more extra tables must be added to the query as a bridge between the two unrelated tables. Data from the bridge tables need not be displayed in the query result. For example, to retrieve fields from the PuppyParadise Customer and OrderDetails tables, the Orders table would be included as a bridge because it is related to each of the tables containing the desired data.

Records that don't have matching join field values can be either included or excluded from the query result. An ***inner join*** specifies that a row is created in the query result only when the join values of both tables match. For example, joining the PuppyParadise Customer and Orders table using the default inner join will return rows only for customers who have placed orders. If any customers have not placed orders, they will not be included in the inner join query results.

As an example, you will create the query that will join all of the tables in the PuppyParadise database using the relationships built in the previous session. The result will contain only customers who have placed orders and will be used to create invoices in the Multitable Report topic.

Creating a multitable query, InvoiceJoin:

1. Verify that the **AC06PuppyParadiseRelationships.mdb** database is open
2. Select the **Queries** object and click **New**
3. Select **Design view** from the New Query dialog box and click **OK**
4. Add **Customer, Orders, OrderDetails,** and **Products** tables to the query design

tip: *Although the position of the tables in the Design window is not important, the order shown is the most effective way to view the relationships. If needed, drag the tables to the positions shown*

5. Close the Show Table dialog box
6. From the Customer table add **FirstName, LastName, Street, City, State,** and **ZipCode** to the QBE grid
7. From the Orders table, add **OrderDate**
8. From the Products table add **ProductDescription** and **ProductPrice**
9. From the OrderDetails table add **QuantityOrdered**

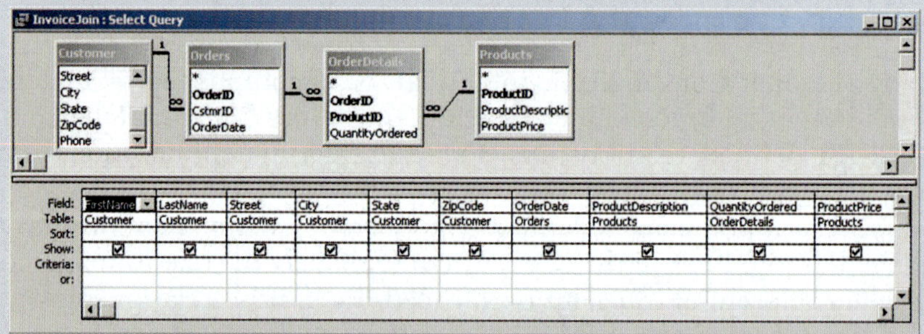

FIGURE 6.12
Select query joining all of the PuppyParadise tables

10. Click the **Run** [!] button to view the query results

InvoiceJoin : Select Query

FirstName	LastName	Street	City	State	ZipCode	OrderDate	ProductDescription	Quantity	ProductPric
Sam	Wagoner	5480 Alpine Lane	Sterling	CO	88661	15-Dec-2002	PoochPouch- no pattern	1	$35.99
Sam	Wagoner	5480 Alpine Lane	Sterling	CO	88661	05-Feb-2003	PoochPouch- no pattern	25	$35.99
Eliza	Calahan	2140 Edgewood Roa	Grand Lake	CO	80446	04-Dec-2002	PoochPouch- no pattern	1	$35.99
Shiela	Monarch	431 Phillips Road	Coatesville	IN	46611	27-Mar-2000	PoochPouch- no pattern	50	$35.99
Thomas	Calahan	840 Cascade Road	Coatesville	IN	80464	03-Feb-2003	PoochPouch- no pattern	10	$35.99
James	Lake	701 East Street	Grandby	MI	49571	03-Mar-2001	PoochPouch- no pattern	1	$35.99
Alto	Smith	114 Lexington Ave.	Granby	CO	49302	05-Apr-2001	PoochPouch- no pattern	1	$35.99
Bridgett	Chinn	400 Salmon Street	Ada	MI	49301	18-May-2001	PoochPouch- no pattern	25	$35.99
Ben	Katz	56 Foursone Road	Detroit	MI	49505	30-Jul-2001	PoochPouch- no pattern	100	$35.99
Monica	Gray	3915 Hawthorne Lan	Richmond	OH	43603	17-Mar-1999	PoochPouch- no pattern	45	$35.99
Monica	Gray	3915 Hawthorne Lan	Richmond	OH	43603	16-May-2000	PoochPouch- no pattern	50	$35.99
Ramona	Rivers	37 Queue Highway	Lacota	MI	49063	12-Nov-2002	PoochPouch- no pattern	1	$35.99
Sandy	Amstont	95 Bay Boulevard	Jenison	CO	80428	22-Dec-2001	PoochPouch- no pattern	1	$35.99
James	Hill	5365 Bedford Trail	Eagle Poin	CO	80031	31-Jan-2000	PoochPouch- no pattern	22	$35.99

Record: 1 of 72

FIGURE 6.13
Inner join results

11. Save the Query as **InvoiceJoin**

Inner joins are also called equi-joins because the values of the join fields must match for a row to be created in the query result. Remember that when there is a Customer table record with no orders, there will be no entry in the query result. To verify this, Judy Johnson is CstmrID 105 in the Customer table. Since there is no order for this customer in OrderDetails, her record does not appear in the result of InvoiceJoin.

Outer Join

There are two types of outer joins. The ***left outer join*** selects all of the records from the first (left) table and joins them to values that match the other table. A left outer join would display all of the records from the previous inner join example, plus Judy Johnson's record since it is in the left table.

The ***right outer join*** selects all of the records from the right table and only those with matching values from the left table. For example, in the Customer/Orders join, a right outer join would show all orders whether or not they are associated with a customer. This relationship can't be demonstrated with PuppyParadise because the referential integrity rules selected when the table relationships were built preclude this type of entry.

Creating a PuppyParadise left outer join query:

1. Verify that the **AC06PuppyParadiseRelationships.mdb** database is open
2. Select the **Queries** object and open the **InvoiceJoin** query in Design view
3. Use the **Save As** option of the **File** menu to save the query with the name **InvoiceLeftJoin**
4. Delete the OrderDetails and Products tables from the top of the query design

tip: *This action automatically removes the fields from the design grid previously selected from these tables*

5. Double-click the relationship line between the Customer and Orders tables to open the Join Properties dialog box
6. Select option button **2: Include ALL records from 'Customer' and only those records from 'Orders' where the joined fields are equal** and click **OK**
7. Run the query to view the results

tip: *If your results do not show the record for Judy Johnson, return to Design view and repeat steps 5–7*

8. Leave the query open in Design view for the next series of steps

Left and right outer joins can involve only two tables, so the OrderDetails and Products tables were removed from the previous example. If other tables need to be included in the final result, a second query

FIGURE 6.14
Setting join properties

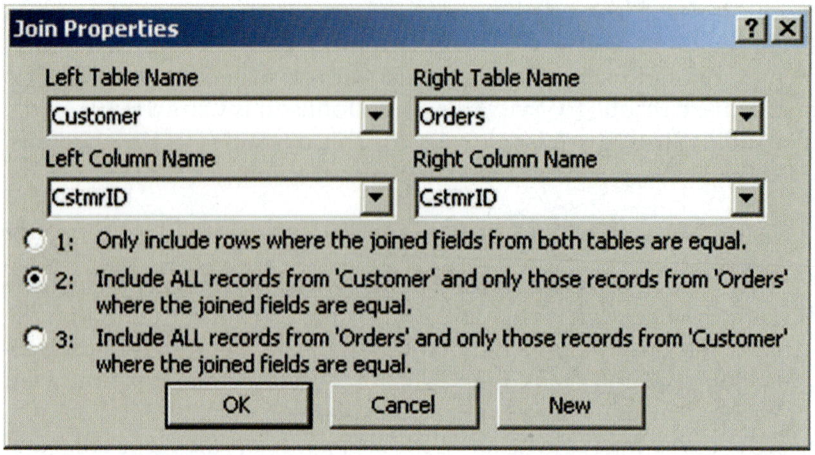

Join Properties

Left Table Name: Customer
Right Table Name: Orders
Left Column Name: CstmrID
Right Column Name: CstmrID

1: Only include rows where the joined fields from both tables are equal.
2: Include ALL records from 'Customer' and only those records from 'Orders' where the joined fields are equal.
3: Include ALL records from 'Orders' and only those records from 'Customer' where the joined fields are equal.

OK Cancel New

FIGURE 6.15
Left outer join results

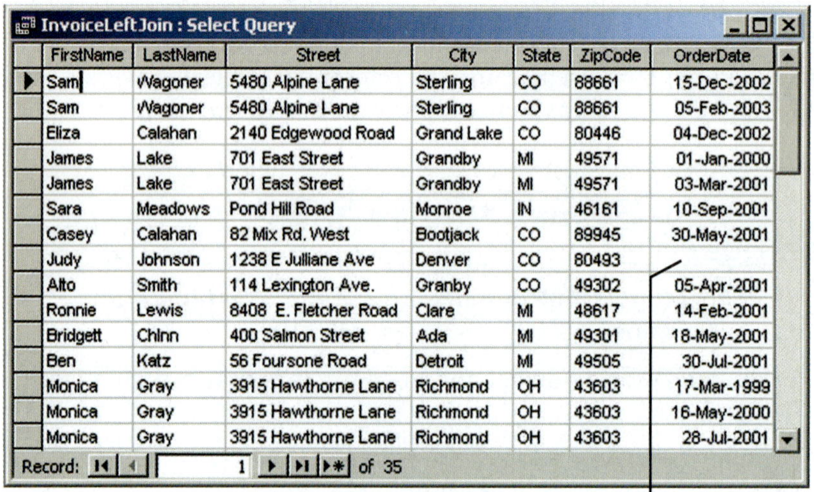

InvoiceLeftJoin : Select Query

FirstName	LastName	Street	City	State	ZipCode	OrderDate
Sam	Wagoner	5480 Alpine Lane	Sterling	CO	88661	15-Dec-2002
Sam	Wagoner	5480 Alpine Lane	Sterling	CO	88661	05-Feb-2003
Eliza	Calahan	2140 Edgewood Road	Grand Lake	CO	80446	04-Dec-2002
James	Lake	701 East Street	Grandby	MI	49571	01-Jan-2000
James	Lake	701 East Street	Grandby	MI	49571	03-Mar-2001
Sara	Meadows	Pond Hill Road	Monroe	IN	46161	10-Sep-2001
Casey	Calahan	82 Mix Rd. West	Bootjack	CO	89945	30-May-2001
Judy	Johnson	1238 E Julliane Ave	Denver	CO	80493	
Alto	Smith	114 Lexington Ave.	Granby	CO	49302	05-Apr-2001
Ronnie	Lewis	8408 E. Fletcher Road	Clare	MI	48617	14-Feb-2001
Bridgett	Chinn	400 Salmon Street	Ada	MI	49301	18-May-2001
Ben	Katz	56 Foursone Road	Detroit	MI	49505	30-Jul-2001
Monica	Gray	3915 Hawthorne Lane	Richmond	OH	43603	17-Mar-1999
Monica	Gray	3915 Hawthorne Lane	Richmond	OH	43603	16-May-2000
Monica	Gray	3915 Hawthorne Lane	Richmond	OH	43603	28-Jul-2001

Record: 1 of 35

Customer record without an order

joining the InvoiceLeftJoin query results to other tables would be built. As was demonstrated, the results of the query can differ depending on the type of join and the order in which the joins are performed.

To fully understand how Access determines which is the left or right table, we need to take a look at the underlying SQL. Recall that SQL (structured query language) is the standard language used to query relational databases. The QBE (query by example) grid that has been used to create queries is a GUI that generates SQL statements executed by Access.

Viewing the SQL for the InvoiceLeftJoin query:

1. Verify that the **AC06PuppyParadiseRelationships.mdb** database is open and that the **InvoiceLeftJoin** query is in Design view
2. Click the down arrow to the right of the View button to drop down the view list
3. Select **SQL View**
4. Close the SQL View

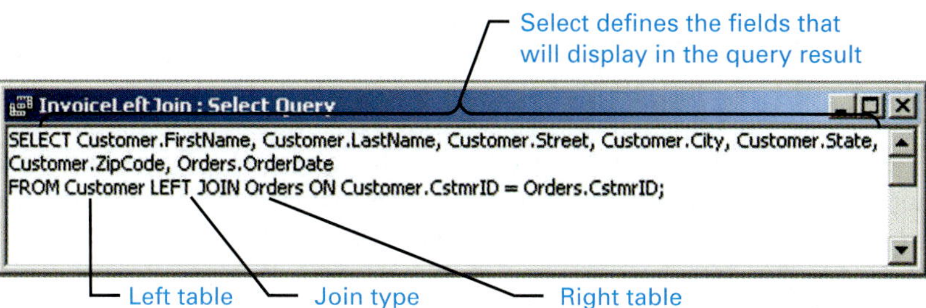

FIGURE 6.16
SQL View of InvoiceLeftJoin

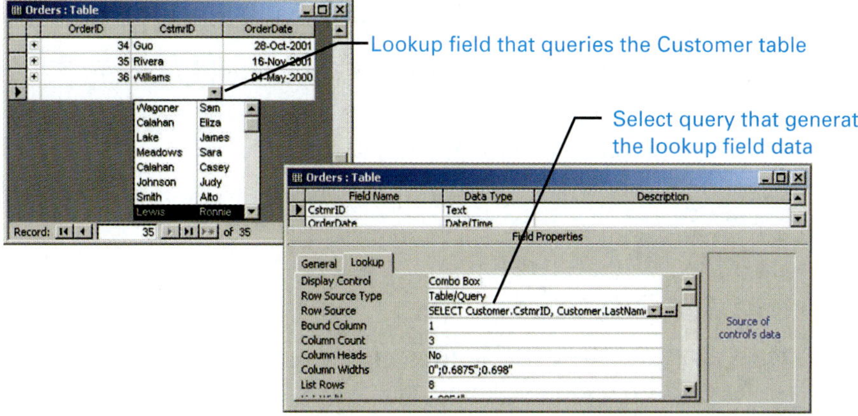

FIGURE 6.17
CstmrID lookup field and query

The order in which tables are added to the design pane of the QBE grid determines their order in the resulting SQL statement. Since tables can be moved in the design grid, the order in which they appear is not always indicative of which was added first. When a left or right outer join is specified, it will be based on the order in which the tables were added to the query and to the order in which they appear in the SQL statement in the SQL pane. It is always best to check the SQL to be sure of the query results.

DEVELOPING MULTITABLE FORMS

To create a multitable form, a relationship between the tables must be defined first. Since the relationships in the PuppyParadise database have already been set, it is ready for multitable operations.

Creating a Lookup Field

The Lookup Wizard data type has already been used to create a lookup field in the Orders table. When table relationships are set, a lookup field provides a list of valid values used when entering data. This makes data entry easier and ensures the consistency of the data in that field.

The relationship defined between the Customer and the Orders tables forces the user to enter the CstmrID for a customer that is already in the primary (Customer) table. In Chapter 4, a lookup field was created to retrieve the customer's last and first name from the Customer table and display it in a drop-down list for the user. A lookup field can get its list of values from a table or query, or from a fixed set of values provided when it is created.

Figure 6.17 shows the Orders table in both Datasheet and Design views. In Datasheet view, the user sees the result of the lookup field. In Design view, the query developed by the Wizard to look up the CstmrID is visible.

Lookup fields also can display a fixed list of possible values. This is effective when there is a limited set of valid values for a field. A good example would be the salutation used for customers in correspondence. A Salutation field with values of Ms., Mrs., and Mr. would be an effective way to add these data to a table. Other uses for such a lookup field would be the departments of an organization, sales regions, or book classifications. In other words, any field with limited values should use a lookup field to improve data integrity.

Creating a fixed-list Customer lookup field:

1. Verify that the **AC06PuppyParadiseRelationships.mdb** database is open
2. Open the Customer table in Design view
3. Insert a row in the field design after CstmrID and before LastName
4. Name the new field **Salutation** and make its data type **Lookup Wizard**
5. Select **I will type in the values that I want** from the Lookup Wizard dialog box and click **Next**

tip: *The other option, I want the lookup column to look up the values in a table or query, was used to create the list of customers from the Customer table when you click in the CstmrID field of the Orders table*

6. Type **Mr.** as a value in the cell of the lookup column
7. Type **Ms.** in the next cell, **Mrs.** in the third cell, and click **Next**
8. Click **Finish**

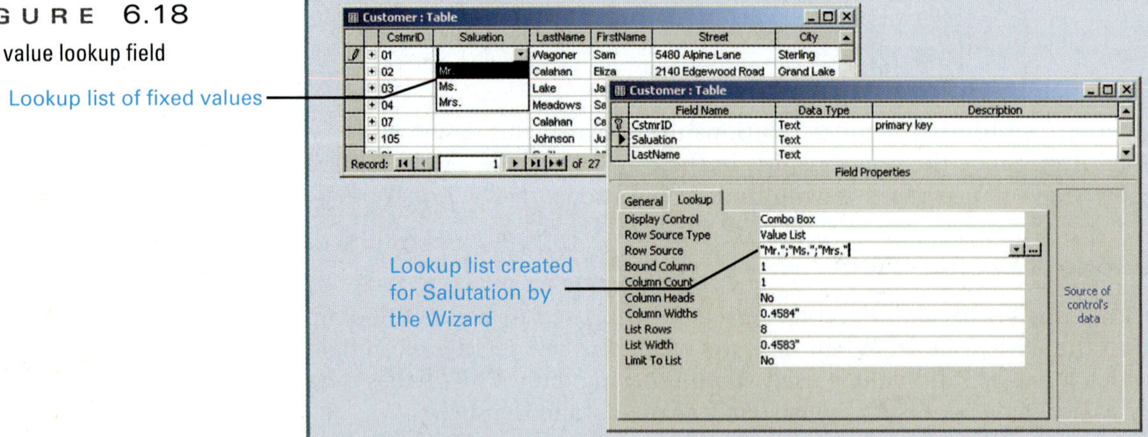

FIGURE 6.18
Fixed value lookup field

9. Select **Salutation** and then click the **Lookup** tab in the bottom portion of the screen to view the lookup criteria created by the Wizard
10. Click the **Datasheet** view button and save your changes
11. Click in the **Salutation** field to drop-down the lookup list
12. Close the Customer table

Of course, a lookup list can be created by typing the values in the Row Source property of the Lookup tab using the format shown. Alternatively SQL can be used to compose queries that will pull data from related tables such as the Customer table previously demonstrated. The Lookup Wizard simply ensures the validity of the syntax.

Lookup fields can be very powerful in improving data integrity and increasing data entry efficiency. Consider the time that is saved by the phone number lookup employed by pizza delivery organizations. The customer provides a phone number, which is used to look up an address and in some cases an order history. All the person taking the order has to enter are a phone number and any changes to the current order. This saves typing and greatly reduces errors. Another example is entering a zip code in an Internet form that is used to look up the correct city and state. The rule of thumb is, if the data exist or can be derived, don't have the user reenter them.

Displaying Related Data in a Subdatasheet

When the relationships between tables are set in a database, the related table data can be viewed from the primary table. Again the PuppyParadise Customer table provides a good example. The Customer table is the primary table in the relationship between the Customer and the Orders tables. Clicking the plus (+) sign in a Customer record will display the related Orders record (see Figure 6.19). Further, the Orders table is primary in the relationship between the Orders and the OrderDetails tables, so the associated OrderDetails can be viewed by clicking the plus (+) sign in the Orders record. The final relationship in the chain, the Products table, cannot be viewed because OrderDetails is the related (not the primary) table in this relationship.

To view related records in this fashion, nothing beyond setting up the table relationships was required. The PuppyParadise database has had this ability since relationships between the tables were built.

Creating a Main Form and SubForm

While subdatasheets are a fast and effective way to view related data, they are busy and sometimes confusing. Forms that show only a single record from the primary table and all of the related records provide better clarity.

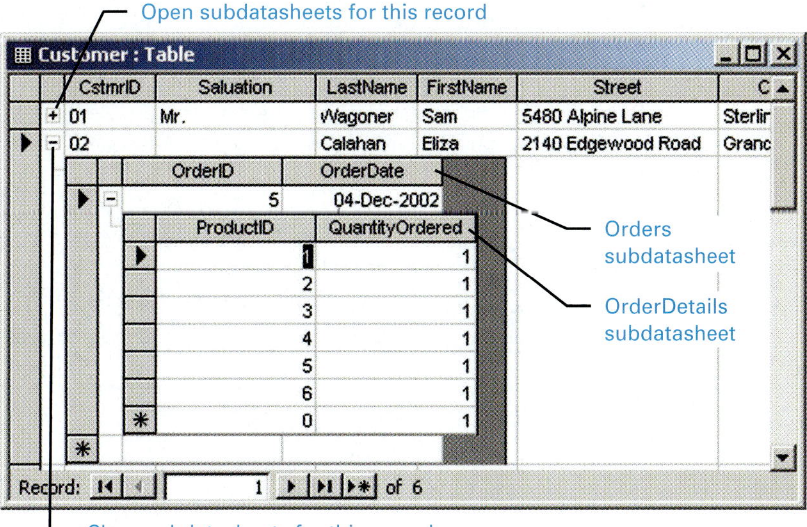

FIGURE 6.19
Customer table subdatasheets

One way to accomplish this is to use a ***main form*** to display the primary table data with a synchronized ***subform*** to display the related data from the second table. The subform is inserted into the main form to display data from a related table. Form/subform combinations also can be referred to as hierarchical forms, master/detail forms, or parent/child forms.

The Form Wizard is a fast way to create main form/subform combinations. As you know, forms and reports created using Wizards can be customized in Design view to improve their appearance and effectiveness. When using the Wizard to select data for the form, the primary table fields are selected first and then the related table fields. If the form is to be used to maintain table data, each table should appear in its own form or subform.

Creating a PuppyParadise main form/subform:

1. Verify that the **AC06PuppyParadiseRelationships.mdb** database is open
2. Select the **Forms** object and click **New**
3. Select **Form Wizard,** choose **Customer** as the record source for the form, and click **OK**
4. Select **all fields** from the Customer table
5. Select the **Orders** table from the drop-down list
6. Select **all fields** from the Orders table and click **Next**
7. Select **by Customer** as the way to view data and click **Next**
8. Select **Tabular** as the layout for your subform and click **Next**
9. Choose **Ricepaper** as the style and click **Next**
10. Verify that the form title is **Customer** and click **Finish**

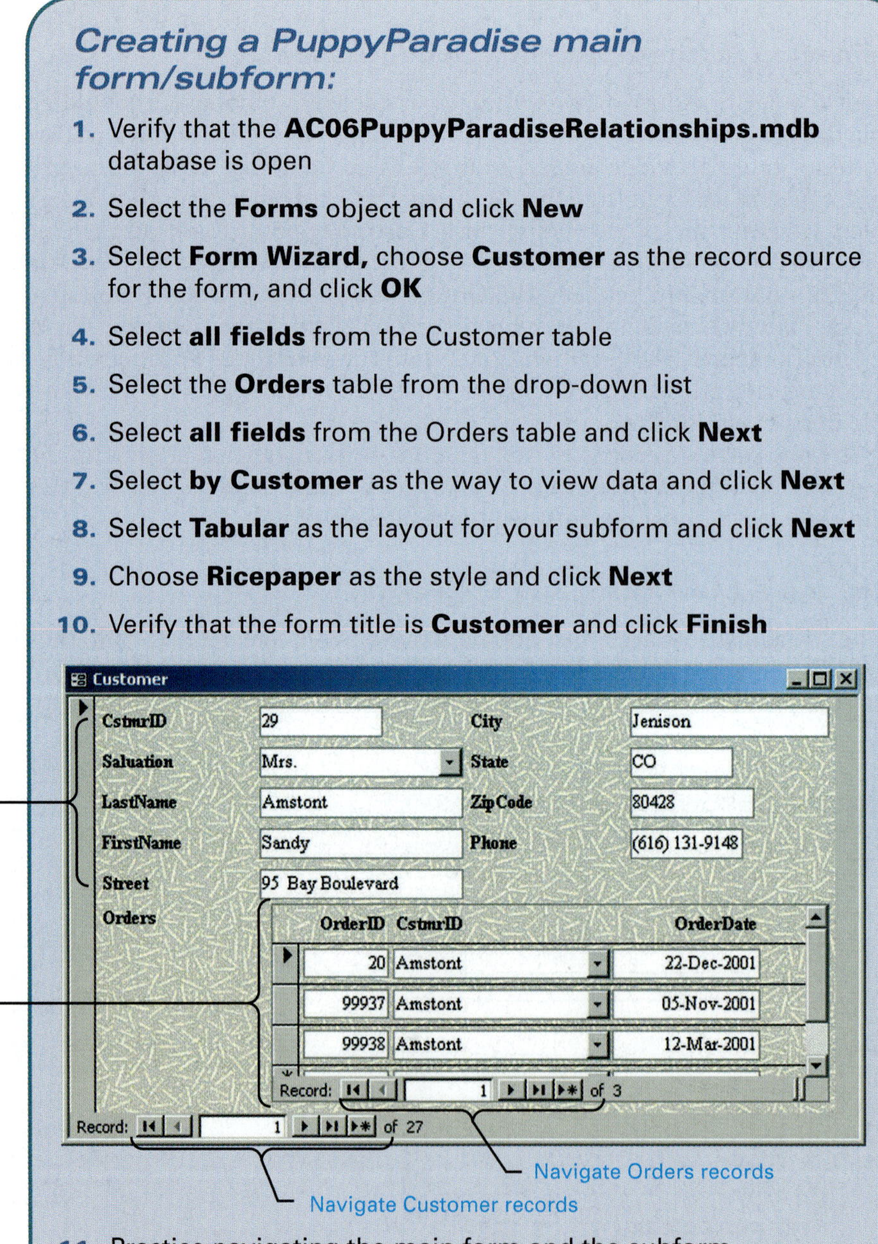

FIGURE 6.20
Customer form with a subform

11. Practice navigating the main form and the subform

This form could obviously benefit from customization. At a minimum, the size and alignment of existing fields should be adjusted to fit the data.

Customizing the PuppyParadise main form/subform:

1. Verify that the **AC06PuppyParadiseRelationships.mdb** database is open with the **Customer** form in Design view
2. Use the **Size** option of the **Format** menu to adjust the size of each label to fit its contents

tip: *You can select all of the Label controls by holding down the Shift button*

3. Move each Text Box closer to its associated Label and arrange them as shown in Figure 6.21.

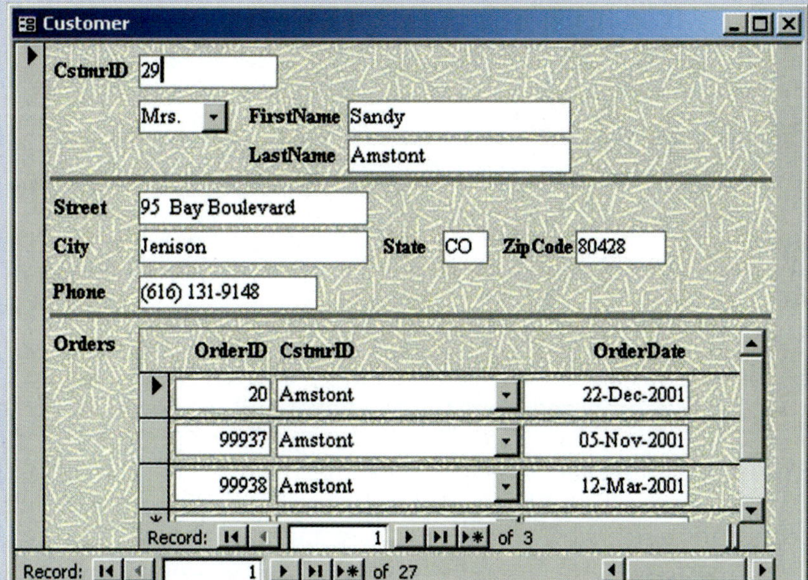

FIGURE 6.21
Customized Customer form with a subdatasheet

4. Adjust the position of the subform

tip: *When you click the subform label, the label and subform each displays a move handle since they are linked (like a bound text box and its label)*

5. Use the Line tool to draw the lines that separate the areas of the form
6. Adjust the headings and compress the field width for the three subform columns as shown in Figure 6.21
7. Use the **Form view** button to preview your changes

tip: *You will be prompted to save both the form and the subform*

8. Close the form and save your changes

FIGURE 6.22
Main form/subform save

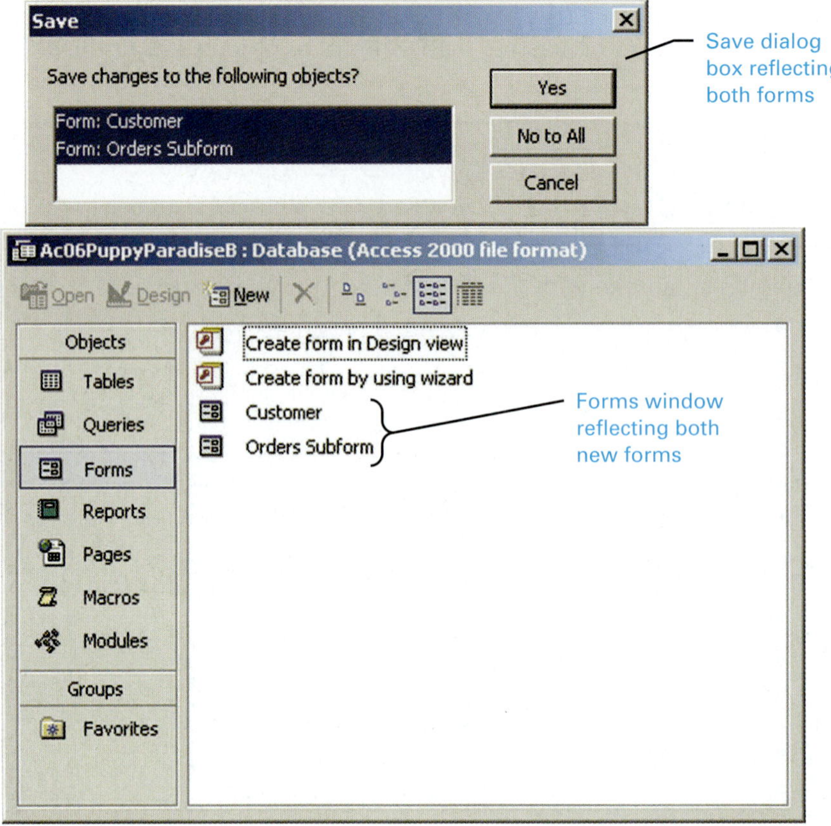

When a main form/subform pair is built, it is actually creating two forms, both of which are listed in the Forms object window. Figure 6.22 shows the save prompt reflecting the two forms and the Forms object window after the save is complete. The Orders Subform is in reality a form that has been embedded into the Customer form. Double-click Orders Subform, and it will open independently. The subform also can be viewed and edited in Design view without the Customer form being open.

When the Customer form is opened, both this form and the embedded subform display. Forms are used to view and update the data in the underlying record source. Since this form involves four tables, we will demonstrate its update capabilities.

Using a Main Form/Subform

Users typically don't care about the technical details of how their applications work; they just want them to be effective. The Customer main form/subform just created is very efficient for the user to view all of the orders a particular customer has placed and is visually more appealing than the default subdatasheet.

All of the techniques used to order and find data on a single table form can be used on the multiple tables involved in this form. The default display order for data in a main form/subform is controlled by the primary table, Customer in this case. If no other order is specified, data will display ordered by the primary key of the primary table. The user can select a field and use the sort buttons to sort by that selection. The Find button can be used to search for a particular value, such as a LastName of Rivera. Filters can be applied to retrieve and manipulate a subset of the data (see Figure 6.23) and new records can be created. Remember to remove any applied filters before proceeding.

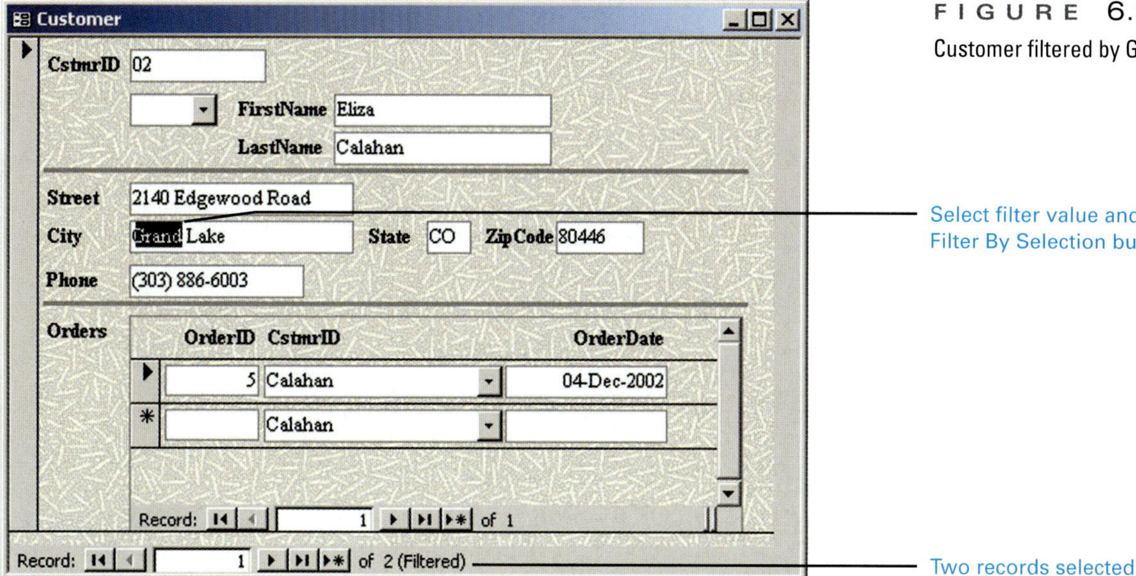

FIGURE 6.23
Customer filtered by Grand

Using the PuppyParadise main form/subform:

1. Verify that the **AC06PuppyParadiseRelationships.mdb** database is open
2. Select the **Forms** object and double-click the **Orders Subform**
3. Navigate through the orders
4. Add a new order for **Thomas Calahan** with today's date

tip: *OrderID is an AutoNumber field and will be generated*

5. **Close** the Orders Subform
6. Open the **Customer** form
7. Navigate through the customers using the lower navigation buttons
8. Add yourself as a customer with CstmrID **328**
9. Add two orders for yourself
10. **Close** the form

Multitable forms can be used to update data only when they represent one-to-many relationships. The main form is the primary side of the relationship and the subform is the related table. When forms are nested, each subform must be nested in its primary table's form (see Figure 6.24).

It is usually most effective to have one subform for each table involved. The main form can have as many subforms as are needed to represent the data. Subforms also can contain subforms—up to seven layers deep. Figure 6.24 shows three levels of nested subforms. The outer form is the Customer table data, which contains the Orders table subform, which in turn contains the OrderDetails table subform.

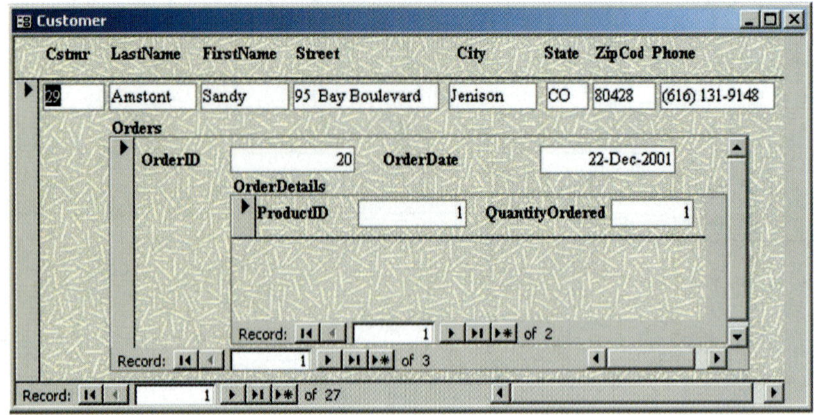

FIGURE 6.24
Nested subforms

SPECIFYING MULTITABLE REPORTS

Unlike forms, which are built to interact with the data, multitable reports retrieve data and report on them without further interaction. Because of this reports are typically based on queries that retrieve the required data so that the report is only responsible for formatting.

Selecting Data from Multiple Tables

Although queries are commonly the foundation for reports, the Report Wizard can help create a report without first creating a query. As with other "automatic" things that we have looked at, a SQL query is being built and submitted behind the scenes.

To demonstrate the use of queries, an invoice report will be created without using a query as its data source and then the same report will be created with a query. The restriction of not using a query is that the report will display all of the data returned by joining the tables—a subset cannot be specified. When a query is used, a subset of the data can be retrieved for the report. For example, only invoices for customers who have made purchases in the last month could be printed. The invoices query would select those records and make them available to the invoice report for formatting.

Building the PuppyParadise Invoice report without a user-defined query:

1. Verify that the **AC06PuppyParadiseRelationships.mdb** database is open
2. Click the **Reports** object and select **New**
3. Choose **Report Wizard** and click **OK**
4. Add all of the fields from the **Customer, Orders, OrderDetails,** and **Products** tables to the Selected Fields list and click **Next**
5. The default by Customer is appropriate for this report, but explore the other options and then return the selection to **by Customer**
6. Add two levels of grouping, **Customer.CstmrID** and **Orders.OrderID,** and click **Next**

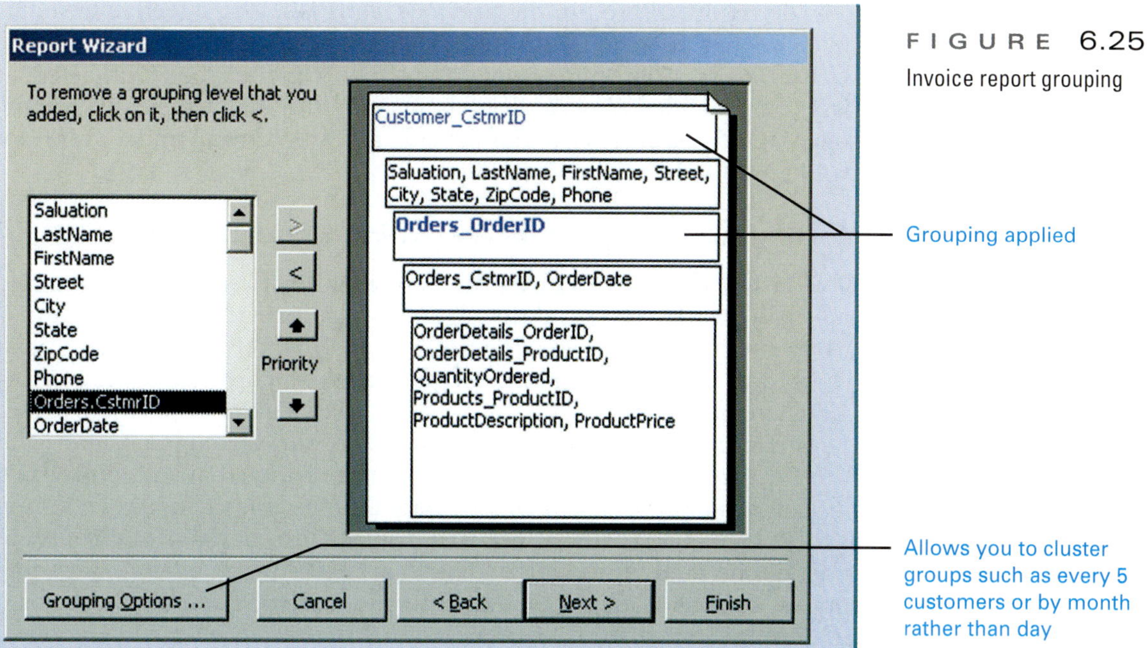

Report Wizard
To remove a grouping level that you added, click on it, then click <.
Salutation
LastName
FirstName
Street
City
State
ZipCode
Phone
Orders.CstmrID
OrderDate
Priority
Customer_CstmrID
Salutation, LastName, FirstName, Street, City, State, ZipCode, Phone
Orders_OrderID
Orders_CstmrID, OrderDate
OrderDetails_OrderID, OrderDetails_ProductID, QuantityOrdered, Products_ProductID, ProductDescription, ProductPrice
Grouping Options ...
Cancel
< Back
Next >
Finish
Grouping applied
Allows you to cluster groups such as every 5 customers or by month rather than day

FIGURE 6.25
Invoice report grouping

7. Select **OrderDetails_ProductID** as the only sort field and click **Next**

tip: *No summary options are applied, because there is no detail line item total to sum since we did not use a query as the record source*

8. Choose **Align Left 1** as the Layout style, **Landscape** as the page Orientation, and click **Next**
9. Select **Formal** as the Style and click **Next**
10. Name the Report **InvoicesNoQuery** and click **Finish**

InvoicesNoQuery
InvoicesNoQuer
Customer_CstmrI 01
Salutation Mr.
LastName Wagoner
FirstName Sam
Street 5480 Alpine Lane
City Sterling
State CO
ZipCode 88661
Phone (303) 161-5545
Orders_OrderID 3
Orders_OrderID 4
Page: 1

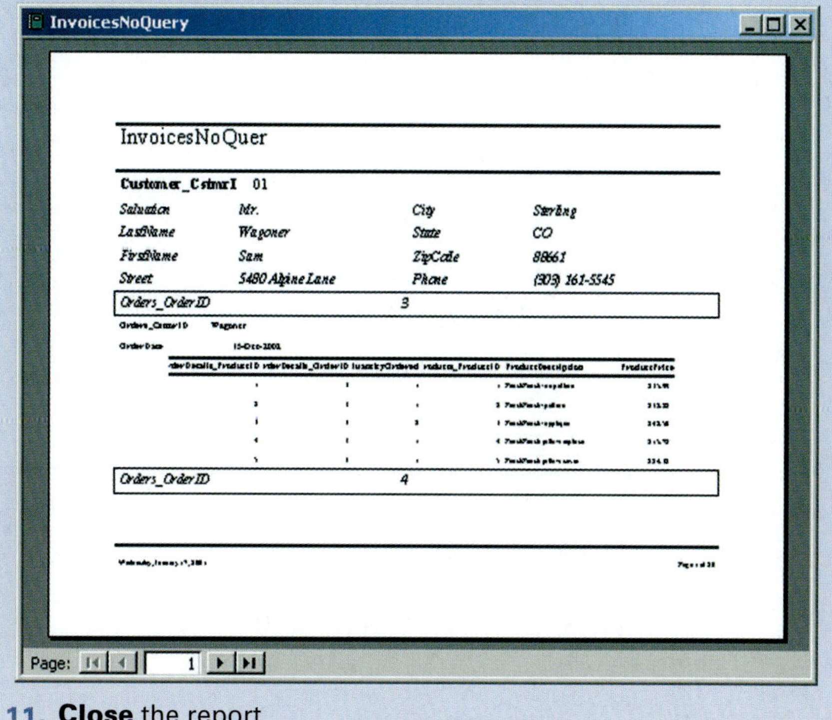

FIGURE 6.26
InvoicesNoQuery report

11. **Close** the report

The report created in the previous steps is a very effective first cut at invoices, but it needs considerable customization. The company logo needs to be added, the alignment of the labels and text boxes adjusted, and page breaks added between each invoice. Additionally, the calculations to total each detail line item and provide an invoice total and a grand total would need to be added manually.

Sorting, Grouping, and Calculating Report Data

Obviously the Report Wizard provides the ability to sort, group, and calculate data in the record source. Queries also provide the ability to sort, group, and calculate. The question then is "How do I know where to sort, group, and calculate when using a query as the record source for a report?"

There are probably as many answers to this question as there are people working with databases. There are no absolutes, and many approaches are effective. For many the best approach is the one that will minimize the customization needs of the report. With that in mind, a good rule of thumb is to sort and place calculations that display with each row of data, such as a detail line total, in the query. That leaves grouping and summary calculations, such as invoice total and report total, to be added in the report.

To try this reporting approach, the InvoiceJoin query created earlier will be modified to include sorting and the detail line calculation. This updated query will be used as the data source for the Report Wizard.

anotherway

. . . to create InvoiceJoinWithCalc

If you prefer working with lists of table fields rather than the QBE grid, it might be easier to create a new query rather than extensively editing the InvoiceJoin query. You could use the Query Wizard to select and order the fields from the related tables and then use the QBE grid to add the calculation.

Modifying the InvoiceJoin query:

1. Verify that the **AC06PuppyParadiseRelationships.mdb** database is open
2. Click the **Queries** object
3. Choose **InvoiceJoin** and click the **Design** view button
4. Double-click on **Customer.CstmrID** and **Orders.OrderID** to add them to the query since they will be needed on the invoice
5. Drag the fields to the order that will be used in the invoice by clicking the bar above each Field Name to select a column. Then drag the selected column to the correct position. The final field order should be OrderID, OrderDate, CstmrID, FirstName, LastName, Street, City, State, ZipCode, QuantityOrdered, ProductDescription, and ProductPrice
6. Use the **Save As** option of the **File** menu to save your changes with the name **InvoiceJoinWithCalc**
7. In the first empty column add the expression **ItemTotal:QuantityOrdered*ProductPrice**
8. Add the **Between #7/1/2001# And #7/31/2001#** selection criteria to OrderDate so that only orders for July of 2001 will be invoiced

tip: *Access will add the # signs if you do not type them*

9. Use the **Run** [!] button to view the query results. Verify the column order, the calculation, and the selection
10. Close the query saving your updates

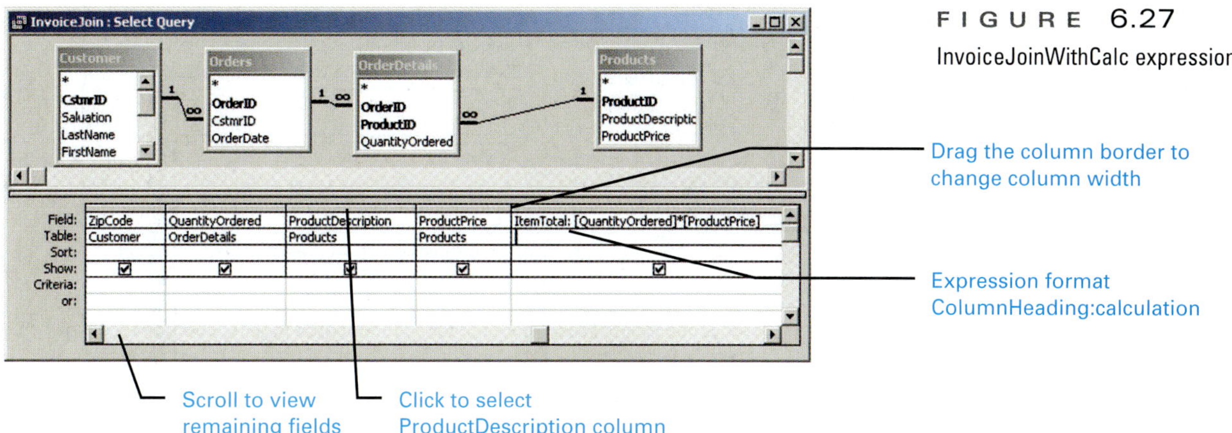

FIGURE 6.27
InvoiceJoinWithCalc expression

Besides simplifying the customization that will need to be done on the invoice report, creating the InvoiceJoinWithCalc query also allows the organization, calculation, and selection of data to be verified prior to report generation. It is helpful to know that the correct data are going into your report since that directly impacts the validity of the report result.

InvoiceJoinWithCalc report:

1. Verify that the **AC06PuppyParadiseRelationships.mdb** database is open
2. Select the **Reports** object and Click **New**
3. Select **Report Wizard,** and **InvoiceJoinWithCalc** as the data source, and click **OK**

tip: *If an empty report opens in Design view, close it and repeat steps 2 and 3, being sure to select the Report Wizard*

4. Move all of the fields of InvoiceJoinWithCalc to the Selected Fields box and click **Next**
5. Add grouping for **OrderID** and **CustmrID** and click **Next**
6. Sort by **ProductDescription** and click **Summary Options**
7. Check the **Sum** calculation for QuantityOrdered and ItemTotal to calculate group totals on these fields
8. Click **OK** and then **Next**
9. Select **Align Left 1** as the layout and **Landscape** as the page orientation, and click **Next**
10. Choose **Formal** as the report style and click **Next**
11. Click **Finish** to preview the report

This report is very similar to the one created without the query, but it has the advantage of already having the calculations in place. Customizing this report is a matter of adding a logo and title, reorganizing the fields to the correct report section, and then adding the page break.

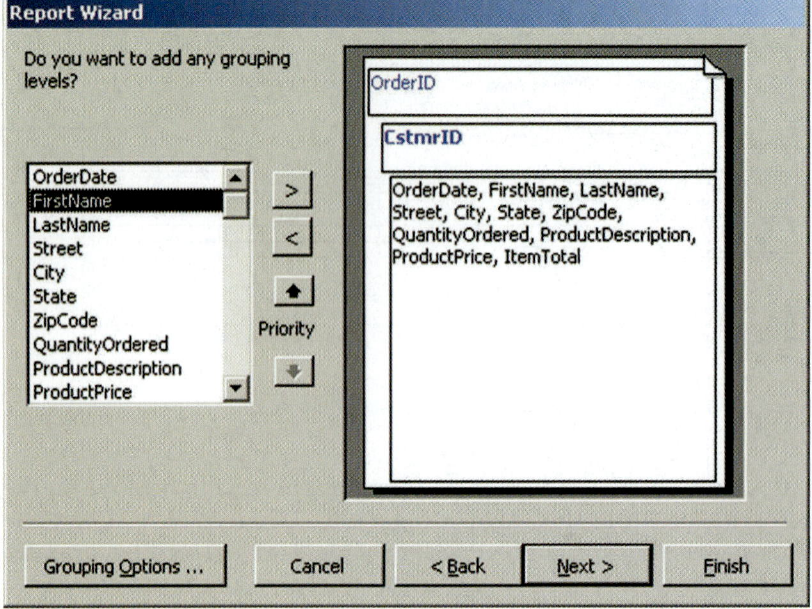

FIGURE 6.28
Grouping added to InvoiceJoinWithCalc report

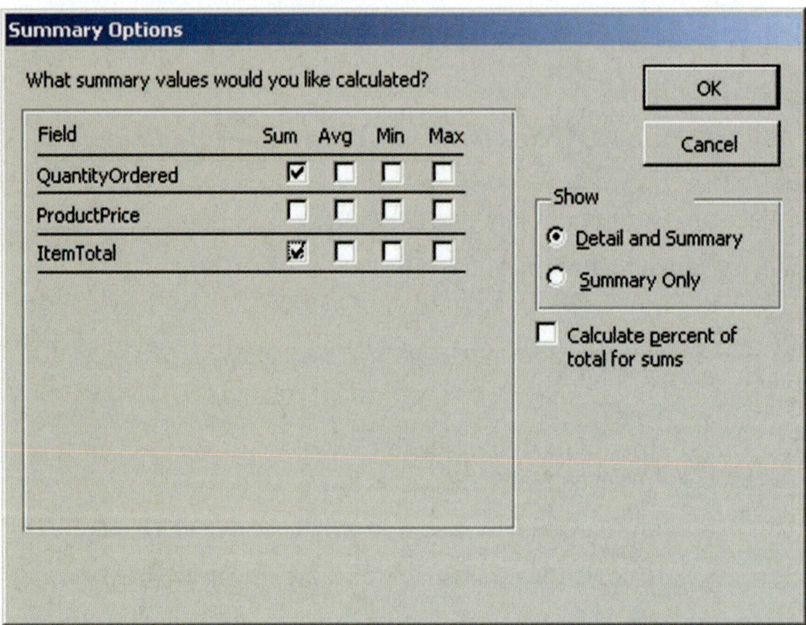

FIGURE 6.29
Adding group calculations to InvoiceJoinWithCalc report

To print on each invoice page, the logo and report title need to be in the Page Header section of the report. The GrandTotal of all invoices would print on the last invoice page, so it will be deleted. The simplest way to accomplish this is to remove the Report Header/Footer sections, which also will remove all controls they contain.

Creating a logo and title for the InvoiceJoinWithCalc report:

1. Verify that the **AC06PuppyParadiseRelationships.mdb** database is open with the **InvoiceJoinWithCalc** report open in Design view

2. Select **Report Header/Footer** from the **View** menu to remove those sections of the report
3. Answer **Yes** to the prompt informing you that this operation is not reversible
4. If the Field List is open, close it since it won't be needed
5. Use the OrderID Header bar to expand the space in the Page Header
6. Select the **Image** tool from the toolbox and click in the Page Header
7. Navigate to the **AC06PupLogo.tif** file and select it

tip: *You may need to change the Type of File in the Open dialog box to Tag Image File Format or All Files*

8. Position the logo in the top left corner of the Page Header and use the OrderID Header to adjust the size of the Page Header until it is just large enough to hold the logo
9. Select the **Label** tool and click in the Page Header just to the right of the logo
10. Type **Invoice** in the Label and set its properties to Times New Roman, 48 point, italic

FIGURE 6.30
PuppyParadise logo and report title

11. Use the **Properties** button to open the Properties window and set the Fore Color property Hue to **28,** Sat to **166,** Lum to **104,** Red to **187,** Green to **141,** and Blue to **34,** click **Add to Custom Colors,** and click **OK**

tip: *Click in the Fore Color property and then click the ellipse to the right of Fore Color and use the Define Custom Colors button*

12. Preview and save your changes

The most arduous reorganization tasks involve moving fields the Wizard placed in the Detail portion of the report. The first field that we'll address is OrderDate. The OrderDate only needs to appear once per order and most reasonably should be in the OrderID Group Header.

Modify the OrderID Header of the InvoiceJoinWithCalc report:

1. Verify that the **AC06PuppyParadiseRelationships.mdb** database is open with the **InvoiceJoinWithCalc** report open in Design view
2. Select the **OrderDate** label in the CstmrID Header, click the **Cut** button on the toolbar, click the **OrderID Header,** and click the **Paste** button on the toolbar
3. Move the label to the right of the existing OrderID Header contents
4. Select the **OrderDate** text box in the Detail section, click the **Cut** button on the toolbar, click the **OrderID Header,** and click the **Paste** button on the toolbar
5. Narrow the OrderID label and text box, add a space between the words in the label, and reposition them as shown in Figure 6.31

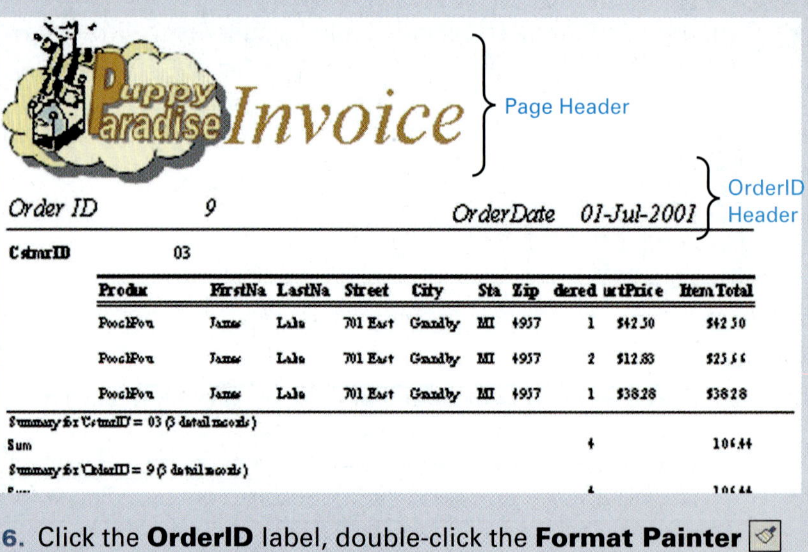

FIGURE 6.31
PuppyParadise OrderID Header

6. Click the **OrderID** label, double-click the **Format Painter** button on the toolbar, and click both the **OrderDate** label and text box to transfer the format to them

tip: *Double-clicking the Format Painter allows you to paint the format of the current object to multiple other objects. Clicking the Format Painter again turns it off*

7. Click the **Format Painter** button to turn it off
8. Resize the OrderDate controls and position them as shown in Figure 6.31
9. Hold down the **Shift** key while using the **Line** tool to draw a line under the fields of the OrderID Header
10. Preview and save your updates

The customer name and address needs to appear only once per invoice and belongs in the CstmrID Group Header. The process of moving and formatting them is very similar to that just performed to modify the OrderID; however, only the text boxes need to be moved since the labels are already in the CstmrID Group Header.

Modify the CstmrID Header of the InvoiceJoinWithCalc report:

1. Verify that the **AC06PuppyParadiseRelationships.mdb** database is open with the **InvoiceJoinWithCalc** report open in Design view
2. Drag the Detail section border to increase the height of the CstmrID Header section
3. Select the labels for ProductDescription, QuantityOrdered, ProductPrice, and ItemTotal in the CstmrID Header section by holding down the Shift key and dragging them to the bottom of the section
4. Move the lower pair of divider lines to lie just above the labels from step 3
5. Arrange the FirstName, LastName, Street, City, State, and ZipCode labels as shown in Figure 6.32

FIGURE 6.32
PuppyParadise CstmrID Header

6. Edit the ZipCode caption to read Zip and add spaces to the Captions of the other labels
7. Cut each text box for FirstName, LastName, City, State, and Zip from the Detail section. Paste it into the CstmrID section, and move it to the right of the appropriate label

tip: *Work on one control at a time. When you paste a control into the CstmrID Header section, it will be pasted in the top left corner*

8. Set all of the Text Box controls to display 10 point

9. Right-align the text in the Quantity, Product Price, and Item Total labels
10. Preview the report and adjust the size of the controls to display all of the data
11. Use the Format menu to finalize control alignment in the CstmrID Header section
12. Preview and save your updates

The Wizard added a Group Footer section for both OrderID and CstmrID. Both footers contain the same information, so the CstmrID Footer needs to be eliminated. After this footer is removed and the Detail section sized and aligned, the Page Break tool will be used to print one invoice per page.

Modify the Detail and Footer sections of the InvoiceJoinWithCalc report:

1. Verify that the **AC06PuppyParadiseRelationships.mdb** database is open with the **InvoiceJoinWithCalc** report open in Design view
2. Select the Text Box controls in the Detail section and set them to 10 point
3. Select Quantity, ItemPrice, and ItemTotal text boxes and select Right Alignment so that the numbers will line up
4. Align the Text Box controls in the Detail section with their corresponding Label controls in the CstmrID Header section

tip: *The numeric fields need to right-align and the text fields need to left-align*

5. Click the Sorting and Grouping button, select the CstmrID row, and click the Group Footer off
6. Respond **Yes** to the prompt and close the Sorting and Grouping dialog box
7. Delete the text box in the OrderID footer containing = "Summary for " &. . .
8. In the OrderID Footer, select the Sum label and the two text boxes with total calculations and set them to 10 point bold
9. Edit the Sum label to read **Count of items sold** and add a Label controls for the other text box containing **Order Total**
10. Set the Format for the sum of ItemTotal to **currency**
11. Add a line above the Footer contents and organize them as shown in Figure 6.33
12. Click the Page Break tool and click below the contents of the OrderID Footer

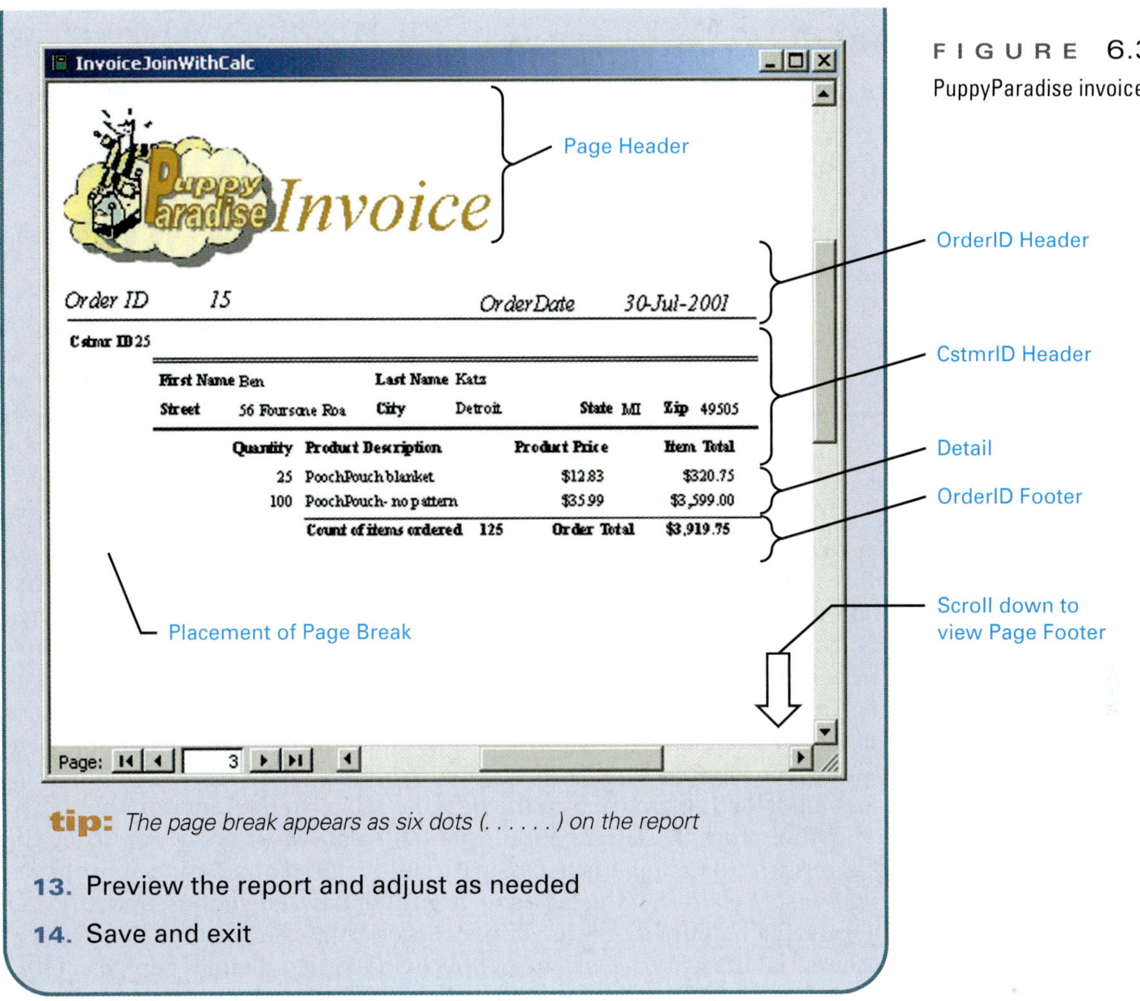

FIGURE 6.33
PuppyParadise invoice

tip: *The page break appears as six dots (. . . . . .) on the report*

13. Preview the report and adjust as needed
14. Save and exit

anotherword

. . . on Modifying Database Objects

In this chapter you have modified queries, forms, and reports. Sometimes the modification was to improve the functionality. Sometimes it was to improve the visual impact. Regardless of why you are modifying an object, it is always wise to keep the original object as a backup. When making large numbers of changes, you should create intermediate backups also. A copy of the original design can be made using copy and paste in the Objects list before opening the object. You can use the Save As option of the File menu to save intermediate work under different names. Attaching sequential letters or numbers to the file name works well (InvoicesNoQuery1, InvoicesNoQuery2, and so on). Rename the final file and delete all unneeded files when you are done.

The PuppyParadise Invoice is a complex report involving four tables, two levels of grouping, detail line calculations, and summary calculations. No matter how this report is approached, it will be time consuming to develop, but once it is completed it can be used over and over again. The way this report is implemented, Evan will need to edit the selection criteria of the query before each report run. A more efficient methodology using Parameter queries will be introduced in later chapters.

SESSION 6.2

making the grade

1. How would you decide whether to use an inner join or one of the outer join queries?
2. Why would you want to see the SQL generated by a query that you create in the QBE grid?
3. How do you know which table to open when you want to view related data in a subdatasheet?
4. Why would you consider adding indexes to your database tables?
5. Why would you use a query as the record source for a form?

SESSION 6.3 SUMMARY

To reduce data redundancy and increase data validity, database data are stored in multiple tables. Multiple tables reduce data redundancy because data that are common to multiple records are stored only once and then joined to each related row using a query. Data validity is improved because there is only one place to add or update each piece of data.

Only one-to-one and one-to-many relationships can be defined in a relational database. Many-to-many relationships use a junction table containing the key fields of both original tables, so that a one-to-many relationship is built from each of the original tables to the junction table.

While properly designed multiple-table databases greatly enhance the reliability of the data, it is necessary to understand and define appropriate relationships between the tables to control updates, deletions, and joins for output. Each defined relationship has properties that control its behavior. Referential integrity rules control how data in related tables can be entered and updated. Referential integrity rules can be turned off, enforced, or partially enforced. Double-click a relationship line in the Relationships window to set these options. In general, database data are more reliable when all referential rules are enforced.

When creating a multitable query, the relationship lines can be double-clicked to set the join properties. The default, inner join, returns records when the join field values of both tables match. A left outer join returns all of the rows from the left table and rows from the right table with a matching foreign key value. A right outer join returns all of the rows from the right table and rows from the left table with a matching foreign key value.

Data from multiple tables can be updated using the default primary datasheet and related subdatasheets. To open a subdatasheet, click the plus sign in the primary datasheet row. Related table data also can be displayed in a main form/subform combination. Data from the primary table are displayed in the main form and those from the related table are displayed in the subform.

Visit www.mhhe.com/i-series/ to explore related topics.

MOUS OBJECTIVES SUMMARY

- Create one-to-many relationships—AC2002-6-1
- Enforce referential integrity—AC2002-6-2
- Establish many-to-many relationships—AC2002-5-2

task reference roundup

Task	Page #	Preferred Method
View table relationships	AC 6.4	• Click the **Relationships** button on the Database toolbar
		• If relationships exist, they will be displayed. If there are no current relationships, you can add tables and build relationships between them
View relationship properties	AC 6.7	• Click the **Relationships** button on the Database toolbar
		• If relationships exist, they will be displayed. If there are no current relationships, you can add tables and build relationships between them
		• Double-click the relationship line that you would like to view
		• The Edit Relationships dialog box displays the properties of that relationship
Create a relationship	AC 6.8	• Click the **Relationships** button on the Database toolbar
		• If relationships exist, they will be displayed
		• Click the **Show Table** button on the toolbar
		• Select the table that you want to relate and click the **Add** button. Repeat this process for each table to be related
		• When you have added all of the necessary tables click **Close**
		• Click the primary table field of the relationship and drag to the secondary field to initiate the relationship
		• Select the referential integrity options in the Edit Relationships dialog box
		• Click **OK** to close the Edit Relationships dialog box
		• Repeat this process for any other relationships to be built
		• Close the Relationships window
Index a table field	AC 6.14	• Open the table in **Design view**
		• Select the field to be indexed from the Field Name column
		• Set the Indexed field property to **Yes (Duplicates OK)** or **Yes (No Duplicates**)
		• Close the table design and save the changes
Delete an index	AC 6.15	• Open the table in **Design view**
		• Select the field whose index is to be removed from the Field Name column
		• Set the Indexed field property to **No** (this does not impact the field or its data)
		• Close the table design and save the changes
View the indexes of a table	AC 6.15	• Open the table in **Design view**
		• Click the **Indexes** button of the toolbar
		• Click an index to review its properties

NOTES

review of terminology

CROSSWORD PUZZLE

Across

5. Where relationships are defined.
6. Deletes all children when the parent is deleted.
7. Accessed by clicking the plus sign before a datasheet record.
10. The maximum number of fields that can be in a multifield index.
12. Field type that lists values for the user to select.
13. The table on the many side of a relationship.
14. Retrieves records with matching foreign key values.
15. The table on the one side of a relationship.

Down

1. Retrieves all records in the first table and records with matching foreign keys in the second table.
2. Updates all children if the value of the parent's related field is changed.
3. A lookup table that improves sorting and searching.
4. Indexes are automatically created for this type of key field.
8. The number of relationship types that can be defined in a relational database.
9. The inner form displaying related data.
11. The outer form containing data from the primary table.

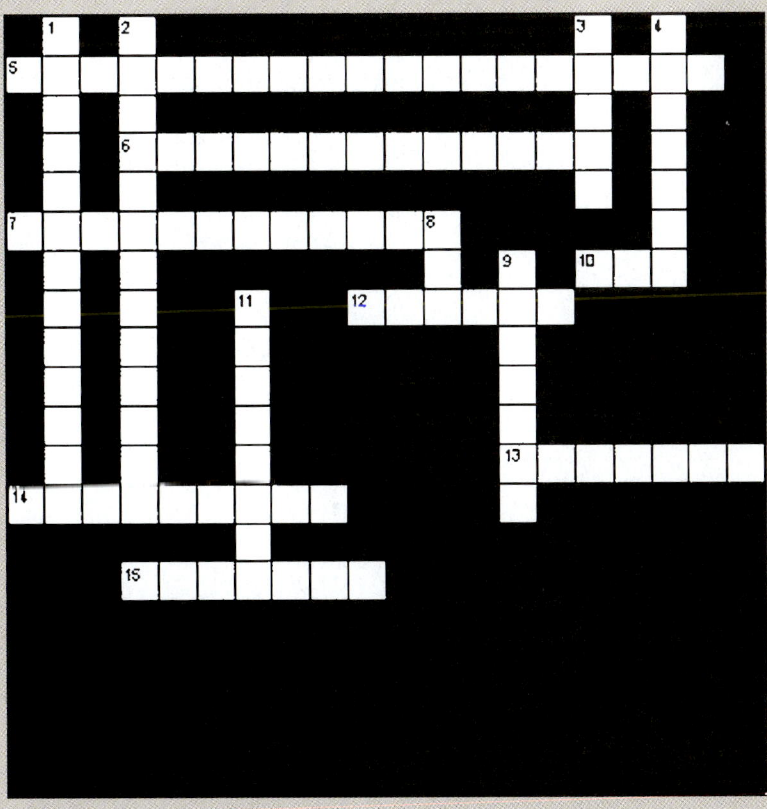

review of concepts

FILL-IN

1. Indexing is accomplished in ____________ view.
2. A ____________ retrieves all of the records in the second table, but only rows of the second table with matching foreign key values.
3. The ____________ menu option is used to align multiple selected controls.
4. The ____________ menu option causes a Label control to adjust to the size of its Caption property.
5. The ____________ table is on the many side of a one-to-many relationship.

REVIEW QUESTIONS

Each of the following topics should be addressed in one to three paragraphs.

1. Give an example of a one-to-many relationship between tables and explain how it might be used.
2. Describe the relationship line notations in the Relationships window and how they can impact the construction of a main form/subform.
3. How are many-to-many relationships handled?
4. How would you delete a relationship that was built in error or is no longer needed?
5. What is the importance of cascade updates and deletes?

CREATE THE QUESTION

For each of the following answers, create the question.

ANSWER	QUESTION
1. Yes (No Duplicates)	____________
2. SQL View button	____________
3. Lookup fields	____________
4. The report or form section and all of the controls it contains are permanently deleted	____________
5. The Sorting and Grouping dialog box	____________

FACT OR FICTION

For each of the following, determine whether the statement is fact, fiction, or both and present your arguments for that conclusion.

1. Calculations must always be completed in a query before creating a report.
2. Both a Group Header and a Group Footer must exist on a report for each defined group.
3. For the best database performance, index every field in a table.
4. To create a new relationship, you must drag from the primary table to the related table.
5. You can drag and drop controls from one form section to another.

practice

Altamonte High School Booster Club Donation Tracking—Part I: Setting Table Relationships

Altamonte High School Booster Club is an organization of students, teachers, parents, and community members who sponsor high school activities. The Boosters are using an Access database to track donations.

1. Start Access and open **AC06AltamonteBoosters.mdb**
2. Use Figure 6.34 to create and populate the **DonationClass** table depicted in the figure
3. Close the DonationClass table and use the **Relationships** button to open the Relationships window
4. Add the **Boosters** and **DonationClass** tables to the Relationships window
5. Drag a relationship from **DonationClass.Class** (Class in the DonationClass table) to **Boosters.DonationClass** (DonationClass in the Boosters table)
6. Close the Relationships window, saving your updates
7. Open the Donations table in Design view
8. Use the Lookup Wizard to create a Lookup field for Booster that retrieves the Name field from the Boosters table

tip: *To test the Lookup field, open the Donations table in Datasheet view. A drop-down list of names should be available in the Booster column*

9. Open the Relationships window and add the Donations table

tip: *You may need use the **Show Table** button to display the Show Tables dialog box*

10. Adding the Lookup field created a relationship between the Donations table and the Boosters table without any attributes (no notation on the lines)
11. Double-click the Donation/Boosters relationship line
12. Click on all of the Referential Integrity options
13. Verify your table relationships using Figure 6.35
14. Close the Edit Relationships dialog box
15. Add the data in Figure 6.36 to the Donations table
16. Open the DonationClass table in Datasheet view
17. Add yourself as a booster in Class 1
18. Use the subdatasheets to add two donations for yourself dated last month and this month for $15 and $25, respectively
19. Close the AltamonteBoosters database and exit Access if your work is complete

FIGURE 6.34

DonationClass table

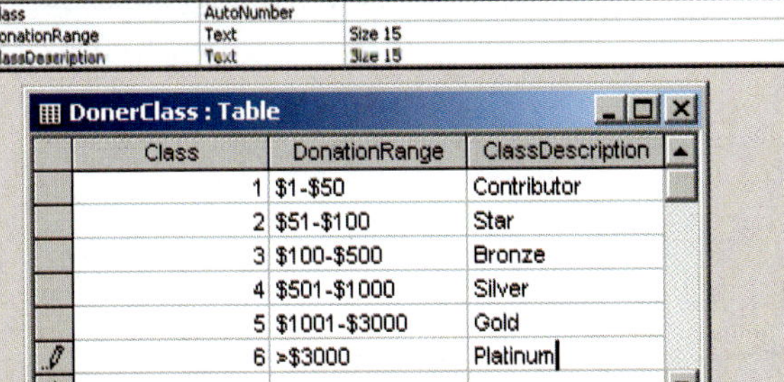

Field Name	Data Type	Description
Class	AutoNumber	
DonationRange	Text	Size 15
ClassDescription	Text	Size 15

DonerClass : Table

Class	DonationRange	ClassDescription
1	$1-$50	Contributor
2	$51-$100	Star
3	$100-$500	Bronze
4	$501-$1000	Silver
5	$1001-$3000	Gold
6	>$3000	Platinum

Record: 6 of 6

FIGURE 6.35

AltamonteBoosters table relationships

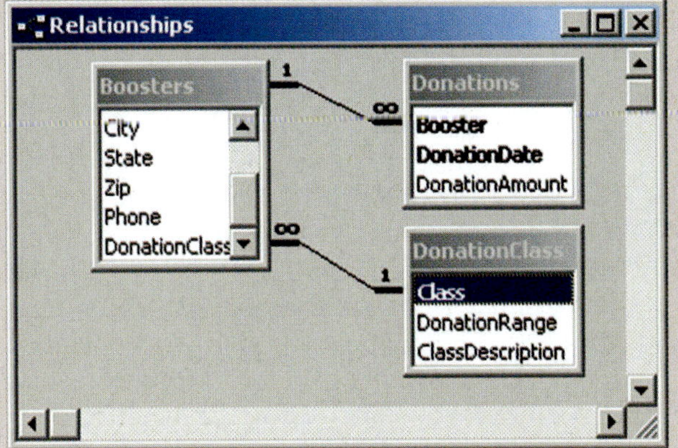

challenge!

Altamonte High School Booster Club—Part II: Using Related Tables

1. Start Access and the **AC06AltamonteBoosters.mdb** database

   tip: *If you did not complete the Practice assignment, you will need to do so now*

2. Use the Form Wizard to create a main form/subform
   a. The main form should display all of the Boosters table fields
   b. The subform should display all of the Donations table fields
   c. Set the data to be viewed **by Boosters**
   d. Use the **Tabular** layout for the subform
   e. Use the **Blueprint** style
   f. Name the form **BoostersDonations**
   g. Refer to Figure 6.36 and customize the main form and subform so that all of the labels display and the field sizes are appropriate
3. Use the form to add another donation for Matthew Hoff for the current date and **$700.** Change his DonationClass to **6**
4. Close the form, saving your changes
5. Create a query that
   a. Selects **Boosters.DonationClass, Boosters.DonationName, Donations.DonationDate,** and **Donations.DonationAmount**
   b. Selects all of the donations for October 2001
   c. Save the query as **Oct01Donations**
6. Use the Report Wizard to create a report using **Oct01Donations** as the record source
   a. List data by DonationClass
   b. Group the data by DonationClass
   c. Sort the data by **DonationDate**
   d. Total **DonationAmount**
   e. Use **Block** format and **Casual** style, and name it **BoostersOct01Donations**
7. Customize the report using Figure 6.37 as a guide
   a. Change title to **Altamonte HS Boosters**
   b. Add a Label control under the report title with a Caption property of **October 2001 Donations report,** teal color, bold, and a point size of 14
   c. Adjust the Labels and Text Boxes so that all of the data display
   d. Adjust the first group summary Label so that it is indented
   e. Delete the Group Footer Sum label
   f. Add a Text Box control in the Group Footer. Add the following expression **="Total for Class" & [DonationClass]**
8. Close the AltamonteBoosters database and exit Access if your work is complete

FIGURE 6.36

BoostersDonations form

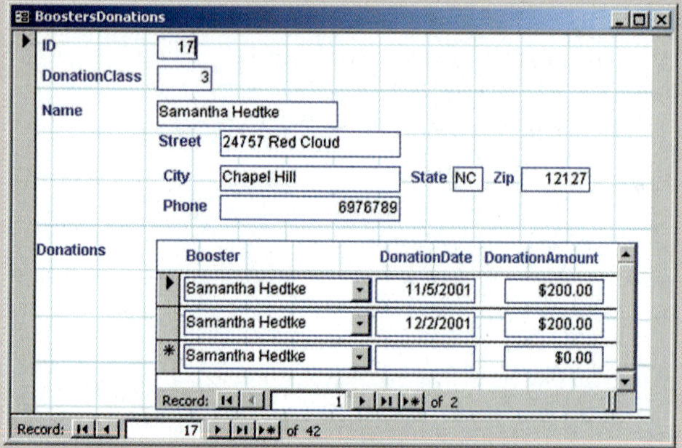

FIGURE 6.37

Customized October 2001 Donation report

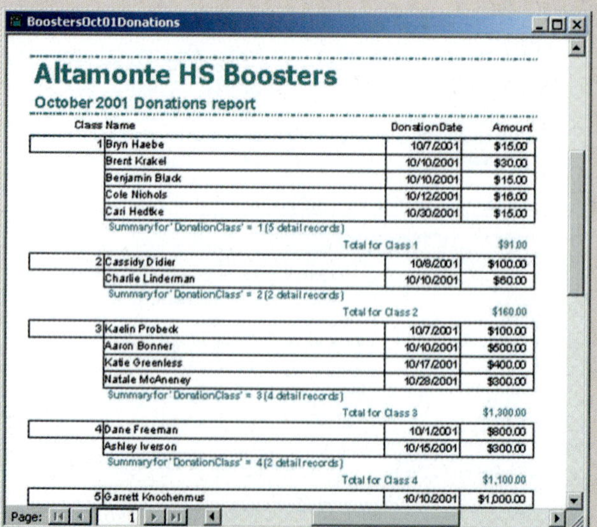

on the web

Academic Software Multitable Relationships and Reports

Academic Software, as the name implies, is a clearinghouse for educational software. You are improving its existing Access database.

1. Use a search engine to find at least three academic software titles and prices for the K–12 environment. Find at least three free download titles
2. Open the **AC06Software.mdb** database
3. Open the Relationships window and review the relationship between tblVendor and tblSoftware
4. Open the Edit Relationships dialog box and click on Cascade Updates and Deletes
5. Close the Edit Relationships dialog box and the Relationships window
6. Users have reported significant delays when searching by tblSoftware.Category. Index this field to try to address these issues
7. Open tblVendor and use the subdatasheet to add the three software titles that you found to the Edusoft Inc. vendor. Add a new vendor named **Web Downloads** with a VendorCode of **WD**
8. Open a new query in Design view and put both tables on the QBE grid
    a. From tblSoftware add **Category, Name, Quantity, Price,** and **VendorCode**
    b. From tblVendor add **Name, Address, City, State, ZipCode,** and **Phone Number**
    c. Run the query
    d. Save the query as **SoftwareByCategory**
9. With the Report Wizard, create a report using the SoftwareByCategory query
    a. Use the **by tblSoftware** option
    b. Group by **Category**
    c. Sort by **tblSoftware.Name**
    d. Select the **Portrait** page orientation and **Stepped** layout
    e. Choose the **Soft Gray** style
    f. Name the report **SoftwareByCategory**
10. Customize the report using Figure 6.40 as a guide

FIGURE 6.38
SoftwareByCategory query

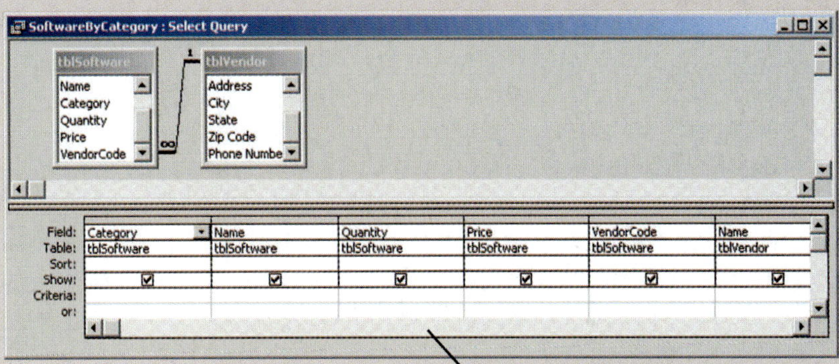

FIGURE 6.39
SoftwareByCategory report

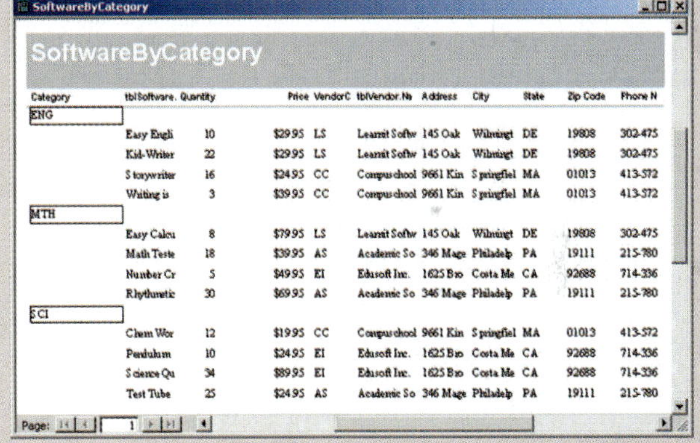

SoftwareByCategory

Category	tblSoftware.	Quantity	Price	VendorC	tblVendor.Na	Address	City	State	Zip Code	Phone N
ENG										
	Easy Engli	10	$29.95	LS	Learnit Softw	145 Oak	Wilmingt	DE	19808	302-475
	Kid-Writer	22	$29.95	LS	Learnit Softw	145 Oak	Wilmingt	DE	19808	302-475
	Storywriter	16	$24.95	CC	Compuschool	9661 Kin	Springfiel	MA	01013	413-572
	Writing is	3	$39.95	CC	Compuschool	9661 Kin	Springfiel	MA	01013	413-572
MTH										
	Easy Calcu	8	$79.95	LS	Learnit Softw	145 Oak	Wilmingt	DE	19808	302-475
	Math Teste	18	$39.95	AS	Academic So	346 Mage	Philadelp	PA	19111	215-780
	Number Cr	5	$49.95	EI	Edusoft Inc.	1625 Bro	Costa Me	CA	92688	714-336
	Rhythmetic	30	$69.95	AS	Academic So	346 Mage	Philadelp	PA	19111	215-780
SCI										
	Chem Wor	12	$19.95	CC	Compuschool	9661 Kin	Springfiel	MA	01013	413-572
	Pendulum	10	$24.95	EI	Edusoft Inc.	1625 Bro	Costa Me	CA	92688	714-336
	Science Qu	34	$89.95	EI	Edusoft Inc.	1625 Bro	Costa Me	CA	92688	714-336
	Test Tube	25	$24.95	AS	Academic So	346 Mage	Philadelp	PA	19111	215-780

FIGURE 6.40
Customized SoftwareByCategory report

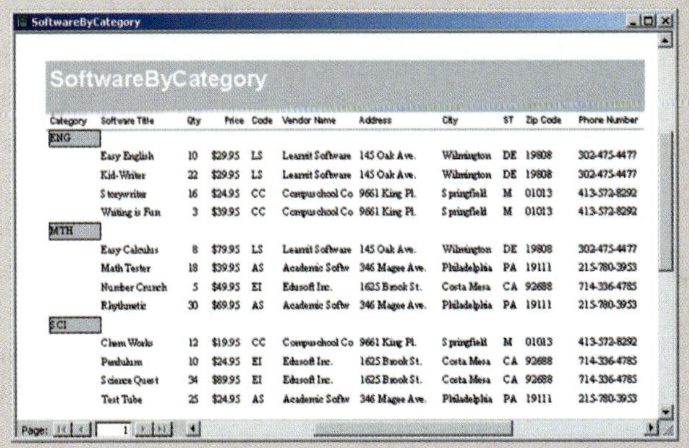

SoftwareByCategory

Category	Software Title	Qty	Price	Code	Vendor Name	Address	City	ST	Zip Code	Phone Number
ENG										
	Easy English	10	$29.95	LS	Learnit Software	145 Oak Ave.	Wilmington	DE	19808	302-475-4477
	Kid-Writer	22	$29.95	LS	Learnit Software	145 Oak Ave.	Wilmington	DE	19808	302-475-4477
	Storywriter	16	$24.95	CC	Compuschool Co	9661 King Pl.	Springfield	M	01013	413-572-8292
	Writing is Fun	3	$39.95	CC	Compuschool Co	9661 King Pl.	Springfield	M	01013	413-572-8292
MTH										
	Easy Calculus	8	$79.95	LS	Learnit Software	145 Oak Ave.	Wilmington	DE	19808	302-475-4477
	Math Tester	18	$39.95	AS	Academic Softw	346 Magee Ave.	Philadelphia	PA	19111	215-780-3953
	Number Crunch	5	$49.95	EI	Edusoft Inc.	1625 Brook St.	Costa Mesa	CA	92688	714-336-4785
	Rhythmetic	30	$69.95	AS	Academic Softw	346 Magee Ave.	Philadelphia	PA	19111	215-780-3953
SCI										
	Chem Works	12	$19.95	CC	Compuschool Co	9661 King Pl.	Springfield	M	01013	413-572-8292
	Pendulum	10	$24.95	EI	Edusoft Inc.	1625 Brook St.	Costa Mesa	CA	92688	714-336-4785
	Science Quest	34	$89.95	EI	Edusoft Inc.	1625 Brook St.	Costa Mesa	CA	92688	714-336-4785
	Test Tube	25	$24.95	AS	Academic Softw	346 Magee Ave.	Philadelphia	PA	19111	215-780-3953

e-business

Curbside Recycling

Curbside Recycling is enhancing its Web presence so customers can view their current account status and the profit position of the organization.

1. Open the **AC06CurbsideRecycling.mdb** database
2. Open the Relationships window and review the relationship between the Customer and the CustomerRecords tables
3. Open the Edit Relationships dialog box and click on all of the referential integrity options
4. Close the Edit Relationships dialog box and the Relationships window, saving your changes
5. Users have reported significant delays when searching by LastName and FirstName. Create a multicolumn index called **Name** to try to address this issue
6. Use the Form Wizard to create a main form/subform for maintaining table data
   a. Include all fields from both tables
   b. View the data **by Customer**
   c. Use the Datasheet view for the subform
   d. Select the **Standard** style
   e. Name the form **CustomerRecordsUpdate**
7. Customize the form to improve its functionality
   a. Narrow the subform to about 3.5 inches
   b. Add spaces to the form and subform labels
   c. Change to Form view and drag the subform column widths to display the column headings and data

tip: *You cannot change the width in Design view because you have chosen a Datasheet for the subform*

8. Use the Report Wizard to create a report
   a. Select **CstmrNmbr, LastName,** and **FirstName** from the Customer table
   b. Select **SrvcDate, WeightPaper,** and **WeightOther** from the CustomerRecords table
   c. View the data by **Customer**
   d. Sort the data by **SrvcDate**
   e. Sum both weight fields
   f. Use **Block** format
   g. Use **Compact** style
   h. Name the report **CustomerPickups**
9. Customize the report
   a. Add spaces to the labels
   b. Adjust the field widths to fit the size of the column headings and labels
   c. Change the label for the sum to **Total Weight**
   d. Preview and save your changes
10. If your work is complete, exit Access; otherwise continue to the next assignment

FIGURE 6.41
Updating table relationships

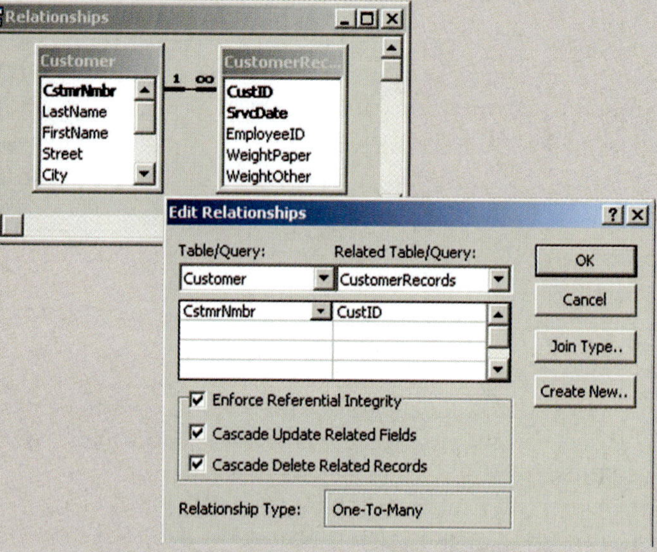

FIGURE 6.42
Customized CustomerRecordsUpdate form

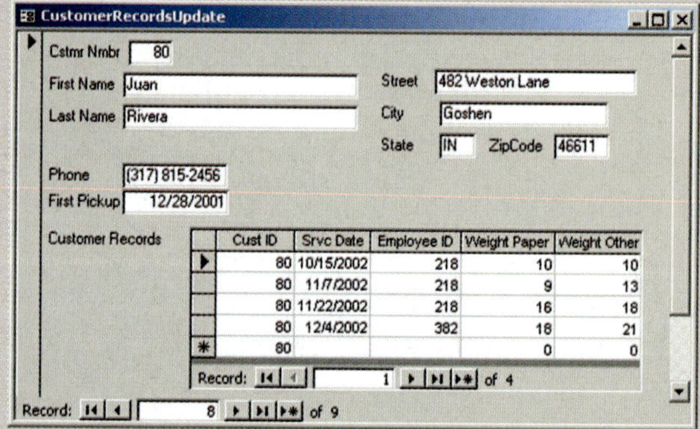

around the world

TechRocks Seminars Forms and Reports

TechRocks Seminars provides onsite technical training to large businesses around the world. You will build the Table relationships and test the multitable abilities.

1. Start Access and open the **AC06Seminars.mdb** database
2. Open the Relationships window
   a. Use the **Show Tables** button to add the Facilitators table to the Relationships window
   b. Open the Facilitators/Seminars relationship and enforce all referential integrity rules
   c. Open the Seminars/Enrollment relationship and enforce all referential integrity rules
   d. Use Figure 6.43 to verify your relationships and then close the Relationships window
3. Create a mulitable query
   a. From the Seminars table select **SeminarID, Description, Date, Time, Hours,** and **Place**
   b. From the Facilitators table select **LastName, FirstName,** and **Phone**
   c. From the Enrollment table select **Student Number, Last Name, First Name,** and **Student Phone**
   d. Select **Detail** query
   e. Save the query as **StudentListing**
4. Use the StudentListing query to create a report listing the students currently enrolled in each seminar
   a. Initiate the Report Wizard
   b. Select the **StudentListing** query as the data source
   c. Select all of the fields from the query
   d. Select **by Seminars** as the way to view the report
   e. No additional grouping is necessary
   f. Select **Align Left1** as the layout
   g. Select the **Bold** style
   h. Name the report **StudentListingBySeminar**
   i. Save the report as **StudentsBySeminar**

FIGURE 6.43

Seminars table relationships

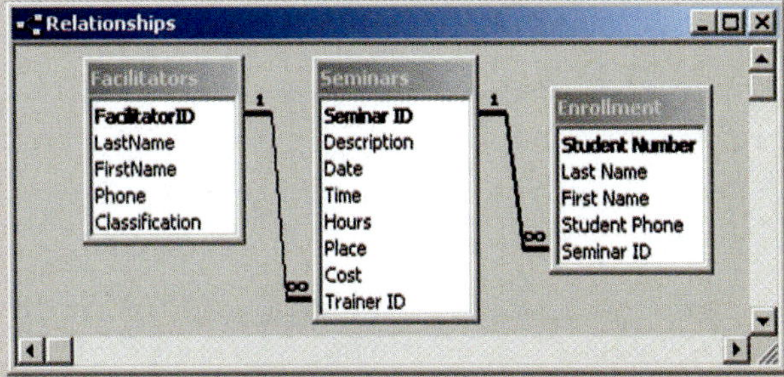

FIGURE 6.44

Customized StudentListingBy Seminar report

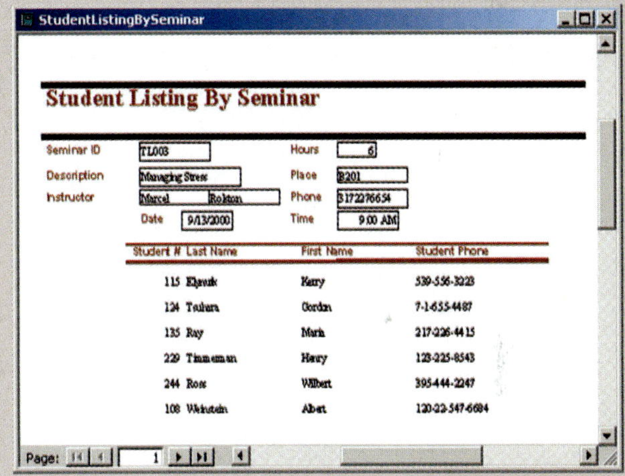

5. Customize the StudentsBySeminar report. Refer to Figure 6.44
   a. Change the column headings as shown
   b. Adjust the size of labels and text boxes
   c. Rearrange the Seminar ID Header fields as shown
   d. Adjust the length of the lines above and below the header (there are two above and two below even though it looks like one line each)
   e. Activate the Sorting and Grouping dialog box and add a Group Footer for Seminar ID
   f. Insert a Page Break in the Seminar ID Footer section
   g. Preview and save your work

running project: tnt web design

Custom Forms and Reports for TnT

As TnT grows, so does the complexity of its database. Tori and Tonya now have over 65 employees and several hundred customers. Employees and projects are spread across the United States, so it is becoming critical to have simple data entry and reporting.

1. Start Access and open the **AC06TnT.mdb** database. Familiarize yourself with each table if necessary
2. Open the Relationships window
   a. Drag the tblCustomers/CustomerSites relationship
   b. Enforce all referential integrity rules
   c. Close the Relationships window and save your changes
3. Use the Query Wizard to create a query listing fields from each table
   a. From the tblCustomers select **cstName** and **cstAddress**
   b. From CustomerSites select **URL**
   c. From Employees select **LastName** and **FirstName**
   d. Save the form as **CustomerWebSites**
4. Use the Report Wizard to create a report with all of the fields of CustomerWebSites
   a. No additional sorting or grouping is needed
   b. Choose **Stepped** layout
   c. Select **Soft Gray** style
   d. Save the report as **CustomerWebSite**
5. Customize the CustomerWebSite report
   a. Put spaces in the report title
   b. Remove the "cus" prefix from the Customer table fields
   c. Change the LastName label to **Development Manager**
   d. Delete the FirstName label
   e. Expand the URL label and text box
6. If your work is complete, exit Access; otherwise continue to the next assignment

FIGURE 6.45
TnT Relationships

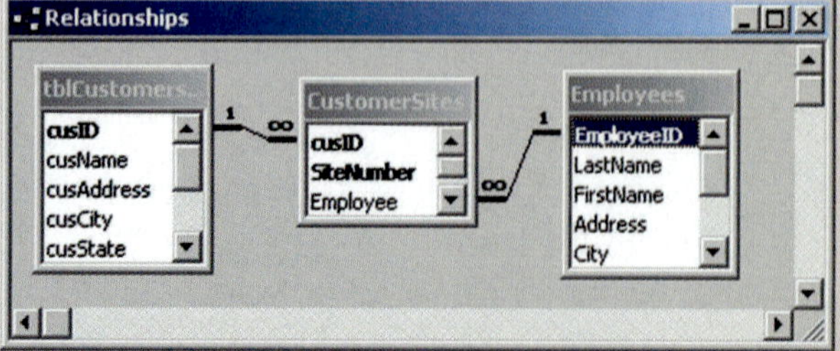

FIGURE 6.46
CustomerWebSites report

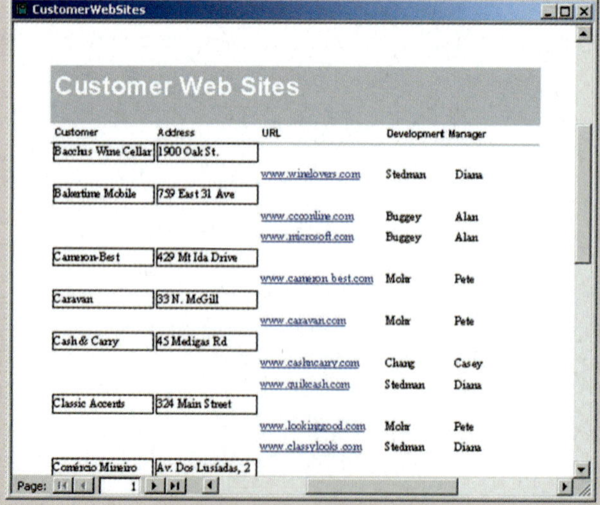

did you know?

playing *cards were originally invented by the Chinese.*

the *average human has over 1,500 dreams every year.*

"for *every complex problem, there is a solution that is simple, neat, and wrong."—Henry L. Mencken*

Victoria *Woodhall became the first woman to run for president of the United States in 1872.*

the *largest nerve in the human body is the sciatic nerve, which is about 2 cm wide and runs from the spinal cord down the back of each leg.*

corporations *and government agencies report that the average cost to investigate, repair, and secure computer systems that have been hacked is $1 million per intrusion.*

the *average person laughs _____ times per day.*

Chapter Objectives

- **Use data validation criteria to ensure data accuracy—AC2002-1-1**
- **Create and modify custom input masks—AC2002-1-4**
- **Add user permissions to a database—AC2002-7-5**
- **Set database passwords—AC2002-7-5**
- **Use database replication to synchronize multiple copies of a database—AC2002-7-6**
- **Apply database encryption to secure data—AC2002-7-3**
- **Use the Database Splitter to protect databases from modification and to create a front and back end—AC2002-8-2**

CHAPTER 7

seven

Maintaining Databases

chapter case

PuppyParadise

Evan has been using the PuppyParadise database for several months and believes that it is time to reevaluate its design. When the database was built, PuppyParadise had just six products, Evan was the only user, and he was not familiar with databases. Now there are 20 products and more than three times as many sales per week. Over the past months he has learned to build queries, forms, and reports for himself. He has even changed table design and built indexes to improve performance. In addition, the organization has grown to have three employees, each with different database requirements.

It is getting sloppy for Evan and each employee to create their own versions of reports and queries. There are too many database objects, which slows performance. More data entry errors are cropping up due to individual style and preference issues. Finally, sharing a computer is not efficient. There is a real need to share the database using multiple copies or a network.

The first step of a design review is to gather known issues and problems with each database object. Evan did this by talking to each user of the database about the problems they were encountering and any suggestions they could offer on improving it. Some of the issues discussed include

- Data entry errors need to be reduced
- The Phone Input Mask is not providing the desired results
- Consistency in the capitalization of data would improve the data's value

FIGURE 7.1

Potential improvements to PuppyParadise

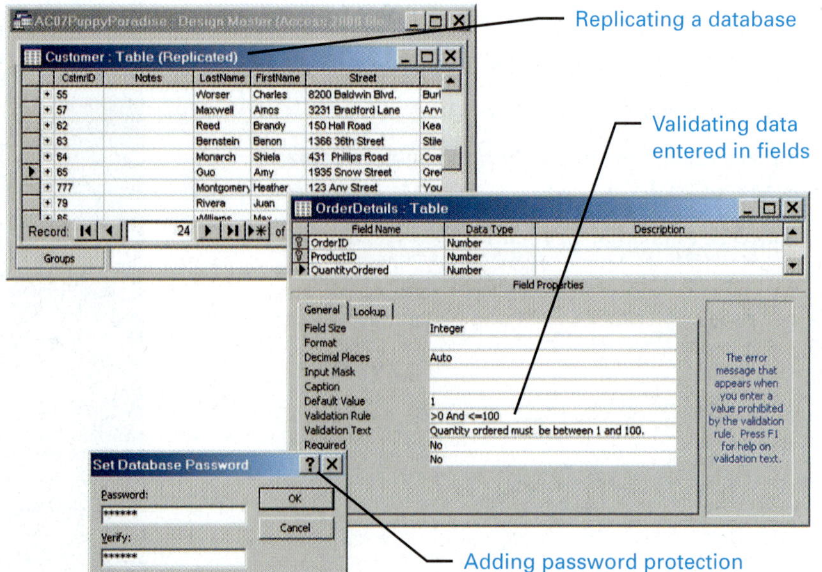

- Many fields could benefit from default quantities
- Some of the fields that are now blank should not allow blank values
- A more effective way of sharing the database is desirable
- Security of the data is becoming an issue because PuppyParadise is now in shared office space

Since issues with the current performance of the database have been identified, the next logical step is to evaluate the various ways that Access can address each issue. Evan again asks you to help in this process given that it is not his area of expertise.

SESSION 7.1 REFINING TABLE DESIGN

CHAPTER OUTLINE

The design of any database needs to be reviewed periodically to ensure that the user's needs are being appropriately met and that it is optimized for performance. Databases are designed to fit the needs of their users at a given point in time. Over time these needs change for a number of reasons. Change is fundamental to the growth and success of any organization or business, so over time data and data analysis needs can change dramatically. It is also true that the more people use a database, the more they want from the database. Users become more familiar with their data over time and recognize additional touches that would improve the usability of the database.

Add to the mix that you get better at designing, developing, and supporting databases, and it is easy to see that leaving a database alone is dooming it to failure. On the system optimization side, databases that are not optimized become slow and hog system resources. Disk space and seek time are wasted by storing records that could be archived because they are never accessed in the active database. Besides impacting other applications on the system by not sharing resources, these issues also can impact user satisfaction.

Don't panic. If the original database design was sound, most of these concerns can be addressed by adding tables to hold the new data, adding fields to existing tables, refining indexes, archiving unused records, and building new queries, forms, and reports. The more heavily a database is used, the more critical this review is. This is where spending the time up front to design sound tables pays off.

It is sometimes difficult to see the need for maintenance on a functioning system. Think about what it would cost the organization if this database failed. How much happier and more efficient could the users be with an optimized database? Maintaining a database is like changing the oil or tuning up your car. It significantly decreases the likelihood of a major disaster.

BUILDING INPUT MASKS

Input masks were introduced in Chapter 2 as a way to improve data entry by providing a template like (___)___-____ for the user to follow when entering data. Input masks are field properties and can be set for Text, Date, Number, and Currency field types. Input masks make what needs to be entered clear to users and reduces their keystrokes.

Reducing input keystrokes always improves the likelihood of valid data. In the case of a phone number, using an input mask cuts out three keystrokes ((,), and -) that otherwise would be necessary for the phone number to display in the desired format.

Consider building input masks for any table data that have a repetitive component. Repetitive components include punctuation such as parentheses, dashes, periods (decimal places), slashes, at signs (@), and so on. Cutting out a keystroke or two may not seem like much, but remember that keystrokes add up when multiple fields and records are considered.

When using an input mask with repetitive components, mask properties control whether or not those fixed values are stored with the data. Typically they are not, since it would require extra disk space, and the Format property allows control over how stored data display. Using the Format property, it is easy to display repetitive components without storing them.

In general, the Input Mask property and display Format property should match on the data entry forms because it is less confusing to the user. When they do not match, the user enters the data using the Input Mask template and when he or she moves to another record, the entry is displayed using the format. Avoiding such visual ambiguities will lead to happier users. Remember that setting the Format property of the field's text box on a form or report can control the display format for that output. Output formats are covered in the next topic.

To create an input mask, provide Access with a string outlining what is to be presented to the user, what will be accepted as valid input, and what will be stored. Figure 7.2 lists the valid mask characters. Any character not listed in Figure 7.2 becomes a literal when included in an input mask. Characters in the list must be preceded by a backslash to literally appear in the mask.

The Input Mask Wizard is great for creating default masks, but like most wizards lacks the flexibility to effectively create complex or uncommon masks. Figure 7.3 depicts some of the masks that could be applied to a 15-character field with an explanation of their results.

In the PuppyParadise Customer table, the Input Mask property of the Phone field was set in Chapter 2 with the Wizard for a standard phone number. Users often do not like this mask because it makes it difficult to not enter the area code. Even though the area code does not have to be entered, the user must space by the first three characters of the input mask. If your data always include the area code, this setup is satisfactory. If, however, your data do not include the area code a significant amount of the time, the area code should be split into another field that the user could tab past.

Evan was not happy with the Phone input mask for PuppyParadise data so it has been removed. Evan has noticed that he is inconsistent in capitalizing customer's names and decides that a mask for the Name fields is in order. State and Zip Code also need input masks to reduce entry errors.

Character	Description
0	Required digit (0–9), no plus (+) or minus (−) sign
9	Optional digit, no plus (+) or minus (−) sign
#	Optional digit, plus (+) or minus (−) sign allowed
L	Required letter (A–Z)
?	Optional letter (A–Z)
A	Required letter or digit
a	Optional letter or digit
&	Required character or space
C	Optional character or space
.,:;-/	Placeholders and separators
<	Causes all characters that follow to be converted to lowercase
>	Causes all characters that follow to be converted to uppercase
!	Causes input mask to display from right to left
\	Used to display any of the characters in this table as a literal
Password	Creates a password entry text box with all entries displayed as *

FIGURE 7.2
Input Mask definition characters

Input Mask	Sample Display	Explanation
00000-999;;_	_____-____	Zip Code mask created by the Wizard. 0s are required positions, 9s are optional positions. Both require digits for valid data. The dash is a literal that will not be stored due to the;; notation. The _ notation sets that as the character that displays to the user.
000-00-0000;;_	___-__-____	SSN mask created by the Wizard. All 0s represent required digits. The dashes display as literals and ;;_ causes the literal characters (-) not to be stored. The _ notation sets that as the character that displays to the user.
!(999) 000-0000;;_	(___) ___-____	Phone Number mask created by the Wizard. 0s are required digits, 9s are optional digits, the dashes and parentheses are literals that will not be stored due to the ;;_ notation. The ! causes the field to display from right to left. The _ notation sets that as the character that displays to the user.
>L<?????????		The first letter entered will be converted to uppercase before it is stored. The remaining nine characters are optional but, if entered, will be converted to lowercase before being stored.

FIGURE 7.3
Input Mask examples

Customizing the Customer table input masks:

1. Start Access and open **AC07PuppyParadise.mdb**
2. Open the **Customer** table in Design view
3. Select the **LastName** field. This is a 25-character text field that should always begin with a capital letter, followed by up to 24 lowercase letters
4. Click the **Input Mask** property of LastName and type **>L<????????????????????????**

tip: *>L< followed by 24 question marks*

5. Click the **FirstName** field. This is a 15-character text field that should always begin with a capital letter, followed by up to 14 lowercase letters
6. Click the **Input Mask** property of FirstName and type **>L<??????????????**

tip: *>L< followed by 14 question marks*

7. Click the State field. This is a 2-character text field that should always contain two uppercase letters

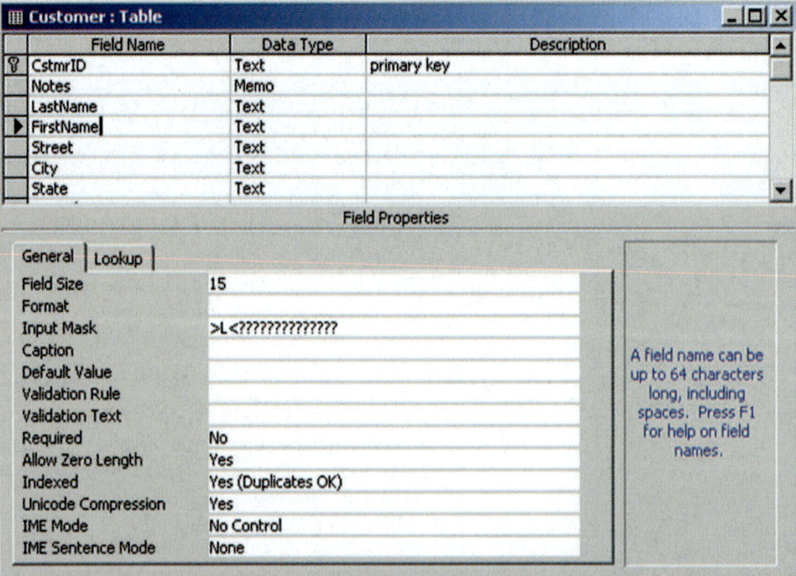

FIGURE 7.4
FirstName input mask

8. Click the **Input Mask** property of State and type **>LL** to force the entry of two uppercase letters
9. Click in the ZipCode field. This is a 5-digit required field
10. Click the **Input Mask** property of ZipCode and type **00000**
11. Switch to Design view, saving your changes
12. Make up the data for two new customers. Enter the first record in all lowercase and observe the result. Enter the second record in all uppercase and observe the result

Input Masks are a simple way to improve data validity and user satisfaction without negatively impacting performance. It is important to be sure that the masks don't get in the user's way (like the phone number example). Adding, editing, or deleting an input mask has no impact on existing table data, since the template is only activated on input. Input masks do impact editing existing data because newly entered data must meet the mask criteria.

DEFINING OUTPUT FORMATS

Output formats were introduced in Chapter 2 as the way to control how a value displays. Output formatting is controlled by the Format property of a field. The Format property set in table design becomes the default format of that field in queries, forms, and reports. As was mentioned in the input mask discussion, the Format property set in table design should match the Input Mask property.

Evan is not satisfied with the Orders.OrderDate (OrderDate field of the Orders table) input mask/format combination. It works great for data entry when the input mask ___/___/_____ is displayed. The problem arises when editing an existing date. The Format property is set as dd-mmm-yyyy, so when Evan selects a portion of a date (such as the dd component) and enters a new value, the input mask generates an error because it doesn't know what to do with the dashes generated by the Format property. Since Evan has indicated that he would be satisfied with a dd/mm/yyyy format, you will update the table.

Customizing the Orders.OrderDate field format:

1. Verify that Access is running with **AC07PuppyParadise.mdb** as the open database
2. Open the **Orders** table in Design view
3. Select the **OrderDate** field and review the current Input Mask and Format properties

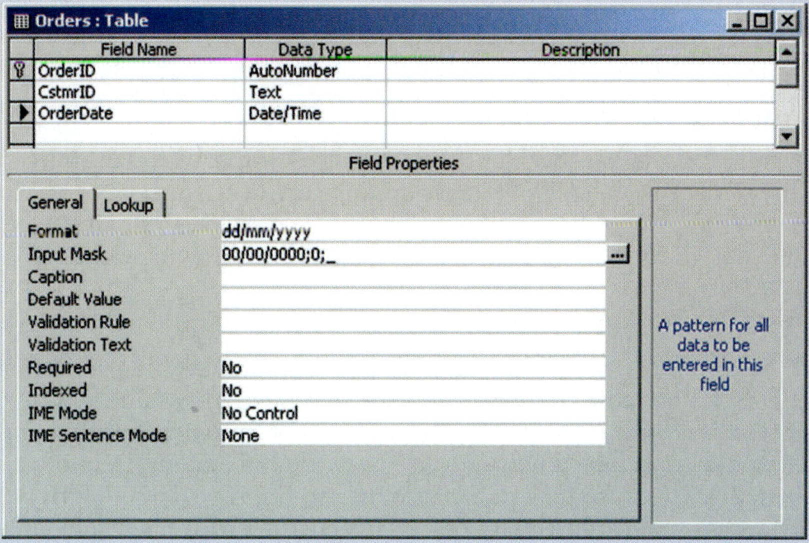

Orders : Table

Field Name	Data Type	Description
OrderID	AutoNumber	
CstmrID	Text	
OrderDate	Date/Time	

Field Properties

General | Lookup

Format	dd/mm/yyyy
Input Mask	00/00/0000;0;_
Caption	
Default Value	
Validation Rule	
Validation Text	
Required	No
Indexed	No
IME Mode	No Control
IME Sentence Mode	None

A pattern for all data to be entered in this field

FIGURE 7.5
Orders.OrderDate properties

4. Click the **Format** property of OrderDate and type **mm/dd/yyyy**
5. Move to Datasheet view, saving your changes
6. Add orders for Sara Meadows and Juan Rivera with today's date (OrderID is an AutoNumber field and will be generated) to observe the effectiveness of your changes
7. Edit the day on each of these new records to yesterday's date

tip: *If the change has been correctly applied, you should be able to select and change the day portion of the date successfully*

When custom forms and reports are created, Design view is used to set the Format property of the Text Box control displaying the field. This action does not impact the field and what it stores, or change the Format set in table design, but simply applies a template altering how a field is displayed on that particular form or report. The Text Box Format property overrides the Format property set in table design and is applied only to that text box. In both form and report design, the ***Format Painter*** is available to copy formats from one control to another.

When setting a Format property, selections can be made from a list of predefined formats for AutoNumber, Number, Currency, Date/Time, and Yes/No data types or a custom format can be defined. Text data types do not have any predefined formatting. Formats cannot be applied to OLE Object data types.

Number and date data types have predefined formats displayed in a drop-down list. To improve consistency among applications, the regional settings from Microsoft Windows Control Panel are used for the predefined Number and Date/Time formats. Changing the Windows format does change the display but does not perform conversions. This can cause problems when moving between computers with different regional settings. For example, the value 5.47 displayed with currency format would result in $5.47 in the United States and 5,47kr on a computer set for Denmark. One or both of the displayed currency values would be inaccurate since no conversion was performed. In such cases, a custom format should be entered representing the true currency of the data. Custom formats override the Windows settings.

USING DATA VALIDATION

Data validation is another area that can often improve the usability and validity of database data. Validation settings are used to check the accuracy of data entered by the user. Several of the field properties that can be set in table design to validate data are covered in the following topics.

Default Value Field Property

Each field in a Microsoft Access table has a Default Value property that can be set to the most common value for that field. This value will display in that field for new records. The user can accept this entry by tabbing past it or can stop and type a new entry to override the default. Default values are beneficial because they reduce typing and improve data integrity.

Evan has determined that most of his customers are in Michigan and he would like MI to be the default state value. Since most orders are for the current date, he would also like that default added to the Orders table. The default order quantity was set to 1 when the table was developed and is working well.

Adding default values to the PuppyParadise database:

1. Verify that **AC07PuppyParadise.mdb** database is open
2. Open the **Customer** table in Design view
3. Select the **State** field
4. Click the **Default Value** property of State and type **MI**

tip: *Access will add double quotes around this string value, resulting in "MI"*

5. Change to Datasheet view and test the default value by adding records for yourself and a friend. For your record accept the default value. For your friend's record set the State to NM
6. Close the Customer table
7. Open the **Orders** table in Design view

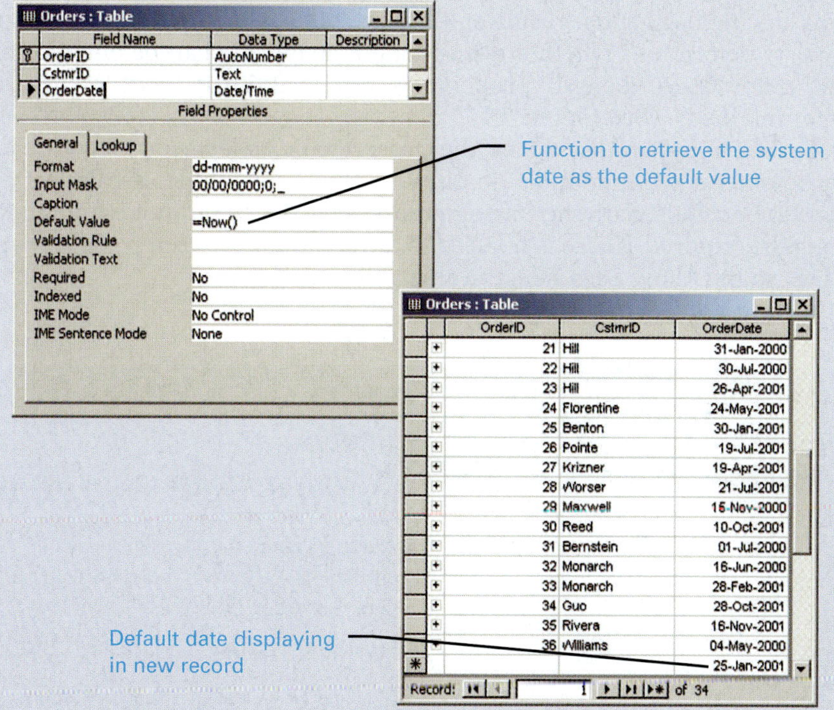

FIGURE 7.6
Adding a default value for OrderDate

8. Click in the **OrderDate** field and type **=Now** in the Default Value property

tip: *Access will convert it to =Now() since the parentheses are required for correct function syntax*

9. Switch to Datasheet view and add an order for yourself and your friend. Accept the default of today's date for your order. Set the date from your friend's order to tomorrow

Default values are not limited to fixed quantities such as 1 or "MI" but can also use expressions like =Now(). An expression can be either typed, as was done in the steps, or built using the Expression Builder. An ellipsis (. . .) will appear to the right of the Default Value property after it is clicked. Clicking the ellipsis will activate the Expression Builder.

Required and Allow Zero Length Field Properties

The Required and Allow Zero Length field properties work together to control the types of blank values allowed in a field. Microsoft Access differentiates between ***null*** values and ***zero-length strings.*** A null value indicates missing or unknown data. A field is null when nothing has been entered. A zero-length string can be used to indicate that no data are supposed to be in a field. The user creates a zero-length string by typing two double quotes with nothing between them ("").

Sometimes it is important to differentiate between when a data value is not known and when it does not exist. For example, if a fax number field was added to the customer table, a null value could indicate that the fax number is not currently known, while a zero-length string would indicate that the customer does not have a fax. While there is nothing visual to differentiate these values, queries searching for nulls will not return zero-length strings and vice versa.

The Required property of a field determines whether it can be left blank during data entry, resulting in a null value. The Allow Zero Length property determines whether a zero-length string ("") can be entered in a field. Allow Zero Length property is only valid for Text, Memo, or Hyperlink fields. (See Figure 7.7)

In the PuppyParadise tables, the OrderDetails table needs to require the user to enter a product and a quantity. In the Orders table, the OrderDate needs to be required. In the Customer table everything but notes and phone should be required. There is no need to differentiate between types of blank values, so the Allow Zero Length value will remain No.

FIGURE 7.7

Combinations of Required and Allow Zero Length values

Required	Allow Zero Length	Result
No	No	Allows blank values when you don't need to distinguish blank values that indicate unknown data from blank values that indicate you know there's no value
Yes	No	Prevents users from leaving a field blank
Yes	Yes	Allows blank values in a field only when you know that there are no data. In this case, the only way to leave a field blank is to type double quotation marks with no space between them, or press the Spacebar to enter a zero-length string
No	Yes	Allows both types of blank values so that you can distinguish blank values that indicate unknown data from blank values that indicate you know there are no data

task reference

Controlling Blank Data Values

- Open the table in Design view
- Click the field whose blank values you would like to control
- Set Required to **Yes** to disallow blank values (Allow Zero Length should be set to No)

Requiring fields in the PuppyParadise database:

1. Verify that **AC07PuppyParadise.mdb** database is open
2. Open the **Customer** table in Design view
3. Click in **LastName** and double-click the **Required** property to change it to **Yes**
4. Repeat this process for **FirstName, Street, City, State,** and **ZipCode**
5. Close the Design view of Customer, saving your changes and validating existing data

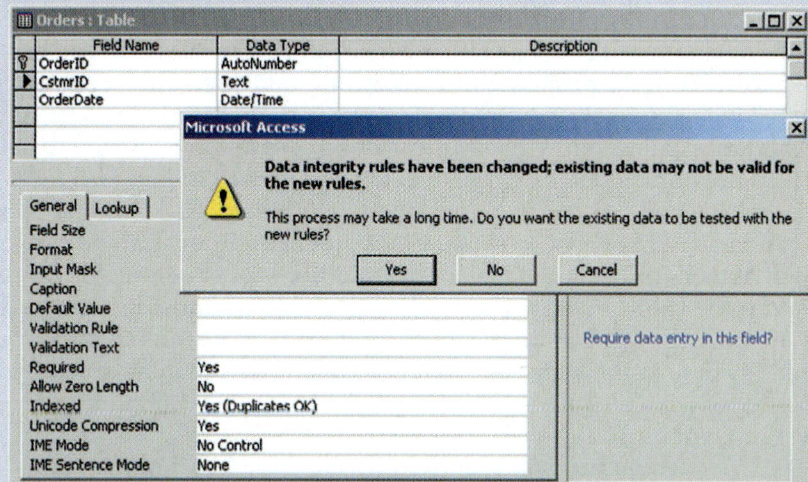

FIGURE 7.8
Checking existing data for missing values

6. Open **OrderDetails** in Design view and set the Required property of **QuantityOrdered** to **Yes**

tip: *ProductID does not have to be set to Required because as a key field it is already required*

7. Close the Design view of OrderDetails
8. Open **Orders** in Design view and set the CstmrID and OrderDate fields to Required
9. Close the Design view of Orders

The Required property of a field can only be set in Design view, but it is applied throughout all database objects (datasheets, forms, and reports). When the table design is saved after updating a Required property, Access presents the option of checking existing records for compliance. Entry can be required in future records whether or not there are currently blank fields.

Validation Rules and Validation Text Field Properties

The Validation Rule and Validation Text properties work together to help verify the data values entered by users. Validation rules are based on expected data values. For example, when accepting credit card payments, expired cards are not valid. In such a case, the validation rule would be >=(=now()). Recall that =now() is a function that will return the current system date and time. The function is enclosed in parentheses to separate it from the relational operator, >=. The expression >=(=now()) says that the date entered must be greater than or equal to today's date.

Validation text contains the message that will display to the user when the data entered do not meet the validation rule. Continuing with the credit card expiration date example, the Validation text might be *Expired Credit Card. Check the expiration date or choose another card* (see Figure 7.9). If, for example, an expiration date of 1/01 is entered, the Validation text would be displayed and the user must either enter data that pass the validation or abandon their changes. Validation rules cannot be overridden, so be very sure of the rules created.

Validation rules and their associated Validation text are most effectively added to the field properties of table design. Like other field properties, validation rules can be set in a form or report, but it is ineffective to validate data entry only on specific forms. Validation rules and text can be added to table field properties at any time, and then the rules will be enforced by all controls for that field (even those created before the rule).

Validation rules follow the syntax rules of expressions. String data are enclosed in double quotes (""), Date data are enclosed in pound signs (##), and numeric data are not enclosed in any character. All relational operators can be used (>, <, >=, <=, <>). Compound conditions can be connected with And or Or. Use And when both conditions must be true for the data entered to be valid. Use Or when only one condition must be true for the data to be valid. For example, >=#1/1/2001# And <#1/1/2002# would accept any date in the year 2001, but the Validation Text dialog box would be issued for any date outside this range. Other sample validation rules are shown in Figure 7.10.

Figure 7.10 contains validation expressions for text, number, and date data types with the appropriate delimiters. The use of And and Or to create compound conditions for validation is demonstrated, as is the use of wildcards. The wildcards ?, *, and # can be used to create match values for data validation in the same fashion that they were used to create filter and query criteria.

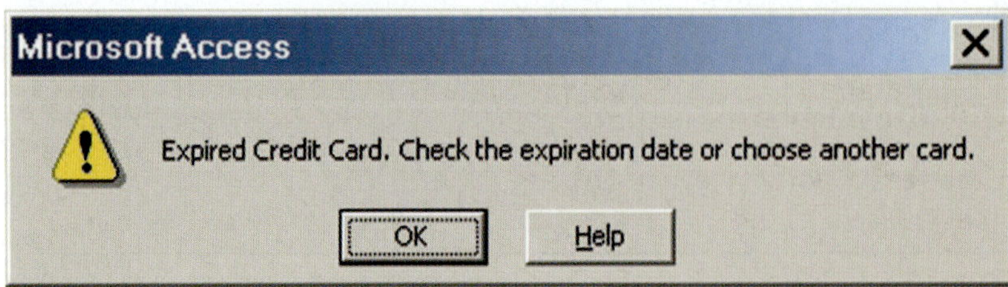

FIGURE 7.9
Validation text displaying

Evan has determined that his customers always need to order 100 or fewer units of each invoice item. PuppyParadise can't deliver larger volumes and current distributors can't handle them either. OrderDates also need to be the current date or later (backdating is not allowed). Adding these validation rules will help reduce errors in orders and improve customer satisfaction.

task reference

Defining Field Validation Rules

- Open the table in Design view
- Click the field that will be monitored by the validation rule
- Select the **Validation Rule** property for that field
- Type the validation expression or use the Expression Builder by clicking the ellipsis to the right of the Validation Rule text box
- Click the Validation Text property box for the same field and enter the text that is to display when the validation rule is broken
- Save the table update
  - If the validation rule has been set for a field that already contains data, Access will ask if you want to apply the new rule to existing data
  - If there are no existing data in the field, there will be no prompt

FIGURE 7.10

Sample validation rules

Sample Validation Rule	Sample Validation Text	Result
<>0	Please enter a non-zero value	Validation text will display when a non-zero value is entered
0 Or >25	Please enter zero or a number greater than 25	Validation text will display when values 1 through 24 or a negative number is entered
<=Now()	Date must be earlier than today	Validation text will display when dates equal to or later than the current system date are entered
>100 And <1,000	Please enter a number between 100 and 1,000	Validation text will display when a value of 100 or less is entered or a value of 1,000 or greater is entered
Like "X???"	Please enter a 4-character string beginning with X	Validation text will display when X is not the first character or the text entered is not 4 characters
"M" Or "F"	Please enter M for male or F for female	Validation text will display for any value not equal to M or F. This text is case sensitive
>#10/1/01# And <#10/31/01#	Please enter an October date	Validation text will display for values not between the dates in the condition

Adding field validation to the PuppyParadise database:

1. Verify that **AC07PuppyParadise.mdb** is open
2. Open the **OrderDetails** table in Design view
3. Click the **QuantityOrdered** field
   a. Click the **Validation Rule** property and type **>0 And <=100**
   b. Click the **Validation Text** property and type **Quantity ordered must be between 1 and 100.**

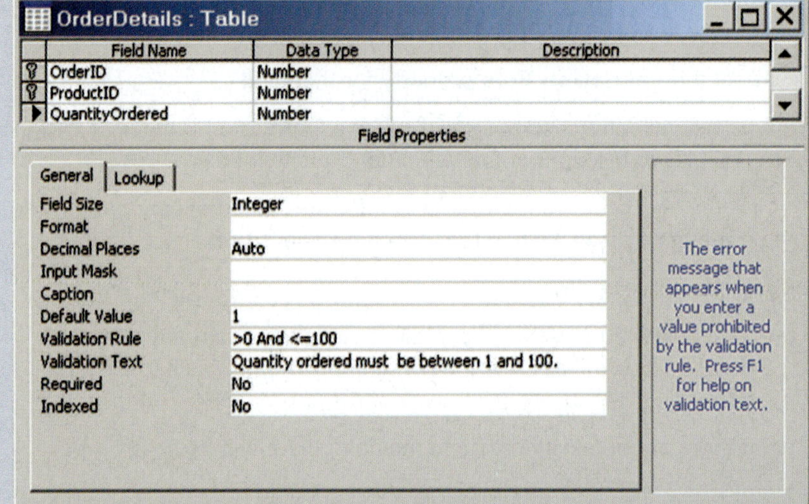

FIGURE 7.11
OrderDetails Validation rule and Validation text

4. Switch to Datasheet view, saving your changes and answering **Yes** to the data integrity prompt
5. Enter an order detail that violates the rule

tip: *Closing the OrderDetails in the next step will allow you to abandon this record*

6. Close OrderDetails
7. Open the **Orders** table in Design view
8. Click the **OrderDate** field
   a. Set the **Validation Rule** property and type **>=(=Now())**
   b. Set the **Validation Text** property and type **Date must be greater than or equal to today.**
9. Switch to Datasheet view, saving your changes and answering **Yes** to the data integrity prompt
10. Enter a record that violates the rule, move to another record to view the validation text, and then respond **OK**
11. Close the Orders table to abandon the erroneous record

Although validation rules and text can be added to tables at any time, difficulty can arise when testing these rules. The only way to check the rules that have been added is to add both valid and invalid data.

When testing validation rules, it is best to use a trait to mark the records so that they can be deleted when testing is complete. For example, customers named Dummy1, Dummy2, and so on could be added to the Customer table, along with Orders and OrderDetails added for those records. When testing is complete, deleting the Dummy? records would remove all of the test data.

Validation rules and text are the simplest tools for validating data, but they lack flexibility and cannot compare data from field to field or across records. Users cannot override the rule and there is no check to ensure that values are internally consistent. For example, a man's medical records should not include pregnancy data, but validation rules cannot check for that condition. Record validation, macros, and Visual Basic code provide the power to perform more extensive validation.

making the grade SESSION 7.1

1. How can you determine whether or not a field should have an input mask?
2. How are Input Mask and Format properties of a field different?
3. How would you determine the default value of a field?
4. Why use validation rules for table fields?

SESSION 7.2 ACCESS DATABASE TOOLS

The Tools menu in Microsoft Access contains a variety of facilities to help maintain and optimize databases. These tools can help to analyze the design and performance of your database, convert to other versions of Access, secure data, and so on. Some of these tools already have been introduced. Convert Database and Compact and Repair Database are examples of tools that already have been explored.

As with the tools already used, each Access tool is designed to satisfy a particular database maintenance need. The tools explored in this session generally relate to sharing databases among several users and securing data.

USING THE DATABASE SPLITTER WIZARD

Access databases can be stored on a network drive and shared by authorized network users. One approach to sharing a database is to separate the user interface, called the ***front-end,*** from the data, or the ***back-end.*** This approach has the advantage of maintaining one data source while allowing each user to control his or her front-end interface. A single data source means that users always have access to the most current data because all updates are made to the same tables. It also reduces network traffic by transmitting only data rather than data with the associated query, form, or report.

The process of splitting a database removes the tables and their data from the open database and places them in the back-end file. The open database becomes the front-end file, with arrow icons in front of the table names to indicate the link to the back-end.

task reference

Splitting a Database

- Back up the database
- On the **Tools** menu, point to **Database Utilities,** and then click **Database Splitter**
- Follow the Database Splitter Wizard instructions

Splitting the PuppyParadise database:

1. Close **AC07PuppyParadise.mdb** if it is open
2. Use Windows Explorer to create a folder for the split database and place a copy of AC07PuppyParadise.mdb in that folder
3. Open the copy of **AC07PuppyParadise.mdb**
4. On the **Tools** menu, point to **Database Utilities,** and then click **Database Splitter**
5. Click **Split Database**
6. Select the folder made in step 2 as the location, accept the default name for the back-end, and click **Split**

tip: *By default _be is included in the back-end file name and the front-end name is not changed. The back-end holding the tables would normally be on a shared network drive*

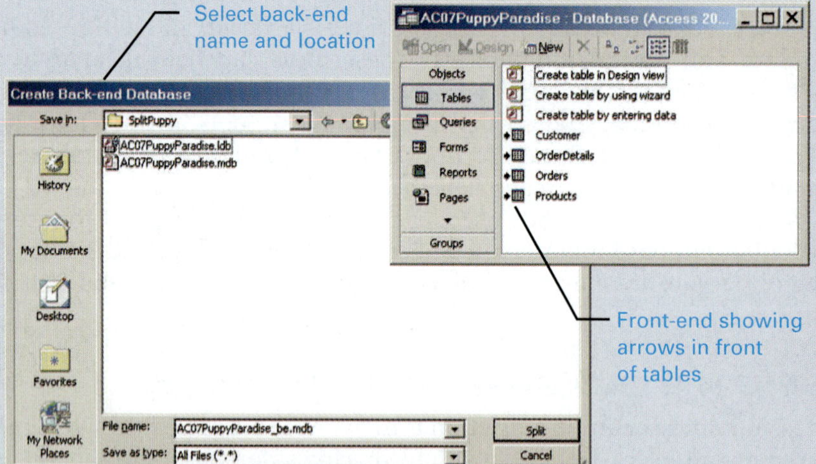

FIGURE 7.12
Creating the back-end

7. Notice the icons in front of each table name indicating that you are now working in a front-end file
8. Save the front-end

The front-end file contains all of the queries, forms, and reports. Each user can store a copy of this file on his or her computer and customize it for his or her needs. One copy of the back-end file containing the data is stored on a shared network drive.

Commercial software developers split databases so that they can implement interface changes without impacting the data stored by clients. Each copy of the front-end has access to the data stored in the back-end, but cannot change table design. Opening the back-end database will allow table design changes to be specified.

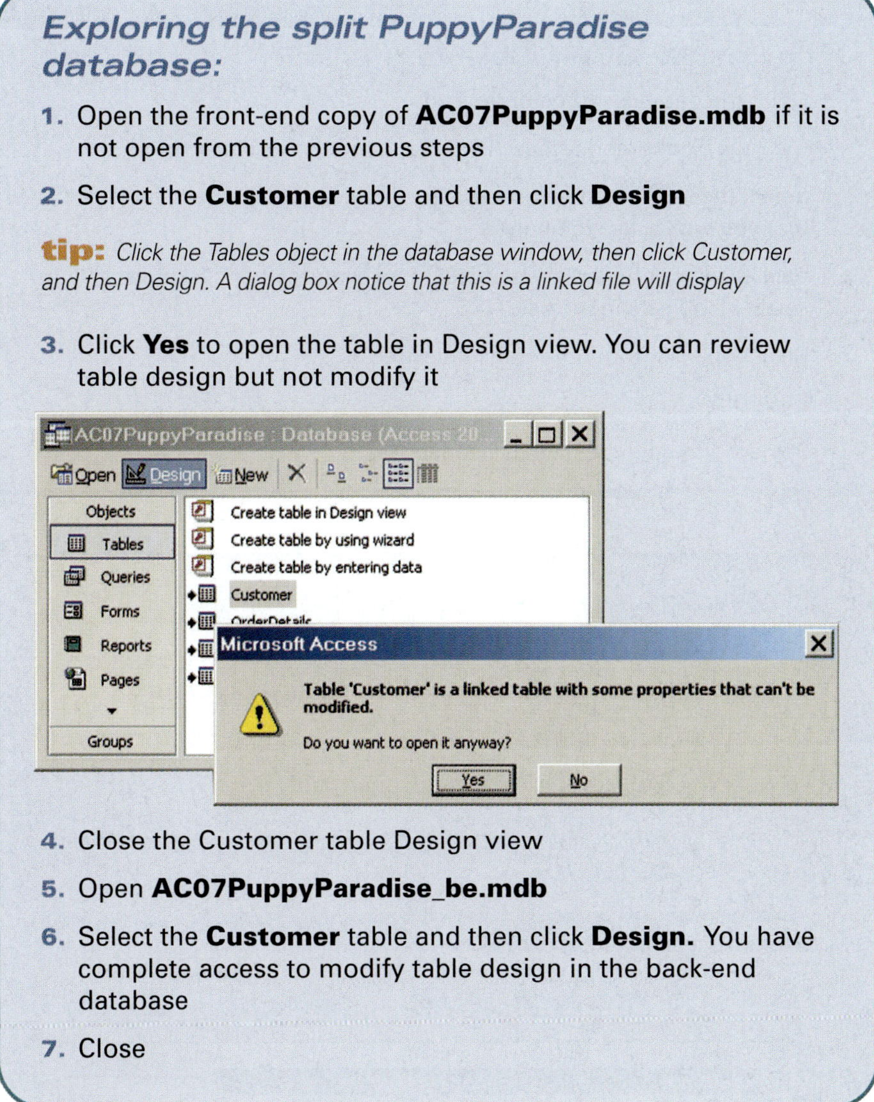

Exploring the split PuppyParadise database:

1. Open the front-end copy of **AC07PuppyParadise.mdb** if it is not open from the previous steps
2. Select the **Customer** table and then click **Design**

tip: *Click the Tables object in the database window, then click Customer, and then Design. A dialog box notice that this is a linked file will display*

3. Click **Yes** to open the table in Design view. You can review table design but not modify it

FIGURE 7.13 Viewing the design of a linked table

4. Close the Customer table Design view
5. Open **AC07PuppyParadise_be.mdb**
6. Select the **Customer** table and then click **Design.** You have complete access to modify table design in the back-end database
7. Close

Once a database has been split, there is no facility for rejoining it. If the back-end file moves to a new drive or foloder, the links in all of the front-ends must be adjusted.

USING THE DATABASE PERFORMANCE ANALYZER

The Database Performance Analyzer is a tool that reviews database objects and suggests improvements. The goal is to optimize database performance, but the performance of Access itself or the computer running Access cannot be evaluated in this manner. When the Performance Analyzer starts, a dialog box used to select database objects for evaluation is displayed. The Analyzer will review the specified objects and recommend changes that could benefit performance.

The proposed changes are classified by their potential benefit (Recommendation, Suggestion, Idea, and Fixed). Items classified as Fixed have already been repaired. Recommendations have the most potential benefit, while Ideas have the least. It is important to carefully review each proposed change in light of the database design and utilization.

task reference

Optimizing Database Objects:

- Open the database to be optimized
- Click the **Tools** menu, then **Analyze,** and then **Performance**
- Select the tab for the database object (table, query, report, form, etc.) that you would like to analyze
- Click the check box of each object to be evaluated or click Select All to select all objects in the list
- Select objects from other tabs if desired
- Click **OK**
- Review and apply results as needed

Optimizing PuppyParadise database objects:

1. Open the original copy of **AC07PuppyParadise.mdb**
2. Click the **Tools** menu, then **Analyze,** and then **Performance**
3. Select the **Tables** tab and check each table

tip: *The check box in front of each table must be checked—selecting a table does not check the check box*

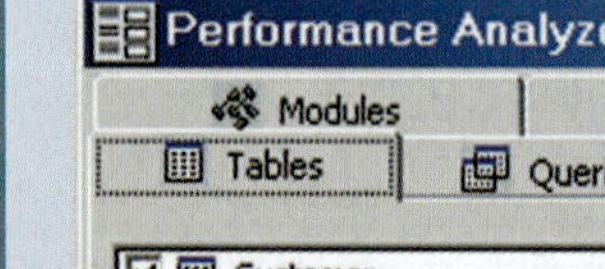

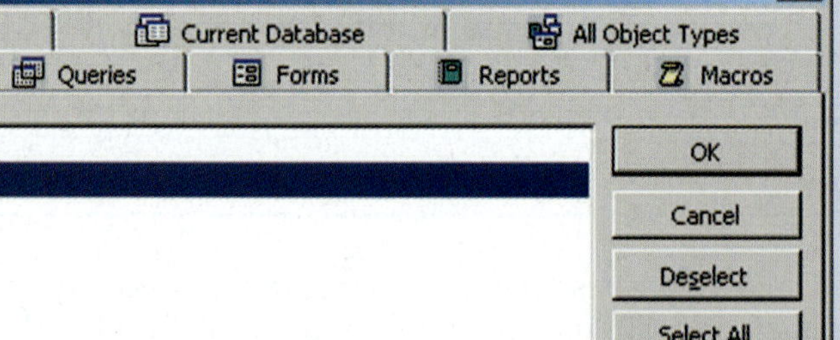

FIGURE 7.14
Selecting objects to be analyzed

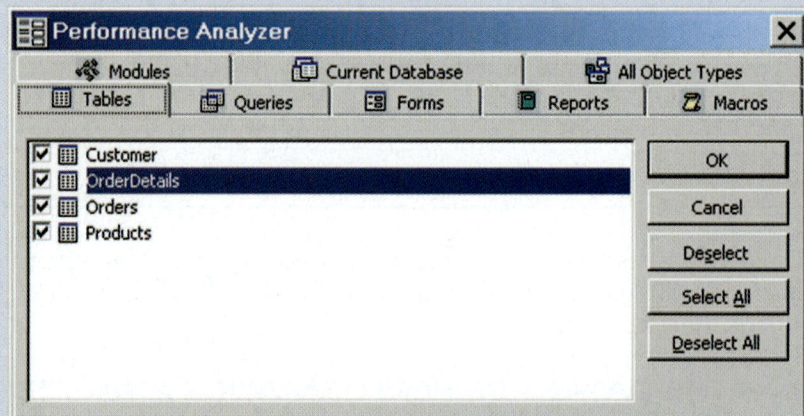

4. Click **OK**
5. Review the suggestions by clicking each and reading the Analysis Notes. None of the suggestions are consistent with the design in this case, so don't apply them

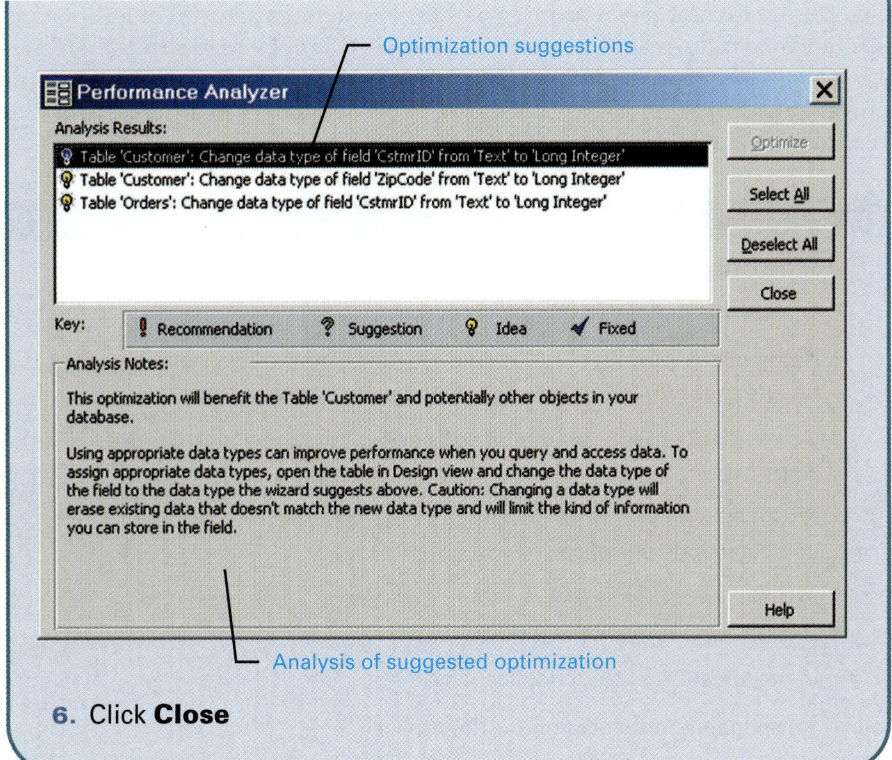

6. Click **Close**

FIGURE 7.15
Optimization suggestions

After reviewing the Analysis Notes, you can elect to have Access perform Recommendation and Suggestions optimizations for you. Click the Recommendation or Suggestion optimizations to be performed and then click the Optimize button. Idea optimizations must be completed manually by following the instructions in the Analysis Notes.

REPLICATING A DATABASE

Replication is a way of sharing database data between computers that may or may not be attached to a network. Creating a ***replica*** of a database produces a full database copy that will track changes made to the data so they can be applied to the original database. Normally each replica is used independently and then synchronized with the other replicas on a scheduled basis. Users of replicas are not guaranteed to have the most up-to-date data, because data can be modified in each replica.

Creating a Replica

The act of creating a replica causes the original database to be marked as the ***Design Master.*** The Design Master and all of its replicas are called the ***replica set.*** The design of existing database objects can be updated in the Design Master, but not in a replica.

Special tables in both the Design Master and replica databases keep track of data changes. The Design Master also tracks changes made to the design of any database object in order to pass these updates to the replicas. These special tables are used in ***synchronization,*** the process of updating the Design Master and its replicas so that all copies reflect the same status.

Each replica created has a priority assigned to using a number between 0 (lowest) and 100 (highest). When conflicting updates are made to different replicas of the database, the priority is used to resolve them.

The Design Master has a priority of 100. The default priority of a replica is 90, but any valid priority can be assigned. Changes made to the Design Master always have precedence over those made to a replica. During synchronization, the priority setting of each replica is evaluated and the record with the highest priority wins in any conflicts.

task reference

Replicating a Database:

- Open the database to be replicated
- Remove any password protection (covered later in this session) and ensure that the database is not open by any other users
- On the **Tools** menu, point to **Replication,** and then click **Create Replica**
- Click **Yes** when prompted with: The database must be closed before you can create a replica
- Answer **Yes** when prompted with: Converting a database into a Design Master results in changes . . .
- In the Location of New Replica dialog box
    - Navigate to the location for the replica
    - Set the **Priority**
    - Check the **Prevent deletes** check box to prevent record deletions in the replica
    - In the Save as type box, select the replica Visibility
    - Click **OK**

Replicating PuppyParadise:

1. Open the original copy of **AC07PuppyParadise.mdb**
2. On the **Tools** menu, point to **Replication,** and then click **Create Replica**

tip: *You will not have enough space on the A: drive to create a replica set, so you will need to use another drive like C:*

3. Click **Yes** to close the database

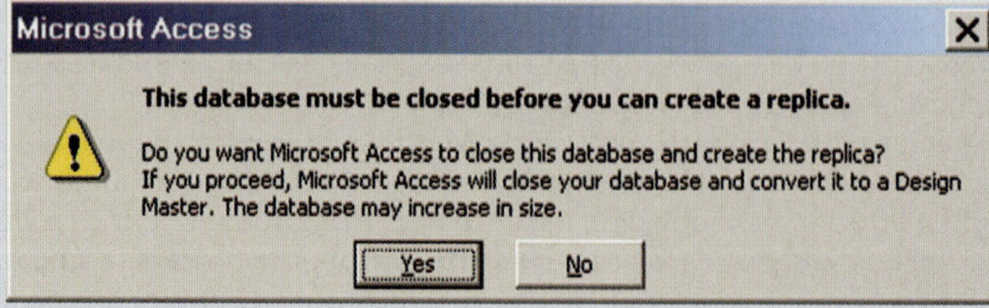
Microsoft Access
This database must be closed before you can create a replica.
Do you want Microsoft Access to close this database and create the replica?
If you proceed, Microsoft Access will close your database and convert it to a Design Master. The database may increase in size.
Yes
No

FIGURE 7.16
Create a replica

4. Click **Yes** when prompted with: Converting a database into a Design Master results in changes . . .

5. Click **OK** in the Location of New Replica dialog box to accept the default location, name, priority, and deletion settings
6. Click **OK** to complete the replication process in the dialog box reading Microsoft Access has converted . . .

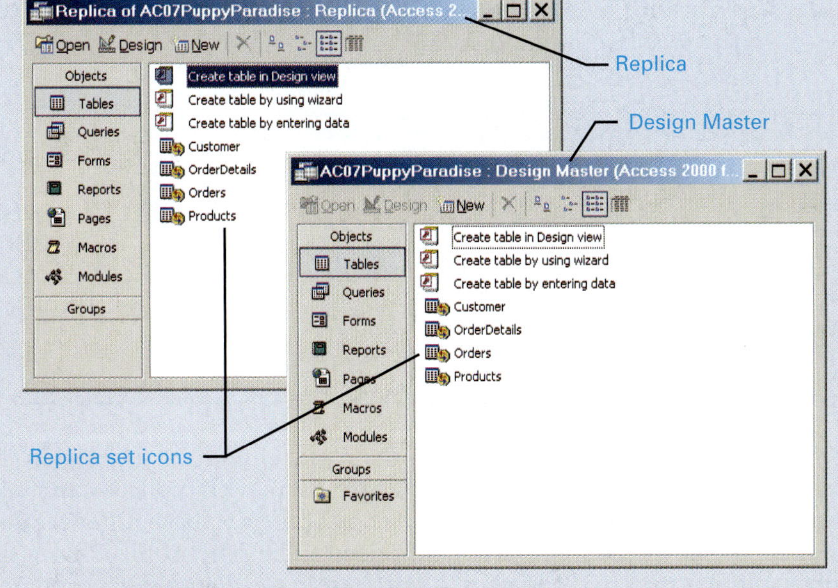

FIGURE 7.17
Design Master and replica

7. Notice that the title bar now says Design Master and the icons to the left of each database object (table, query, form, and report) indicate that this database belongs to a replica set
8. Close the Design Master
9. Open the Replica
10. Notice the word Replica in the title bar and the icons to the left of each database object (table, query, form, and report) indicate that this database belongs to a replica set

When a database is replicated, the Design Master and each replica contain all of the database objects (tables, queries, forms, reports, and so on). Significant changes are made to the database during the replication process. Fields are added to each table, tables are added to the database, and the database properties are changed. Any AutoNumber fields that previously generated sequential numbers will generate random numbers to reduce synchronization conflicts caused by users adding two different records using the same AutoNumber. The overall result is a larger database.

anotherword

. . . on Creating Replicas

Single-copy replicas can be created using My Briefcase. When you want to work on files using another computer, drag the file(s) to My Briefcase and then copy My Briefcase to a floppy disk or link the computers and transfer the files. Use the Update All feature of the briefcase to synchronize the files. This is an ideal way to create a copy of a personal database for use on your laptop while you are away from the office.

The backup created in the replication process has a .bak file extension. It can be used to create an emergency replica set. It will not be possible to synchronize replicas made from the backup with replicas made from the original.

Updating PuppyParadise replica data:

1. Open the **Replica of AC07PuppyParadise.mdb** if it is not still open from the previous steps
2. Open the **Customer** table
3. Add a record for **Heather Montgomery** with a CstmrID of 777 (make up the remaining data)

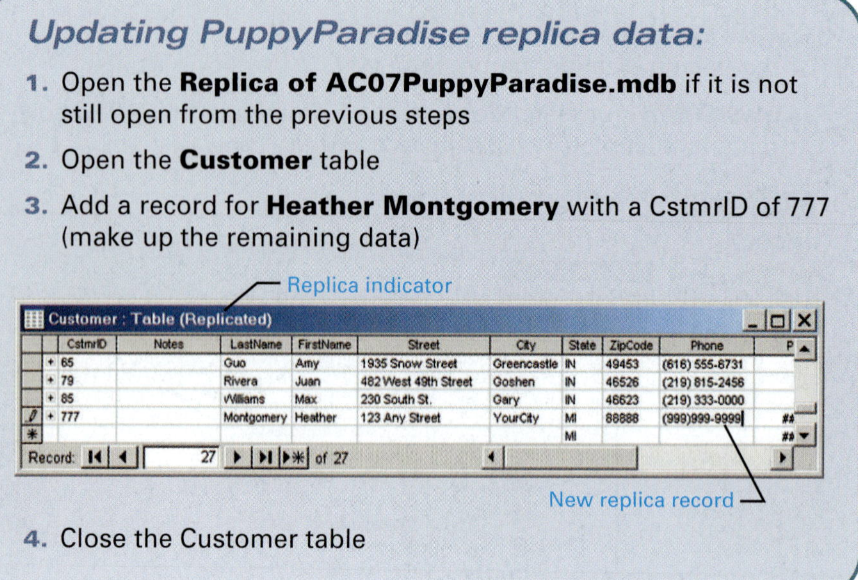

Replica indicator
Customer : Table (Replicated)
CstmrID Notes LastName FirstName Street City State ZipCode Phone
65 Guo Amy 1935 Snow Street Greencastle IN 49453 (616) 555-6731
79 Rivera Juan 482 West 49th Street Goshen IN 46526 (219) 815-2456
85 Williams Max 230 South St. Gary IN 46623 (219) 333-0000
777 Montgomery Heather 123 Any Street YourCity MI 88888 (999)999-9999
Record: 27 of 27
New replica record

FIGURE 7.18
Adding a new customer to the replica

4. Close the Customer table

The new record has been added to the replica but does not exist in the Design Master. As you can imagine, multiple users with replicas can make a significant number of updates to each copy of the database. Changes also can be made in the Design Master that need to be synchronized with the replicas. When multiple copies of a database have high-volume updates, replication may not be the most successful method of sharing data for users who need current information. It can be very effective, however, if synchronization is performed frequently, or if the various users typically update and use different data.

Synchronization

Once replicas have been generated, each database can be updated independently of the others. Exchanging updated records between two or more members of a replica set is called ***synchronization.*** Two replica set members are synchronized, or in sync, when the changes made individually in each have been applied to the other.

The previous steps created one replica and a Design Master for the PuppyParadise database. The new record added to the replica needs to be applied to the Design Master so that the databases are synchronized again.

task reference

Synchronizing Replicated Databases

- Open the replica to be synchronized
- On the **Tools** menu, point to **Replication,** and then click **Synchronize Now**
- Select the other replica set member to be synchronized from the Directly with Replica drop-down list box
- Click **OK**
- Respond **Yes** when prompted to close the database for synchronization
- Respond **OK** when notified that the process has been completed

Synchronizing PuppyParadise:

1. Open the **Replica of AC07PuppyParadise.mdb** if it is not still open from the previous steps
2. On the **Tools** menu, point to **Replication,** and then click **Synchronize Now**

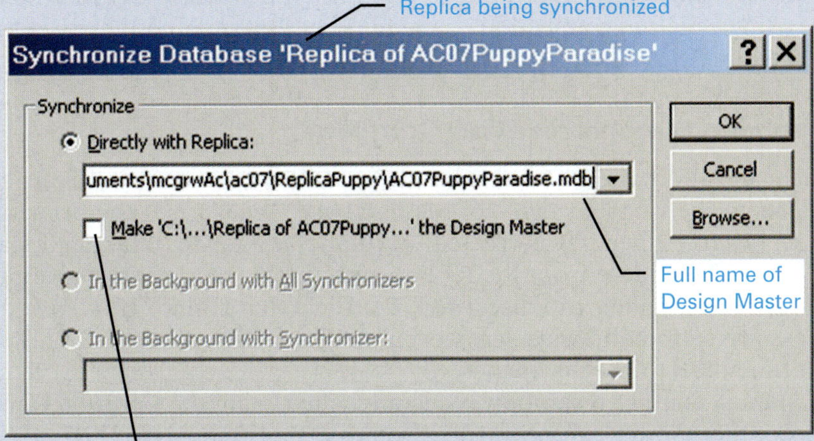

FIGURE 7.19
Synchronize Database dialog box

3. Select the Design Master name from the drop-down list

tip: *If the Design Master name does not display, use the Browse button to locate it*

4. Click **OK**
5. Respond **Yes** when prompted to close the database for synchronization
6. Respond **OK** when notified that the process has been completed
7. Open **AC07PuppyParadise.mdb**—the Design Master
8. Open the Customer table and locate record 777

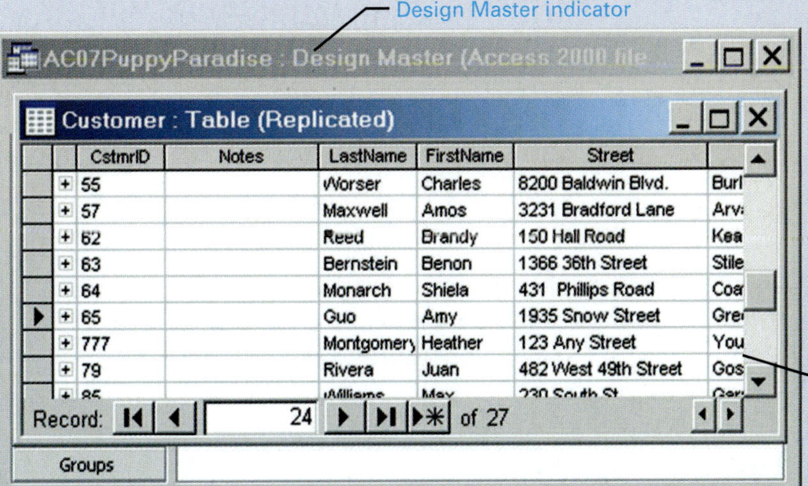

Design Master indicator
AC07PuppyParadise : Design Master (Access 2000 file
Customer : Table (Replicated)
CstmrID
Notes
LastName
FirstName
Street
55 Worser Charles 8200 Baldwin Blvd.
57 Maxwell Amos 3231 Bradford Lane
62 Reed Brandy 150 Hall Road
63 Bernstein Benon 1366 36th Street
64 Monarch Shiela 431 Phillips Road
65 Guo Amy 1935 Snow Street
777 Montgomery Heather 123 Any Street
79 Rivera Juan 482 West 49th Street
Record: 24 of 27
Groups
Record added to replica

FIGURE 7.20
Replica record added to the Design Master by synchronization

9. Close the Customer table

This was a very simple example of adding one record to the replica and then using synchronization to update the Design Master with the same record. Normally synchronization is completed at regular intervals, like the close of business each day or Friday at 4:00 P.M.

The synchronization method demonstrated is called ***direct synchronization*** and is effective for replica sets that are stored on the same computer or in shared folders of a network. The alternate Indirect and Internet synchronization methods can be applied when it is necessary to synchronize using a dial-up connection or the Internet. Both methods are well documented in Access help.

Resolving Synchronization Conflicts

Synchronization of replicas can result in conflicts created by unrestricted updates to the various copies of the database. Access uses the priority of the replica (set when it was created) to resolve as many conflicting updates as it can. The update from the replica with the highest priority is applied and all other updates are discarded. Conflicts that cannot be resolved by Access are stored and the user is prompted to resolve them manually the next time the database is opened.

Manual conflict resolution is accomplished using the ***Conflict Viewer.*** The Conflict Viewer can be opened from the Tools menu (see Figure 7.21) or from the unresolved conflicts prompt that displays when a database containing conflicts is opened. When using the Tools menu, you will be notified when there are no conflicts and the Conflict Viewer will not open. If there are conflicts, possible resolutions will be presented in a selection list.

The most common conflict is a simultaneous update conflict that occurs if changes have been made to the same record in more than one replica set member. Conflicts also can be caused by two or more replicas adding a new record with the same key or applying updates that impact referential integrity. Remember that referential integrity stops parent records from being deleted when there are still child records. If one database deletes a parent and all of its children while another adds a new child,

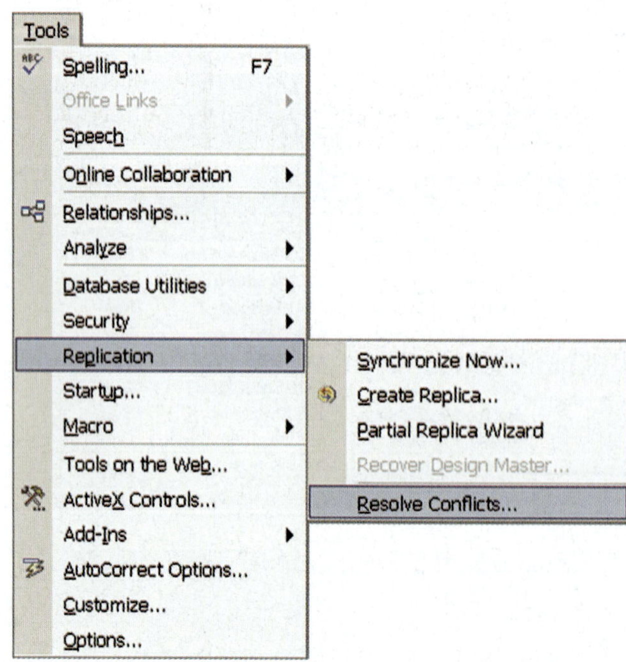

FIGURE 7.21
Initiating the Conflict Viewer

a referential integrity conflict would result. Regardless of the source of synchronization conflicts, it is important to review and resolve them each time synchronization is performed.

Retaining and Deleting Replicas

Each replica that is created has a retention period that controls the number of days nonsynchronized records are kept. The default retention period is 60 days, but any period between 5 and 32,000 days is valid. Set a long retention period if the replicas do not synchronize frequently and a short retention period for frequently synchronized replicas. Shorter retention periods keep replica sizes smaller and improve database performance.

The Design Master and replica must be synchronized within the retention period. If synchronization is not accomplished before the replica expires, the replica will be removed from the replica set when synchronization is attempted. Synchronization must occur whether or not any updates have been made.

Mechanically deleting a replica is the same as deleting any other file in the Microsoft Windows environment. Use Windows Explorer, select the file, and press the Delete key. A Yes response will place the replica in the Recycle Bin until it is emptied. A word of caution, however: deleting a replica without synchronizing will lose any changes that it contains. Deleting the Design Master removes the controlling database of the replica set. The other members of the set cannot be synchronized until a new Design Master is assigned.

It is best not to delete a Design Master, but replicas can be deleted with no impact when they are no longer needed. The Design Master retains all of its attributes and continues to track updates for synchronization whether or not there are any current replicas. New replicas can be created as the need arises.

SECURING AN ACCESS DATABASE

All data stored for business or operational purposes is valuable and needs to be protected from theft, loss, misuse, and unwanted updates. Whether the breech is accidental, mischievous, or malicious, the result of unauthorized database access is usually damaged or destroyed data. Protecting data from unauthorized access requires careful planning. The level of security should match the importance of the data.

Microsoft Access data files can be read by a number of utility and word processor programs, meaning that data can be viewed outside the environment in which it was created. Access supports several methods of controlling access to a database and its objects. These methods range from simple to complex. The simpler methods are less costly and less secure, but are adequate for restricting access to nonessential data. More time and care should be taken with critical data.

Hiding Files

One of the simplest protections is to hide your sensitive files from the casual observer. Microsoft Windows assigns properties to each file that is saved including the Hidden property. A hidden file does not display in a standard file listing like that provided by Windows Explorer. Setting the Hidden property is accomplished by right-clicking on the file, selecting Properties, and clicking Hidden. Even though the file is not visible, it can be manipulated using its name. For example, a hidden file can be opened with the standard Open dialog box by typing its name rather than clicking a name in the file list. Viewing hidden files is also easy; set the folder's properties to Show Hidden Files.

task reference

Hiding a Database

- Open Windows Explorer
- Navigate to the file to be hidden
- Right-click on the file to be hidden
- Click the **Properties** option
- Click the **Hidden** attribute
- Click **OK**

Hiding the PuppyParadise backup:

1. Close the open Access database
2. Use the Start menu to open Windows Explorer

tip: *Usually Start|Programs|Accessories|Windows Explorer*

3. Navigate to the backup of PuppyParadise created during replication, **AC07PuppyParadise.bak**
4. Right-click on AC07PuppyParadise.bak
5. Choose **Properties**
6. Select the **Hidden** check box and click **OK**
7. Click **OK**
8. Press **F5** to refresh Windows Explorer

tip: *AC07PuppyParadise.bak should be grayed out or not listed because it is hidden. If the file does display, the folder options on your computer (steps 9–11) have already been set and you will need to reverse them to see how a hidden file behaves*

9. Click **Tools** and select **Folder Options**
10. Click the **View** tab
11. Click **Show Hidden Files and Folders** and click **OK**

tip: *If AC07PuppyParadise.bak is not visible, press F5*

Setting Show Hidden Files and Folders causes all hidden files and folders to display in the current folder. Selecting the Like Current Folder button, rather than OK, will cause all folders to display hidden files. Since hidden files can be so readily displayed, hiding the file only keeps it out of the hands of people who don't really know how to look.

FIGURE 7.22
File Properties dialog box

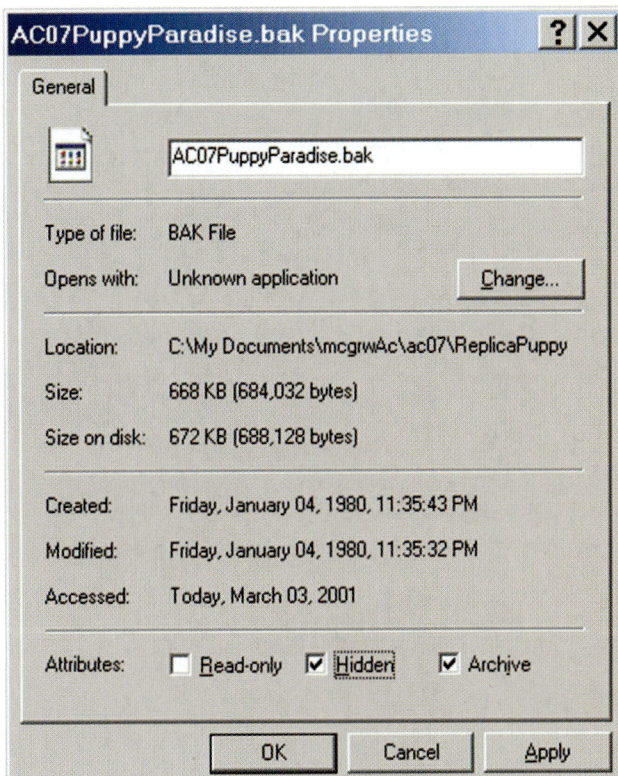

Enabling Data Encryption

Encryption is a simple method of securing a database. Encrypting a database ensures that it is indecipherable to utility and word processor programs. This method is most effective for a database that is being transported on a storage medium or digitally transmitted. Since the process of opening an encrypted database in Access decrypts it, this is not an effective way to stop Access users from viewing and updating the database.

An important component of security is that only specific users can apply and remove database security measures. The person who created a database is its ***owner*** and has full security rights to it. When multiple users or user groups have been defined for a database, the users who have full rights are members of the administrator group called Admins. Only the owner or a member of the Admins group can open the database exclusively so that no other users have access and can set security.

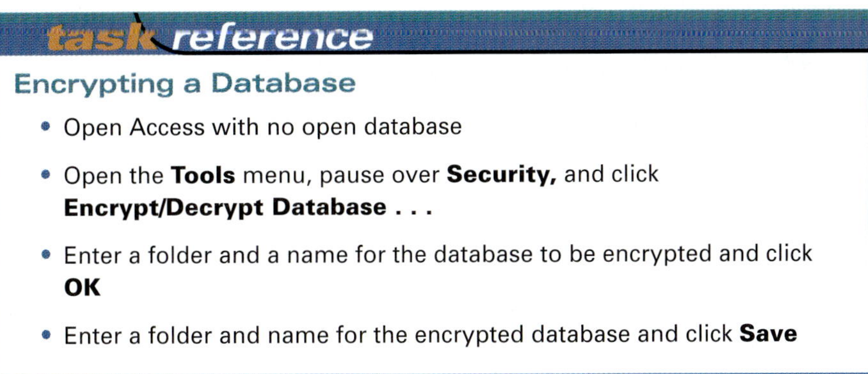

task reference

Encrypting a Database

- Open Access with no open database
- Open the **Tools** menu, pause over **Security,** and click **Encrypt/Decrypt Database . . .**
- Enter a folder and a name for the database to be encrypted and click **OK**
- Enter a folder and name for the encrypted database and click **Save**

Encrypting PuppyParadise:

1. Open Access and close any open database
2. On the **Tools** menu, point to **Security,** and then click **Encrypt/Decrypt Database . . .**

FIGURE 7.23
Encryption menu selections

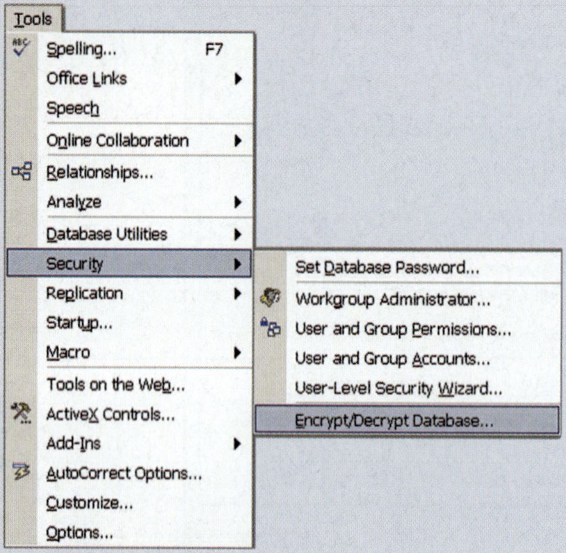

Tools
Spelling... F7
Office Links
Speech
Online Collaboration
Relationships...
Analyze
Database Utilities
Security
Replication
Startup...
Macro
Tools on the Web...
ActiveX Controls...
Add-Ins
AutoCorrect Options...
Customize...
Options...
Set Database Password...
Workgroup Administrator...
User and Group Permissions...
User and Group Accounts...
User-Level Security Wizard...
Encrypt/Decrypt Database...

3. Navigate to the folder containing your files and select **AC07PuppyPardise.mdb** as the database to encrypt
4. Click **OK**
5. Name the encrypted database **EncryptedAC07PuppyParadise.mdb**
6. Click **Save**

When naming the encrypted file, one option is to use the same name as the original file. If the encryption operation is successful, the database is replaced with the encrypted version. If the encryption operation fails, the original file is retained. Data added to an encrypted file are encrypted before they are stored. Data are decrypted by Access before they are displayed to the user. Decrypting a database is the reverse of encrypting.

Continually encrypting and decrypting the data as the database is used can slow database performance. It is best to encrypt the database for transport and decrypt it for use.

SETTING PASSWORD PROTECTION

Evan would like to add a password to the PuppyParadise database to control who has access to the data. Adding a ***password*** or passwords to a database is the simplest way to prevent unauthorized access to the data and other objects it contains. Users will have to provide the password before they are able to open the file. The Password dialog box displays asterisks as the user enters the password to keep others from viewing it.

Opening an Access database in the usual fashion allows ***shared*** access. Shared access means that two or more users can open the same database simultaneously. ***Exclusive*** access is required while setting a password to prevent other users from entering the database.

task reference

Password Protecting a Database

- Open Access with no open database
- Click the **Open** button on the Database toolbar
- Navigate to the folder and select the file to be password protected
- Click the Open button's list arrow and select **Open Exclusive**
- Open the **Tools** menu, pause over **Security,** and then click **Set Database Password**
- Type the password in the Password text box, repeat the same password in the Verify text box, and then press **Enter**

Adding a password to PuppyParadise:

1. Open Access and close any open databases
2. Click the **Open** button
3. Locate **AC07PuppyParadise.mdb** and click it
4. Click the list arrow on the Open button

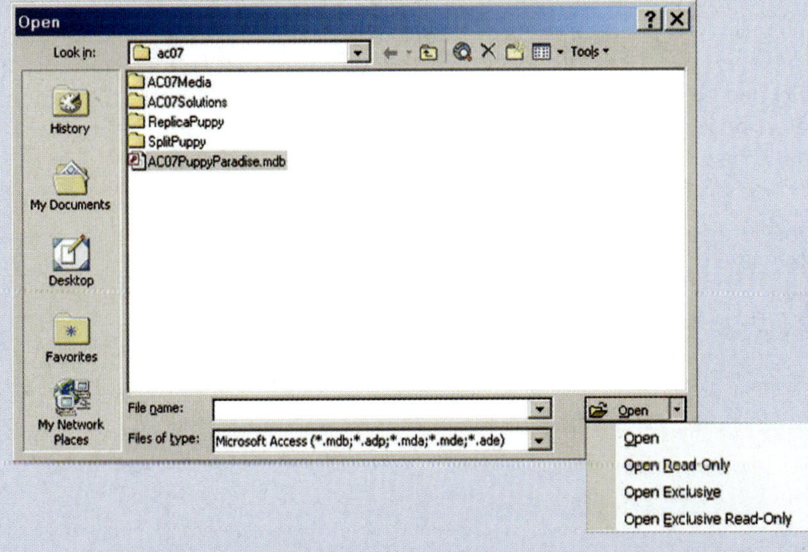

FIGURE 7.24
Open button options

5. Select **Open Exclusive**
6. Select **Tools,** pause over **Security,** and then click **Set Database Password**

tip: *If Set Database Password is grayed out, the database is not exclusively opened. Close it and repeat steps 2 through 5*

FIGURE 7.25
Set Database Password dialog box

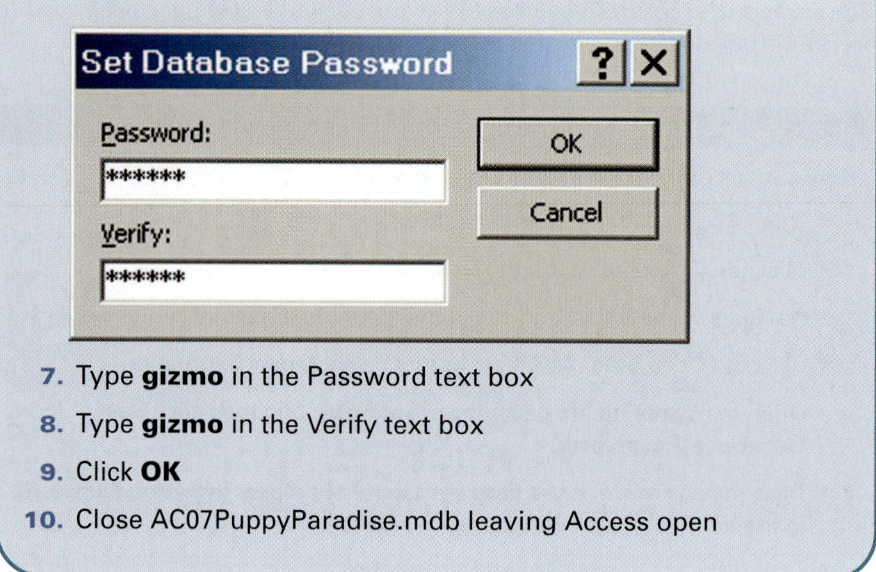

7. Type **gizmo** in the Password text box
8. Type **gizmo** in the Verify text box
9. Click **OK**
10. Close AC07PuppyParadise.mdb leaving Access open

Figure 7.24 displays all of the available open modes. As previously discussed, choosing Open results in shared access and choosing Open Exclusive locks the database so that no other users have access. The ***Open Read-Only*** option allows shared access for reading database objects. Read access allows all actions that do not update any database objects. Examples of allowable read-only operations include printing reports and running queries. The Open Exclusive Read-Only option locks out other users and allows you read access.

A new password must be entered twice to prevent typing errors in the password. Access passwords are case sensitive, so be very careful when entering them. Pick a password that is easy to remember since opening the database is not possible without the password. Replicated databases should not be password protected, since the password halts the synchronization process. Testing the password is accomplished by trying to open the database.

Testing the PuppyParadise password:

1. Click the Open button
2. Locate **AC07PuppyParadise.mdb** and click it
3. Click the **Open** button

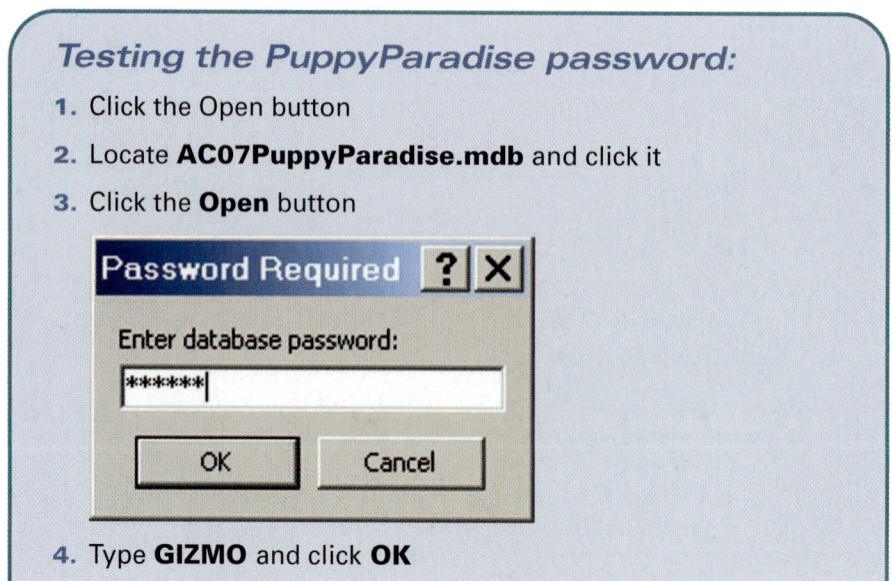

FIGURE 7.26
Password dialog box

4. Type **GIZMO** and click **OK**

tip: *Passwords are case sensitive, so GIZMO will not work*

5. Respond OK to the prompt that you have entered an invalid password
6. Type **gizmo** and click **OK**

Passwords are unencrypted so that they can be viewed by other users from the password file. This can be handy for forgotten passwords, but does not provide the most effective password protection. Encrypted passwords can be set with user-level security.

Removing the PuppyParadise password:

1. Verify that Access if running and that **AC07PuppyParadise.mdb** is open
2. Click the **Tools menu,** then **Security,** and then **Unset Database Password**

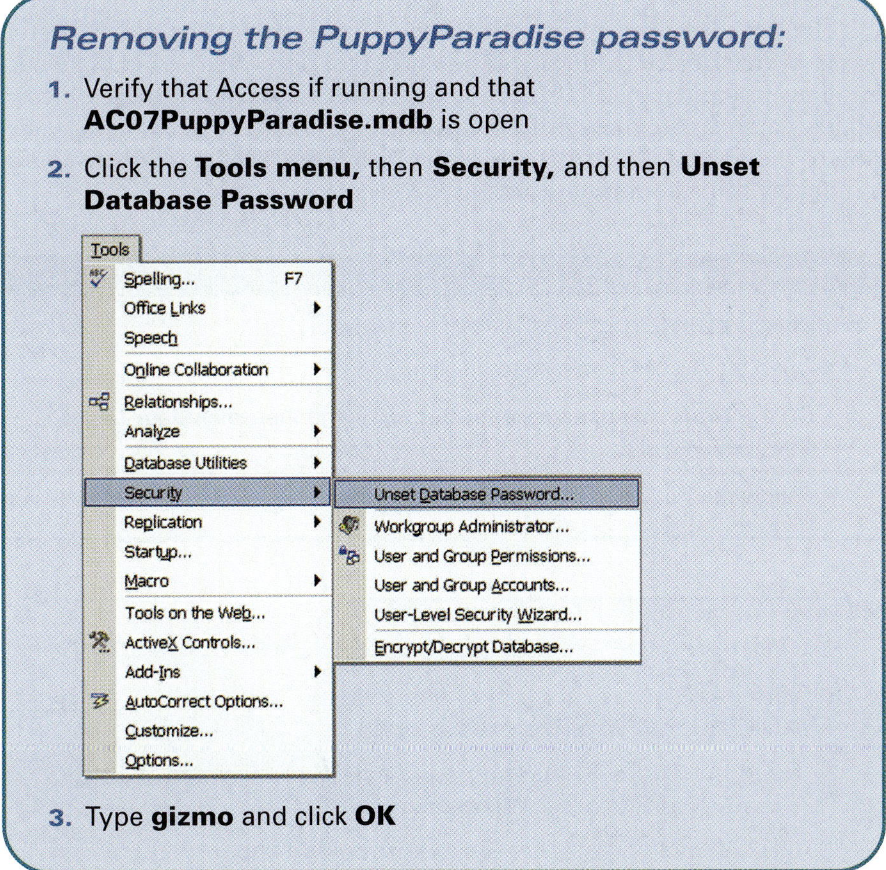

FIGURE 7.27
Removing a password

3. Type **gizmo** and click **OK**

Removing a password from a file is accomplished with the file open. With the Security option of the Tools menu displaying, select Unset Database Password and enter the correct password when prompted. Successfully entering the password will remove it from the file.

User-Level Security

In a multi-user database ***user-level security*** settings can allow some users to have full access to the database while others have restricted access. Restricted access might keep certain users from replicating the database, changing the database design, creating new tables, changing the database password, or almost any other operation.

User-level security provides the most comprehensive security available for an Access database. When user-level security is applied, the user must type a password to enter the database. The password used is matched against a list of users to establish a level of access to each database object called ***permissions.***

Each user has a set of permissions that determine what operations they can perform on each table, query, form, report, and macro. Permissions are either explicit or implicit. ***Explicit permissions*** are granted directly to each user by setting a user account. ***Implicit permissions*** are granted to a user group and inherited by the users belonging to that group.

Permissions can be changed for a database object by

- Members of the Admins group
- The owner of the object
- Any user who has Administer permission for the object

The user who creates a table, query, form, report, or macro is the owner of that object. Additionally, the group of users that can change permissions in the database also can change the ownership of these objects, or they can recreate these objects, which is another way to change ownership of the objects. Access provides the User-Level Security Wizard to aid in implementing common security schemes.

task reference

Setting User-Level Security

- Open the Access database to be secured
- On the **Tools** menu, pause over **Security** and then click **User-Level Security Wizard**
- Follow the Wizard instructions

Setting PuppyParadise user-level security:

1. Verify that Access is running and that **AC07PuppyParadise.mdb** is open
2. Open the **Tools** menu and pause over **Security** and then click **User-Level Security Wizard**
3. Click **Next** to create a new workgroup information file
4. Read and accept the defaults on this Wizard page by clicking **Next**
5. Accept the default of securing all database objects by clicking **Next**
6. Create user groups
   a. Check **Full Permissions** and read the Group Permissions description
   b. Check **Full Data Users** and read the Group Permissions description

tip: *You are creating two unique and encrypted user groups with different permissions. The Administrator group is created by default*

7. Click **Next**
8. Accept the default of not assigning Users group permissions by clicking **Next**
9. Add users and passwords
   a. Add **user1** with a password of **user1**
   b. Add **user2** with a password of **user2**
   c. Click on Administrator and set the password to **gizmo**
10. Add users to the groups
    a. Select **user1** from the drop-down list and click **Full Permissions**
    b. Select user2 from the drop-down list and click **Full Data Users**
11. Click **Next**
12. Name the backup **PuppyParadiseUserSecurityBak.mdb** and click **Finish**
13. Print the Security report

The PuppyParadise database now has three users with unique passwords. The username and password used to open the database determine the operations that can be performed.

Testing PuppyParadise user-level security:

1. Close Access and reopen it
2. Open the **AC07PuppyParadise.mdb**
3. Log on as user2 and try to change the database design

The Administrator username and password will allow full access to the database including altering security settings. Logging on as user1 will allow full access to the database except assigning permissions to other users while user2 will allow data editing, but no updates to database objects.

making the grade

SESSION 7.2

1. What is the purpose of splitting a database?
2. What tool will suggest changes to improve database performance?
3. How is replicating a database different from splitting a database?
4. When should you consider securing an Access database?

SESSION 7.3 SUMMARY

Every database requires periodic maintenance to repair known problems regardless of how well it was designed. Preventive maintenance or design reviews are performed to reduce the likelihood of a serious system failure. The frequency of preventive maintenance is determined by how critical the data are to the operation of the organization.

Periodic maintenance starts with the users evaluating the system and suggesting modifications that would improve usability and performance. User issues typically involve ease of data entry, validity of data, and reporting. Input masks, formats, default values, data validation, and other field properties are usually the way to address such issues. Access also provides the Database Performance Analyzer for monitoring database performance and suggesting areas for object design improvement.

Often design changes are necessary because the organization using the data or the business operations supported by the data have changed. New tables, fields, and reports can be created to support business changes, but organizational changes are more complex. When multiple users need access to the same data, effective methods of sharing must be employed. One alternative for sharing is to create replicas of a database that must be synchronized so that all replicas reflect the same data.

The method chosen for sharing data is determined by whether or not the organization is networked and the level of access needed by each user. Another sharing method splits the database into a front-end and back-end. Each user maintains unique front-end (queries, forms, and reports) with access to the data held in the back-end.

When a database is exposed to risk of violation, it is wise to implement security measures. Security is also needed when there are multiple users with differing levels of responsibility. Encryption can be used to secure a database being transported. A simple password can ensure that only authorized users access the data. End-user security uses permissions to determine exactly what operations a user can perform on each database object.

MOUS OBJECTIVES SUMMARY

- AC2002-1-1—Use data validation
- AC2002-1-4—Create and modify custom input masks
- AC2002-7-5—Assign database security (permissions and passwords)
- AC2002-7-6—Replicate databases
- AC2002-7-3—Encrypt and decrypt databases
- AC2002-8-2—Use the Database Splitter (creating front/back-end and protecting a database from modification)

task reference roundup

Task	Page #	Preferred Method
Controlling blank data values	AC 7.11	• Open the table in Design view
		• Click the field whose blank values you would like to control
		• Set Required to **Yes** to disallow blank values (Allow Zero Length should be set to No)

task reference roundup

Task	Page #	Preferred Method
Defining field validation rules	AC 7.13	• Open the table in Design view
		• Click the field that will be monitored by the validation rule
		• Select the **Validation Rule** property for that field
		• Type the validation expression or use the Expression Builder by clicking the ellipsis to the right of the Validation Rule text box
		• Click the Validation Text property box for the same field and enter the text that is to display when the validation rule is broken
		• Save the table update
		• If the validation rule has been set for a field that already contains data, Access will ask if you want to apply the new rule to existing data
		• If there are no existing data in the field, there will be no prompt
Splitting a database	AC 7.16	• Back up the database
		• On the Tools menu, point to Database Utilities, and then click Database Splitter
		• Follow the Database Splitter Wizard instructions
Optimizing database objects	AC 7.18	• Open the database to be optimized
		• Click the **Tools** menu, then **Analyze,** and then **Performance**
		• Select the tab for the database object (table, query, report, form, etc.) that you would like to analyze
		• Click the check box of each object to be evaluated or click Select All to select all objects in the list
		• Select objects from other tabs if desired
		• Click **OK**
		• Review and apply results as needed
Replicating a database	AC 7.20	• Open the database to be replicated
		• Remove any password protection and ensure that the database is not open by any other users
		• On the **Tools** menu, point to **Replication,** and then click **Create Replica**
		• Click **Yes** when prompted with: The database must be closed before you can create a replica
		• Answer **Yes** when prompted with: Converting a database into a Design Master results in changes . . .
		• In the Location of New Replica dialog box
		• Navigate to the location for the replica
		• Set the **Priority**

task reference roundup

Task	Page #	Preferred Method
		• Check the **Prevent deletes** check box to prevent record deletions in the replica
		• In the Save as Type box, select the replica visibility
		• Click **OK**
Synchronizing replicated databases	AC 7.22	• Open the replica to be synchronized
		• On the **Tools** menu, point to **Replication,** and then click **Synchronize Now**
		• Select the other replica set member to be synchronized from the Directly with Replica drop-down list box
		• Click **OK**
		• Respond **Yes** when prompted to close the database for synchronization
		• Respond **OK** when notified that the process has been completed
Hiding a database	AC 7.26	• Open Windows Explorer
		• Navigate to the file to be hidden
		• Right-click on the file to be hidden
		• Click the **Properties** option
		• Click the **Hidden** attribute
		• Click **OK**
Encrypting a database	AC 7.27	• Open Access with no open database
		• Open the **Tools** menu, pause over **Security,** and click **Encrypt/Decrypt Database . . .**
		• Enter a folder and a name for the database to be encrypted and click **OK**
		• Enter a folder and name for the encrypted database and click **Save**
Password protecting a database	AC 7.29	• Open Access with no open database
		• Click the **Open** button on the Database toolbar
		• Navigate to the folder and select the file to be password protected
		• Click the Open button's list arrow and select **Open Exclusive**
		• Open the **Tools** menu, pause over **Security**, and then click **Set Database Password**
		• Type the password in the Password text box, repeat the same password in the Verify text box, and then press **Enter**
Setting user-level security	AC7.32	• Open the Access database to be secured
		• On the **Tools** menu, pause over **Security** and then click **User-Level Security Wizard**
		• Follow the Wizard instructions

review of terminology

CROSSWORD PUZZLE

Across

7. Must be typed to enter a secured database.
9. A method of rendering files undecipherable.
10. Open mode that will not allow updates.
14. Security that controls access to objects by username.
15. Permissions inherited from a user's group.
16. Complete copy of a database.
17. Database access that locks out all other users.

Down

1. Updating replica set members.
2. Determines the operations a user can perform.
3. Permissions granted directly to the user.
4. The portion of a split database that is customized for each user.
5. Data portion of a split database.
6. The creator of an object.
8. The synchronization method used when replicas have access to each other.
11. Term for nothing entered.
12. The original database of a replica set.
13. Format ________ copies formatting.

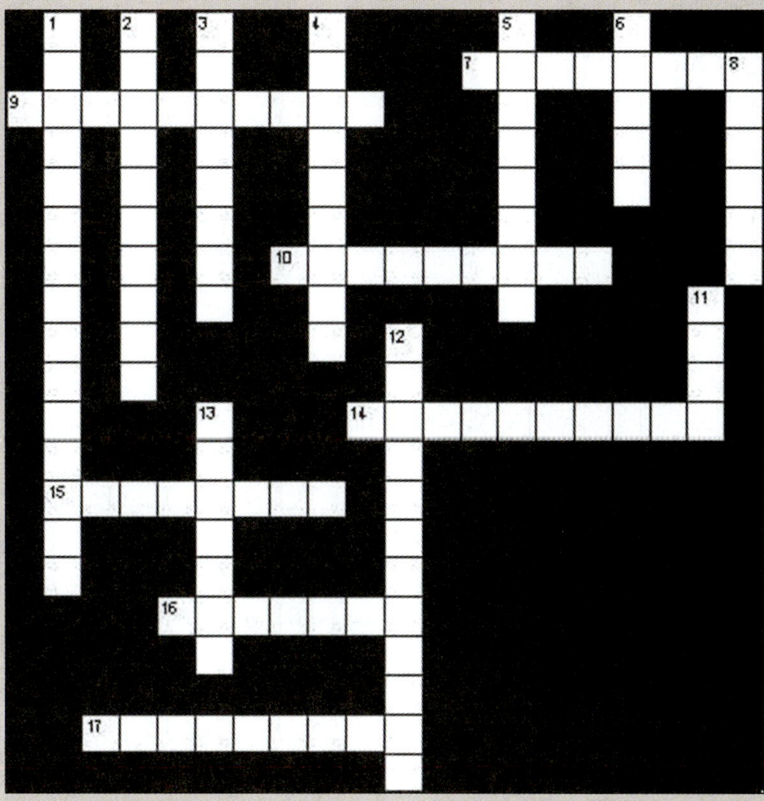

review of concepts

FILL-IN

1. Passwords protect a database from ________ access.
2. The least effective method of securing a database discussed is ________.
3. Administrators and owners can grant ________ to database objects.
4. Encryption is not effective in protecting against people who own ________ software.
5. One of the easiest ways to improve the validity of database data is to reduce ________.

REVIEW QUESTIONS

Each of the following topics should be addressed in one to three paragraphs.

1. Consider the data that your college or university stores about you and suggest some validation rules that would be effective for improving data validity with that type of data.
2. Explain the relationship between validation rules and Validation text.
3. Assume that you have created a database that will track service calls for billing purposes. The minimum service call is 30 minutes. How would you set up and verify the performance of data entry restrictions on the ServiceTime field?
4. Why is it important for split databases to be on a network?
5. If your database resides on a desktop computer and you are taking a business trip with a laptop, what is the most effective way to take your database with you?

CREATE THE QUESTION

For each of the following answers, create the question.

ANSWER	QUESTION
1. ___-___-____	________
2. The Text Box format overrides the format set in the table definition.	________
3. When you can identify a value that is most often entered in a field	________
4. Please enter a value between 1 and 100.	________
5. The back-end	________

FACT OR FICTION

For each of the following, determine whether the statement is fact, fiction, or both and present your arguments for that conclusion.

1. The queries, forms, and reports contained in the front-end file of a split database cannot be updated.
2. You should always follow the suggestions of the Database Performance Analyzer.
3. When you add a record to a replica, the other members of the replica set are automatically updated.
4. Synchronization conflicts that cannot be resolved with the priority must be handled manually with the Conflict Viewer.
5. Deleting a replica does not impact the Design Master or the remaining replicas.

practice

Altamonte High School Booster Club Donation Tracking—Part III: Database Design Review

The Altamonte Boosters have been using their database for several months and are encountering some problems. Since there are no input masks or validation rules, and multiple users, the data are not at all consistent. The capitalization of names is an issue and incomplete data entry occurs too frequently. A database design review has been completed uncovering the need for the updates outlined below.

1. Start Access and open **AC07AltamonteBoosters.mdb**

   tip: *You cannot use your copy of the database from the previous chapter, since there have been modifications for this chapter*

2. Open the **Boosters** table
   a. Make each field required by setting the Required property to **Yes**
   b. Correct the Field Size property of Name to **25**
   c. Change the Data Type of Phone to **Text** and use the ellipsis (. . .) to set the Input Mask to **Phone Number.** Do not store the symbols.
   d. Edit the Phone Input Mask property to be **!(000)000-0000** since the area code in Altamonte is required
   e. Change the Data Type of Zip to **Text** and set an Input Mask of **00000**
   f. Since all of the boosters are in state, the zip code should begin with 27. Enter the validation rule **Like "27???"**
   g. Enter the Validation text **Booster's Zip Code must begin with 27**
   h. Since most of the boosters are in the **27234** zip code, set that as the default value of Zip
   i. Set the Default property of the State field to **NC**
3. Save your changes to the Boosters table and respond yes to the prompt informing you that validation rules have changed
4. To test your updates, change to Datasheet view
   a. Create a new booster record for **Mark Funk** and try to move to another record

   tip: *You should receive a validation record for the missing street address*

   b. Add a Street address for Mark Funk in **Cary, NC**
   c. Leave the Zip blank and try to move to another record
   d. Enter a Zip of **33228** and try to move to another record
   e. Change the Zip to **27228** and try to move to another record
   f. Enter a Phone of **3174382851** and try to move to another record
   g. Set DonationClass to **1** and move to another record

   tip: *Now you have tested and corrected each modification to the database and the record should be accepted for update*

5. Close the Boosters table
6. Exit Access if your work is complete

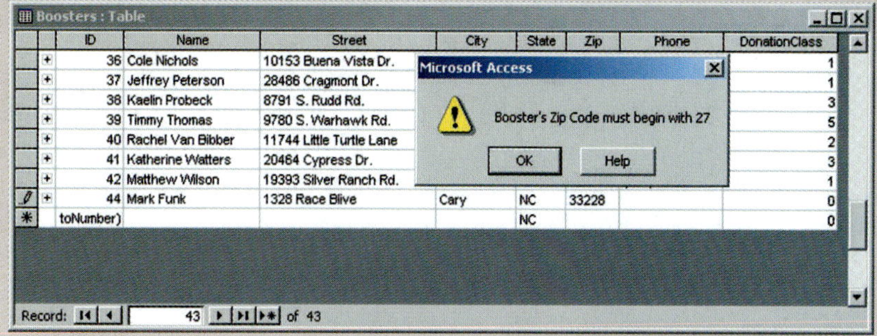

FIGURE 7.28
Testing Boosters design changes

challenge!

Altamonte High School Booster Club Donation Tracking—Part IV: Exploring Alternatives for Sharing the Database

The Altamonte Boosters are preparing for a fund-raising drive and believe that it would be more effective to have a way for multiple members to update the database. Since the computers holding the databases will not be networked, replication will provide the most effective way to share database access. At this point they think that there should be three users: the club president, vice president, and fundraising chair.

1. If you did not complete the previous project, start Access and open **AC07AltamonteBoosters.mdb**

   tip: *You can use your copy of the database from the Practice project in this chapter. You cannot use your copy of the database from the previous chapter since there have been modifications for this chapter*

2. Use the Performance Analyzer to evaluate the performance of all tables in the AlatamonteBoosters database. Document the Analysis Results and outline whether or not the results should be acted on
3. Create a replica set for the three users. The Design Master will be retained by the club president and each of the other users will need a replica
   a. Use the Tools menu to create the first replica with the following attributes:
      i. Name the replica **ReplicaAltamonte1** and save it in a folder named **ReplicaAltamonte**
      ii. Create a backup and close the open database when prompted
      iii. Click on the **Prevent Deletes** check box so that this replica can't delete existing records
   b. Use the Tools menu to create the second replica, named **ReplicaAltamonte2,** with the same attributes as ReplicaAltamont1

   tip: *You will not be prompted to create a back-up in subsequent replications*

4. Passwords cannot be applied to replicated databases, so each user will have to be responsible for securing his or her computer and folders to protect the database. For added security, use Windows Explorer to
   a. Create a folder for each user named **Pres, VPres,** and **Chair**
   b. Move the Design Master to Pres, ReplicaAltamonte1 to Vpres, and ReplicaAltamonte2 to Chair
   c. Hide the Pres, VPres, and Chair folders
5. Exit Access if your work is complete

FIGURE 7.29
AltamonteBoosters Design Master and replicas

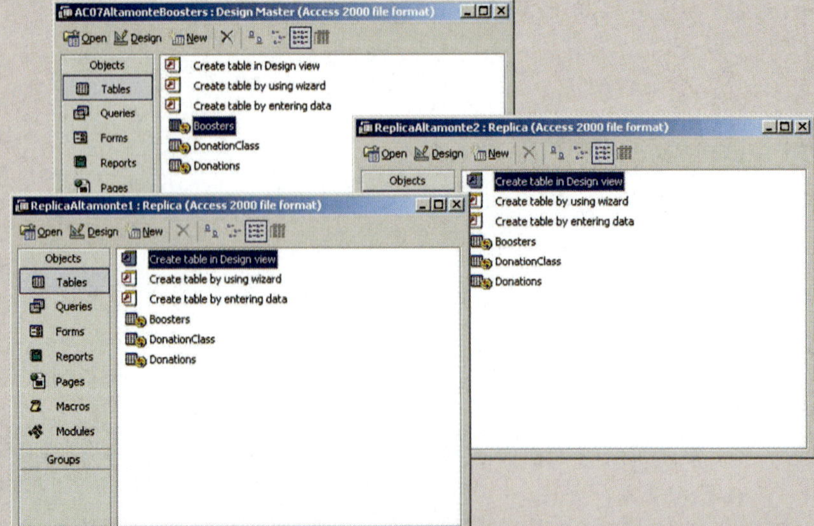

hands-on projects

on the web

Academic Software

The design review for the Access database used by Academic Software has been completed and a list of updates compiled. Additionally, Academic has installed a network and plans to split the database so that the various users can customize their front-end components.

1. Use your favorite search engine to find an Academic software title for the study of chemistry
2. Start Access and open **AC07Software.mdb**

   tip: *You cannot use your copy of the database from the previous chapter since there have been modifications for this chapter*

3. Open tblVendors
   a. Make each field required by setting the Required property to **Yes**
   b. Use the ellipsis (. . .) to set the Input Mask to **Phone Number.** Do not store the symbols
   c. Use Find and Replace to remove the dashes from the current phone numbers
   d. Create a Phone input mask that requires the area code to be entered
   e. Create an input mask for Zip that requires all five digits to be entered
   f. Create an input mask for State that requires both characters to be entered
   g. Test these updates with **RS, Ricks Software, 838 E. Jay St., Indianapolis, IN, 46121, 7518300848**
   h. Close AC07Software.mdb
4. Use Windows Explorer to create a backup of the database named **AC07SoftwareBak.mdb** before splitting it
5. Use the **Database Utilities** option of the **Tools** menu to activate the Database Splitter Wizard
   a. Name the back-end file **AC07Software_be.mdb**

   tip: *This file would normally be placed on a shared network disk so that all of the front-ends would have access to it. The front-end can be copied to any number of computers*

   b. Select **tblSoftware** and click **Design**

   tip: *A message will warn you that this is a linked table, which means that the data are stored in the back-end and you are in the front-end*

   c. Use the Query Wizard to create a query, **tblSoftwareQuery,** displaying Name, Category, and Vendor Code
6. Open **AC07Software_be.mdb**
   a. Open **tblSoftware** and add the Validation Rule **="MTH" Or ="ENG" Or ="SCI"**
   b. Add appropriate Validation Text for the Category field
7. Open **AC07Software.mdb** and add a record to the Software for **NewsNow** with a SoftwareNumber of **6060,** Category of **Che,** and VendorCode of **LS**

   tip: *You should receive the message from the validation rule added to the back-end*

8. Change Che to **SCI** and move to another record to save the change
9. Add a record for the software title that you located on the Internet with a VendorCode of **CC**
10. Exit Access if your work is complete

FIGURE 7.30

Front-end of Software.mdb

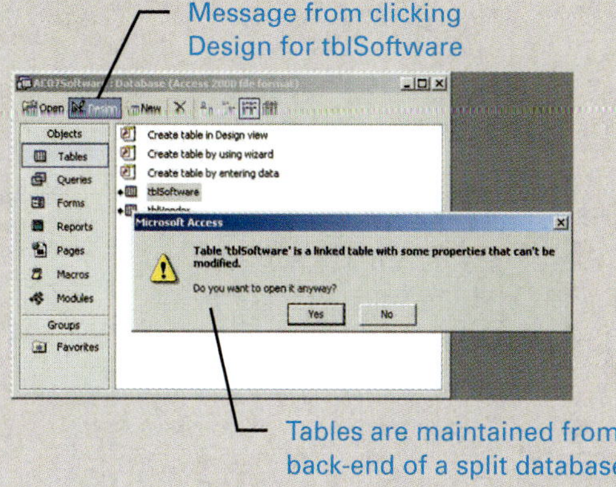

e-business

Curbside Recycling

A design review for the Curbside Recycling Access database has been completed and a list of updates compiled. The updates include adding input masks and default values and replicating the database.

1. Start Access and open **AC07CurbsideRecycling.mdb**

   tip: *You cannot use your copy of the database from the previous chapter since there have been modifications for this chapter*

2. Open the Customer table
   a. Make each field required by setting the Required property to **Yes**

   tip: *CstmrNmbr is the key field and so is already required*

   b. Create a Phone input mask that requires the area code to be entered
   c. Create an input mask for ZipCode that requires all five digits to be entered
   d. Create an input mask for State that requires both characters to be entered
   e. Apply a Short Date input mask to FirstPickup
   f. Based on the current data, set appropriate default values for City, State, and Zip
   g. Test these updates with **Connor McKinsey, 838 E. Jay St., Indianapolis, IN, 46121, 7518300848**
   h. Close the Customer table
3. Use the **Replication** option of the **Tools** menu to create replicas
   a. Create a new folder for the replicas named **Curbside Replicas**
   b. Set the appropriate properties to stop the replica from deleting records and name the replica **Curbside1**
   c. Create a second replica that cannot delete records, **Curbside2,** in the same folder
4. You are in the Design Master where changes to database design should be made
   a. Open the Customer table in Design view
   b. Set an input mask for First Name that causes the first letter to be capitalized
   c. Set an input mask for Last Name that causes the first letter to be capitalized
5. Open Curbside1
   a. Open the Customer table in Design view
   b. Verify that the input masks for First and Last Names do not exist yet in the replica
   c. On the **Tools** menu, point to **Replication** and select **Synchronize Now**
      i. Respond **Yes** to closing open objects
      ii. Select the **Design Master** for synchronization and click **OK**
   d. Open the Customer table in Design view and verify that the input masks for First and Last Names now exist
6. Exit Access if your work is complete

FIGURE 7.31
Curbside replicas

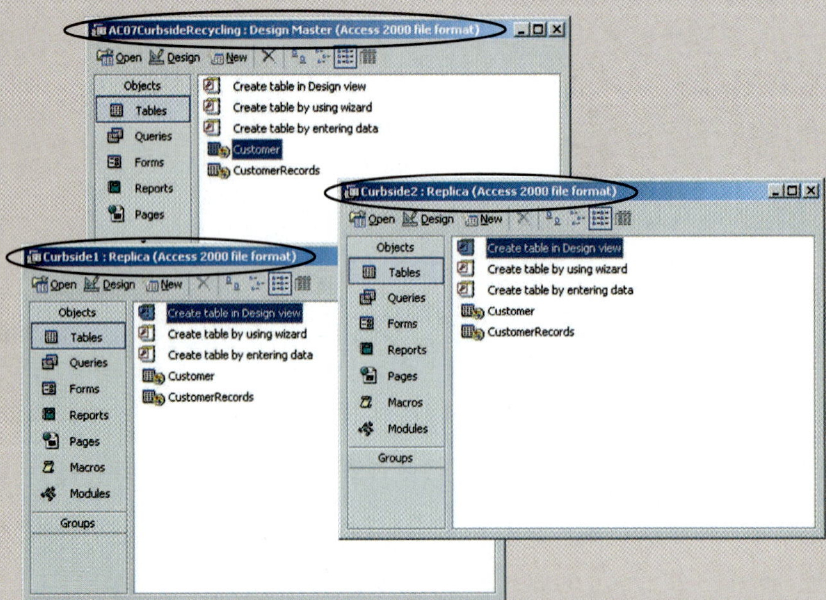

around the world

TechRocks Seminars

The design review for the TechRocks Access database used to track seminars, facilitators, and enrollment has been completed. Several design updates to improve usability have been approved. Additionally, TechRocks enrollment will now be handled from multiple locations around the world, so users in various offices must have access to the data. Since the offices are not networked, replicated databases using Internet synchronization is the planned approach.

1. Start Access and open **AC07SSeminars.mdb**

   tip: *You cannot use your copy of the database from the previous chapter since there have been modifications for this chapter*

2. Open the **Seminars** table
   a. Make SeminarID, Date, Time, and Hours required by setting the Required property to **Yes**
   b. Set an Input Mask for SeminarID that requires the entry of 5 characters (letters or digits)
   c. Set an Input Mask for SeminarTime of **Medium Time**
   d. Set the Default seminar cost to 250
   e. Set a Data Validation Rule to ensure that the Cost entered is between $50 and $2,500. Do not set Validation Text; the default message is sufficient

   tip: *Use the Between comparison operator*

   f. Set a Data Validation Rule to ensure that Hours is between 16 and 80
   g. Use the Datasheet view to test these updates with a new seminar **XX134** and Trainer **5.** Be sure to enter invalid values for each field before settling on valid values
   h. Close Seminars

3. Activate the **Tools** menu, pause over **Replication,** and select **Create Replica**
   a. Create a folder **ReplicaSeminars**
   b. Name this replica **ParisSeminars.mdb**
   c. Create a second replica called **LondonSeminars.mdb** with a priority of **70.** Store this replica in the same folder
4. Open **ParisSeminars.mdb**
   a. Open the **Student** table
   b. Locate record 114 and change the student's name to **Edna**
5. Open **LondonSeminars.mdb**
   a. Open the **Student** table
   b. Locate record 114 and change the student's name to **Evan**
   c. Open the **Tools** menu, point to **Replication,** select **Synchronize Now,** and select **ParisSeminars.mdb** as the database to synchronize with

   tip: *You may need to manually resolve the conflict in favor of the Paris changes, but they should resolve themselves if the priorities were set correctly*

   d. Open the Student table to verify that the Paris change (Edna) was used to resolve the conflict
6. Open the Student table of ParisSeminars.mdb to verify that it still holds the value Edna for student 114
7. Exit Access if your work is complete

FIGURE 7.32

Validation rule violation message

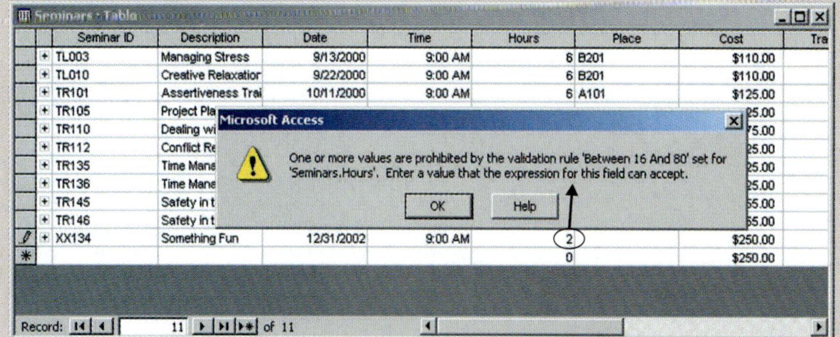

www.mhhe.com/i-series

running project: tnt web design

Database Maintenance and Security

TnT has continued to grow and the database is out of control. In a recent design review, inactive records were archived and a plan for refining table design outlined. Since there are a large number of users who need to be able to view and report on data, but only a few users who need to be able to update data, two user groups will be created.

1. Start Access and open **AC07TnT.mdb**

   tip: *You cannot use your copy of the database from the previous chapter since there have been modifications for this chapter*

2. Open **Employees**
   a. Make each field required by setting the Required property to **Yes**
   b. Create an Input Mask for First Name that will cause the first letter to always be uppercase and subsequent letters lowercase
   c. Create an Input Mask for Last Name that will cause the first letter to always be uppercase and subsequent letters lowercase
   d. Create an Input Mask for State that requires both characters to be entered
   e. Use the ellipsis (. . .) to set the Input Mask to **Phone.** Do not store the symbols.
   f. Create a Phone input mask that requires the area code to be entered
   g. Create an Input Mask for Zip that requires all five digits to be entered
   h. Test these updates with a record for **Bob Willson** with a JobClass of **QA**
   i. Close Employees
3. Activate the **Tools** menu, point to **Security,** and select **User-Level Security Wizard**
   a. Click **Next** on the first panel
   b. Click **Next** again to accept the default names
   c. Click **Next** again to secure all database objects
   d. Check **Read-Only Users** to create a group for the users who can't update the database

   tip: *The Administrators group has full rights to the database and is created automatically*

   e. Click **Next**
   f. Click **Next** to bypass setting permissions for users
   g. Create users
      i. **Tori,** with password **purple**
      ii. **Tonya,** with password **yellow**
      iii. **Readers,** with password of **seeit**
   h. Click **Next**
4. Assign permissions to the users you added
   a. Select **Tori** from the drop-down list and click **Admins**
   b. Repeat this process for **Tonya**
   c. Select **Readers** from the drop-down list and click **Read-Only Users**
   d. Click **Finish**
   e. Print the report
5. Exit Access if your work is complete

FIGURE 7.33
Creating a Read-Only Users Group

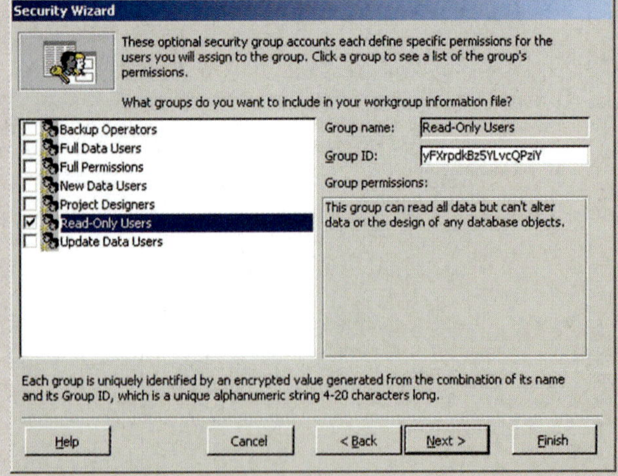

NOTES

did you know?

most *landfilled trash retains its original weight, volume, and form for 40 years.*

a *"jiffy" is an actual unit of time for 1/100th of a second.*

there *are more insects in one square mile of rural land than there are human beings on the entire earth.*

a *chameleon's tongue is twice the length of its body.*

the *Neanderthal's brain was bigger than yours is.*

any *month that starts on a Sunday will have a Friday the 13th in it.*

the *most popular first name in the world is _____.*

Chapter Objectives

- **Use Microsoft Graph to chart data in tables or queries**
- **Import data to Access—AC2002-8-1**
- **Export data from Access—AC2002-8-2**
- **Create a Data Access Page using the Page Wizard—AC2002-8-3**
- **Use Design view to modify a Data Access Page—AC2002-6-1**

CHAPTER 8 eight

Integrating with Other Applications

chapter case

PuppyParadise

PuppyParadise, like most successful businesses, has outgrown its current physical environment, distribution channels, and organizational structure. Products are being back ordered because the existing production facilities can't meet the demand. Orders are not processed on the day that they are received because the volume is more than the current part-time staff can handle. Adding employees and products are reasonable steps, but that will mean an added need for space and money.

Evan has enlisted the help of a marketing research firm to determine the potential of his market and create a diversification plan to protect from business losses. Until now his business has been without risk because Evan's only real investment was the cost to produce his products. The largest expenses were for contract labor and shipping. Now that he is considering hiring full-time employees, acquiring facilities, and securing a business loan, the risk is increasing and the need for planning and reporting is more critical.

Evan lives in Colorado and doesn't plan to leave until he finishes school. Current research indicates that most of PuppyParadises' sales are in Indiana, Ohio, and Michigan. Placing facilities close to the largest demand can reduce overhead, so he is considering producing and distributing products from Indiana. Evan's Aunt Corolla is a CPA who lives in Indianapolis and is willing to champion PuppyParadise in addition to her full-time job.

Accepting, producing, and shipping products from two sites will require new data sharing and communication methods. Evan believes that the Web will provide the needed communication channels. PuppyParadise databases can be replicated and use the Internet for synchronization. In addition Data Access pages can be built for shared reporting.

Before he can finalize a plan, Evan will need to create a sales forecast to determine how many employees and how much space are needed at each location. He will then build a business plan to present to lenders in order to secure the loan necessary to accomplish the goals outlined.

To create a forecast, Evan needs to learn about the charting utility Microsoft Graph so he can analyze the history of sales trends and forecast them into the future. For the business prospectus he will need to integrate existing documents from Word and Excel spreadsheets to appropriately present his business.

Evan does not want to build the data storage, reporting, and sharing infrastructure until he is further along in his business plan. However, he does want to see exactly how the necessary components work before he commits to a plan he will rely on.

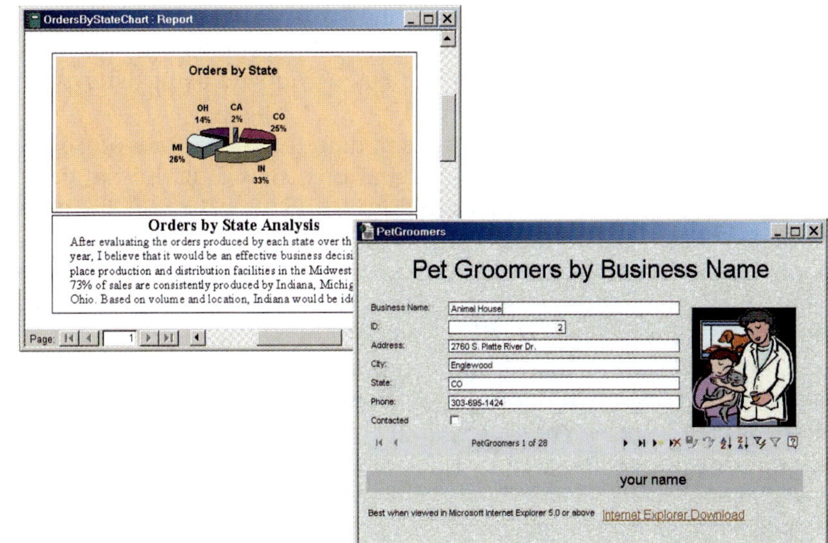

FIGURE 8.1
PuppyParadise Chart and Web report samples

SESSION 8.1 OFFICE INTEGRATION

CHAPTER OUTLINE

A basic tenet of computing is not to recreate anything that already exists. Office products are designed to integrate with each other to avoid recreating documents, data, and formatting when another form of output is needed. Microsoft Office applications are able to import and export multiple Office file formats to facilitate sharing documents across software platforms. The formats of other common documents such as Paradox, DBase, and Lotus 1-2-3 also can be accessed.

Importing and exporting are made possible through the features of ***OLE (object linking and embedding).*** Most programs designed for the Microsoft operating system support some level of OLE. Programs designed for other operating systems typically don't support OLE.

ADDING A CHART TO A FORM OR REPORT

Sometimes it is not necessary to import or export data to obtain alternative formatting. Office products include an array of applets that provide commonly needed features. WordArt is an example of a small application that is available in all office applications that use the Drawing toolbar. Similarly, the Microsoft Graph is a small application available in Access, Excel, and PowerPoint to create charts and graphs based on table data.

Embedding a Chart in a Report

Charts are used to represent numeric data graphically. Graphs can be added to a form or report using the Chart Wizard or imported from Microsoft Excel. The ***Chart Wizard*** steps users through the process of defining a ***chart*** on an Access report. The Chart Wizard can be accessed from the New Report dialog box or by using the Insert menu. An embedded chart is created based on the table data and parameters provided to the Wizard. Once a chart is created, it can be customized using ***Microsoft Graph***.

When a chart involves large quantities of data that do not already exist in Access, when there are complex calculations, or when the data are already in Excel, creating the chart in Excel and then importing it to PowerPoint is more effective than using Microsoft Graph.

Evan believes that charts can enhance the existing forms and reports by graphically displaying data relationships. For example, the Customers by State report could use a chart to show the number of customers from each state, or the Orders report could display a chart of orders by state.

Using the Chart Wizard, the fields to be plotted can be selected from any existing table or query. The chart can be based on all of the data in the table using sums or the chart can depict only the data from the current record. A chart based on a record is called a ***record-bound chart*** and will change as the active record changes. A chart based on all of the data is called a ***global chart.*** By default the Wizard creates a report to hold the chart.

task reference

Create a Microsoft Graph

- Click the **Reports** object in the Database window
- Click **New** to activate the New Report dialog box
- Select **Chart Wizard,** use the drop-down list to select the query or table containing the data to be charted, and then click **OK** to initiate the Chart Wizard
- Follow the instructions to select the field(s) with the data to be charted, select the chart type, specify the layout, and add a chart title

Creating a report with a chart:

1. Verify that Access is running with **AC08PuppyParadise.mdb** open
2. Click the **Reports** object in the Database window
3. Click **New** to open the New Report dialog box
4. Click **Chart Wizard,** select **CustomerStateJoin** from the drop-down list, and choose **OK**
5. Move the **State** and **QuantityOrdered** fields to the Fields for Chart list box and click **Next**
6. Review the available chart types, then select **3-D Pie Chart,** and click **Next**
7. Use the **Preview Chart** button to see a sample of the chart that you are building

tip: *Microsoft Graph displays dummy data for the design process*

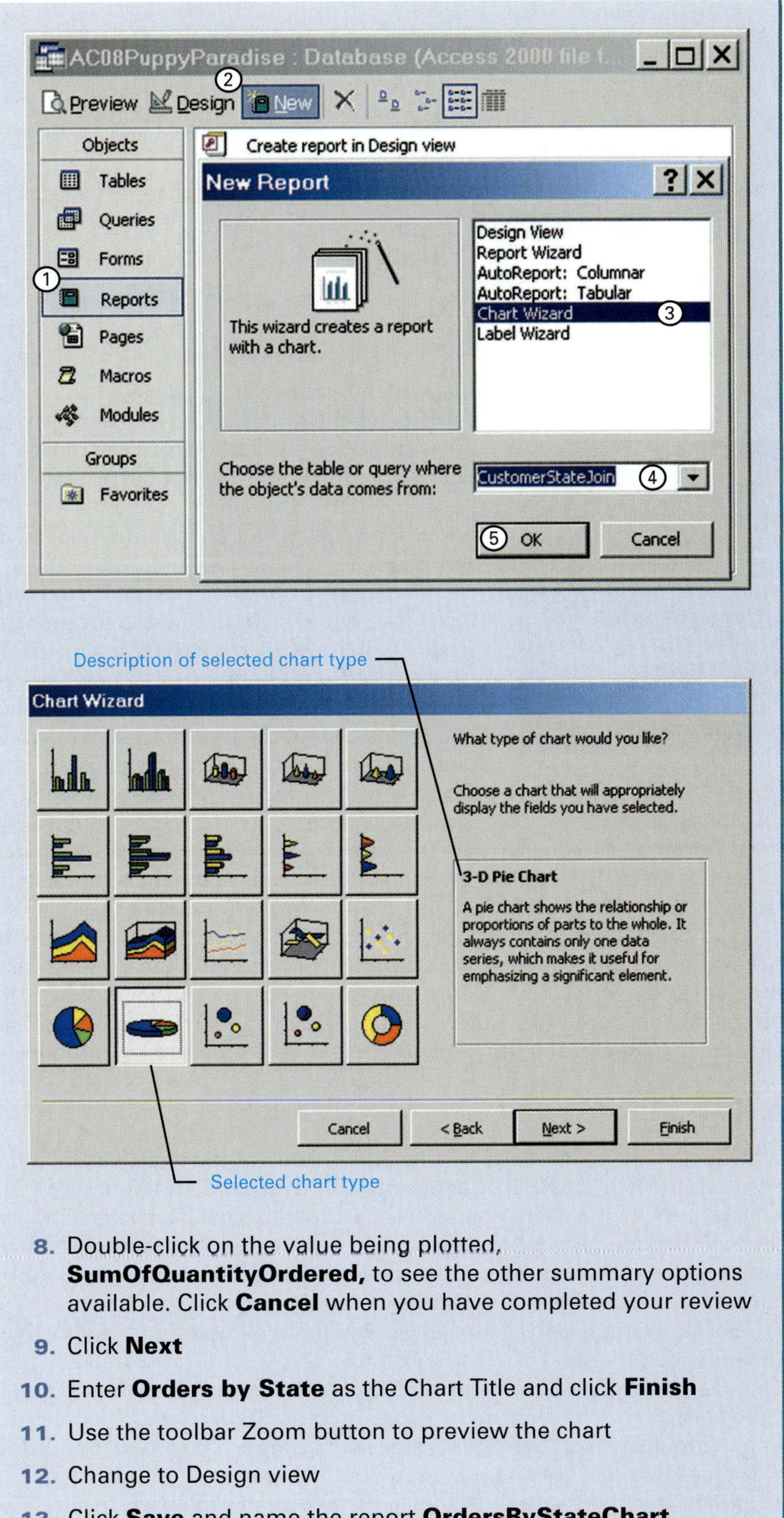

8. Double-click on the value being plotted, **SumOfQuantityOrdered,** to see the other summary options available. Click **Cancel** when you have completed your review
9. Click **Next**
10. Enter **Orders by State** as the Chart Title and click **Finish**
11. Use the toolbar Zoom button to preview the chart
12. Change to Design view
13. Click **Save** and name the report **OrdersByStateChart**

FIGURE 8.2
Initiating the Chart Wizard

FIGURE 8.3
Selecting a chart type

FIGURE 8.4
The OrdersByStateChart report

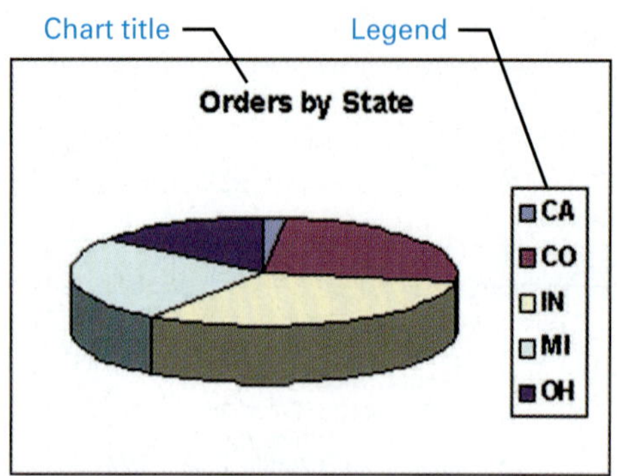

anotherword

. . . on Embedding Charts

Sometimes you will want to add a chart to an existing report or form. This is accomplished by opening the report in Design view and selecting the Chart option of the Insert menu. The pointer will become a chart used to click and drag an area for the chart to display in the report. The Chart Wizard will initiate as soon as an area for chart display is indicated. The advantage of adding a chart to an existing report or form is the ability to display the detailed data beside a graphic representation of the data.

The OrdersByStateChart is a global chart created using the Chart Wizard and based on data from an Access query. The chart is placed in the Detail section of a standard Access report. Changing the data in the underlying tables will change the display of this chart.

The Chart Wizard presented 20 chart types for your selection. These represent the most commonly used chart types available from Microsoft Graph. It is important to select a chart type that best suits the data being plotted and the report audience. When plotting one data series to emphasize how each value in the series relates to the total of all values, a pie or stacked column chart is appropriate. Area and line charts work best to display data movement across time or categories such as a sales trend. Bar and column charts effectively show the relationships between categories of values.

The chart being developed is an object that has been embedded in an Access report. ***Embedded*** objects retain a connection to the program that developed them, called the ***source*** program. The application holding the object, in this case Microsoft Graph, is called the ***destination.*** Double-clicking an embedded object will open the source program in edit mode.

Editing a Chart

Editing a chart involves either altering the look of the chart or changing the data used to create it. Changes to the data need to be made in the table(s) on which a chart is based. The simplest visual change is to adjust the size of the chart on the form or report, which is accomplished by dragging the object borders. Other changes are accomplished by double-clicking the chart to activate Microsoft Graph.

Because Graph is the source program, it has greater functionality than that provided by the Wizard. For example, the Wizard presented 20 chart types while Graph organizes the charts into 14 chart types with at least 2 subtypes each, providing many more options. ***Chart types*** include pie, line, column, and bar. Subtypes define formatting within a type. For example, a pie chart has flat and 3-D subtypes.

When Microsoft Graph is active, its menus and toolbars display. The Graph menu and toolbar are designed for manipulating and formatting the chart. For example, the Chart menu contains options for changing the chart type, setting chart options that control how the data are charted, and controlling the 3-D view.

Editing a chart also involves moving and formatting the various components of the chart. For example, a legend can be moved, a wedge of a pie exploded, the color of a data series changed, and chart titles adjusted. Those familiar with Microsoft Graph from other Office applications will recognize the datasheet and data that display when editing. In other applications, the datasheet is used to enter the data to be plotted. Since Access holds data in tables, the datasheet is not used and any changes that are made there will not be reflected in the chart. That being the case, closing the datasheet frees screen space and avoids confusion about the chart data source.

Evan would like the OrdersByStateChart to have a background consistent with the PuppyParadise color scheme. He also wants each wedge of the pie labeled with the state and the legend eliminated.

Modifying the OrdersByStateChart:

1. Verify that Access is running with **AC08PuppyParadise.mdb** open with the OrdersByStateChart report open in Design view

tip: *The Orders By State chart should be in the Detail section of the report*

2. Click the chart object to select it and then use a sizing handle to make it the width of the report page
3. Double-click on the chart to open Microsoft Graph

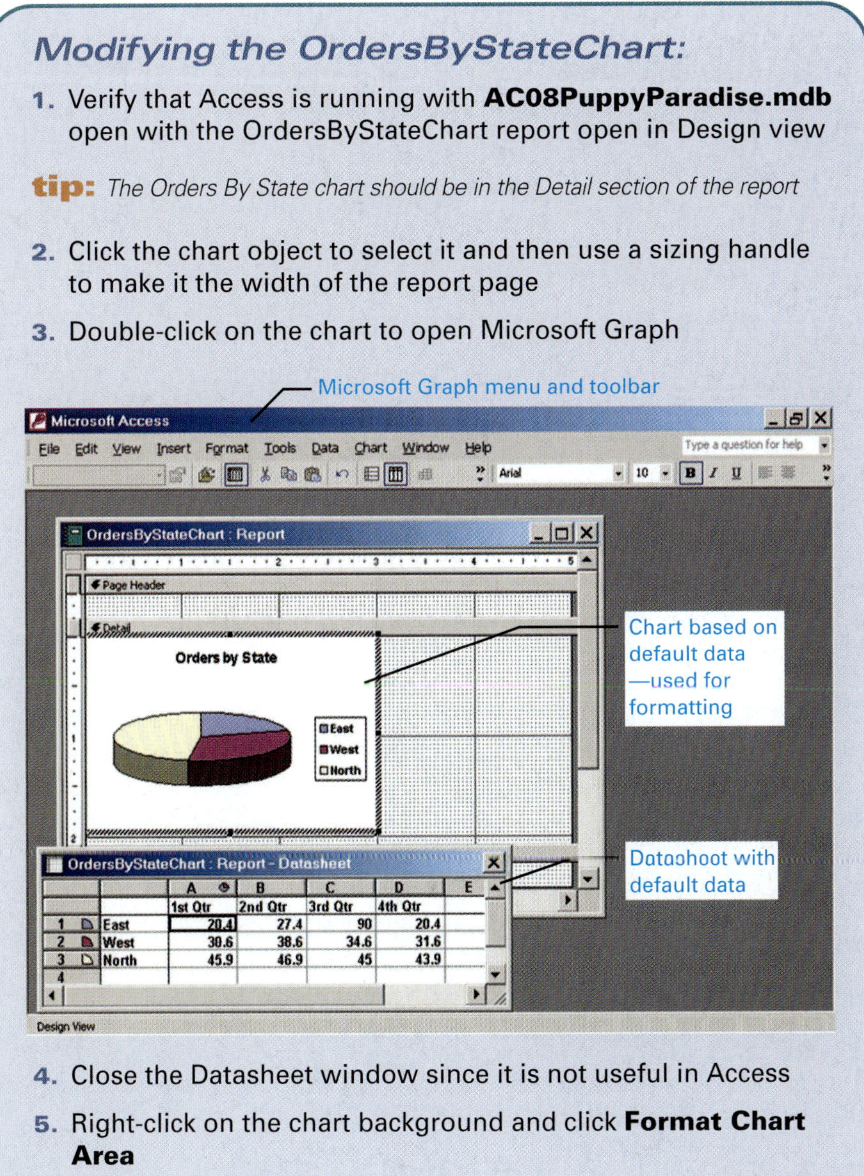

FIGURE 8.5
Microsoft Graph window

4. Close the Datasheet window since it is not useful in Access
5. Right-click on the chart background and click **Format Chart Area**

6. Choose the light tan color square and click **OK**
7. Right-click on the chart background, click **Chart Options,** click the **Legend** tab, and uncheck **Show legend**

tip: *The Office Assistant provides information about these options if it is active*

8. Click the **Data Labels** tab, click **Category name** and **Percent,** and then click **OK**
9. Click off the chart area to leave **Microsoft Graph**
10. Click the **Print Preview** button on the toolbar

tip: *Your chart (rather than the default chart) will display as it will print*

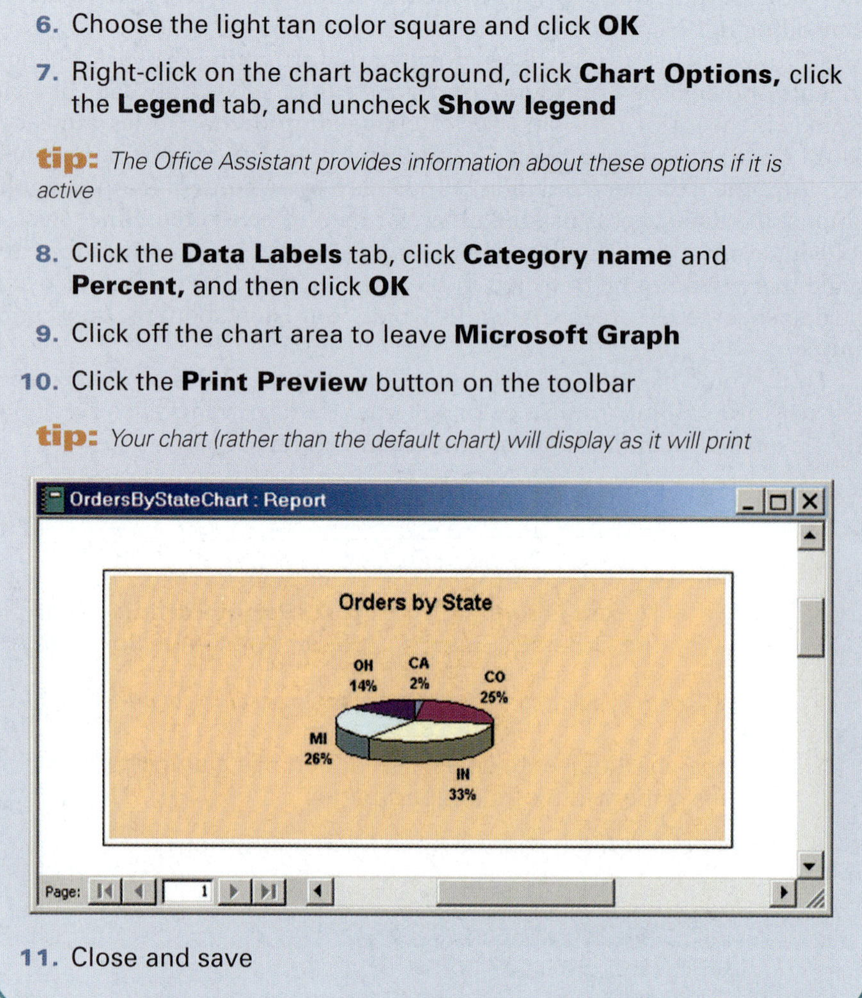

FIGURE 8.6
OrdersByStateChart with formatting

11. Close and save

Evan believes that the pie chart is probably the most effective way to present these data but would like to see some alternatives. It is usually helpful to review charting alternatives before settling on the chart type that best presents the data.

Exploring chart types and subtypes for OrderByStateChart:

1. Verify that Access is running with **AC08PuppyParadise.mdb** open with the OrdersByStateChart report in Design view
2. Double-click on the chart to open Microsoft Graph and close the datasheet
3. Select **Chart Type** from the **Chart** menu
4. Review the current chart type and subtype
5. Select the first subtype for a Column chart and press and hold the button to view the sample
6. Select the **Line** chart type and preview the result
7. Experiment with other chart types and subtypes

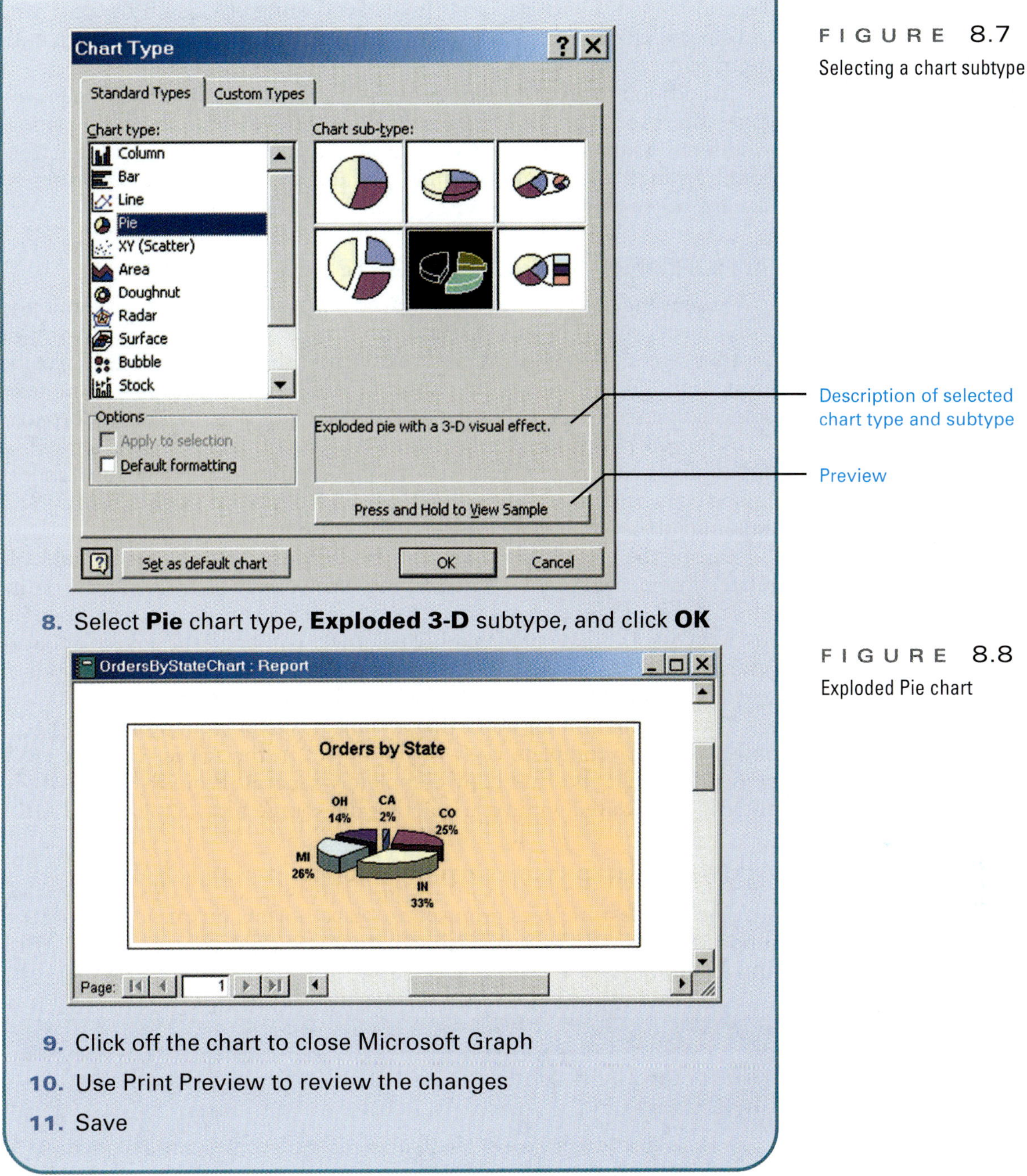

FIGURE 8.7
Selecting a chart subtype

8. Select **Pie** chart type, **Exploded 3-D** subtype, and click **OK**

FIGURE 8.8
Exploded Pie chart

9. Click off the chart to close Microsoft Graph
10. Use Print Preview to review the changes
11. Save

Because a pie chart is being used, there is no need for x or y axis labels. Bar, column, and line charts all use axes that typically need to be labeled using the Chart Options selection of the Chart menu. This option also can be used to modify the chart title.

Chart options allow control of the titles, axes, gridlines, legend, data labels, and data table display. The gridlines behind the chart can be turned off or made finer using the Gridlines tab. The chart legend can be turned off or placed in a new location with the Legend tab. Data labels can be added to the chart displaying the value plotted and the datasheet can be displayed in the slide with the chart.

Each chart object can be selected and modified. Font, size, and orientation can be set for text objects. Shape objects can have fill colors, border colors, and shapes options set. The chart consists of a plot area that holds

. . . to select chart objects

Double-clicking on almost any chart object will open it to edit its attributes.

the graph and a chart area that holds everything else. Both the plot area and chart area can be set to a custom color, fill, or pattern. By default, both are transparent.

In addition to all of the standard chart components that have been covered, Microsoft Graph allows text to be added to a chart by typing. Additional text may be needed to draw out information or emphasize a point. Typing opens a text box that can be moved, modified, or formatted like any other object.

IMPORTING AND LINKING OBJECTS

Oftentimes the data in one or more Access tables will need to be combined with objects stored in an external format such as HTML, Excel, Word, or another Access database. When this occurs, the external objects can be brought into Access using the import facilities. Besides graphics and text, other database file formats such as Fox Pro and dBase can be imported.

An ***imported*** object displays in an Access container such as a table or unbound object on a form or report. For example, an Excel spreadsheet can be converted to an Access table or text from Word can be placed in an unbound object on a report through importing.

During the import process, settings determine how the Access object is related to the original file. When an imported object is just a picture of the contents of a file, it is said to be ***linked.*** Linked files cannot be updated from Access. Double-clicking a linked object will open the source application where edits can be applied. Link the object if it is important to retain one copy of the file with a connection to the source application.

The other option for importing an object is to embed it. Embedding an object places a complete copy of the object in the Access container. An ***embedded*** object is a full copy completely separate from the original file and can be updated without impacting the source file.

Adding Objects to a Form or Report

The simplest imports are used to place objects on an Access form or report. You already have used this method to add graphics to both forms and reports.

task reference

Importing with an Unbound Object Frame on a Form or Report

- Open the Design view of the form or report to contain the imported object
- Click the **Unbound Object Frame** tool in the toolbox
- Click and drag the area on the form or report that will contain the object
- In the Microsoft Access dialog box
  - Click **Create From File**
  - Browse to the file for import
  - Click the Link check box to create a linked object or leave it unchecked to create an embedded object
  - Click **OK**

Linking a Word document to the OrdersByStateChart report:

1. Verify that Access is running with **AC08PuppyParadise.mdb** open with the OrdersByStateChart report in Design view
2. Expand the report Detail section by dragging the Detail border up and the Page Footer border down
3. Click the **Unbound Object Frame** tool in the toolbox and then click and drag the area in the Detail section of the report that will hold the Word object

tip: *Get the size and positioning close to that shown in figure 8.11 of these steps. You can adjust it later if necessary*

4. Click **Create from File,** navigate to **AC08OrdersAnalysis.doc,** check the **Link** check box, and click **OK**

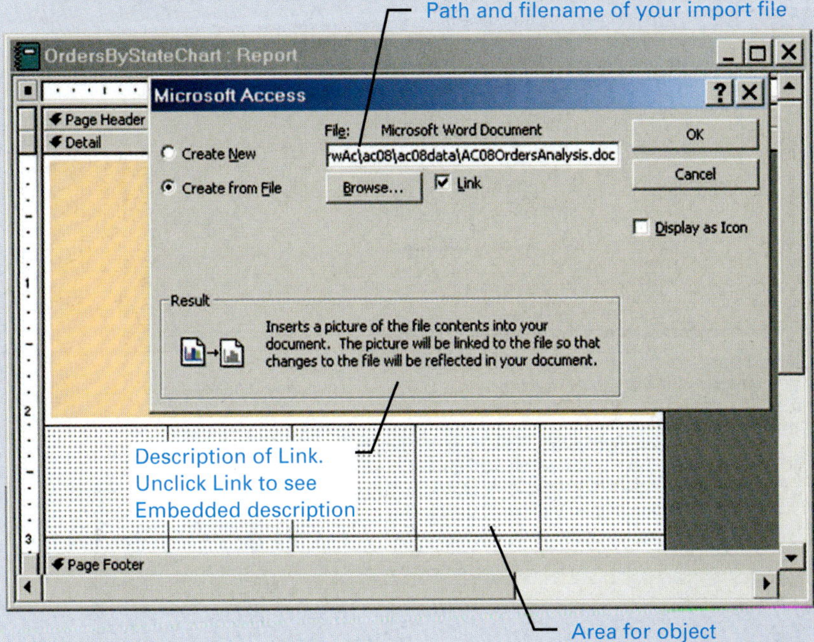

FIGURE 8.9
Linking a Word document

5. Size and reposition the object to resemble Figure 8.11 if needed
6. Double-click the object to open Word
7. In Word
   a. Select all of the text
   b. Use the ruler to adjust the margins for the Access object as shown in Figure 8.10
   c. Save the changes and close Word
8. If your report does not reflect the margin changes, close and reopen Design view to update the link
9. Activate Print Preview to review your changes
10. Save

FIGURE 8.10
Adjusting margins with the Word ruler

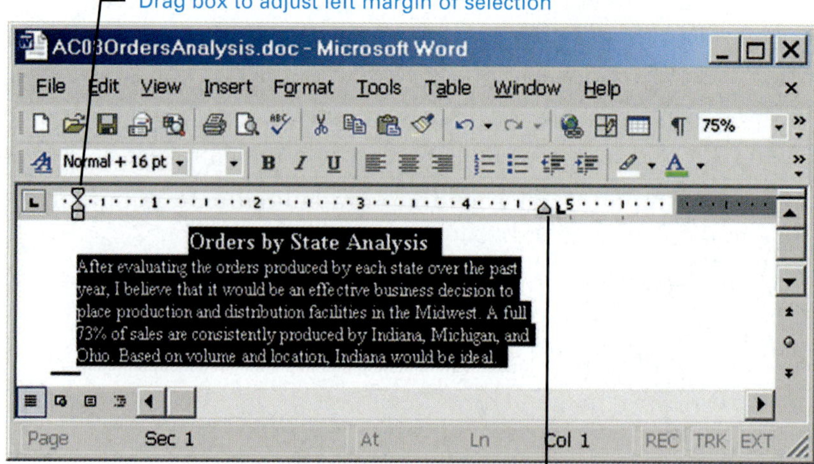
Drag box to adjust left margin of selection
AC03OrdersAnalysis.doc - Microsoft Word
File Edit View Insert Format Tools Table Window Help
Normal + 16 pt
Orders by State Analysis
After evaluating the orders produced by each state over the past year, I believe that it would be an effective business decision to place production and distribution facilities in the Midwest. A full 73% of sales are consistently produced by Indiana, Michigan, and Ohio. Based on volume and location, Indiana would be ideal.
Page Sec 1 At Ln Col 1 REC TRK EXT
Drag to adjust right margin of selection

FIGURE 8.11
Linked object reflecting edits made in Word

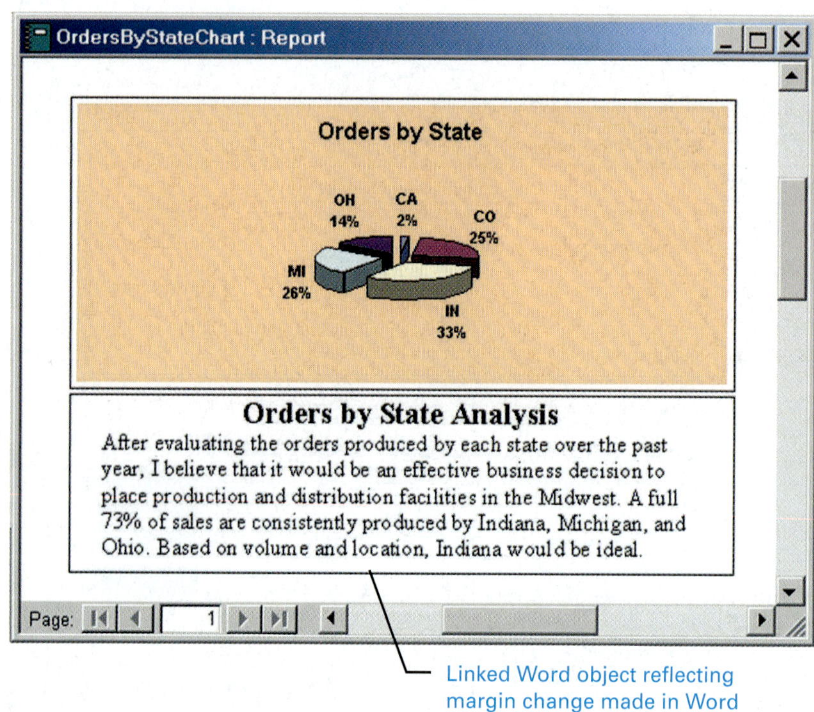
OrdersByStateChart : Report
Orders by State
OH 14%
CA 2%
CO 25%
MI 26%
IN 33%
Orders by State Analysis
After evaluating the orders produced by each state over the past year, I believe that it would be an effective business decision to place production and distribution facilities in the Midwest. A full 73% of sales are consistently produced by Indiana, Michigan, and Ohio. Based on volume and location, Indiana would be ideal.
Page: 1
Linked Word object reflecting margin change made in Word

anotherway

. . . to update linked objects

Linked objects do not maintain continual contact with the source document. Once a report or form is open and displaying a linked object, the object won't change until the link is updated. You can manually update the link using the OLE/DDE Links option of the Edit menu. The dialog box allows you to select a link or links to update and then click the Update Now button.

Because the Linked check box was used in the import process, the Access report holds only a picture of the Word document. Updates to the document are made using Word and are reflected in the Access copy each time the link is updated. By default, the Update option of a linked object is set to Automatic, which will refresh the object each time it is opened.

Of course, if the Linked check box had been left unchecked, the Word document would have been embedded in the Access report. Embedding is the best option when the Access copy of the document needs to be manipulated independently of the Word version of the document. To experience the difference between manipulating a linked and an embedded object, the linked Word document will be deleted and reimported as an embedded object.

Embedding a Word document in the OrdersByStateChart report:

1. Verify that Access is running with **AC08PuppyParadise.mdb** open with the OrdersByStateChart report in Design view
2. Click the Unbound Object Frame containing the Word document and press the Delete key
3. Select the **Unbound Object Frame** tool from the toolbox and then click and drag the area to contain the Word document
4. Click **Create from File,** navigate to **AC08OrdersAnalysis.doc,** uncheck the **Link** check box, and click **OK**

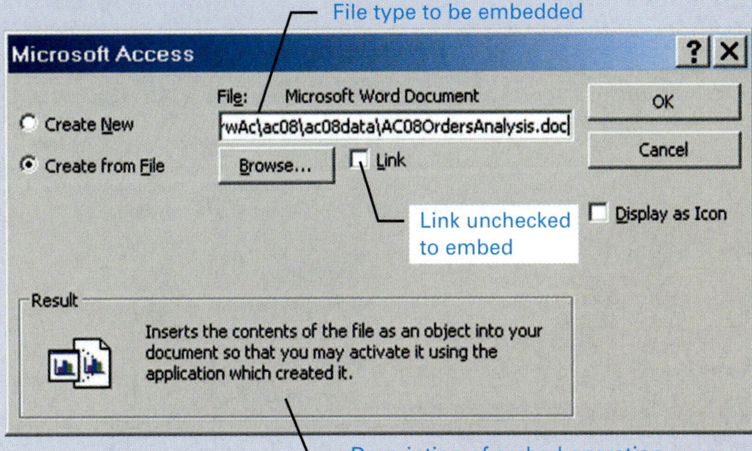

FIGURE 8.12
Embedding a Word document

5. Size and reposition the object to resemble Figure 8.13 if needed
6. Double-click the object to initiate editing

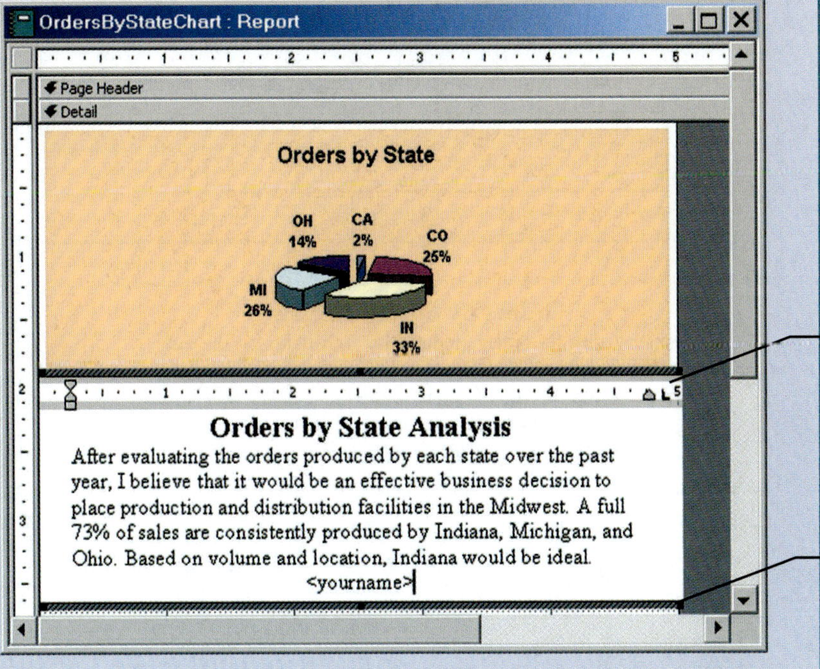

FIGURE 8.13
Editing an embedded Word document

7. Click the cursor after the period in the last line of text and press **Enter**
8. Type your full name and then use the toolbar to center the text
9. Click outside of the Unbound Object Frame object to end editing and save your changes
10. Save the report changes

In the previous steps a linked Word document was edited using a full version of Word, indicating that there is only one copy of the document controlled by Word. In this set of steps, edits were performed on the same Word document that had been embedded. An Edit window provided the same features as Word but indicated that this copy of the document is independently updated by Access. Let's take a look at the Word document to verify that the changes made to the embedded document did not impact it.

Verifying the status of the source Word document:

1. Click the **Start** button on the Taskbar, point to **Programs,** and select **Microsoft Word**
2. Use the Open button on the toolbar to open **AC08OrdersAnalysis.doc**
3. Notice that the margin changes applied to the linked document are saved. Your name, which was added to the embedded version of the document, is not part of the source but is retained in the OrdersByStateChart report

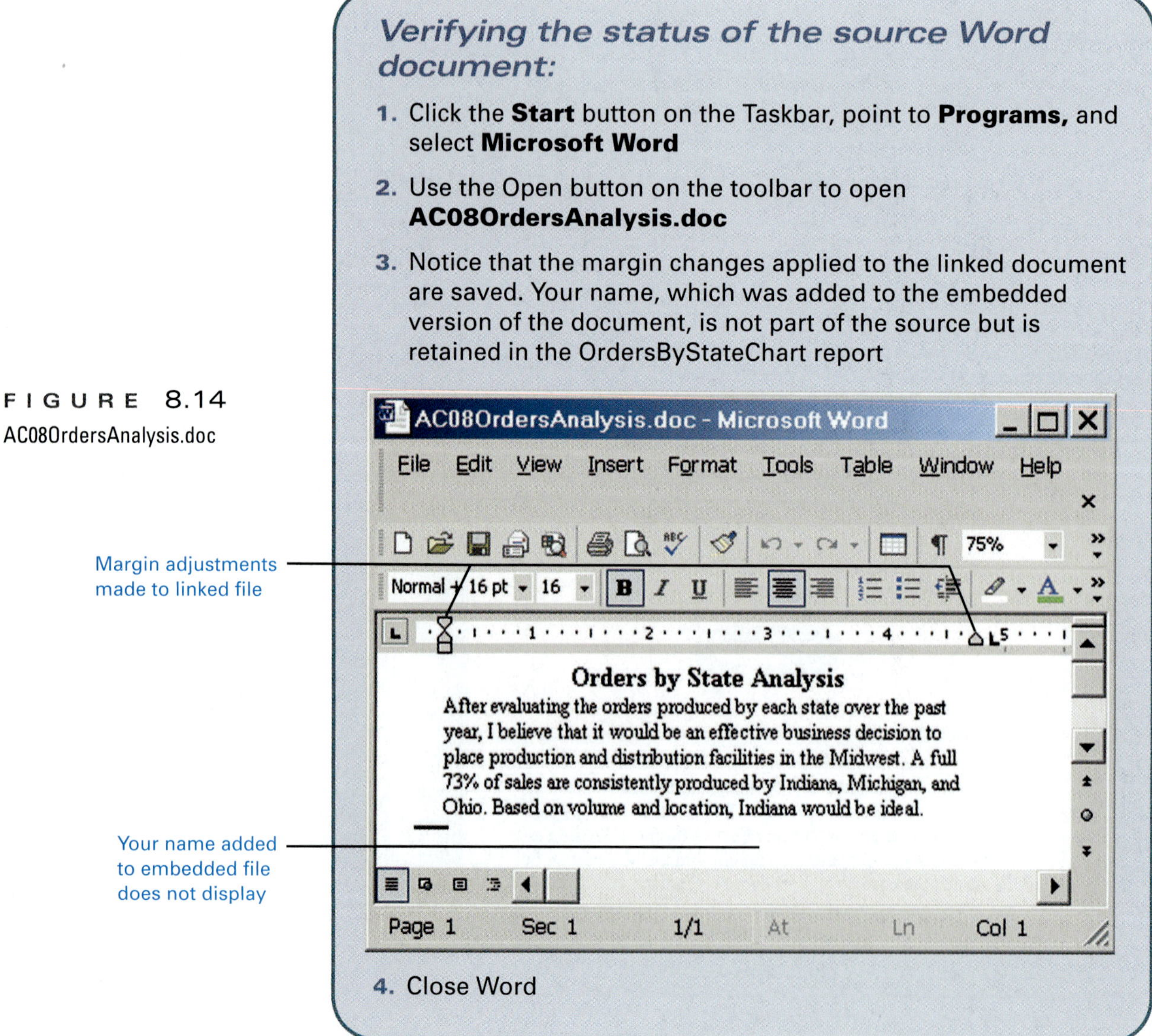

AC08OrdersAnalysis.doc - Microsoft Word
File Edit View Insert Format Tools Table Window Help
Normal + 16 pt 16
75%
Orders by State Analysis
After evaluating the orders produced by each state over the past year, I believe that it would be an effective business decision to place production and distribution facilities in the Midwest. A full 73% of sales are consistently produced by Indiana, Michigan, and Ohio. Based on volume and location, Indiana would be ideal.
Page 1 Sec 1 1/1 At Ln Col 1
Margin adjustments made to linked file
Your name added to embedded file does not display

FIGURE 8.14
AC08OrdersAnalysis.doc

4. Close Word

The same linking and embedding procedures demonstrated can be used to place objects on Access forms. Any OLE-compliant application can be imported. All of the Microsoft Office products support OLE, as do most applications developed by other vendors for the Windows environment.

Using Data from Another Access Database

Sometimes due to a design flaw or change in business practice, it is desirable to use data that are stored in multiple Access database files or in files maintained by another database program. In such cases the data tables can be imported into Access and treated like any other Access table, or linked so that they retain the properties of the original database and can be maintained in the source. The process is very similar to importing application objects, but the result is data that can be used like any native Access table.

Evan has created a PetStores database that he has used to create form letters in Microsoft Word. He would like to incorporate this table into the PuppyParadise database so that he only has to worry about sharing one database file.

task reference

Import or Link to Another Access Database

- Open the Access database that is to contain the imported data
- Open the **File** menu, point to **Get External Data,** and then do one of the following:
  - Click **Import** to create Access tables from the external data
  - Click **Link Tables** to create links to tables that remain in the source location
- In the Import or Link dialog box
  - Use the Files of Type drop-down list to select **Microsoft Access (*.mdb, *.adp, *.mda, *.mde, *.ade)** as the type of file to be linked or imported
  - Use the Look In box to select the drive, folder, and file name of the file to be imported or linked
  - Select the import tables and click **Import**

Importing AC08PetStores.mdb:

1. Verify that Access is open with the **AC08PuppyParadise.mdb** database open and no active object (table, query, form, report, etc.)
2. Activate the **File** menu, point to **Get External Data,** and click **Import**
3. From the Import dialog box select **AC08PetStores.mdb** and click **Import**

tip: *Verify that the Files of type box will display Microsoft Access files for you to select from*

4. On the Tables tab of the Import Objects dialog box, select **Distributors** and click **OK**

tip: *Notice that Queries, Forms, Reports, and other database objects also can be imported*

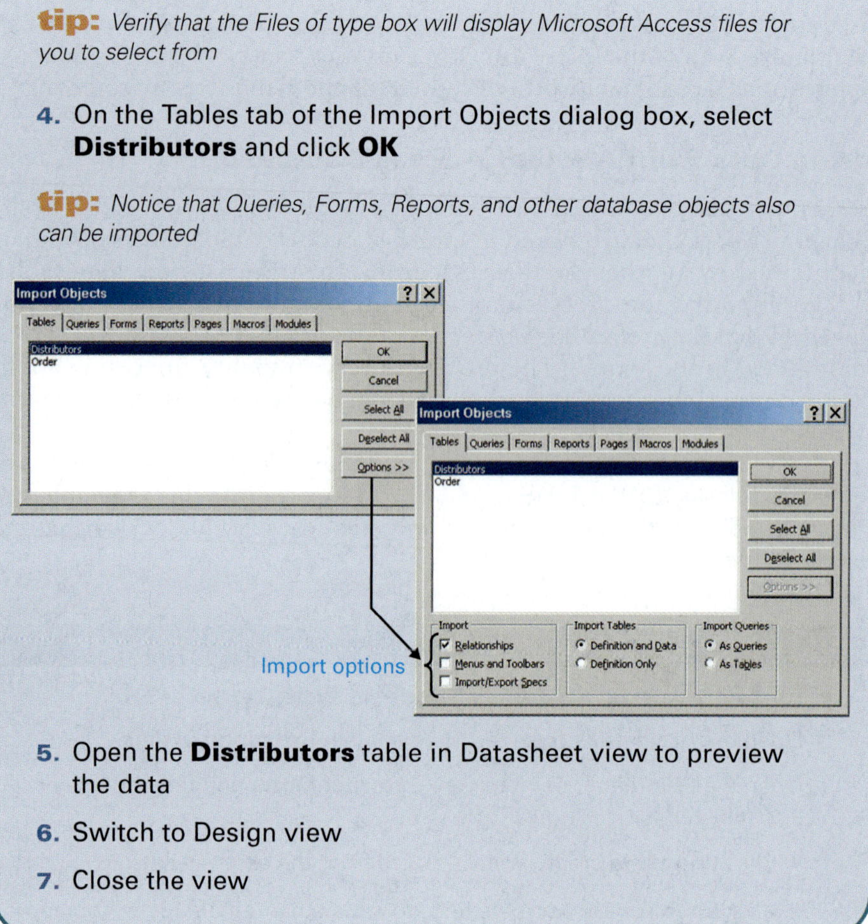

FIGURE 8.15
Import Objects options

5. Open the **Distributors** table in Datasheet view to preview the data
6. Switch to Design view
7. Close the view

When importing data from another Access database, either both the table and its contents or just the definition can be imported, using the options shown in Figure 8.15. The Distributors table now belongs to the PuppyParadise database and you have full control over its design and contents. The original AC08PetStores.mdb is not impacted by changes made in PuppyParadise.

The procedure for linking data is very similar to that used to import data. Evan wants to evaluate the difference between embedding and linking the Distributor database so a linked copy needs to be created.

Linking AC08PetStores.mdb:

1. Verify that Access is open with the **AC08PuppyParadise.mdb** database active with no open objects (tables, queries, forms, reports, etc.)
2. Activate the **File** menu, point to **Get External Data,** and click **Link Tables**
3. From the Link dialog box select **AC08PetStores.mdb** and click **Link**

4. On the Tables tab of the Link Tables dialog box, select **Distributors** and click **OK**

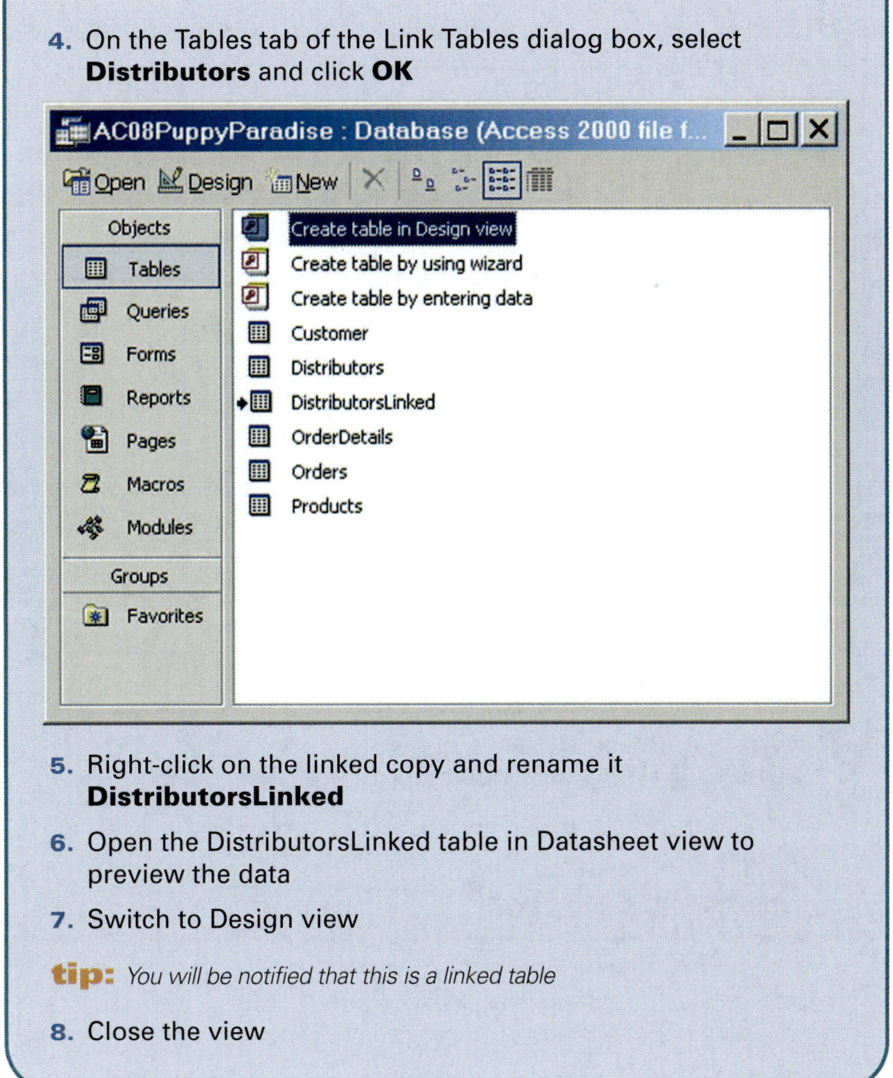

FIGURE 8.16
Imported and Linked Distributors tables

5. Right-click on the linked copy and rename it **DistributorsLinked**
6. Open the DistributorsLinked table in Datasheet view to preview the data
7. Switch to Design view

tip: *You will be notified that this is a linked table*

8. Close the view

For the most part, linked tables behave the same as any other Microsoft Access table. The icon to the left of the table name indicates that the table is linked and a dialog box is a reminder that much of the table design can't be modified outside the original database. Linked tables can be used to create queries, forms, and reports. No changes can be made to the design, but properties can be set to control local behavior.

Importing Data from Excel

Since Microsoft Excel is designed to store and analyze data, many users already have a great deal of valuable data stored in spreadsheet format before learning to use an Access database. The data stored in Excel do not need to be reentered because they can be imported and stored in a table for use in Access.

Imported Excel data can be either linked or embedded. Before beginning the process, it is important to make sure that the data in the spreadsheet are arranged appropriately into fields (columns) and records (rows). Evan has been trying to recruit local pet groomers to distribute PuppyParadise products. He has been tracking his contacts in an Excel spreadsheet that should be incorporated in the PuppyParadise database.

task reference

Import or Link to an Excel Spreadsheet

- Open the Access database that is to contain the imported data
- Open the **File** menu, point to **Get External Data,** and then click **Import**
  - Click **Import** to create Access tables from the external data
  - Click **Link Tables** to create links to tables that remain in the source location
- In the Import or Link dialog box
  - Use the Files of type drop-down list to select **Microsoft Excel (*.xls)** as the type of file to be linked or imported
  - Use the Look in box to select the drive, folder, and file name of the file to be imported or linked
  - Follow the Import Spreadsheet Wizard instructions

Importing AC08Groomers.xls:

1. Verify that Access is open with the **AC08PuppyParadise.mdb** database active
2. Activate the **File** menu, point to **Get External Data,** and click **Import**
3. In the Import dialog box
   a. Use the Look in drop-down list to navigate to the folder containing your files
   b. Set Files of type to **Microsoft Excel (*.xls)**
   c. Select **AC08Groomers.xls** and click **Import**

FIGURE 8.17
Import Spreadsheet Wizard

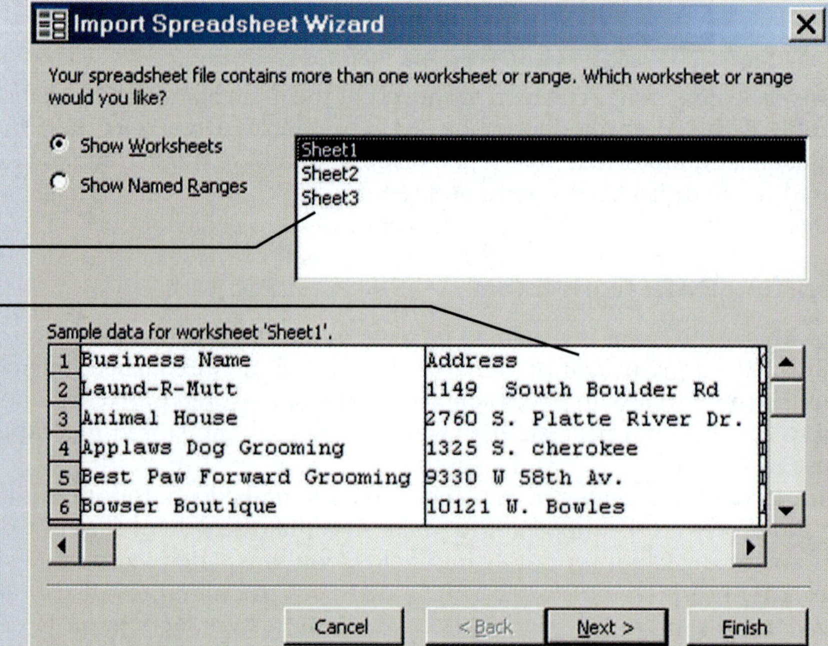

4. Verify that the Import Spreadsheet Wizard selections match those shown in Figure 8.17 and click **Next**
5. Check the **First Row Contains Column Headings** check box so that the Excel column headings will be used as Access field names and click **Next**
6. Verify that **In a New Table** is selected and click **Next**
7. Explore selecting fields to set their properties. Do not set any properties and click **Next**

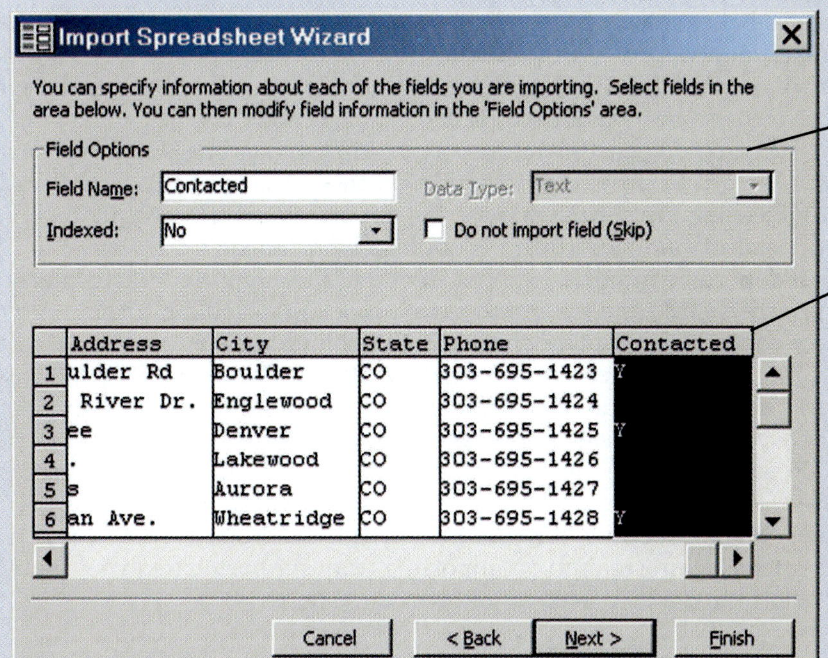

FIGURE 8.18
Setting Import Field Options

8. Verify that **Let Access Add Primary Key** is selected so that Access will add an AutoNumber field to the table for a key and click **Next**
9. Name the table **PetGroomers** and click **Finish**
10. Click **OK** in the Finished Importing message dialog box
11. Open PetGroomers in Design view and change the data type of Contacted to **Yes/No**

PetGroomers : Table

ID	Business Name	Address	City	State	Phone	Contacted
1	Laund-R-Mutt	1149 South Boulder Rd	Boulder	CO	303-695-1423	☑
2	Animal House	2760 S. Platte River Dr.	Englewood	CO	303-695-1424	☐
3	Applaws Dog Grooming	1325 S. cherokee	Denver	CO	303-695-1425	☑
4	Best Paw Forward Grooming	9330 W 58th Av.	Lakewood	CO	303-695-1426	☐
5	Bowser Boutique	10121 W. Bowles	Aurora	CO	303-695-1427	☐
6	Bow-Wow Barbers	9359 S. Sheridan Ave.	Wheatridge	CO	303-695-1428	☑
7	Bubbles and Bows	3224 Lowell Blvd.	Arvada	CO	303-695-1429	☐
8	Canine Creations	5083 E. Colfax Blvd.	Boulder	CO	303-695-1430	☑
9	Clip N Yip Pet Grooming	1006 Wadsworth Blvd.	Englewood	CO	303-695-1431	☐
10	Clean Critter	4943 W 72 Ave.	Denver	CO	303-695-1432	☑
11	Coat & Tails Grooming	270348 E. Iliff Ave.	Lakewood	CO	303-708-8060	☑
12	Dog-O-Mat	5550 W 44th Ave.	Aurora	CO	303-708-8061	☐
13	Doggie Spa	1382 Peoria	Wheatridge	CO	303-708-8062	☐
14	Doggie Do's	2390 S Pearl	Arvada	CO	303-708-8063	☐

Record: 1 of 28

FIGURE 8.19
PetGroomers table

12. Switch to Datasheet view, saving your changes

The import options control whether all of the data from a spreadsheet are retrieved or only data in a named range of cells. Spreadsheet data can be used to create a new table or append to the data already in an existing table. To successfully append the data to an existing table, the spreadsheet column headings must match the Access field names exactly.

Access assigns data types to the import fields based on their content. It is important to review data types and other field properties before using the imported table.

Retrieving Data from Other Applications

Besides being able to import data from Office products, Microsoft Access can accept a variety of other file formats including Lotus 1-2-3, Text files, HTML, Paradox, XML, and dBase. The process to import or link these file types is the same as that used for Excel since each file type can be selected from the Look in box of the Import or Link dialog box. Each file format has a Wizard to provide instruction on the conversion process. Paradox and dBase require special drivers that are provided by Microsoft Technical Support if the native software is not locally installed.

If data to be imported are not in one of the supported file formats, try to use the source application to save it in a supported file format. Almost every database and spreadsheet has the ability to save comma delimited text files that can then be imported by Access. For example, a Microsoft Works database cannot be directly imported into Microsoft Access. Works can save the database as a comma delimited text file that can be imported.

Regardless of the file type being imported, the data must be stored in a format that can be recognized as fields and records. For example, HTML tables can be effectively imported, but lists are less successful. Access Help has extensive information on importing from supported file types that will be helpful if you ever need to perform these tasks.

EXPORTING DATA

Access also has the ability to export database objects to other file formats. While Access has powerful data storage and retrieval capabilities, other applications provide better analytical and formatting capabilities. For example, Access is the ideal tool for gathering sales data, but Excel would be a better choice for using those data to create a model used to forecast future sales.

Organizations often use different database programs that may need to share data. The different programs can be the result of varying needs across the organization or simply a matter of preference. Regardless of why data for the same organization are stored in multiple formats, Access's import and export capabilities usually can facilitate sharing data. Most other database software packages support similar import and export features.

Sharing Access Data with Word Processing Applications

Although Microsoft Access data can be shared with virtually any word processing application, this discussion will focus on Microsoft Word since it provides the simplest and cleanest integration.

Data from a Microsoft Access table can be used in conjunction with Word Mail Merge to create form letters based on data stored in a table or query. This process can use an existing Word document, or create a new merge document if it does not exist.

The second sharing method uses the formatting and publishing capabilities of Word to enhance Access output. The output of any Access datasheet, form, or report can be exported in Rich Text Format (.rtf) that can then be opened and manipulated with Word or any word processor supporting the format. The Rich Text Format preserves fonts, styles, and other formatting.

Evan would like to use the ProductByState crosstab query results as a table in a Word document that he is preparing. You will export it for him.

task reference

Export an Access Object to Microsoft Word

- Open the Access database with the object to be exported
- Select the object to be exported in the Database window (it is best to preview the object before exporting)
- Open the **Tools** menu, point to **Office Links,** and then either
  - Select **Merge It with Microsoft Word** to use an Access table or query as the data source for a Word merge document
  - Select **Publish It with Microsoft Word** to create an .rtf file in the default database folder (usually C:\My Documents or the folder containing the database) with the same name as the exported object

Exporting ProductByStateCrosstab.rtf:

1. Verify that Access is open with the **AC08PuppyParadise.mdb** database active
2. In the Database window select the **Queries** object and open **ProductByStateCrosstab**
3. Activate the **Tools** menu, point to **Office Links,** and click **Publish It with Microsoft Word**

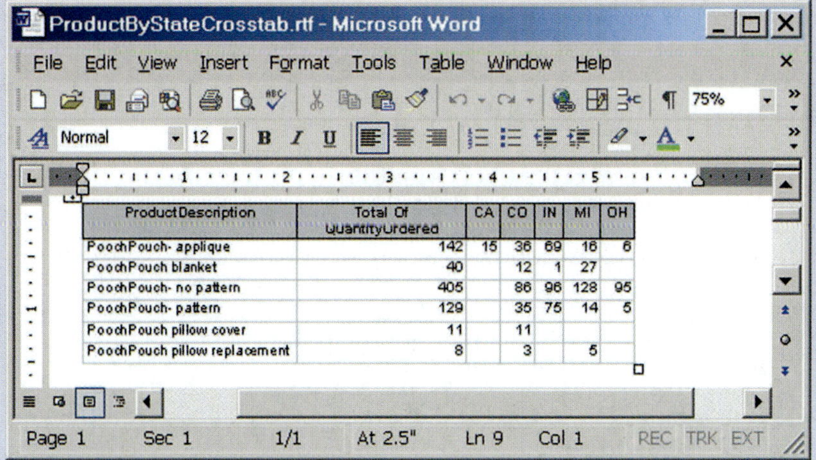

ProductDescription	Total Of QuantityOrdered	CA	CO	IN	MI	OH
PoochPouch- applique	142	15	36	69	16	6
PoochPouch blanket	40		12	1	27	
PoochPouch- no pattern	405		86	96	128	95
PoochPouch- pattern	129		35	75	14	5
PoochPouch pillow cover	11		11			
PoochPouch pillow replacement	8		3		5	

FIGURE 8.20
ProductByStateCrosstab.rtf

4. Add your name to the Word document and save it

When the Office Tools option of the Tools menu is used to export an Access object, Word automatically opens with the exported file displaying. With the document open, Word has full access to it with formatting capabilities that are far superior to those provided by Access. Word supports multicolumn reporting, drop cap text formatting, borders, graphics, and sectioning to apply differing formats to various report components. Word also can be used to create a report based on multiple Access outputs by combining exported data into one document.

Finally, to output a .txt file or control the folder and name of the file, use the Export option of the File menu. The Export To dialog box contains options used to select a folder, file name, and output format for the object being exported. Both .rtf and .txt files can be opened by most word processing applications.

Exporting Access Data to Spreadsheet Applications

Microsoft Access database objects also can be exported to a number of spreadsheet file formats. Spreadsheets enhance datasheet formatting options and provide greater analytical capabilities than Access. Microsoft Excel or any of the other supported spreadsheet formats can provide modeling, forecasting, what-if analysis, and charting capabilities that greatly exceed those available in Access.

The simplest way to apply Excel features to an Access object is to use the Office Links option of the Tools menu just demonstrated to export a word processing file. Evan would like to perform what-if analysis on the orders data generated by the OrderData query.

task reference

Export an Access Object to an Excel Spreadsheet

- Open the Access database that contains the data to be exported
- Select the object to be exported in the Database window (it is best to preview the object before exporting)
- Open the **Tools** menu, point to **Office Links,** and then click **Analyze It with Microsoft Excel**

Exporting OrderData.xls:

1. Verify that Access is open with the **AC08PuppyParadise.mdb** database active
2. In the Database window select the **Queries** object and open **OrderData**
3. Activate the **Tools** menu, point to **Office Links,** and click **Analyze It with Microsoft Excel**
4. Add your name to the Excel worksheet in cell A74 and save it

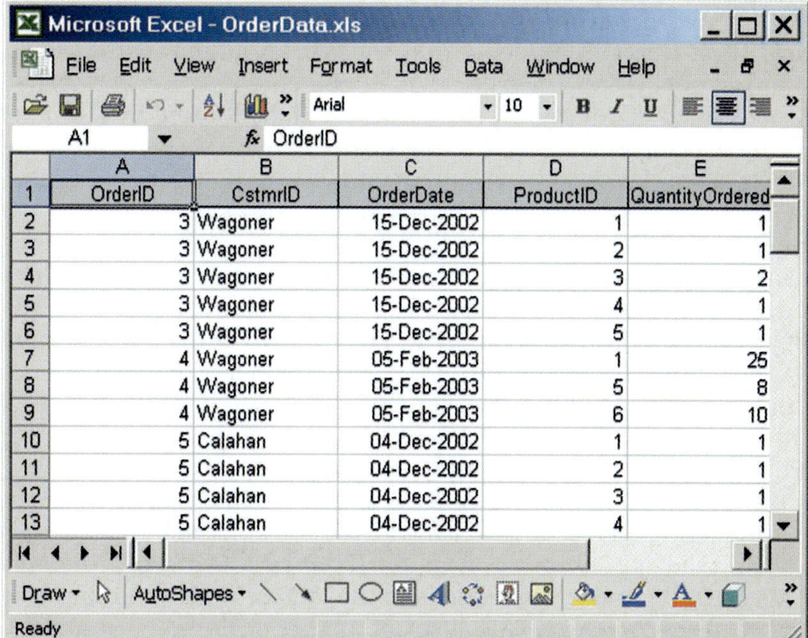

	A	B	C	D	E
1	OrderID	CstmrID	OrderDate	ProductID	QuantityOrdered
2	3	Wagoner	15-Dec-2002	1	1
3	3	Wagoner	15-Dec-2002	2	1
4	3	Wagoner	15-Dec-2002	3	2
5	3	Wagoner	15-Dec-2002	4	1
6	3	Wagoner	15-Dec-2002	5	1
7	4	Wagoner	05-Feb-2003	1	25
8	4	Wagoner	05-Feb-2003	5	8
9	4	Wagoner	05-Feb-2003	6	10
10	5	Calahan	04-Dec-2002	1	1
11	5	Calahan	04-Dec-2002	2	1
12	5	Calahan	04-Dec-2002	3	1
13	5	Calahan	04-Dec-2002	4	1

FIGURE 8.21
OrderData.xls

When the Office Tools option of the Tools menu is used to export an Access object to Excel, Excel automatically opens with the exported file displaying. The exported file will normally be saved in either C:\My Documents or the folder containing the database. The name of the exported object is used as the file name. The OrderData.xls file can now be modified like any native Excel file. The .xls file is not linked to Access and will not reflect database updates.

To output a spreadsheet format other than Excel or control the folder and name of the file, use the Export option of the File menu. The Export To dialog box provides options to select a folder, file name, and output format for the object being exported. Older versions of Excel, Lotus 1-2-3, dBase, and Paradox selections are available from the Save As type drop-down list. The non-Excel options require conversion software that is not included in the typical Access install.

making the grade

SESSION 8.1

1. How are the Chart Wizard and Microsoft Graph related?
2. What is a source application?
3. How do you determine whether to link or embed an object?
4. Why is a chart type important?

SESSION 8.2 WEB PUBLICATION

Access Web technology tools are designed for sharing data, queries, forms, and reports generated from Access using an intranet or the Internet. Access provides an array of Web publication methodologies to meet the differing needs of organizations.

REVIEWING WEB TECHNOLOGIES

The ***World Wide Web (WWW),*** or simply the Web, is an international network of linked documents that share a common computer network called the ***Internet.*** Each computer on the network can be located by a unique address called a ***Uniform Resource Locator (URL).*** These computers are called ***Web Servers*** because they run server software that allows a web of linked documents to be viewed using a ***Web browser.*** Web pages also can be delivered over private networks called ***intranets*** to share documents within an organization or using both Internet and Intranet technology called an ***extranet.***

People who use the Web from work are typically provided continual access through a local server. Most home users who use the Web are not continuously connected to the Internet but, typically, a phone line is used to dial into an ***Internet Service Provider,*** a company that sells the use of its Internet Servers to individuals and businesses.

Regardless of whether the documents are on the Internet, an intranet, or an extranet, they can be viewed using a Web browser such as Microsoft Internet Explorer or Netscape Navigator. ***Hypertext Markup Language (HTML)*** is used to provide instructions to the Web browser outlining how to deliver the page content. HTML instructions are enclosed in <> and are called ***tags.*** As its name implies, HTML was developed to deliver text but it has been expanded to deliver graphics and multimedia content as well. HTML tags set fonts, colors, position, and other formatting characteristics of text. Tags also control what graphic file displays and what other document is opened when a ***hyperlink*** is clicked. Hyperlinks define the paths between Web documents and typically display in a different color than nonlinked text. (See Figure 8.22.)

Figure 8.22 shows an example of a Web page documenting a physics lab assignment created with Office products. The table of data and chart were created in Excel and exported to Word, where the explanatory text was added, and then the page was saved as Filtered HTML (filtering removes Office-specific tags added by the generator). The document was submitted for grading by placing it on the school's intranet. Notice the tags enclosed in <> brackets and the relationship between the <title> tag and the Internet Explorer title bar. While this type of conversion is fast and relatively painless, it may not provide the most efficient HTML code or load times.

BUILDING HTML PAGES

The preferred method of creating HTML pages with new content is to type the tags and text of a page into a basic text editor like Notepad and save the file with an .htm (or .html) extension. When the content for a page already exists, it can be converted by any Office application and many other applications.

Most Web pages are static; that is, their content does not change. Dynamic Web pages contain data that are updated to reflect the current status of something such as the price of a stock. Microsoft Access has the ability to create both ***static Web pages*** and ***dynamic Web pages*** based on database objects.

Static Web pages created from an Access object cannot be updated from a browser and changes made to the data after the static page was generated are not reflected. The content of a dynamic Web page is updated each time that page is viewed so that it reflects the current status of the object. Certain types of dynamic Web pages will allow users to update the Access database object using a Web browser.

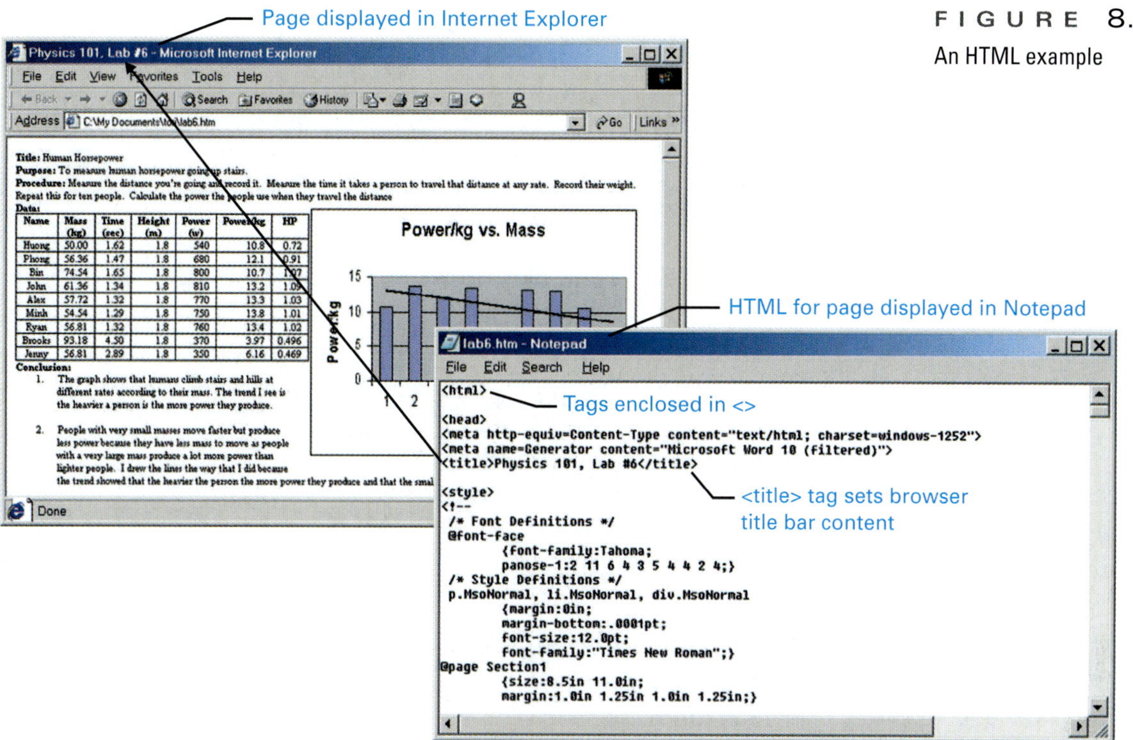

FIGURE 8.22
An HTML example

PuppyParadise will need both static and dynamic Web pages to support sharing information between geographically dispersed locations. Objects from the PuppyParadise database will be converted to HTML and stored on a Web server where they can be viewed and sometimes updated using a Web browser.

Creating a Static HTML Document

The simplest Web pages to generate are static—those that do not update as the data change and cannot be modified by Web users. Static Web pages can be generated from tables, queries, forms, or reports in an existing Access database. Tables, queries, and forms will display as datasheets on the Web page. Reports will appear with HTML versions of the page formatting, which does not always provide ideal conversions. Static Web pages can be viewed using any current Web browser and are best for data that change infrequently.

Exporting PetGroomers.html:

1. Verify that Access is open with the **AC08PuppyParadise.mdb** database active
2. In the Database window select the **Tables** object and open **PetGroomers**
3. Activate the **File** menu and click **Export**
4. In the Export Table PetGroomers To dialog box
   a. Set the Save In drive and folder
   b. Set the Save As box to **HTML Documents (*.html; *.htm)**
   c. Click **Save Formatted, AutoStart,** and **Export**

5. In the HTML Output Options dialog box click **OK**

FIGURE 8.23

PetGroomers.html

The display of Netscape and other browsers will vary slightly

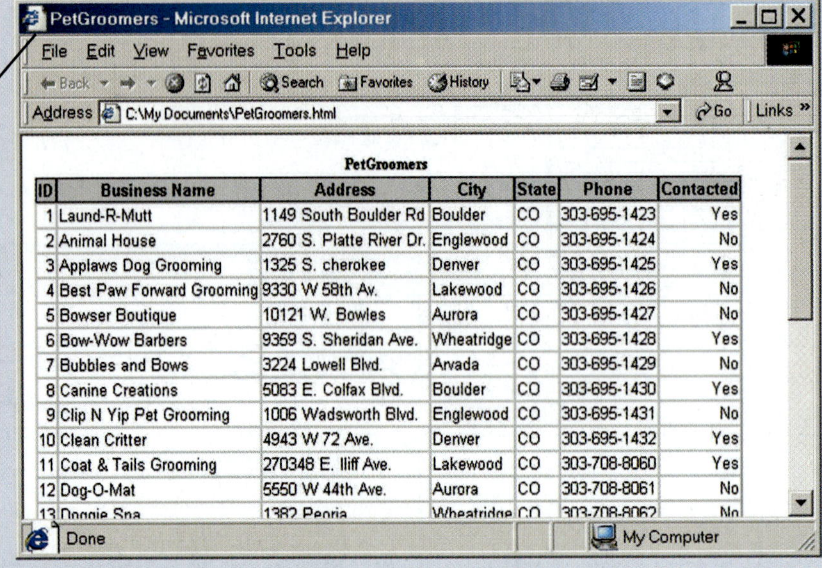

PetGroomers

ID	Business Name	Address	City	State	Phone	Contacted
1	Laund-R-Mutt	1149 South Boulder Rd	Boulder	CO	303-695-1423	Yes
2	Animal House	2760 S. Platte River Dr.	Englewood	CO	303-695-1424	No
3	Applaws Dog Grooming	1325 S. cherokee	Denver	CO	303-695-1425	Yes
4	Best Paw Forward Grooming	9330 W 58th Av.	Lakewood	CO	303-695-1426	No
5	Bowser Boutique	10121 W. Bowles	Aurora	CO	303-695-1427	No
6	Bow-Wow Barbers	9359 S. Sheridan Ave.	Wheatridge	CO	303-695-1428	Yes
7	Bubbles and Bows	3224 Lowell Blvd.	Arvada	CO	303-695-1429	No
8	Canine Creations	5083 E. Colfax Blvd.	Boulder	CO	303-695-1430	Yes
9	Clip N Yip Pet Grooming	1006 Wadsworth Blvd.	Englewood	CO	303-695-1431	No
10	Clean Critter	4943 W 72 Ave.	Denver	CO	303-695-1432	Yes
11	Coat & Tails Grooming	270348 E. Iliff Ave.	Lakewood	CO	303-708-8060	Yes
12	Dog-O-Mat	5550 W 44th Ave.	Aurora	CO	303-708-8061	No
13	Doggie Spa	1382 Peoria	Wheatridge	CO	303-708-8062	No

6. If your browser is Internet Explorer, click **View** and **Source** to review the HTML code for the generated page
7. Close Notepad
8. Close the browser window

task reference

Export an Access Object to a Static HTML Page

- Open the Access database that contains the data to be exported
- Select the object to be exported in the Database window (it is best to preview the object before exporting)
- Open the **File** menu and click **Export**
- In the Export To dialog box
  - Use the Save In box to select the drive and folder for the Web page
  - Set the Save As Type to **HTML Documents (*.html; *.htm)**
  - In the File Name box, enter the name for the Web page (it is best not to use spaces in these names)
  - **Save Formatted** should be clicked to retain the formatting applied to the datasheet in Access and activate the next two options
    - Check **AutoStart** to display the page in your default browser
    - In the HTML Output Options dialog box
      - Apply an HTML template to standardize formatting (Optional)
      - Click **OK**

Once a static page is built, it can be edited outside of Access using Notepad or any other text editor to add links, create additional content, or modify the design. Most browsers have an option on the File menu that will allow a local drive file to be opened so changes can be reviewed.

To make manual changes, update the HTML code in the editor software, save the file, and then refresh the browser screen to see the impact. When the page is complete, it can be loaded into a folder on a Web server where it can be accessed via the Internet. The URL used to retrieve a Web page that has been placed on a Web server is the WebServerAddress+path+filename.

The process for creating static HTML pages from queries, forms, and reports is the same, but the result is slightly different. An Access report creates one HTML file for each printed page of the report numbered sequentially. The CustomersByState-Chart report would create CustomersByState-Chart.html, CustomersByState-ChartPage2.html, CustomersByState-ChartPage3.html, and so on. OLE objects stored in a database, including most graphics, do not display on the HTML page but they can be added manually or using a template file.

Using Access to View and Update an HTML Page

Microsoft Access Web tools integrate well with those of other Microsoft products. The Access Web toolbar is very similar to the Microsoft Internet Explorer toolbar and allows users to modify and view Access-based Web pages without leaving the Access interface. If Microsoft Internet Explorer is not the default browser, you will not be able to complete these steps.

task reference

Use Internet Explorer to View a Static HTML Page

- Open Access
- From the **View** menu, pause over **Toolbars** and then click **Web**
- On the Web toolbar, drop down the **Go** list and select **Open Hyperlink**
- Click the **Browse** button in the Open Internet Address dialog box
- Use the Browse dialog box to navigate to the file to be viewed
- Select the file and click **Open**
- Click **OK**

Using the Access Web toolbar to view PetGroomers.html:

1. Verify that Access is open
2. Open the **View** menu, point to **Toolbars,** and select **Web**
3. Drop down the **Go** list on the Web toolbar and click **Open Hyperlink**
4. Click the **Browse** button in the Open Internet Address dialog box

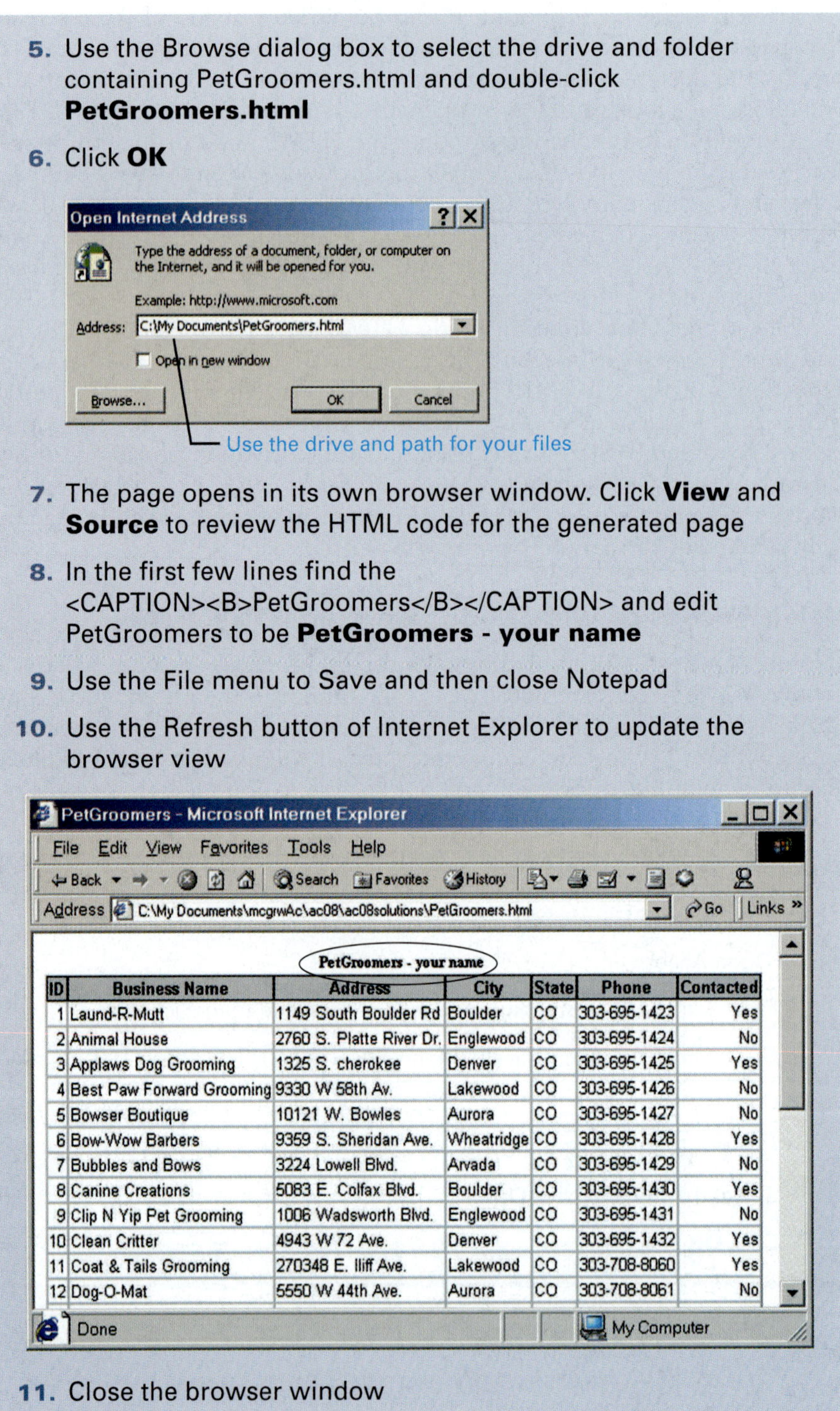

5. Use the Browse dialog box to select the drive and folder containing PetGroomers.html and double-click **PetGroomers.html**
6. Click **OK**

FIGURE 8.24
Open Internet Address dialog box

7. The page opens in its own browser window. Click **View** and **Source** to review the HTML code for the generated page
8. In the first few lines find the <CAPTION><B>PetGroomers</B></CAPTION> and edit PetGroomers to be **PetGroomers - your name**
9. Use the File menu to Save and then close Notepad
10. Use the Refresh button of Internet Explorer to update the browser view

FIGURE 8.25
PetGroomers edited

ID	Business Name	Address	City	State	Phone	Contacted
1	Laund-R-Mutt	1149 South Boulder Rd	Boulder	CO	303-695-1423	Yes
2	Animal House	2760 S. Platte River Dr.	Englewood	CO	303-695-1424	No
3	Applaws Dog Grooming	1325 S. cherokee	Denver	CO	303-695-1425	Yes
4	Best Paw Forward Grooming	9330 W 58th Av.	Lakewood	CO	303-695-1426	No
5	Bowser Boutique	10121 W. Bowles	Aurora	CO	303-695-1427	No
6	Bow-Wow Barbers	9359 S. Sheridan Ave.	Wheatridge	CO	303-695-1428	Yes
7	Bubbles and Bows	3224 Lowell Blvd.	Arvada	CO	303-695-1429	No
8	Canine Creations	5083 E. Colfax Blvd.	Boulder	CO	303-695-1430	Yes
9	Clip N Yip Pet Grooming	1006 Wadsworth Blvd.	Englewood	CO	303-695-1431	No
10	Clean Critter	4943 W 72 Ave.	Denver	CO	303-695-1432	Yes
11	Coat & Tails Grooming	270348 E. Iliff Ave.	Lakewood	CO	303-708-8060	Yes
12	Dog-O-Mat	5550 W 44th Ave.	Aurora	CO	303-708-8061	No

11. Close the browser window

Static HTML pages must be reexported to display updated data. Each time a page is regenerated, any customizations such as added text, graphics, or navigation will need to be reapplied. Because recustomizing is tedious and prone to error, it is a good idea to create HTML templates. An HTML template is a file that contains HTML instructions for creating a Web page and can include text, graphics, and navigation. When a template is applied, Access will place its content based on the instructions, and the remainder of the page is not impacted. In the Export process the HTML Output Options dialog box has an option to specify a template.

CREATING DATA ACCESS PAGES

Data Access pages are built using Dynamic HTML and can be viewed only in browsers supporting that technology (Internet Explorer 5.0 and above). Data Access pages consist of an exported HTML page and a new database object that links the HTML file to a database object. Because this connection is maintained, Data Access pages can be used to view, edit, update, delete, filter, group, and sort live data in the database using a Web browser. Data Access pages also can contain components from spreadsheets, PivotTables, or charts.

Displaying Data and Reports

To make Data Access pages available from the Internet, publish the HTML pages to a Web server. The Access database supporting the pages also must be made available to page users. The best security is provided by placing the HTML pages and the database on the same server. It is a good idea to place the database on a shared server before you create Data Access pages. Moving the database after pages are created will cause the connection between the database and the HTML page to be interrupted.

task reference

Use the Page Wizard to Create a Data Access Page

- Open the database containing the data for the Data Access page
- Click the **Pages** object in the Database window
- Double-click **Create data access page by using wizard**
- Follow the Wizard instructions

Using the Page Wizard to create PetGroomersDataAccess.htm:

1. Verify that Access is running with **AC08PuppyParadise.mdb** open
2. Click the **Pages** object in the database window
3. Double-click **Create data access page by using wizard**
4. Select the **PetGroomers** table and move all of the fields to the Selected Fields list and click **Next**
5. Click **Next** without setting any grouping
6. Choose **BusinessName** for the ascending sort and click **Next**
7. Click **Finish**
8. Click in the Title placeholder and type **Pet Groomers by Business Name**

tip: *If the Title placeholder is not visible, click in the header area*

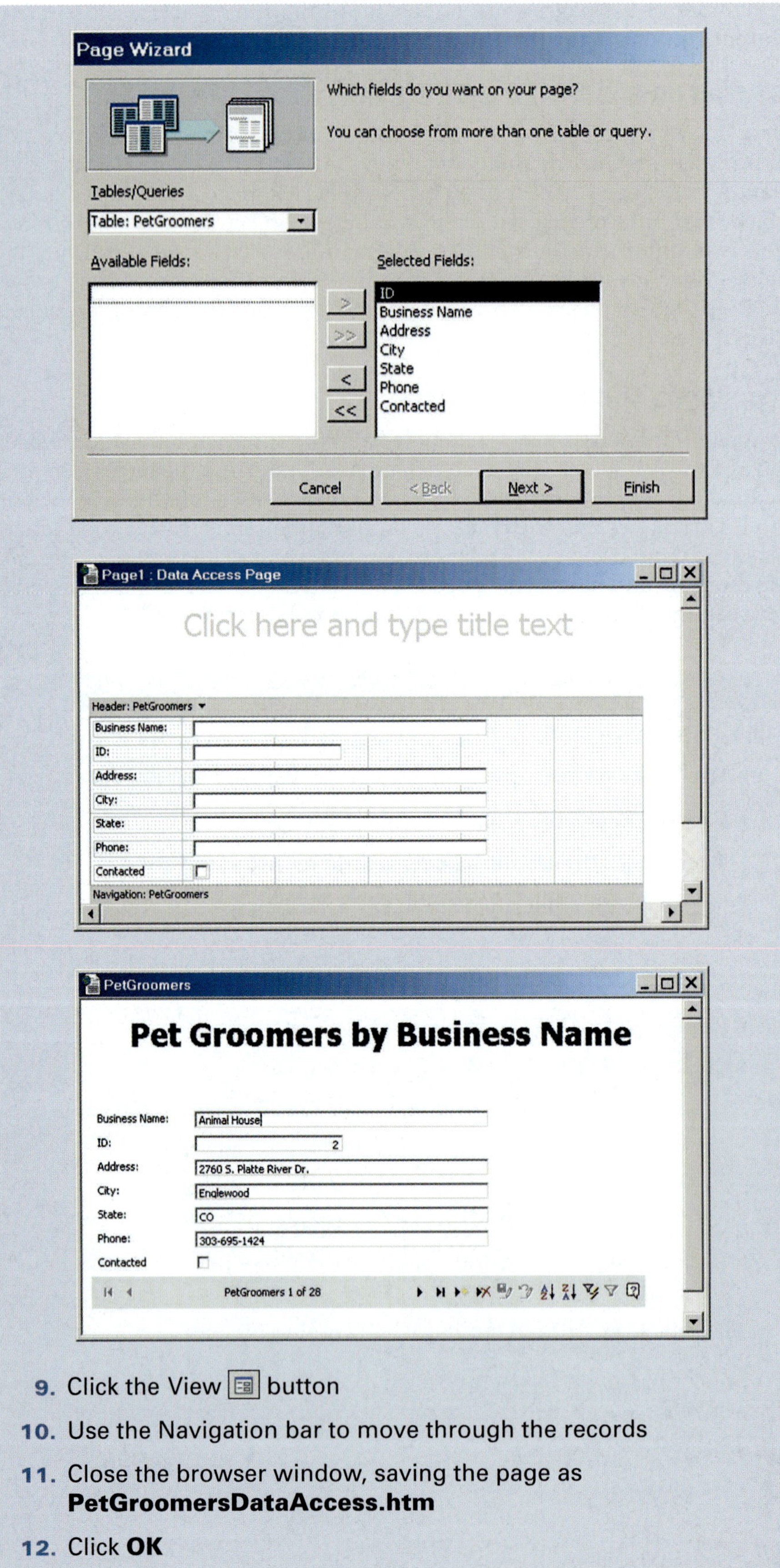

FIGURE 8.26
The Page Wizard

FIGURE 8.27
Data Access Page Design view

FIGURE 8.28
Data Access Page in the browser

9. Click the View button
10. Use the Navigation bar to move through the records
11. Close the browser window, saving the page as **PetGroomersDataAccess.htm**
12. Click **OK**

anotherway

. . . to create a Data Access page

Access provides several options for creating a Data Access page. The steps have covered using the Page Wizard, but a page also can be created from scratch in Design view, created from an existing page, or created in a columnar format. Select the Pages object in the Database window and click New to activate the New Access Data page with all of the page creation options.

- Design view—Create a new page without using a Wizard
- Existing Web page—Use an existing Web page to create a Data Access page
- Page Wizard—Automatically generate a page based on your field selections. You also can specify grouping and sorting options
- AutoPage—Columnar—Creates a default page based on your table or query selection.

You cannot specify fields, grouping, or sorting.

The Pet Groomers Data Access page has an appearance similar to a form displaying one record at a time. In the browser, the ***Record Navigation toolbar*** is used to move from record to record, add new records, delete records, edit records, and sort and filter data. Most of the buttons should be familiar because they appear on other Access toolbars. Screen tips will display for each button when the cursor pauses over it.

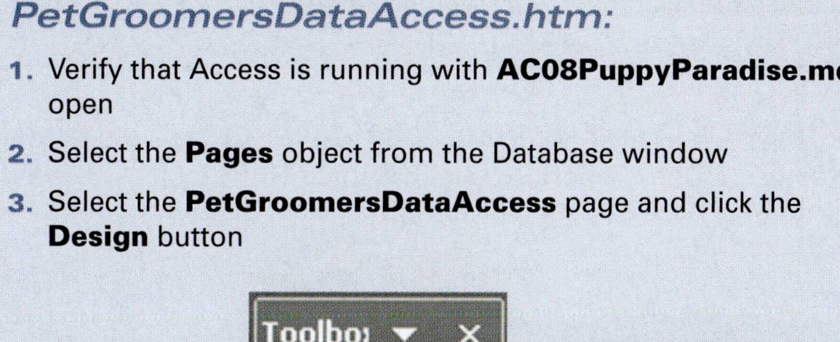

Adding scrolling text to PetGroomersDataAccess.htm:

1. Verify that Access is running with **AC08PuppyParadise.mdb** open
2. Select the **Pages** object from the Database window
3. Select the **PetGroomersDataAccess** page and click the **Design** button

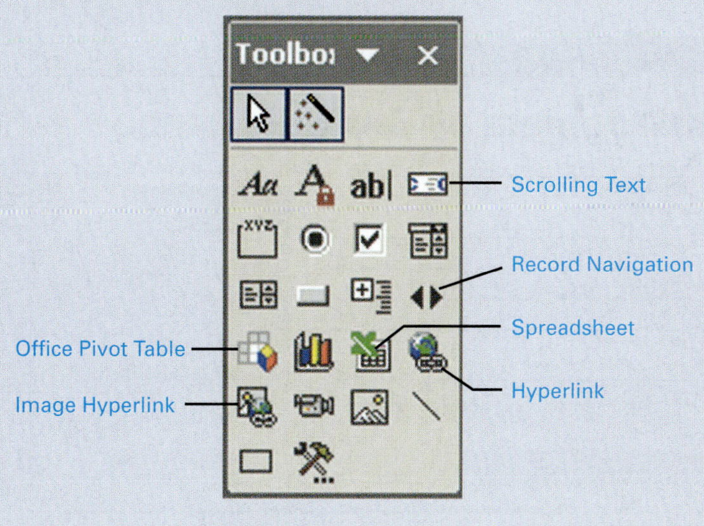

FIGURE 8.29
Data Access Page Design view toolbox

4. Click the **Scrolling Text** tool in the toolbox and drag the area below the Record Navigation toolbar on the Data Access page
5. Select the default Marquee text and type your name
6. Right-click on the Scrolling Text object and select Element Properties
   a. Set Background Color to silver
   b. Close the Properties dialog box
7. Click the **View** button

FIGURE 8.30
Scrolling text

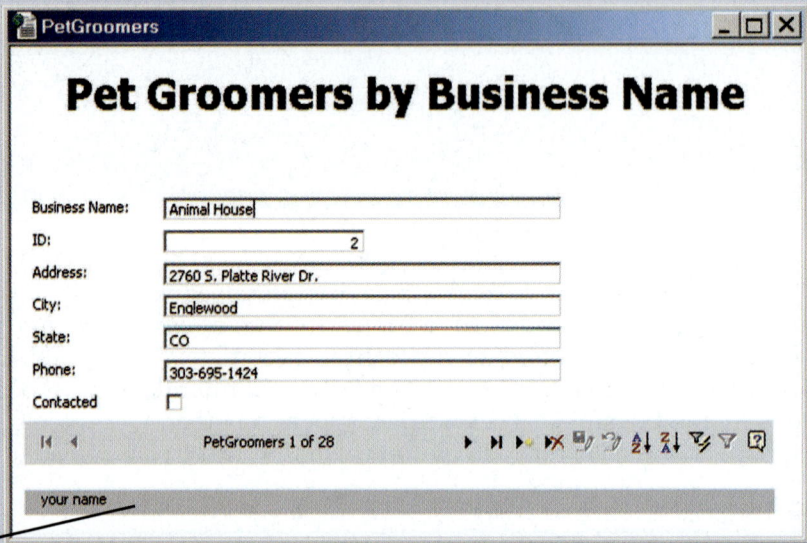

Text entered scrolls

8. Close the window and save the changes

Making edits in the Design view of a Data Access page is very similar to updating a form or report. Notice that some of the toolbox buttons are specific to Data Access pages. The most important differences are noted in Figure 8.29.

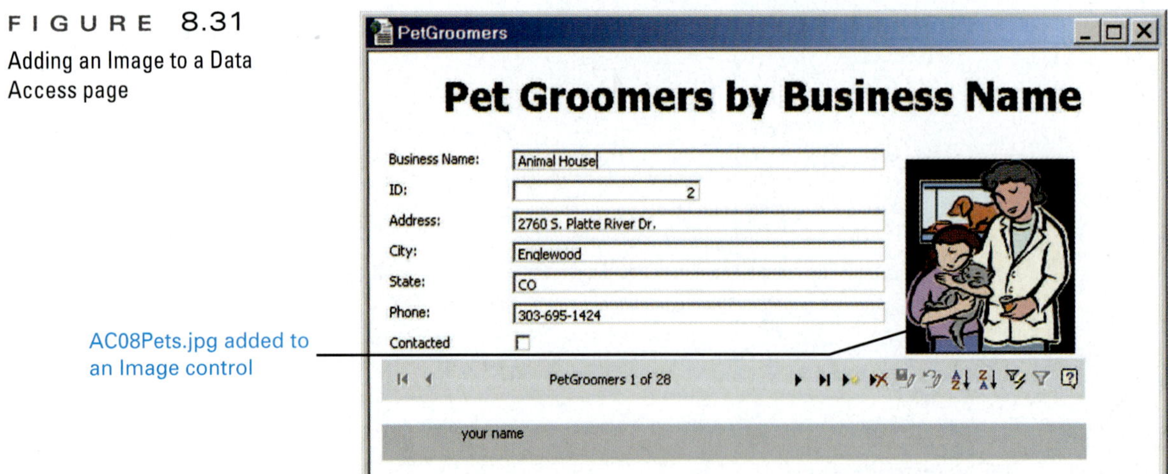

FIGURE 8.31
Adding an Image to a Data Access page

Adding an image to PetGroomersDataAccess.htm:

1. Verify that Access is running with **AC08PuppyParadise.mdb** open
2. Select the **Pages** object from the Database window
3. Select the **PetGroomersDataAccess** page and click the **Design** button
4. Click the **Image** tool in toolbox and drag the area shown in Figure 8.31
5. Navigate to the files for this chapter and select **AC08Pets.jpg**
6. Click the **View** button
7. Close the window and save the changes
8. Use Windows Explorer to view the files in the PetGroomersDataAccess_Files folder
9. Close Windows Explorer

Access provides artistic themes that can be applied to pages for visual impact. Themes are available from the Format menu and can be changed at any time without impacting the presentation.

Applying a theme to PetGroomersDataAccess.htm:

1. Verify that Access is running with **AC08PuppyParadise.mdb** open
2. Select the **Pages** object from the Database window
3. Select the **PetGroomersDataAccess** page and click the **Design** button
4. Open the **Format** menu and select **Theme**
5. Click through the available themes to preview them
6. Select **Sandstone** and click **OK**
7. Click the **View** button to see the page results
8. Close the window, saving the update

Any bullets, backgrounds, or graphics displayed in a Data Access page are stored in a folder that must be moved with the Data Access page. The folder will carry the name of your page with an underscore and the word Files. So the supporting files for PetGroomersDataAccess are stored in a folder named PetGroomersDataAccess_Files. The folder should contain an

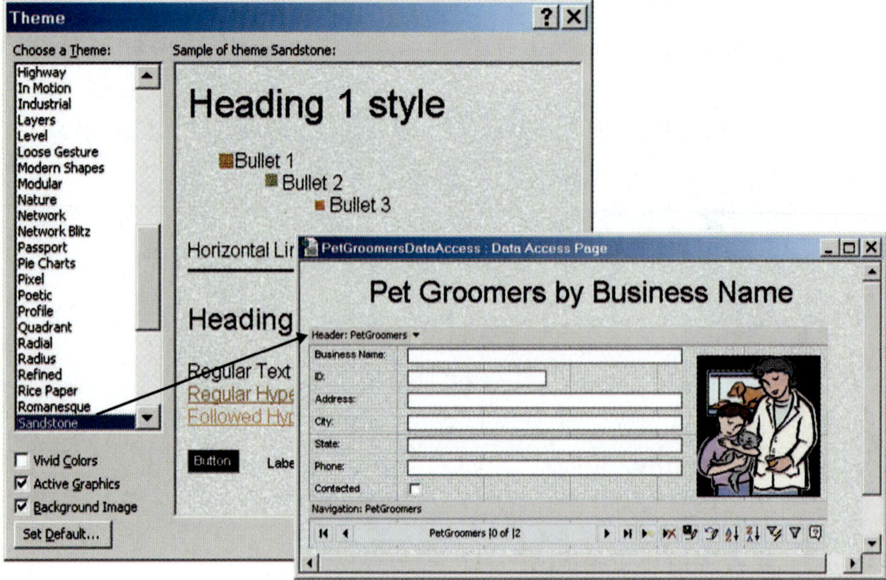

FIGURE 8.32
Applying a theme

.xml file with references to the other objects on the page and the .jpg file containing the image. The remaining files were generated by the theme applied.

Allowing Database Access

When Data Access pages, the supporting files, and the database have been properly loaded on a shared server, live database data can be updated. The process is similar to using a form to update data in an open Access database, but is accomplished from a browser.

Updating the database using PetGroomersDataAccess.htm:

1. Close Access if it is open
2. Use Windows Explorer to navigate to the **PetGroomersDataAccess.htm** file and double-click to open it

tip: *The icon for this file incorporates both the Web page and Access icons. If Internet Explorer is not your default browser, you will need to open IE and use the File menu to open PetGroomersDataAccess.htm. You cannot accomplish these steps with a browser that doesn't support Data Access technology*

3. Move to record 2 and edit the business name to read **Appaws Dog Groomers**
4. Click the **Save** button on the Record Navigation toolbar
5. Move to the Dog-O-Mat record, check the **Contacted** check box, and click the **Save** button on the Record Navigation toolbar
6. Move to the Super Pet Cuts record and use the **Delete** button on the Record Navigation toolbar to delete it

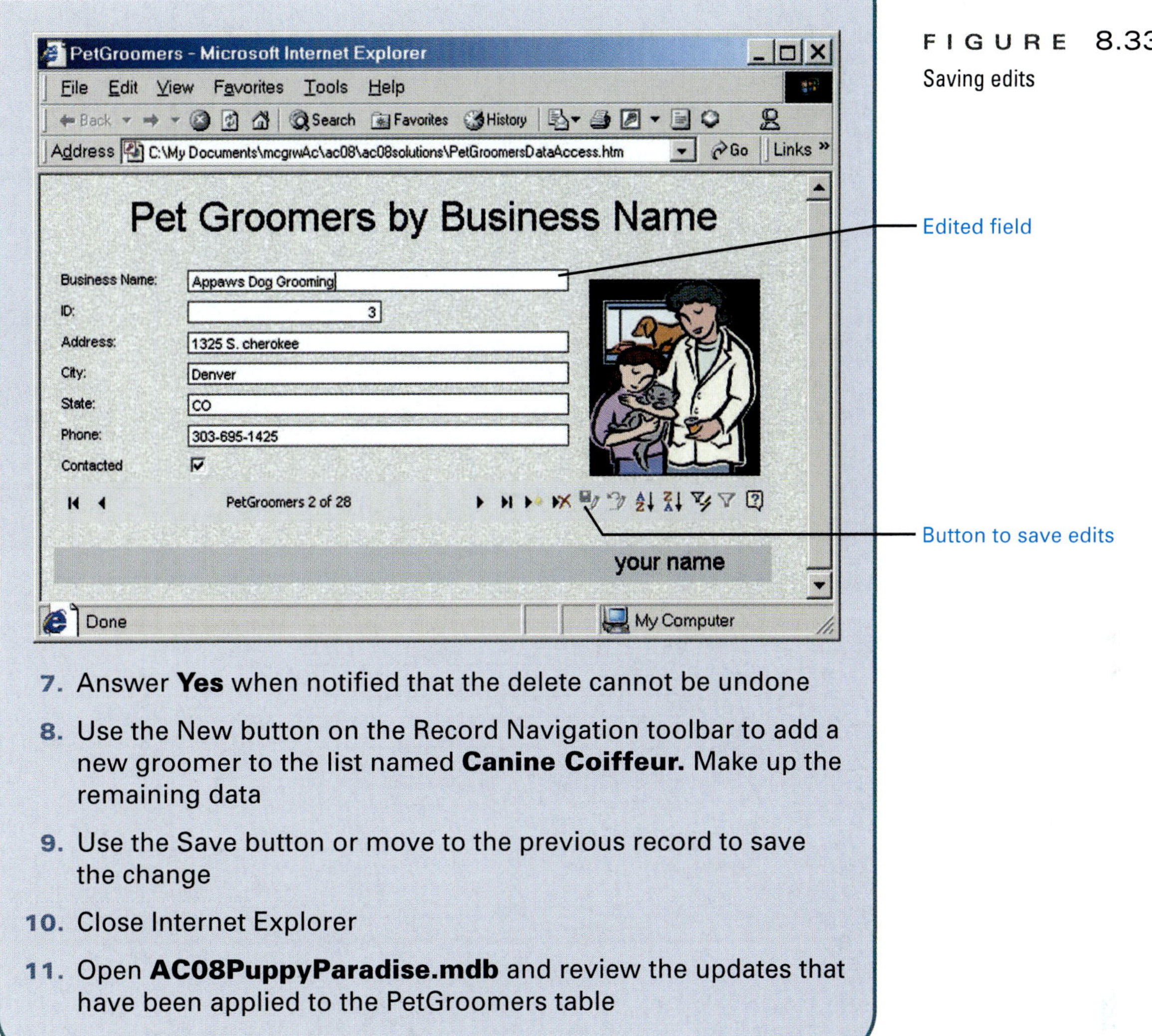

FIGURE 8.33
Saving edits

7. Answer **Yes** when notified that the delete cannot be undone
8. Use the New button on the Record Navigation toolbar to add a new groomer to the list named **Canine Coiffeur.** Make up the remaining data
9. Use the Save button or move to the previous record to save the change
10. Close Internet Explorer
11. Open **AC08PuppyParadise.mdb** and review the updates that have been applied to the PetGroomers table

For demonstration purposes, the steps in this topic are using local files that are not stored on a shared server. Using a Web browser to update a database through a Data Access page will work the same way from an intranet or the Internet as it did with these local files.

Because Data Access pages are based on live data, sorts and filters can be used to control the order of records and what records display. These features work from the Record Navigation toolbar when viewing a page in the browser.

Sorting and filtering PetGroomersDataAccess.htm:

1. Close Access if it is open
2. Use Windows Explorer to navigate to the **PetGroomersDataAccess.htm** file and double-click to open it

tip: *If your default browser is not Internet Explorer, you will need to open IE and use the File menu to open this file*

3. Click in the **City** field and then click the **Sort Descending** button on the Record Navigation toolbar
4. Move through the records to verify the sort
5. Click in the **Business Name** field and then click **Sort Ascending** button on the Record Navigation toolbar to return those data to their original order
6. Select the city **Englewood** and then click the **Filter By Selection** button on the Record Navigation toolbar

FIGURE 8.34
Filter by Selection

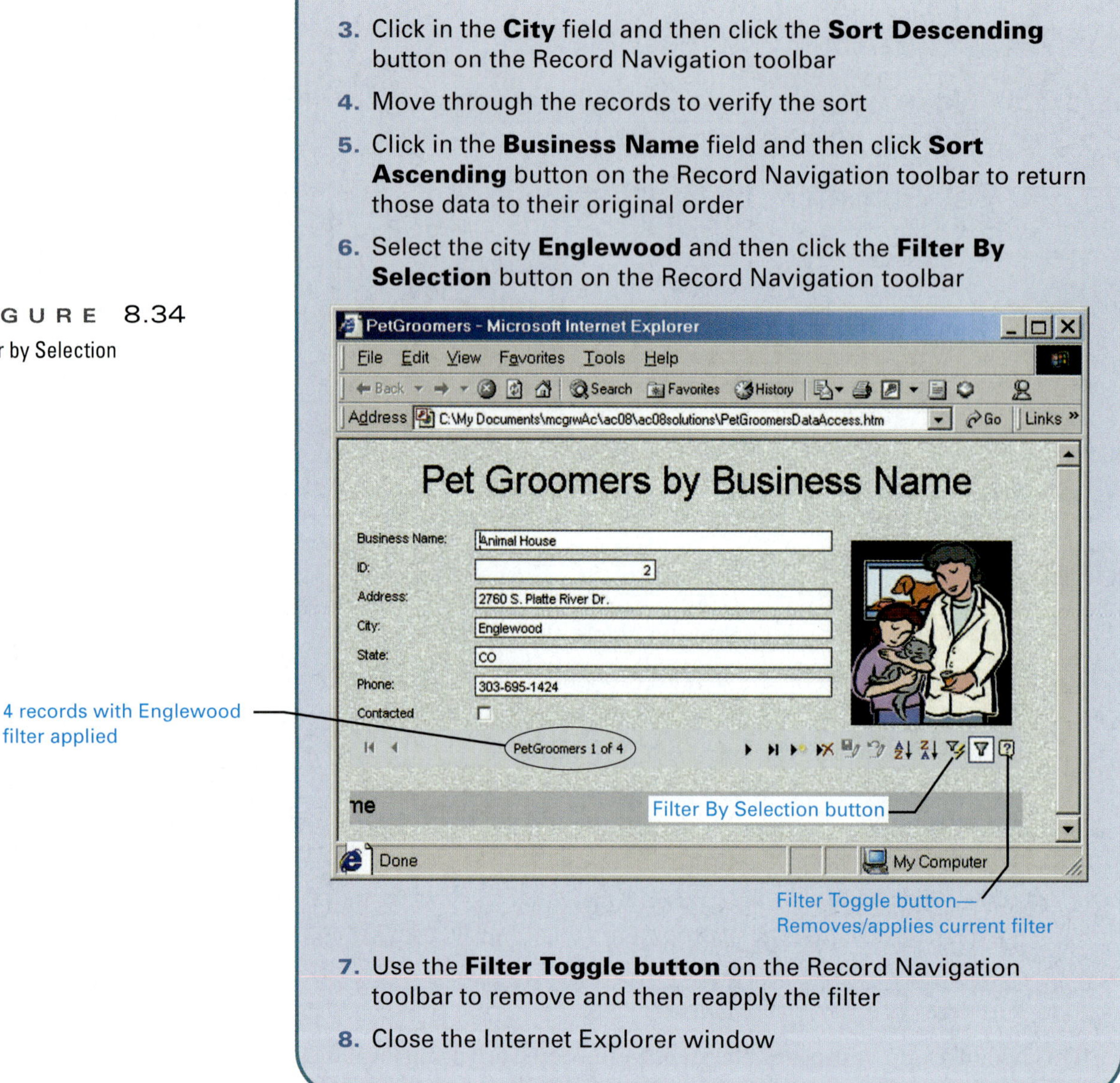

7. Use the **Filter Toggle button** on the Record Navigation toolbar to remove and then reapply the filter
8. Close the Internet Explorer window

Filter by Selection is the only filtering methodology available from a browser. Remember that Filter by Selection supports partial-field filtering but not multiple-field filtering. Selecting the first character of a field retrieves all records starting with that character. Selecting any other character in a field will return all records containing that character.

IMPORTING AN HTML DOCUMENT AS AN ACCESS TABLE

A fundamental concept of database storage is that data should be entered and validated only once. After valid data are stored, they should always be used from that validated source. This principle reduces errors and is more efficient than reentering data each time a new data storage or evaluation technology is needed.

Building an Access Table from a Web Page

To support this concept, Access can use and incorporate data from sources outside itself. Since the World Wide Web is a great informational resource, one of the formats that Access can interpret is HTML. When Web page data are compiled as a table or list, they can be directly converted to an Access table.

Evan has used Web search utilities to locate Web merchants selling pet supplies. His goal is to research and contact these companies as potential distributors of PuppyParadise products. After the page resulting from the search was saved, it was edited in Notepad to remove the unneeded page components such as the search engine and logo. Now the data retrieved can be loaded directly into an Access table.

task reference

Importing an HTML Document as an Access Table

- Open the database to hold the imported table
- Verify that the layout of the data to be imported is either a list or a table
- On the **File** menu, point to **Get External Data,** and then click **Import**
- Select the HTML file for import and click **Import** (be sure to set the Files of Type to HTML documents)
- Complete the Wizard dialog boxes

Importing WebPetSupplies.htm as an Access table:

1. Verify that Access is running with **AC08PuppyParadise.mdb** open
2. Use Internet Explorer to preview WebPetSupplies.htm

tip: *On the Web toolbar in Access click **Go,** then **Open Hyperlink,** and then **Browse***

3. Close the Internet Explorer window
4. On the Access **File** menu, point to **Get External Data,** and then click **Import**
5. In the Import dialog box
   a. Set Files of Type to **HTML Documents (*.html; .htm)**
   b. Navigate to the drive and folder containing files for this chapter, select **WebPetSupplies.htm**, and click **Import**
6. In the Import Wizard
   a. Click **First Row Contains Column Headings** and then click **Next**
   b. Click **Next** to save the HTML import in a new table
   c. Change the Merchants data type to **Hyperlink** and the Description data type to **Memo,** and click **Next**

tip: *You may need to scroll to find these fields*

   d. Click **Next** to let Access assign a primary key
   e. Type **WebPetSuppliers** in the Import to Table box and click **Finish**

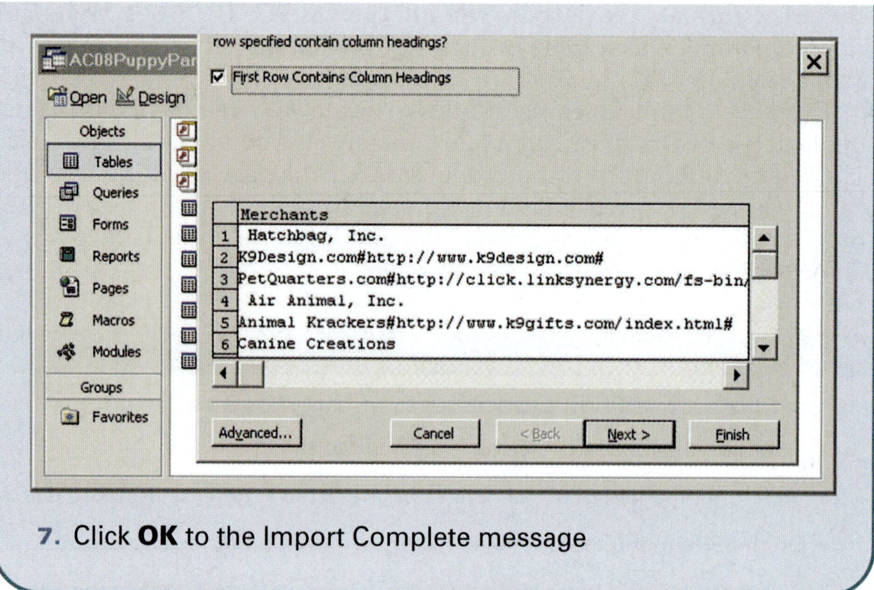

FIGURE 8.35
The Import HTML Wizard

7. Click **OK** to the Import Complete message

The WebPetSuppliers table has successfully been created from the modified HTML document. You should also see an _ImportError table. This table contains a record for each improperly imported row that Access detected. The most common import problem occurs when the data are longer than the field can hold and are truncated in the import process.

Confirming the import:

1. Verify that Access is running with **AC08PuppyParadise.mdb** open
2. Click the **Tables** object in the Database window
3. Double-click the **WebPetSuppliers** table to open it and confirm the import
4. Double-click the column button border for each field to adjust its width

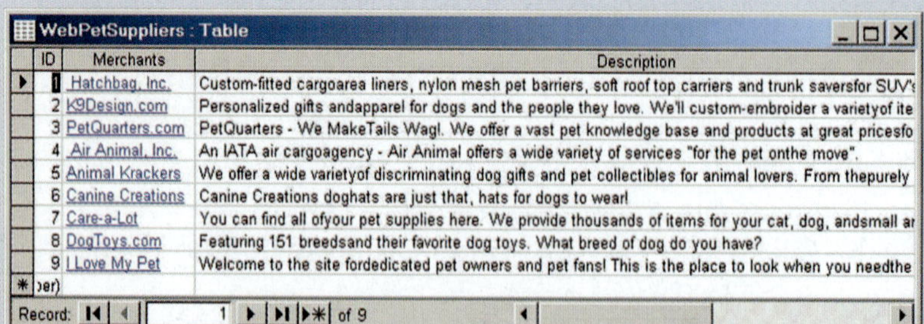

WebPetSuppliers : Table

ID	Merchants	Description
1	Hatchbag, Inc.	Custom-fitted cargoarea liners, nylon mesh pet barriers, soft roof top carriers and trunk saversfor SUV's
2	K9Design.com	Personalized gifts andapparel for dogs and the people they love. We'll custom-embroider a varietyof ite
3	PetQuarters.com	PetQuarters - We MakeTails Wag!. We offer a vast pet knowledge base and products at great pricesfo
4	Air Animal, Inc.	An IATA air cargoagency - Air Animal offers a wide variety of services "for the pet onthe move".
5	Animal Krackers	We offer a wide varietyof discriminating dog gifts and pet collectibles for animal lovers. From thepurely
6	Canine Creations	Canine Creations doghats are just that, hats for dogs to wear!
7	Care-a-Lot	You can find all ofyour pet supplies here. We provide thousands of items for your cat, dog, andsmall ar
8	DogToys.com	Featuring 151 breedsand their favorite dog toys. What breed of dog do you have?
9	I Love My Pet	Welcome to the site fordedicated pet owners and pet fans! This is the place to look when you needthe

Record: 1 of 9

FIGURE 8.36
WebPetSuppliers table

5. Close the window
6. Double-click **Pet Supplies at the All-Internet Shopping Directory_ImportError** to evaluate any import issues
7. Review the errors and close the window

FIGURE 8.37
__ImportError table

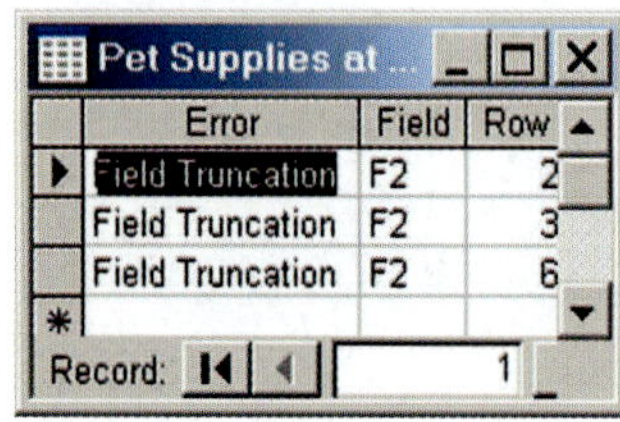

Pet Supplies at ...

Error	Field	Row
Field Truncation	F2	2
Field Truncation	F2	3
Field Truncation	F2	6

Record: 1

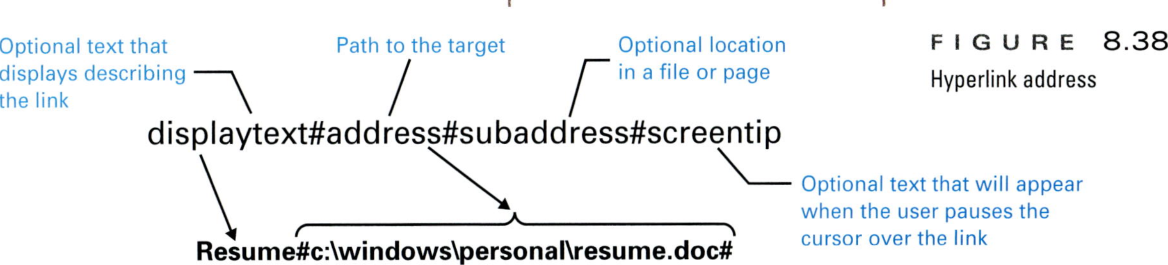

FIGURE 8.38
Hyperlink address

The import errors encountered in this case are in the second field, the hyperlink to the pet suppliers. The links that were truncated will need to be repaired. Additionally, the text in the memo field has some spacing problems, but overall the conversion is good.

Constructing World Wide Web Hyperlinks

Most people associate hyperlinks with Web pages, but since they are really pointers from one object to another object, they can be used to link to pictures, e-mail addresses, or files. The hyperlink itself can display as text or a clickable image.

Hyperlinks can be used to navigate to another file, open another Web page, send an e-mail message, or start a file transfer (FTP). When pointing to text or a picture that contains a hyperlink, the pointer becomes a hand, indicating that it is something that can be clicked. When a hyperlink is clicked, the destination is displayed, opened, or run, depending on the type of destination. For example, a hyperlink to a sound file opens the file in a media player, and a hyperlink to a Web page displays the page in the Web browser.

Access provides a dialog box with the component parts of a hyperlink address (see Figure 8.38). Each address can have up to four parts separated by the number sign (#), but only the address is required.

In an Access table setting the data type of a field to hyperlink allows users to enter any type of a link into the field. When the user enters more than the required address component of a hyperlink, only the display text is visible. This is also true of a text box that is formatted to display hyperlinks. In either case, to see the rest of the entry, click in a cell and press F2.

The error table for WebPetSuppliers indicates that there are problems with the hyperlinks for records 2, 3, and 6. To review and repair these links, the correct URL for the pages must be known. Evan has returned to the Internet and retrieved the correct addresses so that this import can be completed.

Entering and repairing a hyperlink in WebPetSuppliers:

1. Verify that Access is running with **AC08PuppyParadise.mdb** open
2. Click the **Tables** object in the Database window and open **WebPetSuppliers** in Design view
3. Confirm that the Merchants field has a Data Type property of Hyperlink

FIGURE 8.39
Editing Hyperlinks

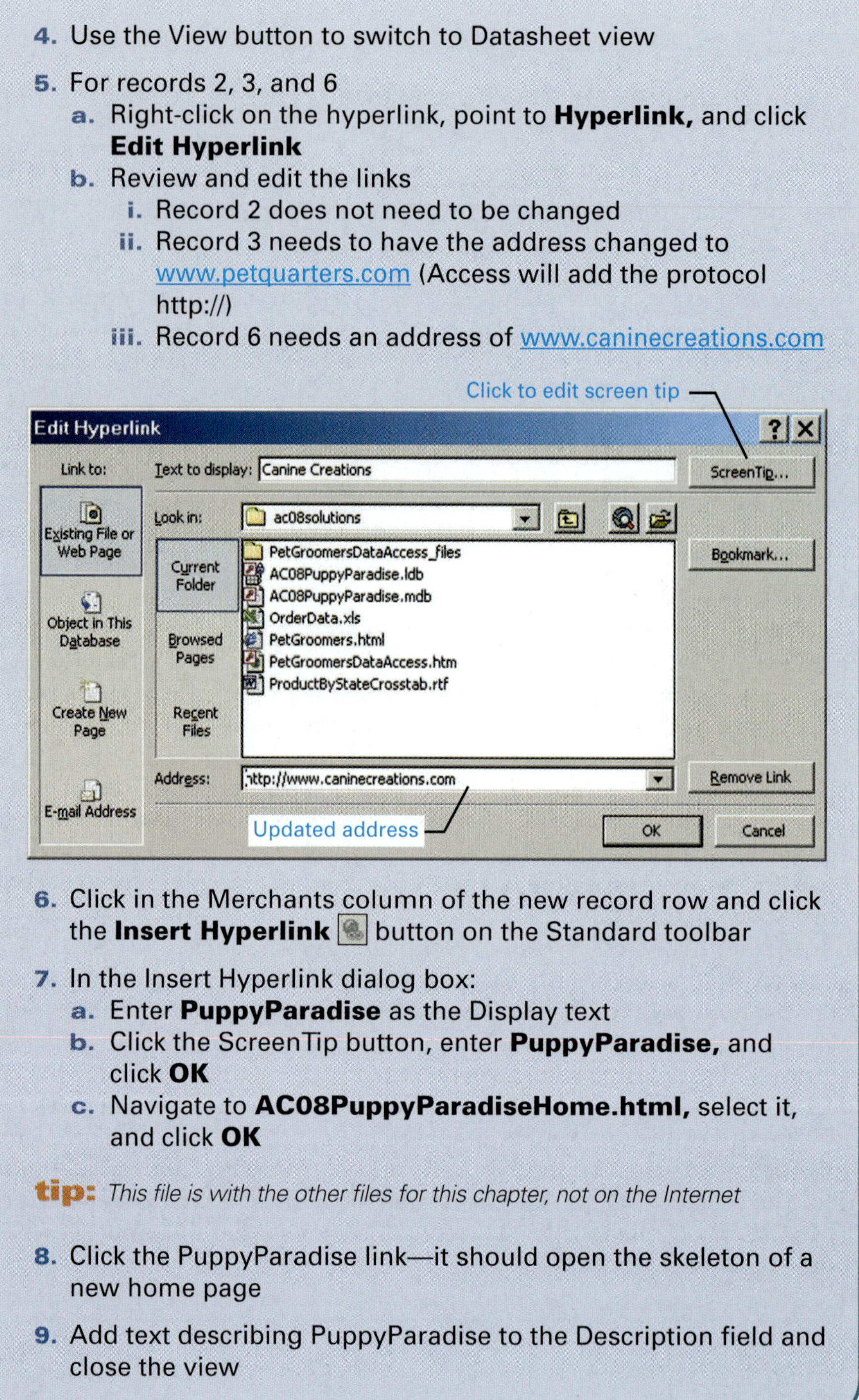

4. Use the View button to switch to Datasheet view
5. For records 2, 3, and 6
   a. Right-click on the hyperlink, point to **Hyperlink,** and click **Edit Hyperlink**
   b. Review and edit the links
      i. Record 2 does not need to be changed
      ii. Record 3 needs to have the address changed to www.petquarters.com (Access will add the protocol http://)
      iii. Record 6 needs an address of www.caninecreations.com

6. Click in the Merchants column of the new record row and click the **Insert Hyperlink** button on the Standard toolbar
7. In the Insert Hyperlink dialog box:
   a. Enter **PuppyParadise** as the Display text
   b. Click the ScreenTip button, enter **PuppyParadise,** and click **OK**
   c. Navigate to **AC08PuppyParadiseHome.html,** select it, and click **OK**

tip: *This file is with the other files for this chapter, not on the Internet*

8. Click the PuppyParadise link—it should open the skeleton of a new home page
9. Add text describing PuppyParadise to the Description field and close the view

The address to a destination object can be either absolute or relative. An ***absolute address*** is said to be fully qualified because it includes all of the information needed to find an object including the protocol (http, ftp, . . .), the server address, the path, and the file name. A ***relative address*** omits some of the address components. When components are omitted, they default to the values of the source object (the object containing the hyperlink). For example if the source document http://www.microsoft.com/index/htm contains a link samples.htm, the source protocol (http) and

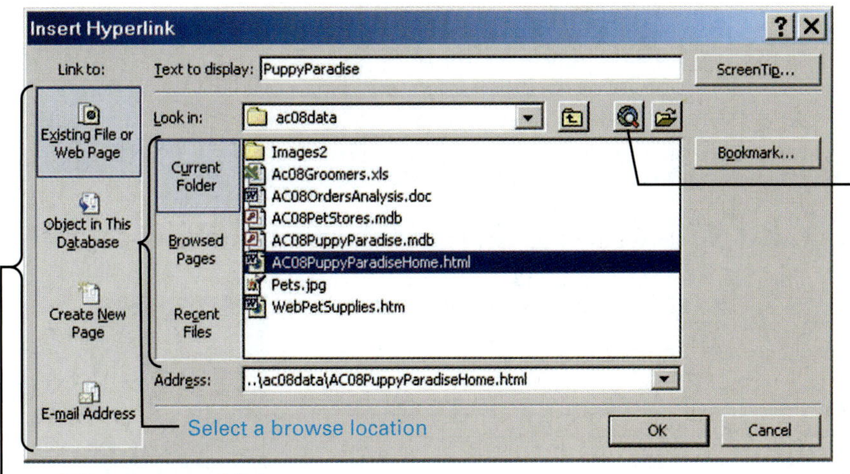

FIGURE 8.40
Adding the PuppyParadise hyperlink

address (www.microsoft.com) are used to determine the full address of the destination, http://www.microsoft.com/samples.htm.

Absolute addresses do not function when files are moved to a new location. Relative addresses will function after files are moved, as long as they are still in the same relative locations (the folders and file names remain the same).

task reference

Construct a Web Page or File Hyperlink

- Open the form, report, or Data Access page in Design view
- Click the Insert Hyperlink button in the toolbox and drag the display area on the form, report, or Data Access page
- In the Insert Hyperlink dialog box
  - Select the type of object to **Link to** (Existing File or Web Page, Object in This Database, Create New Page, or E-Mail Address)
  - Enter the **Text to display** for the hyperlink (if this is blank, the URL will display)
  - Enter the **Screen Tip text** (if this is blank, the URL displays when the user pauses the cursor over the link)
  - In the Address box, type or browse to the path of a file or a URL
  - Click **OK**

Adding a hyperlink to PetGroomersDataAccess:

1. Verify that Access is running with **AC08PuppyParadise.mdb** open
2. Click the **Pages** object in the Database window and Open **PetGroomersDataAccess** in Design view

3. Click the **Label** tool in the toolbox
   a. Click and drag the area shown in Figure 8.41 below the name marquee

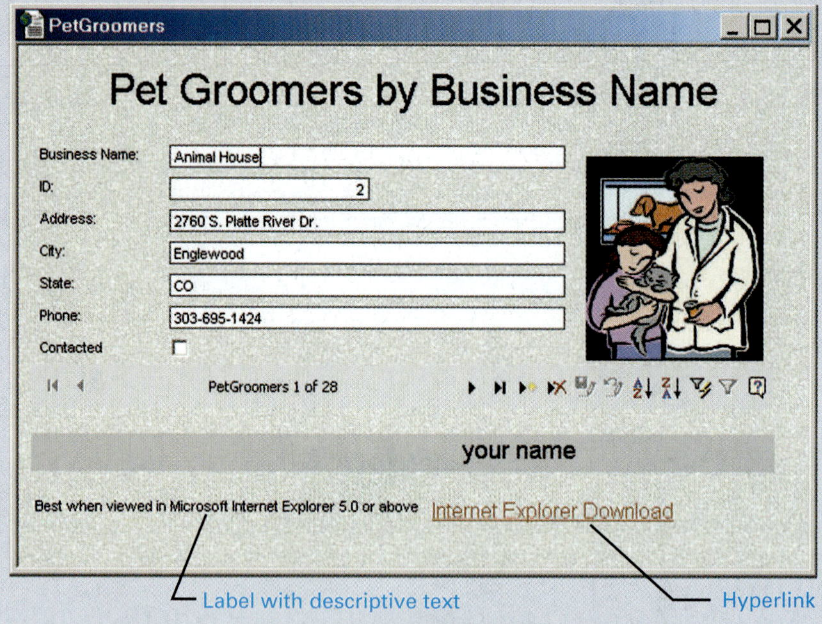

FIGURE 8.41
Hyperlink added to PetGroomersDataAccess

   b. Click in the label and type **Best when viewed in Microsoft Internet Explorer 5.0 or above**
4. Click the **Hyperlink** tool in the toolbox
   a. Click and drag the area shown in Figure 8.41 to the right of the label just created
   b. In the Text to display box type **Internet Explorer Download**
   c. Click the ScreenTip button, type **Newest IE Version!,** and click **OK**
   d. In the address type www.microsoft.com
   e. Click **OK**
5. Click the View button to preview the page
6. Close the window, saving the changes

When adding a hyperlink to a Data Access page, a special Hyperlink control is used. Forms and reports do not have a Hyperlink control, but use labels with the hyperlink information entered into the properties of the label. To test the hyperlink on the PetGroomersDataAccess page, you switched to Page view and clicked the link. When testing a hyperlink stored in a label on a form or report, right-click the label, point to Hyperlink, and then click Open.

Take another look at the Insert Hyperlink dialog box (Figure 8.40) and note the similarities to a standard Open dialog box. Notice also that it contains items specific to locating a file for a hyperlink. The Link to options are used to define the type of link Access should create. We have created links using Existing File or Web Page, but there are also options to link to an Object in This Database, Create New Page, and E-mail Address. The HTML syntax for each of these options is unique, but the process to create them in Access is the same.

The Look In options are used to search the Current Folder, which works like a standard Open File dialog box. Browsed Pages, which will list Internet Explorer's browsing history, also can be used to select a Web address or Recent Files can be used to easily link to a file that was recently opened.

Evan is now satisfied that he understands the import, export, and Web capabilities of Access. He believes that they will help immensely in managing and sharing data in a distributed organization. He will evaluate and begin implementing these features when his business plan is complete.

making the grade

SESSION 8.2

1. What is the difference between a static HTML page and a Data Access page?
2. Why are relative and absolute addresses important?
3. How is the data content of a static Web page updated?
4. What is the Record Navigation toolbar?

SESSION 8.3 SUMMARY

Sharing data is important in reducing data entry and saving time. Allowing multiple applications to have access to the same data allows users to apply the best formatting and analytical tools available in every situation. Access can import data from external sources such as Word, Excel, or another database. Embedded objects belong to the Access database while linked objects remain under the control of their source program.

The Chart Wizard uses Microsoft Graph to create graphs based on numeric data stored in a table. There are a number of chart types that can be created including bar, pie, column, and line. A global chart reflects summaries from all of the table data, while a record-bound chart is based on a single record. Once created, charts can be modified to display other chart types, contain explanatory text, and customize each chart component.

The Access Tools menu contains an Office Links option that automates data sharing with Microsoft Word and Excel. The Export option of the File menu can be used to export other file types such as .txt, HTML, or Paradox. HTML pages created from using the Export menu are static.

Dynamic Web pages called Data Access pages are created using the Pages object in the Database window. An HTML page that can be used to interact with live data is created along with a database object that maintains the connection between the database and the HTML page. Creating and editing a Data Access page is very similar to the Design view of an Access form or report. The Data Access Design toolbar contains controls specifically designed for creating Web pages such as the Scrolling Text control and the Hyperlink control. Data Access pages work best with Microsoft Internet Explorer 5.0 or above.

MOUS OBJECTIVES SUMMARY

- AC2002-8-1—Import data to Access
- AC2002-8-2—Export data from Access
- AC2002-8-3—Create a Data Access page using the Page Wizard
- AC2002-6-1—Use Design view to modify a Data Access page

task reference roundup

Task	Page #	Preferred Method
Create a Microsoft Graph	AC 8.4	• Click the **Reports** object in the Database window
		• Click **New** to activate the New Report dialog box
		• Select **Chart Wizard,** use the drop-down list to select the query or table containing the data to be charted, and then click **OK** to initiate the Chart Wizard
		• Follow the instructions to select the field(s) with the data to be charted, select the chart type, specify the layout, and add a chart title
Importing with an Unbound Object Frame on a form or report	AC 8.10	• Open the Design view of the form or report to contain the imported object
		• Click the **Unbound Object Frame** tool in the toolbox
		• Click and drag the area on the form or report that will contain the object
		• In the Microsoft Access dialog box
		• Click **Create From File**
		• Browse to the file for import
		• Click the Link check box to create a linked object or leave it unclicked to create an embedded object
		• Click **OK**
Import or Link to another Access database	AC 8.15	• Open the Access database that is to contain the imported data
		• Open the **File** menu, point to **Get External Data,** and then do one of the following:
		• Click **Import** to create Access tables from the external data
		• Click **Link Tables** to create links to tables that remain in the source location
		• In the Import or Link dialog box
		• Use the Files of Type drop-down list to select **Microsoft Access (*.mdb, *.adp, *.mda, *.mde, *.ade)** as the type of file to be linked or imported
		• Use the Look In box to select the drive, folder, and file name of the file to be imported or linked
		• Select the import tables and click **Import**
Import or Link to an Excel Spreadsheet	AC 8.18	• Open the Access database that is to contain the imported data
		• Open the **File** menu, point to **Get External Data,** and then click **Import**
		• Click **Import** to create Access tables from the external data
		• Click **Link Tables** to create links to tables that remain in the source location

task reference roundup

Task	Page #	Preferred Method
		• In the Import or Link dialog box
		• Use the Files of Type drop-down list to select **Microsoft Excel (*.xls)** as the type of file to be linked or imported
		• Use the Look In box to select the drive, folder, and file name of the file to be imported or linked
		• Follow the Import Spreadsheet Wizard instructions
Export an Access Object to Microsoft Word	AC 8.21	• Open the Access database with the object to be exported
		• Select the object to be exported in the Database window (it is best to preview the object before exporting)
		• Open the **Tools** menu, point to **Office Links,** and then either
		• Select **Merge It with Microsoft Word** to use an Access table or query as the data source for a Word merge document
		• Select **Publish It with Microsoft Word** to create an .rtf file in the default database folder (usually C:\ My Documents or the folder containing the database) with the same name as the exported object
Export an Access Object to an Excel Spreadsheet	AC 8.22	• Open the Access database that contains the data to be exported
		• Select the object to be exported in the Database window (it is best to preview the object before exporting)
		• Open the **Tools** menu, point to **Office Links,** and then click **Analyze It with Microsoft Excel**
Export an Access Object to a static HTML page	AC 8.26	• Open the Access database that contains the data to be exported
		• Select the object to be exported in the Database window (it is best to preview the object before exporting)
		• Open the **File** menu and click **Export**
		• In the Export To dialog box
		• Use the Save In box to select the drive and folder for the Web page
		• Set the Save As Type to **HTML Documents (*.html; *.htm)**
		• In the File Name box, enter the name for the Web page (it is best not to use spaces in these names)
		• **Save Formatted** should be clicked to retain the formatting applied to the datasheet in Access and activate the next two options
		• Check **AutoStart** to display the page in your default browser
		• In the HTML Output Options dialog box
		• Apply an HTML template to standardize formatting (Optional)
		• Click **OK**

task reference roundup

Task	Page #	Preferred Method
Use Internet Explorer to view a static HTML page	AC 8.27	• Open Access
		• From the **View** menu, pause over **Toolbars** and then click **Web**
		• On the Web toolbar, drop down the **Go** list and select **Open Hyperlink**
		• Click the **Browse** button in the Open Internet Address dialog box
		• Use the Browse dialog box to navigate to the file to be viewed
		• Select the file and click **Open**
		• Click **OK**
Use the Page Wizard to create a Data Access page	AC 8.29	• Open the database containing the data for the Data Access page
		• Click the **Pages** object in the Database window
		• Double-click **Create data access page by using wizard**
		• Follow the Wizard instructions
Importing an HTML document as an Access table	AC 8.37	• Open the database to hold the imported table
		• Verify that the layout of the data to be imported is either a list or a table
		• On the **File** menu, point to **Get External Data,** and then click **Import**
		• Select the HTML file for import and click **Import** (be sure to set the Files of Type to HTML documents)
		• Complete the Wizard dialog boxes
Construct a Web page or file hyperlink	AC 8.41	• Open the form, report, or Data Access page in Design view
		• Click the Insert Hyperlink button in the toolbox and drag the display area on the form, report, or Data Access page
		• In the Insert Hyperlink dialog box
		• Select the type of object to **Link to** (Existing File or Web Page, Object in This Database, Create New Page, or E-Mail Address)
		• Enter the **Text to display** for the hyperlink (if this is blank, the URL will display)
		• Enter the **Screen Tip text** (if this is blank, the URL displays when the user pauses the cursor over the link)
		• In the Address box, type or browse to the path of a file or a URL
		• Click **OK**

CROSSWORD PUZZLE

Across

1. Microsoft ________ software creates charts.
5. A computer that holds documents to be shared.
7. The technology that allows objects to be linked and embedded.
8. A private network for sharing documents.
10. Combines Internet and intranet.
12. An object is ________ when a picture of it appears in another object.
13. An objects is ________ when a copy of it is placed in another object.
14. A graphical presentation of numeric data.

Down

2. A link to navigate between two objects.
3. An object address that does not contain all components.
4. Software used to view a Web page.
6. A world-wide network of computers.
9. An HTML instruction is called a ________.
11. An object address that contains all components.
15. The language used to define Web pages.

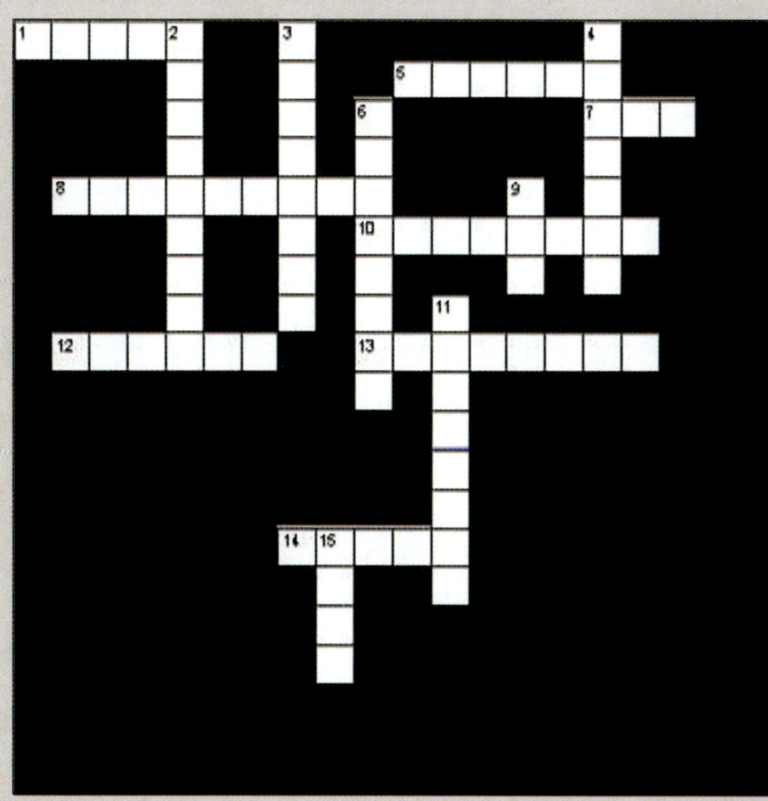

review of concepts

FILL-IN

1. An ________ combines the technologies of an intranet and the Internet.
2. A company that sells the use of its Internet connection is a(n) ________.
3. ________ allow a database table to be updated from a Web browser.
4. HTML instructions are called ________.
5. An HTML ________ can be imported into Access as a table.

REVIEW QUESTIONS

Each of the following topics should be addressed in one to three paragraphs.

1. Why would you use a template when creating Web pages from Access objects?
2. Why is the Access Web toolbar important?
3. Discuss the components of a hyperlink.
4. The address provided in a hyperlink specifies a protocol. What is this?
5. Why are the toolbox tools different for Data Access pages and reports?

CREATE THE QUESTION

For each of the following answers, create the question.

ANSWER	QUESTION
1. Import Wizard	________
2. A column chart	________
3. The legend	________
4. Unbound Object Frame	________
5. The Linked check box	________

FACT OR FICTION

For each of the following, determine whether the statement is fact, fiction, or both and present your arguments for that conclusion.

1. Embedding an object is always the best option when you want to maintain only one copy of the object.
2. Object linking and embedding can be used to import and export all file formats.
3. Imported Excel data can be placed in an Access table or an Unbound Object Frame.
4. The Office Links feature is a simple way to share features of other Office products.
5. The Internet is the only way to share Access forms, reports, and data.

practice

Altamonte High School Booster Club Donation Tracking—Part V: Sharing Database Data

The Altamonte Boosters database has been successfully secured and data validation added to ensure data integrity. Now it is time to look at options for sharing data that do not impact security and integrity. The leadership believes that importing and exporting appropriate file formats will allow them to share data using e-mail attachments. The organization has a secured area on the school's Web server that can be used to share Web documents with authorized members.

1. Start Access and open **AC08AltamonteBoosters.mdb**

   tip: *You cannot use your copy of the database from the previous chapter since there have been modifications for this chapter*

2. Use the Query Wizard to create a query that totals the donations made for each class of donor. These data will be charted
   a. From the **Boosters** table move the **DonationClass** field to the Selected Fields list
   b. From the **Donations** table move the **DonationAmount** field to the Selected Fields list
   c. From the **DonationClass** table move the **ClassDescription** field to the Selected Fields list
   d. Click **Next**
   e. Select the **Summary Option** button and then use the Summary Option button to **Sum** DonationAmount
   f. Click **Next**
   g. Name the query **DonationsByClass** and click **Finish**
   h. Close the Query window after verifying the result
3. Select the Reports object from the Database window
   a. Click the **New** button
   b. Select the **Chart Wizard,** select **DonationsByClass** as the data source, and click **OK**
4. In the Chart Wizard
   a. Select **ClassDescription** and **Sum of DonationAmount** as the fields for the chart and click **Next**
   b. Select **3-D Pie** as the chart type
   c. Preview the chart and then click **Next**
   d. Title the chart **Donations by Class** and click **Finish**
   e. Double-click on the chart to open Microsoft Graph
      i. Right-click in the chart area (not on the pie itself) and select **Chart Options**
      ii. On the Data Labels tab check **Values** and **Percent**
      iii. Click **OK**
5. Close and save the form, naming it **DonationsByClassChart**
6. Open the DonationsByClassChart in Form view to preview your work and then close it
7. Exit Access if your work is complete

FIGURE 8.42
DonationsByClassChart

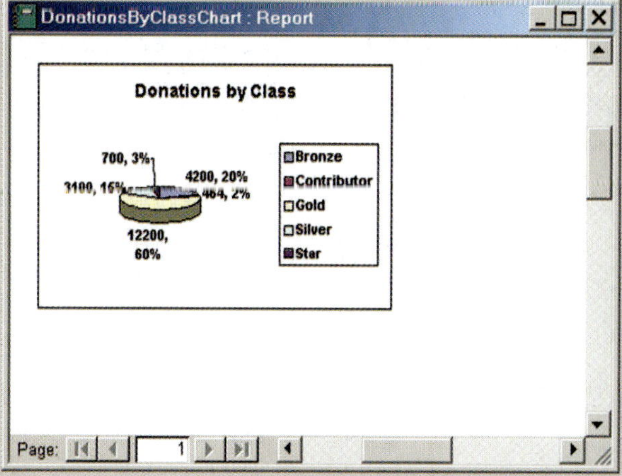

challenge!

Altamonte High School Booster Club Donation Tracking—Part VI: Exploring Alternatives for Sharing the Database

The Altamonte Boosters' fund-raising drive is complete and it is time to publish the results for the next meeting.

1. If you did not complete the Practice project for this chapter, start Access and open **AC08AltamonteBoosters.mdb** and complete it

   tip: *You can use your copy of the database from the Practice project in this chapter. You cannot use your copy of the database from the previous chapter since there have been modifications for this chapter*

2. Review the chart created in the Practice steps and then open Microsoft Word and write a brief (3-4 line) summary of what the chart presents. Save the document as **AltamonteSummary.doc**
3. Open the DonationsByClassChart report in Design view
   a. Enlarge the report by dragging the Detail and Page Footer borders
   b. Enlarge the chart area to fill the width of the form

   tip: *Make sure that your enlargement is proportional. Do not distort the graphic by only adding width*

   c. Use an Unbound Object control to import (embed) AC08AltamonteSummary.doc and position it below the chart
   d. Double-click on the Unbound Object to enter edit mode and adjust the margins to the size of your form

   tip: *You may need to enlarge the form to adjust the right margin and then reduce the size again*

   e. Preview your work, update as needed, and save
4. From the Pages object of the Database window
   a. Use the Page Wizard to create a Data Access page based on the Boosters table named **AltamonteBoosters**
   b. Include all fields from the Boosters table
   c. Sort by Name
   d. Make the title **Altamonte H.S. Boosters**
   e. Use the View button to preview the page

   tip: *Select a DonationClass, then click the + to the left to view the boosters for that DonationClass*

   f. Use the AltamonteBoosters Data Access page to add a record for **Pierre Verrizen** in DonationClass **3.** Supply the remaining data
5. Exit Access if your work is complete

FIGURE 8.43

Fund-raising chart and description from Word

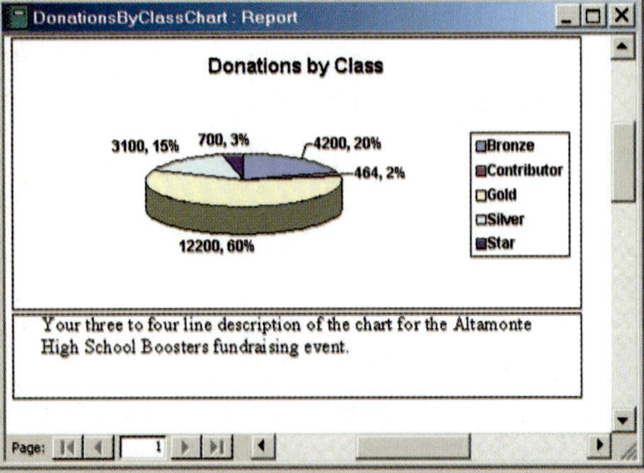

FIGURE 8.44

AltamonteBoosters Data Access page

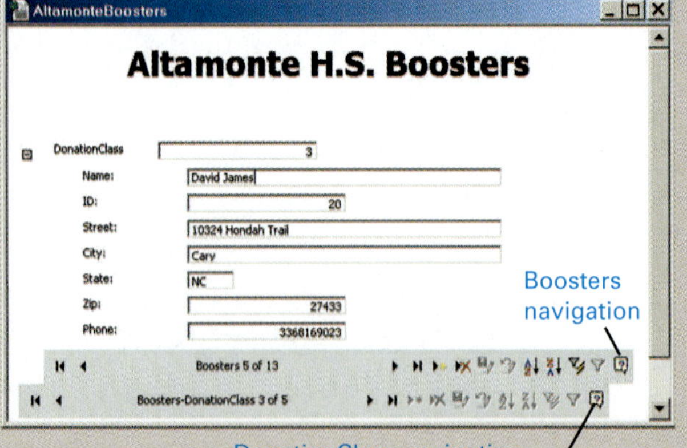

on the web

Academic Software

Academic Software is a fairly large organization with diverse data needs. In the past users have created the data that they needed to complete each job. Now that a functioning database is available, the goal is to use import, export, and Web capabilities to avoid recreating data.

1. Use your favorite search engine to locate two foreign language software titles suitable for academic language study. Be sure to note the prices too
2. Start Access and open **AC08Software.mdb**

tip: *You cannot use your copy of the database from the previous chapter since there have been modifications for this chapter*

3. Several users have been tracking new software titles in an Excel spreadsheet. Use the import capabilities of Access to add these data to tblSoftware
   a. Open tblSoftware to view the existing 12 records
   b. Close tblSoftware
   c. Import **SoftwareTitles.xls**

   tip: *Open it in Excel first to review the content*

      i. The file does have column headings in the first row
      ii. Proceed with the import even if there are warnings
   d. Open tblSoftware to verify the addition of 12 records

   tip: *Only 10 of the 12 records from Excel were imported because the other 2 records violate the validation rule set for Category (="MTH" Or ="ENG" Or ="SCI")*

   e. Add "LNG" to the validation rule and repeat the import

   tip: *Duplicate key violations will keep the 10 records that imported the first time from being duplicated*

   f. Open tblSoftware, verify that the two LNG software titles have been added, and close the table
4. From the Pages object of the Database window
   a. Use the Page Wizard to create a Data Access page based on the tblSoftware table named **Software**
   b. Include all fields from the tblSoftware table
   c. Sort by Name
   d. Make the title **Software Titles by Vendor**
   e. Use the View button to preview the page

   tip: *Select a VendorCode, then click the + to the left to view the titles for that vendor*

   f. Use the Software Data Access page to add a record for the software titles located on the Internet. Add them to VendorCode **EI** with a Category of **LNG**
5. Exit Access if your work is complete

FIGURE 8.45

Software Data Access page

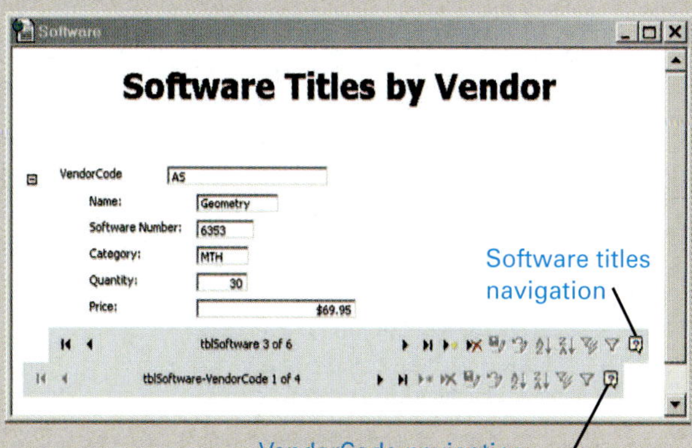

e-business

Curbside Recycling

Earth First, the parent company of Curbside Recycling, is sponsoring a recycling competition between the cities that it serves. The status of the competition will be posted on the Web site and the city that recycles the most will receive a donation earmarked for park renovation.

1. Start Access and open **AC08CurbsideRecycling.mdb**

   tip: *You cannot use your copy of the database from the previous chapter since there have been modifications for this chapter*

2. Use the **Get External Data** option of the **File** menu to import **AC08Competition.xls**

   tip: *Use Excel to preview this file before import.*

   a. There are no headings in the file
   b. Import to a new table
   c. Name Field1 **City** and Field2 **TonsRecycled**
   d. Let Access set the key
   e. Name the table **Competition**
   f. Open Competition to verify the import and then close it

3. Create a Data Access page with a chart based on the Competition table
   a. Click the **Pages** object in the database window and open a new page in Design view
   b. Set the title to **Earth First Recycling Competition**
   c. Click the Office Chart tool in the toolbox and then click an area on the page surface that covers the width of the page
   d. Click the Office Chart to open the Commands and Options dialog box if necessary
   e. In the Commands and Options dialog box
      i. Click **Data from the following Web page item** and then click **DataSource Details** button
      ii. Select **Competition** from the Data member table, view, or cube name drop-down list

      tip: *If you lose the Commands and Options dialog box, click the Chart Wizard button*

      iii. Click the **Type** tab and select **Column** and **3-D clustered**
      iv. Close the Commands and Options dialog box
   f. Use the Field List button on the Standard toolbar if you do not have a Field List displaying
      i. Open the Competition field list using the +
      ii. Drag **City** to the Drop Category Field area of the chart
      iii. Drag **TonsRecycled** to the Drop Data Fields Here area of the chart
      iv. Save the Data Access page as **Competition**

4. Open Competition in Internet Explorer
   a. Drop down the City list and uncheck one to see the chart result
   b. You can change the data in the Drop areas too

5. Exit Access if your work is complete

FIGURE 8.46

Internet Explorer with Competition Data Access page

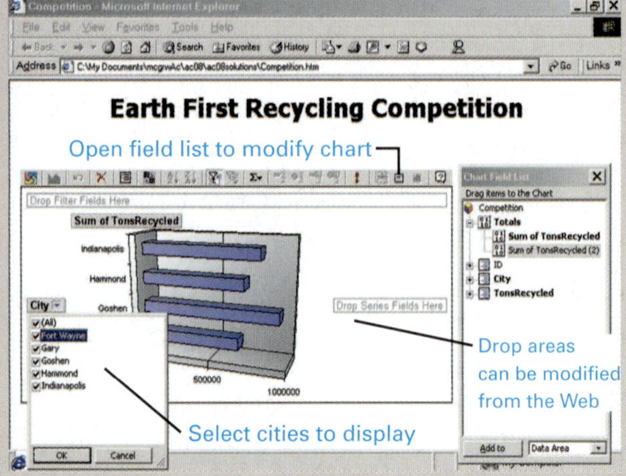

around the world

TechRocks Seminars

TechRocks Seminars is a worldwide organization with requirements to share data, analysis, and update capabilities. Management has decided to try using Data Access pages to allow all of the sites to enter students into a class.

1. Start Access and open **AC08Seminars.mdb**

   tip: *You cannot use your copy of the database from the previous chapter since there have been modifications for this chapter*

2. Activate the **Pages** object in the Database window
   a. Activate the Page Wizard
   b. Set the **Enrollment** table as the data source and move all of its fields to the field list
   c. Group the data by **SeminarID**
   d. Sort by LastName and FirstName
   e. Name the page **Enrollment**
3. In the Design view of the Enrollment Data Access page
   a. Make the page title **Seminar Enrollment**
   b. Use an Image control to add a picture from the collection on your computer positioned as shown in Figure 8.47
   c. Add a scrolling text box below the data area with the text **New Class! Data Access Pages. Limited Enrollment,** and set the Font size to **Medium**

   tip: *Right-click on the marquee and select* ***Element Properties***

4. Open **Enrollment**
   a. Move to seminar TR105
   b. Move through the records and then add two new records for **Kate Whittey** and **Thomas Elliott.** Make up the remaining data
5. Create a Data Access page from the StudentListing query
   a. Activate the Page Wizard and select **StudentListing** as the data source
   b. Use all of the StudentListing fields
   c. Sort by SeminarID, LastName, and FirstName
   d. Select Enrollment as the table to update
   e. Click the check box to apply a theme to the page
   f. Choose **Nature** as the theme
   g. Use the View button to evaluate this design and then save it
6. Exit Access if your work is complete

FIGURE 8.47
Enrollment Data Access page

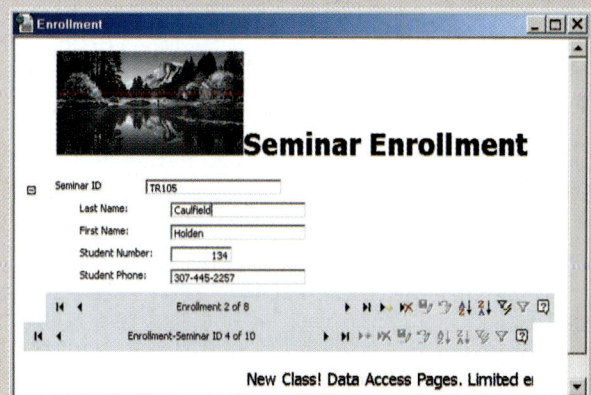

running project: tnt web design

Web Publishing from Access

TnT is continuing in its use of Access to gather and analyze data. It is time to develop the interfaces from the database to the Web site to provide current and accurate data and improve data sharing.

1. Start Access and open **AC08TnT.mdb**

   tip: *You cannot use your copy of the database from the previous chapter since there have been modifications for this chapter*

2. Open the CustomerSites table and use the Hyperlink button on the Standard toolbar to update the following hyperlinks:
   a. MMB Holdings Site 1—Set the display text and screen tip to **MMB Holdings, Inc.**
   b. MMB Holdings Site 2—Set the display text and screen tip to **Your Holdings!**
   c. Omega Distributions—Set the display text and screen tip to **Omega Distributions**

   tip: *While this process should be repeated for all of the links, for brevity we will just pretend that they are all displaying descriptive text*

3. Export the CustomerSites table as a static Web page and then use Internet Explorer to review it. You should notice that the improperly entered hyperlinks display as text not links. The properly entered hyperlinks would work if the Web pages actually existed. This export has other problems we will not address
4. Export the EmployeesByJobClass query as a static Web page and then use Internet Explorer to review it. Notice that two HTML pages are created and that the navigation is automatically added to the bottom of each page. This is the public version of the report that cannot be updated
5. Create a Data Access page based on the Employees table that will reside in a secure area of the intranet to update the Employees table
   a. Use all fields from the table
   b. Group by **JobClass** and sort by **LastName** and **FirstName**
   c. Check the **Apply theme** check box and then apply **Edge**
   d. Set the title to **Employees by Job Classification**
   e. Preview the result
6. Close Access if your work is complete

FIGURE 8.48

CustomerSites.html

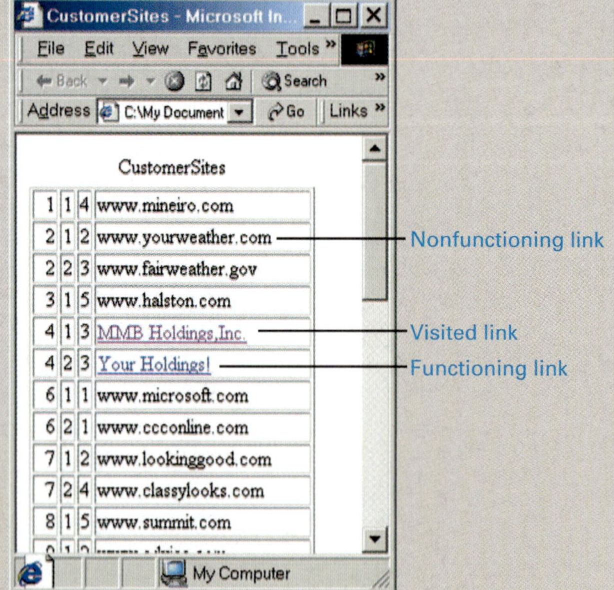

NOTES

reference 1 Access File Finder

Access file finder

Location in Chapter	Data File to Use	Student Saves Data File as
CHAPTER 1		
Opening a blank database		Blank.mdb
Opening a database	AC01Customers.mdb	
Opening a table	AC01Customers.mdb	
Opening a table	AC01CurbsideRecycling.mdb	
Creating a primary key		LittleWhiteSchoolHouse.mdb
On the Web		WHHA.mdb
Create a new database		ExoticFlora.mdb
Create a report	AC01AGC.mdb	
Create a table	AC01TnT.mdb	
CHAPTER 2		
Reorganizing datasheet columns	AC02customers.mdb	
Sorting	AC02customers.mdb	
Find and replace	AC02customers.mdb	AC02customers.mdb
Wildcards	AC02customers.mdb	
Adding new records	AC02customers.mdb	
Deleting a record	AC02customers.mdb	
Using Office Clipboard	AC02customers.mdb	
Hiding and unhiding columns	AC02customers.mdb	
Freezing and unfreezing datasheet columns	AC02customers.mdb	
Building a table	AC02PuppyParadise.mdb	
Setting tab attributes	AC02PuppyParadise.mdb	
Building a table	AC02PuppyParadise.mdb	
Populating a table	AC02PuppyParadise.mdb	
Toolbars		BbsShoes.mdb
Print table design		MedTemps.mdb
Copy records	AC02TempEmployees.mdb	
Comparing records		IRI.mdb

Location in Chapter	Data File to Use	Student Saves Data File as
Comparing with wildcards		SportBabie.mdb
Unique ID		Getz.mdb
Relationships	AC01TnT.mdb	<yourname>TnT.mdb
CHAPTER 3		
Filtering a table	AC03PuppyParadise.mdb	
Excluding records	AC03PuppyParadise.mdb	
Filter by Form	AC03PuppyParadise.mdb	
Filtering with an Or condition	AC03PuppyParadise.mdb	
Filter by Form	AC03PuppyParadise.mdb	
Advanced Filter/Sort	AC03PuppyParadise.mdb	
Creating a table query	AC03PuppyParadise.mdb	
Formatting a table query	AC03PuppyParadise.mdb	
Sorting a query	AC03PuppyParadise.mdb	
Selecting table records	AC03Software.mdb	
Expression Builder	AC03Software.mdb	
Aggregate functions	AC03Software.mdb	
Summarizing grouped data	AC03Software.mdb	
Form Wizard	AC03Software.mdb	
Report Wizard	AC03Software.mdb	
Mailing labels	AC03Software.mdb	
Adding a graphic to InventoryByCategory	AC03Software.mdb	
	(AC03Computer.tif)	
Filters, forms, queries, and reports	AC03CurbsideRecycling.mdb	
	(AC03Curbside.tif)	
Converting spreadsheets		LittleWhiteSchoolHouse.mdb
Importing external data	AC03lwsh.mdb	
	AC03lwsh.tif	
On the Web	AC03IRI.mdb	
	AC03IRI.tif	
Filtering records	AC03Cars.mdb	
	AC03ClassicCars.tif	
Filter by Form	AC03Populations.mdb	

Location in Chapter	Data File to Use	Student Saves Data File as
Filter by Records	<yourname>TnT.mdb AC03TnT.tif	
CHAPTER 4		
Selecting table records	AC04PuppyParadise.mdb	
Selecting table records with In	AC04PuppyParadise.mdb	
Selecting table records with Like	AC04PuppyParadise.mdb	
Selecting table records with compound criteria	AC04PuppyParadise.mdb	
Selecting table records with Not	AC04PuppyParadise.mdb	
Crosstab query	AC04PuppyParadise.mdb	
Adding a memo	AC04PuppyParadise.mdb	
Deleting a field	AC04PuppyParadise.mdb	
Moving a field	AC04PuppyParadise.mdb	
Changing field properties	AC04PuppyParadise.mdb	
Setting a lookup field	AC04PuppyParadise.mdb	
Setting an input mask	AC04PuppyParadise.mdb	
Compacting and repairing	AC04PuppyParadise.mdb	
Backing up a database	AC04PuppyParadise.mdb	
Automatic compact and repair	AC04PuppyParadise.mdb	
Query	AC04Merrill.mdb	
Query	AC04CurbsideRecycling.mdb	
Query datasheet	AC04SportsPix.mdb	
Query	AC04Populations.mdb	
Query and sort	AC04TnT.mdb	
	AC04TnT.tif	
CHAPTER 5		
Creating a form—Design view	AC05PuppyParadise.mdb	
Changing form properties	AC05PuppyParadise.mdb	
Repositioning form controls	AC05PuppyParadise.mdb	
Changing labels	AC05PuppyParadise.mdb	AC05PuppyParadise.mdb
Changing text boxes	AC05PuppyParadise.mdb	
Adding Form Header/Footer	AC05PuppyParadise.mdb	
Adding content to form header	AC05PuppyParadise.mdb	

Location in Chapter	Data File to Use	Student Saves Data File as
Finding form records	AC05PuppyParadise.mdb	
Filtering form records	AC05PuppyParadise.mdb	
Querying an open form	AC05PuppyParadise.mdb	
Customizing AutoReport	AC05PuppyParadise.mdb	AC05PuppyParadise.mdb
Report in Design view	AC05PuppyParadise.mdb	
Editing label Captions	AC05PuppyParadise.mdb	AC05PuppyParadise.mdb
Aligning report controls	AC05PuppyParadise.mdb	
Adding report date and time	AC05PuppyParadise.mdb	
Adding page numbers to a report	AC05PuppyParadise.mdb	
Adding a header to a report	AC05PuppyParadise.mdb	
Adding separators to a report	AC05PuppyParadise.mdb	
Adding a report total to a report	AC05PuppyParadise.mdb	
Adding sorting and grouping to a report	AC05PuppyParadise.mdb	
Adding header/footer content	AC05PuppyParadise.mdb	
Hiding duplicate values	AC05PuppyParadise.mdb	
Forms and reports	AC05Cyberia.mdb	
Sorting and grouping	AC05Cyberia.mdb	
Creating forms and reports	AC05TerraPatrimonium.mdb	
Creating forms and reports	AC05SportsPix.mdb (AC05Sportspix.tif)	
Creating reports	AC05Seminars.mdb (AC05TechRocks.tif)	
Custom forms and reports	AC05TnT.mdb (AC05TnT.tif)	
CHAPTER 6		
Viewing relationships	AC06PuppyParadise.mdb	
Viewing relationship properties	AC06PuppyParadise.mdb	
Building a one-to-one relationship	AC06PuppyParadiseRelationships.mdb	AC06PuppyParadiseRelationships.mdb
Deleting a table and relationships	AC06PuppyParadiseRelationships.mdb	
Building a one-to-many relationship	AC06PuppyParadiseRelationships.mdb	
Indexing	AC06PuppyParadiseRelationships.mdb	AC06PuppyParadiseRelationships.mdb
Viewing table indexes	AC06PuppyParadiseRelationships.mdb	
Setting a multifield index	AC06PuppyParadiseRelationships.mdb	AC06PuppyParadiseRelationships.mdb
Creating a multitable query	AC06PuppyParadiseRelationships.mdb	

Location in Chapter	Data File to Use	Student Saves Data File as
Creating a left outer join query	AC06PuppyParadiseRelationships.mdb	
Viewing the SQL for the InvoiceLeftJoin query	AC06PuppyParadiseRelationships.mdb	
Creating a fixed-list lookup field	AC06PuppyParadiseRelationships.mdb	
Creating a main form/subform	AC06PuppyParadiseRelationships.mdb	
Customizing a main form/subform	AC06PuppyParadiseRelationships.mdb	AC06PuppyParadiseRelationships.mdb
Using a main form/subform	AC06PuppyParadiseRelationships.mdb	
Invoice report/user-defined query	AC06PuppyParadiseRelationships.mdb	
Modifying a query	AC06PuppyParadiseRelationships.mdb	AC06PuppyParadiseRelationships.mdb
InvoiceJoinWithCalc report	AC06PuppyParadiseRelationships.mdb	
Creating a logo and title	AC06PuppyParadiseRelationships.mdb (AC06PupLogo.tif)	AC06PuppyParadiseRelationships.mdb
OrderID Header	AC06PuppyParadiseRelationships.mdb	AC06PuppyParadiseRelationships.mdb
CstmrID Header	AC06PuppyParadiseRelationships.mdb	AC06PuppyParadiseRelationships.mdb
Modify Detail/Footer sections	AC06PuppyParadiseRelationships.mdb	AC06PuppyParadiseRelationships.mdb
Setting table relationships	AC06AltamonteBoosters.mdb	
Using related tables	AC06AltamonteBoosters.mdb	
Multitable relationships and reports	AC06Software.mdb	
Enhancing a database	AC06CurbsideRecycling.mdb	AC06CurbsideRecycling.mdb
Forms and reports	AC06Seminars.mdb	AC06Seminars.mdb
Custom forms and reports	AC06TnT.mdb	
CHAPTER 7		
Customizing table	AC07PuppyParadise.mdb	
Customizing field format	AC07PuppyParadise.mdb	
Adding default values	AC07PuppyParadise.mdb	
Requiring fields	AC07PuppyParadise.mdb	
Adding field validation	AC07PuppyParadise.mdb	
Splitting a database	AC07PuppyParadise.mdb	AC07PuppyParadise.mdb (front-end file)
Exploring split database	AC07PuppyParadise.mdb (front-end file) AC07PuppyParadise_be.mdb	
Database objects	AC07PuppyParadise.mdb	
Replicating a database	AC07PuppyParadise.mdb	
Updating replica data	AC07PuppyParadise.mdb	

Location in Chapter	Data File to Use	Student Saves Data File as
Sychronizing	AC07PuppyParadise.mdb (replica) AC07PuppyParadise.mdb (Design Master)	
Hiding a backup	AC07PuppyParadise.bak	
Encrypting a database	AC07PuppyParadise.mdb	EncryptedAC07PuppyParadise.mdb
Adding a password	AC07PuppyParadise.mdb	
Testing a password	AC07PuppyParadise.mdb	
Removing a password	AC07PuppyParadise.mdb	
Setting user-level security	AC07PuppyParadise.mdb	PuppyParadiseUserSecurityBak.mdb
Testing user-level security	AC07PuppyParadise.mdb	
Database design review	AC07AltamonteBoosters.mdb	
Alternatives for sharing the database	AC07AltamonteBoosters.mdb	ReplicaAltamont1.mdb ReplicaAltamonte2.mdb
Academic Software	AC07Software.mdb AC07SoftwareBak.mdb	AC07Software_be.mdb (back-end file)
Curbside Recycling	AC07CurbsideRecycling.mdb	Curbside1.mdb Curbside2.mdb
TechRocks Seminars	AC07Seminars.mdb	ParisSeminars.mdb LondonSeminars.mdb
Database Maintenance and Security	AC07TnT.mdb	
CHAPTER 8		
Creating a report	AC08PuppyParadise.mdb	
Modifying a chart	AC08PuppyParadise.mdb	AC08PuppyParadise.mdb
Chart types and subtypes	AC08PuppyParadise.mdb	AC08PuppyParadise.mdb
Linking Word document to a report	AC08PuppyParadise.mdb	AC08PuppyParadise.mdb
Embedding a Word document	AC08PuppyParadise.mdb AC08OrdersAnalysis.doc	
Verifying a source document	AC08OrdersAnalysis.doc	
Importing	AC08PuppyParadise.mdb AC08PetStores.mdb	
Linking	AC08PuppyParadise.mdb AC08PetStores.mdb	DistributorsLinked.mdb
Importing	AC08PuppyParadise.mdb AC08Groomers.xls	AC08PuppyParadise.mdb
Exporting	AC08PuppyParadise.mdb	AC08PuppyParadise.mdb
Exporting	AC08PuppyParadise.mdb	AC08PuppyParadise.mdb

Location in Chapter	Data File to Use	Student Saves Data File as
Exporting	AC08PuppyParadise.mdb	
Viewing an HTML page	PetGroomers.html	PetGroomers = your name
PageWizard	AC08PuppyParadise.mdb	
Adding scrolling text	AC08PuppyParadise.mdb	AC08PuppyParadise.mdb
Adding an image	AC08PuppyParadise.mdb AC08Pets.jpg	
Applying a theme	AC08PuppyParadise.mdb	AC08PuppyParadise.mdb
Updating a database	PetGroomersDataAccess.htm AC08PuppyParadise.mdb	AC08PuppyParadise.mdb
Sorting and filtering	PetGroomersDataAccess.htm	
Importing	AC08PuppyParadise.mdb	
Confirming the import	AC08PuppyParadise.mdb	
Hyperlink	AC08PuppyParadise.mdb AC08PuppyParadiseHome.html	
Adding a hyperlink	AC08PuppyParadise.mdb PetGroomersDataAcess.htm	AC08PuppyParadise.mdb
Sharing Database Data	AC08AltamonteBoosters.mdb	
Exploring Alternatives for Sharing a Database	AC08AltamonteBoosters.mdb	AC08AltamonteSummary.doc
Academic Software	AC08Software.mdb (SoftwareTitles.xls)	
Curbside Recycling	AC08CurbsideRecycling.mdb (AC08Competition.xls)	
TechRocks Seminars	AC07Seminars.mdb	
Web Publishing	AC08TnT.mdb	

reference 2

MOUS Certification Guide

MOUS Certification Guide

MOUS Objective	Task	Session Location	End-of-Chapter Location
CHAPTER 1	**Understanding Relational Databases**		
AC2002-1-1	Create Access databases using the Wizard	1.2	AC 1.33
AC2002-1-2	Open database objects in multiple views	1.1	AC 1.33
AC2002-1-3	Navigate among records	1.2	AC 1.33
CHAPTER 2	**Maintaining Your Database**		
AC2002-1-4	Format datasheets for display	2.1	AC 2.35
AC2002-2-1	Create one or more tables	2.2	AC 2.35
AC2002-5-1	Enter and edit records in a datasheet	2.1	AC 2.35
AC2002-5-3	Sort records in a datasheet	2.1	AC 2.35
CHAPTER 3	**Introducing Queries, Filters, Forms, and Reports**		
AC2002-3-1	Creating Select queries using the Simple Query Wizard	3.2	AC 3.38
AC2002-3-1	Adding a calculated field to queries in query Design view	3.2	AC 3.38
AC2002-4-1	Creating forms using the Form Wizard	3.3	AC 3.38
AC2002-4-1	Creating auto forms	3.3	AC 3.38
AC2002-4-2	Modifying the properties of a form and/or specific controls on a form	3.3	AC 3.38
AC2002-5-1	Entering records using a form	3.3	AC 3.38
AC2002-5-4	Filtering datasheets by form	3.1	AC 3.38
AC2002-5-4	Filtering datasheets by selection	3.2	AC 3.38
AC2002-7-1	Creating and formatting reports using the Report Wizard	3.3	AC 3.38
AC2002-7-3	Previewing a report	3.3	AC 3.38
AC2002-7-3	Printing a report	3.3	AC 3.38
CHAPTER 4	**Compound Queries and Database Utilities**		
AC2002-1-5	Use Access tools to maintain and repair databases	4.3	AC 4.30
AC2002-2-2	Add a predefined input mask to field	4.2	AC 4.30
AC2002-2-3	Create lookup fields	4.2	AC 4.30
AC2002-2-4	Modify field properties	4.1	AC 4.30
CHAPTER 5	**Customizing Forms and Reports**		
AC2002-2-1	Create a form in Design view	5.1	AC 5.5
AC2002-4-1	Create and modify reports in Design view	5.1	AC 5.26
AC2002-4-3	Sort and group data in reports	5.2	AC 5.35
AC2002-7-3	Preview and print reports	5.2	AC 5.41

MOUS Objective	Task	Session Location	End-of-Chapter Location
CHAPTER 6	**Defining Table Relationships**		
AC2002-2-3	Create and use multitable custom forms including subdatasheets and subforms	6.2	AC 6.21
AC2002-5-2	Change the properties of table relationships	6.1	AC 6.5
AC2002-6-1	Build table relationships in the Relationships window	6.1	AC 6.3
AC2002-6-2	Enforce referential integrity	6.1	AC 6.5
CHAPTER 7	**Maintaining Databases**		
AC2002-1-1	Use data validation	7.1	AC 7.8
AC2002-1-4	Create and modify custom input masks	7.1	AC 7.4
AC2002-7-3	Encrypt and decrypt databases	7.2	AC 7.27
AC2002-7-5	Assign database security (permissions and passwords)	7.2	AC 7.28
AC2002-7-6	Replicate databases	7.2	AC 7.19
AC2002-8-2	Used the Database Splitter (creating front/back-end and protecting a database from modification)	7.2	AC 7.15
CHAPTER 8	**Integrating with Other Applications**		
AC2002-6-1	Use Design view to modify a Data Access page	8.1	AC 8.31
AC2002-8-1	Import data to Access	8.1	AC 8.10
AC2002-8-2	Export data from Access	8.1	AC 8.20
AC2002-8-3	Create a Data Access page using the Page Wizard	8.2	AC 8.29

reference 3

Task Reference RoundUp

task reference roundup

Task	Page #	Preferred Method
Opening an Access object	AC 1.18	• Click the type of object that you would like to open in the Database window's Objects bar
		• Select the object that you would like to open
		• Click the **Open** button
Activating Access Wizards	AC 1.23	• Click the object (Queries, Forms, Reports) whose Wizard you would like to access in the Database window's Objects bar
		• Click **New** in the Database window's toolbar
		• The available Wizards will be listed
		• Select the Wizard and respond to its questions
Getting Help	AC 1.30	• Click in the Ask a Question drop-down text box in the Access menu
		• Type in keywords relevant to your topic. Full sentences are not necessary and do not improve the performance of the search
		• Press **Enter**
		• Select from the topics provided or adjust the keywords and search again
Finding Specific Data Values	AC 2.6	• Click in the column that you would like to search
		• Click the **Find** button
		• Enter the Find What criteria using the data value that you would like to find. Remember that a question mark (?) can be used as a wildcard for one character and an asterisk (*) is a wildcard for multiple characters
		• Click the **Find Next** button. If multiple rows match the Find What criteria, you may need to repeat this step until the row you are searching for is found
Office Clipboard: Collect Items to Paste	AC 2.14	• Display the Office Clipboard by selecting **Office Clipboard** from the **Edit** menu
		• Select the item to be copied
		• Click the **Copy** or **Cut** button in the Standard toolbar
		• Continue placing items on the clipboard (up to 24) until you have collected everything that you need
Office Clipboard: Paste Collected Items	AC 2.14	• Display the Office Clipboard if it is not already present. If the Office Clipboard option of the Edit menu is not available, you are in an application or view that does not support the Office Clipboard
		• Click or select the area where you want to place items
		• Do one of the following:

task reference roundup

Task	Page #	Preferred Method
		• Select the **Paste All** button to paste the entire contents of the Office Clipboard
		or
		• Select a clipboard item and choose **Paste** from its drop-down menu
Office Clipboard: Remove Items	AC 2.14	When the clipboard is open • To clear one item, click the arrow next to the item you want to delete and then click **Delete**
		• To clear all clipboard contents, click the **Clear All** button
		• Placing more than 24 items on the clipboard will replace existing items beginning with the oldest item
Hiding Datasheet Columns	AC 2.16	• Open a table, query, or form in Datasheet view
		• Click the field selector of the column to be hidden
		• Click **Hide Columns** on the **Format** menu
To Unhide a Column	AC 2.16	• On the **Format** menu, click **Unhide Columns**
		• Select the names of the columns that you want to show from the Unhide Columns dialog box
Freezing and Unfreezing Datasheet Columns	AC 2.16	• Open a table, query, or form in Datasheet view
		• Select the column(s) that you want to freeze or unfreeze
		• To freeze column(s), select **Freeze Columns** on the **Format** menu
		• To unfreeze column(s), select **Unfreeze All Columns** on the **Format** menu
Defining a Table Field	AC 2.26	• Click **Tables** in the Options bar
		• Click the **Design view** button on the toolbar
		• Enter a field name
		• Select a data type
		• Define other field attributes as needed
Filter by Selection	AC 3.4	• Open the table in Datasheet view
		• Select the field and character(s) of the search criteria (see Figure 3.2)
		• Click the **Filter By Selection** **toolbar button to return values matching the selection**
		or
		• **right-click and choose** Filter Excluding Selection to filter the selection out of the data
		• Evaluate the results of the filter
		• Click **Remove Filter** on the Access toolbar
Filter by Form	AC 3.6	• Open a table in Datasheet view

task reference roundup

Task	Page #	Preferred Method
		• Click the **Filter By Form** toolbar button
		• Build the filter criteria by selecting from the drop-down list for a field or typing your own value
		• Click the Filter toolbar button
		• Review the filtered data to be sure it is what you expected
		• Work with the filtered data
		• Click **Remove Filter** on the Access toolbar when you are done
Filter for Input	AC 3.8	• Open a table in Datasheet view
		• Right-click the field to be filtered
		• Type the filter criteria in the Filter For text box using wildcards, operators, and values
		• Press **Enter** to activate the filter
		• Review the filtered data to be sure they are what you expected
		• Work with the filtered data
		• Click **Remove Filter** on the Access toolbar when you are done
Advanced Filter/Sort	AC 3.9	• Open a table in Datasheet view
		• On the **Records** menu, point to **Filter**, and then click **Advanced Filter/Sort**
		• Add criteria fields to the design grid
		• Enter the filter and sort criteria
		• Click the **Apply Filter** button on the toolbar
		• Review the filtered data to be sure they are what you expected
		• Work with the filtered data
		• Click **Remove Filter** on the Access toolbar when you are done
Saving a Filter as a Query	AC 3.10	• Display the filter in either the Filter By Form window or the Advanced Filter/Sort window (recall that any filter can be displayed in these windows regardless of how it was created)
		• Click the **Save As Query** button on the toolbar
		• Type a name for the query and click OK
		• The new query will appear with the other query objects in the Database window
Create a Select Query	AC 3.12	• Select the **Queries** object from the Database window
		• Verify that **Create query in Design view** is selected
		• Click **New** on the toolbar
		• Select the **Design view** button from the New Query dialog box and click **OK**

task reference roundup

Task	Page #	Preferred Method
		• Double-click the name of each table that contains relevant data from the Show Table dialog box
		• Double-click each table field that is to be contained in the query result to place it in the Field row of the design grid. The order of the columns is the order of the output
		• Enter sort criteria in the Sort row of the design grid
		• Enter selections in the Criteria row of the design grid
		• Click the **Datasheet view** button on the toolbar to see the query results
		• Click the **Design view** **button on the toolbar to update the query criteria**
		• **Click the** Save button to save the query criteria
Create an Expression using Expression Builder	AC 3.20	• Click in the Field row of the QBE grid column that will display the calculation
		• Click the **Build** button in the query design toolbar
		• Select expression elements and operators to create the desired calculation
		• Click **OK** to place the calculation in the QBE grid
Modify the Format of a Form	AC 3.28	• Open the form in Design view
		• Click the **AutoFormat** button in the Form Design toolbar
		• Select from the same formats that were available in the Wizard
Modify the Format of a Report	AC 3.31	• Open the report in Design view
		• Click the **AutoFormat** button in the Report Design toolbar
		• Select from the same formats that were available in the Wizard
Add a Graphic to a Report or Form	AC 3.36	• Open the report or form in Design view
		• Select the section that is to display the graphic
		• Select **Picture** from the Insert menu
		• Navigate to the folder containing the image and change the file type selector to the image file type
		• Select the file and click **OK**
		• Move and size image as needed
Create a Crosstab Query	AC 4.10	• Click the **Queries** object in the Database window, select **Create query by using wizard**, and then click **New**
		• Select **Crosstab Query Wizard** from the New Query dialog box and then click **OK**
		• Follow the Wizard's instructions to choose the data source, row heading, column heading, and aggregate functions for the query

task reference roundup

Task	Page #	Preferred Method
		• Name the query and then view the results
Creating a lookup field	AC 4.15	• Verify the relationship between the table that will have the look up field and the table where the field is being looked up. The most likely relationship is one-to-many, where the child (many sides of the relationship) table will lookup the key value of the parent table (one side of the relationship)
		• Open the child table and change the Data Type to **Lookup Wizard**
		• Follow the Lookup Wizard instructions
Creating an Input Mask	AC 4.18	• Open a table in Design view
		• Select the field for which you want to define an input mask
		• From the General tab select the **Input Mask** property and either
		• Click the **Build** button and follow the InputMask Wizard instructions (Text and Date fields only)
		or
		• Type the input mask definition (Numeric and Currency masks must be entered manually)
Compact and Repair the Open Database	AC 4.21	• **On the** Tools menu, point to **Database Utilities, and then click Compact and Repair Database**
Compact and Repair an Unopened Database	AC 4.22	• Access must be running with no open database
		• On the **Tools** menu, point to **Database Utilities**, and then click **Compact and Repair Database**
		• In the **Database to Compact From** dialog box, specify the Access file you want to compact, and then click **Compact**
		• In the **Compact Database Into** dialog box, specify a name, drive, and folder for the compacted Access file
		• **Click** Save
Setting Automatic Compact and Repair	AC 4.24	• Open the Access database that you want to compact automatically
		• On the **Tools** menu, click **Options**
		• Click the **General** tab
		• Select the **Compact on Close** check box
Setting Detect and Repair for Microsoft Office	AC 4.25	• On the **Help** menu, click **Detect and Repair**
		• To restore the program shortcuts to the Windows **Start** menu, make sure the **Restore my shortcuts while repairing** check box is selected
		• Click **Start**

task reference roundup

Task	Page #	Preferred Method
Backup and Restore using Microsoft Windows 2000 Backup and Recovery Tools	AC 4.26	• Click the Windows **Start** button, **Programs**, **Accessories**, **System Tools**, and then **Backup**
		• Select the **Backup Wizard** to walk you through creating a backup of your file(s). Be sure to carefully explore all of the options. The Advanced button will allow you to set the type of backup and the schedule for backups
		• Select the **Restore Wizard** to walk you through restoring all or part of a backup
Open a new form in Design view	AC 5.5	• In the Database window of an open database, click the **Forms** object
		• Click the **New** button on the Database window toolbar
		• In the New Form dialog box, click **Design View**
		• Select the table or query that will be the record source for the form and click **OK**
Select and move form controls	AC 5.9	• Select the control to be operated on by clicking it. The Shift key can be used to select multiple controls
		• Drag the control(s) to the new location. Use the large move handle to independently move components of a bound control
Set control properties	AC 5.11	• Right-click the control to open the pop-up menu
		• Select **Properties** from the pop-up menu
		• Select the appropriate Properties tab (usually Format)
		• Navigate to the property and change its setting
Show Form Headers and Footers	AC 5.14	• Open a form in Design view
		• Select **Form Header/Footer** from the **View** menu
Add Toolbox controls to a design	AC 5.15	• Open a form or report in Design view
		• If necessary, activate the toolbox using the **Toolbox** button on the Form Design toolbar
		• Verify that the toolbox **Control Wizards** button is depressed (a blue outline will show around it)
		• Click the toolbox control that is to be added to the form
		• Click in the Form section that will contain the control
		• Set the control's properties using the Properties pages activated with the Properties button
Query an open form with a saved filter	AC5.20	• Open a form in Form view
		• Click the **Filter By Form** button
		• Click the **Load From Query** button

task reference roundup

Task	Page #	Preferred Method
		• Select the query to be applied and click **OK**
		• Click the **Apply Filter** button
Create a report in Design view	AC 5.26	• In the Database window click the **Reports** object and click the **New** button
		• Click **Design View** as the way to develop the report, select the record source from the drop-down list, and click **OK**
Add page numbers to a report in Design view	AC 5.32	• Display the report in Design view
		• Choose **Page Numbers** from the **Insert** menu
		• Select the formatting, position, and alignment options that you want and click **OK**
Control Sorting and Grouping in a Report	AC 5.37	• Display the report in Design view
		• Click the **Sorting and Grouping** button on the toolbar
		• Use the Field/Expression drop-down list box to select each field that you want to use to sort or group data. Each selected Field/Expression will be on a different line of the grid
		• Select the Sort order for each Field/Expression listed. The order of multiple fields determines their priority in the sort
		• Select the grouping option(s) for each field
		• Close the Sorting and Grouping dialog box
		• Add the necessary controls and content to any Group Headers and Footers created
View table relationships	AC 6.4	• Click the **Relationships** button on the Database toolbar
		• If relationships exist, they will be displayed. If there are no current relationships, you can add tables and build relationships between them
View relationship properties	AC 6.7	• Click the **Relationships** button on the Database toolbar
		• If relationships exist, they will be displayed. If there are no current relationships, you can add tables and build relationships between them
		• Double-click the relationship line that you would like to view
		• The Edit Relationships dialog box displays the properties of that relationship
Create a relationship	AC 6.8	• Click the **Relationships** button on the Database toolbar
		• If relationships exist, they will be displayed
		• Click the **Show Table** button on the toolbar

task reference roundup

Task	Page #	Preferred Method
		• Select the table that you want to relate and click the **Add** button. Repeat this process for each table to be related
		• When you have added all of the necessary tables click **Close**
		• Click the primary table field of the relationship and drag to the secondary field to initiate the relationship
		• Select the referential integrity options in the Edit Relationships dialog box
		• Click **OK** to close the Edit Relationships dialog box
		• Repeat this process for any other relationships to be built
		• Close the Relationships window
Index a table field	AC 6.14	• Open the table in **Design view**
		• Select the field to be indexed from the Field Name column
		• Set the Indexed field property to **Yes (Duplicates OK)** or **Yes (No Duplicates**)
		• Close the table design and save the changes
Delete an index	AC 6.15	• Open the table in **Design view**
		• Select the field whose index is to be removed from the Field Name column
		• Set the Indexed field property to **No** (this does not impact the field or its data)
		• Close the table design and save the changes
View the indexes of a table	AC 6.15	• Open the table in **Design view**
		• Click the **Indexes** button of the toolbar
		• Click an index to review its properties
Controlling blank data values	AC 7.11	• Open the table in Design view
		• Click the field whose blank values you would like to control
		• Set Required to **Yes** to disallow blank values (Allow Zero Length should be set to No)
Defining field validation rules	AC 7.13	• Open the table in Design view
		• Click the field that will be monitored by the validation rule
		• Select the **Validation Rule** property for that field
		• Type the validation expression or use the Expression Builder by clicking the ellipsis to the right of the Validation Rule text box
		• Click the Validation Text property box for the same field and enter the text that is to display when the validation rule is broken

task reference roundup

Task	Page #	Preferred Method
		• Save the table update
		• If the validation rule has been set for a field that already contains data, Access will ask if you want to apply the new rule to existing data
		• If there are no existing data in the field, there will be no prompt
Splitting a database	AC 7.16	• Back up the database
		• On the Tools menu, point to Database Utilities, and then click Database Splitter
		• Follow the Database Splitter Wizard instructions
Optimizing database objects	AC 7.18	• Open the database to be optimized
		• Click the **Tools** menu, then **Analyze,** and then **Performance**
		• Select the tab for the database object (table, query, report, form, etc.) that you would like to analyze
		• Click the check box of each object to be evaluated or click Select All to select all objects in the list
		• Select objects from other tabs if desired
		• Click **OK**
		• Review and apply results as needed
Replicating a database	AC 7.20	• Open the database to be replicated
		• Remove any password protection and ensure that the database is not open by any other users
		• On the **Tools** menu, point to **Replication,** and then click **Create Replica**
		• Click **Yes** when prompted with: The database must be closed before you can create a replica
		• Answer **Yes** when prompted with: Converting a database into a Design Master results in changes . . .
		• In the Location of New Replica dialog box
		• Navigate to the location for the replica
		• Set the **Priority**
		• Check the **Prevent deletes** check box to prevent record deletions in the replica
		• In the Save as Type box, select the replica visibility
		• Click **OK**
Synchronizing replicated databases	AC 7.22	• Open the replica to be synchronized
		• On the **Tools** menu, point to **Replication,** and then click **Synchronize Now**

task reference roundup

Task	Page #	Preferred Method
		• Select the other replica set member to be synchronized from the Directly with Replica drop-down list box
		• Click **OK**
		• Respond **Yes** when prompted to close the database for synchronization
		• Respond **OK** when notified that the process has been completed
Hiding a database	AC 7.26	• Open Windows Explorer
		• Navigate to the file to be hidden
		• Right-click on the file to be hidden
		• Click the **Properties** option
		• Click the **Hidden** attribute
		• Click **OK**
Encrypting a database	AC 7.27	• Open Access with no open database
		• Open the **Tools** menu, pause over **Security,** and click **Encrypt/Decrypt Database . . .**
		• Enter a folder and a name for the database to be encrypted and click **OK**
		• Enter a folder and name for the encrypted database and click **Save**
Password protecting a database	AC 7.29	• Open Access with no open database
		• Click the **Open** button on the Database toolbar
		• Navigate to the folder and select the file to be password protected
		• Click the Open button's list arrow and select **Open Exclusive**
		• Open the **Tools** menu, pause over **Security**, and then click **Set Database Password**
		• Type the password in the Password text box, repeat the same password in the Verify text box, and then press **Enter**
Setting user-level security	AC7.32	• Open the Access database to be secured
		• On the **Tools** menu, pause over **Security** and then click **User-Level Security Wizard**
		• Follow the Wizard instructions
Create a Microsoft Graph	AC 8.4	• Click the **Reports** object in the Database window
		• Click **New** to activate the New Report dialog box
		• Select **Chart Wizard,** use the drop-down list to select the query or table containing the data to be charted, and then click **OK** to initiate the Chart Wizard

task reference roundup

Task	Page #	Preferred Method
		• Follow the instructions to select the field(s) with the data to be charted, select the chart type, specify the layout, and add a chart title
Importing with an Unbound Object Frame on a form or report	AC 8.10	• Open the Design view of the form or report to contain the imported object
		• Click the **Unbound Object Frame** tool in the toolbox
		• Click and drag the area on the form or report that will contain the object
		• In the Microsoft Access dialog box
		• Click **Create From File**
		• Browse to the file for import
		• Click the Link check box to create a linked object or leave it unclicked to create an embedded object
		• Click **OK**
Import or Link to another Access database	AC 8.15	• Open the Access database that is to contain the imported data
		• Open the **File** menu, point to **Get External Data,** and then do one of the following:
		• Click **Import** to create Access tables from the external data
		• Click **Link Tables** to create links to tables that remain in the source location
		• In the Import or Link dialog box
		• Use the Files of Type drop-down list to select **Microsoft Access (*.mdb, *.adp, *.mda, *.mde, *.ade)** as the type of file to be linked or imported
		• Use the Look In box to select the drive, folder, and file name of the file to be imported or linked
		• Select the import tables and click **Import**
Import or Link to an Excel Spreadsheet	AC 8.18	• Open the Access database that is to contain the imported data
		• Open the **File** menu, point to **Get External Data,** and then click **Import**
		• Click **Import** to create Access tables from the external data
		• Click **Link Tables** to create links to tables that remain in the source location
		• In the Import or Link dialog box
		• Use the Files of Type drop-down list to select **Microsoft Excel (*.xls)** as the type of file to be linked or imported
		• Use the Look In box to select the drive, folder, and file name of the file to be imported or linked

task reference roundup

Task	Page #	Preferred Method
		• Follow the Import Spreadsheet Wizard instructions
Export an Access Object to Microsoft Word	AC 8.21	• Open the Access database with the object to be exported
		• Select the object to be exported in the Database window (it is best to preview the object before exporting)
		• Open the **Tools** menu, point to **Office Links,** and then either
		• Select **Merge It with Microsoft Word** to use an Access table or query as the data source for a Word merge document
		• Select **Publish It with Microsoft Word** to create an .rtf file in the default database folder (usually C:\ My Documents or the folder containing the database) with the same name as the exported object
Export an Access Object to an Excel Spreadsheet	AC 8.22	• Open the Access database that contains the data to be exported
		• Select the object to be exported in the Database window (it is best to preview the object before exporting)
		• Open the **Tools** menu, point to **Office Links,** and then click **Analyze It with Microsoft Excel**
Export an Access Object to a static HTML page	AC 8.26	• Open the Access database that contains the data to be exported
		• Select the object to be exported in the Database window (it is best to preview the object before exporting)
		• Open the **File** menu and click **Export**
		• In the Export To dialog box
		• Use the Save In box to select the drive and folder for the Web page
		• Set the Save As Type to **HTML Documents (*.html; *.htm)**
		• In the File Name box, enter the name for the Web page (it is best not to use spaces in these names)
		• Save Formatted should be clicked to retain the formatting applied to the datasheet in Access and activate the next two options
		• Check **AutoStart** to display the page in your default browser
		• In the HTML Output Options dialog box
		• Apply an HTML template to standardize formatting (Optional)
		• Click **OK**
Use Internet Explorer to view a static HTML page	AC 8.27	• Open Access
		• From the **View** menu, pause over **Toolbars** and then click **Web**

task reference roundup

Task	Page #	Preferred Method
		• On the Web toolbar, drop down the **Go** list and select **Open Hyperlink**
		• Click the **Browse** button in the Open Internet Address dialog box
		• Use the Browse dialog box to navigate to the file to be viewed
		• Select the file and click **Open**
		• Click **OK**
Use the Page Wizard to create a Data Access page	AC 8.29	• Open the database containing the data for the Data Access page
		• Click the **Pages** object in the Database window
		• Double-click **Create data access page by using wizard**
		• Follow the Wizard instructions
Importing an HTML document as an Access table	AC 8.37	• Open the database to hold the imported table
		• Verify that the layout of the data to be imported is either a list or a table
		• On the **File** menu, point to **Get External Data,** and then click **Import**
		• Select the HTML file for import and click **Import** (be sure to set the Files of Type to HTML documents)
		• Complete the Wizard dialog boxes
Construct a Web page or file hyperlink	AC 8.41	• Open the form, report, or Data Access page in Design view
		• Click the Insert Hyperlink button in the toolbox and drag the display area on the form, report, or Data Access page
		• In the Insert Hyperlink dialog box
		• Select the type of object to **Link to** (Existing File or Web Page, Object in This Database, Create New Page, or E-Mail Address)
		• Enter the **Text to display** for the hyperlink (if this is blank, the URL will display)
		• Enter the **Screen Tip text** (if this is blank, the URL displays when the user pauses the cursor over the link)
		• In the Address box, type or browse to the path of a file or a URL
		• Click **OK**

reference 4 Making the Grade Answers

making the grade

CHAPTER 1

SESSION 1.1

1. Relational Database Management System.
2. The standardized language used to ask questions of data stored in relational databases.
3. Columns, attributes, fields, or foreign keys each is an acceptable answer.
4. Primary key.
5. A wide range of answers can be considered appropriate for this. There are some key components that all acceptable answers should contain. At a minimum, the answer should contain fields for FirstName, LastName, StreetAddress, City, State, and ZipCode. Better answers would also contain fields for OrderDate, Product, and OrderQuantity and address the need to find a unique key to identify each customer.

SESSION 1.2

1. Any answers from the following list are correct: Tables, Queries, Forms, Reports, Pages, Macros, or Modules.
2. False. The user is prompted to save them when they close the view.
3. One of the features of the Documenter is the ability to create printed documentation about an Access object such as a table. The chapter example used the Documenter to print the Customer table design.
4. The query results should include the customer's full name and complete street address. The records should be sorted by ZipCode.

CHAPTER 2

SESSION 2.1

1. Indicates the new record row.
2. Wildcards are used to set match values for searching text. * replaces any number of characters. ? replaces a single character. [] can be used to include alternate values such as [jf].
3. The Access table file is updated with changes made in a record when the pointer is moved to a new record.
4. The column order is important when sorting because the first field is primary and the second field is secondary—only used to break ties in the first value.
5. False.
6. False.

SESSION 2.2

1. Underline the primary key.
2. False.
3. 255.
4. Default.
5. False.
6. True.

CHAPTER 3

SESSION 3.1

1. If the selection is at the beginning of a field, records that begin with the selected values will be retrieved. If the selection is in the middle of a field, records with the selected characters anywhere in their value will be selected.
2. False. Filtering restricts the rows.
3. Select the value to be excluded, right-click on it, and choose Filter Excluding Selection.
4. False. Filters are cumulative until the Remove Filter instruction is executed.
5. The Or tab in Filter By Form and the Or row in the Advanced Filter/Sort both allow you to enter multiple criteria for the same field.
6. The first benefit is that you can execute the filter again without recreating the criteria. Secondly, the saved filter could be used as the basis for creating a more complex query.

SESSION 3.2

1. The >, >=, <, and <= operators all return a contiguous range of values. Between also could be used.

making the grade

2. False. Relational operators include =, >, >=, <, <=, and <>. The operators listed are mathematical operators.
3. Expression Builder and Zoom box.
4. If there is no grouping, there will be one row of statistics for the entire selection. If there is grouping (i.e, Group by VendorCode or Group by Category), one row of summary will be returned for each group member (i.e., one row for each VendorCode or one row for each Category).

SESSION 3.3

1. A form object is used to create a custom format for input and display of data from tables or queries. A report is used to design printed output from tables and queries.
2. False. The Form Wizard allows you to select fields from multiple tables or queries.
3. Both buttons are used to select fields. The > button selects the current field, while the >> button selects all available fields.
4. Expressions are used to calculate values that are not stored in tables such as gross pay. An expression is entered in the Field row of the QBE grid to create a calculated field.
5. Labels and text boxes are the controls that make up forms and reports. The label contains the heading or descriptive text for the field, while the text box holds the field value from each record.
6. Setting the Grouping in a report is the same as setting the Group By option in a query. Both allow you to select a field or fields that will control summary statistics. For example, to create an inventory report by department, you would want totals for each department, so department would be the group field.

CHAPTER 4

SESSION 4.1

1. The Like operator allows you to use wildcards to set a pattern that retrieved data must match. The question mark (?) wildcard replaces one character. The asterisk (*) wildcard replaces a group of characters. The pound sign (#) replaces one numeral. The Like operator is designed to work on text fields.
2. Placing GME in the Criteria row of the Category field would produce the desired results.
3. Crosstab queries allow you to perform aggregate functions using two controlling fields represented by the row and column headers.
4. The Between operator has two arguments, an upper and lower limit. These arguments specify a range of values to be retrieved that can be any size.

SESSION 4.2

1. When you change to a different view.
2. Lookup.
3. All data stored in that field are also deleted.
4. False.
5. Integers store whole numbers that are smaller than Single formats and cannot keep decimals. Loss of any decimal values is certain. There is also a potential for loss of Single values that are larger than Integer format supports.
6. Subdatasheet.

SESSION 4.3

1. Databases need to be backed up to protect against data loss. Data loss can occur due to user errors such as shutting off the computer without properly exiting Access or computer errors such as a drive failure.
2. A database should not be converted if there is still a need to use it in the older version of Access. Convert it if it won't be used in the older version.
3. Compacting a database reorganizes it so that unneeded space is released. Repairing a database fixes problems with the structure of database objects.
4. Detect and Repair will detect problems with Office software and initiate the steps to repair the problem.

making the grade

CHAPTER 5

SESSION 5.1

1. Open the form in Design view. Select all of the labels to be adjusted by holding down the Shift key while you click. Either use the justification buttons on the toolbar or the Properties pages to change the alignment.
2. Bound controls display data from a table or query and are bound to the field that the control will display. The contents of a bound control change as the user moves through records. An unbound control is not attached to a record source and displays static data.
3. Object properties are set using Properties pages, by resizing the object, by moving the object, or by formatting the object. Properties are settings that control how an object appears or behaves. They are set to change such things as the background color, font, or format of an object.
4. Form Design view allows the developer to have full control over the alignment, layout, and properties of form elements. Often forms developed using a Wizard are customized in Design view.

SESSION 5.2

1. The Detail section of a report is used to define the fields that will be displayed for each row of data in the record source.
2. The frequency of the calculation determines where you place the calculation. If the calculation is to print summary information about the groups on the report, the calculation needs to be in the Group Footer. If the calculation is to summarize all of the records in the record source, place it in the Report Footer.
3. Sizing Handles are smaller and used to resize the control. The large handle at the top left of a control will move joined controls independently.
4. Controls are chosen by what they are to display. Labels hold text that doesn't change such as the title of a report. Text boxes hold calculations and display values from record source fields. Images hold graphics such as a logo.

CHAPTER 6

SESSION 6.1

1. With the database open, click the Relationships button to activate the Relationships window. The properties of each relationship can be viewed by double-clicking the relationship line.
2. The drag operation is from the primary field to the related field.
3. Referential integrity rules govern how data are entered and deleted in related tables. They prevent orphans by requiring that the parent record exist before child records can be added to the related table, and that the parent can't be removed while it still has active children.
4. Access uses indexes to speed sort and search operations. An index is a table that can be used to look up index values and then move directly to the fields containing that value.

SESSION 6.2

1. Inner join queries are used when you want only rows of data where both tables have the same join field value. Use one of the outer joins when you want all of the data in one or the other table, regardless of whether there is a matching value in the other table.
2. You might want to see the SQL to verify which table is the left and which is the right table in the defined relationship. It could also help you learn SQL so that you could type your own queries for operations like lookup fields.
3. Open the primary table. A plus sign displays in front of each record that will allow you to open the related table records.
4. Indexes improve search and sort operations. Candidates for indexing include fields that are frequently used in these operations, are not automatically indexed (like primary and foreign key values), and contain a wide range of values.

making the grade

5. Queries allow you to verify the validity of data selection and calculations before applying formatting in the form.

CHAPTER 7

SESSION 7.1

1. Input masks speed data entry by reducing keystrokes. They also improve reliability by not requiring users to enter repetitive data. Any field containing data with a repetitive component such as punctuation should be considered for an input mask.
2. Both the Input Mask and Format properties are similar since they use the same definition characters. The input mask displays a pattern for the user to enter data, such as (__)__-___. You can choose whether or not the punctuation is stored with the data. If the punctuation is not stored with the data, it will need to be added before displaying data from the field to the user. The Format property is used to add repeating characters to data retrieved from a table.
3. The default value assigned to a field should be the most common data value for the field.
4. Validation rules are designed to improve data validity by ensuring that data entered into a field are appropriate for that field.

SESSION 7.2

1. Splitting a database separates the data from the queries, forms, and reports that use it. This is normally done in a networked environment to share the data while allowing users to have their own custom queries, forms, and reports.
2. Database Performance Analyzer
3. When a database is replicated, there are multiple full copies of the database that have to be synchronized with each other. A split database maintains only one copy of the data in a central location that is shared by all users. With a split database, each user has his or her own front-end (queries, forms, and reports) based on the centralized data.
4. Databases should be secured whenever there is risk of theft, inappropriate use, or unwanted data altering.

CHAPTER 8

SESSION 8.1

1. The Chart Wizard walks you through creating a chart using Microsoft Graph. Microsoft Graph is used to edit an existing chart.
2. The source application is the software that originated a linked or embedded object.
3. Embedded objects are a copy of the original that can be edited independently. Linked objects are just a picture and should be used when you want only one copy of a file.
4. The chart type controls how the data are plotted. Chart types include bar, pie, column, and radial.

SESSION 8.2

1. Static HTML pages cannot be used to update a database and so are not browser specific. Data Access pages allow database updates and require specific browser technology.
2. Hyperlinks use addresses to point to another object. Absolute addresses contain all of the components while relative addresses omit some components. The missing components are assigned the values of the current page.
3. Static Web pages do not maintain any connection to the original data and so must be reexported to display updated data.
4. The Record Navigation toolbar displays on a Data Access page and is used to edit, filter, and move through displayed records.

glossary

Absolute address: An address to a Web page, local file, or other object that contains values for every address component. Moving files will cause an absolute address to be invalid.

Access window: The main window of the Microsoft Access user interface. Other windows display inside it.

Action queries: Queries that update the data in a database in some fashion. For example, to delete a group of records that meet a criterion, to update a group of records, to add records to an existing table, or to add records to a new table.

Active Server Page: A Web page designed to display up-to-date read-only data. The data are selected by the server and displayed in a table format. Opening or refreshing an ASP file from a Web browser causes the page to be dynamically created from current values and sent to the browser.

Advanced Filter/Sort: The most comprehensive filtering method that presents a grid of the table being filtered and allows you to enter record selection criteria.

Aggregate function: Access predefined calculations used to summarize groups of data (e.g., Sum and Avg).

Alternate keys: A table field that could have been assigned as the primary key but was not.

And: The logical operator that combines two conditions that must both be true to retrieve a record.

Back-end: The centralized data storage of a split database.

Between: The relational operator used to select records whose values fall between the stated upper and lower bounds. For example, Between 14 and 18.

Calculated field: A field of a query that contains an expression.

Candidate key: Each table field that could be defined as the primary.

Caption: The table field property that determines what displays as the label for the field in Datasheet and other views.

Cascade Delete Related Records: Referential integrity setting that causes the related records to be deleted when a primary record is deleted.

Cascade Update Related Fields: Referential integrity setting that causes an update in the primary table to also be applied to the related table.

Chart: A graphical representation of numeric data. For example, a pie chart.

Chart Wizard: An Access Wizard that walks you through the process of creating a chart based on table data.

Client/server databases: DBMSs that are designed to support multiple users in a networked environment.

Compact on Close: The database option that causes a database to automatically compact each time it is closed.

Compacting: The process of removing excess space from a database.

Composite key: The result of multiple attributes being combined for the primary key.

Condition: The method of entering selection criteria using operators such as >, <, >=, <=, and <>.

Conflict Viewer: Access tool used to resolve synchronization conflicts in replication sets.

Crosstab queries: Queries that are used to analyze data by grouping data and calculating values for each group.

Crosstab query: A query format that allows data to be tabulated by two variables: a row header and a column header.

Data access language (DAL): RDBMS language for rapidly retrieving and organizing stored data. SQL is the standard.

Data Access pages: Web pages that allow a Web browser to be used to view and update table data via a live connection to the data in your database.

Data definition language (DDL): The language provided by RDBMS for structuring the data tables and their relationships.

Data integrity: A term used to describe the reliability of data.

Data redundancy: Storing the same data such as a customer's last name multiple times. Redundant data increase the likelihood that data will not be updated properly in all locations and so reduce data integrity.

Data Type: The table field property that determines what type of data it can store and how much storage space it will require.

Data validation rules: Rules that verify data entered are within appropriate bounds. For example, Gender should contain only M for male or F for female.

Data value: The intersection of a table row and column containing data pertaining to one attribute of one entity.

Database management system (DBMS): The software used to store data, maintain those data, and provide easy access to stored data.

Database window: The window displaying an open Access database.

Database: A file that organizes Access objects (tables, queries, forms, reports, and so on) that are related to each other.

Datasheet view: The default grid layout used to display Access table data.

Default Value: The table field property that determines the value that will automatically be loaded for the field in a new record. The user can overtype the default value.

Design grid: The form used to specify fields and criteria in a query.

Design Master: The original database of a replica set that keeps track of all replicas.

Design view: The view of an object that is used to change the structure of the object.

Detect and Repair: A facility to detect and repair problems with Office software.

Direct synchronization: The synchronization method used when the replica set shares a network and can directly connect to each other.

Domain: All valid entries for one table attribute (column).

Embedded: A distinct copy of an object placed in a destination document that retains a link to the program that developed them, called the source program. Double-clicking an embedded object will open the source program in edit mode.

Encryption: A method of coding a file so that it is indecipherable without the conversion algorithm.

Entity: A person, place, object, idea, or event about which data are being collected.

Exclusive: A type of database access that locks out all other users. Use the Open button drop-down list to access this mode.

Explicit permissions: Those permissions granted directly to a user account.

Expression Builder: A tool for building expressions by selecting fields from tables, operators, and other calculation components.

Extranet: A combination of Internet and intranet technologies capable of securing and sharing data and information both locally and via the World Wide Web.

Field list: The listing of fields for a table used to select fields to be included in a query.

Field Name: The attribute of a table field that identifies it and is used to refer to it in queries, forms, reports, and modules.

Field selector: The button containing the field name that can be used to select an entire column of a datasheet.

Field Size: The table field property that determines the maximum value that the field can store, how much space is required to store it, and how fast it can be processed.

Field: A table column representing a unique property of an entity such as LastName, BirthDate, or Quantity; it can also be referred to as an attribute.

Filter by Form: A method of filtering or selecting records using an empty version of the current datasheet where you can type match values.

Filter by Selection: The simplest type of filter, which selects records that match the datasheet value you have selected.

Filter Excluding Selection: A method of selecting records that do not meet the stated criteria.

Filter for Input: A filter initiated from the pop-up menu that provides a text box for entering record selection criteria.

Foreign key: The value used to match the attributes from one table to those in another table.

Form view: The view used to manipulate data in a form.

Form Wizard: An Access Wizard that walks you through the process of building a form by selecting fields from multiple tables and queries.

Form: A user-friendly way to view and update data on a computer screen.

Format Painter: A tool available on the Standard toolbar that will pick up formatting applied to text and allow you to paint it onto other text.

Format: The field property of a table definition that controls how data display to the user after they have been entered.

Freezing columns: Keeping the leftmost columns of a datasheet on the screen when scrolling through columns to the right. The leftmost columns would scroll off of the screen if they were not frozen.

Front-end: In a split database, this is the part that is customized for each user.

Global chart: A type of chart that is based on all of the available data. Totals or averages from the data are usually charted.

Group by: Option used to set a field or fields that will be used to calculate subtotals.

Groups bar: A bar in the Access Database window to allow users to group database objects for easier manipulation.

HTML: See Hypertext Markup Language.

Hyperlink: A link between two objects that allows the user to navigate from object to object. Text hyperlinks are usually underlined and a different color. When the cursor is over a hyperlink, it changes to a pointing hand.

Hypertext Markup Language: A tag-based language used to create and link Web pages for delivery on a local computer, the Internet, an intranet, or an extranet.

Implicit permissions: Those permissions inherited from the group to which the user belongs.

In: The relational operator used to select records whose values match those listed. For example, In ("CO", "IN", "CA").

Index: Used to speed data access and sorting by allowing direct access to a specific value. Works like the index of a book.

Indexed: The field property of a table definition that determines whether or not this field indexes the table.

Inner join: A type of table relationship that creates rows in the query answerset when the related fields have matching values.

Internet: A world-wide network of computers used to distribute and share data and information.

Intranets: A local network used to share data and information using Web pages and other Internet technologies.

Joining: The process of using a foreign key from one table to link to the data in another table.

Left outer join: A type of table relationship that creates rows in the query answerset for all of the records in the first (left) table and adds the data from the second table when the related fields have matching values.

Like: The relational operator used to select records using wild cards (*, ?, #).

Linked: A picture of an object displays in the destination document but there is only one copy of the object, which can be maintained only from the source program.

Lookup field: A tool to ease data entry by listing valid values from a related table. Lookup fields are created using a Wizard in table Design view.

Macros: Used to automate repetitive database tasks using a series of actions; a self-contained instruction or command.

Main form: The outer form in a main form/subform pair. The main form typically displays data from the primary table and a subform displays related records.

Many-to-many: A table relationship that exists when one row in the first table matches with multiple rows in the second table and one row in the second table matches with multiple rows in the first table. Many-to-many relationships can't be directly modeled in relational databases, but are broken into multiple one-to-many relationships (abbreviated M:N or ∞:∞).

Microsoft Graph: The application that is used by the Chart Wizard to create a chart.

Module: A collection of Visual Basic statements and procedures that are organized and stored together to be accessed as a unit.

Not: The logical operator that negates the condition that it precedes.

Null: A field is said to be null or contain null values when nothing has been entered. This is used to differentiate between spaces and nothing entered in a field.

Object bar: A bar displaying icons in the Access Database window for each of the objects that can be created for a database.

Object linking and embedding: The Microsoft technology that allows objects to be placed in other objects. Such objects are either linked to the source object or embedded with no link to the source.

Object: Virtually anything—traditional data, a moving image, people talking, a photograph, narrative, text, music, or any combination.

OLE: See Object linking and embedding

One-to-many: The table relationship that exists when one row of the first table matches to multiple rows in the second table (abbreviated 1:M or 1:∞).

One-to-one: The table relationship that exists when one row of the first table matches to one and only one row of the second table and both tables have the same primary key (abbreviated 1:1).

Optimizing: A series of performance-enhancing operations that will result in a more efficient database.

Or: The logical operator that combines two conditions when either one or both of the conditions can be true to retrieve a record.

Owner: The user who created a database object is the owner of that object and has all security rights to that object.

Parameter query: A query that prompts the user for criteria that will be used in selecting data from the database.

Password: A password is used to allow only authorized users to access a database.

Permissions: Permissions establish the level of access a user has to a specific object. The level of permission determines whether the user can see, update, print, modify, and perform other operations on an object.

Personal databases: Systems like Microsoft Access that work best in single-user environments.

Primary key: A table field or fields that uniquely and minimally identify an entity.

Primary sort: The first field that is used to order rows of data.

Primary table: The table on the one side of a one-to-many relationship.

Query Questions that are posed to a relational database using ***structured query language (SQL).***

Read-Only: A type of database access that will not allow updates to the database. Use the Open button drop-down list to access this mode.

Record Navigation toolbar: A toolbar on a Data Access page that will allow you to save edits, delete records, move through the records, and other maintenance tasks.

Record selector: The buttons to the left of records in Datasheet view used to select a row.

Record-bound chart: A type of chart that reflects the data of the current record and changes when another record is active.

Record: One row in a relation (table) representing the unique data for one ***entity*** (person, place, object, idea, or event); it also can be referred to as a tuple.

Related table: The table on the many side of a one-to-many relationship.

Relational Database Management Systems (RDBMS): A type of DBMS that stores data in interrelated tables. Tables are related by sharing a common field.

Relational database: A collection of data relations defined using related tables.

Relational operator: The operators (>, < >=, <=, <>) used to set conditions in queries.

Relationships window: The window used to set or edit table relationships. Accessed using the Relationships button on the toolbar.

Relative address: An address to a Web page, local file, or other object that does not contain all of the address components. The missing components are assigned the values of the current object.

Repair: The process of fixing errors in the structure of database objects.

Replica: A copy of a database that must be synchronized with the Design Master to maintain accuracy among all of the replicas.

Replica set: The Design Master and all of its replicas.

Report: RDBMS object used to format data for printing.

Required: The table field property that determines whether or not the user must enter a value in this field.

Right outer join: A type of table relationship that creates rows in the query answerset for all of the rows in the second (right) table and adds the data from the first (left) table when the related fields have matching values.

Secondary sort: The second field that is used to order rows of data.

Select queries: The most common type of query used to retrieve (select) data from one or more tables.

Shared: A type of database access that allows multiple users to be logged on to the same database simultaneously. The default open mode.

Sort Ascending: Toolbar button used to cause an ascending sort based on the selected column(s).

Sort Descending: Toolbar button used to cause a descending sort based on the selected column(s).

Static HTML: Web pages used to publish a snapshot of the data, which have to be updated manually.

Structured query language (SQL): The language used to pose questions or queries to a relational database; SQL has been standardized by the American National Standards Institute (ANSI).

Subdatasheet: A small datasheet that presents over the main datasheet to display related data. Activated by clicking the plus (+) sign on the main datasheet.

Subform: The inner form in a main form/subform pair. The main form typically displays data from the primary table and the subform displays related records.

Synchronization: The process of retrieving updates from replicas and applying them to the members of the replica set so that they all reflect the same data, queries, forms, and reports.

Table: Rows and columns used to store data in a relational database management system.

Uniform Resource Locator: The address that identifies an object on a computer. An Internet address consists of the protocol, server address, path, and file name.

URL: See Uniform Resource Locator.

User-level security: Complex security such as that found on larger computers. Users belong to user groups that carry permissions for levels of access to each database object.

Validation: The table field property that contains the rule or rules that govern what data are acceptable for that field of a table.

Web browser: The software that allows you to view Internet documents. For example, Microsoft Internet Explorer.

Web servers: Computers that store documents for Internet distribution.

Wizards: Provide the user with step-by-step instructions on common tasks such as creating simple queries, forms, and reports.

World Wide Web: A network of linked documents made available through the Internet.

WWW: See World Wide Web.

Zero-length strings: Entered as " ", this indicates that the field is not supposed to contain data.

Zoom box: An enlarged area for entering long expressions activated by pressing Ctrl+F2.

Glossary for Common Microsoft® Office XP Features

Access 2002: A relational database tool that can be used to collect, organize, and retrieve large amounts of data. With a database you can manipulate the data into useful information using tables, forms, queries, and reports.

Answer Wizard: Located in the Microsoft Help dialog box, it provides another means of requesting help through your application.

Application: A program that is designed to help you accomplish a particular task, such as creating a slide-show presentation or creating a budget.

Ask a Question: A text box located in the top-right corner of your window, it is perhaps the most convenient method for getting help.

Clipboard: A temporary storage location for up to 24 items of selected text that has been cut or copied.

Clippit: The paper clip office assistant.

Excel 2002: An electronic spreadsheet tool that can be used to input, organize, calculate, analyze, and display business data.

F1: The robot office assistant.

Formatting toolbar: Collection of buttons that allows you to change the appearance of text, such as bold, italicize, or underline.

FrontPage 2002: A powerful Web publishing tool that provides everything needed to create, edit, and manage a personal or corporate Web site, without having to learn HTML.

Integrated application suite: A collection of application programs bundled together and designed to allow the user to effortlessly share information from one application to the next.

Links: The Cat office assistant.

Menu bar: Displays a list of key menu options available to you for that particular program.

Office Assistant: Character that will appear ready to help you with your question.

Office XP: The newest version of the popular Microsoft integrated application suite series that has helped personal computer users around the world to be productive and creative.

Outlook 2002: A desktop information management tool that allows you to send and receive e-mail, maintain a personal calendar of appointments, schedule meetings with co-workers, create to-do lists, and store address information about business/personal contacts.

Paste Options button: Button that appears when you paste into your document. When clicked it will prompt the user with additional features such as allowing you to paste with or without the original text formatting.

PowerPoint 2002: A popular presentation tool that allows users to create overhead transparencies and powerful multimedia slide shows.

Professional edition: Office XP version that includes Access, in addition to the Standard version of Word, Excel, PowerPoint, and Outlook.

Professional Special edition: Office XP version that includes Access, FrontPage, and Publisher, in addition to the Standard version of Word, Excel, PowerPoint, and Outlook.

Publisher 2002: A desktop publishing tool that provides individual users the capability to create professional-looking flyers, brochures, and newsletters.

Rocky: The dog office assistant.

Smart tag button: Buttons that appear as needed to provide options for completing a task quickly.

Standard edition: Office XP version that consists of Word, Excel, PowerPoint, and Outlook.

Standard toolbar: Collection of buttons that contains the popular icons such as Cut, Copy, and Paste.

Task pane: This window allows you to access important tasks from a single, convenient location, while still working on your document.

Title bar: Located at the top of each screen, it displays the application's icon, the title of the document you are working on, and the name of the application program you are using.

Toolbar: A collection of commonly used shortcut buttons.

Word 2002: A general-purpose word-processing tool that allows users to create primarily text-based documents, such as letters, résumés, research papers, and even Web pages.

index

u

v

w

y

z